THE MARKETPLACE OF REVOLUTION

BOOKS BY T. H. BREEN

The Character of the Good Ruler (1970)

Shaping Southern Society (1976)

Puritans and Adventurers (1980)

Myne Owne Ground, with Stephen Innes *(1980)*

Tobacco Culture (1985)

Imagining the Past (1990)

American Colonies in an Atlantic World, with Timothy Hall (2003)

The
Marketplace
of
Revolution

How Consumer Politics Shaped
American Independence

T. H. Breen

OXFORD
UNIVERSITY PRESS

OXFORD

UNIVERSITY PRESS

Oxford   New York
Auckland   Bangkok   Buenos Aires   Cape Town   Chennai
Dar es Salaam   Delhi   Hong Kong   Istanbul   Karachi   Kolkata
Kuala Lumpur   Madrid   Melbourne   Mexico City   Mumbai   Nairobi
São Paulo   Shanghai   Taipei   Tokyo   Toronto

Copyright © 2004 by T. H. Breen

First published by Oxford University Press, Inc., 2004
198 Madison Avenue, New York, New York 10016
www.oup.com

First issued as an Oxford University Press paperback, 2005
ISBN-13: 978-0-19-518131-9
ISBN-10: 0-19-518131-X

Oxford is a registered trademark of Oxford University Press

The Library of Congress has cataloged the cloth edition as follows:
Breen, T. H.
The marketplace of revolution : how consumer politics shaped American
independence / by T.H. Breen.
p. cm.
Includes bibliographical references and index.
ISBN-13: 978-0-19-506395-0
ISBN-10: 0-19-506395-3
1. United States—History—Revolution, 1775–1783—Causes.
2. United States—History—Revolution, 1775–1783—Economic aspects.
3. Consumption (Economics)—United States—History—18th century.
I. Title.
E209 .B77   2004   973.3′1—dc22   2003023138

9 8 7 6 5 4 3 2 1

Printed in the United States of America
on acid-free paper

For Lady Susan

Contents

Acknowledgments

My memories of writing *The Market-place of Revolution* are for the most part extremely pleasant. To be sure, there were moments when the muses rebelled. But such frustrations soon passed, and now I look back on many stimulating conversations with colleagues and students, all of whom encouraged me to get on with the project. I learned a lot about the implications of the argument from people who knew how to ask good questions. They also listened to my own thoughts about a revolutionary marketplace, noting politely when I had clearly failed to push the analysis in a persuasive direction.

I want in particular to thank all the people who shared with me the pleasures of a fellowship at the National Humanities Center. There were others who offered similar support and encouragement at the Huntington Library, where I held the Times Mirror Distinguished Research Professorship. Much of the research was completed while I served as the Pitt Professor of American History and Institutions at Cambridge University. I am particularly indebted to the university librarians who provided access to eighteenth-century materials and to the Fellows of Trinity College who did their best to make me feel comfortable at High Table. Later, during a crucial period in the writing, I taught at Oxford University as the Harmsworth Professor of American History. A Fellowship at Queen's College that year made a good posting even better.

I have received much welcome funding for this project from the National Endowment for the Humanities and the Earhard Foundation. I owe a particular debt of gratitude to the Society of Colonial Wars in the State of Illinois. Many years ago, Ron Waud, then the governor of the Society, decided to help underwrite my efforts, and at no time over almost a decade did either he or his generous colleagues ever stop cheering me on. And, of course, if the leaders of Northwestern University had not supported me with time and resources, I might have taken even longer to complete the present volume. Two former deans of the Weinberg College of Arts and Sciences, Lawrence Dumas and Eric Sundquist, deserve special mention. Both administrators made it clear that they saw their mission within the university to be to promote original scholarship, in the classroom and on the printed page. Whatever the environment at other schools may be, Northwestern communicates to its faculty a commitment to academic excellence. I am pleased now to have an opportunity to repay the administration's faith in me.

Several paragraphs in Chapter 1 originally appeared in T.H. Breen, "Narrative of Commercial Life: Consumption, Ideology, and Community on the Eve of the American Revolution," *William and Mary Quarterly*, 3d ser., 50 (1993), 471–501 and are used here with permission of Christopher Grasso, editor *W&MQ*. In some eighteenth-century quotations spelling has been changed to conform to modern conventions.

Many individuals gave timely assistance along the way. Seven friends volunteered—if that is the correct word—to read the manuscript from start to finish, a labor that yielded hundreds of marginal scribbles that I have done my very best to incorporate into the final manuscript. Hermann Wellenreuther, Patrick Griffin, Christopher Hodson, Walter Woodward, Ethan Shagan, Josef Barton, and Lacey Baldwin Smith have saved me from many embarrassments and suggested wonderfully constructive ways to sharpen the argument. Susan C. Breen read every word at every stage and with admirable diplomacy indicated a number of problems along the way. Others helped me to develop the interpretation, occasionally without being aware that they had done so. This vital group includes James Axtell, Jacob Lassner, Edward Muir, James Oakes, Robert (Roy) Ritchie, Carole Shammas, David Shi, Tina Radler, Eric Slauter, John Crowley, Russell Maylone, Susan Stein, Graham Hood, Sir John Elliott, John Styles, Harold Perkin, James Horn, Alan Ryan, Jason Lake, Tony Badger, Bant Breen, Sarah Breen, Maxine Berg, Neil McKendrick, John Robertson, Edmund S. Morgan, and Rebecca Becker. During the difficult process of checking and rechecking the notes, Michael Guenther provided invaluable assistance, often taking the initiative in ways I only slowly came to appreciate. Elzbieta Foeller-Pituch accepted the hard task of obtaining permissions for illustrations, cutting gracefully through a maze of bureaucratic obstructions. Working with Sheldon Meyer has been a constant pleasure. He is a master editor who has won the respect of every author who has had the privilege of doing a book with him. And finally, without Susan C. Breen there would have been no *Marketplace of Revolution*. A single volume cannot adequately thank her for her unfailing support. She knows that the book is as much her creation as my own.

Introduction: The Revolutionary Politics of Consumption

I would be hard pressed to identify the precise moment when simple curiosity about the character of daily life in colonial times became the basis for a book on the coming of the American Revolution. As I now remember it, the inspiration occurred many years ago in the Wallace Gallery, a museum that is part of Colonial Williamsburg. It is located quite literally deep below the surface of the ground, indeed, in the basement of a nineteenth-century hospital. The gallery offers visitors a rare treat. It houses a splendid collection of manufactured goods imported into America from Europe during the eighteenth century. These are not the things that usually draw modern visitors to Williamsburg. Such people seem to prefer spending their time among the craftsmen who tell them how a revolutionary generation made various household items such as furniture or candles. Perhaps these products strike tourists as more authentic, or as more American, than do the imported articles displayed in the Wallace Gallery.

I much prefer the British goods that were shipped so long ago to the colonial markets. In their presence, one senses immediately how a small piece of Staffordshire pottery or a handsomely designed buckle might have brought pleasure into the life of some obscure American consumer. By introducing vibrant colors into the poorly illuminated rooms of colonial houses, imported manufactures made the world of ordinary men and women come alive. Within a few decades during the middle of the eighteenth century, imported goods transformed monochrome spaces into Technicolor. Walking among the display cases containing ceramics and metal ware, textiles and prints, the visitor imagines how these things allowed people whose names have long since been forgotten to fashion themselves in ways that made them feel prettier, more successful, and more informed. Imported goods reflected cosmopolitan tastes and manners, so that an American who managed to purchase a porcelain teacup or a modest pewter bowl could fancy that he or she partook of a polite society centered in faraway places such as London or Bath. These wonderful objects arouse suspicion today that however much local ministers may have once railed against the corrupting influence of luxury, they did not really discourage the members of their congregations from buying goods that yielded so much personal satisfaction.

One item in particular drew my attention. A small teapot—no more than five inches high—told a complex tale. Decorated with a soft cream glaze, it carried a message written in brick-red lettering: "No Stamp Act." Some English entrepreneur during the 1760s—probably a clever potter from the Midlands—had apparently followed a developing political crisis in the colonies, and just in time to help the Americans protest parliamentary taxation without representation, he produced an object that spoke to me of irony and desire, of customary markets that had suddenly become dangerously politicized. For a brief moment, a delicate teapot transported many thousands of miles and sold in a local shop became a vehicle for helping provincial consumers protest the policies of the British government. It survived the violence of war and the abuses of time, reminding those who reflect on such matters today that common goods once spoke to power.

Small, brightly colored teapot produced by an enterprising English potter for colonial American consumers who were organizing resistance to parliamentary taxation. *Courtesy of the Colonial Williamsburg Foundation, Wallace Gallery, Williamsburg, Virginia.*

I

By all odds the American Revolution should be remembered as a relatively minor event in the long history of the British Empire. After all, like the insurgencies of unhappy peoples from Ireland to India, the rebellion in colonial America involved a staggering mismatch between the world's most potent military power and ordinary subjects whose ideological passions often blinded them to the harsher realities of the contest. That the story of the Revolution did not end in crushing disappointment invites modern Americans to revisit a society that so spectacularly defied experience and history. Those who celebrate their achievement might well inquire how the colonists overcame local jealousies and mutual ignorance, profound fear and clashing identities, so that on the eve of independence leaders of the rebellion could speak credibly to strangers scattered over a huge geographic territory about a common political vision.

It is easy, of course, to take popular mobilization for granted or to treat it as an almost providential occurrence. From this perspective the rising of colonial Americans—at least, in sufficient numbers to make good on their challenge to British authority—acquires an almost miraculous character. It is a narrative of freedom-loving men and women coming effortlessly together under the banner of rights, inspired at every turn by brilliant leaders of the sort the country has not seen for a very long time. Even contemporaries marveled at the level of solidarity they witnessed. As the Reverend Charles Chauncy, Boston's most respected minister, remarked in a letter addressed to the English philosopher Richard Price following the first meeting of the Continental Congress, "I cannot but look upon it [as] an occurrence in our favor truly extraordinary, that so many colonies, so distant from one another, and having each their separate interest, should unite in sending delegates to meet in one general body upon the present occasion."[1]

The Marketplace of Revolution explains popular mobilization from an entirely different point of view. In fact, it breaks with most previous accounts of this period, putting forward a new interpretation of what precisely was radical about the politics of the American Revolution. Instead of assuming the existence of political collectivities, it asks how such a dispersed population generated a sense of trust sufficient to sustain colonial rebellion. It explores how a very large number of ordinary Americans came to the striking conclusion that it was preferable to risk their lives and property against a powerful British armed force than to endure further political oppression.

Mobilization on this level did not come easy. Neither luck nor providence had much to do with the story. Over a decade of continuous experimentation, American colonists discovered a means to communicate aspirations and grievances to each other through a language of shared experience. Between 1764 and 1775, they built a sense of mutuality slowly and tentatively, and in the process of reaching out beyond familiar boundaries of class and gender, they developed radically inclusive structures of resistance. They created brilliant forms of collective and extra-legal political action, overcoming discouraging moments of alleged betrayal to bring forth an imagined national community unanticipated at the start of the revolutionary crisis.

Like revolutionaries throughout the world, they had to learn to trust each other. Simply mouthing a vocabulary of rights and freedom was not sufficient to persuade people that they could rely on others about whom they knew very little. Trust was the product of mutual education. It required the free flow of information; it could not be coerced. Although in the early days trust proved distressingly fragile, Americans persuaded themselves by 1774 that other Americans could be counted on to do what they had actually promised to do, quite simply, to make genuine sacrifices for a common cause.

Trust-building involved more than strategic considerations. As ordinary Americans affirmed their trust-worthiness through revolutionary acts that were then quickly reported in the popular press, they discovered that the language of rights and liberty was more than rhetoric. Within a framework of local groups that came to identify with similar groups in distant places, people translated personal sacrifice into revolutionary ideology. The point here is that if we begin an investigation of revolution with ideology—as many historians have done—we inevitably discount the social conditions that energized these ideas for the men and women who stood to lose the most in a conflict with Great Britain.

The purpose in concentrating attention on political mobilization is not to insist that the revolutionary generation possessed virtues demonstrably superior to our own. Of course, they did not. Ordinary people who denied the sovereignty of Parliament and who united in armed resistance against the British Empire were subject to the same doubts and failings found in most human societies, then and now. To transform the colonists into heroic figures—the kinds of patriotic characters who so often appear in the myths that modern Americans tell themselves about a revolutionary world that we have lost—really serves only to diminish their accomplishment. If it could somehow be demonstrated that these particular men and women were in touch with principles and values purer than those of our own society, they would have very little of significance to say to us. We would be reduced to Old Testament Jeremiahs, perpetually lamenting our own fall from political grace.

Analysis of the coming of independence is not a call to worship. It provides an opportunity to comprehend just how colonists who were by turns frightened, bigoted, chauvinistic, ambitious, jealous, proud, and misinformed managed to imagine a larger political community containing people whom they had never met and who at times must have seemed more foreign to their own immediate concerns than did the British. It is in the context of the messy experience of everyday life that they have something to teach a current generation which seems uncertain of its ability to construct meaningful political solidarities. From this earlier narrative of mobilization and resistance we learn something valuable about overcoming the divisions that compromise our own ability to cooperate effectively for the general political welfare, however defined.

The Marketplace of Revolution thus provides a richer intellectual understanding of the capability of ordinary men and women to reform the character of larger political structures, even ones of global dimensions. Against staggering opposition, it is still possible to come together to create powerful collectivities which might ameliorate the conditions of our shared civic lives. At the commencement of the new millennium, therefore, we return to the years before the signing of the Declaration of Independence not to reaffirm myths about national origins but rather to discover something about our own ability to transform political society through collective imagination.

II

A reinterpretation of the coming of the American Revolution must deal with timing. Although it may seem obvious, we should remember that separation from Great Britain occurred at a precise historical moment. However plausible alternative dates may appear with hindsight, it did not happen during the Glorious Revolution of 1688, or at the conclusion of the Seven Years' War in 1763, which removed forever the threat of French encroachment, or, despite the spontaneous street violence associated with the Stamp Act crisis, in 1765. No one seriously advocated independence in 1768, even though Charles Townshend's Revenue Acts provoked hostility throughout the colonies. Nor, in fact, did the Tea Act of 1773 do the trick. What may seem today as irresistible momentum carrying a colonial society toward national independence could at any moment have been halted, diverted, or thwarted. British administrators need not have pursued a policy so doggedly confrontational. By the same token, Americans from different regions could have followed separate paths, concluding, for example, that those who spoke for Boston were troublesome radicals deserving whatever punishments Parliament cared to mete out. Reminding ourselves of the contingency of events is another way of drawing attention to the force of human agency—real people making choices about the politics of empire—in shaping the flow of activities that we lump together as the coming of the American Revolution.

What gave the American Revolution distinctive shape was an earlier transformation of the Anglo-American consumer marketplace. This event, which some historians have called a "consumer revolution," commenced sometime during the middle of the eighteenth century, and as modestly wealthy families acquired ever larger quantities of British manufactures—for the most part everyday goods that made life warmer, more comfortable, more sanitary, or perhaps simply more enjoyable—the face of material culture changed dramatically.[2] Suddenly, buyers voiced concerns about color and texture, about fashion and etiquette, and about making the right choices from among an expanding number of possibilities.

This was surely not a society of self-sufficient yeomen farmers. People purchased the items they most desired at local stores; they often demanded and received liberal credit. Each year the volume of imports increased, creating by 1750 a virtual "empire of goods." England experienced the same consumer revolution as did the American colonists. But there was a major difference. In a colonial marketplace in which dependency was always an issue, imported goods had the potential to become politicized, turning familiar imported items such as cloth and tea into symbols of imperial oppression.[3] And since Americans from Savannah to Portsmouth purchased the same general range of goods, they found that they were able to communicate with each other about a common experience. Whatever their differences, they were consumers in an empire that seemed determined to compromise their rights and liberties.

The Marketplace of Revolution argues, therefore, that the colonists' shared experience as consumers provided them with the cultural resources needed to develop a bold new form of political protest. In this unprecedented context, private decisions were interpreted as political acts; consumer choices communicated personal loyalties. Goods became the foundation of trust, for one's willingness to sacrifice the pleasures of the market provided a re-markably visible and effective test of allegiance.

Before this moment, no massive political movement had organized it-self around the denial of imported goods. In other words, although it does not receive the same acclaim from historians as does the system of checks and balances put forward in the Constitution, the consumer boycott was a brilliantly original American invention. As General Thomas Gage, a British military leader who wanted to nip rebellion in the bud, exclaimed, "I never heard of a people, who by general agreement, and without sumptuary laws to force them, that ever denied themselves what their circumstances would afford, and custom and habit prompted them to desire."[4] But that is pre-cisely what the colonists did. They made goods speak to power in ways that mid-century consumers and merchants had never anticipated.

The term boycott is, of course, an anachronism, since it first came into the language during the nineteenth century in recognition of the activities of an English land agent in Ireland, Charles C. Boycott. Such considerations need not deter us. We are dealing with popular political movements that were boycotts in all but name. Within the structures of voluntary associa-tions formed to enforce non-importation of British manufactures, men and women found that they could judge for themselves whether or not other Americans were in fact fulfilling pledges of mutual support. Failure to com-ply exposed possible enemies who publicly demonstrated by their contin-ued purchase of imported goods that they could not be counted on during a crisis. A strategy of political resistance centered on the marketplace quickly transformed myriad private acts of consumption into self-conscious pub-lic declarations of resistance. The non-importation agreements through-out colonial America provided an effective means for distinguishing supporters from those people who suffered humiliation as "the friends of government." In more positive terms, one's relation to everyday goods be-came a measure of patriotism. "What is true grandeur," asked a writer in the *New-London Gazette*, "but a noble patriotic resolution of sacrificing every other consideration to the Love of our Country. And can he be a true lover of his country . . . who would be seen strutting about the streets, clad in foreign [British] fripperies, than to be nobly independent in the russet grey?"[5]

Commercial rituals of shared sacrifice provided a means to educate and energize a dispersed populace. These events helped participants dis-cover the radical political implications of their own actions, even as those same rituals demonized people who inevitably held back, uncertain and afraid, victims of new solidarities they never quite understood. Indeed, the boycott movement invited colonists traditionally excluded from formal political processes—the election of representatives to colonial assemblies, for example—to voice their opinions in a raucous, open public forum, one that defined itself around subscription lists, voluntary associations, orga-nized protests, destruction of goods, and incendiary newspaper exchanges. What we encounter in colony after colony is a radically new form of politics, a politics practiced out-of-doors, in which women and the poor experienced an exhilarating surge of empowerment. Although during the two decades following the winning of national independence—the so-called constitutional period—well-to-do leaders had second thoughts about encouraging such groups to speak out, we should appreciate the powerfully egalitarian potential of that earlier moment. The non-importers of the 1760s and 1770s were doing more than simply obstructing the flow of British-made goods. They were inviting the American people to reinvent an entire political culture.

III

The book is structured around the politicization of a consumer market-place. Chapter 1 sets forth a general argument about large-scale mobilization, the *sine qua non* of a successful rebellion. Although the analysis starts with the punch line, as it were, I aim to demonstrate not only how shared consumer experience facilitated new forms of collective political action but also why historians have so long downplayed the significance of imported goods on the eve of independence.

Part I, entitled "An Empire of Goods"—chapters 2 through 5—examines in detail different aspects of the new eighteenth-century marketplace, showing among other things how colonial Americans made sense of the flood of imports that found its way into even the most humble provincial households. What should become clear from this discussion is that a spectacularly new material culture provided a social and economic framework—a realm of intensely personal experience—in which people could work out for themselves the implications of core liberal values which we now associate with modernity.

The key element in this mid-eighteenth-century transformation might best be termed the invention of choice. This proposition may seem bizarre. After all, making choices appears to be an expression of the human condition. From a social and political perspective, however, *choice* has a legitimate history. British imports offered American colonists genuine alternatives, real possibilities to fashion themselves in innovative ways. After the 1740s they began articulating status and beauty through choice; it affected the character of relations within family and community. Even more, it introduced dynamic categories of comfort and taste into the lives of middling sorts of people, forcing them to recalculate the allocation of hard-earned family resources. In this social environment, the invitation to make choices from among competing brands, colors, and textures—decisions of great significance to the individual—held within itself the potential for a new kind of collective politics.

Part II, "A Commercial Plan of Political Salvation"—chapters 6 through 8—traces how this private world of personal choice became the foundation for new political solidarities during the decade following the Stamp Act crisis. Effective mobilization was achieved slowly, only after many disappointments and alarms over real and imagined defections. By 1774 people who had come to trust each other proclaimed their common rights and liberties. As these final chapters remind us, the American Revolution was the first large-scale political movement in recorded history to organize itself around the relation of ordinary people to manufactured consumer goods. It was an inspired strategy. Indeed, from this perspective we can see that national independence was in no small measure the consequence of widespread political resistance within a new consumer marketplace, a phenomenon that might best be described as the revolutionary politics of pursuing happiness.

THE MARKETPLACE OF REVOLUTION

1

Tale of the Hospitable Consumer: A Revolutionary Argument

Colonial rebellions throughout the modern world have been acts of shared political imagination. Unless unhappy people develop the capacity to trust other unhappy people, protest remains a local affair easily silenced by traditional authority. Usually, however, a moment arrives when large numbers of men and women realize for the first time that they enjoy the support of strangers, ordinary people much like themselves who happen to live in distant places and whom under normal circumstances they would never meet. It is an intoxicating discovery. A common language of resistance suddenly opens to those who are most vulnerable to painful retribution the possibility of creating a new community. As the conviction of solidarity grows, parochial issues and aspirations merge imperceptibly with a compelling national agenda which only a short time before may have been the dream of only a few. For many American colonists this moment occurred late in the spring of 1774.

Before the Parliament of Great Britain enacted the Boston Port Bill, Americans did not know for certain whether talk of political solidarity involved much more than statements of good intentions. However consoling such rhetoric may have been during earlier imperial clashes—during the Stamp Act resistance of 1765, for example—the situation now demanded a more tangible demonstration of support. Most people understood that failure to come together would mean that colonial Americans would find themselves in a situation much like the eighteenth-century Irish, a subjugated people within the British Empire. The destruction of tea in Boston Harbor had sparked this particular confrontation with Parliament, and while the people of Boston understood full well that the provocation would not go unpunished, they entertained hope that Parliament might show compassion. Like other colonists from Georgia to New Hampshire, they waited. Reports of the Tea Party crossed the Atlantic, king and ministers debated how best to deal with a brazen attack on private property, and in March, after months of uncertainty, the British response finally reached Massachusetts. Its severity shocked even the most sanguine colonists. Parliament closed the great port. All commerce ceased; hundreds of laborers lost their jobs.[1] Boston suddenly found itself a city under siege, seemingly alone and facing a doubtful political future.

The stunning news from England immediately raised another, even more unsettling issue. The problem was not so much occupation by the British army or the collapse of the local economy but rather the reaction of other Americans. No one in Boston could be sure that these distant strangers would in fact come to their aid. For almost a decade men and women scattered along the Atlantic coast had protested against British taxation; some had rioted, others had signed petitions, and a few had written quite eloquently about constitutional and human rights. But this time the political stakes were much higher. Colonists in Virginia and South Carolina, New York and Pennsylvania, could have labeled the citizens of Boston extremists, troublemakers, people unworthy of support at a moment when organized resistance could easily spark full-scale armed rebellion. That view of the events in Massachusetts was widespread in England. As Richard Price, a respected philosopher and friend of America, explained in his *Observations on the Nature of Civil Liberty*, parliamentary leaders believed that "the malcontents in the Colony of Massachusetts were a small party, headed by a few factious men, that the majority of the people would take the side of government as soon as they saw a force among them capable of supporting them, that, at worst, the Colonies in general would never make a common cause with this province, and that the issue would prove, in a few months, order, tranquility and submission."[2] On both sides of the Atlantic the fate of Boston became a crucial trial of American solidarity.

Within weeks of the announced retaliation, an unprecedented outpouring of public support revealed that the inhabitants of Boston need not have feared political isolation. Throughout America ordinary colonists spoke up, pledging generous assistance for a city about which they really knew very little. Connecticut farmers sent livestock to feed the poor people of Boston. The inhabitants of other Massachusetts villages, many of them obscure farming communities, pledged hard currency to assist those "who are suffering by means of the Boston Port Bill." Pennsylvania patriots promised large shipments of grain, while South Carolinians dispatched hundreds of barrels of rice. In Charleston a committee of thirteen gentlemen declared that it had begun collecting "donations for the relief of our distressed brethren in this town [Boston], now suffering for the common cause of all America, under the most cruel, arbitrary and tyrannical act of the British Parliament."[3] From Georgia to New Hampshire, towns raised money, usually through voluntary charitable subscriptions. Some efforts showed unusual imagination. A group identified in a newspaper as the "young" men of Charleston, South Carolina, proposed staging a play entitled *Busiris, King of Egypt*. The producers promised that funds gathered from the sale of tickets—small amounts of rice were accepted in lieu of cash—would go toward the relief of Boston, and advertisements assured those unfamiliar with the plot of *Busiris* that it concerned "an injured gallant people struggling against oppression, resigning their All to fortune, and wading through a dangerous bloody field in search of freedom."[4]

Enthusiastic and spontaneous declarations of solidarity often accompanied these donations. People living in distant communities who could have remained silent chose forcefully to record their conviction that Boston's adversity directly affected their own political freedom. During a meeting held on August 8, 1774, for example, the freeholders of Rowan County, North Carolina, concluded that "The Cause of the Town of Boston is the Common Cause of the American Colonies."[5] The logic of the declaration is noteworthy. The Carolina farmers assumed almost reflexively that they spoke for a national community that in fact existed only in their own imaginations; in response to British oppression they construed an America that included Boston as well as Rowan County.

Everywhere people proclaimed a shared sense of political identity, resolving, as did the freemen and inhabitants of Baltimore County, Maryland, "that the town of Boston is now suffering in the common cause of *America*."[6] The farmers of Harvard, Massachusetts, an isolated community located many miles to the west of the great port, found the pressure of the moment almost insupportable. As the Reverend Joseph Wheeler, moderator for the Harvard town meeting, recorded in the official minutes, the people regarded the Boston crisis "a matter of as interesting and important a nature when viewed in all its Consequences, not only to this Town and Province, but to America in general, and that for ages and generations to come, as ever came under the deliberation of this Town."[7] Like so many of their colonial contemporaries, the people of Harvard found themselves swept up by external events. The experience expanded their political horizons, linking local decisions for the first time not only to an imagined concept called "America in general" but also to future generations who presumably would praise Wheeler and his neighbors for their brave stand in support of Boston.

The flood of public support from so many distant places heightened Boston's resolve. Out of fear and uncertainty had come a sense of confidence about a united effort. The patriot leaders of that city had taken a huge risk when they sanctioned the destruction of the hated tea. But by August 1774 they had discovered that however great their current distress, Boston would not stand alone against the empire. "Notwithstanding all the wicked arts that have been practiced to create division and animosity among the friends of their country," declared "A Tradesman" in the *Massachusetts Spy*, "we have the happiness to see the cause of virtuous freedom, still supported by a continental unanimity. There is scarce a town or city to be found, but what feels for our distress, and is determined to assist us.—Every post who rides, and almost every gentleman who journeys hither, is loaded with such sympathizing expressions and such manly assurances, as cannot fail to inspire us with fortitude."[8] And the Reverend Charles Chauncy declared with pride, "I can't help assuring you as an evidence that the Colonies continue united in supporting the common cause, that they are almost daily sending to this town [Boston] for its relief, flour, Indian corn, beef, pork, mutton, butter, cheese, and in a word every thing necessary for the comfort as well as support of life."[9]

From a modern perspective that takes for granted the mobilization of the American people, impassioned declarations of shared political purpose come as no surprise. We know that the colonists—certainly by the summer of 1774—were on the road to national independence. Reflecting on the events of this period, John Adams declared, "Thirteen clocks were made to strike together," a sentiment that historians have repeated for a very long time.[10] Adams was not alone. Dr. David Ramsay, an officer in the Continental Army and the author of the most insightful contemporary account of the Revolution, explained in 1778, "Our enemies seemed confident of the impossibility of our union; our friends doubted it; and all indifferent persons, who judged of things present, by what has heretofore happened, considered the expectation thereof as romantick." Union was something of a miracle. Only an Enlightenment God could have brought together thirteen separate polities, "frequently quarreling about boundaries, clashing in interests, differing in policy, manners, customs, forms of government, and religion, scattered over an extensive continent, under the influence of a variety of local prejudices, jealousies, and aversions."[11] The Reverend Samuel McClintock of New Hampshire came to share this growing sense of wonder. It was truly remarkable, McClintock explained in 1784, "That people so widely separated from one another by their situation, manners, customs, and forms of government, should all at once be willing to sacrifice their private interests to the public good, and unite like a band of brothers, to make the cause of one state, and even of one town, a common cause."[12] It is precisely this kind of providential language about the construction of a shared sense of political purpose that we should resist. It suggests that the discovery of a "common cause" during the summer of 1774 was somehow inevitable, a kind of divine blessing defying close analysis.

Like the people of Boston who were none too sure about receiving aid from outside Massachusetts, we can easily put forward an alternative narrative, a seemingly counterfactual account of these years in which there seemed no possibility that thirteen separate colonial clocks could be made to strike as one. Indeed, thoughtful contemporaries on both sides of the Atlantic predicted that Americans would never unite in common cause. Not surprisingly, the men who governed the empire took a measure of comfort from such intelligence, concluding on the basis of apparently reliable testimony that profound religious, cultural, and political diversity precluded the creation of effective union. In a 1759 account of colonial society, the English traveler Andrew Burnaby rehearsed what was by then a familiar argument, dismissing out of hand suggestions that Americans might be contemplating independence from Great Britain. He specifically drew attention to "the difficulties of communication, of intercourse, [and] of correspondence," evidence which strengthened his conviction that "fire and water are not more heterogeneous than the different colonies in North America." Left to their own devices, Burnaby declared, "there would soon be a civil war, from one end of the continent to the other."[13]

Thomas Pownall, a former royal governor of Massachusetts and an astute student of political economy, shared Burnaby's general assessment of colonial society. In his widely respected *Administration of the Colonies*, originally published in 1764, Pownall explained precisely why the American people could never hope to form an independent government. Their mental horizons were too narrow, too much the product of local history and culture, for them ever to cooperate with those who happened to live in other provinces. "The different manner in which they are settled," Pownall assured readers, "the different modes under which they live, the different forms of charters, grants, and frame of government . . . will keep the several provinces and colonies perpetually independent of, and unconnected with each other, and dependent on the mother country."[14]

Americans accepted the force of this analysis. In a pamphlet intended to persuade the British government to retain Canada following the Seven Years' War, Benjamin Franklin sounded a lot like Burnaby. And well he might. At the Albany Congress of 1754 Franklin had proposed a loose confederation of mainland colonies, and to promote the spirit of cooperation, he circulated in the provincial press his famed severed-rattlesnake cartoon, which warned all Americans that they should "Join or Die." But to his immense frustration, even the threatening reptile failed to generate union. At the end of the day, not a single colony endorsed Franklin's plan to reconstitute the governance of empire. Writing in 1760 Franklin seemed to have learned from that earlier experience. The colonies, he now informed an Anglo-American audience, "have different forms of government, different laws, different interests, and some of them different religious persuasions and different manners." These conditions served powerfully to inhibit any meaningful union, even for "their common defense and security against their enemies."[15] The Reverend Ezra Stiles, future president of Yale College and an admirer of Franklin, could hardly imagine a meaningful colonial union. In his *Discourse on the Christian Union*, published in 1761, he summarily rejected the proposition that the southern colonies had much in common with their northern neighbors. "As to the three southern provinces," wrote Stiles, "their climate not suiting European constitutions, they will not figure as to numbers for perhaps yet a century or more, until the present race is hardened and get the better of a noxious region."[16] It is no wonder, then, that another of Franklin's correspondents, Dr. William Clarke of Boston, announced that the British colonies would never unite until "we are forced to it, by the Supreme Authority of the Nation," a comment that if nothing else demonstrated Clarke's failure to comprehend the futility of using state power to coerce either loyalty or identity.[17]

Long after Americans had forgotten the Albany Congress, they assumed without much debate that social diversity would overwhelm the creation of a powerful identity separate from that of Great Britain. John Adams, who later would rhapsodize about the synchronization of thirteen clocks, advanced a particularly sober assessment of the mobilization of the American people on the eve of independence. He, too, found it difficult to comprehend the mental process that had allowed virtual strangers to cooperate in a political cause. The colonists' separate histories seemed to have conspired against the formation of a new nation. The American settlers, Adams observed, had evolved quite different constitutions of government. But that was not all. Ethnicity, religion, customs, manners, and habits—all these cultural elements had set the colonists seriously at odds, and if one also took into account the rarity of "their intercourse" and their imperfect "knowledge of each other," one began to appreciate that the achievement of meaningful political solidarity "was certainly a very difficult enterprise."[18] As late as November 1774 Thomas Hutchinson—the royal governor of Massachusetts whom the Americans had forced into exile—was trying to reassure colonial administrators in Great Britain that "a union of the Colonies was utterly impracticable." Experience had taught Hutchinson that "the people were greatly divided among themselves in every colony, and that there could be no doubt that all America would *submit*, and that they *must*, and moreover would, *soon*."[19]

These commentators cannot be faulted for failing to chart accurately the course of late eighteenth-century history. They only seem deficient because we know that Americans did in fact manage to unite in precisely the manner that these men claimed impossible, creating, in the words of David Ramsay, a country "for which we would choose to live, or dare to die."[20] On the topic of social diversity, however, they were right on the mark. Americans who contributed food and currency in support of Boston in 1774 defined themselves in many different ways: as members of distinct communities, as Methodists but not as Congregationalists, as rice planters but not as growers of wheat or as producers of tobacco, as wealthy urban merchants but not as struggling rural farmers, or as persons of German or Scottish but not English heritage. The list of identities could be extended almost infinitely. Diversity characterized everyday life in all the colonies, and even in the self-contained villages of New England, a region celebrated for homogeneity, travelers frequently encountered African Americans and occasionally, in the mid-eighteenth century, Native Americans.[21]

Local perceptions powerfully shaped the colonists' views of an outside world, for, as Adams fully understood, the experience of living in a specific place—a tightly bounded little community where shared genealogies and historically sanctioned customs gave meaning to human existence—crosscut other, larger possibilities for personal identity. And so, at any given moment during the run-up to revolution, men and women were not simply Anglicans, Quakers, or Presbyterians. They were Anglicans from the Northern Neck of Virginia or New York City, the Carolina Low Country or the Maryland Eastern Shore. Colonial Presbyterians may have shared a perspective on church government, but a Presbyterian living outside Boston probably did not have a lot in common with a newly arrived Scots-Irish Presbyterian in central Pennsylvania or North Carolina. A Quaker from Rhode Island was not quite the same social being as a Quaker from Philadelphia. These competing senses of self were woven into the fabric of mid-eighteenth-century America, sometimes generating severe strains and ongoing jealousies, sometimes coexisting as people of diverse interests and backgrounds went about their normal business. It is important to remember, therefore, that the fabrication of broader forms of political identity during this period—indeed, the ability to imagine total strangers as a "band of brothers"—occurred against the background of persistent diversity. The rhetoric of common cause, however defined, had constantly to struggle against feelings of distrust and suspicion fueled by cultural and social difference.

Adams's remarks—as well as those of so many of his contemporaries—focus attention on another perplexing aspect of popular political mobilization. It happened quite swiftly. Colonists who had previously been strangers developed over a relatively short period of time—little more than a decade—a self-conscious commitment to a common cause, to a set of shared principles and strategic goals that energized resistance. Explaining the speed of the process represents a major challenge for anyone studying the coming of independence. At mid-century such unity struck bright, well-informed observers as highly improbable, even impossible. By 1774, however, the unthinkable had become reflexive, something that large numbers of Americans could imagine. By that time few questioned that the cause of Boston was genuinely the American cause. The invention of identity was a collective act of self-discovery that intensified over a decade of tumultuous confrontation with Great Britain. And although it is tempting to explain this achievement with arguments based on a shared history and environment, political mobilization on this vast scale does not seem in fact to have owed much to the formative experiences of the seventeenth-century European settlers or to the mythic qualities of the free air of the New World or to the rigorous demands of living on the frontier. The ability successfully to imagine oneself as part of a larger political community developed precisely because ordinary men and women working with the cultural resources at hand willed that community into existence.

These observations suggest that a persuasive explanation of political mobilization on the eve of the American Revolution must meet certain criteria. First, it must map out in some detail the process of political imagining that allowed strangers in Britain's mainland provinces to reach out to each other and form new collectivities.[22] Second, it must take into account the huge number of people who in one form or another participated in this movement. It may seem self-evident that political mobilization involved a large segment of the population. In point of fact, however, historians sometimes treat a few articulate colonial leaders as proxies for the mass of forgotten people who had to learn within their own little communities and extended clans the meaning of political trust. Convincing these ordinary colonists to cooperate was no easy task. Nevertheless, as we should continually remind ourselves, it was they who sustained the possibility of winning independence, and if frightened, sometimes deeply conservative men and women had not found a way to translate the experiences of family and neighborhood into a broader political context and a language of mutual responsibility, Boston would have received no meaningful assistance in its protest against the policies of Great Britain.[23] As a writer in the *South-Carolina Gazette* noted in 1770 with considerable insight: "The greatest difficulty lies, in setting a huge massy body in motion. To point out to mankind their real interest, is easy enough; but to convince them of their duty, and to persuade those who are activated by different views, and subject to different passions, to lay aside their prejudices, to give up a strong attachment to their immediate interests, and to act in mutual concert, for the good of the whole, is an arduous task."[24] Unless an interpretation of the coming of the American Revolution comprehends the political mobilization of that "huge massy body," it does not tell us very much at all.

II

These interpretive issues have, of course, received scholarly attention. The most appealing explanation for the mobilization of the American people is simply that they came to share a powerful but loosely defined bundle of ideas about liberty and property, what might best be labeled a compelling political ideology. When Parliament threatened to tax the colonists without representation, they sensed almost instinctively how to respond, and, as the familiar narrative runs, during moments of grave imperial crisis they drew upon commonly held ideas about the abuse of power and the decay of virtue to sustain popular resistance.

Recently, intellectual historians have defined the content of these popular notions with greater rigor, insisting that what was at stake in popular mobilization was not a set of everyday notions about rights and freedom but rather a complex political ideology that the colonists allegedly borrowed from eighteenth-century opposition figures in England such as John Trenchard and Thomas Gordon. Early in Sir Robert Walpole's administration—during the 1720s—these writers began warning their readers of authoritarian forces plotting to undermine Great Britain's traditional balanced constitution. Unless virtuous citizens came forward in the manner of a Cato or Cincinnatus—allegedly selfless Roman republicans—to preserve the country's ancient liberties and unless they forswore luxury and self-indulgence, rapacious ministers in the central government would surely gain total power over the people, becoming virtual tyrants. Trenchard and Gordon listed the danger signs: substitution of a standing army for local militias, state censorship of a free press, and efforts by stock-jobbers and financiers to corrupt the common good in the name of private commercial gain. This conspiratorial ideology, often labeled "republicanism" or "civic humanism," condemned liberal values frequently associated with individualism and modern capitalism, and, according to some leading historians, it provided disgruntled Americans from colonial Georgia to New Hampshire with a consistent package of "assumptions, beliefs, and ideas—the articulated world view—that lay behind the manifest events of the time."[25]

The ideological interpretation has stimulated a fruitful debate among historians of political thought, some of whom have concluded that Lockean liberalism and reformed Protestantism contributed as fully to the colonists' "articulated world view" as did the civic humanism of writers such as Trenchard and Gordon.[26] Whatever the precise character of popular political ideas may have been, the intellectual explanation for mobilization—indeed, for the creation of a broadly shared political identity—evades hard issues. It does not, for example, effectively address questions of diversity, process, or timing. As we have already noted, communication among scattered colonists developed over a period of little more than a decade. It involved imagination and mutual discovery. Only after a series of crises provoked by an increasingly aggressive Parliament did Americans manage to achieve the degree of mutual trust required to sustain a successful bid for independence.

Intellectual historians seem to take for granted a key element in popular political mobilization, an ability to reach out across boundaries of space and class to establish a larger, more formidable solidarity. Moreover, the presence of certain ideas in a society, no matter how widely or passionately held, does not necessarily generate specific forms of political resistance. It is one thing to believe that corrupt placemen controlled the British Empire and quite another to translate that conviction into a broadly shared strategy for collective protest. And finally, ideological historians tend to reify assumptions and beliefs, assigning extraordinary powers of motivation to abstract ideas without first demonstrating how these ideas provided an emotional link between the experiences of everyday life in diverse communities and families and the larger collectivity of Americans who actually achieved independence from Great Britain.[27] The goal is not to drain a popular resistance movement of intellectual content. The colonists understood why they challenged traditional authority and risked their lives. But to transform local grumbling into full-scale rebellion they had first to assure themselves that in an emergency distant strangers would come to their support. Abstract principles—the stuff of popular political ideology—made sense within a framework of trust, a vast web of assumed reciprocities that required time and patience to negotiate.

One can appreciate the appeal of the ideological interpretation. After all, studies of the material experience of everyday life in colonial America have yielded even less insight into the dynamics of political mobilization. No doubt, various free, white Americans believed that they had in some measure been wronged by economic practices that paid them less than they thought they deserved for their labor or crops. But however irritating these issues may have been, they do not appear to have shaped significantly either the character or intensity of political commitment beyond the boundaries of the local community. Loyalists and patriots came from all social and economic backgrounds.[28] What passed for class consciousness in the colonies was more likely to divide people than to generate a meaningful sense of solidarity. It is not that pocketbook concerns did not count for something in colonial America; they surely did. But they did not count for something in any systematic way. We must conclude, therefore, that it would have been very hard for Americans to have forged the kind of mutual trust that political mobilization requires solely on the basis of perceived economic grievance.

For the ordinary colonist, of course, the challenge of sorting out his or her relationship to the material culture involved more than a calculation of narrow work-related interests. Historians have begun to appreciate that during this period Americans of all sorts struggled to incorporate a flood of British manufactured goods into their daily lives. How they interpreted these artifacts—often small personal items promising beauty, comfort, and status—figures centrally in the construction of an entirely new explanation of revolutionary mobilization. What needs to be stressed at this point in the discussion of consumer politics is that the literature of material culture in colonial America tends to treat the purchase of these goods as evidence of the extension from Europe to the American mainland provinces of the conditions of a "polite" society, or as essential elements in defining new bourgeois rules of etiquette, or as aspects of a much larger story of the rise of middle-class gentility.[29]

Without question, as Americans acquired these goods, they also acquired knowledge of how polite, tasteful middle-class people in London as well as Boston, Charleston, and Philadelphia were expected to use them. We know that the rituals of self-presentation changed dramatically during the last half of the eighteenth century. The problem that these studies raise for the analysis of political mobilization is that the spread of gentility and refinement—indeed, all the major attributes of middle-class society—did not in any clear way depend on the Revolution. Even if the colonists had failed utterly in their bid for independence, they presumably would still have worried about how to appear in public without committing an embarrassing *faux pas*. From the perspective of the history of gentility, goods were largely devoid of political meaning, and efforts to link the private pleasures of possession to large-scale mobilization would seem a non-starter.[30]

III

Considering the apparent divorce between politics and material culture, it comes as something of a surprise to discover that the colonists themselves took a quite different view of the politics of the relationship. For them the goods of the new marketplace invited an imaginative response that among other things helped explain the sudden change in imperial policy that had occurred following the conclusion of the Seven Years' War. Americans spun out an inventive story that might be called the "Tale of the Hospitable Consumer." It was a profoundly anthropological project, one that effectively linked the interpretation of a new consumer marketplace to collective politics. Although the exact origins of popular explanations are difficult to isolate, we can with reasonable confidence begin the investigation of the new commercial narrative in the early 1760s. It was during this period that colonists first focused attention on why British authorities had redefined the rules that had governed the empire for as long as anyone could remember. In this context, the Sugar Act of 1764 seemed so precipitate, so destructive to the normal flow of trade, so ill-conceived that it defied easy explanation. But Americans accepted the interpretive challenge, probing connections between parliamentary oppression and the consumption of British goods.

The first version of the story appeared in Boston. Although the author of the anonymous pamphlet of 1764 entitled *Considerations upon the Act of Parliament* did not proclaim a full-blown conspiracy, he suggested that Americans themselves somehow bore responsibility for deteriorating relations with England. During the Seven Years' War, the colonists not only had lived too well but had done so too publicly. Their opulent consumption of British manufactures strongly impressed "the gentlemen of the army and others, at present and lately residing in the maritime towns." These genial outsiders learned that Americans "spend full as much [on] the luxurious British imports, as prudence will countenance, and often much more."[31]

The next year, the consumer interpretation of parliamentary taxation took on fuller definition. John Dickinson, a respected Pennsylvania lawyer, traced the imperial crisis in part to a stunning misinterpretation in Great Britain of American buying habits. "We are informed," Dickinson noted in *The Late Regulations*, "that an opinion has been industriously propagated in *Great-Britain*, that the colonies are wallowing in wealth and luxury." That conclusion, he insisted, represented a pernicious misreading of colonial culture. Whatever English scribblers might claim, the streets of America were not paved with gold, and in any case, impoverished colonists could not possibly pay new taxes. During the Seven Years' War, European visitors had witnessed an abnormally prosperous economy, artificially fueled by large military expenditures. Americans, Dickinson claimed, were ordinarily and mostly quite poor. British observers had been misled because the colonists, "having a number of strangers among us," were too generous and hospitable for their own good. The Americans had "indulged themselves in many uncommon expences." This "imprudent excess of kindness" was simply an ill-conceived attempt to impress British visitors.[32]

Like Dickinson, Benjamin Franklin could not tolerate what he came to see as gross British misrepresentations of colonial American culture. Few polemicists could match Josiah Tucker, dean of Gloucester, for his ability to irritate Franklin. Tucker achieved a modest reputation as a political economist, and although some of his writings anticipated the work of Adam Smith, he was known chiefly in America during this period as an outspoken defender of Parliament's colonial policy. In one particularly provocative piece published in 1766 entitled *A Letter from a Merchant in London to His Nephew in North America*, the dean belittled American protests against taxation without representation. "Remember, my young Man," explained Tucker's imaginary merchant, "the several Expostulations I had with your deceased Father on the prodigious Increase of American Luxury. And what was his Reply? Why, that an Increase of Luxury was an inseparable Attendant of an Increase of Riches; And that, if I expected to continue my North American Trade, I must suit my Cargo to the Taste of my Customers; and not to my own old-fashioned Notions of the Parsimony of former Days, when America was a poor Country."

The entire patronizing performance angered Franklin, who was then living in London. In the margins of his personal copy of Tucker's *Letter,* the American scribbled comments such as "This is wickedly false," "An absolute Falsehood," and "A Fib, Mr Dean." When he came to the passage abrading the colonists for high living, however, Franklin adopted a more moderate tone. "This should be a Caution to Americans how they indulge for the future in British Luxuries," he jotted on the edge of the page. "The People who have made you poor by their worthless, I mean useless Commodities, would now make you poorer by Taxing you," warned Franklin, but as he did so, he admitted that the colonists themselves bore some of the blame for Tucker's condescending analysis. After all, he concluded, echoing a central theme of the tale of the misunderstood American consumer, "The Luxury of your Tables, which could be known to the English only by your hospitable entertaining, is by these grateful Guests now made a Charge against you, & given as a Reason for taxing you."[33]

Other American writers soon took up the consumer narrative, adding innovative elements of their own. In 1768 an anonymous New York pamphleteer situated Anglo-American consumer experience within a larger historical framework. Readers of *The Power and Grandeur of Great-Britain*—one of the more impressive political discussions of this period—learned that the original New World settlers had overcome "a thousand discouragements" and only recently had managed to establish themselves as "a numerous people." Whatever hardships they endured, the struggling colonists had contributed generously to English prosperity. As loyal consumers on a distant shore, they purchased "merchandize of an almost infinite variety, numberless useful and useless articles [that] are now yearly furnished to three millions of people." The profits of this trade inevitably flowed back to England. Even during the mid-century wars against France, commercial revenues increased. For the privilege of obtaining these goods, uncomplaining colonists ransacked "the seas and the wilds of America . . . to make payment for them, and the improved lands are cultivated chiefly for the same purpose." Like other colonial authors, the New Yorker described the Seven Years' War as the crucial moment in the development of an empire of goods. In its aftermath, Britain turned the ingenuity of American consumers into a justification for parliamentary taxation, based on the reports of visitors "who saw a great display of luxury, arising from the wealth, which many had suddenly acquired during the war."[34]

At this point, the author added a sociological dimension to an evolving consumer explanation of political crisis. It was not so much that the reports of extravagant American market behavior had been erroneous. Rather, the colonists were parvenu consumers who had failed to master the etiquette of a polite society. "It is an old observation," the pamphleteer confessed, "that those who suddenly plunge into unexpected riches, in ostentation greatly exceed those who either derive them from their ancestors, or have gradually acquired them by the ordinary course of business." Contemporary imperial policy, therefore, was the product of shoddy cultural anthropology. The British refused to appreciate that, despite their superficial glamour, eighteenth-century Americans remained provincial bumpkins too poor to pay parliamentary taxes and too untutored to display their wealth tastefully.[35]

In 1768 William Hicks of Philadelphia heightened the conspiratorial element in the developing narrative. It was no accident, he announced, that ordinary English people accepted inflated estimates of colonial prosperity as truth, for, as he could testify, unnamed sources had made it their business to disseminate distorted reports of economic conditions in colonial America. Hicks protested that "the estimates of our wealth which have been received from ignorant or prejudiced persons, are, in every calculation, grossly erroneous. These misrepresentations, which have been so industriously propagated, are very possibly the offspring of political invention, as they form the best apology for imposing upon us burthens to which we are altogether unequal." This interpretive framework—what was becoming for Hicks a consumer conspiracy—carried extremely sinister implications for the colonists' happiness within a commercial empire. Boldly linking consumption and politics, Hicks asked American readers to remember exactly how Parliament had first reacted to the false reports of colonial wealth. Had that body not immediately imposed new taxes? Were not these revenue acts an ominous hint of future assaults on American rights? The plot was self-evident. The British wanted to keep the Americans poor, marginal consumers just able to pay the rising taxes but never "suffered to riot in a superfluity of wealth." Industrious colonists could surrender their dreams of the good life, in other words, their just expectations of sharing the splendid material culture of Britain. "Whatever advantages may hereafter present themselves, from an increased population, or a more extended trade," lamented Hicks, "we shall never be able to cultivate them to any valuable purpose; for, howmuch soever we may possess the ability of acquiring wealth and independence, the partial views of our selfish brethren, supported by the sovereignty of Parliament, will most effectually prevent our enjoying such invaluable acquisitions."[36]

Narratives of commercial misunderstanding—by this time a fluid assemblage of popular notions about consumption and politics—resonated through the colonial newspapers, indicating that the tale of the naively hospitable American consumer and the insensitive British visitors, of luxury and poverty in a rapidly changing provincial economy, had become a staple of popular culture on the eve of independence. Writing for the *New-London Gazette*, "Incutius Americanus" reminded readers that the Seven Years' War had been responsible for "an insatiable itch for merchandizing; and the folly and extravagance of the people in imitating the customs and dress of foreigners." Self-indulgence had been the colonists' undoing. "Our extravagant dress and luxury had this fatal effect . . . that Europeans concluded we were a people abounding with wealth, and well able to furnish largely for defraying the national debt."[37] The *Boston Evening-Post* noted that the British belief in "our being in affluent and flourishing circumstances, was grounded upon a mistake or the misrepresentation of travellers or others."[38] By 1771 the argument for disjuncture between appearance and reality had become standard fare in the colonial journals. "A Friend of the Colony of Connecticut" explained in the *New-Haven Post-Boy* that "a large consumption of unnecessary foreign articles . . . has given us the false and deceitful appearance of riches, in buildings, at our tables, and on our bodies. Which has attracted the attention if not raised the envy of our neighbors, and perhaps had its influence in making the late grievous unconstitutional revenue acts."[39]

Even as the challenge to British authority intensified and the possibility of armed conflict loomed, Americans still maintained that the imperial crisis was somehow related to their own enthusiastic participation in a new Anglo-American marketplace. One striking example appeared in 1774. The Reverend Ebenezer Baldwin of Danbury, Connecticut, published a short sermon explicitly directed to ordinary farmers living in isolated communities, who were therefore "not under the best advantages for information from the news papers and other pieces wrote upon the controversy." How had it come to pass, Baldwin asked this rural audience, that Americans were contemplating armed resistance against the British Empire? For answers one needed to look no further back in time than the Seven Years' War. "As America was much the seat of the last war," Baldwin recounted, "the troops sent here from the mother country, opened a much freer communication between Great Britain and the Colonies, [and] the state of the colonies was much more attended to in England, than it had been in times past."

Sustained contact and conversation with British visitors during this period seemed to present a real possibility for them to learn how colonial American culture actually worked. In fact, however, familiarity generated only superficial observations. The outsiders failed singularly to appreciate just how much the social dynamics of America differed from those of England. "In a country like this," Baldwin reminded the farmers, "where property is so equally divided, every one will be disposed to rival his neighbor in goodness of dress, sumptuousness of furniture, &c. All our little earnings therefore went to Britain to purchase mainly the superfluities of life." Baldwin should be credited with a highly original insight. Economic leveling in the colonies stimulated status competition; consumer goods were the primary means by which men and women sorted themselves out in an open society. "Hence the common people here make a show, much above what they do in England," Baldwin asserted. Here was the source of a profound cultural misunderstanding. "The luxury and superfluities in which even the lower ranks of people here indulge themselves," the Connecticut preacher explained, "being reported in England by the officers and soldiers upon their return, excited in the people there a very exalted idea of the riches of this country, and the abilities of the inhabitants to bear taxes. The ministry [in Great Britain] soon conceived hopes that a large revenue might be raised from America."[40] Whatever their former excesses as consumers may have been, Baldwin thought that Americans could still save the political situation. All they had to do was reform their buying habits, putting aside the imported goods that had made them seem richer than they were. The moment had arrived for the "lower ranks" of provincial society to appreciate that their private decisions in the consumer marketplace had helped to precipitate and could influence the greatest political event of their lives.

Versions of this commercial narrative enjoyed strong popular appeal even on the eve of independence. In 1774, for example, "A Citizen of Philadelphia" submitted a story of ingenuous American consumers to several urban newspapers. This form of the evolving story was both more elaborate and less sophisticated. To be sure, the writer recounted, the Seven Years' War brought British troops to America. These men had not been average soldiers, however, for, as "A Citizen" explained, the officers came from England's upper class, "many of them sons of the best families." But the tale included an innovative element. Other eminent Englishmen who might today be described as amateur anthropologists accompanied the military to the New World. It was an extraordinary group. "Gentlemen on their travels extended their routes to America," "A Citizen" assured colonial readers, "and even Peers of the realm landed on our shores." Sudden attention from such distinguished personages flattered the grateful Americans, who worked hard to make a favorable impression on their elite guests. They really outdid themselves. "A Citizen" recaptured their effusive hospitality: "We lavished the fruits of our industry, in social banquets—We displayed a parade of *wealth,* beyond the bounds of moderation and prudence; and suffered our guests to depart, with *high ideas of our riches.*" As the prodigal Americans soon learned, these socially prominent officers and gentlemen lost no time informing well-connected friends in England about the affluent consumers they had encountered in the colonies. Perhaps these reporters meant no harm; perhaps they did not consciously engage in conspiracy. There was no disputing, however, that as England "was oppressed with a heavy load of debt, ... how natural then was it for Parliament to hunt out fresh resources?"[41]

The narrative of consumer display survived the Revolution, receiving yet another reformulation in David Ramsay's *History of the American Revolution.* Published in 1789, this impressively researched account of the War for Independence strove to avoid the shrill partisan tone that marred so many early patriot histories. Like other Americans who reviewed the conflict with Great Britain, the South Carolina physician and army veteran found it difficult to understand why Parliament decided to tax the colonists in the first place. He located the answer in Britain's willingness to accept "exaggerated accounts" of the visible prosperity of the American people. "It was said," Ramsay explained, "that the American planters lived in affluence, and with inconsiderable taxes, while the inhabitants of Great-Britain were borne down." The source of this serious misunderstanding seems to have been British soldiers serving in America. "Their observations were founded on what they had seen in cities, and at a time when large sums were spent by government, in support of fleets and armies, and when American commodities were in great demand." Generous colonists spared no expense in welcoming their British allies during the long struggle against France. "To treat with attention those, who came to fight for them," Ramsay asserted, "and also to gratify their own pride, the colonists had made a parade of their riches by frequently and sumptuously entertaining the gentlemen of the British army." The failure of these strangers to comprehend the realities of everyday life in America was probably predictable. After all, these officers, "judging from what they saw, without considering the general state of the country, concurred in representing the colonists, as very able to contribute, largely, towards defraying the common expenses of the empire."[42]

What may have been the final rendering of the tale of the misunderstood consumer appeared in Jeremy Belknap's *History of New-Hampshire*. Despite its somewhat parochial title, Belknap's splendid study offered a well-researched and wide-ranging interpretation of the coming of the American Revolution. The second volume, published originally in 1791, expanded on Ramsay's account of effusive colonial hospitality during the Seven Years' War. "The military gentlemen of Britain," Belknap observed, "who had served here in the war, and on whom a profusion of grateful attention had been bestowed, carried home reports of our wealth." Although he apparently found no evidence of "Peers of the realm," Belknap insisted that the British visitors were not the only ones responsible for creating confusion in England about American affluence. Colonial travelers in Europe also bore some of the blame. "The sons of our merchants and planters, who went to England for their education," Belknap wrote, "exhibited specimens of prodigality which confirmed the idea." But however inappropriate the students' behavior may have been, the fact remained that the great contest against France had transformed the appearance of provincial society. Too many American consumers suddenly acquired too many British manufactures. "During the war," the historian concluded, "there had been a great influx of money; and at the conclusion of it, British goods were largely imported; by which means, the cash went back again with a rapid circulation."[43]

These various versions of the consumer narrative joined other more familiar, sometimes competing discourses that Americans invented to explain to themselves why relations with Great Britain had soured so suddenly. Although such other tales circulated widely throughout the colonies during this period—for example, stories of pervasive political corruption in England—this largely overlooked account of eager, misunderstood colonial consumers possesses unusual interest. It represents an imaginative, often entirely plausible response to two distinct crises in the Anglo-American world of the mid-eighteenth century. The colonists had to accommodate not only the demands of a new consumer marketplace that inundated the homes of free men and women with alluring imported manufactures, but also an aggressive Parliament that threatened to destroy a delicate commercial system that made it possible for Americans to pay for these goods.

The consumer narrative that enjoyed such popularity for over two decades effectively linked these separate challenges. For one thing, it established a shared chronology, a sense of timing that helped to explain why the American Revolution occurred at one historical moment rather than another. Commercial change accelerated during the Seven Years' War, setting the stage for a cultural misinterpretation so profound that the Americans could never again persuade Parliament that they were in fact impoverished. The account turned on the consumption of English manufactures by ordinary Americans who were overly hospitable, remarkably self-indulgent, and socially insecure. Versions of the story came from all regions of the continent, from different classes and backgrounds, from people who seemed in retrospect to have felt a little guilty that their own excesses had broadcast such confusing signals. The narrative of consumer life insisted that it was not the goods themselves that undermined American liberty but rather their misuse; not the acquisition but the vulgarity. And most important, it suggests how for the members of a revolutionary generation the experience of participating in an exciting new material culture may have been connected to political mobilization.

It is not surprising that references to the hospitable consumer quickly disappeared from popular accounts of the coming of the American Revolution. An event so fundamental to how the people of a struggling new republic defined themselves as a culture and society seemed to require heroic explanations that stressed the colonists' deep commitment to principle, God's special affection for the new nation, and the remarkable capacity of democratic institutions to protect individual rights and liberties. During the nineteenth century, these various interpretive strands were woven into a compelling patriotic interpretation of national independence. Stories of colonial consumers falling all over themselves in an effort to impress upper-class visitors from Great Britain flew in the face of the egalitarian rhetoric that in Jacksonian America heralded the arrival of the common man.

The overly eager colonial consumer went missing from the pages of history for other reasons. The dominant figure in this particular narrative ran afoul of an even more compelling mythology. The self-sufficient farmer is a romantic character that still exercises great influence over how Americans distinguish themselves from the members of other cultures, presumably those less committed to free enterprise and individualism. Although Thomas Jefferson was surely not the first writer to champion the self-sufficient yeoman, he gave this legendary cultivator a powerful boost, and as Americans enshrined the small independent agrarian—a virtuous freeholder who stood apart from the allegedly corrupting influence of commercial capitalism—the notion of revolutionary consumers as somehow centrally involved in the protests against British rule must have seemed increasingly bizarre. In more recent times, the concept of self-sufficiency has attracted ideological support, from the right as well as the left, with some commentators extravagantly praising economic self-sufficiency and others labeling consumption a vacuous, wasteful activity that somehow embodies the more objectionable features of modern capitalism. Neither perspective has much tolerance for eighteenth-century colonists who shamelessly lived beyond their means.[44]

Although economic historians have not celebrated the myth of self-sufficiency, they too have made it even harder to appreciate the social and political importance of consumption in the period before the Revolution. For a long time scholars in this field concentrated almost wholly on problems associated with production. The organization and recruitment of a colonial labor force, the rates of return on capital, and the costs of disposing American exports on a world market have seemed far more enticing than has the merchandising of European goods in the New World. The so-called staple model reflects this interpretive prejudice. It currently provides the most sophisticated framework for analyzing how eighteenth-century Americans situated themselves in a world export market, showing among other things how they calculated profits and losses within a commercial system designed fundamentally to supply European buyers with staples such as tobacco, rice, and naval stores.[45]

Only within the last several decades have economic historians begun to take more seriously the significance of the growing demand for manufactured goods not only in defining broad market relations but also in providing powerful incentives for increasing worker productivity. They have established that even eighteenth-century households enjoying modest income levels apparently found ways to purchase new articles. As Jan de Vries, a leading economic historian, was able to document persuasively, in early modern Europe demand for these goods stimulated supply, and peasant behavior suggests that willingness to work harder was a function of personal desire. Ordinary men and women decided to participate aggressively in an economic system that suddenly offered them—and not just a few aristocratic buyers—the pleasures of a richer material culture. Indeed, according to de Vries, production strategies were "integrally related to consumption decisions."[46] Agricultural families in the Netherlands and England responded creatively to opportunities presented by an expanding system of exchange, adding, whenever possible, "new goods to their range of consumption."[47]

American historians have come to similar conclusions about the character of the eighteenth-century economy. Like their counterparts in Europe, colonial farmers and planters seem to have accommodated themselves as quickly as possible to the imperatives of a burgeoning world market that offered a broad range of consumer goods in exchange for agricultural surplus. After surveying the colonial marketplace of the eighteenth century, economic historians John McCusker and Russell Menard concluded, "The colonial populace participated in the economy by both producing and consuming, by getting *and* spending."[48] To describe this complex international system as "pre-industrial"—as critics of modern capitalism have done—only compounds the general interpretive confusion. The term is not meant to point out the obvious absence of factories in colonial America but rather to convince modern readers that pre-industrial Americans somehow resisted the encroachment of commercial capitalism and, in the process, managed to preserve a system of communal values fundamentally at odds with economic individualism. The merits of this proposition will be considered in another section. It is sufficient here simply to observe that pre-industrial economies are not usually associated with large-scale consumption.

And finally, we must remind ourselves that focus on production at the expense of consumption raises an additional problem for the study of political mobilization. Within colonial American society, production was inevitably a divisive category. Each staple had its own calendar, its own marketing system, its own technical vocabulary, and its own way of organizing labor.[49] Separate work experiences reinforced local cultural difference, and if, for example, the American Revolution had depended on the ability of the great planters of the Chesapeake colonies to communicate with New England husbandmen about difficulties of marketing tobacco, or on discussions between Carolina rice planters and Pennsylvania wheat farmers about the morality of unfree labor, it is unlikely that independence would ever have been achieved, at least not in the unified form that we have come to take for granted.

IV

Reflections on "getting *and* spending" in late colonial America encourage a quite different interpretation of the "Tale of the Hospitable Consumer." The provincials who so generously entertained British visitors during the Seven Years' War made a strikingly original contribution to the history of organized political protest. Everyone who has studied the American Revolution knows something about the destruction of tea in Boston Harbor. But general accounts of the coming of independence often ignore the massive non-importation movement that had commenced a decade earlier and had gradually broadened and intensified, so that by 1773 the experience of being a consumer in Britain's great empire of goods provided a powerful link between everyday life and political mobilization. Later Americans who translated republican theory into a viable constitutional government usually receive high marks for political invention. And well they should. The so-called Founding Fathers not only put republican government on a firm footing—something that classical theorists had thought impossible—but also brilliantly recast an ancient debate about the balance of power. But the colonists who are the object of our attention deserve similar credit for advancing a genuinely innovative strategy for promoting communication and mutual trust among so many persons of different regions and backgrounds. Although a few isolated boycotts may have taken place in other countries before this period, the Americans were the first to appreciate the extraordinary capacity of ordinary consumer goods—in this case, durables and semi-durables—to bring strangers together in common cause. It was a spectacularly successful new form of political action. The colonists' creative political engagement with commercial capitalism made the American Revolution a truly modern event.

Consumer protest swept colonial society in three waves, each crest breaking with greater force. Americans first employed non-importation to oppose the Stamp Act during the winter of 1765–66. Since the British quickly retreated from this form of taxation, the colonists did not have sufficient time to organize a large-scale boycott, and as a result of inexperience and unreliable communication, the initial early effort to politicize the marketplace seemed somewhat tentative, a number of local experiments rather than an example of coordinated resistance. The strategy had much to recommend it, however, and few doubted that if the British again taxed the colonists without representation, Americans would disrupt the flow of commerce. The second major imperial crisis arrived sooner than most contemporaries anticipated. Passage of the so-called Townshend Acts in 1767 sparked enthusiastic renewal of non-importation, as colonists from Boston to Charleston intensified pressure on local merchants to close the American market to British exports. Although the boycott did not operate as effectively as many participants had hoped, it successfully mobilized large numbers of ordinary consumers in a popular movement that expanded their political horizons.

In 1770 Britain's rulers tried once again to mollify the colonists. With repeal of most Townshend duties, the entire American boycott lost momentum, and for a brief moment it appeared as if cooler heads on both sides of the Atlantic would prevail. Tranquility was short-lived. The Tea Act of 1773 again focused American attention on the politics of consumption, and during this final phase of non-violent protest ever larger numbers of colonists expressed their political solidarity with other Americans by rejecting British goods. By this time, they fully understood what Samuel Adams meant when he warned the Virginian Arthur Lee that the cause of liberty depended on the ability of the American people to free themselves from "the Baubles of Britain."[50]

Over a decade of ever more serious confrontations with Parliament, the boycott had become the distinguishing mark of colonial protest, what cultural anthropologists would call its signature. Within this provincial society a consumer market defined political resistance. The protests of 1774, however, differed strikingly from those of the Stamp Act period. The early boycotts demanded the *non-importation* of common consumer articles. During this phase, the colonists put pressure on local merchants to proscribe the sale of British exports, to keep the desired goods off the streets, as it were. But following the closing of Boston Harbor, ordinary Americans realized that they could not safely delegate the policing of the marketplace to a professional group whose very livelihood depended on continued consumption. During the final months before the battles of Lexington and Concord, *non-consumption* replaced non-importation, and revolutionary consumers took charge of their own market behavior.

The centrality of the boycott to the coming of the American Revolution should put to rest lingering doubts about late colonial self-sufficiency. Only a people thoroughly involved in a complex market economy could possibly have appreciated the capacity of consumer goods to mobilize strangers in political protest. Appeals for non-importation certainly did not represent a rejection of eighteenth-century commercial capitalism. Indeed, even as they organized ever more effective boycotts of British goods, colonists called for investment in American manufacturing. They wanted the "Baubles" that made daily life more comfortable. The problem, alas, was that the best, most desirable items came from Great Britain, and their purchase carried heavy political burdens in the form of unconstitutional taxes and regulations.

V

In the absence of consumer desire, rejection of British goods would have had no political sting. The boycotts worked so effectively as a vehicle for large-scale mobilization precisely because they linked two separate eighteenth-century revolutions, one economic, the other political.[51] The first of these predated the clash with Parliament by at least three decades. Importation of British manufactures took off sometime during the 1740s. The alluring marketplace for cloth, ceramics, and metal goods presented colonists with an unprecedented range of choices. The process of self-fashioning suddenly became more challenging as Americans selected from among competing colors, textures, and weights. Shopkeepers offered easy credit, and eager consumers took the bait. In fact, however bitterly Americans complained about the alleged misrepresentation of their buying habits, it seems likely that the British visitors during the Seven Years' War accurately described the material culture that they had encountered in the New World. The boycott movement presupposed this broad experience of defining self within a social environment of accelerating consumption.

Growing reliance on imported consumer goods at mid-century heightened the colonists' shared sense of identity with Great Britain. They had many reasons, of course, to celebrate their Britishness, not the least of which was Britain's military successes against the French. Historians sometimes describe these eighteenth-century expressions of provincial loyalty as "colonial nationalism" or as "British nationalism."[52] Within this mental framework American farmers and planters could claim a limited measure of legislative autonomy without thereby threatening their standing within the larger imperial structure. To be sure, personal relations within small communities remained the primary source of social meaning for most colonists. But beyond the local level, Americans generally subscribed to what might be called a semiotic order of empire, a system of political symbols that included the Hanoverian monarchy, the balanced constitution, and the common law. Indeed, it was possible for mid-eighteenth-century Americans to imagine themselves in a genuine partnership with England that provided all subjects with commercial prosperity, military security, and individual liberty.[53] For ordinary people, the palpable experience of participating in an expanding Anglo-American consumer market bolstered these often inchoate feelings of identity. Even colonists of modest means copied British fashions, following as best they could at a distance of several thousand miles what the people of London were currently acquiring.

Nothing about the colonial American experience with British exports distinguished it at mid-century significantly from that of Scotland or Ireland, parts of the British Empire that participated just as enthusiastically in the new consumer market. The Scots provide a particularly instructive comparison on how an economically and politically dependent people accommodated themselves to a sudden flood of English manufactured goods. Like some Americans discussed later in this volume, Scottish writers initially greeted the explosion of consumer opportunities with dismay. William Mackintosh remembered, for example, that at the beginning of the century a visit to a friend's house early in the day would result in an offer of a "Morning Drought." But by 1729 expectations and customs had changed, and Mackintosh, who obviously enjoyed a good whiskey, lamented, "I am now ask'd if I have yet had my Tea." It was not unusual for members of his generation to blame such silliness on the Union of 1707, which had promised general commercial prosperity in exchange for the surrender of national sovereignty.[54]

But others, including most of the brilliant political economists identified with the Scottish Enlightenment, viewed the challenge of the consumer marketplace more positively. They wove material progress into a four-stage evolutionary theory that explained the development of modern society from the dawn of time to the modern commercial age. Rather than rejecting the new consumer goods, they associated them with the rise of civility and politeness, key indices of human advancement. As one historian of eighteenth-century Scotland observed, "It was the historic achievement of the Scots to have created a philosophical and literary culture of great complexity which was designed to explain the metaphysical, moral, political, religious and historical foundations on which commercial civilization itself was founded and would teach men and women how to live virtuous and happy lives."[55] Abundant English goods sparked in Scotland a "revolution in manners" rather than political upheaval, and instead of resisting commercial intrusion, enterprising landowners and improving lairds tried to increase agricultural productivity so that they could more readily participate in the world of English fashion.[56] Consumer goods also transformed the material culture of Ascendancy Ireland, where per capita consumption rose at least 50 percent during the eighteenth century. Jonathan Swift and other so-called Irish patriots railed against public displays of imported luxury items, which they attributed largely to "Irish women," but however much English manufactures made the Protestants of Ireland love what they "ought to hate," these goods only occasionally acquired symbolic importance in Irish opposition to London's firm political hand.[57]

Colonial Americans took a different course. Indeed, during the 1760s and 1770s something unprecedented occurred in Britain's mainland colonies. In response to parliamentary taxation, Americans managed to politicize common consumer goods and, by so doing, suddenly invested manufactured items with radically new symbolic meaning. Had it not been for a crisis in the imperial constitution, the story of American consumer experience could well have paralleled Scotland's, becoming little more than a narrative of manners and politeness. In this particular provincial setting, however, the very commodities that were everywhere beginning to transform traditional social relations provided a language for popular political resistance. British imports became political emblems, markers of semiotic change.[58] As an anonymous South Carolina writer recounted in 1769, Americans had once looked upon Great Britain as the source of valued manufactured goods, and because of this historic connection they called England "by the endearing epithet, mother." During that earlier period of mutual respect and cooperation, "we went to the merchants' stores with pleasure, and purchased there the manufactures of Great-Britain, with no grudging hand," but unhappily Parliament had chosen to disrupt the era of good feelings, and "now, we look upon her wares, in a manner as poison to us . . . [which] must be used very sparingly, and with the utmost caution.[59] Such a profound shift in the perception of everyday material culture—an entire visual environment of transformed meanings—served in the words of one economist to awake "the public citizen who slumbers within the private consumer."[60]

It is important to establish that we are documenting a key moment in the history of liberal thought. Within the framework of the new consumer market, Americans worked out a genuinely radical political ideology, an achievement for which they seldom receive proper credit. They managed to situate a complex discourse about rights and liberties, virtue and power, within a familiar material culture. The goods themselves did not generate these ideas. Concepts long associated with John Locke and his many students were already present in this provincial society, the product of local histories and intellectual borrowing, and by the 1760s colonists everywhere took for granted certain assumptions about constitutional government, common law, and the contractual origins of social and political authority. What they did not know, however, was whether other Americans shared these beliefs or, if they professed to do so, shared them with the same sincerity. This element of doubt might be called the problem of the distant stranger.[61] One knows the person is out there, but not whether he or she shares a bundle of core values passionately enough to be counted as an ally.

The point is that the successful mobilization of ordinary people required communication of conviction, a credible means of voicing the intensity of personal commitment. In this context, the language and experience of the consumer marketplace helped strangers persuade each other—and perhaps themselves as well—that they were worthy of trust.[62] Indeed, Americans found that they had repeatedly to demonstrate ideological zeal through organized public sacrifice, through the denial of the "Baubles of Britain." By transmitting news of local boycotts to distant colonists, they proved themselves true patriots, "Sons of Liberty," and plausible members of a larger imagined community. As in religious structures, participation in public rituals could be interpreted and communicated as authentic evidence of belief. This close connection between ideology and the forms of protest, between interpretation and strategies of resistance, helps explain why leaders of a colonial rebellion insisted that patriotism required the rejection of British imports. Action had to accompany principle. It is not hard to find examples of Americans grounding political ideas in the rhetoric of consumer sacrifice. In a speech published in 1774, the South Carolinian Christopher Gadsden drew attention to a powerful emotional link between ideology and behavior. The people of South Carolina—and those in other colonies who happened to read Gadsden's printed text in the newspapers—claimed that they loved freedom. But how much? How intense was their commitment? Would they be willing in order to advance the liberty of other Americans whom they had never met to "forego the elegancies and luxuries of life" if by so doing they liberated "posterity" from political slavery "to the end of time?" Like other Americans of his generation, Gadsden declared it self-evident that "a non-importation agreement will . . . prove a means of restoring our liberty."[63]

The rituals of non-consumption did more than simply transmit from region to region, city to city, the seal of ideological conviction. They radicalized American political culture on the eve of independence in ways that no one at the time could have foreseen. The unintended results of the boycotts were perhaps more significant—and the least appreciated aspect of consumer mobilization. Colonial politics had long been an aspect of public life restricted to white male property owners, and although this group of potential voters was surprisingly large by contemporary European standards, it represented at mid-century only a fraction of the free adult population. Moreover, before the Revolution, no one seriously advocated a more open and inclusive system.[64] The boycott movement, however, shifted the basis of political participation, not in legislative elections or in choosing town officials but rather in the extra-legal structures established throughout America to discourage the purchase of British manufactures.

In this extraordinary political environment it quickly became apparent that if efforts to restrict the sale of imported goods were to have any chance of success, they would need the support of *all* consumers, women as well as men, poorer sorts as well as wealthy lawyers and merchants. Focusing attention almost exclusively on formal electoral politics, on the response of the various colonial legislatures to the demands of royal governors and British administrators, for example, obscures the development of a new kind of popular politics, one that encouraged ordinary consumers—precisely because they were consumers—to take a public stand on the most pressing issues of the day.

The Anglo-American consumer economy of the eighteenth century was in many ways strikingly egalitarian. Anyone with money could purchase what he or she desired. From the very beginning, women played a central role in the expansive world of goods, and after 1764 it became absolutely essential to enlist their enthusiastic participation in the boycotts. To be sure, market sacrifice was more difficult for women than for men. As wives and mothers, they had families to clothe and not a lot of free time to devote to spinning and weaving. It was certainly much easier for them to purchase imported British fabric from the local shopkeepers. Whatever inconvenience the non-importation movement may have presented, however, the invitation to redefine private household decisions as public political acts seemed an exciting prospect for women of all classes and backgrounds. They sensed that they had gained a measure of real power in the public sphere. As three women writing in the *Boston Gazette* in 1767 observed, the traditional rhetoric of politics had changed, "The Ladies of America having been diverse Times addressed as Persons of Consequence, in the present œconomical Regulations."[65]

The creation of so many committees to enforce the boycotts also raised hard questions about the constitution of political authority in a liberal society. These were for the most part voluntary bodies functioning outside the structures of formal government, and during the early stages of the protest against parliamentary taxation the colonists expected the merchant community to organize the non-importation effort. By the late 1760s, however, ordinary men and women were taking a more active role in controlling the consumer market, and as they came forward in ever larger numbers they triggered a far-reaching debate about democratic procedure. How could a movement that claimed to speak for the "people" demonstrate persuasively that it did in fact enjoy popular support? Elections sponsored by colonial officials were out of the question. Crown appointees would never have sanctioned such potentially treasonable organizations.

The answer turned out to be the simple but ultimately deeply radical act of signing subscription rolls. Signing one's name to subscription lists was not in itself a new phenomenon; documents of this sort had a long history in England and colonial America. In this context, however, expressions of support for economic resistance of British policy amounted to a plebiscite, a bold, even courageous recording of the popular will. People who were ineligible to vote in colony elections affixed their names and marks on papers carried from house to house or posted in public gathering places. Numbers, of course, mattered, for the lists of signatures collected in Charleston, New York, and Boston legitimated the rhetoric of protest leaders who insisted that they spoke for the "people." As anyone who has ever signed a petition knows, adding one's name to a list that will be scrutinized by friends and neighbors is not an act lightly taken. Indeed, it amounts to a declaration of ideological commitment, and for ordinary people, who were seldom asked to sign political documents, participation in the subscription drives—in communal pledges of self-denial—facilitated the transition from private unhappiness to public resistance. With a stroke of the pen they exchanged the comfort of anonymity for identification with the common good.

After 1773 such lists circulated in small country towns and at rural county courthouses, as new converts joined the boycott movement in the name of the rights and liberties of the American people. Their decision to sign a piece of paper gave the non-consumption movement a transforming force that no one could have predicted during the Stamp Act crisis. Signers became enforcers, and the first major order of the Continental Congress of 1774 was the establishment of the Association, a huge network of local committees charged with halting once and for all the purchase of England's "Baubles." Comparisons with other eighteenth-century revolutions immediately suggest themselves. Citizen groups in America did not assassinate prominent loyalists. Nor did they incite angry farmers to destroy the homes of the ruling gentry. In this distinctively bourgeois rebellion, the ideological police ferreted out hidden canisters of tea and suspicious pieces of cloth.

Out of these collective experiences colonial Americans forged new political identities. The process was always about to come undone, but the people who joined the boycott movement gradually expanded their personal horizons. In the rhetoric accompanying non-importation, one encounters ever bolder self-descriptions as organizers and participants addressed their "Brethren of the Continent" and announced in local statements that they spoke in the authentic "voice of all America" or for the "whole body of the people." If these sentiments were not yet the stuff of full-blown nationalism, they forcefully reveal that the process of mobilization involved a rethinking of political self-identity, something that occurred well before the winning of national independence.[66] Put another way, the spirit of nationalism was as much a cause as a result of revolution.

By the same token, the discovery of solidarity and the fabrication of mutual trust created deep divisions as former friends and neighbors who refused to aid the boycotts and who thereby exposed their ideological unsoundness found themselves reviled in public as "enemies of America." The formation of a larger imagined community forced men and women to draw boundaries, to construct mechanisms capable of distinguishing them from those who were not full members of the new community, and in this painful sorting out of us and them, a person's relation to the imported consumer goods determined where others marked the line of exclusion. By 1773 the mere possession of British imports signaled possible disloyalty to the common cause. As one writer who called himself "A Consistent Patriot" explained in the *Massachusetts Spy,* "The importation and use of Tea, abstractedly considered, may be innocent; and he who in ordinary times, has an inclination to import or use it, has a right to the protection of the laws." But, of course, no one considered consumption abstractly. Only enemies of the people now used tea, for "when the importation is connected with the ruin of government, its trade—and what is infinitely more valuable, its liberty;—when it is designed for that purpose and will infallibly have that effect, we ought to consider and treat it as we would THE PLAGUE."[67]

VI

An argument about popular mobilization on the eve of independence raises an obvious question about method, about a plan of attack. Where exactly does one look for revolution? For radical politics? What counts for evidence? These are issues of some importance since this book explores the everyday experiences of ordinary people—the kinds of men and women who joined in revolutionary protests—during a period of accelerating social and economic change. It focuses on how these Americans struggled first to comprehend a consumer-oriented market and then, during the 1760s and 1770s, to resist the powerful empire that for half a century had brought beauty and comfort, pleasure and convenience, into their lives. Although the "Tale of the Hospitable Consumer" includes the testimony of wealthy and privileged persons, it concerns itself for the most part with persons of more modest means who were caught up in two separate revolutions, one commercial, the other political.

This interpretation of the coming of the American Revolution owes less to modern theorists than to Samuel Johnson, the famed eighteenth-century writer who on a journey to the Western Islands of Scotland asked how largely invisible men and women on the margins of empire made sense of their lives. How, in fact, did they participate in history? His reflections were as relevant for the American colonists as for the Scottish crofters. "It must be remembered," Johnson observed, "that life consists not of a series of illustrious actions, or elegant enjoyments." For most people, the challenge of surviving from day to day was more difficult, more problematic, a seizing of little joys along the way. "The greater part of our time passes in compliance with necessities," he reflected, "in the performance of daily duties, in the removal of small inconveniences, in the procurement of petty pleasures." Indeed, such prosaic activities suggested to Johnson a generalization about human society: "The true state of every nation is the state of common life." Although Johnson expressed only passing interest in American affairs, he understood that those who fail to take proper account of the "small inconveniences" and "petty pleasures" of life can never persuasively explain great events.

> The manners of a people are not to be found in the schools of learning, or the palaces of greatness, where the national character is obscured or obliterated by travel or instruction, by philosophy or vanity; nor is public happiness to be estimated by the assemblies of the gay, or the banquets of the rich. The great mass of nations is neither rich nor gay: they whose aggregate constitutes the people, are found in the streets, and the villages, in the shops and farms.[68]

Where best to locate the "true state of common life" has, of course, presented historians of the American Revolution with a difficult problem. Much of what we have learned about the imperial crisis and the colonists' reaction to it comes from carefully crafted pamphlets that learned men, many of them lawyers, prepared in defense of American rights and liberties. These rich discussions of constitutional law, republican theory, and ancient history—together with the scores of sermons that have survived—provide useful insights into the various strands of political ideology that colonial writers wove together in coherent explanations of why the British Parliament at this particular moment in time decided to oppress the American people by taxing them without consent. But as valuable as these formal essays may be in reconstructing assumptions about law and power, they seldom spoke directly to the everyday experiences of colonists in local communities, in other words, to ordinary men and women for whom political mobilization meant linking consumption to resistance and who often in a messy, provisional way worked out the implications of their political ideas within the context of heated debates over non-importation.

These creative conversations about trust and identity took place largely in the colonial newspapers. Anonymous contributors to the weekly journals engaged each other as well as their many readers in far-reaching discussions about political mobilization in the marketplace. The papers captured the tensions and uncertainties of the day. Angry letters condemning luxury and debt often appeared next to alluring advertisements for the latest British goods. Appeals for ever more rigorous local enforcement of the boycott frequently accompanied reports of the failure of other colonists to hold the line against importation. It was in this popular forum that Americans most passionately stated their expectations, shared doubts and fears, and called upon all consumers to demonstrate true political virtue by denying themselves the "Baubles of Britain." The arguments were not aimed at a professional class or at university graduates. The target audience was always that large group of Americans who wanted material pleasure as well as political rights and who struggled as long as they could to have both. As Silas Deane of Connecticut wrote in 1776, almost all free colonists had "some Education," and even "the very poorest" consulted "Gazettes & political publications, which they read, observe upon and debate in a Circle of their Neighbors."[69] During this period Isaiah Thomas, editor of the *Massachusetts Spy*, learned a lesson about reaching the people who one day would fight the British: "Common sense in common language is necessary to influence one class of citizens, as much as learning and elegance of composition are to produce an effect upon another."[70] Like other American editors with newspapers to sell, Thomas put his money on the appeal of common sense.

VII

The next section of this book, "An Empire of Goods," sets the stage for the revolutionary boycotts, reviewing in Chapter 2 the various kinds of evidence that document the huge quantities of British imports that suddenly inundated American ports sometime after 1740. Chapter 3 shows how imperial policy makers and British writers on trade tried to make sense of this vast consumer market. An unintended result of this popular commercial literature was a growing conviction throughout the colonies that the Americans actually sustained British prosperity, indeed, that without their continuing purchases the English economy would suffer grievous harm. Chapter 4 takes a close look at the marketing of consumer goods, a complex system linking British manufacturers to colonial buyers. Bold new forms of advertising and generous access to credit energized this remarkable merchandising network. The final chapter in this section probes cultural meanings in the American colonies, arguing that the availability of so many British imports profoundly influenced ongoing debates about morality and gender, about luxury and class, and, most significant, about the importance of allowing people to make whatever choices happened to strike their fancy.

What we encounter long before Thomas Jefferson penned the Declaration of Independence is ordinary Americans busily pursuing happiness, a personal quest for comfort and pleasure that assumed that all free colonists had a right to spend their money however they pleased. As one New England writer explained in a passage comparing religion and consumption at mid-century—a statement that reflects the kind of popular thinking that Isaiah Thomas came to see as "common sense"—"Religion, like Trade, ought to be free. It is best dealing at an open market; by that means we have a more reasonable choice, and at a more reasonable rate. . . . Why should not every man chuse for himself in spirituals, as well as in temporals, and buy those wares he likes best, or thinks he has most need of, seeing he must pay for them."[71] Only with hindsight can we appreciate that this private world of consumer desire held within itself the potential to redefine popular politics.

Part One

An Empire of Goods

2

Inventories of Desire:
The Evidence

An interpretive journey to the frontiers of the empire of goods might best begin by joining Dr. Alexander Hamilton on a personal adventure that started inauspiciously on May 30, 1744. That particular day was so inclement that Hamilton and his African American slave Dromo elected to take the Patapscoe road out of Annapolis rather than to risk crossing the Chesapeake Bay by boat. The weather as well as their spirits improved as they made their way north. The tour eventually carried the two men as far as Maine, then still a part of Massachusetts Bay. Hamilton, a Scottish-born physician in his early thirties and no relation to the more famous secretary of the Treasury, claimed that he traveled "for health and recreation."

Hamilton kept a journal—entitled the *Itinerarium*—in which he recorded impressions of the ordinary and not so ordinary Americans encountered along the colonial roads. Other British gentlemen of the period produced similar works—Samuel Johnson's account of the Scottish Highlands, for example—and like these eighteenth-century imperial writers, Hamilton wanted to entertain as well as to inform, blending erudition and wit in a manuscript designed ultimately to win the admiration of readers

Mid-eighteenth-century self-caricature of Dr. Alexander Hamilton. He commented extensively—usually, negatively—on the manners of colonial Americans he encountered on his travels. *Courtesy of the Maryland Historical Society, Baltimore, Maryland.*

of his own class and background. Most entries in the *Itinerarium* ridiculed well-meaning provincials who seemed intent on dazzling Hamilton with their learning or converting him to evangelical Protestantism. The doctor pronounced the learning shallow, the religion repugnant. Only an occasional exchange with cultivated men and women in Boston, Philadelphia, and New York saved the enterprise from utter disaster.

After staying some days in New York City, Hamilton and a new acquaintance, the Reverend John Milne of New Jersey, decided that they would like to see Albany. The two men engaged a sailing vessel for the voyage up the Hudson River. Unhappily for them, they had to share quarters with a group of hard-drinking Dutch speakers who seemed not the least impressed by the accomplishments of the Scottish physician. On June 23, contrary winds forced the little ship to drop anchor, and since spending any more time with the Dutch passengers was more than Hamilton and Milne could endure, they went ashore "near a small log cottage on the west side of the river inhabited by one Stanespring and his family."

The travelers did not quite know what to make of Stanespring's world. The seven children who rushed out to greet the strangers initially seemed "wild and rustick." Hamilton claimed that it was the sight of his "laced hat and sword" that eventually quieted these ill-mannered boys and girls. What other family members made of the self-styled aristocrat and his clerical friend is not clear. They apparently believed that proper gentlemen might enjoy a basket of fresh blackberries. It may have been while the Stanesprings were out gathering fruit that the visitors decided to assess the quality of material life on this frontier farm. Like early-twentieth-century anthropologists, they supposed that they had discovered a primitive, even Edenic culture.

What they found in the "small log cabin" disturbed the two men. The consumer market had already violated paradise. Milne pointed out that these poor people living on the edge of civilization "showed an inclination to finery." Indeed, as he explored the house, he kept discovering "superfluous things." The New Jersey minister expressed surprise at a "looking glass with a painted frame." And then, as they poked among the family's belongings, other tell-tale signs of a weakness for luxury drew the visitors' attention: "half a dozen pewter spoons and as many plates, old and wore out but bright and clean, a set of stone [stoneware] tea dishes, and a tea pot." Such goods, Milne announced, were not only superfluous but also "too splendid for such a cottage."

In case Hamilton did not understand just where the Stanesprings had gone wrong, Milne launched into a short lecture on practical morality, sounding much like other mid-century well-to-do Americans who railed against other people's alleged luxury.[1] The hospitable husband and wife, he explained, ought immediately to sell the offending articles and from the money they received should "buy wool to make yarn." One suspects that Milne was reacting to the Stanespring children, who must have appeared before the inquisitive strangers in garments made of imported British fabric. As for the mirror, "a little water in a wooden pail might serve." The family could certainly do without the pewter spoons and ceramic plates, for "wooden plates and spoons would be as good for use and, when clean, would be almost as ornamental." The "tea equipage" had no place in this humble household. Milne allowed only one concession to a consumer market. The Stanesprings owned a musket, which as any sensible person knew "was as usefull a piece of furniture as any in the cottage." In a show of provincial *noblesse oblige* Hamilton and Milne distributed "a handful of copper halfpence" among the children. The visitors also bought a pail of milk, which they carried back to the boat, an incidental purchase that surely helped fund another trip to the local store.[2]

What is most curious about the tone of the Reverend Mr. Milne's analysis is how modern it sounds. Historians today sometimes seem surprised—occasionally disappointed—when they encounter eighteenth-century colonists buying painted mirrors, pewter spoons, and colorful stoneware, not to mention the combs and ribbons that Milne would no doubt have uncovered had he probed the Stanesprings' household more thoroughly.[3] As we look over his shoulder, we find ourselves trying to make sense of the family's behavior. Were they exceptional? Perhaps most American farmers of the period really did make do with wooden plates and wooden pails full of water. Without condemning the search for greater material comfort, we might ask how many British imports actually reached colonial Americans before the Revolution.

Evidence of consumer behavior falls into six major categories. First, travelers and government officials described the colonists' changing market behavior. The value of these reports should be obvious. It would be hard to make a case for the existence of a new consumer culture without showing that contemporaries were fully aware of the effect of imported goods on the lives of people such as the Stanesprings. Second, if we want to interrogate the British imports themselves, especially the colorful plates and tea services that shocked the Reverend Mr. Milne, we turn to modern museums where these articles still proudly document an expanding world of goods. Third, since we know that some possessions were thrown away, victims of accidents and hard usage that often befell the most cherished items of everyday life, we consult archaeologists who help us interpret the physical remains of eighteenth-century comfort and pleasure. Fourth, when colonists died, these manufactures sometimes showed up in probate records. Fifth, customs officers monitored the flow of exports through English and Scottish ports. And sixth, colonial newspapers carried long, detailed advertisements announcing the availability of the latest British imports. No single source, of course, captures the full dimensions of the consumer market. The detective must examine each one separately, noting as the investigation unfolds the possible biases, exaggerations, and misrepresentations that complicate the interpretive task.

II

Contemporaries had a lot to say about economic change. Colonial governors had no choice in the matter. British administrators in London expected them from time to time to respond to official questionnaires about the state of local affairs. Since the governors never had adequate staff to gather the relevant data, the answers were necessarily impressionistic. A series of reports submitted by the governors of New York testify to a sudden mid-century take off of an American consumer market. The documents discussed many different aspects of imperial commerce, but the manufacture and trade of cloth was a continuing concern throughout the period. In 1705, Governor Lord Cornbury surveyed the New York economy, noting that the colonists were eagerly trying to find new sources of income so that they could afford the British imports they desperately desired. Cornbury warned his superiors in London that entrepreneurs in Connecticut and Long Island appeared to be on the verge of "setting up a Woollen Manufacture." Indeed, the governor claimed to have seen "Serge made upon Long Island that any man may wear."[4]

Although these manufacturing activities were in their infancy, Cornbury regarded them as a serious threat. If Americans really did find ways to fulfill basic consumer needs, they might soon decide that Great Britain did not have much to offer. "I declare my opinion to be," the governor announced, "that all these Colloneys, which are but twigs belonging to the Main Tree [England] ought to be Kept entirely dependent upon & subservient to England." Cornbury and other crown officials sensed that they would have no end of trouble maintaining royal authority if the Americans conflated economic and political equality.

On this point the governor should be credited with developing an ingenious argument. "If they are suffered to goe on in the notions they have," he continued, "that as they are Englishmen, soe they may set up the same manufactures here as people may do in England," the colonists would surely start thinking of political independence. "For the consequence will be that if once they can see they can cloath themselves, not only comfortably but handsomely too, without the help of England, they who are already not very fond of submitting to Government would soon think of putting in Execution designs they had long harbored in their breasts." Cornbury must have known that his rhetoric might sound hyperbolic to London bureaucrats. He ended his statement, therefore, with the curious declaration that "this will not seem strange when you consider what sort of people this Country is inhabited by."[5] Not until the eve of revolution would Americans fully appreciate the link that Cornbury made between consumer demand and colonial politics.

In 1705 crown officials in New York still perceived the most pressing commercial challenge to be how best to supply Americans with basic British goods while at the same time helping them develop the means to finance this trade. When Governor Robert Hunter completed the Board of

Trade questionnaire in 1715, he echoed much that Cornbury had written. "The Planters and poorer sort of Country people" still wore clothing "of their own manufacture." To be sure, what they wove in their homes was mostly coarse material, but whatever its character, the production of so much cloth threatened to make major inroads into a consumer market that properly belonged to English workers. "I know [of] no way to prevent it," Hunter confessed, "than by encouraging them to go on [with] some manufactures that may be useful to England & beneficial to themselves, for few that are able to go to the expense of English manufacture do wear home spun, and a law to oblige such as are not able to go to the expense to do it, under penalties, would be equivalent to a law to compel them to go naked."[6] Hunter repeated Cornbury's central assumption about American buyers. The colonists wanted English goods; they certainly knew the difference between finer imported fabrics and the heavy "home spun" material that only their relative poverty forced them to accept.

In 1723 Cadwallader Colden, a member of the governor's council in New York, reported to the Board of Trade that conditions had not changed much since Hunter's time. But instead of stressing the dangers of colonial manufacturing to British workers, Colden emphasized pent-up consumer demand. Ordinary people in New York still could not figure out how to cover the cost of what they dreamed of ordering from England. "It is evident," Colden explained, "that the whole Industry, Frugality & Trade of this Province is employed to ballance the Trade with England & to pay for the goods they yearly import from thence, & therefore it is undoubtedly the Interest of Britain to encourage the Trade of this Province as much as possible." If New Yorkers could participate more productively in the imperial marketplace, they would be able to buy even more British goods. As Colden informed London administrators, "if the people here could remit by any method more money or Goods to England[,] they would proportionably consume more of the English Manufactures." Commercial opportunity knocked, if only the members of the Board of Trade would listen. After all, British officials were in a position to tap the central values of the Protestant ethic—industry and frugality—to bring colonial consumers more firmly under their control. But Colden was not optimistic that his advice would make much difference, for, as he explained, "It may be that many in England are not so well informed what their Colonys are able to produce."[7]

If we jump forward to 1774, we immediately sense an extraordinary change. It is as if we have entered a new consumer society. New Yorkers of all classes seem by this time to have been fully integrated into a vast Anglo-American marketplace. In an extensive analysis of the local economy, Governor William Tryon declared flatly that "more than Eleven Twelfths of the Inhabitants of this Province both in the necessary and ornamental parts of their Dress are cloathed in British Manufactures, except [for] Linen from Ireland and Hats and Shoes manufactured here." Even in an impressionistic account, the 90 percent figure is arresting. But cloth for garments was only part of the story of the visual transformation of New York. "The same

proportion of Houses are in like manner furnished with British Manufactures, except Cabinet & Joiner's work, which is Generally made here." Instead of complaining about frustrated consumer demand, Tryon expressed
considerable amazement at the vast range and qualities of goods that the
merchants offered for sale. Like so many other commentators, the royal
governor of New York simply listed general categories of imports, for by
the 1770s, it was impossible for any single observer to provide more than a
rough summary of British goods found in the colonies. "Besides the Articles necessary for cloathing and Furniture," the governor reported, "there
are imported from Great Britain, large Quantities of all kinds of East India
Goods . . . Ironmongery, Arms, Gunpowder, Lead, Tin, Sheet Copper, Drugs,
Brimstone, Grindstones, Coals, Chalk, Sail Cloth, Cordage, Paints, Malt Li-
quors & Cheese." The task of putting together a complete inventory soon
overwhelmed Tryon, and he concluded, "There are indeed few articles the
British Market affords, but what are in some proportion imported here."[8]

The governors of other mainland colonies recorded a similar transformation in consumer behavior. During the early decades of the century, they
too reported that the fulfillment of American demand seemed to have run
against two serious obstacles. First, if these crown officials are to be believed, British imperial administrators were a little slow to appreciate the
intensity of colonial desire. And second, even if English manufacturers had
shipped tons of imports across the Atlantic, it was not clear before the 1740s
that ordinary Americans could have afforded the items they claimed most
to want. In 1733 Governor Samuel Ogle of Maryland, for example, observed
that "The Inhab[ita]nts still supply themselves with what Manufactures are
needful for them f[ro]m G:Britain only, so far as they can possibly find
means to purchase the same." Ogle added, "the exceeding Poverty of the
People in general, occasion'd by the low price of Tobaco, hath driven the
poor Familys to make some few course Woollens & Linnens, to cloath themselves, without which they must go naked." Nothing in this statement indicates that the small farmers of Maryland aspired to self-sufficiency, at least
not in regard to the garments they wore.[9]

As in New York, the consumer trade in Maryland apparently soon heated
up.[10] It did so in other American colonies as well. The precise moment at
which the consumer market took off varied from region to region, but the
comments of the governors suggest that it occurred sometime during the
middle third of the century. In the late 1740s Governor James Glen encountered a robust market for consumer goods in South Carolina. In a detailed
analysis of the local economy, Glen declared his intention "to show how *far*
we contribute to the Prosperity of our Mother Country by the Consumption of such Commodities and Manufactures as she produces or supplies
us with." What he found shocked the governor. Sounding a little like the
Reverend Mr. Milne, Glen censured a popular material culture. "I cannot
help expressing my surprise and Concern," he wrote, "to Find that there are
annually imported into this Province, considerable quantities of Fine
Flanders Laces, the Finest Dutch Linens, and French Cambricks, Chints,

Hyson Tea, and other East India Goods, Silks, Gold and Silver Lace, &c."[11] The locals in South Carolina were living beyond their means, and they were doing it in style.

Earlier in the century governors had complained that colonists could not find adequate sources of income to pay for the imports they so clearly desired. Now suddenly in the 1740s the argument shifted. The British goods created poverty. "By these means," Glen insisted, "we are kept in low circumstances." It does not seem to have occurred to Glen that what he regarded as inappropriate consumption contributed to the "Prosperity of the Mother Country" as much as did the other less flashy forms of buying. The governor set about providing an inventory of the imported articles. He made an energetic try at mastering the flow of goods—listing "Cloth of every Kind, from Cambrick to Osnabrigs"—but the task was too difficult. "I am enabled to say thus much," he asserted, "that in general the Quantity seems to be too great, and the Quality of them too fine, and ill calculated for the circumstances of an Infant Colony." And lest anyone in London conclude that Glen was responsible for the explosion of desire, he added smugly, "I have always endeavored to correct and restrain the vices of Extravagance and Luxury by my own example."[12]

Governors of other colonies alerted the Board of Trade to the colonists' growing mid-century dependence on British imports. They usually managed to avoid Glen's didactic tone, but it was clear that an ever expanding assortment of manufactured goods was reaching American ports. Governor Jonathan Law of Connecticut dutifully answered the Board's questionnaire, noting that "our inhabitants take annually of the British manufactures all Sorts of woolen cloath, Silks, Scythes, naills, glass, pewter, brass, firearms & all Sorts of cutlery ware, the quantity we cannot ascertain."[13] A much more detailed accounting came in 1763 from Virginia, a colony that had forged closer ties with the mother country than had Connecticut. Francis Fauquier, the lieutenant governor of Virginia, explained to colonial administrators in London that "The Inhabitants of Virginia import from Great Britain, woollen Goods and Linnens of all Sorts for their Clothing and the Furniture of their Houses." Fauquier, who apparently had a trained eye for textiles, mentioned an impressive array of woven goods from "Negro Cottons and plains" to "Silks of all kinds." Anyone could see how this rising tide of consumption affected the very appearance of ordinary white Virginians. "These Imports," insisted the lieutenant governor, "daily increase, the common planters usualy dressing themselves in the Manufactures of Great Britain altogether." The amounts of goods shipped to Virginia from England and Scotland exceeded Fauquier's descriptive abilities, and, like so many other governors of this period, he simply threw up his hands. "It is next to impossible to ascertain the Quantities imported, the Entries being always made in this manner (viz.) Sundry European Goods by 10, 15 or 20 Cocquets as it happens. But the Quantity is now so great and increases so fast, that it is now almost beyond a Doubt that it exceeds in Value the Tobacco exported."[14]

The mainland colonies also attracted a number of European travelers, some of whom proved astute observers of eighteenth-century American society. Their comments in diaries and letters immediately strike us as more lively and spontaneous than those recorded by the governors. Like the formal bureaucratic reports, however, the personal accounts reinforce a sense that people at the time were fully conscious of the extraordinary impact that consumer goods had had on the character of American society. How much the travelers actually knew about colonial life before they sailed for the New World is almost impossible to discern. Whatever their preparation may have been, they seem to have assumed that in comparison with contemporary England and Germany the colonists would appear less cosmopolitan, perhaps even a little out of touch with contemporary Continental fashions.

Rusticity of manners was most assuredly not what the travelers encountered. Rather, they discovered striking similarities with the world they had left behind. Indeed, in some respects American consumers seemed quite capable of holding their own with their European counterparts. That was certainly Gottlieb Mittelberger's opinion. He traveled to Pennsylvania in 1750 to assess the possibilities for a new German settlement. In his published account, Mittelberger informed prospective migrants that in terms of material comfort the region represented no real sacrifice. The consumer marketplace was well developed, providing colonists with manufactures such as "fine china vessels, Dutch and English cloth, leather, linen cloth, fabrics, silks, damask, velvet, etc." The "etc." was a nice rhetorical touch. Instead of suggesting that Mittelberger had grown tired of the inventory, it invited eager German readers to engage their imaginations. Whatever they might demand at home, they could surely find in America. "Already it is really possible to obtain all the things one can get in Europe in Pennsylvania, since so many merchant ships arrive there every year."

IMPORTED in the laſt Ships from LONDON, by

Samuel Abbot,

And to be ſold by wholeſale or retail, cheap for caſh, treaſurer's notes, or ſhort credit, at his ſhop near the town-dock, BOSTON,

A Large aſſortment of Engliſh and India goods, ſuitable for all ſeaſons ; among which is a great variety of linnens of all ſorts, cambricks, lawns, gauzes, &c. a fine aſſortment of callicoes, chinces, patches, diapers, table cloths, dimoties, thickſetts, &c. cutlery ware, earthen and glaſs ware by the crate and box, ſtarch by the caſk, beſt of French indigo, Kippen's ſnuff by the caſk or dozen, ſpices of all ſorts, dry caſks, &c. with too many other articles to be here enumerated.

Said *Abbot* has to ſell two Houſes, Land, &c.

Samuel Abbot offered customers in Boston a large selection of imported consumer goods as well as convenient credit. *Boston Gazette*, 29 June 1761. *Courtesy of the Massachusetts Historical Society, Boston, Massachusetts.*

Mittelberger apparently expected the colonists to dress in a distinctive manner, in other words, to look like Americans. Perhaps he anticipated they would wear homespun. Whatever he may have thought, the people he actually encountered in the Philadelphia region strongly resembled eighteenth-century Europeans. "Throughout Pennsylvania," wrote Mittelberger, "both men and women dress according to the English fashion." The women proved to be particularly accomplished consumers, appearing in public in the latest London styles. In this section of his account, Mittelberger provided Germans with an almost sensuous celebration of imported fabrics, capturing in loving detail an alluring range of fibers and textures.

> Women do not wear hoop skirts, but everything they do wear is very fine, nice, and costly. . . . Skirts can be parted in front. Under them women usually wear handsomely sewn petticoats trimmed with ribbon. But the outer long skirts have to reach down to the shoes, and are made of cotton, chintz, and other rich and beautiful material. All the women wear fine white aprons every day, on their shoes generally large silver buckles, round their throats fine strings of beads, in their ears costly rings with fine stones, and on their heads fine white bonnets embroidered with flowers and trimmed with lace and streamers. Their gloves are made of velvet, silk and similar kinds of material, also generally trimmed with silver or gold lace, or beautifully embroidered. Their neckerchiefs are made either of velvet or of pure silk, and are likewise richly embroidered.

Mittelberger warned that if "our women" saw the colonial bonnets, "they would at once want to have them for themselves." If, in comparison to the women, the men of Pennsylvania were less splendidly dressed, they still insisted on apparel "made of excellent English cloth or similar material." And Mittelberger explicitly observed that "this applies to farmers as well as to the other ranks."[15]

In 1759 the Reverend Jonathan Boucher took up residence in Port Royal, Virginia, a small tobacco community on the Rappahannock River. Boucher had just come from the north of England, and soon after his arrival the young man wrote a series of letters to an old teacher, describing his initial impressions of his new home. Like Mittelberger, the clergyman seemed surprised by the splendor of the colonists' apparel. Indeed, Boucher felt a little awkward in the company of these well-dressed Virginians. "I assure you," he explained in remarks specifically directed to his teacher's wife, "the common Planter's Daughters here go every Day in finer Cloaths than I have seen content you for a Summer's Sunday." His friends had sent Boucher off to the New World with a "Sattin Wastecoat," a garment suitable for almost all social gatherings in provincial England. But in the American colonies, he discovered, "I'm noth'g amongst the Lace and Lac'd fellows that are here. Nay, so much does their Taste run after dress that they tell me I may see in Virginia more brilliant Assemblies than I ever c'd in the North of Engl'd, and except Royal Ones p'rhaps in any Part of it."[16]

Boucher eventually moved to Annapolis, where he accepted a comfortable living as rector of St. Anne's Parish. It was in Maryland's capital that Boucher made the acquaintance of another ambitious Englishman who had recently traveled to America in search of new opportunities. During the several years that William Eddis lived in Annapolis, he penned a series of epistolary essays, later published as a little book, shrewdly depicting the customs of the local society. Like his friend Boucher, Eddis sensed immediately how much this colonial community depended on British manufactures. In a piece dated December 24, 1771, Eddis declared that "The quick importation of fashions from the mother country is really astonishing. I am almost inclined to believe that a new fashion is adopted earlier by the polished and affluent American than by many opulent persons in the great

metropolis [London]." No doubt, he exaggerated the speed at which consumer news was disseminated throughout the empire, but probably not all
that much. Later, after he had learned more about the Maryland economy,
Eddis concluded, "At present, it is evident that almost every article of use or
ornament is to be obtained on much more reasonable terms from the mother
country than from artisans settled on this side [of] the Atlantic. It is also as
certain that goods of every kind produced or manufactured in England are
greatly superior to the produce or manufactures of this continent."

There was no doubt whatsoever in Eddis's mind that the people of
Maryland, even those who lived in the rural countryside, were willing to
work hard to obtain British goods. He explained exactly how consumer
desire had taken hold of the colonial imagination. In fact, the acquisition of
British goods served as an index of change itself, as the key element in a
narrative of material progress. "To supply the real and imaginary necessities of those by whose persevering efforts and penetrating genius immense
uncultivated tracts became flourishing establishments," Eddis recounted,
"storekeepers of various denominations were encouraged to pursue the path
which industry had pointed out. Warehouses were accordingly erected, and
woolens, linens, and implements of husbandry were first presented to the
view of the laborious planter. As wealth and population increased, wants
were created, and many considerable demands, in consequence, took place
for the various elegancies as well as necessaries of life."[17]

Boucher, Eddis, and Mittelberger—as well as other less articulate commentators—remained outsiders. At the end of the day, all of them returned
to Europe. Because they situated their observations about American consumers within a comparative framework, the element of surprise in these
accounts comes from the discovery that in terms of material culture the
colonists looked a lot like the inhabitants of the Old World. The Americans
may have been overly inquisitive or politically rebarbative, but at least most
of them dressed like proper English people.

One did not have to cross the Atlantic, however, to appreciate the growth
of consumer demand. Colonists who had little direct contact with Continental societies were conscious of how much the recent importation of common British goods altered the fundamental appearance of everyday life. No
one seemed more amazed by the acceleration of change than John Wayles,
a trusted Virginia agent for Farell and Jones, English tobacco merchants.
Wayles also happened to be Thomas Jefferson's father-in-law. During the
summer of 1766 he experienced unusual difficulty collecting debts owed to
his employers. Strained credit relations, not to mention the bankruptcy of
several leading planters, sparked a sudden awareness of how much consumer demand had transformed Chesapeake society. Reflecting on conditions only a quarter century earlier, Wayles observed that personal income
as well as expenditures had risen very fast, so that "Within these 25 Years
£1000 due to a Merchant was looked upon as a Sum imense and never to be
got over. Ten times that sum is now spoke of with Indifference & thought
no great burthen on some Estates." But Virginians heard the sirens of the

good life, and instead of moderating their purchase of British imports, they ordered ever more exciting and colorful manufactures. "In 1740," Wayles explained, "I don't remember to have seen such a thing as a turkey Carpet in the Country except a small thing in a bed chamber, Now nothing are so common as Turkey or Wilton Carpetts, the whole Furniture of the Roomes Elegant & every appearance of Opulence."[18]

New Yorkers also commented on the mid-eighteenth-century flood of consumer goods. Like Wayles and the others, they were certainly aware that these imports had somehow altered the character of provincial society. The editors of the *Independent Reflector,* an experimental newspaper that enjoyed a brief run in 1753, insisted that "Our extraordinary Success during the late War [King George's War], has given Rise to a Method of living unknown to our frugal Ancestors."[19] A major contributor to this journal, William Smith, accepted the notion that imperial war stimulated colonial consumption, but in his analysis the socially transforming conflict was the Seven Years' War rather than King George's War. As this respected jurist explained in his 1762 history of New York, "In the city of New-York, through our intercourse with the Europeans, we follow the London fashions; though, by the time we adopt them, they become disused in England. Our affluence, during the late war, introduced a degree of luxury in tables, dress, and furniture, with which we were before unacquainted." The sudden surge of buying apparently made Smith a little uneasy, for instead of praising New Yorkers for their show of finery, he observed that "we are not so gay a people as our neighbours in Boston, and several of the southern colonies."[20]

The Reverend Jared Eliot shared Smith's ambivalence about a rapidly changing consumer culture. Eliot lived in Connecticut and produced during the middle decades of the century a number of well-informed essays promoting agricultural improvement. Like other Americans of this period, he worried that excessive reliance on British manufactures might undermine the strength of the local economy. But such concerns did not blind Eliot to the highly visible signs of general prosperity. However much Connecticut farmers needed to learn about scientific cultivation, they were living better. They were purchasing more imported goods. And this remarkable development had occurred within living memory. "The Country may be considered as Improving & Advancing very much," Eliot noted in 1749; "there is now a great deal of Silver & Gold in the Country; we have better Houses, publick & Private, richer Furniture, better Food and Cloathing; better Bridges & Highways, fatter Cattel and finer Horses, and Lands bear a higher Price."[21]

The personalities thus far encountered, governors and travelers as well as colonists, testified to the creation of a new consumer society. They bore witness to a change in the character of provincial material culture that had taken place within the span of their own lives, and the very speed of the transformation of the provincial marketplace sparked a range of responses: astonishment and anticipation, curiosity and fear. Americans such as Eliot and Wayles seem to have been bright, reflective, and responsible observers. They certainly had no reason to fabricate a commercial phenomenon of this type. And they were by no means the only commentators who noted a sudden intensification of consumer activity throughout colonial society. Many contemporaries whom we shall consider in more detail in a later section adopted a much shriller tone than did Eliot and Walyes, insisting among other things that the acquisition of so many British manufactures encouraged a debilitating and universal love of luxury. Soon colonists from New Hampshire to Georgia, they warned, would follow the ancient Romans down the fatal path to effeminacy and idleness. The strident moral condemnation of imported goods is itself a significant aspect of our investigation. The noisy complaints about sin and pride in the marketplace represent strong evidence that the governors and travelers probably knew what they were writing about. At mid-century a lot of people in different regions would appear to have discovered the comforts and pleasures of consumption.

For the detective of material culture, however, our informants raise as many questions as they answer. Their comments about the centrality of imported cloth remind us that first-person reports of the flood of consumer goods were highly impressionistic. Assessing the accuracy of traveler accounts represents a particularly difficult methodological challenge. They recorded what they claimed to have seen in colonial America, often stylish young persons dressed remarkably like well-to-do Europeans. But we do not know what these contemporaries failed to observe. Perhaps, in their eagerness to tell readers about "Lac'd fellows," they ignored many ordinary colonists who wore homespun garments. Or perhaps, because they only had eyes for the cosmopolitan gentry, they systematically overestimated the effect of so many consumer goods on how humble men and women fashioned themselves or experienced everyday society.

We must also consider the possibility that our witnesses exaggerated the pace of change. After all, if one searches hard enough in the records of almost any society, one will find someone grumbling about how much the world has changed in only a single generation. Without additional support from other eighteenth-century sources, arguments affirming the rapid creation of a broad-based consumer society in colonial America—indeed, one that affected the great majority of the provincial population—remain suggestive rather than persuasive.

III

We have other interpretive options. We can subpoena the physical evidence, real teapots and fabric, and test them against the letters and reports of contemporaries. After all, the imported articles that so many observers believed had transformed the visual landscape of eighteenth-century America have not disappeared. The survivors of this early consumer marketplace have become the objects of desire for modern collectors. Many have found their way into museums, where they offer colorful and alluring testimony that sometime before the Revolution the colonial material culture took on a very dif-

ferent appearance, and no one strolling amongst the ordered rooms that usually distinguish time periods in modern galleries can fail to appreciate the
contrast between sparsely furnished, often starkly ornamented seventeenth-
century exhibits and the brighter eighteenth-century reconstructions that
challenge viewers to comprehend competing styles and complex textures.[22]

These objects bring us directly into contact with a late colonial world
that may be less distant from our own than we sometimes imagine. The
variety of imported ceramics is a case in point. The rich holdings of museums document how an Anglo-American market responded to an accelerating demand for ever harder, more beautiful, and technically more
sophisticated items, most of them products of the new and ambitious potteries of the English Midlands. Indeed, anyone who today examines collections in different parts of the country—certainly along the eastern
coast—experiences a form of visual *déjà vu*. One encounters the same designs, the same manufactures, the same selection of bowls, cups, and plates.
However little New Englanders may have had in common with Chesapeake
planters, they seem to have accumulated goods of almost identical shape
and color.

In the more imaginatively planned exhibits such as the Wallace Gallery
in Colonial Williamsburg, one can almost literally journey through consumer time. One starts with the often crudely painted earthenware pieces
of the early 1700s. The viewer then moves to the more dazzling stoneware
goods of the middle years of the century which were fired at much higher
temperatures so that they could accommodate very hot liquids. These pieces
are an example of technological innovation helping to sustain a consumer
fad, in this case drinking tea. Finally, the time traveler confronts the late
colonial porcelain items, some of which were transported to America from
Asia, others manufactured by brilliant English entrepreneurs such as Josiah
Wedgwood. We note the increasing frequency of matched sets, evidence
not only of the determination of provincial Americans to obtain the finest,
most fashionable imports but also of their ability to keep informed about
new and fluid European styles. Other categories of possessions communicate the same general market development. These visual presentations seem
to confirm the impressions of eighteenth-century commentators. Like the
reports filed by governors and visitors, displays found in modern museums
suggest that a major change in the character of consumer culture occurred
sometime during the middle decades of the eighteenth century. The quantity of goods is as significant as is quality for this argument. As one historian of early American material culture explained, "many more beautiful
things" have survived from the eighteenth century than from the seventeenth, "as if America's aesthetic sensibilities were suddenly awakening in
those years."[23]

Period rooms—either in restored old homes or in twenty-first-century
galleries—remind us of an unintended consequence of heightened consumer activity. The acquisition of so many ceramic goods created a major
problem for the colonist. These purchases had to be kept in a safe place, at

the very least out of the reach of curious children and pets. For this purpose the closed chests found in seventeenth-century homes might have functioned well enough. But eighteenth-century consumers also wanted to display their imported treasures, showing visitors that their hosts could afford fine English plates and bowls. No doubt, it was this kind of thinking that contributed to the "Tale of the Hospitable Consumer." The answer to the problem of display and storage was a new piece of case furniture commonly known as the formal cupboard. Often colonial craftsmen constructed these to fit neatly into the corners of rooms where food was served. Before the 1740s cupboards remained relatively rare. After that time, however, their number and geographic distribution expanded rapidly, a dramatic indication that even in modest households British manufactures were making demands of their own on provincial consumers. One of them was Mrs.

The corner cupboard appeared for the first time in ordinary American households during the mid-eighteenth century. This invention provided colonial consumers a way to display colorful imported goods in relative safety. *Painted Corner Cupboard, Accomack County, Virginia, Yellow Pine, 1750–1760. Collection of the Museum of Early Southern Decorative Arts, Winston-Salem, North Carolina.*

George Gilmer, wife of Williamsburg's apothecary. As her husband explained in a letter to a Bristol merchant, "Mrs. Gilmer is perfectly satisfied with your conduct about her China and desires you will take your own time. I have just finished a closet for her to put it in as agreed on before you left us."[24]

The Gilmers' highly visible acquisitions may well have impressed Virginians who dined with the local apothecary and his family. While we can guess at their reaction, we do not know for sure what they thought. It is certain, however, that the dinner guests encountered many more British goods in the Gilmer home than we normally see in the modern collections of colonial objects. To understand the biases of museums—that is, if we are attempting to reconstruct the fullness of an eighteenth-century consumer society—we should think in terms of what might be called "the risk of survival." When we find ourselves in a beautifully appointed period room of the 1740s or 1750s, we should ask ourselves what goods were most at risk of surviving to our own times and, therefore, of being incorporated into the historic displays that allegedly tell us what it was really like to live in colonial times.

The solution to this actuarial problem seems to be that the more expensive the original purchase—the more money the colonist actually spent—the greater the odds of its appearing today in a restored room. Porcelain always had a better chance of inclusion in modern collections than did the cheaper pieces of stoneware and earthenware. Special plates depicting colorful or romantic scenes, for example, were probably hung on walls as ornaments or placed in cupboards as markers of conspicuous consumption soon after their arrival in the household. The colonists who acquired these fine objects and who handed them down to their children and their children's children normally ate off cheaper, more utilitarian ware, much of which no doubt met with unhappy accidents or was given away after showing evidence of abuse. For this reason, everyday goods of all sorts are generally underrepresented in museum displays.

This bias in the presentation of a lost material culture is especially a problem with eighteenth-century cloth. Textiles suffered far more from heavy usage than did ceramics or metal articles. Garments faded, decayed, went out of style, and became permanently soiled, all of which helps explain why they were likely—more at risk—to end in the trash pit or be recycled in the manufacture of paper rather than handed down from generation to generation. One has a far greater chance of viewing a Staffordshire teapot or a Wedgwood plate today than of encountering an imported piece of eighteenth-century linen or cotton fabric. Unless we calculate the odds of survival, we might be tempted to generalize about the character of the consumer marketplace from what we see in museums. And since cloth seems to have been relatively rare, it would appear on the basis of this evidence alone not only that contemporaries such as Walyes and Mittelberger greatly exaggerated the importance of imported textiles but also that colonists only went shopping for British manufactures when they wanted a very special item that they could not possibly produce for themselves.

Evidence encountered in modern museums can distort our understanding of the consumer marketplace in other significant ways. It should come as no surprise, for example, that even the most thoughtful presentations of eighteenth-century

Imported from *London* in Capt. *McTaggart*, And to be Sold by

Edward Wigglesworth,

At his Shop in *Marlboro'-Street*, being the second Shop of English Goods Southward of the Sign of the Three Golden Doves, by Wholesale or Retail, as cheap as can be bought for Cash at any Shop or Store in Town, the following Articles, *viz.*

Superfine black, blue, scarlet and cloth colour'd broad cloths; middling ditto; magareen, blue, black and cloth collour'd thicksetts; London duroys; dy'd pillows: white, strip'd and flower'd dimothys; cotton gowns; 3 & 4 thread black and crimson worsted patterns; black & olive colour manchester velvet; india nankeens: black allapine and bombazine; callicoes and chinces; strip'd cotton hollands; taffaties and persians; silk crapes; black pelong sattin; yard wide sarsnett; handkerchiefs; bengals: 3-4 and 7-8 and yard wide garlix: 3-4 7-8 and yard wide irish linnens; 3 4, 7-8, yard wide, yard and 3-8, and 6-4, checks; long lawns; clear lawns, flower'd ditto; cambricks; tiffany; stay crape; womens white and colour'd bath lamb mitts; womens white & black glaz'd gloves; shammy ditto; mens ditto; belladine sewing silk: silk knee garters; woodstick fans; ebony and bone ditto, black paper ditto, bamboe ditto; russia linnen and diaper; shalloons, durants; buttons, silk and hair twist; dowlass; stock tape; quality binding; silk ferretts; ribbons; bandanoes; romalls; culgee silk handkerchiefs, check linnen ditto, past work ditto; pins and tapes; crimson english damasks; dresdenetts; half-yard venetian poplins; strip'd stuffs; mens grey and black worsted hose, thread and cotton ditto; womens pink green, white & colour'd worsted ditto; womens ruffel shoes; letter'd gartering; white flannel; strip'd swanskin; oznabrigs; black horn buttons; stay cord, braids, gallooms and buckram; yellow holland; brown buckram; Scotch and colour'd threads; choice Bohea Tea, &c. &c. &c.

Edward Wigglesworth's newspaper advertisement revealed the extraordinary range of choices available to colonial American consumers of imported English cloth. *Boston Gazette*, 29 June 1761. *Courtesy of the Massachusetts Historical Society.*

material culture devote most attention to the possessions of the well-to-do, in other words, to goods once owned by the elite families who entertained inquisitive visitors such as Boucher and Eddis. In terms of risk, we are far more likely to discover in an interpretation of colonial life an article associated with a Byrd or a Carter than with an obscure farmer such as Stanespring. Another, even more subtle bias in reconstructions of eighteenth-century material culture is the systematic overemphasis of articles originally produced in the colonies. The celebration of American artisans—the furniture makers of Philadelphia or the silversmiths of Boston seem to head the honor roll—has served to deflect public interest away from British manufactures, many of them of higher quality than those of colonial origin. In fact, concentration on the work of local craftsmen only obscures our appreciation of the stunning impact that imported goods made on the character of domestic landscapes throughout the colonies.[25]

IV

From museums, we move to trash. No matter how much British Americans may have cherished certain consumer items, they inevitably faced a day when the objects of original desire had to be discarded. Most articles simply broke and could not be repaired. Each shattered possession probably represented a small domestic tragedy. Whatever personal event marked its end as a beautiful or useful artifact, it usually found its way to the family trash pit, an unsightly hole dug in the ground not far from the main house.

Over the years the pit gradually filled up with everything from fragments of teacups and rusty bits of metal to the bones of various animals that once graced the dinner table. And in time someone covered the pit, out of concern as much for safety as sanitation, a decision that unwittingly transformed a jumble of refuse into a record of early American consumer habits that now requires a trained archaeologist to interpret. From these sources such scholars have unlocked a great deal of detailed information about the material culture of the mid-eighteenth century, some of which can be found in no other surviving colonial record. After all, the garbage pits of the past were remarkably democratic; every colonial family had one, rich and poor, rural and urban, white and black.

Archaeologists add an important dimension to our understanding of the social and geographic distribution of British manufactured goods. Digging in the Chesapeake soil, for example, they find many of the same items—albeit in less than perfect condition—that we encountered in the period rooms of the museums. Almost every research site reveals a broad selection of imported ceramics, and archaeologists working in different regions report that over the course of the eighteenth century colonists acquired not only more British pottery but also items of higher quality.[26] While the shards of pottery, especially the ubiquitous fragments of clay pipes, survived well in the ground, and therefore have become the archaeologist's major source of knowledge about the human landscape of late colonial society, other categories of imported goods are regularly unearthed, too. Long-abandoned wells and trash pits served to preserve damaged bottles, broken tools, splinters of glassware, and dozens of personal objects, all of them reminders of the demands that even poor-to-middling householders once made on the Anglo-American consumer market. The soil has also yielded a few surprises. A large amount of imported ceramics, some pieces originally quite costly, clearly came into the possession of slaves. We can only speculate on the life cycle of a Staffordshire bowl. Perhaps masters retired slightly damaged objects from the main dining room and gave them to the bondsmen and women whose hard labor had made it possible to purchase fashionable matched sets of imported ware in the first place.[27]

Among other findings, archaeological research suggests that rural Americans may have depended on articles manufactured in Great Britain as heavily as did their more urban neighbors. Of the many sites that have been recently interpreted, few reveal the impact of the flood of British goods more dramatically than Fort Massachusetts, a defensive post constructed in 1744 on the colony's far western frontier. The structure was part of a so-called line of forts, designed to halt incursions into New England by French and Indian forces. For almost a decade this isolated log fortification housed about two hundred members of the colonial militia, local farmers, for the most part, who served several months and then went home. These men—as well as a few women and children—struggled valiantly against boredom. While in residence, they purchased supplies from stores owned by the powerful Williams family on the Connecticut River, and although the transportation costs were high, the colonial soldiers seem to have been able to obtain most of what they desired. And then disaster struck. A small army of French and Indian troops directed by Rigaud de Vaudrieul overran Fort Massachusetts, taking most of the Americans prisoner. After the debacle, government authorities in Boston decided to decommission an outpost that had proved incapable of discouraging surprise attacks. By 1754 the living quarters and major buildings of the fort had already fallen into sad disrepair.

What the militiamen left behind now engages our curiosity. The American soldiers ate, drank, and entertained themselves, waiting more or less patiently for replacements to relieve them from an impossible assignment. When the nineteenth-century historian Francis Parkman visited Fort Massachusetts, he could find almost no sign of the military structure. It is "now a meadow by the banks of the Hoosac [River]," Parkman wrote. "Then [during the late 1740s] it was a rough clearing, encumbered with the stumps and refuse of the primeval forest; whole living hosts stood grimly around it, and spread, untouched by the axe, up the sides of the neighboring Saddleback Mountain."[28]

A fort built at the edge of a "primeval forest" would appear an extremely unpromising spot to unearth evidence of a robust Atlantic consumer marketplace. That is certainly what a team of archaeologists thought when it began excavating the Hoosac River site that Parkman had surveyed a century earlier. But what the carefully sifted soil offered amazed everyone. Researchers uncovered metal, glass, and ceramics "astonishing in their refinement." The colonial militiamen, people who were not by any standard wealthy, discarded fancy metal buttons, shoe and knee buckles, and a brass snuffbox. We can now state with confidence that these soldiers smoked pipes manufactured by "the Robert Tippet firm in Bristol, England," drank imported wine in British "baluster-stemmed wine glasses," sipped tea from British white saltglaze cups, ate with British "two-tined forks," "spatulate knives," and pewter spoons, fired British guns, kept records on British paper, wrote with British ink, wore clothes made from British cloth. It is no wonder that the leading interpreter of Fort Massachusetts concluded, "We find that there is hardly any difference between the material culture of the Line of Forts, way out in the boondocks, and that of central London in the mid-eighteenth century. You could take a print of Hogarth, such as his *Rake's Progress* series, and find a great many of the artifacts from the forts in something like his Rose Tavern, a great bawdy house in contemporary London."[29]

Excavations in other colonies have yielded remarkably parallel results, indicating that a well-developed consumer economy supplied basically the same types of goods to buyers in Virginia and Georgia as in New England. According to James Deetz, who oversaw archaeological investigations at a large Virginia plantation known as Flowerdew Hundred, "It is no surprise that virtually all of the ceramics found at Flowerdew Hundred are of English origin (German stonewares being the sole significant exception), and that they are almost identical to those found on sites from New England to the Deep South."[30] A similar collection of manufactured items appeared in the trash pits and dirt-filled cellars of Kingsmill, another Virginia plantation that has been the subject of especially painstaking analysis.[31]

Like the other types of evidence that we have evaluated—contemporary observations and museum displays—archaeological reports provide a slightly distorted perspective on a changing mid-eighteenth-century cultural landscape. To be sure, the quantity of imported goods seems to have increased markedly over earlier levels of colonial consumption. Nevertheless, data obtained from field excavations tend to underestimate consumer activity in at least two ways, one far more significant than the other. As we have discovered, contemporary governors and visitors called attention to the Americans' growing reliance on textiles produced in the mother country. One commentator estimated that as much as "Eleven Twelfths of the Inhabitants . . . are cloathed in British manufactures."[32] Even if we discount this highly impressionistic figure, we still have to account for a huge amount of imported fabric. And for this challenge, the archaeological research is of little assistance. Unlike fragments of teacups and pieces of glass bottles, cloth quickly disintegrates in the moist ground. Another research anomaly is the relation between pewter and ceramics, both imported artifacts. If one relied solely on probate inventories—the next category of consumer evidence we shall examine—one might conclude that the colonists owned almost as many pewter pieces as ceramic items. The archaeologists, however, find almost no pewter in the trash pits. The solution to the puzzle seems to be that colonists purchased large quantities of pewter *and* ceramics, but since pewter was more durable, intrinsically more valuable, and capable of being recycled, it was less at risk to be buried with the broken dishes.

V

Only someone unfamiliar with colonial probate records could state without a sense of irony that death is a great equalizer. If nothing else, the rich leave behind a lot more stuff than do their less affluent neighbors. And it all must be evaluated. Let us consider a single case. Late in the autumn of 1741 York County officials toured the home of John Pasteur, a recently deceased member of their Virginia community who in terms of material wealth had done quite well for himself. The visitors went from room to room, compiling a detailed inventory of Pasteur's many possessions. One can easily imagine how the appraisers conducted their business. Item after item had to be examined, handled, passed from person to person, its character and quality debated until the probate officers arrived at a fair assessment. In this manner, the men recorded a "small brass Kettle," some dishes of no particular distinction, an interesting "Tea Table," and a large selection of sheets and pillows. The "looking Glass" had special value, as did the "2 China bowls," the "8 pictures in frames," and the impressive assemblage of Pasteur's clothing, including "1 German Serge Waistct.," "1 black Cloth Coat waistcoat and 2 pr. Breeches." The inventory mentioned a few books by title and a huge amount of pottery, some of it labeled simply as "Earthen," an indication probably of its common quality. Other goods had obvious utility: a chocolate pot, a coffeepot, a basin, plates, wine and beer glasses, mugs, bowls, teaspoons, and, finally, four chamber pots.[33]

Appraisals of this type occurred thousands of times throughout late colonial America. Each fully inventoried estate yielded a list of goods, many of them describing objects encountered in other eighteenth-century sources. As modern historians have discovered, however, the probate records present unusually difficult interpretive problems. For one thing, not all estates were inventoried, and the process of translating the possessions of the deceased into a specific monetary value varied considerably from colony to colony, even from town to town. Moreover, the records raise hard issues associated with the analysis of class and gender. The estates of richer colonists, for example, were much more likely to be inventoried than were those of the lower orders. The records contain a disproportionately large number of older, white males.[34] We should also remember that these lists are like still photographs; they capture a specific moment in time. But for people like Pasteur, the accumulation of consumer goods was a lifelong process. Personal possessions came and went; they were given away or discarded. We must consider the possibility that the decedent may have owned a lot more objects when he was younger. Perhaps the person who died had helped establish children in independent households, donating sheets, tableware, and furniture. Certainly, the inventories underrepresented the acquisition of cloth. We know only of garments and linen cataloged during the final inventory.

Such technical concerns need not detain us. The scholars who have analyzed this extraordinarily rich vein of information have taken these methodological problems into account. For our purposes, the lists provide another perspective on the development of a provincial consumer society. We now know that John Pasteur's estate—and for our purposes he was chosen at random—was not particularly exceptional. Historians who quantify probate data have firmly demonstrated a broad increase after the 1730s in the ownership of personal amenities, in other words, the incidence of imported items such as linen and tableware that are used to assess long-term improvements in the general standard of living. This research provides no compelling evidence that colonists felt hesitant about participating in the Anglo-American marketplace. The same categories of British manufactures show up in rural as well as urban inventories. To be sure, less well-to-do families may have substituted cheaper goods for more expensive ones—decorative stoneware for porcelain, for instance—but whatever the quality of the artifacts, they almost always came originally from industrial centers in Great Britain. More to the point, the estate inventories strongly support those contemporaries such as John Wayles who believed that the cultural landscape of colonial America changed perceptibly during the middle decades of the eighteenth century.[35]

The most ambitious investigations of colonial probate records rely on Chesapeake archives. Drawing upon thousands of inventories compiled between the middle of the seventeenth century and the eve of the American Revolution, these studies reveal striking shifts in consumer behavior. During the early period—for these purposes the years before 1716—the planters of Virginia and Maryland managed to obtain certain luxury goods such as fine ceramics, clocks, and silver plate, but the number of these articles appearing in the inventories did not show much increase over several decades. Ordinary farmers lived a fairly constrained material existence. Some inventories for the early years do not even mention basic items such as knives and forks. Sometime after the 1730s, however, patterns of consumption in the Chesapeake colonies changed swiftly as manufactured goods inundated the households of people of all classes. No one disputes the far-reaching impact of this transformation on ordinary men and women. Scholars working with probate records have characterized the broad rise in consumer spending as "rapid and unprecedented." Another researcher claimed, "By the middle of the eighteenth century, the range of domestic props that gentlefolk found desirable exploded." The members of less well-to-do families followed along behind their social betters, adding a "touch of elegance" to their lives. These people aggressively entered the consumer market, demanding amenities that richer neighbors now took for granted. Soon thereafter, the tell-tale signs of consumer desire began appearing even in very modest inventories.[36]

The probate records of eighteenth-century New England tell a similar story. Although the surviving inventories for this region do not indicate an explosive moment when people of different classes suddenly entered a market for imported British goods, they do document a steady increase in the variety and value of items owned at the time of death. The New England economy experienced a gradual rise in household prosperity during this period, and by the middle decades of the century families of modest income levels were purchasing manufactured articles, many of them connected to the tea service, which was itself a recent innovation. Even in rural communities one discovers evidence of New Englanders adding knives and forks as well as many kinds of imported tableware. To be sure, these consumer items first appeared in major port cities such as Boston and Salem, but they were soon taken up by farmers living in more rural settings such as Worcester County. Moreover, within a particular geographic area, the analysis of probate inventories over time indicates that the ability to acquire high-quality ceramics such as porcelain teacups spread quickly from elite to less affluent families. One of the more thorough quantitative studies argues that the probate evidence from eighteenth-century New England reveals "a radically altered life-style among the modestly propertied."[37]

VI

Newspapers heralded the arrival of a vast new consumer culture. Creatures of the marketplace, they carried messages about exciting goods of every sort. Mordecai Yarnall could hardly have survived in business without them. In September 1752 he informed potential consumers that his fall shipment of dry goods had arrived from England. Anyone interested in viewing the selection was welcome to visit his store, located "at the sign of the Handsaw, in Second-street, near Black-horse-alley." Yarnall's modest, one-column advertisement appeared on the third page of the *Pennsylvania Gazette*. A small woodcut—perhaps a picture of a sailing vessel—might have enhanced the visual impact of Yarnall's notice, but he apparently chose to devote the space entirely to an item-by-item enumeration of articles "just imported in the last ships from London." He provided no prices; no article received special descriptive treatment. Indeed, Yarnall's advertisement seems more like a shipping invoice or routine shelf inventory than an effective means of generating consumer desire.

But such a reading would probably misinterpret the text. Yarnall understood colonial merchandising strategies better than we. The advertisement invites the imagination to contemplate variety. His list sparked excitement precisely because it held out the possibility of consumer choice. The newspaper notice surveyed the imported goods, starting with an impressive selection of fabrics: linens, cambrics, lawns, muslins, taffetas, silks, and calicoes. By employing the plural form—linens, not linen—Yarnall suggested that his range of imports was in fact much greater than a single advertisement could ever communicate. He managed to conjure up different colors, weights, and qualities. Yarnall then moved to "silver watches," "shoe and knee buckles," and "cutlery." After mentioning over fifty items of European origin, the Philadelphia merchant concluded abruptly, promising customers that they would find in his store "sundry other goods, too tedious to mention."[38] Yarnall's list—like those of hundreds of other small eighteenth-century merchants from New Hampshire to Georgia—reveals an extraordinary assortment of goods at the moment of presentation. They have not yet been chipped, broken, or discarded; their owners have not recently died. The cloth has not yet been transformed into shirts or dresses. These are goods in transit, items about to become personal possessions. And in the aggregate, they provide powerfully persuasive evidence of the creation of a new consumer society.

Provincial newspapers such as the *Pennsylvania Gazette* served the needs of an expanding commercial empire.[39] In 1720 only three journals were published in colonial America. By 1760 the number had risen to twenty-two. These weekly papers regularly reprinted essays and other news items, many of which had originally appeared in the British press. From time to time, they reproduced royal proclamations. Editors sometimes ran pieces written by local authors—poems or letters, for example—but for the most part printers avoided controversial topics, especially anything having to do with disagreements between royal governors and colonial assemblies. Involvement in such partisan matters threatened lucrative printing contracts that struggling printers needed to remain solvent. Editorial neutrality coupled with out-of-date European stories gave the American weeklies a bland quality, and one suspects that if they had not carried shipping news and other commercial correspondence, they would have had a hard time selling subscriptions.[40]

As dry-goods merchants such as Yarnall well understood, colonists looked to the journals for intelligence about consumer opportunities, in his case, for a listing of what had been "just imported in the last ships from London." Pressruns seem to have averaged about a thousand copies, but the actual readership—in other words, the statistic of greatest interest to potential advertisers—was much larger. Papers were passed around in taverns and coffeehouses.[41] William Parks, a publisher of the *Virginia Gazette,* appreciated the journal's commercial capabilities. In October 1736 he established his rates for advertising, pledging "as these Papers will circulate (as speedily as possible) not only all over This, but also the Neighboring Colonies, and will probably be read by some Thousands of People, it is very likely they may have the desir'd Effect."[42] For colonial printers, newspaper advertising represented a substantial source of income. One man just establishing himself in the trade informed Benjamin Franklin, "I get but few Advertisements yet, which are the Life of a Paper."[43] Franklin, of course, appreciated such business matters, and his *Pennsylvania Gazette* always contained a large number of consumer announcements.

Colonial advertisements can be divided into three broad categories, two of which require only passing comment. Some notices had nothing to do with imported consumer goods, for example, appeals for the capture of a runaway servant or descriptions of land or farm animals for sale. Another category included declarations by colonial artisans—silversmiths, joiners, and the like—offering their services to the public. By far the largest group of advertisements, however, was of the type Yarnall placed in the Philadelphia journal. During the middle third of the eighteenth century—in other words, during a period of increasing importation of British manufactures—the size, location, and appearance of the merchant notices changed remarkably. Before the 1750s advertisements were generally small, one-column texts, but after mid-century it was not uncommon to encounter two-column spreads, announcing newly arrived consumer goods. To be sure, the core copy still consisted of a long list of items, often running into the hundreds, but by mid-century advertisers began to pay greater attention to layout, ornamental borders, and creative variations in type size. And as the number of advertisers in any given issue of a colonial newspaper multiplied, these design features helped to distinguish one merchant's wares from those of his or her competitors, some of whom now specialized in particular kinds of British imports, such as jewelry or medicines.[44] By the eve of revolution, one occasionally saw advertisements for sundry dry goods filling an entire page.[45] Moreover, in a few journals the commercial notices migrated forward, appearing ever more frequently in the left-hand column of the front page. After 1760 the total space assigned to advertising generally equaled or exceeded that given over to the news of the day, and some publishers issued special supplements that were overwhelmingly devoted to commercial notices.[46]

Colonial newspaper advertising presents the possibility of constructing what might be called an "index of consumer choice." This measure of change holds immense significance for an interpretation of the politicization of everyday goods during the American Revolution. After all, what ultimately separated the modern period from traditional history was the ability of ordinary men and women to establish a meaningful and distinct sense of self through the exercise of individual choice, a process of ever more egalitarian self-fashioning that was itself the foundation of a late eighteenth-century liberal society. We shall return to the relation between market experience and political ideology. It is sufficient here to observe that examination of imported goods advertised in the major provincial newspapers between the 1720s and the 1770s provided strong evidence of a mid-century take-off in the number of different British manufactures sold in the colonies. We should accept immediately that an inevitable fuzziness attends the construction of an "index of consumer choice." Advertisers listed hundreds of goods, identifying them by color, size, and quality. But all too frequently the announcements for imported items contained bundling phrases such as "a large Assortment," "goods of all sorts," or simply a string of "etc., etc., etc." These space-saving conventions served systematically to conceal the number of goods that were in fact on offer at a merchant's shop.

Even a conservative enumeration of durable or semi-durable goods—in other words, an advertising count that excludes imported foodstuffs and

><><><><><><><><><><><><><><><><><><><><
>IMPORTED in the laſt Ships from *LONDON*
>
># By John Leverett & Co^y
>
>And ſold at their ſtore No. 5. the ſouth ſide of the
>town dock, by wholeſale, cheap for caſh, treaſurer's
>notes, or ſhort credit, *Viz.*
>
>RUSSIA duck, ozenbrigs, garlix, Ruſſia linnen, Ruſſia diaper, huckabuck, buckrams, clouting diapers, table cloths, callicoes, nankeens, taffities, perſians, cambricks, lawns, women's black ſilk gloves and mitts, men's and women's white kid and lamb gloves, black gauze handkerchiefs, ſilk and linnen handkerchiefs, checks, cotton hollands, thick ſetts fuſtians, velvet ſhapes, women's ſtays and petticoats, ribbons, men's and women's thread, cotton, and worſted hoſe, worſted and ſilk patterns for waiſtcoats and breeches, allapeens, crapes, tiffanies, callimancoes, ſhalloons, tammies, camblets, women's velvet, luteſtring, allamode, black and blue pelong ſattin ; ſcarlet, blue and cloth colour'd broad cloths, German ſerges, kerſeys, buttons, twiſt, bellandine ſewing ſilk, qualities, gartering, pins, braid, galloom, cord, fans, looking glaſſes, men's and boys felt hats, neſts of gilt trunks, ſieve bottoms, ſtarch, lead, ſhot, pipes ; writing, printing, cartridge and brown paper, ink powder, accompt books, &c.
>
>N. B. Sugar by the hogſhead, and barrel coffee.

Customers who visited John Leverett's store on Boston's town dock knew in advance that they would encounter a wide selection of the latest imported English goods. *Boston Gazette*, 29 June 1761. *Courtesy of the Massachusetts Historical Society.*

beverages such as wine and beer—yields impressive results. A survey of New York City newspapers revealed, for example, that during the 1720s and 1730s local merchants seldom mentioned more than five or six British goods in any given issue. By the 1770s, however, it was not uncommon during some busy months for New York journals to list between 350 and 1,000 separate imported consumer items per issue. In New York City—as in the other provincial commercial centers—imported fabrics made up over half of all advertised British goods. The extraordinary quantity of cloth listed in the newspapers suggests why historians of consumer culture cannot rely on a single source such as archaeological site reports, since in that particular set of records they would find little to document what was clearly the major category of Anglo-American trade. The trend was much the same in other newspapers. In 1733 the *South-Carolina Gazette* of Charleston mentioned about fifty British goods per issue. By 1773 the number had risen to about four hundred. Since many of the colony's wealthiest rice planters ordered goods directly from England, the newspaper figure underestimated the number of consumer choices being made in this region. In 1736 the *Boston Evening-Post* carried advertisements each week for about ten manufactured items; by 1773 the June issues mentioned over five hundred British goods. The *Pennsylvania Gazette* averages between 1733 and 1773 jumped from ten per issue to around four hundred.

As the number of advertised items expanded—the really significant jump occurred during the 1750s—the descriptive categories for consumer goods became much more elaborate. It is hard to tell whether colonial merchants were responding to domestic demand for greater variety or were employing the new products to entice men and women into their shops. Whatever the case may have been, we can document how the lexicon of the consumer marketplace became more complex, challenging both buyers and sellers to keep up with a changing commercial vocabulary.

A few examples suggest how difficult it may have been for ordinary colonists just to keep up with the fluid language of commerce. During the 1740s New York advertisers simply offered "paper." By the 1760s, however, they listed seventeen varieties of paper distinguished by size, function, and quality. Someone entering a store could now request products such as "Demy Paper," "Post Paper," "Writing Paper," "Vellum Paper," or "Foolscap." An announcement for "satin" appeared in the *New-York Mercury* in 1733, but it was not until 1763 that the consumer could select from among eight different kinds of satins. Color seems to have been the most important attribute. Merchants stocked satin in black, blue, crimson, green, pink, red, white, yellow, and spotted. The same escalation of choice transformed the market for carpets. No carpets of any sort were mentioned in the New York advertisements before the early 1750s, but by the 1760s stores offered carpets labeled Axminster, Milton, Persian, Scotch, Turkey, Weston, and Wilton, an indication if nothing else that colonists had acquired a discerning eye for regional patterns and weaves.

The trade in other kinds of imported goods developed in much the same way. Before mid-century the New York newspapers seldom listed gloves. During the 1750s general all-purpose categories of gloves began to appear: "Men's Colored Gloves," "Men's Gloves," "Women's Gloves," and "Women's Worsted Gloves." A decade later customers confronted over thirty-five choices, including purple gloves, flowered gloves, orange gloves, white gloves, rough gloves, chamois gloves, buff gloves, "Maid's Black Gloves," "Maid's Lamb Gloves," and a curious line in "Men's Dog Skin Gloves." In 1773 New York advertisers distinguished among forty-four different types of dishes, offering potential customers everything in this line from "Queen's Ware" to "Coarse Ware."

LATELY IMPORTED, and TO BE SOLD BY
Samuel Hughes *in Queen-Street,*

HOgsheads of Earthen and Glass Wares, Boxes of Pipes, Cartridge Paper, Yorkshire Ale, Currants, Starch, Pump and Sole Leather, Flannels, Swanskins, Colchester and Drapery Baize, Shag and striped Duffels, Blankets and Rugs, Callimancoes, Tammies, Durants, Shalloons, Broad Cloths, Irish and Manchester Linnens, Ozenbrigs, Ticklinburgs, Ravens and Ruffia Duck, Dowlass, broad Diapers, Tin Plates, colour'd Threads, Mackrel Lines and Hooks, Ironmongery and Cutlary Wares; Anchors, Cables, Sails and Rigging fit for a Ship of 200 Tons.

Samuel Hughes, who had come to appreciate the importance of fashion in the American marketplace, featured goods "Lately Imported." *Boston Gazette,* 29 June 1761. *Courtesy of the Massachusetts Historical Society.*

Fashionable colonists were tempted by gold watches during the 1730s, by silver watches during the 1750s, and by "toy watches" during the 1770s.

After mid-century various strange and alarming home cures began to appear more frequently in provincial newspapers. By 1773 at least twenty-two different remedies imported from Great Britain were advertised in the New York journals. Of all the goods listed in the weekly publications, only these informed consumers what to expect if they actually purchased a certain pill, powder, or tonic. One could demand "Ormskirk," for example, a product which declared itself a "Certain Cure for the Bite of a Mad Dog," adding that "No family should be without it in the house, tho it costs 16s[hillings]." Chemists offered "Ladies' Balsam for Nervous Disorders" and "Greenock's Tincture for Teeth and Gums." Advertisers apparently took for granted the efficacy of "Jesuit's Drops" and "Godfrey's Cordial." "Keyser's

Genuine Pills" merited a fuller explanation in the June 14, 1774, issue of the *New-York Mercury*. According to James Rivington, this miraculous medicine, which had "just arrived from London," guaranteed "the most effectual Cure of the *Secret Disease*. EVERY PERSON by taking these PILLS, and conforming to the printed directions, may become THEIR OWN DOCTOR, in the most private and personal manner." The afflicted person who turned to Keyser's Pills could take a measure of confidence from the testimonial that the product has cured "thirty-seven thousand soldiers and poor persons, of both sexes . . . as is certified by some of the most eminent physicians and surgeons upon Earth." Keyser's Pills appeared in other major provincial cities at roughly the same time they arrived in the New York market. But wherever American consumers lived, they had to be careful. One advertisement warned those who relied on "Dr. Hill's very celebrated Medicines" that the public should be on the alert for "counterfeit" offerings. The only way the prudent New Yorker could be assured of results—specifically relief from "Scurvy, Headaches, Low Spirits, Vapours, and Melancholy"—was to demand a container of the "Essence of Water Dock," prepared by Dr. Hill and "by him autographed."[47]

In less busy commercial centers such as New Haven, Annapolis, and Portsmouth, newspapers did not contain as many consumer possibilities as one found in Boston, Philadelphia, or New York. But even in the smaller provincial cities, the number of items advertised rose impressively after mid-century. Throughout colonial America the lists of colorful and exciting goods that appeared in the journals assumed the existence of a commercial public, anonymous men and women who had learned to distinguish among goods of different origin and quality. Consumption was thus an active process; it implied creative engagement. The advertisements invited anyone with money or credit to enter into an open conversation. No announcement spoke only to the rich or well-born; anyone could imagine himself or herself acquiring something in this marketplace, if not directly from shops such as the one owned by Mordecai Yarnall, then through other less reputable means we will discuss at greater length in another section. Many goods listed in the advertisements would eventually be given away or resold, and as the index of choice expanded, so too the dreams of possession flourished. Choice was not just a commercial fact; it was also a state of mind.

Newspaper advertising revealed an important characteristic of the new consumer marketplace not found in other sources. The same choices appeared in all regions of colonial America at roughly the same time. Journal announcements published in Boston, Charleston, Philadelphia, and New York were almost indistinguishable. They listed identical categories, and even though the absolute number of artifacts grew sharply after mid-century, the actual market selection as well as the wording of the advertisements themselves seems virtually interchangeable. In Charleston and Williamsburg one encounters local newspaper notices for special items such as "Negro Cloth," but even in the southern colonies the range of choice paralleled that in the North. This development meant that as the colonial import markets expanded, they also experienced remarkable congruence. Consumer choice and regional standardization went hand-in-hand in this eighteenth-century empire of goods, so that whatever elements distinguished the different areas of colonial America—one thinks of different agricultural staples and labor systems—consumer experience does not seem to have been one of them. Several explanations for product standardization immediately spring to mind. Wherever they lived, American merchants placed orders with known groups of British suppliers, and it would have been highly surprising to discover lines of cloth or pottery in Charleston that were not also available in Boston or New York. In an effort to achieve greater efficiency in production, the manufacturers themselves adopted standardized tools and procedures, so that white saltglaze cups or maid's lamb gloves made in one English location looked pretty much like those made in another. Moreover, competitors followed each other closely, copying each other's designs.[48]

VII

The detective of an eighteenth-century consumer culture stumbles finally upon the richest source of them all: British customs records, the product of sedulous, overworked British bureaucrats. In 1696 William Culliford accepted an impossible assignment. The commissioners for "managing and causing to be Leavied and Collected his Majesty's Custom's Subsidies and other Duty's" appointed Culliford to the newly created post of Inspector-General of Imports and Exports. Official instructions spelled out his primary responsibility, keeping "a particular, distinct, and true account of the importations and exportations of all commodities into and out of this kingdom." Culliford may not have viewed himself as a pioneer in what became known as "political arithmetic," but, in point of fact, collecting data of this sort for the purpose of informing government policy had no real precedent. These imposing registers represented a bold attempt to bring quantitative precision to the nation's balance of trade. Assisted by a small staff, Culliford began systematically to gather statistics on the foreign commerce of England and Wales—Scotland was not added to the project until much later—and as the figures poured into the London offices of the inspector-general, clerks dutifully entered the sums into massive ledgers, a separate volume for each year. And for this enterprise, Culliford treated the mainland American colonies no differently from the Baltic Ports or Russia; they were all busy commercial entrepôts where customers and producers generated numbers whose meaning scholars are still debating three centuries later.[49]

Culliford wanted the ledgers to reflect actual market values. For several years he translated units of commerce—yards and dozens, for example—into current prices, an extremely difficult task since trade figures varied regionally and seasonally. Although the challenge of collecting accurate information nearly overwhelmed Culliford's assistants, they managed remarkably well to record significant market fluctuations. At least, they did so while

Culliford remained as inspector-general. After he retired from service early in the eighteenth century, his successors—many of whom regarded the post as a sinecure—compromised Culliford's grand scheme. While they still compiled detailed intelligence on the quantities of imports and exports, they no longer bothered with changing prices. Indeed, for the entire eighteenth century, the registers described the flow of imperial commerce in terms of numbers frozen in 1702.[50]

Such recording practices have discouraged many people attempting to make sense of the British customs ledgers, contemporary interpreters as well as modern. The obstacles have, of course, seemed quite formidable. Various inspectors-general not only ignored current market values but also failed to take into account the impact of smuggling on gross trade balances. And that was not the end of it. Overworked clerks sometimes entered incorrect figures, merchants occasionally misled crown officials about the quantities of goods transported to distant ports, and Scottish trade statistics remained spotty until the middle of the eighteenth century.[51] Nevertheless, as it turns out, none of these problems seriously undermines the usefulness of the customs registers for the study of colonial American consumption of durable and semi-durable goods. The 1702 prices have been recalculated to reflect real eighteenth-century market conditions. Moreover, we now know much more about Scottish trade with the mainland colonies—a particularly important piece of information for anyone reconstructing Chesapeake commerce—and in belated fulfillment of Culliford's original ambitions, it is possible to provide fairly precise monetary figures for the British manufactures exported to the American provinces.[52]

What the Customs House registers do provide, therefore, is powerfully compelling evidence of a sharp mid-century expansion of consumer demand throughout the colonies. During the mid-1740s Great Britain exported to the mainland American ports merchandise valued at £871,658. By the 1760s this figure had risen by roughly 130 percent, and during the extraordinary year of 1771 when well-organized boycotts of British manufactures collapsed, thus opening colonial markets to a sudden flood of goods, the annual total reached a pre-revolutionary high of £4,576,944.[53] The inspector-general's reports divided the mainland colonies into six separate districts—New England, New York, Pennsylvania, the Chesapeake (Virginia and Maryland), Carolina, and Georgia—and although all regions experienced striking advances in the consumption of British exports between the 1740s and 1760s, some rose much faster than others. Pennsylvania, for example, recorded a spectacular jump of almost 380 percent during this period. By comparison, New England's doubling of British exports seemed modest. Other trends are of interest. During the 1740s a lion's share of the exports went to Maryland and Virginia. These colonies alone received almost 43 percent of the British goods shipped to the mainland colonies. By the 1760s, however, their share had dropped to about 30 percent of the American total, a clear indication of the rapid economic development of the other regional markets such as Pennsylvania, New York, and Carolina.[54]

From a British perspective the customs volumes tell a somewhat different although equally impressive story about the expansion of the American consumer market. By 1773 the colonists purchased almost 26 percent of *all* domestically produced goods that were exported out of the mother country. This was a very significant development. At the beginning of the century the colonists received only 5.7 percent of England's total exports. Traders carried most of their merchandise to the Continent.[55] But as the focus of the market shifted to the New World, American consumers acquired greater importance for British manufacturers, major merchant houses, and imperial planners. Certain categories of goods poured into the mainland provinces. It is estimated, for example, that by mid-century the colonists purchased about half of the ironware, earthenware, silk goods, printed cotton and linen, and flannels that English merchants sold abroad. Indeed, American buyers accounted for almost three-quarters of all nails that British manufacturers exported during this period of commercial expansion.[56]

However impressive these aggregate trade statistics may appear, they take on even greater significance when interpreted in the context of a growing colonial population. Long before the Revolution, Franklin observed how rapidly the American population seemed to be expanding. In a brilliantly imaginative essay that greatly influenced Thomas Malthus, the famed British demographer, Franklin posited that because the colonists married younger than did contemporary Europeans, they produced more children. Franklin calculated that the total population was doubling approximately every twenty-five years, a performance which Malthus later announced was probably "without parallel in history." The rate of increase may have been even greater than Malthus understood. Franklin only considered natural increase. He excluded "strangers," presumably the thousands of Scots-Irish and Germans who were then flooding into the middle colonies.[57] Although the provincial governments did not systematically collect census data, they did generate various lists that today make it possible to estimate with reasonable confidence the total population of the American mainland colonies. The actual growth rate turns out to be very close to Franklin's original guess. Between 1700 and 1770 the colonial population, black as well as white, increased by more than eightfold, from roughly 250,888 to 2,148,076. Between 1740 and 1770—the period of greatest concern for the development of a consumer society—the population grew an astonishing 137 percent.[58]

Within this demographic context, rising per capita consumption of British exports actually exceeded the rate of population increase. By any standard, this was a truly remarkable market performance. Although international wars sometimes interrupted the flow of Atlantic commerce, we now know from the inspector-general's ledgers that ever more Americans were purchasing ever more goods from the mother country. Between 1720 and 1770 per capita consumption of British exports grew nearly 50 percent; even more startling, the rate of increase seems to have been accelerating during the period 1750 to 1770. The most striking numbers came from the middle colonies. The Carolinians also recorded a major surge of buying, but even New Englanders posted a 25 percent leap in per capita consumption of British exports.[59] One historian has calculated that the per capita income of colonial Americans in the late 1760s was about £12, and while we should recognize that this figure represents a very rough estimate, it suggests that every man, woman, and child in this society spent about 10 percent of annual income on the "Baubles of Britain."[60] If nothing else, this stunning reliance on imported goods reveals widespread prosperity among the white colonists. Franklin certainly believed that rising personal wealth accounted for the extraordinary quantities of consumer goods that were reaching provincial America. In 1766 he visited a leading professor in Germany, Gottfried Achenwall, and after the two men had discussed the amazing growth of consumption in Pennsylvania, the German observed, "Even if [domestic] manufacturing increases, it cannot keep pace with the increase of population and the demand for goods [comparing 1725 to 1757]. . . . Four times the population uses much more than four times, really seventeen times more goods, because the population grows more rapidly in wealth than in numbers."[61]

Although the Customs House ledgers fail to break down the various categories of British exports as finely as did the colonial newspaper advertisements, they still provide strong testimony to the expanding range of consumer choices that confronted the provincial shopper in mid-century. To be sure, the great registers ignored attributes such as color and pattern. They did, however, list scores of different articles, including many encountered in other eighteenth-century sources.[62] Some categories were more surprising. The inspector-general's staff carefully noted, for example, the "Bugle great" and "Beads Amber" bound for New York, both items representing only a single pound sterling in Great Britain's total annual export. They included as well the "Alphabets" and "Human Hair" that merchants transported to Pennsylvania. The lists averaged about one hundred separate categories of exported goods. One entry in particular reminds us of how difficult it must have been for the clerks to monitor a fast-growing world market. After recording general types of cloth, metalware, and pottery, they seemed almost relieved to describe the remaining sundries simply as "Goods, several sorts," a wonderfully all-purpose label that must have incorporated new products and curiosities as they first made their journey across the Atlantic.[63] As one economic historian explained, "The process of industrialization in England from the second quarter of the eighteenth century was to an important extent a response to colonial demands for nails, axes, firearms, buckets, coaches, clocks, saddles, handkerchiefs, buttons, cordage, and a thousand other things."[64]

The annual summaries of the inspector-general confirmed the preeminence of textiles in Britain's colonial trade. Various kinds of finished cloth made up over half of all manufactured goods transported to the American mainland during the eighteenth century. Of these, woolens represented by far the largest share, but the colonists also purchased huge quantities of fabric which the customs clerks listed only as silk, cotton, or linen. In addition, the ledgers mentioned a constantly expanding supply of calico, satin, gingham, damask, and taffeta. Some fabric came originally from Continental markets in Russia and Germany, usually coarse linens, and were then transhipped to the colonies. Increasingly, however, the textiles exported to America had been produced in Great Britain. Whatever their source, the same basic range of textiles seems to have been carried to all regions of the mainland. In other words, the registers provide no persuasive evidence that consumer experience in Charleston or Williamsburg differed significantly from that of Boston, or for that matter, New York or Philadelphia.

The ledgers suggest that the royal governors who reported that the colonists regularly dressed in British cloth knew what they were writing about. Although ordinary Americans may have spun some fibers into thread and then woven this material into cloth, their domestic activities hardly dented a robust trade in British cloth that literally affected how the colonists presented themselves in public.[65] Imported textiles became the badge of eighteenth-century empire. As the anonymous author of a 1753 pamphlet published in Boston exclaimed about British cloth, "our Beds, our Tables and our Bodies are covered with it."[66] And in time, of course, it came to signify their political and economic dependence on the mother country, something that they were slow to appreciate and even slower to protest. In 1769 a writer who styled himself "A Son of Liberty" informed readers of the *Connecticut Journal, and New-Haven Post-Boy* that "one Half, if not Two-Thirds, of all the Woollen Cloths worn in English America, are imported from Great-Britain." Could the colonists ever overcome this "Subjection," he asked, and then, answering his own question, responded, "We may then project, resolve, vapour and threaten, as much as we please; 'tis all in vain, and we make but a ridiculous Figure, while we are dependent upon Great-Britain for a warm Coat to save us from Freezing in the Winter."[67]

But as "A Son of Liberty" understood, the colonists loved their "Subjection" so long as it carried no obvious political disabilities. The newspapers that often fulminated against luxury in dress also advertised products that protected and preserved imported cloth. "Fine Crown Soap," for example, was just what the colonist needed for washing "fine Linens, Muslins, Laces, Silks, Chinces, [and] Calicoes."[68] And John Atkins, who had just arrived from Dublin, sensed immediately how the importation of so much cloth had created an opportunity for a new service industry. He set himself up as a "Dry-Scourer"—really America's first dry cleaner—and promised "if employed, [to] take out all Spots, Stains and Filth, to the greatest Perfection, and most reasonable Rates, out of all kinds of Men or Womens Apparel." Atkins was especially confident of his ability to "Clean Scarlet Cloaks and Dye them also."[69]

Since the history of eighteenth-century consumption involves the making of choices in an expansive new marketplace, it is important to stress the almost unique relation in colonial America between popular consumer demand and demographic structure. In a population growing as rapidly as did that of Britain's mainland provinces, about half of the people alive at any given moment were necessarily children under the age of sixteen. No doubt, these boys and girls engaged in consumer activities insomuch as they wore garments made of imported cloth, ate from British plates, and worked the fields with British tools. But the decision to purchase one item rather than another, to give preference to a certain color or weight, remained largely the prerogative of adults. The swift transformation of imperial commerce put pressure on parents to learn how to hold their own as consumers, discovering as much as they could about current prices, opportunities for credit, and relative qualities of competing products. In this unprecedented commercial environment, mid-eighteenth-century parents found themselves teaching their children how to be successful consumers, a task which for earlier generations would have been of pressing concern only to gentry families. The population figures also included large numbers of slaves, dependent workers who, like the children, used imported British goods but did not have a significant voice in their actual selection.

What considerations of age and race suggest—and these were major factors differentiating the American consumer society from that developing in contemporary Britain—was that a surprisingly small percentage of the total colonial population, perhaps no more than 30 percent in 1770, controlled the acquisition of imported manufactures.[70] These people energized the entire consumer market. Many were persons of modest means, members of a large and growing middle class, who associated their own freedom and prosperity with improvement in their standard of living. If we consider only the members of this group, then the per capita figure for consumption of British goods was really much higher than the aggregate population statistics revealed, a remarkable phenomenon since those numbers were already very high.

Culliford's grand project sparks one final observation about the broader social implications of eighteenth-century export statistics. After the 1740s competition among British manufacturers translated into lower consumer prices.[71] This long-term trend allowed colonial buyers to acquire ever more goods over time for the same amount of money. In other words, greater efficiencies in merchandising, production, and transportation meant that ordinary Americans enjoyed more choices in the marketplace. Since some items such as teacups and saucers were generally more durable than others, they did not have to be replaced very often, and if they remained in fashion they could be handed down to children. The same conditions pertained for tools and cutlery, indeed, for most metal articles. But other goods, especially imported textiles, obviously wore out. Nevertheless, even within this large category of consumer spending, one quickly met basic needs. A family could only own so many linen napkins, for example, before problems of storage eroded the pleasures of possession.[72] As we have seen, neither lower prices nor fulfillment of demand lessened consumer activity during the period before the American Revolution. Rather, provincial buyers redirected their expenditures, purchasing more and more articles which an earlier generation of Americans might reasonably have defined as luxuries or, in poorer households, substituting new cheaper products for expensive ones.[73]

VIII

The eighteenth-century Anglo-American world compiled its inventories of desire from many different perspectives. Sometimes ordinary men and women showed no awareness that they were creating records of consumer life. They unthinkingly threw shattered dishes and broken knives into the nearest trash pit. Personal correspondence was more self-conscious about changing consumer behavior. It testified to a new world that appeared to contemporaries even newer because of the acquisition of so many imported goods. Other lists represented more formal and official attempts to gain insight into the great transatlantic flow of British manufactures. But whatever the character of the sources, whatever the intentions of their makers, the six major categories of evidence support a common set of conclusions.

For a very long period, perhaps for the entire first century of European settlement in mainland America, the colonists led relatively simple lives. They attended to necessities. Only the wealthy acquired luxury goods from the mother country. English visitors would surely have regarded the material culture of these insecure plantations as stark, dull, and, by cosmopolitan standards, primitive.[74] But at some moment during the middle of the eighteenth century, free Americans entered a new era, a distinct colonial period as different in terms of material culture from the years of initial conquest as our times are from the late nineteenth century. Indeed, the transformation of the colonists' standard of living came so rapidly that people at the time commented on the speed of change. For them, the domestic landscape of everyday life seemed to have taken on an unfamiliar appearance.

It was not consumption itself that so impressed contemporaries or set them apart from earlier generations. The rich and well-born had been buying imported goods from distant lands for as long as societies have kept records. Rather, what was new about the mid-eighteenth-century consumer marketplace was the range of choices that it offered and the ability of ordinary men and women to participate. Some persons, of course, purchased more goods than their poorer neighbors. They also had the means to acquire better, more expensive items. But almost everyone had an opportunity to become a consumer.[75]

And wherever they lived, American consumers confronted not only an accelerating quantity of exports from Great Britain but also an ever greater selection—colors, textures, and patterns—at cheaper rates. The experience of shoppers in the Carolinas and the Chesapeake was not significantly different from that of New Yorkers or New Englanders. All of them had to learn an unfamiliar vocabulary—queen's ware, not china; Wilton carpets, not rugs; maid's lamb gloves, not gloves—that defined an expanding consumer culture. In this sense, the Anglo-American market standardized everyday experience, and even though southern planters did not know—or, for that matter, did not much care—that they were choosing from among the same range of British goods as were northern or middle-colony farmers, no one could deny that they were all being incorporated into a great Anglo-American commercial empire in remarkably similar ways.

With so many consumers demanding so many British goods, one cannot avoid asking why Americans did not produce competing items of their own. They certainly seemed to possess the basic natural resources needed to sustain commercial potteries or glass houses. The same could be said of the manufacture of cloth and paper. Many political commentators on the eve of revolution advocated just these kinds of projects. One of them, an author who published a piece in the 1767 *Connecticut Courant*, explained, "The way then to get redress for our wrongs is to render ourselves unprofitable to Great Britain, by industry. We must begin sooner or later, the increase of the inhabitants of this country being so great as to put it out of the powers of Great Britain to cloath us a century hence."[76]

However much sense plans for domestic manufacturing made in theory, they never achieved the intended results. Many obstacles presented themselves. The primary one, however, was an utter lack of enthusiasm by ordinary colonists. By their own lights, they had transferred to America not to become mere laborers but rather to establish themselves as independent yeomen farmers. Working in urban areas for wages held almost no appeal. On this point colonists of an entrepreneurial turn of mind agreed. During the 1730s Cadwallader Colden, an astute commentator on economic and political affairs, despaired of recruiting an adequate labor force for New York. Some of his colleagues had apparently counseled the importation of large numbers of slaves, but Colden declared the scheme too expensive. The obvious alternative did not seem all that promising. However much New York needed free white workers, the migrants stubbornly refused to cooperate:

> The hopes of having land of their own & becoming independent of Landlords is what chiefly induces people into America & they think they have never answer'd the design of their coming till they have purchased land which as soon as possible they do & begin to improve ev'n before they are able to maintain themselves. This they never fail to do notwithstanding that they every day & every where see the miserable state in which these new Settlers live & that they cannot get in many years the tenth part by their labour on their own lands what they can by wages if they would work for others.[77]

Other frustrated planners echoed Colden's complaint. In 1762 William Smith, colonial New York's most talented historian, blamed the abundance of inexpensive land for the Americans' inability to compete successfully with the British manufactures. "It is much owing to the disproportion between the number of our inhabitants," claimed Smith, "and the vast tracts remaining still to be settled, that we have not, as yet, entered upon scarce any other manufactures than such as are indispensably necessary for our home convenience."[78]

Widespread unwillingness to work for employers drove up the cost of free labor, making it even harder for persons willing to risk capital in manufacturing ventures to flourish even in local markets. Importing indentured servants from Europe did not provide a satisfactory answer. New York's Governor Henry Moore informed the Board of Trade in 1767 that no sooner did servants fulfill the conditions of their contracts than "they immediately quit their masters." They insisted on independence in America.

[They] get a small tract of Land, in settling which for the first three or four years they lead miserable lives, and in the most abject Poverty; but all this is patiently borne and submitted to with the greatest cheerfulness, the satisfaction of being Landholders smooths every difficulty, & makes them prefer this manner of living to that comfortable subsistence which they could procure for themselves and their families by working at the Trades in which they were brought up.[79]

The words "cheerfulness" and "satisfaction" remind us of the industrious members of the Stanespring family whom Alexander Hamilton met on his trip to Albany, happy peasants who somehow managed to purchase the very items that others expected them to produce for themselves.

One of Benjamin Franklin's most endearing talents was his ability to restate commonplace beliefs in unexpectedly amusing and positive ways. On the matter of America's recalcitrant labor force, he turned weakness—if not outright resistance—into a virtue. In 1760 he assured British manufacturers that their many colonial customers would never become competitors; or if they did so, it would not be for a very long time. The reason was simple. "Manufactures are founded in poverty," Franklin observed. "It is the multitude of poor without land in a country, and who must work for others at low wages or starve, that enables undertakers to carry on a manufacture." This rhetoric was not exactly flattering, but perhaps Franklin had learned how to appeal to hard-nosed eighteenth-century businessmen. In America such conditions were sadly absent, for "no man who can have a piece of land of his own, sufficient by his labour to subsist his family in plenty, is poor enough to be a manufacturer or work for a master. Hence while there is land enough in America for our people, there can never be manufactures to any amount or value."[80]

As Franklin noted with characteristic irony, from time to time English workers who possessed advanced industrial training actually moved to America. It was only to be expected, he observed, that members of this small, highly skilled group would quickly set up in the colonies as "brasiers, cuttlers, and pewterers," but when they reached the New World a curious transformation occurred. They gradually dropped "the working part of their business, and import[ed] their respective goods from *England*, whence they can have them cheaper and better. . . . They continue their shops indeed, in the same way of dealing, but become *sellers* of brasiery, cutlery, pewter, hats &c. brought from *England*, instead of *makers* of those goods."[81] For most migrants, therefore, the trip to America took them back to the land, to husbandry; for a few, the journey turned skilled workers into shopkeepers. Thomas Jefferson and others of his agrarian mentality praised this phenomenon. They wanted to keep industrial wage earners out of America as long as possible, thus preserving the yeoman republic from poverty and corruption and allowing free farmers—and a few industrious merchants—to consume foreign imports without thereby compromising their sense of personal independence.[82]

Not surprisingly, when colonial Americans attempted to produce consumer goods of British quality, they almost always came up short. To be sure, they turned out beautiful furniture and silverware. But in the main categories of imported items regularly advertised in the provincial newspapers, colonial craftsmen clearly failed local buyers. Indeed, to take one obvious article, British potteries in the Midlands were able to manufacture various lines of stoneware, creamware, and china and transport them to major English commercial centers, usually by canal or turnpike, where they were crated and shipped to America, then unpacked, displayed in colonial stores, and ultimately sold at prices as low as or lower than those of rival domestic ceramics. The British artifacts were not only more finely executed, more colorfully decorated, and more fashionably conceived, they were also widely affordable. It did not matter that the American potters had abundant supplies of clay and forests of trees to turn into charcoal for their kilns. Except for the cheapest earthenware, they simply could not compete.[83]

Colonial experiments in glassmaking yielded no more satisfactory results. In 1768 William Franklin, royal governor of New Jersey and Benjamin's son, reported to Lord Hillsborough that "A Glass House was erected about Twenty Years ago in Salem County, which makes Bottles, and a very coarse Green Glass for Windows, used only in some of the Houses of the poorer Sort of People."[84] It was this unimpressive record of industrial achievement that discouraged writers such as John Dickinson during the protests of the 1760s. In his *Letters from a Farmer in Pennsylvania*, he admitted that colonial attempts to produce paper and glass had come to nothing. Since American consumers regarded quality goods as "requisite for the comfort of life," and since they could not begin to fulfill their own demand, they inevitably found themselves caught in an impossible market situation, for "the seller has a plain advantage, and the buyer *must* pay the duty."[85]

Although Americans made some cloth, they regarded it as inferior to the fabrics exported to the colonies from Great Britain. In New England the production of homespun seems to have supplemented the larger consumer market.[86] But these efforts never amounted to much. In Connecticut the problem was cost of labor. As "A Well-Wisher to His Country" explained in 1767, "More especially this appears to be very much the Case with Spinners, to the great Discouragement of domestic Manufactures. For the Farmers who are able to raise the Wool and Flax, for their own use and to spare others, are discouraged trying to make any more Cloth than what their Families can spin; which in many Instances is not half so much as they have Occasion to consume."[87] Whenever possible, ordinary people purchased yard goods from local merchants. As Governor William Pitkin of Connecticut reported to the members of the Board of Trade in 1766, "The Inhabitants of this Colony are chiefly Employ'd in subduing and Improving Land, [and] do nothing more at the Woolen & Linen Manufactures than to supply the Deficiencies of what our produce Enables us to purchase of Great Britain." The homespun that one encountered in Connecticut on the eve of independence was "principally of the Courser Sort for Labourers & Servants which is done by particular Families for their Necessary Use."[88] Other sources from the period support Pitkin's assessment. Studies of probate inventories indicate that fewer than half of the households in late eighteenth-century

Massachusetts owned spinning wheels, an artifact which modern interpreters of early America and antique dealers seem to have transformed into an ubiquitous symbol of domestic enterprise. Even more telling was the fact that only one in ten New England families had looms.[89]

Cloth production may have been more common in New York. According to Governor Moore, in New York City projectors experimented with

Imported in the Sally, Captain William Barber, from Glasgow, and sundry Vessels from London, Liverpool and Briftol, and sold wholesale and retail, by
MAGDALEN DEVINE,
In Second-ftreet, between Market and Cheftnut-Streets, within a few doors of the Quaker Meeting house, the following goods, viz.

BLACK, blue and cloth coloured India and English paduafoys, black, blue, pink, white and cloth coloured fattins and pelongs, blue, yellow and brown English damafks, black, pink, and blue figured mode, ftriped luteftrings, green, blue, brown and pink coloured ducapes, brown and changeable 3-qr. and half ell wide mantuas, black English taffeties, blue, black, ftriped and cloth coloured ell wd. India perfians, blufh, blue and white half yd. perfians, white half yd. and half ell wd. farfnet, womens filk cloaks, cardinals and fhades, ftriped and flowered ribbons, mens and womens filk velvets, a variety of cotton ditto, mens black, green and cloth coloured filk breeches patterns, worfted two, three and four threaded ditto, ftriped filk and cotton ginghams and Damafcus, mens and womens filk hose of various colours, mens filk and worfted ditto, mens white and brown knit ribbed ditto, mens, womens, boys, maids and girls cotton, thread and worfted ditto, womens, maids and girls filk and thread mitts and gloves, of various colours, bardance and remal handkerchiefs, Irifh and Barcelona coloured and black ditto, kenting, long lawn, ftampt linen, and check ditto, Barcelona cravats, plain and ftriped Englifh and Scotch gaufes, thread and blond laces, a large affortment of light ground pompadour, two purple, yellow and dark ground chintzes, and cotton chintzes, light, dark and two purple ground ftamped cottons and calicoes, light and dark ground printed linens, a neat affortment of figured India and Manchefter demities, Ruffia diapers, tablecloths, double and quadruple filafia, India nankeens, jeans, fuftians, 5-qr. 6-qr. and yd. wd. muflins and humhums, 7-8ths and yd. wd. cambricks and lawns, long lawns, 7 8ths and yd. wd. Irifh linens, brown and white Irifh, Lancafhire and Ruffia fheetings and dowlas, Britifh and German ozenbrigs, Ruffia drillings, 3 qr. 7-8ths, yd. wd. and yd. 3-8ths wd. linen and cotton checks, a large affortment of tammies, fhaloons, durants, dorfetteens, calimancoes, crapes, ruffels, hairbines, hair graxets, meffinets, half yd. and yd. wd. popiins, fpotted montees, yd. wd. ftarrets, bombazines, camblets, faggathies, Mecklenburghs, fingle and double worfted damafks, 6-qr. naps, plain and napped halfthicks, 6 and 7-qr. broadcloths, from 6 to 10 qr. green, blue and mottled rugs, rofe blankets, large and fmall floor carpets, beft Wilton bed-fide carpets, yd. wd. haircloth for maitfters and brewers, green tea, mahogany tea chefts, womens fhoes, ivory and wood ftick fans, paper for rooms, Scotch threads, tapes, bindings, garterings and ferritings, and fundry other goods, too tedious to infert, all of which fhe will fell at reasonable rates, for ready money or fhort credit.

Innovative advertisers learned quickly how to catch the attention of potential customers. Magdalen Devine included a small woodcut in her newspaper announcement, depicting several new textile patterns and designs to be found in her Philadelphia shop. *Pennsylvania Gazette*, 1 August 1765. *Courtesy of the Northwestern University Library, Evanston, Illinois.*

the manufacture of linen and woolens, but while these activities provided for "several poor families," the overall results were disappointing. A notable exception was the "Custom" of making "Coarse Cloths in private families [which] prevails throughout the whole province, and almost in every House a sufficient quantity is manufactured for the use of the Family, without the least design of sending any of it to market." "Swarms" of children, Moore reported, were "set to work as soon as they are able to Spin and Card, and as every family is furnished with a Loom, the Itinerant Weavers who travel about the Country, put the finishing hand to the Work." But most consumers had no more interest in "Coarse Cloths" than they had in coarse glass, and if Moore is to be believed, even at the height of the Stamp Act protests, when Americans often boasted of their ability to dress themselves fully in homespun fabric, the patriots "never cloathed themselves with the work of their own hands." These New Yorkers did what they had done for at least a generation; they "bought English Cloth for themselves and their families."[90]

IX

None of these examples will definitively dispel the enduring myth of early American self-sufficiency. We want to believe that the colonists were somehow different from those of us who find ourselves living in a modern commercialized world. We insist that these hearty yeomen somehow stood apart from the economic forces that so radically transformed the face of eighteenth-century British and Dutch society.[91] No doubt, ordinary farmers aspired to economic independence. And for most white men and women, most of the time, it was possible to maintain a healthy sense of their own personal freedom in the marketplace. Like other people in other cultures who have worked the soil for a living, they worried about feeding and housing their families, about making it through a hard winter, and about the need to set aside enough seed for next year's crops. They helped out neighbors; favors were exchanged on the community level without anyone demanding monetary compensation. No one questions that such practices defined human relations, especially in the northern and middle colonies.[92]

But arguments that celebrate—even implicitly—the colonists' self-sufficiency cannot possibly comprehend the massive mid-century importation of British goods.[93] The ground holds too many shards; the archives yield too many detailed lists. However much Americans during the run-up to revolution may have advocated turning their backs on consumer opportunity, they knew firsthand how much the new goods had affected the character of their lives. As "A Friend of This Colony" announced in a newspaper in 1767, "since the floods of English goods have been poured in upon us . . . family œconomy is at an end."[94]

The revolutionary generation's attempts to organize large-scale consumer boycotts were so difficult precisely because earlier Americans had so enthusiastically endorsed British manufactures. People of humble means were just as concerned as elite Americans with the articles that were advertised in the local journals. William Roberts, for example, arrived in Maryland as an indentured servant, but unlike Benjamin Franklin, Roberts discovered that ambition and diligence did not ensure personal success in America. As a free person, he struggled to make a living in "plantation work," which in his case meant growing a little tobacco. During one fleeting moment in 1767 when his prospects seemed to improve, this poor farmer decided "to go to house keepin." Recognizing the constraints of his meager resources, Roberts prudently listed what he anticipated would be his basic needs.

Roberts's private inventory of desire reveals just how thoroughly ordinary Americans had been incorporated into an empire of goods. Roberts wanted "a Bed tick, bolster and two pillows, one Rugg, two Blankets and a pair of Sheats, one four gallon Pott and a Eight Gallon one, a dozen of pewter Plates, four dishes of different sizes, a gallon Bason and a half one, four tinn pans, two half ones and two of a Gallon, half a dozen of knifes and forks, a Pint pewter pott and a quart pott, a Couple of candelssticks, Six Pewter spoons, a grid Iron, Box Iron, he[a]ters, and a frying Pann, one Handsaw, a Adge, a drawing knife, a Broad Axe, Narrow Axe, one Inch Auger and a half Inch, a gouge, [and] half a dozen of Gimblets of all Sizes." Roberts concluded that if he managed to acquire all "these things" from Great Britain, he surely would be able to "make my plows."[95]

Other poor people in provincial society apparently welcomed the chance to fashion themselves in exciting new ways. Consider the colorful description of two female servants that appeared in a Virginia newspaper. One woman was attired in "fine Pink coloured Worsted Stockings" along with a brown petticoat, a checked apron, and a striped bed gown, while the other wore a black hat, "an old red Silk Handkerchief round her Neck, an old dirty blue Stuff Gown, with check Linen Cuffs, old Stays, a black and white strip'd Country Cloth Petticoat, an old blue quilted ditto, a check Linen Apron and a brown Linen Shift."[96] We shall never know, of course, what the two women or the recently freed Roberts thought of the concept of self-sufficiency. They certainly desired personal independence in America. They also wanted to be comfortable and appealing, prosaic goals perhaps, but dreams easily fulfilled by the consumer marketplace of the mid-eighteenth century.

3

Consumers' New World: The Unintended Consequences of Commercial Success

Eighteenth-century writers seemed uncertain how best to describe Britain's relation to its many overseas possessions. Only tepidly did they employ the concept of "empire," since for them it carried uncomfortable intellectual baggage from ancient history. The traditional usage suggested that control over distant colonies and expansion into new regions depended on military might. But the notion that Great Britain was a modern-day Rome, dispatching powerful legions to conquer the world, did not sit well with a people who celebrated liberty and rights, the blessings of living under a balanced constitution. From the perspective of free modern subjects, what appeared to distinguish Britain's empire from that of Roman times was commerce, a continuing source of prosperity and stability.

The problem with this line of thought was that commerce itself required precise definition. After all, the English had engaged in large-scale trade for many centuries, certainly long before they laid claim to having an empire. The innovative element in the eighteenth-century discourse was not long-distance trade but rather a commerce organized around an expanding market for British manufactured goods. In this sense, Great Britain broke with the past by creating something genuinely new, an empire of consumer colonies.[1]

The rapid growth of a consumer-oriented economy sparked curiosity on both sides of the Atlantic Ocean. Americans looked at eighteenth-century England with new eyes, admiring its cosmopolitan culture. In turn, the English assessed with heightened intensity the role of the colonies in a burgeoning world system. Few contemporaries had given the changing character of Britain's empire more thought than Edmund Burke. His reflections on Atlantic trade informed a dramatic speech he gave before the House of Commons on March 22, 1775. In support of his "Resolutions for Conciliation with the Colonies," Burke delivered a long, brilliantly constructed set piece that represented one final attempt to avoid armed conflict. He was not sanguine about the prospects for peace. Lord North's majority clearly intended to force the issue of parliamentary supremacy. "Clouds indeed, and darkness, rest upon the future," Burke observed, sensing how critical the situation had become and fearing perhaps that neither reason nor rhetoric would save the day. "We are therefore called upon, as it were by a superior warning voice, again to attend to America," Burke explained. "To attend to the whole of it together; and to review the subject with an unusual degree of care and calmness."[2]

Burke invited Parliament to consider the nation's own best commercial interests. A firm stand on constitutional principle might mollify Englishmen who associated American rights with political anarchy, but such a course would almost certainly destroy the colonial trade that for at least a century had promoted general prosperity throughout the empire. Burke reminded Lord North's followers of the wisdom to be found in the great ledgers stored in the offices of the inspector-general, the same volumes we encountered in the previous chapter. Anyone who bothered to compare the customs records for 1704 with those of 1772 could see immediately that the continued health of the entire economy depended on the export of domestic manufactures. According to Burke, the value of "the whole trade of England" in 1704 was about the same amount as the "Export trade to the colonies alone in 1772." Burke did not explain how he calculated these numbers. Such details probably did not much matter. After all, as with all statistics, it was the interpretation that commanded attention. "The trade with America alone," Burke announced, "is now within less than £500,000 of being equal to what this great commercial nation, England, carried on at the beginning of this century with the whole world!"[3]

Edmund Burke understood the growing importance for Great Britain of the American consumer market better than did most other members of Parliament. *Print in possession of the Lewis Walpole Library, Farmington, Connecticut.*

Burke had spoken in the House of Commons often enough to sense the limits of statistical arguments. Audiences soon grew tired of figures. Burke required another, more personal device to dramatize the commercial transformation of the British Empire. And for that purpose he turned to a colleague in Parliament, Lord Bathurst (1684–1775), a long-lived Tory peer who happened to be the father of the current lord chancellor. The senior Bathurst had enjoyed a distinguished political career in his own right and over the first three-quarters of the eighteenth century had witnessed what Burke termed the "growth of our national prosperity." The man's adult experience conveniently bridged the span between 1704 and 1772, the dates of the two customs registers that Burke had so carefully reviewed. In this context Bathurst suddenly became a representative figure for a great commercial empire. After all, he had seen "all the stages" of Britain's progress, and for the sake of Burke's presentation in 1775, it seemed safe to assume that in 1704 Bathurst had been old enough "*acta parentum jam legere, et quae sit poterit cognoscere virtus* [to read the acts of his forebears and to recognize what virtue is able to accomplish]." Considering that the lord would then have been twenty years of age, he would have had to be a very dull lad indeed not to have comprehended "such things."[4]

For pure theater it was an arresting moment. Burke projected before the members of Parliament a kind of rhetorical holograph, a virtual Bathurst just setting out in 1704 on a long public career. Unlike most young people, however, Burke's imagined Bathurst had known from the very start what the future would bring. He comprehended the history of the entire eighteenth century before it ever occurred. How did he come to possess such prescience? What was his secret? The answer was that during the reign of Queen Anne, Bathurst had had a conversation with an angel of commerce, an annoyingly loquacious spirit intent in 1704 on telling the youthful nobleman how important the American colonies would be for the next sixty-eight years of English economic development.

One might have expected divine messengers of this sort to carry more weighty news, perhaps hints about the Second Coming, but apparently commercial intelligence in Great Britain was heady stuff. In any case, the young Bathurst listened politely as the angel drew back the curtain of time, exposing him to "the rising glories of his country." Gazing at least four generations into the future, the young man properly focused attention on the "commercial grandeur of England." While he contemplated the nation's splendid prospects, the angel pointed to "a little speck" on the globe. As Bathurst struggled to grasp the meaning of the speck, the angel proclaimed impatiently, "Young man, there is America." Lest that revelation cool his interest, the spirit of commerce laid out the course of eighteenth-century British history.

> [T]here is America—which at this day serves for little more than to amuse you with stories of savage men, and uncouth manners; yet shall, before you taste of death, show itself equal to the whole of that commerce which now attracts the envy of the world. Whatever England has been growing to by a progressive increase of improvement, brought in by varieties of people, by succession of civilizing conquests and civilizing settlements in a series of seventeen hundred years, you shall see as much added to her by America in the course of a single life!

If such a conversation had actually taken place in 1704, Burke wondered, would Bathurst have believed the angel of commerce? Probably not, the speaker concluded. The vision was too grand for the "credulity of youth."

It was fortunate, therefore, that the real Bathurst, a gentleman known to the members of Parliament, had lived to see the fulfillment of the prophecy. No one in 1775 could doubt how much American trade had contributed to the rising glory of eighteenth-century England.[5]

Although it persuaded Lord Bathurst, the angel apparently made little impression on a parliamentary majority bent on punishing the colonists. The House of Commons handily defeated the conciliatory motions. Burke's entire speech might well have been forgotten had it not been for a felicitous phrase that he employed to describe an earlier, less confrontational period of imperial history. Before the British government insisted on taxing Americans, it had encouraged a policy of "salutary neglect."[6] The words took on a life of their own, and in the process, created some confusion about the character of the empire that Burke was trying to save. Today, the phrase seems to recall an era of political and economic laissez-faire.[7] By allowing the distant provinces the freedom to develop within a loose framework of authority, Parliament allegedly encouraged the colonists to think of themselves as something different, indeed, as Americans. Such a reading of the speech misses the central thrust of Burke's argument. By "salutary neglect" he intended only to suggest that eighteenth-century Americans had managed to escape intolerable interference by the representatives of an *ancien régime*. British soldiers had never enforced colonial law; rapacious governors had not ridden roughshod over the local populace. The absence of coercion, however, did not mean that Americans were free to do as they pleased or that they defined their own interests as separate from those of Great Britain. The point was that commerce brought most Americans into a closer, more harmonious relationship with the mother country than could naked coercion. Salutary neglect was a velvet policy that bound scattered villages and plantations to a great imperial structure; it reaffirmed the colonists' fundamental Englishness without the threat of force. And with each passing decade, the commercial ties became stronger. American trade "swelled out on every side," Burke exclaimed. "It filled all its proper channels to the brim. It overflowed with a rich redundance . . . breaking its banks on the right and on the left." Sustaining the flood of commerce depended little upon the formal actions of the British government. Thousands of merchants and manufacturers—autonomous agents striving to advance their own private interests—almost unwittingly benefited the entire empire, so that, in Burke's words, "When we speak of the commerce with our colonies, fiction lags after truth; invention is unfruitful, and imagination cold and barren."[8]

Like many British contemporaries, Burke's angel of commerce celebrated the birth of "an empire of goods," a phrase that more accurately captures a mid-century world of trade than does "salutary neglect." The empire of goods was a vast commercial system driven largely by a phenomenon that William Douglass, a Boston physician, cleverly termed a "Galloping Consumption."[9] The new conditions forced the crown's widely dispersed subjects on both sides of the Atlantic to situate themselves within a larger conceptual framework, where mutual imagining, the product of rumor and exaggeration, fantasy and fact, spawned new perceptions of empire. People in the mother country had to decide just how distant provincials fit into an evolving political and commercial order. For Americans, the interpretive challenge was even more basic. They had to establish exactly what it meant for colonists to call themselves British.

II

Accounts of the colonial period often depict America's England as somehow frozen in amber, as a monolithic, unchanging "world we have lost," populated by dashing Elizabethan courtiers and persecuting bishops. To be sure, such a society had once dispatched thousands of Puritans and adventurers across the Atlantic. As colonists born in America as well as later migrants from the British Isles understood quite well, however, the mother country of 1700 or 1740 bore little resemblance to the late medieval regime of the Tudors and early Stuarts.[10] Meanings of empire that had made sense at an earlier moment no longer did so. Ordinary eighteenth-century white colonists suddenly became conscious that their England was not the England of their fathers. As subjects of an empire of goods, they faced economic and political challenges unknown during the seventeenth century. And, of course, many people who had come from other European countries had no memory of English folkways. The Scots-Irish and German migrants who moved in large numbers to eighteenth-century America accommodated to the demands of a commercial New World as best they could, relying as much as possible on their own ethnic resources.

Interpretation took place, therefore, within a specific context. It was the metropolitan core of the British Empire, not the struggling New World settlements, that first experienced the intellectual, religious, and political changes now associated with the development of modernity.[11] After a long civil war that briefly transformed England into a republic, after enduring many other domestic risings and rebellions, and after establishing once and for all the sovereignty of Parliament in the British constitution, the mother country emerged from the Glorious Revolution of 1688 stronger and more self-confident than it had been when its sons and daughters first traveled to the American shore. A troubled court society had brought forth a mighty fiscal-military state. No doubt, a good many fox-hunting country gentlemen weathered the change; the landed oligarchy preserved its political dominance for a very long time. And, although they surrendered many prerogatives so dear to the Stuarts, the Hanoverian monarchs remained central figures in any analysis of the political structure of the empire. What was different in the eighteenth century was that these familiar characters now shared the historical stage with an articulate and powerful middle class, and when colonial Americans took the measure of the mother country, they confronted a vibrant consumer economy, a complex state bureaucracy, a proliferation of new manufacturing centers, and a political culture comfortable with its own exuberant nationalism. Dynamism, growth, and power suddenly appeared the most appropriate terms with which to describe a not-so-traditional England of the mid-eighteenth century.[12]

Colonial Americans, of course, viewed these developments from afar. Distance alone deprived them of detailed information about many aspects of the English situation. Many were probably unaware, for example, of the stubborn survival of the Tories in some county communities until well into the Georgian era. Nor, for that matter, did ordinary Americans seem to know much about how the remarkable growth of provincial towns was changing the human landscape of Great Britain.[13] The army and navy were different matters. Perhaps more than any other element of change, Britain's military strength directly shaped how provincials imagined themselves within a new Anglo-American world. During the long eighteenth century, the British not only waged almost constant warfare against France and Spain but also usually emerged victorious. In other words, they were remarkably good at defending their expanding commercial and political interests.[14] Americans came to appreciate the imperial government for what it was, "the supreme example in the western world of a State organized for effective war-making."[15] It had not always been so. As recently as the 1660s the Dutch navy had presented a formidable threat to the commerce of its imperial rival. Dutch ships appearing in the James River threw the rulers of Virginia into a panic, and they wrote to London claiming that poor planters and unhappy white servants might rise up and join the enemy forces.[16] But less than a century later, British forces demonstrated convincingly that they could hold their own against ambitious and powerful Continental rivals.

England's spectacular military success depended only marginally on the brilliance and courage of the fighting men. Rather, unlike its great European adversaries, the nation had learned how to pay for large-scale war without bankrupting its citizens and, thereby, without sparking the kinds of internal unrest—peasant rebellions against taxation, for example—that destabilized other *ancien régime* monarchies. Although the process of strengthening and integrating local tax gathering had begun to accelerate during the late seventeenth century—changes thought necessary for the creation of modern bureaucratic states—it was not until Great Britain experienced a far-reaching "financial revolution" during the early decades of the eighteenth century that it found itself able effectively to defend and govern a worldwide colonial empire. In a word, British rulers discovered the secret of fighting on credit. Along with innovative banking and financial institutions such as the Bank of England, legions of new collectors and inspectors appeared throughout the realm. These busy new figures in the English countryside served as constant reminders of the establishment of "an impressively powerful central state apparatus."[17]

Economic and military transformation fed what for the mid-century American colonists would surely have been another arresting feature of the age, a sudden burst of British nationalism. Perhaps the Britons of this period did not experience what we might recognize as the advent of a full-blown nationalism, certainly not of the type of romantic nationalism that one encounters in nineteenth-century European states such as Germany. Whatever label one employs, however, it now seems apparent that sometime during the 1740s English men and women of all social classes began to express a sentiment that might be described variously as a dramatic surge of national consciousness, a rise of defiant patriotism, or a greatly heightened affirmation of national identity. To be sure, during the period of the Armada English people took intense pride in the defeat of the hated Spanish, and distinguished Elizabethan writers celebrated the blessings of being English. The Georgian experience was quite different. Even if the eighteenth-century development represented an intensification of an imaginative project with ancient roots, it nevertheless involved a much broader percentage of the population. It was now sustained and amplified by a new commercial press that brought stories of imperial might to urban coffee-houses and country taverns.[18]

Why a sudden intensification of "Britishness" occurred precisely at this particular moment remains unclear.[19] If the social foundations of a heightened sense of national identity are in doubt, however, no one questions the character of the swelling patriotic movement in the mother country. Ordinary people—laboring men and women as well as members of a self-confident middling group—who bellowed out the words to the newly composed "Rule, Britannia" and who responded positively to the emotional appeal of "God Save the King" gave voice to the common aspirations of a militantly Protestant culture. Or, stated negatively, they proclaimed their utter contempt for Catholicism and their rejection of everything associated with contemporary France. It is probably true, as some have suggested, that English aristocrats initially greeted the spread of popular nationalism with muted enthusiasm.[20] But in time, even members of the traditional ruling class came to appreciate the symbolic value of John Bull in mobilizing a population in support of war and monarchy. For most English people— the very men and women whom Americans would have encountered as travelers—the expression of national identity seems to have been quite genuine. Indeed, by noisy participation in patriotic rituals, the middling and working classes thrust themselves into a public sphere of imperial politics.[21]

In their reevaluation of the metropolitan culture, colonial Americans would almost certainly have taken note of the activities of a new social group in Great Britain, the so-called middle class. Whether the men and women who made up the "middling sort" actually represented a self-conscious class or were merely a loose amalgam of economically successful people busy thrusting their way into the public sphere is not, for our interests, of critical significance. We might pause, however, to address another interpretive problem. Since the middle class allegedly has been on the rise throughout recorded history—much like the perpetual growth of religious toleration or representative government—it may seem misguided to situate its arrival so confidently in mid-eighteenth-century England. But, on closer reflection, the issue turns out not to be all that arbitrary. While no one denies the

The TRIUMPH of BRITANNIA.

Between 1761 and 1763 Francis Hayman executed four historical canvases commemorating recent British military successes throughout the world. *The Triumph of Britannia*, now known only through this Simon F. Ravenet engraving (1763), depicts sea nymphs bearing the portraits of victorious British admirals. They follow in the wake of Britannia, who is seated majestically in Neptune's chariot. Thousands of ordinary Londoners saw Hayman's mid-century celebration of British nationalism. *Courtesy of the Yale Center for British Art, Paul Mellon Collection, New Haven, Connecticut.*

existence of other middle classes in the development of other nations—the Netherlands, for example—the British situation argues strongly for the invention of a distinct middle class in Georgian England. Educated, professional, and prosperous people with no claim to inherited privilege established, for the first time in the history of the mother country, a "polite and commercial" society. They articulated a claim to respected standing in the class structure in dramatically visible new ways. Not surprisingly, those who have studied the phenomenon claim that "the vigour, wealth, and numerical strength of the 'middle sort' . . . [was] the most important social feature of the age."[22]

This burgeoning middle class industriously copied the manners of its betters, fashioning self in ever more colorful and elaborate ways, celebrating consumer fads, purchasing the novels now marketed in large numbers, and populating the trendy spas and resort towns. Perhaps most remarkable, even as it redefined the character of English popular culture, the new middling group never seriously challenged the traditional landed oligarchy for the right to rule the nation.[23] And it was those men and women who most often entertained visiting Americans. The colonists abroad encountered English families headed by lawyers, merchants, and doctors, who regularly proclaimed that the freest nation in the world was also the most prosperous. For the provincials, it was an exciting and convincing display.

As any colonist would also have soon discovered, the members of this self-confident middle class of England energized an impressive new consumer marketplace. Economic historians are quick to insist that mid-eighteenth-century England had not yet entered an industrial revolution. Still, even without the benefit of major technological breakthroughs, small manufacturing centers managed to turn out consumer items in unprecedented quantities, and those alluring goods—the simple sundries of daily life—flowed from specialized production sites to scattered stores along the newly constructed canals and turnpikes. Prosperous English men and women, much like their American counterparts, bought what they had seen advertised in an expanding commercial press. And, significantly, people of more modest means also participated in that vibrant marketplace.

In some works published in Great Britain during this period, authors wove industrial geography into a narrative of national pride. They mapped out splendid tours of major manufacturing centers. The readers of *The Advantages of the Revolution Illustrated, by a View of the Present State of Great Britain* learned, for example, "Another undeniable Instance of the Advantage which has accrued to this Nation by the [Glorious] Revolution is the vast Increase and flourishing Condition of our Manufactures; and if Industry is a Characteristic of Liberty, I may venture to affirm that no Country in *Europe* can at this Day produce such glorious Proof of being in Possession of this valuable Blessing as *Great Britain*." The domestic traveler could witness "the admirable Progress of the *Silk Manufacture* in and about Spitalfields, which, within 60 Years, from almost nothing, is now, by the Ingenuity, Application and Expense of the Master-weavers, become the greatest and best in *Europe*." In the North of England "the *Woollen Manufactures* are wonderfully multiplied, improved and enlarged," and no one could dispute that Manchester's recent history revealed "How advantageous the *Cotton Manufacture* is to this Nation." The industrial route through England took the tourist to the metal works of Birmingham and Sheffield, the brass foundries of Bristol, the tin-plate factories in Monmouthshire, and the great porcelain potteries "at *Chelsea, May-fair, Brentford, Worcester, Bristol, Bow, &c.*"[24]

Visiting colonists occasionally really did follow the manufacturing tour. During the early 1770s one struggling Maryland merchant traveled Britain's new industrial countryside in search of bargains. Joshua Johnson believed that he could purchase goods directly from producers and thereby avoid London wholesalers who drove up the cost of doing business. But the scattered centers, each identified with a different specialty, did not fulfill Johnson's expectations. "I have been to many of the manufacturing towns . . . ," he wrote in 1772, "amongst which the following were the most capital, Gloucester, Tewkesbury, Bromsgrove, Birmingham, Coventry, and Woodstock." When he arrived in one of these cities, Johnson looked for huge warehouses filled with articles ready to be shipped to America. But, as he soon discovered,

> it was quite the reverse and the business [is] conducted as follows. The agents who reside in these towns employ the poor men and their families for ten or a dozen miles round them. . . . [T]hey deliver them as much iron etc. as they can work up in a week which is returned on Saturday night when they are paid for their labour, which is hardly sufficient to find them milk and bread, much more meat. In all light work I find the women and children preferred, the men being more inactive and much ad-dicted to drunkenness. . . . The agents, as soon as they collect a load, send it immedi-ately to their principal or correspondent in London, Bristol, etc.[25]

Although Johnson found the human misery in the new industrial towns revolting, he revealed something extraordinarily significant about the eighteenth-century consumer economy. The "Baubles of Britain" came not from factories in any modern sense. They represented the work of thousands of separate individuals, each turning out a few yards of cloth or beating a few pieces of metal into the desired shape, and what was so remarkable was that these poor, often displaced men and women could produce such a huge quantity of articles. A putting-out system had been recorded in England as early as the sixteenth century. What was new was the intensity and quantity of production. A generation before the so-called Industrial Revolution, English manufacturers found ways—some of them oppressive—to meet the sudden demands of a world market.

Perhaps describing the sudden economic transformation of England as a "consumer revolution" overstates the pace of change. Nevertheless, one authority in the field argues persuasively that "more men and women than ever before in human history enjoyed the experience of acquiring material possessions. Objects which for centuries had been the privileged posses-sions of the rich came, within the space of a few generations, to be within the reach of a larger part of society than ever before."[26] Josiah Tucker, dean of Gloucester during the late eighteenth century, would have readily ac-cepted this assessment of the changing character of English material cul-ture. People of all classes, declared Tucker in 1757, "have better Conveniences in their Houses, and affect to have more in Quantity of clean, neat Furni-ture, and a greater Variety (such as Carpets, Screens, Window Curtains, Chamber Bells, polished Brass Locks, Fenders, &c., &c.) (Things hardly known Abroad among Persons of such a Rank) than are to be found in any other Country in *Europe, Holland* excepted." In fact, Tucker believed "that almost the whole Body of the People of *Great Britain* may be considered either as the Customers *to,* or the Manufacturers *for* each other: A very happy Circumstance this."[27] What Tucker reported about the buying habits of the English, others said about the colonial Americans. Like their counterparts in the mother country, they had tasted comfort and luxury and increas-ingly called it happiness.

By mid-century, therefore, provincial Americans confronted what must have seemed a radically "new" British consciousness. It radiated outward from the metropolitan center, providing officials of a powerful, prosperous, and dynamic state with an effective vocabulary for mobilizing popular patriotism.[28] It was in this fluid, uncertain context that colonists on the periphery attempted to construct their own imagined identity within the empire. Although the process of defining identity had begun as soon as European settlers arrived in the New World, the conversation across the Atlantic Ocean changed dramatically at mid-century. Again, with due respect to Edmund Burke—and to the many colonial historians who have echoed the phrase—"salutary neglect" fails utterly to describe the complexity of the changing American situation. Although the number of crown officials in the colonies was always small, Britain aggressively intruded itself into the colonial world of the mid-eighteenth century: the metropolitan center spoke insistently through the flow of consumer goods that transformed the American marketplace, through the Red Coats who came to fight the French and Indians along the northern frontier, through celebrity itinerants such as the Reverend George Whitefield, who brought English evangelical rhetoric to anxious dissenters, and, for most literate colonists, through a commercial press that depicted the mother country in the most alluring terms, indeed, as the most polite and progressive society the world had ever seen.[29] As one American pamphleteer proudly announced, "Britain seems now to have attained to a degree of wealth, power, and eminence, which half a century ago, the most sanguine of her patriots could hardly have made the object of their warmest wishes."[30]

III

Within the imaginative structure of a powerful and prosperous empire, distant colonists not only spent a lot of time taking stock of contemporary English society, they also wondered what the English might think of them. It was not always a rewarding exercise. Provincial Americans worried that the English generally held them in low regard. Indeed, they came to suspect that from the perspective of a cosmopolitan capital such as London the colonists might appear an inferior class of people, perhaps like the Scots or the Irish, a bit uncivilized.[31] It was always possible, of course, to find Englishmen writing about the New World in precisely such unflattering terms, and in response to real or alleged slights, Americans occasionally compensated for their own feelings of cultural inferiority by poking fun at the English.

The provincials liked to tell stories, for example, of how little the English actually knew about the character of colonial society.[32] One such person was the Reverend John Barnard, a Harvard graduate who became the Congregational minister for Marblehead, Massachusetts. Born in 1681, Barnard survived to celebrate his eighty-ninth birthday. In a pithy autobiography completed in 1766 he enthusiastically chronicled the commercial progress of his local community. Indeed, during the years of his ministry, Marblehead had transformed itself from a rough fishing village into a prosperous trading center.[33] As a young man Barnard had visited England, and although he remembered a series of largely positive experiences, he enjoyed relating the story of an "aged gentlewoman" who sought him out one evening after a church meeting. "She asked me if all the people of my country were white, as she saw I was," Barnard recollected, "for being styled in the general West Indians, she thought we were all black, as she supposed the Indians to be." Barnard set the woman straight on matters of race and geography, but, as he quickly discovered, she was just warming to the interrogation. "She asked me how long I had been in the kingdom," he wrote. "When I told her a few months, she said she was surprised to think how I could learn their language in so little time; 'Methinks,' said she, 'you speak as plain English as I do.'" The traveler from America assured his questioner that "all my country people, being English, spake the same language I did," and over the course of a long career in Marblehead, he found that Americans accepted his report of an embarrassing moment in England as entirely plausible.[34]

The incident probably amused revolutionary New Englanders, who protested that they possessed the same rights as persons who happened to have been born in England.[35] One of them, James Otis, a brilliant lawyer and popular leader of the Boston town meeting, announced that government officials in the mother country knew next to nothing about the American colonies. In a trenchant political pamphlet entitled *The Rights of the British Colonies Asserted and Proved* (1764), Otis insisted that an important English imperial administrator who had recently died was uncertain whether Jamaica "lay in the Mediterranean, the Baltic, or in the moon." Otis assured American readers that the man described New England as an "*island*," consisting of "two provinces and two colonies, and according to the *undoubted* bounds of their charters, contain[ed] more land than there is in the three kingdoms."[36] Again, by pointing out these alleged "geographical blunders" Otis drew attention to his own generation's suspicion that no one in England cared enough about the American colonies to learn the difference between imagined islands and a real continent.

However credible such tales of gross ignorance seemed to the Americans, they really got it all wrong. Of course, many contemporary English authors described everyone who had had the ill fortune to be born outside the realm as inferior, but it was most certainly not the case that people living in the mother country ignored the possessions that Great Britain had acquired throughout the world. Rather, they thought about them within a mental framework in which precise cultural and social detail did not count for much. Contemporary English men and women who made "geographical blunders" perceived the American colonies as a vast, somewhat ill-defined field of commercial opportunity. To be sure, scholars and jurists sometimes discussed the status of the British colonies within an obscure language of international law, and in learned treatises they drew upon noted European authorities such as Hugo Grotius and Samuel Pufendorf to describe and defend an empire that by the early eighteenth century had come to rival those of France and Spain.[37] Whether the British system more closely resembled the empires of ancient Rome or Greece—a subject of contemporary scholarly debate—did not seem particularly compelling for the likes of Josiah Wedgwood, a marketing genius who regarded Americans as potential consumers of goods manufactured in England. In a 1766 letter Wedgwood asked a business associate, "What do you think of sending Mr. Pitt [the British prime minister] upon Crockery ware to America[?] A Quantity might certainly be sold there now & some advantage made of the American prejudice in favour of that great Man."[38] The new empire of goods provoked entrepreneurial imagination. Indeed, when Wedgwood contemplated the possibilities of American trade, he could hardly contain his enthusiasm. "I am rejoyced to know that you have shipped off the Green and Gold [china]," he reported to a colleague. "May the winds and seas be propitious and the *invaluable* Cargo be wafted in safety to their destined Market, for the emolument of our American Brethren and friends. . . . The demand for this said *Cream colour,* Alias *Ivory* still increases. It is really amazing how rapidly the use of it has spread almost over the whole globe, and how universally it is liked."[39]

Since the end of the seventeenth century, English authors who explored what would today be called "economic behavior" had marveled at the fluidity of an entirely new business climate. These commentators tried to make sense of the swirl of goods and capital as it moved from merchant to merchant, from country to country, propelled along its way by innumerable anonymous transactions, each reflecting the private and selfish interests of specific agents but in totality generating a transfer of commodities and money so massive that it quickly rendered obsolete traditional modes of explanation.[40] Many writers did not sharply distinguish between domestic and foreign markets. They keenly appreciated that rising popular demand within England was initially responsible for the accelerating velocity of economic activity. As Daniel Defoe, a shrewd observer of the great circulation of goods as well as an early novelist, declared in *The Complete English Tradesman,* "in all these manufactures, however remote one from another, every town in England uses something, not only of one or other, but of all the rest: every sort of goods is wanted everywhere; and where they make one sort of goods and sell them all over England, they at the same time want other goods from almost every other part." Defoe pointed to Norwich as an example of how trade redefined the relationship between previously isolated communities. The weavers of Norwich produced woollens, but however prosperous they seemed, these people depended on external sources of raw materials and coal—in other words, on resources that connected regions of the kingdom to each other in unprecedented ways. "From London," Defoe noted, "the goods go chiefly to the great towns, and from thence again to the smaller markets, and from those to the meanest villages; so that all the manufacturers of England, and most of them also of foreign countries, are to be found in the meanest village, and in the remotest corner of the whole island of Britain; and are to be bought, as it were, at everyone's door."[41]

Within this global frame of analysis, the colonies became an entirely plausible extension of a burgeoning domestic commerce. As the velocity of internal trade accelerated, British manufactured goods simply broke free of locally defined circuits and were carried to distant colonial ports by the centrifugal force of trade. John Campbell, a popular writer whom Samuel Johnson once described as "the richest author that ever grazed the common of literature," explained in his *Political Survey of Britain* that "in our days the value, utility, and importance of the colonies in respect to this Island have been by the evidence of facts put beyond all dispute. The British inhabitants in them draw some of the necessaries and many of the conveniences of life from hence. The supplying them with these is a new and very great source of industry, which by affording employment to multitudes, cannot but have an effect in augmenting the numbers as well as contributing to the ease and happiness of our people at home."[42] As English markets became saturated, merchants and manufacturers who viewed the empire much as Wedgwood did, sought out new colonial buyers, anticipating huge profits in the fulfillment of growing provincial demand.[43]

Richard Rolt commented extensively on this buoyant commercial outlook. His testimony is especially interesting because Rolt was a figure of a new eighteenth-century "public sphere," an imagined discursive space in which authors without traditional court patronage spoke to and for the members of a rising English middle class.[44] In other words, like Campbell, Rolt made a career within a highly commercialized society; to survive he had to sell whatever he produced, be it popular songs, light opera, superficial histories, or in this case *A New Dictionary of Trade and Commerce* (1756). And perhaps not surprisingly, he recycled commonplace observations, as if by some rhetorical alchemy the density of platitudes might yield timeless wisdom. In *A New Dictionary,* Rolt claimed that alleged authorities such as Pufendorf had conjectured that "England was weakened by planting the several colonies in America; and that it would have been more advantageous, to have employed the colonists at home, in manufactures, and in the herring fishery." On matters of world trade, however, the German philosopher clearly did not know what he was talking about. According to Rolt, Pufendorf should have considered "that the commodities and manufactures of a country have a certain limit, beyond which it is impossible they should extend, without an alteration of circumstances; or, when they are carried so high, as that no markets are to be found, domestic industry can proceed no further." The opening of a new American market had allowed Great Britain to avoid an anticipated "stagnation in trade," for, as Rolt reminded his readers, "the colonists established there take off much greater quantities of the national commodities and manufactures than if they had remained at home."[45] It is important to remember that these were very recent developments—current events, as it were—and not changes that had occurred in some dim Elizabethan past. Rolt was trying as best he could to explain to contemporaries a situation that had no precedent. Another English writer, who signed his work "B. G., Esq.," expressed the same point in more direct prose: "[T]he principal *Cornucopia* of *Great-Britain's* Wealth, are its *Colonies in America*, which furnish the most profitable Succour to their Mother Country, and which must every Year increase."[46]

According to a chorus of admirers, the British commercial empire, unlike those of its major European competitors, had acquired the characteristics of a splendidly ordered Newtonian system. It struck contemporaries as being natural, rational, and, most worthy of praise, balanced.[47] Like the famed balanced constitution—crown, lords, and commoners—which Englishmen and many French visitors endlessly described as a source of liberty and prosperity, the empire of goods gained strength from equipoise. The interests of the colonies complemented those of the metropolitan core; the producers of raw staples became the consumers of articles manufactured in other places. As Rolt observed, "commerce is that tie by which the several, and even the remotest, parts of the British empire, are connected, and kept together."[48] Everyone benefited from the circulation of trade as goods moved through the arteries of commerce. Malachy Postlethwayt, whose massive volumes describing the state of commerce achieved widespread popularity, explained in the *Universal Dictionary of Trade and Commerce:* "Our manufactures are prodigiously increased, chiefly by the demand for them in the plantations, where they at least take off one half, and supply us with many valuable commodities for exportation, which is as great an emolument to the mother-kingdom as to the plantations themselves."[49]

Like other writers of the period, Benjamin Franklin applauded the elegance of the system's design. He consciously adopted what he perceived as the British perspective on commerce. Living at the time in London and trying to pass himself off in the public journals as an authentic Englishman, Franklin analyzed the state of imperial trade with almost scientific detachment. Why, he asked readers of a metropolitan paper, had Spain been unable to challenge successfully the productivity of British manufacturers? "The Reasons are various," Franklin acknowledged, but the central explanation for Spain's industrial stupor was the failure of its rulers to recognize that,

> [a] Manufacture is Part of a great System of Commerce, which takes in Conveniencies of various Kinds, Methods of providing Materials of all sorts, Machines for expediting and facilitating Labour, all the Channels of Correspondence for vending the Wares, the Credit and Confidence necessary to found and support this Correspondence, the mutual Aid of different Artizans, and a thousand other Particulars, which Time, and long Experience, have gradually established. A Part of such a System cannot support itself without the Whole.[50]

Thomas Pownall, an acquaintance of Franklin's who had been elected a member of Parliament, echoed this conventional wisdom. In his influential 1764 essay entitled *The Administration of the Colonies*, Pownall inquired— as perhaps did some of his political colleagues—of what use were the colonies to England? What function did they serve? Not unexpectedly, the answer was that they complemented the English economy. They helped maintain a proper balance between producer and consumer. Indeed, as Pownall argued, however troublesome the American provinces may have appeared in 1764, Parliament should resist the temptation to tinker with a commercial system that had evolved over the course of the eighteenth century, for "In the establishing [of] colonies, a nation creates people whose labour, being applied to new objects of produce and manufacture, opens new channels of commerce, by which they not only live in ease and affluence within themselves, but, while they are labouring under and for the mother country . . . become an increasing nation, of appropriated and good customers to the mother country. These not only increase our manufactures, encrease our exports, but extend our commerce; and if duly administered, extend the nation, its powers, and its dominions, to wherever these people extend their settlements."[51]

English newspapers and the popular press carried many examples of this kind of commercial analysis. To rehearse the general argument in all its variant forms would serve no useful purpose. One instance, however, merits special attention. During the early 1720s John Trenchard and Thomas Gordon produced a series of journal essays known collectively as "Cato's political letters." The authors excoriated the policies of Robert Walpole, the leading cabinet member during this period, for undermining Britain's balanced constitution, for corrupting popular liberties, and for abusing the freedom of the press. Although Trenchard and Gordon remained marginal figures within England, they enjoyed a broad following in the American colonies, where their shrill, almost conspiratorial commentary found a sympathetic audience.[52] But on the topic of England's commercial system, the two writers sounded remarkably complacent, repeating notions about imperial trade that few readers would have found objectionable. They energetically promoted commercial growth. In one "letter" (1721) provocatively entitled "Arts and Sciences the Effects of Civil Liberty only, and ever destroyed or oppressed by Tyranny," Trenchard and Gordon declared—again, with an eye on Britain's imperial rivals—that Spain and Portugal only weakened their domestic economies by sending colonists to the New World. How much superior the balanced British system appeared.

> [Spain and Portugal] lost their people by sending them away to dig in the mines; and we, by making the manufactures which they want, and the instruments which they use, multiply ours. By this means every man that they send out of their country is a loss to it, because the reason and produce of their labour goes to enrich rival nations; whereas every man that we send to our plantations, adds to the number of our inhabitants here at home, by maintaining so many of them employed in so many manufactures which they take off there; besides so many artificers in shipping, and all the numerous traders and agents concerned in managing and venting the produce of the plantations, when it is brought hither, and in bringing it hither. So that the English planters in America, besides maintaining themselves and ten times as many Negroes, maintain likewise great numbers of our countrymen in England.[53]

Whatever other lessons the American colonists may have taken from "Cato's political letters," they did not learn from these pages to distrust mercantile capitalism or to cherish economic self-sufficiency.

Much of the self-congratulatory rhetoric about commerce ignored the fact that the British system had developed within a complex statutory framework known as the Navigation Acts. These trade regulations reflected the kind of mercantile—or more precisely, in this case, protectionist—thinking that Adam Smith excoriated in his *Inquiry into the Nature and Causes of the Wealth of Nations* (1776). During the middle decades of the seventeenth century, Parliament approved legislation designed primarily to prevent other European nations—most notably the Dutch—from trading with the American colonies. The major Navigation Acts of the 1660s contained two essential features. First, Parliament ruled that merchants could transport certain enumerated commodities—tobacco and naval stores, for example—only to the mother country on English ships manned largely by English sailors. The idea was not only to prohibit the Dutch from trading in American waters but also to encourage the training of common seamen whom the navy could press into military service during times of war. Second, the Navigation Acts denied the colonists direct access to European markets. All Continental goods they purchased had to pass through an English port before being dispatched to the New World, a cumbersome procedure that added greatly to the cost of these items and effectively discouraged Americans from forming strong commercial ties outside the British Empire. Although the colonists initially attempted to circumvent these restrictions on free trade, they soon discovered that obeying the laws brought more profit than did the alternative.[54]

Whatever ends the economic planners of the seventeenth century may have had in mind, they certainly did not have much to say about the significance of the colonies as a privileged market for the manufactures of the mother country. A hundred years later, however, English writers increasingly justified the Navigation Acts in terms of American consumer demand. British merchants found themselves in control of what has been described as a huge "free-trade zone."[55] In other words, they were free to trade English goods anywhere in the empire without having to worry about European competitors. They enjoyed a commercial monopoly. This was ordinarily a term of opprobrium in English politics, but since the American demand for British exports was so lucrative, commentators usually took the high road, stressing the extraordinary advantages to be derived from an empire of consumer colonies. As an anonymous author in the *Gentleman's Magazine* proclaimed, "We [the people of England] reap from our Colonies the compleat Benefit of Subjects, of free and rich Subjects, not by Taxes and Tribute, but by Means of our *Act of Navigation*." The protectionist legislation had paid off in a wholly unexpected manner. It guaranteed that American wealth "terminates here in the Purchase of our costly Manufactures."[56]

The Navigation Acts encouraged a kind of contractual view of the function of commerce in the empire. Since the colonists never actually voted on trade legislation, their role in this relationship was at best tenuous. For the English, however, the system implied a certain rough reciprocity. On their part, the people of the mother country generously provided good government in the colonies as well as defense from foreign enemies such as the French. In return for these considerations, the Americans agreed—at least implicitly—to respect England's commercial monopoly. They were the consumers of goods, not manufacturers; they were Britain's customers, not its competitors. Thomas Pownall reduced this line of thinking to a few blunt propositions: "As it is the right, so it becomes the duty of the mother country to nourish and cultivate, to protect and govern the colonies: which nurture and government should precisely direct its care to two essential points. 1st, That all the profits of the produce and manufactures of these colonies center finally in the mother country: and 2dly, That the colonies continue to be the sole and proper customers of the mother country."[57]

To be sure, the contractual defense of the commercial empire sparked dissent. Adam Smith, for example, protested that commentators such as Pownall exaggerated the economic value to the mother country of a protected American market. In *Wealth of Nations,* Smith observed, "A great empire has been established for the sole purpose of raising up a nation of customers who should be obliged to buy from the shops of our different producers, all the goods with which these could supply them. For the sake of that little enhancement of price which this monopoly might afford our producers, the home-consumers have been burdened with the whole expense of maintaining and defending that empire."[58] But Smith's was a solitary voice, and a late-sounding one at that. At mid-century informed English opinion firmly believed that the Navigation Acts benefited all the crown's subjects, even those who lived in America.

But at the end of the day, celebration of balance and reciprocity within a new British empire—what Rolt enthusiastically termed "mutual benefit . . . [and] mutual dependence"—approached intellectual dishonesty, something that the system's many apologists must surely have understood.[59] The ultimate justification for protectionist legislation was always the greater prosperity of the mother country. Notions of commercial reciprocity dissolved rather swiftly when they came into conflict with English economic interests, and however much the popular authors of the period lavished praise on a monopolistic system of trade, their loyalties remained thoroughly English. Campbell, for example, revealed how easily people who wrote about imperial commerce could abandon notions of "mutual dependence." When summarizing the dramatic effects of the Americans' growing consumer desire on the British economy, he insisted that "it is incontestibly evident, that they [the colonists] have contributed greatly to increase our industry, and of course our riches, to extend the commerce, to augment the naval power, and consequently to maintain the grandeur and support the prosperity of the mother country."[60] No one reading Campbell's analysis could seriously doubt that "our riches" meant English riches. Even Pownall, who fancied himself a friend of the colonies, merged the language of trade and empire in a way that drew attention to the possessive adjective "our." The American provinces, he concluded, "not only increase our manufactures, encrease our exports, but

extend our commerce; and if duly administered, extend the nation, its powers, and its dominions, to wherever these people extend their settlements."[61]

The tone of this mid-eighteenth-century commercial literature strikes
the modern reader as blunt to the point of insensitivity. In their desire to
assure England's expanding middle class that the British Empire worked
almost providentially to fulfill the economic and political ambitions of what
Adam Smith famously called "a nation of shopkeepers," popular writers
risked insulting all those American consumers who had in fact infused the
entire system with new energy. One example was particularly revealing. In
1748 Robert Dodsley published *Preceptor: Containing a General Course of
Education*. By the standards of the day this two-volume work was an extremely successful venture, reappearing in several new editions over the next
quarter century. Dodsley was no hack writer. He enjoyed a modest reputation as a poet and dramatist; he was a patron of Samuel Johnson. Moreover,
he founded a highly regarded London bookstore. We can assume, therefore, that his views "On Trade and Commerce"—a long section in *Preceptor*—reflected informed opinion in the mother country.

Dodsley began by urging readers to view the colonists with a kinder
eye. He found it inexcusable that "even People of better Figure" regularly
expressed "Disdain and Contempt for their Countrymen in those Parts, as
if their Interests were as far removed from them as their Persons." Such an
attitude, Dodsley argued, merely signaled that so-called educated men and
women did not fully comprehend how radically the Americans had transformed the face of eighteenth-century England. Consumption of British
goods in a colony such as Virginia translated directly into domestic employment. America was the great marketplace. Sounding a lot like the various royal governors who attempted to list all the British goods carried to
the New World, Dodsley explained that consumer demand in Virginia,

> must be supplied from those Handicrafts and Mechanics that have most Hands in
> their Service, such as Weavers, Shoemakers, Hatters, Ironmongers, Turners, Joiners,
> Taylors, Cutlers, Smiths, Bakers, Brewers, Ropemakers, Hosiers, and indeed all Me-
> chanics in *England*. . . . These Commodities sent thither, besides Linen, Silks, *India*
> Goods, Wine, and other foreign Manufactures, are, Cloth, coarse and fine Serges, Stuffs,
> Bays, Hats, and all Sorts of Haberdashers Ware; Hoes, Bills, Axes, Nails, Adzes, and
> other Iron Ware; Cloaths ready made, Knives, Biscuit, Flour, Stockings, Shoes, Caps
> for Servants, and in short, every Thing that is made in *England*.[62]

The lesson of Virginia repeated itself in each separate American colony.
If the provincials stopped buying manufactured goods, English society as a
whole would suffer. One did not have to like the colonists—something
Barnard and Otis discovered—but at least one should treat them with civility. This is the point in Dodsley's analysis of the empire of goods where
condescension betrayed arrogance, and appeals to mutuality and understanding rang hollow. For however much English readers believed that Virginians "live exactly as we do," they also knew that the purpose of the new
consumer colonies was to serve the mother country, in other words, "to
take off the Commodities and Manufactures, to employ the People, to in-

crease the Shipping, and to extend the Trade of this Nation." Dodsley may not have intended to treat the provincials with disdain, but he informed them in no uncertain terms that it was their lot to "undergo all the Drudgery and Labour" so that middle-class Englishmen—the "we" of this account—might "draw from thence annually immense Profits, in which the People of the Plantations have no Share whatsoever. Such are the Prerogatives of a Mother-Country, and such and so great the Benefits she reaps by being so!"[63]

IV

To a remarkable degree eighteenth-century Americans agreed with the likes of Dodsley. Even colonists unfamiliar with the works of Campbell and Rolt—in other words, the great majority of the population—would have characterized the economic and political arguments that the English writers put forward as accurate. After all, this commercial literature generally packaged platitudes about trade as insights, and any modestly informed provincial would have accepted it as an article of faith that the British Empire owed much of its military strength and recent prosperity to commerce. Other empires, they thought, had not been so fortunate. Those systems had coerced obedience, exploiting natives and settlers for short-term returns. But blessedly, eighteenth-century Great Britain was different, perhaps, in the long history of mighty empires, unique, for it nurtured loyalty by inviting colonists to participate in trade. As an anonymous author in the *New-York Mercury* insisted, colonial Americans believed that the mother country "had laid the Foundation of the greatest Empire that ever existed: An Empire the more glorious, as it was not to be founded on the Ruin and Destruction of our own Species, but what is in the highest Degree laudable, the cultivating and peopling [of] an immense Wilderness." It is no wonder, then, that this writer concluded, "We think ourselves at present the happiest people (with respect to government) of any people under the sun, and really are so." Eighteenth-century Americans found themselves in a truly splendid situation, for England not only protected freedom and property but also generously allowed the colonists "so much trade as the wisdom of the nation has tho't proper to permit, as consistent with the interest of the whole."[64]

Grateful provincials sometimes outdid themselves, claiming that commerce in itself was a positive social good. It sparked innovation as well as hard work. Indeed, within an empire of trade people discovered that by attending to their own personal well-being they promoted the general welfare. At least in theory, that is how commerce affected social behavior. Sounding much like his English counterparts, Amicus Reipublica—a Boston pamphleteer writing in 1731—announced that "*Trade* or *Commerce*, is an Engine of State, to draw men in to business, for the advancing and ennobling of the Rich, for the support of the Poor, for the strengthening and fortifying of the State." As his authority on this point, he cited not contemporary English authors but rather Solomon of the Old Testament, a prescient patriarch who apparently appreciated the benefits of "free and liberal *Commerce*." In case New England readers did not fully grasp the central proposition, Amicus Reipublica insisted "*That Trade or Commerce is principally necessary to a Peoples* [sic] *flourishing in the World*." It gave direction to diligence, for, in the author's cascading logic, "Labour will not be improved to any considerable degree of Wealth, without the advantage & encouragement of a profitable *Commerce*. In all Labour there is profit, because none will Labour, but with a fore-sight of Profit, for Profit is the final Cause of Labour . . . so Commerce is the Cause of Profit by Labour."[65] In 1753 the *Independent Reflector* pushed the economic analysis, insisting that commerce was the fundamental key to social progress. Provincial New York, it seemed, had "just emerged from the rude unpolished Condition of an Infant Colony." The future looked promising, however, for within an empire that secured liberty and property, "*Commerce* stretches forth its golden Arms to our Merchants; and our Situation is so pre-eminently advantageous for Navigation, that I am persuaded it will be our own Faults, if we do not extend and increase our Trade beyond our Neighbours and Competitors."[66]

Again, like popular English writers of the day, Americans commended the new British commercial system—the foundation of a free and happy empire—as balanced, natural, and rational. What is more, they also knew their proper place within this intricate structure. They were consumers. That was their major function in the grand design, a condition that they seem to have found not the slightest bit demeaning. It had not always been so. The first settlers struggled merely to survive. But the logic of historical development transformed them into eager and knowledgeable consumers, in other words, into people who worked the fields and plantations of the New World so that they could purchase the manufactured articles that in turn sustained England's prosperity. As George Mason, an extremely well read Virginian, explained to his less studious neighbor George Washington, "Our supplying our Mother-Country with gross Materials, & taking her Manufactures in Return is the true Chain of Connection between us; these are the Bands, which, if not broken by Oppressions, must long hold us together, by maintain[in]g a constant Reciprocation of Interest."[67]

In his highly influential *Letters from a Pennsylvania Farmer* (1768), John Dickinson explained exactly how such "a constant Reciprocation" had developed. Long ago—certainly before commerce had become so significant in shaping human affairs—colonies were established "by warlike nations to keep their enemies in awe; to relieve their country, over-burthened with inhabitants; or to discharge a number of discontented and troublesome citizens." But within a period of living memory, the entire justification for colonies had changed, at least within Great Britain. Dickinson postulated that "in more modern ages, the spirit of violence being in some measure . . . sheathed in commerce, colonies have been settled by the nations of *Europe* for purposes of trade. These purposes were to be attained, by the colonies raising for their mother country those things which she did not produce herself; and by supplying themselves from her with things they wanted. These were the *national objects,* in the commencement of our colonies, and have been uniformly so in their promotion."[68] The *Letters* were published, of course, during a moment of intense imperial crisis, but however great their anger at parliamentary taxation, Dickinson and Mason could still appreciate how in theory colonial commerce was supposed to operate, a self-sustaining balance of the interests of buyers and sellers, of consumers and producers. And in point of fact, the imperial system had worked almost as smoothly as Dickinson claimed. For the most part, mid-century Americans obeyed the Navigation Acts, and while smugglers have captured the imagination of some modern historians, most merchants carried American staples to the mother country and English manufactures to the colonies in British ships manned by British crews.[69]

V

Within a standard imperial rhetoric celebrating the glories of commerce, the Americans stressed several themes that figured only marginally in English writings. Perhaps as a way to rationalize their obvious dependence on the manufactures of the mother country, the colonists attempted to transform necessity into a virtue. Whatever the motive, Americans depicted consumption within the empire as in some measure a demonstration of loyalty to Great Britain. To be sure, buying English goods could expose the colonists to serious debt, and it was a constant challenge for the Americans to raise enough money to participate in this new eighteenth-century marketplace. Nevertheless, a commercial empire providing so many military and political benefits certainly merited personal sacrifice; American consumption—even when it clearly compromised one's own economic interests— became, in fact, a seal of imperial patriotism.

This is exactly what the Reverend Jared Eliot, a Connecticut minister who badgered ordinary New England farmers into adopting more efficient agricultural techniques, argued in an essay on "Field-Husbandry" published in 1759. Eliot advised local cultivators to experiment with the production of silk, an endeavor that Americans had been contemplating with no practical results ever since the English first arrived in the New World. Why, Eliot's readers must have wondered, had he bothered to revive such an unpromising enterprise? Anticipating the force of popular skepticism, the minister observed, "We labour under such difficulties to make returns for goods imported [from England], that many have tho't it would be best that we should make our own clothes, and by this means lessen our importation, which, indeed, would be better than to run into an endless and irrecoverable debt." But self-reliance of this sort created a major ethical problem—at least, it did for Eliot. Within the British commercial system, colonial production of cloth "would make us less useful to *England,* from whom we derive; and from whom we have receiv'd such favours and assistance." No truly patriotic farmer, Eliot insisted, would knowingly set himself up as a competitor to the weavers of the mother country. Silk, however, was another matter. By producing this valuable material, the Americans might even "increase our importation." According to Eliot's calculations, "the same cost, labour, and time" the farmers currently expended to obtain one yard of English cloth might, if rechanneled into the production of a saleable item like silk, "procure two yards of the same sort of cloth." For the loyal colonist, more income meant more consumption.[70]

The minister employed the same curious patriotic logic to develop a highly original attack on slave labor. Eliot objected to slavery not on moral grounds, as did contemporary Quakers, but rather because unfree workers were by definition limited consumers and, as such, failed to advance the greater commercial welfare of the British Empire. "As slaves spend but little," he explained, presumably to an American audience that extended beyond the boundaries of New England, "there will not be a proportionable demand for *English* goods." Freedom was not only intrinsically good, it also strengthened the entire economy. "People of a free condition," reasoned Eliot, "live at an higher rate, spend more, and consequently their demand for *goods* will be larger: If these free people raise, and export, so much, as to pay for *them*, they will be so much more useful, to the mother country."[71]

At least one provincial writer regarded arguments in favor of the patriotic imperial consumer as utterly fatuous. If nothing else, William Douglass's fierce determination to counter this line of thinking suggests just how popular it had become in the colonies. Douglass, a Scottish doctor living in Boston, complained in his ill-tempered history of the "British Settlements" that "Encouraging of a great Consumption of *British* Goods by Luxury and extravagant Equipage in our Colonies, is thought by some wrong-headed Men to be a Benefit to the Mother Country." Such a claim, Douglass asserted, amounted to little more than self-serving twaddle. Indeed, it was "a grand Mistake." Patriotic consumption was one thing, foolish luxury quite another. "Industry and Frugality in all Subservients is requisite," he told American readers, who probably did not appreciate being labeled "Subservients." "Otherways they [the provincials] cannot long afford to continue this Consumption reckoned a Benefit to *Great-Britain.*"[72] Eliot would not have taken issue with this proposition. After all, bankrupt colonists could not do much to advance the interests of the empire.

However the colonists construed loyalty to the British Empire—and the impulse to define consumption as a form of patriotism seems to have been the product of a peculiar and unprecedented set of historical conditions—they shared with English writers a conviction that commerce implied reciprocity. A lot of Americans repeated this commonplace, but none warmed more enthusiastically to the task than Stephen Watts, one of four finalists in Philadelphia for the 1766 "Mr. Sargent's Prize-Medal." Each contestant spoke to an assigned topic, "The Reciprocal Advantages of a Perpetual Union Between Great-Britain and Her American Colonies." Ignoring altogether the question of imperial patriotism, Watts—about whom almost nothing is known—concentrated on the expectation of profit. Empire was not a matter of emotional identity; it was a business relationship, best analyzed in terms of costs and benefits. "I hope therefore to make it appear," Watts explained, "that a reciprocal emolument will arise from a perpetual union between *Britain* and her *American* Colonies." Emolument here meant, of course, return on investment. The mother country could anticipate a great enlargement of "her trade and commerce," thus guaranteeing that it would "become still more rich and powerful." The colonists' side of the imperial bargain was the assurance of military protection and, perhaps more interesting in this context, the prospect of being "supplied with the conveniences of life at a cheaper rate, and of a better quality than if manufactured by themselves." According to Watts, even though "it is from *Great-Britain,* that the Colonies import almost every thing, requisite for cloathing, agriculture, and other uses," the empire was still for the Americans a very good deal.[73]

However appealing the prospect of better goods at lower prices, Watts's argument for commercial reciprocity failed to address what was for many colonists the most difficult issue. The partners in this commercial relationship were not by any stretch of the imagination equals, and because of the obvious disparity in power, Americans sometimes found it hard to explain exactly how over time they proposed to uphold their side of the imperial compact. How could they pretend that claims to "mutual dependence" meant anything other than their own commercial inferiority and, by extension, their political vulnerability? Although the possibility of a continuously expanding colonial consumption appeared the most persuasive response, the discourse of commercial mutuality—unlike that of commercial patriotism—expressed itself in the language of American generosity rather than obligation, of common expectations in the imperial marketplace rather than on blind colonial obedience. From the perspective of profitable trade-offs, it seemed prudent for the uncertain provincial partner to remind the English not only that the Americans purchased huge quantities of manufactures but also that they would surely be wanting more in the future. Rising consumption was not so much a proof of imperial patriotism as it was an indication of the colonies' potential economic leverage within a developing commercial system.

John Dickinson made this point in a pamphlet entitled *The Late Regulations Respecting the British Colonies* (1765). Somewhat disingenuously, he observed that "The *American* continental colonies are inhabited by persons of small fortunes who *are* so closely employed in subduing a wild country, for their subsistence . . . that they have not time nor any temptation to apply themselves to manufactures." Necessity, not patriotism, kept these diligent frontiersmen from making the items that they obtained from England. It required no great insight to see that these imported goods exceeded anything the colonists could produce "in workmanship and cheapness." Dickinson, of course, invented a population of American "subsistence" farmers to lay claim to genuine commercial reciprocity. "Hence arises the importance of the colonies to *Great-Britain,*" he wrote. "Her prosperity depends on her commerce; her commerce on her manufactures; her manufactures on the markets for them; and the most constant and advantageous markets are afforded by the colonies."[74]

Americans such as Dickinson always sounded somewhat defensive, even querulous, when advancing arguments for genuine commercial reciprocity. Their tone seemed to betray a secret suspicion that the consumer's plea for mutual respect might not make a deep inpression on the English. Earlier in the eighteenth century, for example, a Boston newspaper assured its anxious subscribers that Americans would certainly be more highly esteemed within the empire "if they at Home were rightly inform'd of the Value and Benefit this Country is to the Trade and Manufactories of *Great Britain*." In an attempt to prove that the colonies really counted for something in the larger imperial scheme, that they deserved respect, this anonymous author did what so many other American writers did during this period; he transformed himself into a commercial booster for the underappreciated Americans. "It is supposed," he announced, "that this Country pays to *Britain* for the manufactures [*sic*] consumed here upwards of *Two Hundred Thousand Pounds* a Year Sterling; a pretty Customer, for an Infant Colony."[75] The not so subtle message, of course, was that if "an Infant Colony" like Massachusetts could perform so impressively, then a mature one might creditably present itself as indispensable to the continuing prosperity of the mother country. Genuine commercial reciprocity was on the imperial horizon. The inaugural issue of Andrew Bradford's *American Magazine* (Philadelphia), one of the first periodicals published in the colonies, declared as a matter of fact in 1741 that England owed its recent economic success to the colonial demand for manufactured goods, and then, as if heroic consumption were not a sufficient contribution to the triumph of the empire, added defiantly that it is "likely to be much more so."[76]

As one might anticipate, Benjamin Franklin played masterfully on the theme of infinite consumer promise. In his ingenious demographic essay entitled "The Increase of Mankind" (1751), he too held out the growth of colonial demand as the proper index to the Americans' standing within the British Empire. If the upward trend continued—and he had no doubt that it would—then the very concept of "mutual dependence" might take on new meaning. At mid-century true commercial parity was still a possibility, a promise, rather than a reality. But for future Americans, Franklin believed, consumption would be the way to ensure British respect. "In Proportion to the Increase of the Colonies," he observed, "a vast Demand is growing for British Manufactures, a glorious Market wholly in the Power of Britain, in which Foreigners cannot interfere, which will increase in a short Time even beyond her Power of supplying, tho' her whole Trade should be to her Colonies."[77]

As part of this mid-century assemblage of assumptions and beliefs about commerce in the empire, Americans insisted that trade could not possibly flourish unless consumers and producers, buyers and sellers, experienced in their everyday lives maximum political freedom. The notion that commerce required liberty did not originate with the colonists. English writers often praised Britain's famed balanced constitution as a source of general economic prosperity. Trade despised tyranny; arbitrary rule invited corrupt officials to interrupt the smooth flow of goods and staples. And, of course, the crucial incentive in making money—in putting capital at risk— was the knowledge that the law protected private property. "Industry hath its foundation on liberty," Rolt observed in his *New Dictionary of Trade and Commerce*, "and those men, who either are actual slaves, or have reason to believe their freedom precarious, will never succeed in trade; which thrives and flourishes most in climates of liberty and ease."[78] Rolt merely repeated what contemporaries would have identified as cliché.

However common the language of trade and freedom, it resonated particularly strongly in the colonies. In his *Observations on the Importance of the Northern Colonies* (1750), Archibald Kennedy, a Scotsman who moved to America in the late seventeenth century and became an important figure in the political affairs of New York, affirmed as a given that where people "are numerous and free, they will push what they think is for their Interest, and all restraining Laws they have no Hand in contriving or making of will be thought Oppression; especially such Laws, as according to the Conceptions we have of *English Liberty*."[79] Some years later, Dickinson repeated the point in his popular *Letters*, claiming that "all history" demonstrated that "trade and freedom are nearly related to each other."[80] Even Americans who wrote letters to the local newspapers took it for granted that commerce would fail if deprived of liberty. An excellent example of what became a reflexive colonial belief was provided by a Connecticut author who identified himself in print only as "X." He began his piece with a totally unobjectionable observation:

> The experience of every age, and nation from the remotest knowledge, down to the present-day, join in asserting this fact; that no nation, ever became rich or poor, but in proportion to the increase, or decrease of their trade, and what is of vastly more consequence, commerce; [it] has thro' every period, gone hand in hand with liberty; rose, flourish'd and declin'd together.[81]

Although mid-century Americans appreciated the many benefits that flowed from imperial commerce—after all, they fancied themselves as the freest and most prosperous European colonists in the New World—they frequently grumbled that they found it much harder to participate fully in this so-called balanced system of trade than it did their English partners. British manufacturers, the colonists claimed, could count on American consumer demand; all they had to do was fill colonial orders. But for the provincial consumers, the purchase of huge quantities of British exports put them at such an economic disadvantage that they occasionally questioned the logic of mutual dependence and mutual benefits. The problem resulted from a chronic imbalance of payments. Since the English never spent as much on American products as Americans spent on British manufactures, the colonists had to scramble to find additional sources of cash to cover a serious shortfall in the Anglo-American consumer trade. Colonial merchants responded to the challenge with great initiative, opening up new markets, which in fact helped generate the specie needed to pay for all the cloth, ceramics, and metal items that Americans received from the mother country. The provincials, no doubt, underestimated the business risks confronting English merchants and manufacturers. Bankruptcies were not infrequent; even major London commercial houses felt extremely vulnerable to sudden calls on credit.

Nevertheless, from the colonial perspective, it seemed that Americans had to work ever harder just to maintain a fiction of commercial reciprocity within the empire. "Our importation of dry goods from England is so vastly great," explained William Smith, a leading political figure in New York City, "that we are obliged to betake ourselves to all possible arts to make remittances to the British." The busy merchants in his colony imported "cotton from St. Thomas's and Surinam; lime-juice and Nicaragua wood from Curacao; and logwood from the bay, &c.," and yet, no matter how cunningly they schemed to finance the consumer trade, they always seemed to come up short. The demand for British manufactures, Smith insisted, "drains us of all the silver and gold we can collect."[82] Like Smith, Archibald Kennedy thought that commercial reforms might reduce some of the structural tensions within the empire, but he did not sound optimistic. "In Debt we are," he announced in 1750, "and in Debt we must be, for those vast Importations from *Europe*; and as we increase, so will our Debts without, from the present Prospect of Things, ever being able to make suitable Returns." At the end of the day, it was possible to imagine the Americans becoming "Bankrupts."[83]

It was not that the colonists rejected the basic protectionist assumptions that underlay the British mercantile system. Rather, they insisted that commercial reciprocity implied a kind of pragmatic fair play, for, as seemed obvious to them, it made little sense in the long run to encourage colonial consumption unless the provincials could expect realistically to pay for what they had purchased. A short essay first published in the *New-York Mercury* in 1764 betrayed what might be called a general feeling of ambivalent gratitude; that is, the colonists were at once thankful to be part of a great commercial empire and worried about their economic ability to hold their own. "We are not a rich people," this anonymous writer observed, "[but] we enjoy advantages equal to the richest and most opulent, having the necessaries of life in great abundance; and though, in order to procure one of them (*to wit*, Cloathing) and many conveniencies, we are obliged to send abroad all the cash we acquire, and as fast as we acquire it." Just as his tone suggested the possibility of genuine anger, the American author retreated, protesting that even as the colonists sent their money to England, they recognized that the mother country "secures to us every thing else that is valuable in life, [and thus] we have no reason to repine."[84]

VI

By the middle of the eighteenth century, Americans had cobbled together various assumptions and beliefs about imperial commerce. The mental process followed no clear logic. The colonists borrowed concepts from European sources, what we might today call "macro" explanations for economic behavior. They also recast ideas about consumption and trade in light of local experience. Whatever their intellectual merits, these shared notions provided a framework that helped colonists make sense of a radical and sudden transformation of the character of the Atlantic trade. For them, the interpretation of imperial commerce spilled over into other topics, into discussions of liberty and patriotism, into the meaning of reciprocity between colonies and mother country.[85]

In fact, commerce provided Americans with a fluid language of imperial identity as well as a persuasive means for negotiating change. However difficult it may have been for some Americans to accommodate to new market conditions, they made no attempt—at least not on the level of public rhetoric—to restore an earlier, simpler age. The challenge for ordinary colonists was not how best to resist the imperatives of the mercantile system but rather how most effectively to gain a measure of control over a huge consumer-driven marketplace that had no historical precedent. They sometimes analyzed their situation with a tough-mindedness that a later age would associate with modernity. None had fewer illusions about the nature of eighteenth-century commercial society than a Pennsylvania essayist known only as "Colonus." He contrasted the intense religiosity of the Middle Ages with the more enlightened Anglo-American world of the eighteenth century. "But now," concluded Colonus, "religious, or indeed any other principles are little regarded, any where, but as they can be made instruments, directly or indirectly, to promote trade; commercial principles alone, seem to be uppermost every where. All the states of Europe, in short all the world, appear at this time to be made after trade. . . . [It is] the only means to acquire wealth."[86]

Unlike shrill warnings about the spread of political corruption—the type of conspiratorial rhetoric found in the writings of Trenchard and Gordon—the commercial discourse that we have examined provided colonists with a more positive sense of themselves within an exciting, expanding, and mighty empire of goods. The commercial assumptions of the day certainly did not persuade Americans that they were the hapless victims of dark market forces beyond their control. Indeed, these arguments sanctioned an active engagement with a world of trade, for within this new system consumption presented itself as an opportunity enthusiastically to be embraced.

It is not surprising, therefore, that provincials who shared these assumptions and beliefs came gradually to regard themselves as indispensable to the genuine interests of the mother country. The British respected the colonists—at least in theory—precisely because the Americans had demonstrated themselves to be loyal consumers. And thus, by demanding so many manufactured articles, they inevitably reinforced a growing feeling of empowerment within a commercial empire. Their market decisions really did matter. To be sure, reciprocity brought the colonists comfort and pleasure.

But, as they fully appreciated, it also ensured the continuing prosperity of the ordinary people of England.

Even during this earlier period, it is not hard to appreciate that commonplace notions about reciprocity provided the colonists with potent intellectual resources that could under certain political conditions generate resistance rather than encourage accommodation. The literature of consumption flattered the Americans; it reminded them how much strength they had within a new, rapidly growing empire of goods. The colonists were bound to conclude that if, in fact, American consumption played such a significant role in the prosperity of the mother country, then any interruption of that trade was likely to discomfort England's rulers.

At mid-century no colonist pushed the logic of consumer patriotism and reciprocity in this subversive direction. But for Americans who had come to believe that trade without liberty represented a form of slavery, who insisted that an empire that impoverished, even bankrupted, its own best customers betrayed their trust, and who interpreted the concept of commercial balance as truly guaranteeing "mutual benefits" and "mutual dependence," the manufactures of England had a high potential at moments of stress to become politicized. Reciprocity betrayed required explanation. "It was the interest of Great-Britain to encourage our dissipation and extravagance," David Ramsay insisted in 1778, "for the two-fold purpose of *increasing the sale of her manufactures,* and of *perpetuating our subordination.* In vain we sought to check the growth of luxury, by sumptuary laws; every wholesome restraint of this kind was sure to meet with the royal negative: While the whole force of example was employed to induce us to copy the dissipated manners of the country from which we sprung."[87]

Ramsay's reflections on the empire of goods came after the decision for independence had been made. Before the final break, however, we obtain a sense of the significance of the issue of mutual dependence. The townsmen of Harvard, Massachusetts, called an emergency meeting on February 18, 1773. A political crisis loomed; they feared violence. According to their moderator, the Reverend Joseph Wheeler, they insisted "That any Disputes with our Parent Country is what we take no pleasure in, and would be glad [they] might be avoided if possible consistent with fidelity to ourselves and mankind in general." At this crucial moment, the farmers of Harvard also poignantly reminded the British Parliament to remember—before it was too late—that "our Forefathers' coming into the Wilderness, in leaving His Majesty's Dominions and Encreasing the Commerce of Great Brittain [*sic*] has tended more to the Emolument of the Mother Country than if they had remained in their native land; and that the profit which Great Brittain annually receives from us in the way of trade is more than we receive from them."[88] A few months later these same colonists voted to send aid to their neighbors in Boston, who had just destroyed the famed shipment of tea. Within the empire of goods, these Americans reluctantly concluded that they were no longer receiving value for money.

Only a people who had come to take "galloping consumption" for granted could fully have comprehended the revolutionary implications of an organized disruption of the imperial market. As we shall discover, Americans like the writer who signed his essay Colonus would turn the language of commerce on its head, reminding an unhappy generation, "When therefore the Americans consider their situation, in all its circumstance, and know themselves to be the best customers Great-Britain has, for her wares: When, instead of that protection, they reasonably expected from her, as a return for the custom they find themselves most grievously oppressed . . . [w]hat more natural, more justifiable method could they pursue, than to resolve to set about manufacturing themselves and not to import a farthing of British goods they can possibly do without?"[89]

4

Vade Mecum: The Great Chain of Colonial Acquisition

A *vade mecum* is a small guidebook whose Latin name might best be translated "go with me." For many centuries merchants carried such manuals along unfamiliar roads to distant places where strangers calculated weights and measures according to local custom. In 1731 the Reverend Thomas Prince, a Boston minister, produced the first *vade mecum* for a region of colonial America. Despite its ambitious title—*The Vade Mecum for America*—the publication seems to have been intended only for "Traders and Travellers" eager to do business in New England.

Prince provided tables for computing interest and values, a directory of major towns, a description of principal roads, a list of Britain's kings and queens, and, most unexpectedly for a Congregational stronghold, a schedule for the General Meetings of the Baptists and Quakers. In a short introduction, Prince trumpeted the "great Usefulness" of his handbook for "the *British Provinces* in AMERICA." In fact, the entrepreneurial minister noted that a work that could be easily fitted into a jacket pocket had been "long desired." For Prince, the initial pressrun represented only a start. In future editions he planned to improve the guide by reaching out to other mainland British provinces. As he explained, "[We] should with Pleasure have Proceeded to *South-Carolina,* if we cou'd have gotten due Intelligence."[1]

Prince never produced a second edition. His failure, however, should not discourage us from attempting to do so. In fact, the original project invites us to reimagine the muddy, often impassible country roads that tested the resolve of so many mid-eighteenth-century commercial travelers. As darkness overtook them, they may have consulted a *vade mecum,* hoping desperately to reach an inn or ordinary before nightfall. Perhaps over a rum drink late in the evening they asked local farmers how selling imported goods to Baptists or Quakers differed from dealings with Congregationalists. These were conversations within and about a new consumer market-

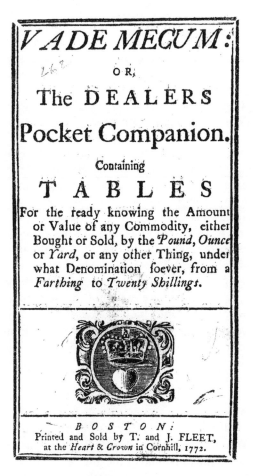

Frontispiece of "The DEALERS Pocket Companion," a *vade mecum* for commercial travelers published on the eve of American independence. *Courtesy of the John Carter Brown Library, Brown University, Providence, Rhode Island.*

place. They occurred in rural settings, in stores, in the offices of country merchants. Such exchanges—themselves provincial expressions of an empire of goods—represented the human face of a great chain of acquisition stretching from the new manufacturing centers of the mother country to eager colonial consumers. We are concerned in our own *vade mecum* with more than informative lists of names and places. Eighteenth-century peddlers and traders—as well as the less peripatetic storekeepers—converted the dreams of colonial consumers into reality, into objects that they could actually see, smell, and touch. As brokers of material change on this intimate level, they bid us to compose a *vade mecum* sensitive to the cultural nuances of an expanding consumer market. Unlike the second edition that Prince once planned, our guidebook will reconstruct a complex and innovative system of merchandising, exploring different sites of distribution throughout the Atlantic World as we follow the "Baubles of Britain" from bustling ports to rural villages, from stores to consumers, and sometimes even from legitimate buyers to gangs of thieves. It will introduce a world of easy credit and clever advertising, of chain stores and massive public auctions, of largely anonymous men and women in search of what one contemporary felicitously called "cheap bargains."[2] Our new guide to colonial merchandising depicts an eighteenth-century colonial society strikingly more modern than the one that we may have expected.

The guide adds another key piece to the overall argument. We have reviewed evidence that testifies to the *quantity* of British manufactures shipped to America at mid-century. We have also seen that the "consumer colonies" forced themselves onto the *consciousness* of policy makers and commercial writers, thus sparking a radical reappraisal of the relation of commerce to empire. But a central element in the analysis is still missing. We need to know more about how the new consumer market actually operated, about the *availability* of imported goods. The reason should be obvious. If most Americans could not in fact have purchased what they desired, or if inadequate personal resources or primitive marketing conditions obstructed the flow of goods into modest households scattered from New Hampshire to Georgia, then it will be very hard for us to link colonial consumers to the political rebels who later demanded independence.

II

Our discussion of distribution and merchandising begins—a bit arbitrarily perhaps—not with the merchant houses of Boston, Charleston, and Philadelphia but rather at the other end of the great chain of acquisition, where we encounter the burglars and shoplifters who understood as well as any of their contemporaries the wonderful new opportunities presented by an empire of goods. Throughout history, persons of a larcenous turn of mind have responded imaginatively to economic change. For such people, innovative technologies redefine the possibilities of crime. It does not romanticize wrongdoing to observe that thieves—like established storekeepers and their regular customers—closely monitor evolving popular tastes in material culture. They know as well as honest businessmen what a community values; they develop a keen eye for quality and authenticity, even if, for reasons of their own, they do not participate in legitimate channels of distribution. As one legal casebook entitled *Pleas of the Crown* (1788) explained, England's "increase of commerce, opulence, and luxury" had spawned a "variety of temptations to fraud and rapine."[3] Not surprisingly, the robbers of late-colonial America accommodated themselves to the sudden flood of British manufactured goods, demonstrating once again that men and women on the margins of society fully appreciate how the mainstream defines desire in a consumer marketplace.

BURGLARY !

TWELVE DOLLARS REWARD·

ON the Night of the 26th Inftant the 'hop of the fubfcriber in Canaan was broke op·en, and the following Articles of Goods were ftolen, viz, Four Doz. black Barcelona Handkerchiefs, three Doz. blue Tapeftry ditto, one Doz. Check Silk ditto, one Piece black Perfian, one Piece black Sattin, twelve Pieces Ribbon different Colours, three Packs Pins, fundry Pair Worfted Stockings, about twenty Yards very fine white Holland, half a Pound of cloth colour'd fowing filk, fundry Pieces of Callico one Doz. of Rafors, together with fundry other fmall Articles, and about twenty fhillings in Cafh, in fmall filver and coppers. Whoever will apprehend the Theif, with faid Articles, and him fecure, fo as he may be bro't to Juftice fhall be entitled to the above Reward, and all neceffary Charges paid, by

Benjamin Sedgwick.

Canaan, June 27, 1772.

An announcement of a "Burglary" in Connecticut suggests that colonial thieves kept up with the latest fashions in imported goods. *Connecticut Courant*, 27 January 1772. *Connecticut Historical Society, Hartford, Connecticut.*

Thomas Dwyer was the colonial shopkeeper's nightmare. An Irishman who found himself in Massachusetts Bay, Dwyer possessed equal measures of cunning and charm, and during the late 1730s he often visited Boston stores, striking up conversations with proprietors while carefully assessing the different yard goods on offer. Even though some colonists later depicted him as a "strolling Fellow," nothing about his physical appearance initially seems to have put obliging clerks on their guard. A newspaper described him as "a lusty full fac'd Fellow of pale Complection, having long strait black Hair." Dwyer took advantage of the storekeeper's eagerness to please, developing a distinctive mode of criminal operation that earned him the disarming sobriquet "Velvet Merchant." According to one account, Dwyer entered local shops "under the Pretense of buying; but while he was inspecting or bargaining for [certain goods] . . . improv'd any Opportunity that presented [itself] to convey what lay most convenient for his Purpose under his great Coat or into his Pocket, and then, after usual Compliments, walk off with his Booty."

Predictably, the Velvet Merchant always demanded quality goods. Even his victims marveled at Dwyer's audacity. On one occasion, he purloined an entire bolt of black velvet—the best cloth in town—but instead of fleeing the scene of the crime, as any prudent thief would have done, Dwyer "carry'd it to a Taylor's in Town, in order to make a Suit of Clothes for himself, and insist'd upon being present while it was cut up, lest any of it shou'd be cabbag'd." At this time "cabbage" meant to pilfer or to appropriate surreptitiously, a fraud almost always associated with tailors who apparently secreted away odd bits of fabric while making garments. Perhaps if the Velvet Merchant had been of a more trusting character he would have avoided arrest. When he came before the magistrates of Suffolk County in 1738, charged with theft, it was reported that "A Variety of Goods were found in his Custody." The inventory of loot included "Sundry Handkerchiefs, sundry Pieces or Remnants of Garlick, sundry Remnants of Persian, a Piece of Blue Stuff, Buttons, Pins, a new pair of Leather Breeches, etc." Dwyer protested that he had purchased "most of them," but a stream of shopkeepers came forward to identify items that had recently gone missing. The court sent the culprit to the Boston jail, a building unable to hold such a clever prevaricator, and within days the Velvet Merchant broke out with eight other men, including "*John Baker*, (an Indian) and a Negro Fellow named *Jocco*." Even then, the editor of the local newspaper found reports of Dwyer's infamous greatcoat amusing. This talented Irishman, the journal observed, "tho' in nothing else worthy [of] our Imitation, yet is certainly a Pattern of Frugality and good Husbandry, if we may depend upon what is affirmed in the Advertisements for apprehending him, where, after his Person is described, 'tis said, *He had on when he went away, a dark blue Coat, about* TWENTY FIVE *Years of Age.*"[4]

John Williams, another careful student of consumer society, died young. In a short account of his life composed on the eve of execution in 1767 when he was only nineteen, Williams explained to those who might learn from his own misadventures that he had come originally from a "middling Family" in Bilesford, a small village located a few miles outside Derby, England. Whatever support his parents may have provided—and this did not include, in Williams's opinion, a proper "Education"—he found himself "a Vagabond in the Streets." Things swiftly went from bad to worse. As a boy of only twelve he traveled the low road to London, "thieving all the Way," and after a series of personal disappointments, in crime and love, the quick-witted teenager decided it was time for a fresh start in the colonies. Once again Williams misjudged the situation. Without prospects in legitimate trade, he became a "strolling Fellow"—much like Thomas Dwyer—and had since then "been constantly strolling, in all Parts from New Hampshire to Georgia, robbing, stealing, pilfering, when ever Opportunity offer'd."

Although he would not have described himself in precisely these terms, Williams was an articulate representative of a burgeoning commercial empire, just as were the British soldiers and itinerant ministers who traveled the same roads. Passing himself off to strangers as an honest peddler, Williams knew full well that the colonists were so eager to acquire British imports that they would never scruple to challenge his credentials. In his pack he carried an impressive assortment of "Needles, Pins, Garters, Buckles, Laces, Fans, &c.. acquired by stealing." By his own admission, Williams took advantage of "Country Girls." A "Present" usually won their confidence, and while they were contemplating his selection of goods, Williams reconnoitered the house for "any Thing valuable that he could conveniently carry off." The next step required only a demonstration of charm. Williams would request lodging, informing his hosts during the course of the evening that he intended to depart well before dawn. As the family slept, Williams made off with small items. Sometimes his victims pursued him, but, ever lucky, he always escaped, pushing north through Virginia, Pennsylvania, and New Jersey. In Albany he ran off with "the Wife of an honest Man." But New York City proved Williams's undoing. Arrested for theft and sentenced to the gallows, the young man entertained local authorities to the end. "A Vein of Humour and Pleasantry runs thro' his whole Account," noted one minister, but then, realizing the danger of turning a seductive peddler into a popular hero, he added, "Yet at the last he [Williams] says, that since he must enter into Eternity, he is sorry for his Misdeeds."[5] Like the curious "Country Girls," the Derby peddler had simply wanted to share in a new material culture that he could never quite afford.

If contemporary mid-century accounts are to be believed, John Morrison and his confederates terrorized consumers throughout the Philadelphia area. The gang of robbers came into existence sometime during the winter of 1750, an event made strikingly manifest "by the unusual Frequency of *Robberies, Thefts,* and *Burglaries.*" Morrison, a recent arrival from Ireland, seems to have masterminded the group's criminal activities. He had come to America seven years earlier as an indentured servant. After obtaining his freedom, Morrison began appearing in the streets of Philadelphia as an urban peddler, "selling Limes and Onions from House to House." This modest business provided a convenient cover for his real interests. As the good citizens of the city soon discovered, his hawking of limes and onions "gave him an Opportunity of observing how the Windows and Doors were fastened, where he purposed to make his Attempts; and of pilfering out of Entries, &c. when he had knock'd and no body appear'd." Morrison recruited several associates, most of them former servants. Each person brought a specific skill to the gang. Several specialized in fencing stolen goods; others actually participated in the break-ins. None was more valuable than Elizabeth Robinson. Months later, after her arrest, Morrison declared—a backhanded compliment from an Irish male—that "she was as true-hearted a Woman as ever lived, tho' an English Woman, and was better than any two Men for his Work, being able to go up and down a Chimney very dextrously." Robinson also seduced one of her accomplices, a piece of sexual gossip used against her at the trial.

The members of the Morrison gang might have escaped detection if they had been able to keep quiet. But success went to their heads; they talked a little too freely in local taverns. The display of consumer objects that one would never have expected a former servant to own raised suspicion. The entire scheme came undone after magistrates questioned Francis McCoy, an Irish Protestant, about stolen goods. Although he protested his innocence, authorities decided to arrest the man, and as McCoy was "taking off his Shoes to put on the Irons, a stolen Necklace was found in one of them, [and] he was struck dumb, being exceedingly confounded." Suddenly, faced with the possibility of capital punishment, other accomplices decided to confess, or, as we might say, to turn state's evidence. To be sure, one of the confederates claimed hotly that he had actually purchased the many fine objects found hidden in the gang's hideout. When the arresting officers asked him exactly how much he had paid for these items, he mentioned amazing bargain rates, so low indeed "as render'd it very suspicious." A law-abiding person would surely have known how much fine cloth and metal goods should cost in a proper store. The magistrates who policed an expanding commercial society certainly did.

What gang members had to say in court confirmed the worst fears of the good people of Philadelphia. At first, Morrison had been content to steal only "Turkies and Ducks." One thing led to another, however, and soon the group began breaking into shops and houses, taking "some Wearing Apparel, two Silver Spoons and a Silver Tea-Tongs." As the local authorities reported, "At length scarce a Night pass'd without an Attempt on one or more Houses, and some of the Robberies were attended with Circumstances that show'd a Boldness and Dexterity in the Actors, really surprizing." The busy criminals even had to obtain a special bag to carry their ever larger hauls of "Booty."

What most seemed to impress local authorities—other than the suggestions of lewd sex—was how well informed Morrison and his friends were about consumer fashion. Early on, the leader had insisted that the gang concentrate whenever possible only on "the best Shop Goods." A pamphlet published soon after three of the robbers had been hanged recounted in unusual detail the various items that Morrison and the others had taken. Sections of this publication read almost like contemporary newspaper advertisements, a predictable phenomenon since some of these objects had only recently migrated from the shelves of local stores to back-of-the-tavern fencing operations. Morrison remembered, for example, having "robb'd Mr. R——d's House of two Silk Gowns, two other Gowns, three fine Aprons, a Tea Chest, some Cambrick Handkerchiefs and other Things, which one of his Companions carried to New-York for Sale." The criminal's narrative included teakettles, pewter basins, silver utensils, a wide selection of cloth, a pair of stays, a calico gown, a silk waistcoat, and a scarlet long cloak. "Mrs. G——h's House" yielded "a Camblet Cloak, a Pot of Butter, a blue Cloth Jacket, a pair of black Silk Stockings, two pair of Pumps." These goods found a ready market in Lancaster, Pennsylvania, some miles outside Philadelphia.

In the end a colonial court saw no option other than executing such hardened criminals. When he heard the sentence, Morrison "rav'd and swore and curs'd." On the way to the gallows, a great procession of townspeople accompanied the condemned thieves, who were ghoulishly forced to drag empty coffins along the path. Clergymen offered soothing words. At the last moment, the governor of Pennsylvania pardoned one member of the gang. Poor Elizabeth Robinson was not so favored, even though she thought that she had been saved when the rope broke. The hangman repeated the operation, and on the second attempt she died. So too did McCoy and Morrison. Before Morrison's execution, he offered an apology for the group's activities. "To support our selves in *Idleness,* and maintain our expensive Vices, we *plundered* the *Honest* and *Industrious; we robbed* even the *Poor* of their *Little,* which they had gained with *hard Labour,* and hoped to enjoy with *Comfort*."[6] It would have been improper form, of course, for Morrison at that moment to have expressed satisfaction at having distributed so many consumer goods at low prices to ordinary people who hoped—like the members of the gang themselves—to acquire the newest material comforts of the age.

Like John Morrison, Isaac Frasier was a good judge of the latest British imports. He almost always worked alone, however, and for several years during the 1760s this troubled young man traveled the main roads of New England, from Salem to New Haven, breaking into stores and houses. At the time of his execution in 1768 Frasier's life seems to have spun out of control. He simply moved from place to place, in a frenetic search for imported goods. Frasier himself expressed surprise that he had fallen so far so fast. He had been born in 1740 to a hardworking Rhode Island family, and his major handicap was poverty. His father died during the famous Louisbourg campaign of 1745—the New Englanders' great victory over the French in Canada—and although his mother tried to provide the rudiments of education, Frasier later confessed, "I was learned no more than just to know my letters, and write my name, which I have since entirely forgot." Apprenticed to an extremely unpleasant shoemaker, Frasier struggled to master a legitimate trade, but at age sixteen he decided that he could no longer tolerate his overbearing employer. He ran away to join the army, a mistake, since military service seems only to have

The "Boldness and Dexterity" of the Morrison gang frightened the hard-working consumers of mid-century Philadelphia. *Courtesy of the Rosenbach Museum and Library, Philadelphia, Pennsylvania.*

schooled him in the techniques of breaking and entering. Lacking both money and a home, Frasier sensed that if he did not quickly reform his behavior he would come to an unhappy end.

Love appeared to hold the solution. When a woman in rural Connecticut agreed to marry Frasier, he resolved to take up farming. But since he brought no material resources to the union, not even elementary agricultural tools, he knew that he would be forced to open an account at the local store. His desire to provide his new wife with the basic comforts of domestic life proved his undoing. As Frasier explained, "Our attention was then employed in procuring necessary articles for house-keeping. Now my resolution taken at my first coming to this place failed me, and Satan overpowered my feeble fortitude." Driven by an "avaricious temper," Frasier wanted to become a consumer without the burden of payment. He stole from "the shop of one Trueman Hinman" consumer goods valued at almost £80, a sum so large that one wonders how Frasier carted all the loot back to the farm. Not surprisingly, he was detected in the act, and although he managed to escape punishment by making restitution to the owner, he alienated the object of his affection. Without prospect of marriage, Frasier "gave a rein to my covetous disposition, being extremely desirous to be rich."

From that moment, Frasier's ill-fated life became an unceasing journey of acquisition, a kind of commercial pilgrim's progress without promise of redemption. Whereas other people of his generation organized autobiographies around major events—the birth of children or participation in a crucial battle—Frasier narrated his story largely in terms of the quality and quantity of the goods that he stole. At times the pace of his movement seemed almost frenzied, a nervous motion with no certain goal. "I then went to Boston," Frasier observed in a typical passage, "stealing at several places on the road. From Boston, I returned to Middletown, in Connecticut, where I committed four burglaries in one night, *viz.* Widow Wetmore's house, of £3 or 4 cash, a merchant's shop of 2 or 3 dozen handkerchiefs, a watch, a gun, and several other articles. A taylor's shop of a new coat. A shoe-maker's of 3 pair of shoes and a calf-skin, and went off undiscovered, and sold the effects." Then he traveled to New York, before returning to Norwalk, Connecticut, "where I broke Mr. Gould Hoit's store and robbed it of 2 pieces of velvet, 2 pieces chintz, some silk handkerchiefs and sundry other articles, to the amount of £50 and was not detected."

Frasier's narrative of crime contains scores of passages just like these. It presented a tale of an eighteenth-century consumer gone bad. Like the honest people of New England, Frasier knew the value of ribbons and breeches, knee buckles and beaver hats, coats and stockings. Indeed, even confronting execution for his many robberies, Frasier took a kind of perverse pride in his accomplishments, drawing the reader's attention to "feats worthy of notice." The man who recorded Frasier's life story—probably a local minister—explained that "the articles taken from each store, are particularly mentioned at his [Frasier's] desire, that the owners may know the articles taken by him, in order to exculpate others."[7] It was a generous gesture on the eve of execution, but one suspects that a more pressing consideration was Frasier's insistence on receiving proper credit for a notable career.

People like Frasier expose an underworld of consumer life.[8] That other colonists took these crimes seriously is revealed not only by the crowds that attended the executions but also by the popularity of the published confessions.[9] Like modern swindlers and thieves who have found a niche on the Internet, mid-eighteenth-century burglars seized upon opportunities presented by the empire of goods. They understood the new fashions, the new language of desire, and although fencing was not an accepted form of merchandising, it brought fashionable objects to men and women who could not otherwise have participated in this alluring material culture. But, of course, most people never dealt with these shady figures, giving their custom instead to honest merchants and peddlers, factors and chapmen. It is to their experience as consumers that we now turn our attention.

III

For representatives of the provincial underworld as well as for legitimate buyers of imported goods, the great chain of acquisition most likely began in a major colonial port such as Charleston, Boston, Philadelphia, or New York. During the eighteenth century these urban centers came to symbolize America's growing commercial prosperity within the British Empire, and colonists described long-distance trade as a divine blessing. In *God's Marvellous Kindness,* for example, a sermon of thanksgiving delivered in 1745, the Reverend Jared Eliot reminded a congregation that King Solomon himself had advocated "the Eastern Trade." Exchange with various remote nations helped explain ancient Israel's "Power and Wealth." And so it would for Britain's mainland colonists. They bore witness to the wisdom of the Old Testament. "It may be laid down as a Rule," exclaimed Eliot, "that ordinarily no Kingdom, State or Province will ever advance to any considerable Degree of temporal Greatness, Polity, Power and Influence, without Trade and Navigation."[10]

The story was much the same from South Carolina to New England. Provincial ports bustled with activity. Ships arrived from metropolitan centers such as Bristol, London, and Liverpool carrying cargoes of manufactured goods. Other vessels anchored in American harbors were bound for the West Indies or for lesser colonial markets, key destinations in an increasingly complex commercial system that struggled to find ways to pay for the flood of new consumer goods. In 1774 a foreign visitor recounted the scene that greeted him along the "majestic *Delaware*," the river that served as Philadelphia's commercial highway to the ocean. "The voice of industry perpetually resounds along the shore," he wrote, "and every wharf within my view is surrounded with groves of masts, and heaped with commodities of every kind, from almost every quarter of the globe."[11]

Considering the economic importance of the major port cities, it is not surprising that during the middle decades of the eighteenth century American artists began turning out prints depicting the various urban waterfronts. Works of this sort were common in England, and some sold an impressive number of copies. One of the first people to appreciate the need for colonial prospects was Thomas Penn, the proprietor of Pennsylvania. He wanted

Like those who lived in other colonial American ports, the people of Charleston took pride in the rising volume of commerce connecting them to metropolitan centers such as Bristol, London, and Liverpool. *Watercolor, Charleston Harbor by Bishop Roberts, ca. 1740. Courtesy of the Colonial Williamsburg Foundation.*

Part of Charter Town

Imperial commerce dominated this popular
eighteenth-century prospect of Boston. *"A
Northeast View of Boston," ca. 1723, attributed to
William Burgis. Courtesy of the Peabody Essex
Museum, Salem, Massachusetts.*

his English friends to view for themselves the flourishing capital of the colony that bore his family's name. In 1750 he wrote to Richard Peters, his agent in America, demanding "a perspective view of the City." Peters showed little initial enthusiasm for the project, noting that "Philadelphia will make a most miserable Perspective for want of steeples." But Penn was not to be put off, and after several false starts by others, George Heap produced an illustration that pleased the proprietor. A few years earlier a man known as B. Roberts completed a handsome prospect of Charleston. William Burgis performed the same service for New York City and Boston.[12]

Although Peters had a point about the missing steeples in Philadelphia, he overstated their importance in the composition of a colonial prospect. In other ports church spires—many of them financed by new eighteenth-century mercantile wealth—dominated the horizon, but in all the visual interpretations of American cities the artists focused the viewer's attention on the paramount importance of commerce, indeed, on the centrality of "the groves of masts."[13] The prints captured the energy of mercantile life, depicting the arrival and departure of huge oceangoing transports, the off-loading of British goods onto smaller vessels, and the density of the docks and warehouses. In Burgis's prospect of New York, for example, the foreground ships formed a wall of hulls and sails so thick that it almost completely obscured the city itself. Roberts provided more precise architectural detail for Charleston, but like Burgis and Heap he celebrated the explosion of maritime commerce. In his print, dozens of sailors can be seen rowing small boats among the larger vessels anchored along the waterfront. The message was, of course, not hard to comprehend. Without long-distance Atlantic trade, American ports such

George Heap's "An East Prospect of the City of Philadelphia, under the Direction of Nicholas Skull (London, 1 September 1754)," reflected the rising importance of imperial commerce to the life of the community. *Detail of larger print reproduced with permission of the Historical Society of Pennsylvania.*

as Charleston could not have emerged from their former "rude unpolished Condition." Commerce brought civilization. It sustained the steeples and the warehouses; it made America worthy of British attention.

Nestled among the more prominent structures of the port cities—perhaps on crowded streets just beyond the docks—one would have encountered the stores that linked ordinary consumers to the great British merchant houses which had originally transported the manufactured goods to America. However modest these shops may have appeared in comparison to the soaring church spires, they were no less important in the lives of the colonists. It was in these stores that honest people as well as lowlifes such as the Velvet Merchant personally experienced the new Atlantic economy. In all the major port cities newspaper advertisements invited potential buyers to examine the inventories of the large retail businesses, many of them owned by women.[14] Each establishment offered a slightly different range of stock. The majority of colonial storekeepers, however, never bothered with notices in the local journals. A survey conducted in 1771 revealed that Boston, a city of about sixteen thousand people, supported over five hundred separate shops. Several smaller port towns in Massachusetts also reported surprisingly large numbers. Although Salem had a population only half that of Boston, it listed 172 stores, while nearby Charleston, a modest farm community, boasted of ninety-nine retail outlets.[15]

Stores in New England and the middle colonies—we shall examine merchandising in the Chesapeake in a later section—generally received their stock of dry goods from large American wholesale merchants who maintained close commercial ties with British correspondents. Although the majority of these suppliers worked out of London, some of the more specialized

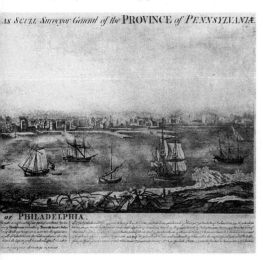

As Scull Surveyor General of the PROVINCE of PENNSYLVANIA.

of PHILADELPHIA.

British firms—those concentrating on metal goods, for example—often routed American orders through western English ports such as Bristol.[16] Colonial wholesalers preferred what they described as "sundry merchandize," in other words, assortments of different kinds of British goods from ceramics to cloth. Putting together a proper bundle of consumer items was no easy task, since it required English exporters to maintain direct contact with various manufacturers scattered throughout the country.

British exporters tried to anticipate the colonial markets, knowing in advance that most shipments would depart England in two great waves governed by prevailing weather systems, one in January, the second in mid- to late summer.[17] They also had to attend to specific American requests, a challenge that sometimes strained relations among the various parties involved in transatlantic trade. American wholesalers, for example, occasionally set a limit on the prices that they were willing to pay for certain English goods. Such instructions—written months before they reached London or Bristol—could effectively cut English merchants off from their normal suppliers. In 1759 a correspondent complained to James Beekman, then New York City's leading wholesale merchant, "I find your limitations in the price of China ware is almost intirely a prohibition of Sending any."[18] At other times, the problem was the low quality of the articles on offer, or simply their availability. One English firm apologized for a selection of hats that did not meet American expectations. The hats, it explained, were not "so fine as [we] could have wished ... Owing to the wickedness of our Jurnimen [Journeymen] in not doing their work as it should be."[19] Bad weather as well as political conflicts in distant places could interrupt the normal flow of commerce. The partnership of Pomeroys and Hodgkin confessed to Beekman in 1757 that "troubles in the country where our saxon linnens are made have rendered them very scarce."[20]

Whatever the obstacles, both sides in these exchanges worked hard to avoid conflict. The almost insatiable demand in the colonies for these sundry goods helped to reduce tensions. After all, the British houses generally received a handsome commission for their services.[21] During the middle decades of the eighteenth century, relations between American wholesale merchants and their English correspondents were usually stable and, indeed, frequently cordial. The British firm of Peach and Pierce could hardly have been more polite about an overdue American bill. "We must with Justice Acknowledge your Punctuality in remitting [funds] and it is with Chearfullness we Submit to waite the time when it will suit you to remit farther and hope it will be more to your Advantage than at Present."[22] One way or another, Anglo-American businessmen learned whom they could trust, who offered the best-quality manufactures at the lowest prices, and who provided liberal terms of credit.

We should be alert, of course, to the possibility that commercial geniality concealed real insecurity. Although American wholesalers frequently described British trading partners as friends, they must have recognized the potential in these relationships for disappointment, even betrayal.[23] The cheerful rhetoric served only to mask the logic of capitalism. During the long decade before independence, aggressive London exporters apparently decided that they could obtain even higher rates of return from the American market by going around the established colonial wholesale firms and dealing directly with retail businesses. In 1768 Francis Bernard, royal governor of Massachusetts, informed Lord Shelburne that the character of transatlantic trade had changed substantially in recent years. In former times, Bernard claimed, American merchants were "importers and Dealers by wholesale & by no means retailers." This traditional arrangement pleased all parties, and the London houses promised their Boston contacts "a reasonable profit." Suddenly, however, a different set of commercial under-standings had come into play. "For some Years past the London Merchants for the sake of advancing their Profits have got into dealing immediately with the Retailers, and have thereby abolished the Distinction of Merchants at Boston: so that at present every Merchant is a Shopkeeper & every Shop-keeper is a Merchant. Hence instead of dealing with Respectable and Cred-itable Houses, the London Merchants are engaged in a great Number of little Shops."[24]

We should probably not place too much interpretive weight on Bernard's observations. His strongest political allies included large wholesale mer-chants such as Thomas Hutchinson and his sons. Nevertheless, although Bernard may have exaggerated the structural shift in merchandising, he clearly appreciated the vulnerability of American wholesale firms within the great chain of acquisition. The wholesalers resented any suggestion that they were mere retailers. The character of one's business distinguished the owner's place in society; function as well as size translated into claims of class. John Hancock, the famed signer of the Declaration of Independence and leading Boston merchant, complained when an English export firm injured his professional pride. "I look on myself [as] a Man of Capital," he thundered, "& am not to be put on a footing with every twopenny Shop-keeper that addresses you."[25]

The large colonial merchants—those who dominated the commerce of the major northern ports—faced an even more daunting set of problems with their own customers, usually small retailers. They not only had to sup-ply the shopkeepers with the kinds of goods that ordinary buyers demanded, but they also had to provide generous credit. During the best of times, re-ceiving timely payment for the British imports proved exceedingly diffi-cult. The retailers complicated matters by constantly haggling over prices.[26] The colonial economy also suffered from a chronic shortage of hard cur-rency, and since the British export firms demanded returns in specie or the equivalent in the form of negotiable bills of exchange, the American whole-sale merchants were hard put to obtain sufficient cash to sustain the trade. The stores often collected payment in regional agricultural products such as livestock, which the wholesale merchants then sold in the West Indies for hard money. This secondary trade helps explain the prominence in con-temporary urban prospects of ships bound for the Caribbean. Currency pressures sparked other highly innovative strategies, especially in the north-ern colonies. Often American wholesale merchants supplied their British correspondents not only with raw materials—whale oil and naval stores, for example—but also with the vessels that actually carried these products to market. This so-called invisible commerce in colonial-made ships—it is not clear that government officials understood the nature of the arrange-ment—helped balance the books. At the end of the day, however, it was always a struggle for the Americans to meet their obligations as consumers, and over the years their debts to the English export firms steadily mounted.[27]

IV

Country stores played a huge role in the rapid expansion of the new consumer marketplace. If this statement seems hyperbolic, it is perhaps because Frederick Jackson Turner, the influential historian of the American West, has instructed us to imagine the frontier as an exceptional space inhabited largely by self-reliant men and women. The development of global merchandising has no place in this familiar story that we tell ourselves about our own past. During the middle decades of the eighteenth century, however, a different account resonated among the colonists. It stressed the centrality of consumer opportunity in bringing what contemporaries called civilization to inland towns and small villages. William Eddis, an astute English observer who traveled to Maryland, advanced a quite different version of the frontier thesis in which storekeepers played a dominant role. "To supply the real and imaginary necessities of those by whose persevering efforts and penetrating genius immense uncultivated tracts became flourishing establishments," Eddis explained, "storekeepers . . . were encouraged to pursue the path which industry had pointed out. Warehouses were accordingly erected, and woollens, linens, and implements of husbandry were first presented to the view of the laborious planter." Opportunity to purchase manufactured goods excited ever greater demand. Frontier retailers became the agents of social change. "As wealth and population increased," wrote Eddis, "wants were created, and many considerable demands, in consequence, took place for the various elegancies as well as necessaries of life."[28]

Eddis told a tale of market accommodation, rather than resistance; of expanding communication, rather than isolation. People living in the more inaccessible areas of Connecticut would have understood this perspective. Like Thomas Prince, who published the *Vade Mecum for America*, they sometimes measured progress in terms of the construction of serviceable roads. One florid petition sent to the colonial magistrates by the townsmen of Kensington and Southington in 1762 complained that existing highways were "attended with bad mountains, miry swamps, steep hills and ledges together with many turnings and crooks which render it exceedingly difficult travelling and costly carting or transporting the produce of the country to s[ai]d river [Connecticut River]." Lest obtuse legislators miss the point, the signers noted that "as there is great increase of inhabitants[,] so consequently of traveling, trade and business . . . [we are] retarded for want of convenient roads."[29]

Few contemporaries seemed quite certain how best to describe the small retail businesses that sprang up along the back roads of empire. According to Sarah Kemble Knight (her pen name was simply Madam Night), an English visitor who traveled from Boston to New York City early in the century, the colonists "gave the title of merchant to every trader."[30] Some decades later another visitor, Nicholas Cresswell, observed that "what they call stores in this country are Shops in England."[31] Whatever name one employed, however, the village stores that transformed the social landscape of late colonial

America depended on passable roads to link them to the larger port cities where their owners exchanged local products for imported British articles. The Connecticut petitioners who complained that mountains, swamps, and ledges hindered the flow of commerce, for example, relied on suppliers in Boston and New York. Fisher Gay of Farmington, the village's most successful shopkeeper, obtained his inventory from New York, while his competitors, John Patterson and Samuel Cowles, who defined themselves as "traders in company," transported goods such as cloth, hosiery, gloves, and books from Boston.[32] Similar merchandising networks became common throughout the northern and middle colonies. Country merchants in New Jersey looked either to New York or Philadelphia for popular consumer items. In western Pennsylvania and the Shenandoah Valley of Virginia the desired manufactured goods generally came from Philadelphia or, after mid-century, from one of the newer commercial centers such as Baltimore or Falmouth.[33]

Commercial relationships along the entire chain of acquisition tended to replicate themselves. The country dealers looked upon their urban American suppliers much as the great city merchants viewed the British export firms that had assembled the original cargoes. Each link in these expanding networks sustained expectations of reciprocity, which achieved a certain legitimacy through a commercial language of shared interests and mutual respect. Everyone knew, of course, that the new merchandising system spawned little fish as well as large ones, but a fiction of rough equality informed the new consumer marketplace. Thomas Hancock, the Boston wholesale merchant, understood these assumptions as well as any of his competitors. He encouraged village shopkeepers, many of whom ordered only small amounts of dry goods during a single year. "I shall be Glad to Supply you with any Sort of Goods," Hancock assured one correspondent, "and upon as Good Terms as any body, whenever you may have occasion."[34] Moreover, the wholesaler listened carefully to their grousing about quality and quantity, about color and style. When some country merchants grumbled about the poor selection of paper they had received, Hancock immediately informed his London contact: "[I] must Request you always to procure for me the other sort [of paper] which please my Country Chaps much better then [*sic*] what you now Sent."[35] The firm of Jackson and Bromfield in Newburyport, Massachusetts, sounded as if it were being tyrannized by the shopkeepers who were in fact their customers. The partners wrote to a large Bristol house, announcing, "[Y]ou'll please to put up [a cargo] of good quality & cheap as can possibly be afforded, for our Business has got to such a Pass that every petty Shopkeeper will set himself up a Judge of English Goods."[36] And to make matters worse, carefully nurtured relations could suddenly turn sour, for however hard the wholesalers tried to please the small retailers, they often found that displays of attention could not ensure loyalty. Just as the major London export merchants sought to bypass the American wholesale firms, the small country shopkeepers attempted from time to time to circumvent their suppliers in New York or Boston by dealing directly with English companies.[37]

News of the arrival of large trunks filled with imported goods drew curious American consumers to local shops. *Colonial trunk. Courtesy of the East Hampton Historical Society, East Hampton, New York.*

Moreover, although the language of merchandising may occasionally have sounded solicitous, the settling of accounts strained goodwill. Bills had to be paid. Urban merchants demanded compensation for the "small parcels of European goods" dispatched to the many inland communities.[38] As we have seen, this side of the business presented a severe challenge, for village shopkeepers seldom could obtain sufficient hard currency to cover their obligations. From their customers—almost of all of whom were middling farmers—they accepted agricultural products in lieu of cash. No one liked these arrangements. Local exchanges seemed to take on the character of an elaborate barter economy. But in this instance appearances were deceptive. The proprietors of the small stores knew as well as the farmers who gave them their business the full market value in currency of each cow or bushel of grain offered in payment for the flood of British manufactures. Often calculations became extremely complex, a reminder that only an extremely robust colonial market for British imports could have justified such difficult financial arrangements. One visitor explained the bargaining process as practiced in Connecticut stores. The shopkeepers rated

> their goods according to the time and specie they pay in: viz. Pay, money, pay as money, and trusting. *Pay* is grain, pork, beef, &c. at the prices set by the General Court that year. *Money* is pieces of eight, rials, or Boston or Bay shillings (as they call them) or good hard money, as sometimes silver coin is termed by them; also wampum, viz. Indian beads, which serve for change. *Pay as money* is provisions, as aforesaid one-third cheaper than the Assembly or General Court sets it. And *Trust* as they and the merchant agree for time.[39]

In New England, the consumer economy sparked important structural transformations that further complicated the great chain of acquisitions. During any single year, for example, the owner of a family farm might safely sell off only one or two head of cattle. Other animals were needed for breeding or to feed dependents. At some appointed time—usually in the autumn—drovers would sweep through the countryside, picking up a few cows from each village and then driving the entire herd to Boston or New York, where the cattle supplied shoemakers with leather or naval contractors with salted meat for the British fleet. On the eve of independence, a new group of middlemen appeared in the towns that formed a ring around Boston. These entrepreneurs intercepted the cattle drives and then, after butchering the animals, sold meat and leather to the artisans and contractors of the city, an innovation that raised prices and greatly annoyed Boston's shoemakers.[40] Other market strategies depended on the nearly insatiable needs of the Caribbean sugar planters. In 1731 Governor Joseph Talcott of Connecticut informed the Board of Trade, "Horses and lumber are exported from hence to the West Indies, for which we receive in exchange, sugar, salt, molasses and rum. What provisions we can spare, and some small quantity of tar and turpentine, are sent to Boston and New York, and Rhode Island, for which we receive European goods."[41] Country traders sometimes packed local pork in barrels and carted it off, together with the corn and wheat they had taken in, to the cities. Long Island shopkeepers sent whale oil, and even the hides of small game that their customers had killed.[42]

V

Our *vade mecum* of mid-eighteenth-century colonial merchandising must take into account the strikingly different networks of exchange that developed in the Chesapeake, a region that included Maryland, Virginia, and much of northern North Carolina. Tobacco provided the engine driving this provincial economy. To be sure, during the previous century the price that the American staple fetched on the European market fluctuated wildly, and boom times often gave way to depressions so severe that impoverished workers and desperate servants sometimes rose up in rebellion against crown authorities in Virginia.[43] As income from tobacco gradually improved, however, political tranquility replaced chronic unrest. Not surprisingly, the examples of an opulent material culture that draw modern tourists to Williamsburg and the surrounding area—a style of life expressed most powerfully by the Palladian mansions constructed by the great Tidewater planters—date from this period.

Providing a persuasive explanation for the extraordinary social transformation of the Chesapeake colonies has attracted a number of able scholars.[44] Although the topic remains contested, it seems clear that the prosperity and stability of the region resulted from a number of separate factors: the growth of an unfree African labor force, the establishment of a government-controlled system of tobacco warehouses, which carefully monitored the quality of the crops exported to Great Britain and the Continent, and the sale by enterprising Scottish merchants of huge amounts of Chesapeake tobacco on the French market.[45] At mid-century growers in Virginia and Maryland still complained about the prices their crops fetched on the world market, but a steady demand for tobacco throughout Europe meant that those with access to land and slaves could make an acceptable return, which was, of course, the ticket to participation in the new empire of goods. In this commercial environment, the major Scottish syndicates—John Glassford and Co., William Cuninghame and Co., and Speirs, Bowman, and Co., for example—did quite well for themselves. In fact, the leading partners in these companies came to be known as "tobacco lords" or "tobacco aristocrats," and one can still visit the impressive estates around Glasgow that they financed from profits in the Virginia trade.[46] The larger point is that, unlike the small farmers of New England, the Chesapeake planters were fully integrated into a complex Atlantic economy from the very beginning of settlement. For them, the question was never whether to resist the marketplace but rather how best to take advantage of the opportunities that this commercial system presented.[47] And, for most eighteenth-century tobacco planters, the possibility of obtaining British manufactures proved most alluring.[48]

Long before aggressive Scottish firms acquired a dominant share of the Chesapeake tobacco, elite Tidewater planters had consigned their crops directly to London merchants. For a commission, these agents not only sold the tobacco but also filled orders for specific English goods. Moreover, they performed quasi-banking services, arranging for shipping, negotiating for insurance, and dealing with customs officials.[49] These commercial relations often lasted for several decades, taking on a highly personal character. The great planters—those possessing hundreds of slaves and immense tracts of land—sometimes referred to the consignment merchants as "friends." The Americans trusted these distant businessmen, most of whom they knew only through commercial correspondence, to sell their tobacco at the best price and to purchase British manufactures at bargain rates. Although the annual consignment trade represented no more than a third of the total Chesapeake crop, it has received extremely close analysis. The reason is not hard to discern. The most familiar names of eighteenth-century Virginia— George Washington, Thomas Jefferson, and William Byrd II, for example— relied on the consignment system to furnish their splendid homes and dress their families in the latest London fashions. After the 1730s the demand for consumer goods among the local gentry rose sharply. In fact, these gentlemen regularly ran up huge debts to their English representatives, a painful reminder of their dependence on relative strangers who were more concerned about maintaining their own solvency than about underwriting planter extravagance.[50]

Elite spending on imported goods only partially explained the dramatic mid-century surge in consumer activity in the Chesapeake. A striking change in marketing strategy suddenly afforded thousands of less affluent planters access to British manufactures. The plan owed everything to the Scots. Sensing that they would have a hard time breaking the great planters of their traditional reliance on the London consignment merchants, the Glasgow firms decided to focus their operations directly on the smaller producers, growers who often owned only a couple of slaves and a few acres of arable land but who nevertheless accounted for over two-thirds of the tobacco produced in Virginia and Maryland. After 1740 Glasgow houses opened scores of American stores—often called "Scotch stores"—staffed by employees hired in Britain. These resident factors collected small parcels of tobacco and, in return, supplied the less affluent planters of the region with a variety of imported goods.

The stores represented a brilliant innovation. As a contemporary observed, the factors opened up the Atlantic economy to "the common People . . . who make up the Bulk of the Planters."[51] By any standard, the explosion of business sites along the navigable rivers of the Chesapeake was impressive. Even personnel who operated the stores could hardly keep up with the rapid expansion. In 1742 Francis Jerdone exclaimed that "there are 25 stores within 18 miles round [in lower Hanover County, Virginia] which is 13 more than at Mr. Johnson's death [in 1740] and 4 or 5 more expected next year."[52] The Glasgow companies established separate chains of stores, and their American agents communicated regularly among themselves about the prospects for future harvests and about the prices they would have to offer the local planters for tobacco. But what seemed most to concern the storekeepers was competition from other Scots, for no sooner did one firm set up for business than another would open its doors. By 1739 the rivalry had become so intense that one harried factor complained, "[T]his river at present is so crowded with stores that its very difficult to make a purchase [of tobacco], and every year grows worse & worse."[53]

The dramatic quickening of the consumer marketplace in the Chesapeake was more a function of generous credit allowances than of the convenient location of the new Scottish stores. In modern terminology, the small planters discovered that they could buy now, pay later, and this liberating invitation brought them to the shops in droves. Long-term credit greatly expanded the working capital of the smaller producers, allowing them to enjoy desirable British imports many months before they had to settle accounts.[54] The system also worked to the storekeeper's advantage, for the planters were far more likely to sell their tobacco to those factors who had treated them most generously. A broad selection of manufactured goods helped cement these local relationships. John Mair, a Scotsman who in 1736 published *Book-Keeping Modernized or Merchant-Accounts by Double Entry, According to the Italian Form*, counseled his countrymen on how best to conduct business in the Chesapeake. "These merchants or storekeepers generally sell their goods on trust, or time," Mair explained, "and receive payment, not in cash, but in tobacco, as the planters can get it ready." Such a colonial venture required precise planning. "Before a merchant opens a store in this retail way," he continued, "it is his interest to have it well provided with all sorts of commodities proper for clothing and family-use; and the greater variety he has, the better; for where-ever planters find they can be best suited and served, thither they commonly resort, and there dispose of their tobacco."[55] Such advice was well placed. Like other commercial relations in the great chain of acquisition, these market arrangements from the very first had the potential quickly to come unraveled. After all, however canny the Scots may have been in their daily operations, they remained Scots, outsiders in a provincial society, and when consumer desire itself became a contentious political topic, it was easy for the planters to blame the foreigners for a number of ills not of their own making.

The moment of crisis did not occur until the eve of independence. Indeed, the Scots spent considerable time and energy ingratiating themselves to their Chesapeake customers. The remarkably complete papers of one leading firm—William Cuninghame and Company—document how closely the Glasgow merchants attended to the operation of the new stores. In the autumn of 1767 a Cuninghame partner in Scotland wrote to a factor who had just arrived in Virginia. "I suppose by this time you have got your store fixed out," the employer observed, "which I daresay the assortment of goods will encourage as it will be a very complete one after you have received the whole [cargo] intended from here and some cutlery." Bennet Price, the Virginia factor, had to act fast, however, for the company expected him to recruit a large number of local customers "before Martin Pickett opens [his] store in the spring after which your endeavour will be attended with double trouble."

Of course, as veterans of this competitive business climate, the Scottish merchants instructed Price exactly how to avoid "double trouble." First, he had swiftly to judge the character of the small tobacco planters, erring as much as possible on the side of generosity. "If a man be good it is not material if he cannot pay you any thing next year," explained the Glasgow correspondent. "By selling goods to such men you no doubt increase your debts, but at the same time, you will extend your influence." Second, the novice factor should remember that Cuninghame authorized him to order whatever goods he needed to win the battle of the stores. Quantity made no matter. As Price's contact noted, "I daresay from the quality of the goods and the moderate prices they are charged, you will be enabled to give general satisfaction to all your old customers and to engage a good many new ones." To achieve this target, the Scottish employer counseled, "Try if you can to hook in some of the River people."[56] And finally, Price should learn basic merchandising tricks. Company representatives had discovered, for example, that neat shelving and regular rotation of stock made a favorable impression on customers. Another inexperienced factor was told to "take care to have all your goods in the store in proper order, which greatly contributes to make them sell well. The oftener they are taken down and new [ones] tried, so much the better."[57]

Presented with the possibility of good profits—often as much as a 6 percent return on investment—indigenous Chesapeake merchants soon joined the field. One man who had originally migrated to Maryland as a footman for a local gentry family captured the entrepreneurial spirit that burst forth suddenly at mid-century, and in an effort to launch a small retail business, he begged English relatives to ship him "some knives, some buckles and butens and any thing you think proper, for I can make money here." Of course, for an American just getting started, it helped to possess independent capital. Annapolis shipbuilders and tanners usually had more personal resources than did former footmen, and they took advantage of rising consumer demand. Between 1745 and 1753 the number of dry-goods stores in Annapolis jumped from three to twelve.[58] Other merchants living in Norfolk, Virginia, were soon drawn into this lucrative trade. Unlike their Scottish competitors, who concentrated on tobacco, the colonial business-men also purchased wheat and flour, Chesapeake products that after 1750 did well in southern Europe and underwrote the cargoes of British goods transported back to Virginia.[59]

In Charleston, South Carolina, where the demand for British manufactures was even greater than in other parts of colonial America, the majority of the local merchants maintained accounts with the leading London firms. For a commission, established houses exchanged Carolina rice and indigo for parcels of dry goods.[60] Robert Pringle, who started his career as a factor for a London West Indian merchant, provides insight into the South Carolina consumer market. He operated a modestly successful business in Charleston. His commercial letterbook has a querulous quality, as if he could never quite persuade himself that British correspondents rightly understood the character of local demand. In an order dispatched in 1738, Pringle told them exactly how things worked. "This province," he lectured, "takes off yearly a great Quantity of all manner of dry goods from Europe & Ports in England that are chiefly supply'd from London, Bristol, Topsham, & Liverpool & our manner of Trade in Dry goods is by giving the Planters Credit from Crop to Crop." Worried that the London merchants would attempt to fob him off with goods inappropriate for the Charleston market, Pringle provided them with a detailed list of "Goods proper for So Carolina."

> Vizt. Course Cloths & Heavies, Camblets of all sorts & Colours & Silk Camblets, Linnen & Cotton Checks, Huckaback [a rough linen fabric often for towels] for Tables & Napkins, Diapers & Damask for ditto. Sheeting Linnen. Bagg & Gulix [fine linen for good shirts] & Holland Cambricks. Gun Powder. A Large Quantity 3/4 & 7/8 Garlix low pric'd. Brown Osnaburggs, Dowlas [coarse linen] & Russian Linnen. Indian Trading Guns with two Sights & Gun Flints. . . . White, Blue, & Green plains for Negro Cloathing. Sagathy & Duroys & worsted Damask, Ship & Duffill Blanketting. Ruggs for Negroes Beds. Bed Blanketts fine. Strouds blue & Red. Felt hatts for men & Boys. Course Worsted stockings for Negroes. Course Leather Shoes. . . . China Ware and Punch Bowls. Earthen Ware in crates.

The catalogue contained many other imports; indeed, almost nothing seemed unlikely to sell in South Carolina, even the surprising last item,

"Cheshire cheese." The problem was that London correspondents never fulfilled Pringle's expectations. The calicoes were "very Old and Unfashionable." Other items did not strike him as "fresh and Good in quality." The Italian gauze came in the wrong color. The velvet "happens not to be a Right Sort for this Place," and when he opened a crate of ceramics, he discovered "You omitted in the China Ware to send Dishes as well as plates."[61] Reading between the lines of Pringle's letters, we sense that the Charleston consumers were just as fussy about their purchases as were those of the Chesapeake and New England.

The small but widely scattered planters of North Carolina presented the new retailers with another inviting consumer market. After all, the colony's royal governor, William Tryon, reported as late as 1767 that he had not heard "of a Piece of Woollen or Linnen Cloth being ever sold [in North Carolina] that was the Manufacture of this Province."[62] Tryon probably exaggerated the colony's dependence on external trade. No one, however, questioned the rising demand in this region for British imports. The problem plaguing store owners throughout North Carolina was poor roads. Because the colony lacked deep rivers penetrating far into the interior, many goods had to be laboriously transported overland. Like the eager farmers of Connecticut, the merchants of North Carolina as well as their customers asked the colonial government to improve the highways as well as the navigational facilities along the coast. By the third quarter of the eighteenth century, Scottish stores had begun to appear along the colony's border with Virginia, and manufactured articles flowed to the Moravian settlements in the Piedmont along the Great Wagon Road, a vital commercial link connecting communities such as Salem, Salisbury, and Bethabara with Philadelphia to the north and Charleston to the south.[63]

One other change in how imported goods reached colonial consumers merits attention. Although much of the merchandise that appeared in small retail outlets throughout the South came directly from Great Britain, storekeepers turned increasingly for their stock to suppliers sailing out of major American ports like Boston and Philadelphia.[64] Successful colonial merchants such as Boston's Thomas Hancock supported a fleet of small vessels called coasters which carried British manufactures to correspondents located as far away as Charleston, South Carolina. Perhaps not surprisingly, Robert Pringle seemed no more pleased with the goods he received from Hancock than he did with those coming from London. During the spring of 1742 Pringle accepted a consignment of ribbons from his Boston correspondent, but after four months without recording a single order, he declared that "they happen to be in no manner of Demand here at present, & are entirely unsaleable, The Town being very full of them. I have try'd most of the Shopkeepers for them, but Cannot dispose of them or no part at any Rate." The following year Pringle complained that he could find no market for Hancock's axes or iron pots; still unhappy about the earlier shipment, he added, "[A]lso a Good part of your Ribbons still unsold."[65] Misunderstandings of this sort should not obscure the broader importance of an expanding coastal consumer trade. It not only offered an alternative system of distribution but also established a new form of communication linking Americans with other Americans. No one imagined the tiny coasting vessels as having much political significance, at least not at mid-century. But they carried messages from other colonies, and quite unwittingly commercial innovation opened the possibility for later discussions about resisting king and Parliament.

Reviewing how the empire of goods opened up so many new channels of trade, we can understand perhaps why one business historian of an earlier generation described the flow of British imports in almost lyrical language. "In our mind's eye," he declared, ". . . we may watch cottons from India and nails from England creeping slowly round the coast and up the waterways, over pack-horse trails, past the furthest villages, and so at last into the hands of frontiersmen."[66] In such matters, one tries not to exaggerate the degree of change or project back onto a "world we have lost" a dynamic commercial economy that in fact had not yet come into being. No doubt, stores operated by the likes of Robert Pringle and Bennet Price would strike us as a little sleepy. Nevertheless, however we characterize these marketing developments, we can assert with confidence that during this period colonial Americans experienced a greatly expanded access to British goods.

VI

The formal commercial ledgers that chronicled how merchants interacted with other merchants—suppliers with shopkeepers—can carry us only so far in the construction of a new *vade mecum* designed as a guide to the highly personal character of eighteenth-century merchandising. What usually goes missing from such accounts is the actual consumer. But it was, in fact, during conversations between buyers and sellers—what we might call the culture of doing business—that ordinary men and women negotiated market expectations with storekeepers eager to make a sale. These were the crucial exchanges in the new consumer marketplace.

To paraphrase the poet Carl Sandburg, in the life histories of obscure Americans the consumer revolution came to the mainland colonies on little cat's feet. The market drew energy from countless small transactions. A review of some account books that have survived in New England suggests that consumers typically made quite modest purchases. In these volumes, the columns of carefully entered sums indicate that colonists generally entered a village store looking for specific items—an ivory comb, some pins, a piece of cloth, for example—and the charge for these goods seldom exceeded several shillings.

Allen MacLean served such people. He operated a general dry-goods store in Hartford, Connecticut, and maintained a precise record of all sales from 1741 to 1746—in other words, the period when the consumer economy was beginning to transform the material face of the Anglo-American world.

We know the names of those who came to MacLean's shop; we witness what they purchased. Most customers demanded the same range of household goods. They took home shoe buckles and snuffboxes, knee buckles and pen knives, iron kettles and writing paper. MacLean sold a lot of cheaper fabrics. The most expensive items on offer seem to have been books, and on one particularly memorable day he received the immense sum of three and a half pounds for a "large Bible." And on May 10, 1742, we read that one Elizabeth Loveland indulged herself by buying a pair of gloves, some ribbon, a girdle, garters, and a fan, the entire bundle costing her just under two and a half pounds.[67]

How much attention MacLean gave to what we might call innovative merchandising techniques is impossible to ascertain. No doubt, he realized that he should familiarize himself with his customers' idiosyncratic needs. Unlike some storekeepers in Philadelphia, however, MacLean does not appear to have tried to lure customers into his shop with offers of free coffee

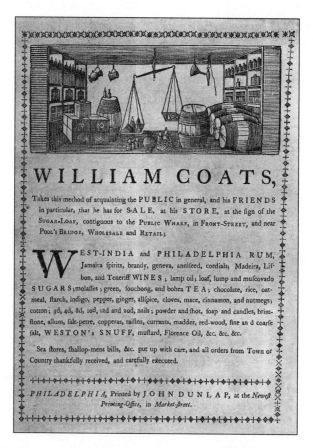

A handbill distributed by William Coats, a general merchant in Philadelphia, depicts the actual layout of a colonial store. *Courtesy of the Library Company of Philadelphia.*

and food.[68] Nor does the Hartford merchant seem to have constructed a special glass window "such as are commonly used in large Towns and Cities by Milliners, Stationers, Watch-Makers, &c. in order to expose their Merchandise for Sale, to the View of Passengers, passing and repassing the Streets." On one of his trips MacLean may well have seen one of these new display windows designed to entice strolling shoppers. It probably would not have surprised him to learn that a New York grand jury condemned these windows as unwarranted "Incroachments" on the city's streets.[69]

Whatever MacLean's retail skills may have been, he could be certain that visitors such as Elizabeth Loveland would scrutinize his behavior. Unlike modern Western economies in which no one cares much about the character of the clerks who fetch goods and ring up the bill, early modern American society judged its shopkeepers in highly moral terms. As "Agricola" informed the subscribers of the *Boston Evening-Post*, colonial consumers expected "Merchants and Shopkeepers" to make "Use of Conscience."[70] In 1732 an irate citizen warned readers of the *South-Carolina Gazette* that "there are a great many Retailers, who falsely imagine that being Historical (the modern Phrase for Lying) is much for their advantage; and some of them have a Saying, That 'tis a Pity Lying is a Sin, it is so useful in Trade." The writer demanded "fair Dealing."[71]

Accounts of actual shopping during this period are extremely rare. The fullest description of such activities came from the pen of Madam Knight, an English traveler who seems to have found the simple colonists a source of amusement. However condescending she may have been, Knight recounted in detail a conversation that occurred in a general store in New Haven, Connecticut. She reported that the first question the shopkeeper asked his potential customer concerned the intended method of payment. This opening query may sound insulting, but the retailer was not suggesting that the person standing before him lacked the resources required to make a purchase. At issue was the medium to be employed, for example, Spanish, Massachusetts, or Native American money. Some consumers arrived with agricultural products; others expected to negotiate on credit. Once the shopkeeper had this information, he could quote the appropriate prices for the various goods on display. A so-called sixpenny knife might cost as much as twelve pence if the customer offered pork or beef instead of specie. The proprietor preferred hard money, of course, especially silver coin, and gave the best deals to buyers who reduced his operating cost.

Having learned the basic conventions of retail trade in New Haven, Knight pounced on an American customer with the fervor of a modern anthropologist doing fieldwork. "In comes a tall country fellow, with his alfogeos [saddlebags] full of tobacco," she recounted. To her horror, Knight discovered the tobacco was for "chewing and spitting," and during his conversation with the storekeeper he shocked the English woman by occasionally leaving "a small shovelful of dirt on the floor." After remaining silent for some minutes, "staring round him like a cat," he blurted out, "Have you any ribbons for hatbands to sell, I pray?" Trying his best to accommodate the man, the proprietor presented what he regarded as a likely choice. The buyer rejected the ribbon out of hand, exclaiming, "It's confounded gay." Only then did the real customer enter the building. The man's wife immediately approved the "gay" ribbon and then inquired about "hood silk." The storekeeper brought out cloth that pleased her. Finally, she asked, "Have you any thread silk to sew it with?" Satisfied with the thread, the couple paid for the items and departed.

Knight apparently witnessed other transactions. Before dropping the topic, she observed of American consumers that "they generally stand after they come in a great while speechless, and sometimes don't say a word till they are asked what they want, which I impute to the awe they stand in of the merchants, whom they are constantly almost indebted to."[72] Had she been an anthropologist, Knight might have explored structures of market dependency or commented on consumer gender roles. After all, in contrast to her husband's spitting and stammering, the country wife seemed confident and knowledgeable about the imported goods on offer. A factor in Maryland warned that storekeepers ignored women at their peril. "You know the influence of the Wives upon their Husbands," he wrote, "& it is but a trifle that wins 'em over, they must be taken notice of or there will be nothing done with them."[73] But such questions would have ruined Knight's fun, and without further comment she left New Haven in search of other colonial peasants.

Many colonial storekeepers would probably have dismissed Knight's conclusions. They would have been particularly skeptical about their alleged ability to command deference. As they well knew, customers made demands. If they did not find what they wanted, they turned to competitors. Proprietors had to entice buyers into their shops, a process that began when they ordered their stock. Northern stores wanted summer goods to arrive in late spring, the season for lighter linens and also for general household articles. One Philadelphia merchant instructed a British correspondent, "[T]he spring is the best time for iron mongery, cutleryware, furniture for furnishing houses, and all other brass and iron work."[74] Southern merchants expected the summer imports to reach the colonies in February or March.[75] A second merchandising season occurred in mid-autumn.[76] The winter market emphasized heavier cloth, usually woollens. When a shipment arrived, the storekeeper could anticipate a sudden spurt of business, but within a month or two much of the new inventory had been sold. Because of the cyclic character of the consumer market, storekeepers regularly suffered periods of greatly reduced commercial activity. In 1742 one struggling Philadelphia retailer complained to his patron Thomas Penn, "I have not sold any thing to speak on for this month past and sitt several days together without having one Person to ask a question . . . in short, I am almost dull & stupid."[77]

During peak months, therefore, storekeepers tried to leave as little to chance as possible. They learned from hard experience that quality as well as variety could determine success or failure in this competitive marketplace. Cutting corners invited disaster. Well-informed buyers recognized inferior goods when they spotted them in the local shops. Moreover, they expected to be offered a selection of weights and colors. Henry Callister, a Maryland factor, quickly assessed the challenges confronting the colonial retailer, explaining in 1749 to his Scottish employer that he needed British imports "suited to the situation of the Store and *Fancy* of the Customers."[78] In other words, Callister had to take account of ordinary planters who simply wanted to look around the store. Such people reacted to the stimulus of the actual goods, and if they had a mind at that moment to treat themselves, they might well seem to behave in a whimsical and unpredictable manner. In 1725 one Philadelphia retailer informed a British correspondent in a wonderful abuse of the language that American consumers wanted goods "more nice" than did English buyers. The message coming out of the colonies, in fact, was that "the people here will have everything the newest and best of their kind."[79] Another ambitious factor who operated a tobacco store in Falmouth, Virginia, understood the concern about attracting independent-minded men and women who could, of course, take their business elsewhere. He insisted on having a "good assortment in order to keep my customers to myself without allowing them to go to my neighbors for trifles."[80] A South Carolina merchant reminded a supplier that a store that did not offer the latest fashions would not long remain in business. After all, he took for granted that "fresh assortments of those things [would] Constantly [be] coming in by every Ship from London."[81]

As a result of such pressures, prudent storekeepers had to anticipate the capriciousness of some buyers while at the same time maintaining a stock of basic goods—iron ware or cutlery, for example—for which there was always a steady demand. Thomas Hancock of Boston developed a marketing strategy designed to minimize the risk of customer dissatisfaction. Everyone expected him to carry hosiery; it was a feature of his standard inventory. But within this general category, he promoted variety. When ordering stockings from Britain, he asked for "a Suitable Sortment for this Country & I believe [this] will answer here next Spring if the hose be fresh & Good and the Colours well Sorted."[82] The firm of James and Drinker in Philadelphia would not even consider dealing with an English supplier who was not thoroughly acquainted "with the Patterns and colours best suited to this Market."[83]

Storekeepers found it almost impossible to fool customers. If the items on offer had no appeal, if they did not compare well in terms of color and pattern with those found in other shops, they did not sell. Hancock had to discount entire bundles of hose because they "were very badly sorted for sale here, & much moth-eaten and I believe had they laid much longer [I] should not have been able to have sold them at any price. I tried the whole town; no body would look at them."[84] Philadelphia book dealers had something of the same experience. They were greatly annoyed whenever British correspondents sent them "rum books," so called because volumes that found no buyers in England were dumped on the Jamaica market in exchange for rum. As one storekeeper noted sarcastically, a title dealing with the technical details of military gunnery did not excite many readers in the mainland colonies. Indeed, this sort of book "moves very slowly here, except it be some Thing of an extraordinary Character."[85] Customers were just as demanding in the South. When the Scottish chains situated a new outlet not far from an older, more established store, they deliberately ordered inventories different from those found at the original location. They took this precaution after discovering that the local planters "imagine that one store made out of another must be made up of Remnants or refused Goods."[86] If nothing else, the attention paid to such marketing details suggests that colonial consumers had already come to appreciate the value of comparison shopping.

Everyday language struggled to keep pace with change in this consumer marketplace. Ordinary buyers—the men and women studied by Madam Knight—knew what they wanted. At least, they could picture it in their imaginations. The problem was actually describing the objects of desire to the storekeeper. He found himself regularly passing local definitions up the chain of acquisition, no doubt well aware of the high probability for misunderstanding. Each item generated a special market vocabulary. By the mid-eighteenth century fabrics and ceramics—two of the more popular British exports—came in a variety of colors, shapes, and designs. Confronted with an unprecedented range of choice, one frustrated English firm begged an American merchant to use words with greater precision. General orders for pieces of china, for example, only created confusion. One had "to describe them by round or long common Dishes for Meat, Soup Dishes, or deep Sallad or Pudding Dishes, [for] otherwise [we are] at a Loss to know what [you want]."[87]

Provincial storekeepers tried as best they could to facilitate these transatlantic negotiations. Customers spoke in an insistent but vague voice; British manufacturers offered an expanding, often unpredictable selection of goods. The solution to the problem of description seemed to be pattern books. These convenient listings allowed Americans to review manufacturer's samples and then place orders with confidence that they might actually receive what they wanted. In 1756 a representative of a major English export firm explained to a Philadelphia merchant: "There is no way to send goods with any certainty of sale but by sending Patterns of the several colours in vogue with you in the several kinds of stuff ordered . . . & the number of pieces of every colour writ against each of the patterns."[88] The marketplace encouraged a kind of interactive process unprecedented in the history of merchandising. In this particular example, the colors were already "in vogue"; they were distinctive Philadelphia colors. But now, aided by the pattern books, Philadelphia buyers could match color with pattern, local taste with British fashion.

Shopkeepers occasionally referred to the samples as "pattern cards." Competing cloth manufacturers put together cards reflecting their own offerings, and British export houses would then provide American correspondents with as many as four different pattern books. This innovation helped focus consumer desire. Jackson and Bromfield, dry-goods merchants in Newburyport, Massachusetts, thought that sample books could even stimulate new demand. The American might come into a store looking for a particular article but then, seeing examples of colorful patterns, order something entirely different. "We wou'd be glad you'd send us," they wrote, "the patterns of Silks & Silk mixtures, you mentioned in your last [letter], as it may be the means of our finding a Vent for what we might otherwise not be acquainted with."[89] Thomas Hancock regarded the pattern books as a marvelous invention. For him they invited constructive discussions about wallpaper. "Pray Send me Some Patterns of Role paper," he informed an English correspondent, "with the price Affixt both [for] Flock work & others of Lively Colours & Good figures. [I]f you could send a yard of a sort . . . [it] may do just to Give the figure and Colour. [I]t would be a Great Advantage to you & me in the Sale here for our People then would Suit themselves with Colours & Figure & then I shall have a Certain Sale for what I write for."[90] Other American merchants accepted the logic of Hancock's argument.[91] Some quickly discovered, however, that British product lines changed so rapidly that the sample books were out of date before the customer ever made a decision.[92] As one of Beekman's suppliers confessed, "Fashions alter so soon that many fancy Patterns are out of Make in 12 Months which renders sending Patterns of all sorts useless."[93]

Storekeepers exploited other imaginative strategies to entice potential customers into their shops. During this period advertisers developed a strikingly new commercial language of allurement. Retailers came to appreciate how newspapers could be used to spark curiosity and desire, indeed, to communicate with strangers about the latest British imports. From this perspective, advertising copy might best be seen as fragments of cultural conversations linking ordinary colonists to a larger Atlantic economy. The commercial announcements generally took the form of long, detailed lists of goods, suggesting, of course, that colonial consumers were receptive to news of variety and choice.[94] But colonial retailers did not rely solely on published inventories. After all, other merchants could match them item for item. In this climate the rhetoric of advertising began to stress fashion, change, and fluidity. Reports of the arrival of a ship from England carrying a cargo of dry goods alerted everyone that stores would soon display fresh colors and designs. These were important events in provincial communities, moments of public entertainment and personal pleasure. Many people were probably impatient for fresh shipments of standard household articles. As the wording of the advertisements revealed, however, others were drawn to the stores in anticipation of the sheer excitement of discovering what was on offer. To heighten the attraction, clever merchants hinted at the possibility of finding lower prices. No one advertised special sales in the modern sense; merchants did not mark down prices for holidays. Rather, they tried to persuade comparison shoppers that even during the busiest weeks of merchandising, they would in fact encounter genuine bargains.

Hard-Ware Goods.

S. and S. Salisbury,

Continue Importing from

LONDON, BRISTOL, BIRMINGHAM
and *SHEFFIELD,*

A large and compleat Assortment of

HARD-WARE GOODS,

Which they sell very CHEAP, by Wholesale and Retail, at their Shop at BOSTON, two Doors Southward of Dr. Silvester Gardner's in Marlborough-Street.

And at their Shop at WORCESTER, upon the West Side of the Bridge near the GOAL.

N. B. They desire it as a Favour of all Persons, that want any kind of HARD-WARE, that they would call at either of their Shops and satisfie themselves as to the Quality and Cheapness of their Goods.----

PERSONS living in the Country, that go to *Boston* to buy Goods, may, by purchasing of them at their Shop at *Worcester*, save themselves the Trouble and Expence of Transportation.

They have also to sell at their Shop at *Worcester*, a very elegant Assortment of Looking Glasses---An Assortment of Glass, White-Stone, Delph, Brown and Cream-Colour'd Ware---Best Bohea Tea---Brown and Loaf-Sugar--Flax--Sheeps Wool, Cotton Wool--Red-Wood and Log-Wood---Copperas, Allum, Brimstone, Chalk, Rosin--Green Coffee, Chocolate, Molasses, Salt Fish, Rice, Ginger, Pepper, Alspice, Mace, Cloves, Nutmegs, Cinnamon, Figs, Raisons, &c. &c.
☞ Bees Wax, Old Pewter, Brass and Copper, will be received as CASH.

In their advertisement S. and S. Salisbury not only described for the public "a large and compleat Assortment" of recently imported goods, but also drew attention to a second store in Worcester that saved country customers in search of "Quality and Cheapness" a long trip to Boston. *Courtesy of the American Antiquarian Society, Worcester, Massachusetts.*

Contemporary newspapers yield thousands of examples. A single one makes the point. Bremar and Neyle informed readers of the *South-Carolina Gazette* that they had a wonderful selection of goods "just imported, in the *Alexander,* Capt. Curling, from London, and the latest Vessels from Bristol, to be sold VERY REASONABLE, at their Store on the Bay." Bremar and Neyle appealed to a tough market. Ten other Charleston retailers placed advertisements in the same issue of the newspaper. Most proclaimed the arrival of the best goods "just imported" or "a fresh assortment of EURO-PEAN GOODS, proper for the season, to be sold at the lowest prices."[95]

Few retailers manipulated the language of allurement more cleverly than John Paul Grimke, a Charleston jeweler who boldly placed his advertisements on the front page of the *South-Carolina Gazette.* In one notice that appeared in February 1753, Grimke demonstrated how a merchant could create with words alone an exciting commercial environment. First, he declared that he had on hand items "just imported from London, in the *Martha,* Capt. Bell." The new objects on display were unlike any that the people of the city had ever before seen. The advertisement pledged "the following curious new-fashioned goods, made in the neatest and most elegant taste, which, for the sale of ready money, will be sold on very low rates in his house in *Broad-street.*" Second, Grimke guaranteed that all prices would be clearly marked. The customer had no reason to fear that he or she would be obliged to haggle over money, a process that could well put the inexperienced consumer at a disadvantage. Third, the jeweler stressed unprecedented variety. Indeed, "the public may depend on seeing far greater choice in this branch of trade, and in all kinds of gold and silver work, than has at any time heretofore been exhibited for sale in this part of the world." Fourth, although one might predict that a colonial jeweler would direct his message chiefly to the rich and well-born, of which Charleston had many, he decided instead to stress a kind of rough commercial equality. In his shop everyone was welcome; all buyers could anticipate personal attention. The members of the public were assured that they would be "treated in the most just and upright manner, the lowest price being fixed on each article, and those that are not judges will be served equally as if they were." Even suspicious customers could see for themselves that all Grimke's silver carried "the *London* hall mark." Fifth, people who responded to the advertisement could have their purchases "engraved *gratis.*" And finally, the jeweler promised customers who might not want to carry a package through the streets of Charleston that they "may be waited on with their goods at their houses." The advertisement then listed scores of British imports, including clocks and watches, candlestick holders and tea strainers, and a "Great variety of trinkets for ladies."[96] Grimke had mastered the art of communication through advertising.

Some innovative retailers experimented with an entirely different form of advertising that linked the seller directly to the consumer. No sooner had a ship arrived from Britain carrying dry goods than these merchants published their own broadsides. Precisely how they distributed the handbills is not known. Perhaps employees walked the streets of the town, spreading news of fashion and choice to anyone willing to accept a commercial flyer. A broadside designed by the Boston firm of Joseph and Daniel Waldo looked much like the advertisements that appeared in the local newspapers. But, of course, the virtue of the new medium was that the Waldos did not have to share the announcement with competitors. They focused attention solely on the goods "Imported from London," to be sold in this case at the "Sign of the Elephant."[97] John Appleton, a Salem merchant, issued a broadside heralding marvelous goods "Imported in the Last Ships From London." He assured local consumers that they would find at his store "A Fine Assortment of English and India Goods." Appleton even bragged that he sold dry goods—over seventy-five different types of cloth were listed on his handbill—at prices "as low as can be bought at Boston, by Wholesale or Retail."[98] This was a brazen claim, and one wonders whether people from Salem actually bothered to compare Appleton's prices with those of Boston.

However significant advertising and the imaginative presentation of goods may have been to the small retailer's success, everyone knew—customers as well as storekeepers—that the robustness of the new consumer marketplace depended ultimately on an extraordinary expansion of credit throughout the entire Atlantic world. It was a necessary rather than a sufficient cause of change, for within the empire of goods it provided the lubricant allowing buyers and sellers all along the great chain of acquisition to negotiate purchases that would otherwise have been out of reach. Without impressive sources of credit the large export houses in Britain could not have filled American orders.[99] In turn, these merchants extended credit to the colonial wholesalers; they then distributed British manufactures to small retailers on credit. And finally, the ordinary consumer purchased on credit—creating what were called "book debts"—often without having to worry about making interest payments for six months or a year following the initial transaction. Colonial Americans fully appreciated how credit connected them to larger economic structures. As a Rhode Island debtor wrote in 1754 from a Newport jail, "Trade, we know, is supported by Credit; and Credit is to Trade, what the Blood is to the Body; If credit fails, Trade stagnates."[100] We have already observed in our *vade mecum* how expectations of credit and problems related to punctual repayment strained conversations among British export merchants and American wholesalers. Here we are concerned with ordinary consumers and local retailers, in other words, with a bundle of mutual, often conflicting perceptions about the workings of a market economy.

Although small colonial traders eagerly appealed in newspaper advertisements for "ready cash"—offering handsome discounts to those who paid for goods with hard currency—they knew that their business depended on a generous offer of credit as well as a pledge of patience in the settlement of accounts. Philadelphia records indicate that dry-goods merchants sold as much as 90 percent of their goods on credit. In the Chesapeake colonies, where the Scottish factors fell all over themselves granting credit to new customers, the figure was about 80 percent. New England storekeepers apparently followed the same practice.[101] Most American consumers seem to have welcomed the invitation to buy on credit. In an economy that suffered from a chronic shortage of specie, it allowed farmers to obtain whatever goods they wanted in advance of the sale of their crops. But credit represented something more than a convenience. It stimulated desire not directly connected to need. As one writer explained, " '[T]is well known how Credit is a mighty inducement with many People to purchase this and the other Thing which they may well enough do without."[102]

Although small colonial retailers could not have prospered without credit, they viewed it with nervous ambivalence. For them credit was more than a financial or legal obligation; it was a set of professional values, a manner of self-presentation upon which their very survival depended. They were caught between their suppliers—major wholesale merchants who often lived in the same community—and their regular customers. If shopkeepers did well for themselves, treating themselves and members of their families to the British imports that flowed through their own stores, they risked public embarrassment. Suppliers interpreted visible success as evidence of a healthy income, perhaps even as a sign of a large supply of cash on hand, and therefore they had no compunction about pressuring the storekeeper to settle long-standing debts. By the same token, hints of affluence suggested to the ordinary customer that the small merchant might be making too much profit, thereby taking advantage of a neighbor who had trusted the trader's sense of fair dealing. And then again, the good life might have meant that the shopkeeper who lacked proper restraint was spending himself into poverty. As one Boston commentator lectured the harried retailers, "In *London* a Merchant or Tradesman making a more than usually splendid Appearance, is frequently a Fore-runner of Bankruptcy."[103]

In this insecure commercial environment, appearances could determine a merchant's solvency. Indeed, the kinds of values most often associated with the so-called Protestant ethic—thrift, diligence, honesty, and modesty—were forced upon the colonial shopkeeper as a condition of doing business. Whatever his or her personal beliefs may have been, the retailer had to appear energetic and trustworthy. A new consumer marketplace transformed seventeenth-century religious mandates into eighteenth-century bourgeois concerns. At stake was a public reputation, a kind of social capital that one squandered at one's peril. And given the bankruptcy laws of the period, a sudden demand for the settlement of debts could lead to disaster. A creditor could insist on obtaining hard currency. It made no matter that the merchant himself may have been owed sums well in excess of the amount being importuned.[104] From South Carolina "Honestus" protested that a small merchant's "reputation" must be maintained at all costs. He apparently had learned that "Credit is undone in Whispers. . . . [A]n ill Word may change Plenty into Want."[105] The Rhode Island debtor who styled himself "An Impartial Hand" put the point even more bluntly: "[W]hen a Man in Trade breaks his Agreements . . . so that there can be no well grounded

Dependence upon him, he is soon discovered, hunted down, undone, and perhaps cast into Prison."[106]

Few colonists appreciated the force of these concerns better than Benjamin Franklin. Although he did not write his much quoted *Advice to a Young Tradesman* with small storekeepers such as Allen MacLean specifically in mind, Franklin's counsel was right on the mark for anyone hoping to succeed in the dry-goods business. He advised ambitious traders to be punctual and thoughtful. From him they learned that "*Time* is Money." Maintaining one's "*Credit*" was vital in the marketplace. By credit, Franklin did not refer simply to accounts payable. The wise tradesman had to look credible to gain popular trust; credit demanded a commercial mask that may or may not have been in conflict with the clerk's true self. "The Sound of your Hammer at Five in the Morning or Nine at Night, heard by the Creditor," Franklin observed, "makes him easy Six Months longer." Anyone could put these principles into practice. Summing up his own argument, Franklin reminded commercial readers that "The Way to Wealth, if you desire it, is as plain as the Way to Market. It depends on two words, INDUSTRY and FRUGALITY."[107]

The theme of merchant virtue became a staple in colonial newspapers. On their part, retailers complained that they had to endure constant scrutiny. One slip could bring ruin. Their customers were spies, gossiping behind the storekeeper's back. In a curious article that originally appeared in South Carolina and was later picked up by a New York City journal, "Philander" whined that "A Merchant's *Credit* and a Virgin's *Virtue* ought to be equally sacred from the Tongues of Men." The author insisted that few people missed an opportunity to disparage merchants. "The Tea-Table among the Ladies," he grumbled, "and the Tavern among the Men seem to be places of new Invention for a Depravation of our [the merchants'] Manners and Morals, Places devoted to Scandal." No one paused to consider the hurtful consequences of such unguarded conversation. The women were as dangerous as the men in this regard. "On these Accounts it is . . .," argued Philander, "that a Merchant walks in continual Jeopardy, from the Looseness and Inadvertency of Men's Tongues, ay, and Women's too." The lesson for shopkeepers was not difficult to discern. In the retail business the loss of a trader's "Money or Goods is easily made up, and may be sometimes repaired with Advantage, but the Loss of Credit is never repaired."[108]

Judging from other articles published during this period, not a few retailers ignored such advice. The most common charge against them was that they put on airs. They did not look like proper merchants. The editor of the *Boston Evening-Post* reprinted an essay originally submitted by "Plautus" to the *New Universal Magazine* (England) which railed against the alleged excesses of "young shopkeepers." These ambitious businessmen overreached themselves, dressing like dandies rather than sober merchandisers. Such public behavior could only lead to the obvious end. "Should the young and unexperienced shopkeeper," intoned Plautus, "once find that his laced waistcoat, ruffles, gold watch and snuff box [have] frighten'd his customers away, on the wise presumption that they must contribute thereto in the price of his goods; there is no doubt but he would soon reduce himself and family to the stile and simplicity of our forefathers." The American editor justified running this English piece on the grounds of its relevance to recent colonial experience. "These Observations," he noted, "tho' calculated chiefly for the Kingdom of Great Britain, may, without sensible Error, serve the Province of the Massachusetts-Bay; and, we have Reason to believe, many other Parts of North America."[109] Only a few years earlier the same newspaper had exposed this kind of moral corruption in the heart of Boston. The problem once again was "our young Merchants." They apparently waited on customers dressed "more like foppish Officers . . . than Men of Business, with their Scarlet and Silk lac'd Wa[i]stcoats and Breeches, and *French* Cambrick Ruffles down to their Fingers Ends, &c. which looks very little like the Dress of Men of Business."[110] No wonder that one New England writer concluded that merchants—however wealthy they may have been— were well advised to "live more upon a level with [their] Neighbours."[111]

Another colonist, writing as "Incultus Americanus," suggested that retailers persuaded consumers to purchase more than they really needed. He placed the blame squarely on a profligate extension of credit. Had not the merchants encouraged "the people to purchase their commodities, with a promise of long credit, insinuating that payment would be easily made, and that the articles were much cheaper imported than manufactured among us"?[112] At the end of the day, credit was something to be controlled rather than rejected. As one almanac counseled under a section entitled "Necessary hints for those who would be rich," unless the customer was "willing to pay interest, and interest upon interest," he should pay cash for "any unnecessary household stuff, or any superfluous thing." Even the simplest customer should know that "he that sells upon credit, expects to lose five per cent by bad debts; therefore he charges on all he sells upon credit, an advance that shall make up that deficiency. Those who pay for what they buy upon credit, pay their share of his advance."[113]

Perhaps too much has been made of the tensions and strains generated by the sudden expansion of a mid-eighteenth-century consumer marketplace. Buyers and sellers alike were anxious about reputation, about avoiding temptation, and about staying abreast of new challenges associated with advertising and credit. While it is valuable to interpret relations between customers and retailers as a kind of fluid cultural conversation, one in which ordinary people negotiated the rules of conduct as they went along, we should not lose sight of the fact that stores in this social context were sites of imagination. If we overlook the capacity of merchandising to entertain and please, we miss the powerful insight that Samuel Johnson had during a journey with James Boswell to the Western Islands of Scotland. As he discovered,

> In Col there is a standing shop, and in Mull there are two. A shop in the Islands, as in other places of little frequentation, is a repository of every thing requisite for common use. Mr. Boswell's journal was filled, and he bought some paper in Col. To a man that

ranges the streets of London, where he is tempted to contrive wants for the pleasure of
supplying them, a shop affords no image worthy of attention; but in an island, it turns
the balance of existence between good and evil. To live in Perpetual want of little things,
is a state not indeed of torture, but of constant vexation.[114]

By 1750 most Americans had discovered that they did not have to live in
"want of little things," and, like the leading figures of the Scottish Enlightenment, they came to regard this freedom from "constant vexation" as
progress.

VII

From the perspective of less affluent Americans, two additional mercantile
activities must be included in our *vade mecum*. Vendue sales and peddling
may have brought more British manufactures into colonial homes than did
urban shops and country stores. We shall never know for certain the volume of business conducted within these segments of the market. Neither
form of marketing generated the kinds of records that we associate with
established merchants. The silences of the archives, however, do not provide a reliable index to the extent to which these enterprises touched the
lives of marginal although honest men and women. It was while attending
the vendue sales—perhaps best imagined as a combination of modern flea
market and wholesale auction—and while examining the mysterious contents of a peddler's pack that many Americans first discovered the pleasures
of owning an ivory comb or colorful piece of ribbon. For the buyer who
possessed limited financial resources, these were challenging moments, si-
multaneously alluring and threatening, and, as we have noted in our recon-
struction of conversations between shopkeepers and customers, without
some prior knowledge of the rapidly changing character of commerce—
assumptions about products and pricing, for example—the eager colonists
risked disappointment in the marketplace.

Americans often referred to vendue sales simply as auctions. They had
a long history in the colonies, dating back to the late seventeenth century,
but as with most forms of marketing, the size and complexity of the vendues
expanded to keep pace with the consumer economy. During the early decades of the century, they provided a means for merchants quickly to clear
off damaged or unpopular items. By 1750 they functioned as a major outlet
in the great chain of acquisition.[115] Madam Knight, whom we encountered
in a small store in New Haven, Connecticut, visited a vendue sale in New
York City. She was in search of high-end Dutch writing paper, apparently in
much larger quantity than could be obtained in the regular shops. The vendue price struck her as a bargain, eight or ten shillings for about ten reams
of paper. Perhaps more intriguing was the social aspect of the auction. "At
the vendue," Knight recounted, "I made a great many acquaintances amongst
the good women of the town who courteously invited me to their houses
and generously entertained me."[116]

No doubt, vendues did serve as a form of public recreation. Colonial authorities recognized that the auctions might draw less savory persons than the women who spoke with Madam Knight. Larger port cities appointed "vendue masters" who were expected to maintain order and honest dealing. A variety of sellers appeared at these events. Most visible were the established merchants who dumped slow-moving stock at auction. To be sure, they took a loss on such transactions, but a swift return was preferable to holding on to stale inventories, which they may have purchased on credit. That was precisely what the Charleston retailer Robert Pringle did in 1744 with a shipment of dull goods he had received from Thomas Hutchinson and Thomas Goldthwait of Massachusetts. "Shall sell of the Ribbands, Potts, & Axes at Public Vendue as you Direct as soon as I Can have an Opportunity," he informed his Boston correspondents.[117] Like the storekeepers, vendue sellers advertised in colonial newspapers. Although they did not provide as much detail about weights and colors as did their competitors, they too promised large selections of dry goods. In fact, it is highly likely that some smaller shopkeepers and peddlers were among the bidders. In this sense, the vendue confused the marketplace, blending wholesale transactions with retail sales.[118] To cite a single example, in 1737 the *New-England Weekly Journal* (Boston) carried notice of a "publick Vendue" that would be offering not only books but also "a large variety of English Goods, Haberdashery and Cutlery Wares, and choice Piggs [iron blocks], with divers other sorts of Goods." The same issue also announced that Joseph Lewis would auction off a huge assortment of cloth "at the Sign of the red Cross and Crown." In addition to the seven textiles listed by name, Lewis would be dispensing "Men's Hose, sundry sorts of Cutlery and Haberdashery Ware, with sundry other Things."[119]

More than other forms of merchandising, the vendue sales generated sharp controversy. Defenders insisted that the public auctions represented a marvelous innovation that served the interests of everyone involved. These arguments reveal how thoroughly the colonists had accommodated themselves to the new consumer marketplace. Commentators praised the vendue for providing much-needed jobs in the cities, for helping the small merchants obtain hard currency during slow periods, and, perhaps most interesting, for keeping the established merchants from charging usurious prices. Modern markets implied open competition. One writer publishing under the name "A Planter" sounded much like a promoter for a modern discount outlet: "Vendues are the places where people may get cheap bargains; and they are the means of obliging the shopkeepers in general to sell their goods cheap; so the country is well supplied on reasonable terms, while the shopkeepers and store-keepers are kept within due bounds."[120]

In a broadside entitled *A Few Reasons in Favour of Vendues,* another colonist pushed this line of reasoning. "If it be granted," he explained, "that the importation of British manufactures is necessary, and of advantage to the country, then those persons that introduce and dispose of them on the lowest terms, must be confessed the best friends to the community, and deserve their countenance and encouragement." This is a splendid example of the kind of insistent bourgeois rhetoric that greeted the new consumer marketplace. The common interest was defined as the preservation of bargain prices and not, as some historians have declared, a turning back of the economic clock to some simpler age. In fact, the writer believed that the citizens of Philadelphia should give "great encouragement to strangers trading among us." After all, these strangers—apparently speculative traders from England and Ireland who relied on the vendues for immediate sales—"have kept the country well supplied [with British goods]; and in return, have taken off large quantities of our produce." It made no sense to this American to levy heavy taxes on vendue transactions. Apparently some people had suggested such a policy, but if they ever succeeded in their silly plan, they would force ordinary people who did not have much cash on hand to patronize "Pawn-Brokers, as in London."[121] The message was clear. Unfettered access to consumer goods best served the public good.

As the vendues became more popular, they sparked more vocal criticism. Although the large public auctions supplied some small retailers with British imports at lower prices, the proprietors of larger stores complained about unfair competition. After all, they had to factor into their prices substantial overhead costs. Like the evangelical itinerants who drove the established parish ministers to distraction during this period—the Reverend George Whitefield, for example—the vendue merchants seem to have worked out of doors. To control the proliferation of these discount markets, storekeepers regularly appealed to local government authorities, demanding that auctioneers pay license fees and special taxes. In 1769 Governor Moore, the royal governor of New York, reported that the city council insisted on reining in the vendue trade. The members of this body wanted "to put a stop to the pernicious practice, which had prevailed here for some time past of putting up every thing to Auction, as well, dry goods, as Rum, sugars, wines, etc., by which the number of Vendue Masters was greatly increased to the prejudice of the shopkeeper."[122]

The denunciation of the vendue markets echoed noisily in the popular press of Philadelphia. Antagonists faulted the auctions for diverting laborers away from proper agricultural pursuits. Moreover, the vendues promoted idleness, for "people go to them without any real necessity, merely to pick up bargains." It was asserted as fact, for example, that consumers might spend an entire afternoon searching for a specific item, and after wasting so much time, "they often buy nothing." Bargain hunters traveled from one vendue to another, often simply to examine the various British imports on offer. Consumer curiosity also encouraged dishonesty, for, as thieves such as the members of the Morrison gang had discovered, it was not all that difficult to purloin desirable objects and then sell them at unregulated markets. The most troublesome moral issue—at least in the eyes of a critic writing in a Pennsylvania newspaper—was the scandalously low prices encountered at the public auctions. "Vendues," claimed one author, "are the means of lowering the price of goods in the shops; this is also a temptation for people to buy articles which they otherwise might have made at home, or done without."[123] In other words, this undisciplined outlet for cheap consumer goods had taken on a commercial life of its own, and by providing an exciting new form of public entertainment, it encouraged ordinary men and women to spend their money however they pleased.

Benjamin Franklin appreciated both the allure and the temptation of the vendue markets more fully than did most of his contemporaries. For him, the sale of so many imported articles to so many ordinary colonists raised moral concerns, but unlike those who wanted to legislate the auctions out of existence, Franklin knew that the popular will could not easily be restrained. In a wonderful tongue-in-cheek piece published as *Father Abraham's Speech,* Franklin recounted how this revered figure who exemplified an earlier, simpler, more self-sufficient culture gave a short lecture before the start of a large vendue sale. Abraham told the shoppers impatiently waiting for the gates to open, "Here you are all got together at this Vendue of *Fineries* and *Knicknacks.* You call them *Goods,* but if you do not take Care, they will prove *Evils* to some of you." According to this sage man, the problem was not the goods themselves—no, not necessarily even the fineries or knickknacks—but rather the likelihood that buyers would spend beyond their means. "Many a One," intoned Father Abraham, "for the Sake of Finery on the Back, have done with a hungry Belly, and half starved their Families. *Silks and Sattins, Scarlet and Velvets, have put out the Kitchen Fire.*" He understood, of course, the psychology of vendues. The sudden accessibility of British goods blinded some consumers to hard financial logic. They made purchases simply because the goods "look pretty." Father Abraham warned that invitations to buy on credit only made the situation more dangerous. "We are offered," he explained, "by the Terms of this Vendue, *Six Months Credit;* and that perhaps has induced some of us to attend it, because we cannot spare the ready Money, and hope now to be fine without it." But debt represented a loss of liberty, a compromise of virtue, even an invitation to imprisonment. The people queuing up for the vendue listened to the advice more or less politely, but it was clear that Father Abraham's words made no lasting impression. As soon as the sale commenced, they acted "just as if it had been a common Sermon; for the Vendue opened, and they began to buy extravagantly." Only "Poor Richard" learned the lesson, leaving the vendue without purchasing "Stuff for a new Coat."[124] No one seemed to have noticed his personal sacrifice. They were too busy rooting through the merchandise in search of bargains.

Peddlers made their way along the back roads of empire from Georgia to New Hampshire. They were mysterious, ubiquitous figures. They arrived in little communities as strangers, and while colonial authorities viewed their comings and goings with suspicion, farm families welcomed their arrival. Sometimes called hawkers or petty chapmen, peddlers linked those who could not conveniently reach country stores with an exciting European marketplace. As one commentator in Massachusetts reported in 1769, peddlers were "People who carry Goods into the remotest Corners of the

Country, and sell to Inhabitants at a great Distance from Stores, and who without such Supplies carried to them by Pedlars, wou'd content themselves with such poor Commodities, as they could manufacture with their own Hands."[125]

Dr. Alexander Hamilton discovered firsthand in 1744 how peddlers generated an almost insatiable curiosity among people who might normally have been expected to show more reserve. According to Hamilton, one evening in Bristol, Rhode Island, "I and my company were taken for pedlars." No sooner had Hamilton opened his "portmanteau" to rearrange some personal belongings than a person who "mistook my portmanteau for a pack" approached the physician and "would have chaffer'd [bargained] with me for some goods." A few days later Hamilton and his slave Dromo experienced an unusual reception in Newport. As the doctor explained, it was "betwixt seven and eight att night, a thick fog having risen so that I could scarce find the town." In the heavy mist the two travelers became separated. "When within a quarter of a mile of it [Newport], my man [Dromo] upon account of the portmanteau, was in the dark taken for a pedlar by some people in the street who I heard coming about him and enquiring what he had got to sell."[126] It apparently did not strike either Hamilton or the residents of Newport as odd that an unfamiliar black person carrying a heavy trunk in the night would be mistaken for a peddler. They were more interested in the contents of the case than in the stranger's life history.

Like the people who turned out to interrogate Dromo, we too are curious about the contents of the peddlers' packs. For all the excitement that they generated, the cases or trunks were probably small. After all, these travelers generally transported their goods on their backs. A few may have had sufficient resources to purchase a horse. We know that travelers from the Piedmont brought pack animals to Urbanna, Virginia, where they negotiated for goods with Scottish factors.[127] But however large their trunks, peddlers seem to have offered consumers the same general range of British imports found in the more established stores. When the New York peddler Robert Gregg died, for example, his estate included sundry dry goods, carpenter's rules, razors, fiddle strings, some books, and "Spectakles." Another peddler who concentrated on the Connecticut Valley market carried items on one trip valued at only £8, among which were lace, buttons, necklaces, ink, rough cloth, jackknives, and Jew's harps.[128] His pack brings to mind John Williams, the rascally Derby peddler who pleased the "Country Girls" with an assortment of enticing baubles. Like the honest peddlers of the period, Williams had on offer "Needles, Pins, Buckles, Laces, Fans, &c."

The success of the peddlers greatly annoyed the country storekeepers. They complained loudly about the competition, sounding much like those who wanted to legislate the vendue markets out of existence. If the authorities of the various colonies are to be believed, peddlers spread disease to inland communities, trafficked in stolen goods, and took business away from resident merchants who contributed to the general welfare by paying taxes. One Virginia county went over the top, accusing peddlers of undermining the entire regional economy. In 1760 the angry petitioners informed the House of Burgesses "of the great Disadvantages to which the Trade of this Colony is subject, by the Practice of Pedlars and traveling Merchants, in the Interior Parts of the Country, who import large Quantities of Goods by Land from *Pennsylvania* and *Maryland,* and dispose of them there, and in Return carry away great Sums of our Paper Currency, and all the Gold and Silver they can procure."[129] One imagines that the peddlers fervently wished that the charges were true, for if they could have amassed great sums of money, they could have retired from peddling, a calling that seldom made anyone rich. Other critics claimed that peddlers exposed American consumers to irresistible "Lawns, Cambricks, Ribbons, &c." and thereby tempted "women, girls, and boys with their unnecessary fineries."[130]

Most colonial legislatures passed—and then repassed—statutes designed to control the peddlers.[131] Some assemblies tried to restrict the hawkers, petty chapmen, and peddlers to certain underpopulated areas. In other words, they could not do business within the corporate limits of a major city. Far more common were fees and licenses. During the early decades of the eighteenth century, the government of Massachusetts Bay went a step further, declaring peddling a crime and announcing that "all taverners, alehouse keepers, common victuallers and retailers are hereby strickly forbidden to receive or give any entertainment to any hawker, peddler or petty chapman . . . under penalty of twenty shillings." One has the impression after reading the legislative records that no one paid much attention to these regulatory acts. Often lawmakers approved statutes that repeated almost in the same words bills that had passed only a few years earlier. In 1750 the *New-York Mercury* begged the elected representatives of New Jersey to enforce a licensing act that they had accepted twenty years earlier. Failure to collect fees from peddlers meant that "the Number of that sort of People are greatly increased in the Province."[132] In neighboring Connecticut, one town threatened to apply rough justice to the peddlers. After all, insisted the citizens of Ashford, it was well known "that peddlers who without law or license go about the country selling wares are a nuisance to the public, and, if in our power, shall be picked up and put to hard labor."[133] Nothing of this sort was done, of course; too many people regarded the colonial authorities as a greater nuisance than the peddlers.

Surviving colonial records reveal very little about the men and women who actually peddled British goods for a living. They must have been marvelous talkers. An anonymous peddler whom Hamilton observed charming a potential buyer in a country inn at the end of Long Island, New York, was such a person. Displaying "some linnen by candle light," the salesman informed his customer that "he would be upon honour with him and recommend to him the best of his wares, and as to the price he would let him know the highest and lowest att one word." A "Scotch Irish" peddler encountered in Stonington, Connecticut, had a gift for "palaber" and was able to sell "some dear bargains to Mrs. Williams."[134]

Not all peddlers remained nameless, of course. We would like to know more about Sarah Abbot, who merited an obituary in a leading Boston newspaper. According to this journal, Abbot had died recently in Ipswich "in the Ninetieth Year of her Age." She received praise as "a notable Peddler in Goods through the Course of many Years of her Life in that and the Neighbouring Towns of this Government."[135] Abbot built up a solid local reputation. Other peddlers, especially those of Scots-Irish background, had to travel many miles to find customers. Jonathan Trumbull Sr., a member of one of Connecticut's leading political families, regularly recorded the licenses he issued to peddlers. On January 6, 1758, for example, he certified that "license is hereby granted to Gideon Prior to trade, traffick, & deal in this Colony as a Peddler, Hawker or Petty Chapman, for one full year." Another person traveled all the way from Londonderry, New Hampshire, to Trumbull's home in Lebanon to obtain a license.[136] Most peddlers seem to have been younger, marginal men, in search of economic opportunity. Occasionally, one of their number managed to put together a modest estate. Robert Gregg did so. For more than two decades, Gregg peddled his wares through the small towns of New York and New Jersey, and when he died colonial authorities valued his property at £134, a sum that indicated that the hardworking Gregg had risen to the middle class.[137]

VIII

William Moore brings our *vade mecum* full circle. This unfortunate "Pedler or Petty Chapman" was not a thief; he posed no threat to the New England communities where he displayed the small objects he had originally purchased in Boston. Nevertheless, he ran afoul of Massachusetts law. His problems began during a visit to Berwick, a village located in Maine, then a province of Massachusetts. Moore arrived in 1721, just in time for the Christmas season. Although he had not bothered to purchase a license to trade, he felt secure enough to enter the home of Phillip Hubbard and there "Expose to Sale & Sell Sundry goods and Merchandize." Local magistrates got wind of Moore's activities. They hauled him before the Berwick court, confiscating his "bagg or pack of goods." After taking depositions from the villagers, officials convicted Moore of traveling without proper license "from town to town" and selling "sundry goods . . . to sundry persons."

However much we may sympathize with Moore, our attention in this case is drawn to the men and women of this isolated frontier settlement who were so eager to examine the goods he carried in his pack. Daniel Goodwin was one. He informed the magistrates that he had "bought of Wm Moore a yard and halfe of Stuff for handcarchiefs." Most of Moore's customers were women. Sarah Gooding deposed that she had gone to the Hubbard house three days before Christmas and had purchased "Three Quarters of a yard of muslin and a yard & a half of firritting [ferreting: tape or edging material] and a yard and Quarter of Lase for a Cap and for fine thread 12 pence, in black silk 9 penne worth." Patience Hubbard acquired "a pare of garters" and "sundry other goods." And finally, Sarah Stone confessed to have taken home "one penne worth of smole trifeles."[138]

None of these purchases amounted to more than a few pennies. That is precisely the point. What we encounter in Hubbard's house is a moment of excitement and entertainment, a gathering of humble neighbors in their capacity as consumers of British manufactured goods. The new marketplace presented the Sarah Stones and Patience Hubbards of colonial America with unexpected opportunities; it compelled such people to compare prices, follow the advertisements, and weigh the personal risks of buying on credit. From the great wholesale merchants, the alluring articles reached the urban shops and country stores. Peddlers distributed them; colonists sought them out at the vendue markets. Everyone in this society had a chance to acquire something. For elite colonists, the flood of British imports quickly transformed an entire material culture. For most Americans—for those upon whom a colonial rebellion would ultimately depend—the empire first entered their lives as "smole trifeles."

5

The Corrosive Logic of Choice: Living with Goods

Eighteenth-century consumers had choices to make. Sometimes they found the results pleasing, sometimes disappointing. But whatever their decisions, they frequently expressed irritation at the market behavior of other people whose choices seemed presumptuous, even vulgar. The people who inhabited the Moon were a case in point. On the eve of independence, an amateur sociologist from Massachusetts took a trip to Lunar City, and what he encountered there revealed just how corrosive consumer choice could be to the proper ordering of society.

Surprising as it may seem to modern readers, this early space traveler showed almost complete indifference to the technical aspects of the feat. As he explained in a published report entitled *News from the Moon*, a person intent on taking such an adventure simply had to follow the correct highway and, from time to time, to ask other travelers for directions. The journey required no unusual equipment, not even special supplies of food and water. Moon research did, however, take considerable courage. For one thing, the satellite was densely populated, and while the adventurous colonist assumed that Moon people looked much like ordinary Americans, he expressed no little anxiety about the state of their culture. A trip to Lunar City, he discovered, exposed him to the manners and customs of a modern consumer society that a person of his background found utterly shocking.

Everything went well at the start. The traveler reached "the World on this side [of] the Moon" with remarkable ease. Even without the assistance of a proper *vade mecum*, he sensed that he had gained the outskirts of Lunar City when he encountered a sign over a tavern owned by a certain "Mr. Sharper." The advertisement struck him as odd, however, for instead of proclaiming a familiar drinking establishment such as the King's Arms or the Whitehart—as one would have found in Boston—it pictured "one Man picking another Man's Pocket." And sure enough, a short time later, someone robbed him of his belongings. From this unpleasant experience the colonist concluded that Moon people, like some colonial Americans, must be "knaves and rogues." More unpleasant moments awaited the intrepid researcher.

The traveler soon began to gather data. He stumbled quite by chance on an honest innkeeper. After providing him with a tasty chicken dinner and a comfortable "feather bed"—the Moon seemed to have evolved a curious parallel universe in which people appreciated chicken dinners and warm beds—the proprietor told the visitor from Earth in more detail what he could expect to encounter when he finally reached Lunar City. The prospects were daunting. Since the local economy was depressed, Moon people were finding it difficult to "get money to trade with, and all commodities were dear and nothing cheap." When the colonist expressed surprise at such a sorry state of affairs, his host informed him that the local merchants were largely to blame, for they employed unsavory business practices designed to fleece Lunar workers of hard-earned currency. The next morning the resolute New Englander, now fortified by a breakfast brandy, set off for Lunar City. As he departed, the innkeeper provided him with a rough map of the commercial district, warning emphatically that the colonist should under no condition stray from "Honest Dealing-street."

The advice went unheeded. The Earth traveler simply could not resist the temptation to explore other streets. A stroll down "Proud-lane" confirmed his apprehension about the moral health of Lunar City. Everywhere he saw "men and women dressed up in the best clothing and newest fashions there were in the Lunar world." But it was not the face of luxury that the visitor found most disconcerting. Everything was topsy-turvy, like the convoluted plot of a Mozart opera. Nothing conformed to what the outside researcher regarded as the correct order of society. When he entered Lunar homes, for example, he "could not tell the maids from the mistress by their apparel; the mistress was patched and painted, and so was the maid." Things got worse. "The mistress was clothed in her scarlet cloak and jockey-cap and her fine pattoons; and when I came to see the maid, she likewise was dressed up in her scarlet cloak and her jockey-cap and fine pattoons and her silk gown." The males of the Moon contributed to the chaos. "The servant man," the traveler learned, "must go in his wig and banjan equal to his Master."

It was the women of Lunar City, however, who seemed most responsible for the confusion so conspicuous on Proud-lane. They ruined their husbands "by spending so much upon [themselves] in Pride." The wives of tradesmen demanded "silk gowns and scarlet cloaks and fine pattoons, and have chocolate or Tea or Coffee for their breakfasts." This sybaritic environment corrupted Moon children. The daughters suffered most visibly.

> There is many men in Proud-lane who have—it may be—half a dozen fine daughters who must go in the newest fashions, so spruce and neat that they may get husbands.... [M]any young women in the Moon are so proud, they will go fine in cloths, [even] if they undo their parents. They will not only have fine Cloths, but if they are not fair by nature they will endeavour to make themselves fair by art.

The contagion spread from class to class. Indeed, as the American discovered, "it is grown so common in the Moon that every servant wench must have fine calamanco or chintz gowns who has hardly a smock to her back."

The investigation of the streets of Lunar City quickly turned into a nightmare. The consumers of the Moon were out of control; their excesses in the marketplace had poisoned commercial relations. The urban tour included the frightening spectacle of daily life on "Tattling-street" and "Prodigal-lane," "Whispering-street" and "Lying-lane street." It brought the traveler to "Envy-street," where Moon citizens regularly indulged themselves in public fits of jealousy. These horrific neighborhoods sustained the retail shops located nearby on "Stealing-lane," "Over-reaching-street," and "Cheating-street." Here, no one even attempted to mask the disintegration of civil society. The Lunar City market encouraged the adulteration of goods and the use of false weights and measures. "The Shopkeepers in Cheating-street," observed the Earth visitor, ". . . will sell Moth-eaten or damnified Cloth to cheat ignorant people who know no better."

Cheating-street was the last straw. The Lunar traveler could take no more. As he retraced his steps, he encountered a person who inquired whether Moon people differed "from the inhabitants of my country." The response was predictable. "I told him no," confessed the colonial space traveler. "They did and acted just like the people in my country."[1] At the end of the day, Lunar City was just another Boston, or New York, or Philadelphia. To paraphrase the wisdom of another age, the colonial explorer had confronted an alien culture and recognized it as his own.

To disparage *News from the Moon* as simply a clumsy dystopia would be a mistake. In his own heavy-handed style—and one picks up echoes of John Bunyan's *Pilgrim's Progress*—the author addressed the pressing concerns of his own generation. The flood of British imports that we have chronicled in detail invited colonists to fashion themselves in bold new ways. Within their own communities, they wanted to appear prettier, or more successful, or perhaps merely different from other people with whom they came into contact. But, as they rapidly discovered, the goods of this expanding marketplace were never just goods, things never just things. Consumer objects demanded cultural interpretation; they were the stuff by which a society experiencing what it perceived as accelerated change sorted itself out. Whatever the purchaser's original intentions may have been, store-bought items spoke to contemporaries of class and gender, of character and identity. The process of defining meaning and significance was, of course, always a matter of individual perspective. What one person saw as innocent pleasure, another labeled as sinful indulgence.

In this context personal decisions about how best to spend one's own money inevitably sparked heated cultural controversies in which appeals to traditional morality and proper behavior were employed to preserve an older social order in which women and children—indeed, ordinary colonists of all sorts—allegedly knew their place. If nothing else, the visit to Lunar City demonstrates that debates over the freedom to acquire British manufactures rested ultimately on conflicting claims to power, and it is for this reason that we should see mass participation in an eighteenth-century empire of goods as at once wonderfully liberating and deeply threatening. It was, in fact, what the poet Wallace Stevens might have called "the imagination's new beginning."[2]

The challenge for the modern visitor to colonial society is to avoid becoming caught up in a moral vocabulary of the eighteenth century. We have no interest in keeping servants and maids in their place. It surely serves no constructive purpose to try to pin down luxury with great precision or to determine whether a certain type of fabric represented an extravagance or a necessity. Such distinctions only divert attention from the social conditions that so thoroughly discredited a language of goods inherited from medieval church fathers and Renaissance republicans. What generated an undeniable sense of instability was the huge number of ordinary men and women who so visibly engaged in making choices about the character of their everyday lives. This was a genuinely new phenomenon. And, what is more, the people who most concern us welcomed making choices. As colors, textures, and designs proliferated, such decisions became even more meaningful. For many of them—and one thinks of the poor farmers who purchased "smole trifeles" from the peddler in Maine—the act of choosing could be liberating, even empowering, for it allowed them to determine for themselves what the process of self-fashioning was all about. As one of them declared on the eve of independence, "I, for myself, choose that there should be many Stores filled with every Kind of thing that is convenient and useful, that I might have my choices of Goods, upon the most reasonable or agreeable Terms; whether foreign or homemade; I would have Liberty of either, and to Deal as I judge best for myself. And I wish the same Privilege to all my Friends and Neighbors."[3]

It should not come as a surprise that for such men and women choice in the consumer marketplace gradually merged with a discourse of rights, so that efforts by the British Parliament that seemed to curtail participation were interpreted not only as an annoyance, but also as an attack on basic human rights. Men and women discovered at such moments that the choices that had brought them so much pleasure could be recast during market boycotts into choices for political freedom.

II

While humans may not have an innate desire for various familiar comforts, they surely define their needs within specific historical contexts, so that the actual choice before them may not have been crates or chairs but rather chairs of this or that design.[4] Eighteenth-century writers fully understood this point. Francis Hutcheson, a leading figure in the Scottish Enlightenment who also happened to be popular in the colonies, explained that "the world has so well provided for the support of mankind, that scarce any person in good health need be straitened in bare necessaries. But since men are capable of a great diversity of pleasures, they may be supposed to have a great variety of desires, even beyond the necessaries of life." Human beings were by nature industrious and inventive, and for Hutcheson—as well as for many contemporary Americans—it seemed merely rhetorical to ask, "What man, who had only the absolute necessaries of meat and drink, and a cave or a beast's skin to cover him, would not, when he had leisure, labour for farther conveniencies?"[5]

Fashion provided the catalyst necessary to transform normal human desire into a powerful social force capable of driving the new consumer marketplace. The word itself is associated with a long history of moral controversy, suggesting to censorious commentators a vacuous chasing after glitter while to others it signified a quite unobjectionable aspect of social behavior. One does not expect to find the second, more accommodating perspective on fashion in eighteenth-century writings. But, in fact, authors were able to discuss fashion without losing self-control. Richard Rolt, a British author on the topic of trade, regarded it as a legitimate engine of commercial prosperity. He advised merchants of the empire that "the term *fashion* is . . . applicable to new stuffs, which pleasing by their colour, their design, or their manufacture, are first eagerly sought for, but give way in their turn to other stuffs that have the charms of novelty." Rolt, of course, was not saying anything that the anxious Scottish factors of the Chesapeake or the harried shopkeepers of Boston had not already learned through experience. He deserves credit, however, for describing fashion as something other than a moral threat. "The word *fashion*," Rolt explained in the pragmatic language of business, "is therefore used with regard to every particular that enters the commerce of wool, and silk, either for clothing, ornament, or furniture, or even things in no respect relative to commerce." Rolt conjured up an ordinary consumer casually sorting through imported goods while noting that "the colour of this cloth is the fashion," "this damask is a new fashion," or "this design is new, but the fashion will not continue long." It is hard to conjure up a shopkeeper so dull-witted that he had to be reminded that "a stuff is said not to be in fashion when there is no call for it." But Rolt revealed a powerful insight into a rapidly changing market culture driven by choice by counseling, "[I]t is certainly advantageous for a tradesman to invent new fashions of stuffs, or silks, if he can have a prompt sale for them."[6]

Rolt aside, it was far more common for essayists on both sides of the Atlantic to heap abuse on the "charm of novelty." In their condemnation of an incessant pursuit of anything new, they drew upon a vocabulary of sickness. Other societies, including our own, have equated public behavior that mainstream critics find repellent with disease. Actions that transgress moral boundaries are seen as evidence of a spreading contagion. Thus, when an eighteenth-century writer such as the Englishman John Brown contemplated the rising tide of fashion, he sputtered about "a craving," a "Rage," an "Itch," and an "unmanly Dissipation." The consumer marketplace promoted "effeminacy" and "Impotence." Brown's *Estimate of the Manners* provided

Americans who feared that servants might pass for masters with a full catalogue of corruptions directly attributable to fashion.[7]

The colonists did not really need Brown's assistance. When fashion was
the topic of discussion, they warmed to the task. One Pennsylvania scribbler who appropriately took the pen name "Tim Gruff" announced in a
newspaper, "[T]here is nothing [that] influences mankind (and by mankind here I would be understood to mean woman kind also) so much as
fashion—Let a thing be ever so preposterous or inconvenient, 'it's the fashion,' is sufficient to make it admired."[8] In 1750 a Boston writer identified
simply as "M. F." insisted that only extraordinary self-control could possibly save New England from "Wild-Fire *Fashion.*" He devised an extremely
clever argument in his crusade against consumer madness. The society would
have to innoculate itself, so that anti-fashion would become fashionable.
Even assuming the leadership of the local gentry in this project, the prospects were not all that promising, for, as M. F. complained, "it is *now fashionable* to live great, to indulge the Appetite, to dress rich and gay."[9] And in
New York an avowedly dispassionate writer informed readers how fashion
could destroy a hardworking farm family in only a single generation. A son
without self-discipline invited almost certain doom. In this moral exercise,
the good farmer dies,

> and his Son succeeds to the Estate; but being a fashionable Gentleman, he must have
> Claret and Madeira; he cannot drink his own Malt Liquor, but must have it from
> *England*; the Linen made of his own Flax is home-spun, he therefore cannot endure it,
> but supplies himself with that of *Holland* and *Ireland*. He cannot sleep in a Bed with
> his own Linen, or Stuff Furniture, but he must have that of Chintz, which are more
> genteel; and nothing but a China Damask is fit for a Morning-Gown for him to wear.
> By this Means he soon spends the ready Money his Father had saved.[10]

No one in colonial America seriously contemplated anything remotely
like—to adopt Hutcheson's examples—wearing the skins of wild animals
or returning to life in caves. M. F. gave the game away when, after excoriat-
ing the evils of fashion, he protested, "I would by no Means be understood
to be a Favourer of a close, mean, niggardly Way of Living."[11] The problem,
in other words, was to determine who in society was best equipped to handle
the temptations of consumer novelty. The glib answer, of course, was the
rich and well-born. Unfortunately, for those who wanted to contain the
contagion, conventional wisdom about class and manners did not speak
effectively to the issue of containment. Everyone assumed that novelty in
the marketplace spread—again like a kind of infectious disease—through
mimicking. The lower orders took their cues about fashion from their supposed betters, so that a consumer decision made by a highly visible person
of influence would in time inevitably capture the imagination of middling
and lower groups, the very people allegedly least able to acquire these goods
without succumbing to vice and degeneracy.

No one who bothered to write on the topic questioned whether the goods
of the marketplace served as the external markers of class; they surely did so,
on the Earth as well as on the Moon. But if people perpetually copied each

other, it became nearly impossible to tell where in the traditional social order a person properly belonged. Such concerns had been raised in earlier times—during the reign of Elizabeth I, for example—but now a far greater percentage of the population was engaged in the process. The author of an English tract explained as well as anyone the unusual potential for an open, consumer-oriented society to abrade customary notions of hierarchy. "A strong emulation in all the several stations," he explained, sparks "a perpetual restless ambition in each of the inferior ranks to raise themselves to the level of those immediately above them. In such a state as this, fashion must have an uncontrolled sway. And a fashionable luxury must spread through it like a contagion."[12] Such apparently irrefutable logic echoed through the provincial press. The Reverend Nathaniel Potter thundered in a sermon published as *A Discourse on Jeremiah* that "men naturally emulate those above them, and study to equal or resemble their Superiors in the Luxuries and Superfluities of Life, from the highest Favourite to the meanest Footman."[13]

No one grasped better how Americans communicated claims to social status through possession of the newest fashions than Benjamin Franklin. In his *Autobiography* he recounted the manner in which market novelty first entered his own Philadelphia household. The culprit in this consumer confession was Franklin's wife. She was the one who wanted to acquire the fashionable objects she had encountered in the homes of her neighbors. But instead of whining about Franklin's failure to provide the family with the goods that would properly reflect his rising social status—after all, he had become one of the richest men in Pennsylvania—she cleverly manipulated her proud husband. Despite his mild protest, Franklin seems to have been fully complicit in this mutual experience of self-fashioning. As Franklin remembered the moment,

> my breakfast was a long time bread and milk (no tea), and I ate it out of a twopenny earthen porringer, with a pewter spoon. But mark how luxury will enter families, and make a progress, in spite of principle: being call'd one morning to breakfast, I found it in a China bowl, with a spoon of silver! They had been bought for me without my knowledge by my wife, and had cost her the Enormous sum of three-and-twenty shillings, for which she had no excuse or apology to make, but that she thought *her* husband deserv'd a silver spoon and China bowl as well as any of his neighbors. This was the first appearance of plate and China in our house, which afterward, in a course of years, as our wealth increas'd, augmented gradually to several hundred pounds in value.[14]

However developed Mrs. Franklin's sense of fashion may have been, it did not come close to matching her husband's. He knew that correctly interpreting the cues of this new material culture was a key aspect of social mobility. One had to be self-conscious about one's buying habits; consuming British goods could be hard work. In a marvelous letter that Franklin wrote from London to his wife soon after the "China bowl" incident had occurred, he gave an account of his frantic efforts to keep up with or, in this case perhaps, keep ahead of his provincial neighbors. Describing the contents of two large shipping crates dispatched to America, he explained that since he wanted "to show the Difference of Workmanship[,] there is something from all the China Works in England." An itch for "Fancy" compelled him to purchase a china basin "of an odd Colour" as well as four ladles of the "newest, but ugliest, Fashion." Just think, he seemed to suggest, how friends and rivals in America would react when they saw the "little Instrument to Core Apples" and "another to make little Turnips out of great ones." Franklin admitted that he could not resist picking up "56 Yards of Cotton printed curiously from Copper Plates, a new Invention." But the central piece—an example of eighteenth-century schlock—was a china jug for beer. "I fell in Love with it at first Sight," Franklin told his wife, "for I thought it look'd like a fat jolly Dame, clean and tidy, with a neat blue and white Calico Gown on, good natur'd and lovely, and [it] put me in mind of—Somebody."[15] One wonders whether Mrs. Franklin appreciated her husband's consumer joke.

Franklin was, of course, precisely the kind of self-made man whom later generations of Americans have found so appealing. Within the context of the mid-eighteenth century, however, upwardly mobile figures such as Franklin seemed much more problematic. They were men out of place; they defied traditional notions of social class. The source of the difficulty was not ambition, for, in point of fact, every free person in this society aspired to economic independence, whether that meant purchasing a few more acres of productive farm land or establishing oneself as a skilled tradesman.[16] What stirred apprehension was the propensity of quite unobjectionable ambition to spin out of control, becoming for some people little more than an expression of envy. Franklin may have successfully portrayed the acquisition of china and pewter as relatively harmless acts, but contemporaries—especially those who viewed self-made men as a threat to their own social standing—insisted that the celebration of novelty betrayed a deeply flawed character, perhaps even the presence of vice. As one colonial newspaper warned, "there is always, an Emulation most dangerous to the Community when every one beholding the *Finery* of his Neighbours pines to see himself outdone—burns with Envy—Or perhaps ruins his own Fortune and Credit to keep with him in those things that excite his Envy."[17]

Colonists who trooped so enthusiastically to the local stores professed to believe in a divinely sanctioned social hierarchy in which each person had an assigned position. During the seventeenth century this Renaissance concept still had considerable purchase, and men and women attempted to sort themselves out as best they could according to different ranks supposedly acquired at birth. Social mobility represented a direct challenge to God's cosmic plan. Within this older theological framework, certain rights and privileges pertained to each class. Magistrates could not, for example, subject a proper gentleman to corporal punishment; only malefactors recruited from the lower orders deserved the sting of the lash. External evidence of wealth—the display of expensive cloths, for example—did not reveal one thing or another about a person's genuine status. Rather, as clergymen in the Chesapeake as well as New England repeatedly explained in a kind of circular logic, only someone whose position in the community had already been established could legitimately wear the garments that one would associate with a man or woman of that particular status.[18] By the end of the seventeenth century, this static model had come under heavy attack. The leading figures of the Enlightenment systematically undermined the assumptions that had for so long sustained inherited religious notions of class and status. John Locke and Isaac Newton played major roles in the demolition, but scores of lesser-known writers in Britain and America began to reassess just how much God cared about maintaining a precisely calibrated social hierarchy.[19]

At the time when Mrs. Franklin decided that her husband merited a new breakfast set, the debate over how best to describe the structure of society remained unresolved. The sudden torrent of imported consumer goods after 1740 only exacerbated an ongoing controversy, for as more and more quite ordinary people purchased British manufactures, they inevitably transgressed the older boundaries of class and status. They increasingly made what we might call choices out of bounds. This situation had a curious effect on popular discussions about the character of the new marketplace. Those who took it upon themselves to speak for the common good generally decried the apparent erosion of a divinely ordered society. They spoke nostalgically of a world that they had lost in which the lower orders knew their place. But usually these same commentators passionately defended their own right to acquire goods that allegedly brought them so much happiness. Without openly admitting what was happening, they took onboard the concept that status was somehow dependent on display—indeed, on the spectacle of fashion—and once they had entertained the idea that the ordering of society turned on one's visible possessions rather than on innate qualities, they had to face the unsettling possibility that money alone determined the character of the social order.[20]

In this unstable intellectual environment, imported goods took on an especially heavy cultural burden. In most societies around the world, people spend a lot of time interpreting the belongings of other men and women with whom they come into contact. These objects are the props of everyday life, and by defining sacred and secular rituals, they powerfully reinforce the social order. At mid-century, however, these normal hermeneutic processes short-circuited.[21] The availability of so many goods confused shared meanings about hierarchy. The *Boston Gazette* complained, "We run into . . . Extremes as to Dress; so that there is scarce any Distinction between Persons of great Fortune, and People of ordinary Rank."[22] It probably would not have consoled this writer to learn that the same blurring of social boundaries had also occurred in Lunar City. Another journal exclaimed that "no age can come up to the present, when by their dress, the clerk, apprentice, or shopman, are not distinguishable from their master; nor the servant maid, even the cook-wench, from her mistress."[23] Everywhere a frenetic chasing after fashionable goods had generated disorder. Even Connecticut, styled by some contemporaries as "the land of steady habits," seemed in danger. According to "Intonsus Cato,"

The People throughout our King's Dominions, seem to vie with each other, in Extravagance. Throughout the Whole, there are zealous Efforts in every single Person to imitate
the person next above him, and in every Town to equal [the] next [highest] in Wealth,
Popularity and Politeness. Thus by a [spread] of the most ridiculous Mimickry, the Fashions of London are communicated to the poorest, meanest Town in Connecticut.[24]

Although the rhetoric seems at times hyperbolic, popular commentators
worked themselves into a frenzy over the impending anarchy. "Mentor," for
example, announced that "the lowest rank of men would pass for a middle
sort; and every one lives above his condition . . . to make a shew of their
wealth. . . . Thus a whole nation falls to ruin; all conditions and ranks of
men are confounded; [and] an eager desire of acquiring wealth to support
a vain expense, corrupts the purest minds."[25]

The striking newness of it all amplified the shrillness of complaint. The
perception of living at a moment of rapidly accelerating social change—a
condition by no means unique to this generation—convinced many colonists that they were in fact confronting a crisis without historical precedent. The Reverend William Tennent, an evangelical minister, betrayed a
general sense of temporal discontinuity during a sermon delivered in
Charleston, South Carolina. Tennent claimed that in the past—as recently
as the late seventeenth century—each social group had indulged in vices
peculiar to itself. In other words, in those times the poor and middling
classes may have been corrupt, but they were corrupt in ways that separated
them clearly from those above and below them. "Formerly Vices were described by the Classes of Mankind to which they belonged," lectured Tennent.
The most heinous examples, of course, were "confined chiefly to the Channel of the Court." Tennent insisted that the "middle and lower Classes of
People" as well as "the Inhabitants of Villages and Country Places" had escaped the truly dissolute practices associated with Charles II. But, by the
same token, the minister announced that a different sociology was now in
place, for his contemporaries had witnessed a curious democratization of
vice. Objectionable practices, Tennent observed, have "spread themselves
so universally among all Ranks in the *British* Empire, that we can no longer
describe them in that Manner." In the new consumer age, "our common
and Country People seem to vie with the first Classes of Mankind in Vices,
which were formerly peculiar to them alone."[26]

The analysis reveals something about Tennent's own confusion about
the structure of late-eighteenth-century society. He never doubted that human beings sorted themselves out according to class and status; he issued
no call for social leveling. Like many other Americans, however, he had lost
the ability to decode the rules of the hierarchy. Status and class were supposed to coincide, so that if a man was accepted as a gentleman by others,
he was expected to look like a gentleman. But in the new order almost anyone of moderate means seemed capable of presenting himself, at least in
terms of material possessions, as a gentleman or lady. The middling orders
found themselves similarly vulnerable to incursions by the poor. Judged on
the basis of innate character, of course, the poor were still the poor, the

middling sorts still middling sorts, but the elements that made them so seemed unhappily obscure. Put another way, choice in the consumer marketplace had begun to uncouple status and class. Dr. William Douglass, a Boston physician, would have had little good to say about Tennent's evangelical preaching style, but he too understood how rampant emulation had destabilized the social order. "It is true," Douglass confessed with a bow to Locke, that "all Men are naturally equal, but Society requires subordination."[27] And fearful "Simplicius Honestus" of Philadelphia called attention to the "quick advancement" of fashion in "this young city." "This pernicious distemper," he cried, "not only discovers itself in people of high rank amongst us, but is infecting those of an inferior class."[28]

III

Controversy over the social impact of fashion focused chiefly on clothes. Imported fabrics introduced Americans to a stunning range of consumer choice. After 1740 the market suddenly became alive with possibilities. One could purchase different textures and weights; shopkeepers offered an unprecedented selection of colors and designs.[29] The fact that men and women of all backgrounds could so easily acquire the latest styles incensed conservative commentators who insisted that other people dress appropriately to their stations in life. As the plaintive rhetoric of the period suggests, the realities of daily life no longer harmonized with the discourse of self-restraint. Ordinary Americans were actually demanding the same new weights and colors, designs and variety, that members of the colonial elites concluded ought rightly to distinguish them from the lower orders. A pamphlet calling for reforms in the political economy of New England pinned the region's monetary woes squarely on the democratization of fashion in apparel. "Our Gentry," observed the essayist, "yea our Commonalty, must be dress'd up like Nobles, nothing short of the finest Broad-Cloaths, Silks, &c. will serve."[30]

Other writers pursued this critique. "Plautus," for example, whose reflections on the blurring of class and status appeared in a Boston newspaper, noted, "[D]ress is grown of universal use in the conduct of life; even so far that a stranger of tolerable good sense dressed like a gentleman, is frequently better received by those of quality above him, than one of much better parts, whose attire is regulated by the rigid notions of œconomy." The nettlesome issue was not the articulation of difference through styles of dress. Rather, the grievance was against those of middling and lower orders with a few extra shillings in their pockets who successfully fobbed themselves off as *real* gentlemen. "Dress," lectured Plautus, ". . . is a necessary qualification in life; but then it must be suitable to the station and even to the age, and capacity of the person, that puts it on." The wanton disregard for the symbolic rules of apparel threatened to subvert the reflexive displays of public deference that the members of each class were expected to show to superiors as well as to inferiors. If etiquette no longer reinforced the structures of power, then the entire order of things might come tumbling down like Humpty-Dumpty. Plautus posed a series of questions that surely troubled his readers, especially those rendered insecure by the changing face of provincial material culture. "If a promiscuous use of fine cloaths be countenanced, who, that is really deserving of our respect and reverence, can be distinguished from the profligate and base born miscreant, that lies in wait to deceive under the disguise of noble garb?" Would not such pretenders attempt to worm their way into the hearts of the daughters of leading families? And how, this author whined, "must we distinguish the young gentleman ... from the journeyman taylor or barber, and it may chance the more artful and dangerous footman; who have had the impudence to dress like men of quality"?[31]

If we examine the erosion of traditional deference from the perspective of the "uppity" sorts rather than from that of a defensive elite, we begin to appreciate that those men and women who elected "gaiety" over "sobriety" were more concerned with the private pleasures of dressing fashionably than with the preservation of social order. They could always judge for themselves how they looked, no doubt envisioning themselves at these moments as prettier, younger, or more successful than they were in fact. During this period many colonial shopkeepers began carrying mirrors, especially small, affordable looking-glasses employed in personal grooming. This may have been the first generation of Americans who could conveniently check how they actually appeared in public. They decided whether they looked better in yellow or red, stripes or solids, light cottons or heavy woollens. They could monitor the process of self-fashioning anytime they pleased.[32]

The pressure to make the right choices from among so many contending possibilities must have been considerable. Even chance encounters in public—a greeting after a church service or a short conversation in a tavern—became occasions for placing other colonists within a social order now increasingly defined through clothes. Not surprisingly, Americans of this generation developed a sharp eye for textiles. It is impressive how often their descriptions of other people drew attention to the quality and color of garments. These word-pictures sometimes amounted to little more than commentaries on contemporary fashion. Philip Fithian was not a person whom one would expect to have noticed such things. This religious young man, a recent graduate of Princeton, served as a tutor for the children of Robert Carter. Fithian kept a private journal of his experiences at Nomini Hall, one of the largest plantations in Virginia. One summer evening in 1774 he met Miss Betsy Lee. "She wore a light Chintz Gown," Fithian recounted, "very fine, with a blue stamp; elegantly made, & which set well upon her—She wore a blue silk Quilt—In one word Her Dress was rich & fashionable." On another occasion he explained that when they attended church, "Almost every Lady wears a red Cloak; and when they ride out they tye a white handkerchief over their Head and face."[33] It was not only outsiders who made such observations. The Virginians commented extensively on the cut of Fithian's garments. When John Bartram, one of America's first botanists, set off in 1737 to visit two of Virginia's most influential planters, a friend advised him to purchase a new set of clothes, "for though I should not esteem thee less, to come to me in what dress thou will,—yet these Virginians are a very gentle, well-dressed people—and look, perhaps, more at a man's outside than his inside."[34]

When Bartram's friend used the word *outside,* in all probability he was not referring to the botanist's physical features. It was clothes that mattered. To be sure, Americans took note of an individual's height and weight. They spotted obvious deformities. But when called upon to describe another colonist, they inevitably concentrated on the color and quality of the person's garments. One sees this sensitivity to textiles expressed most arrestingly in the frequent advertisements for runaway servants. These descriptions contained general information about hair color and body type. It was clothes, however, that received the most detailed attention. An advertisement that ran in the *Virginia Gazette* announced that when William Smith disappeared, "He had on . . . a light coloured broad cloth coat, which is broke at the elbows, and with very few buttons on it, a pail blue duroy waistcoat, a pair of deep blue sagathy breeches, coarse shoes, several pair of stockings, steel buckles, coarse felt hat, a *Newmarket* coat of light bath coating, not bound, but stitched on the edges, with death head buttons on it, a pair of wrappers, rather of a darker colour than the *Newmarket* coat . . . he likewise carried off with him a black sattin capuchin, a piece of new *Virginia* cloth, containing eight yards, striped with blue and copperass."[35] Such advertisements for servants appeared in newspapers throughout the colonies, indicating if nothing else that the consumer revolution touched the lives of even the most humble eighteenth-century Americans. During the Seven Years' War, military authorities attempting to track down deserters employed virtually the same descriptive language. When John Thomas left Captain Thomas Shaw's Company of New Jersey Provincials, he "had on . . . a white Drugget Jacket, and Breeches of the same, a Calico under Jacket, check Shirt, grey Worsted Stockings and new Shoes, with large Brass Buckles in them."[36]

The incessant reading of cloth for cultural meaning extended even to the paintings that colonists commissioned to hang in their homes. Eighteenth-century portrait painters understood the symbolic significance of textiles for the Americans, resulting in a heightened awareness of textures and weights perhaps unmatched until the Asian Indians, another colonial people dependent upon British exports, defined their own nationalist aspirations around the use and production of cloth.[37] The faces of the prominent colonists who were captured on canvas seem by modern aesthetic standards disappointing. They appear flat, repetitious, totally lacking in personality. They have nothing of the imaginative depth that one associates with later, more technically skilled painters such as John Singleton Copley. And yet, despite their anatomical crudeness, sitters and members of their families extravagantly praised the works of prolific painters such as John

Newspaper announcements appealing for the return of runaway servants and slaves often focused on the clothes that the person was wearing when last seen. Even these marginal laborers managed to obtain colorful and fashionable garments. *Connecticut Courant*, 3 July 1772. *Connecticut Historical Society.*

RUN away laſt Monday night from Wethersfield a tranſient perſon who ſays his
name is William Johnſon, an old countryman,
about 5 feet 9 inches high about 25 years of
age, wore his own light colour'd ſhort, curl'd
hair, well built, has a ſore on his right leg,
had on when he went away, a ſhort blue coat,
red double breaſted waiſtcoat, black knit
breeches, had with him a pair long ſtrip'd trow-
ſers and had one white ſhirt, and two ſtriped
linen ditto. He ſtole and carried with him
the following articles viz: one check linen
ſhirt, a pair worſted ſtockings, a pair of thin
ſhoes a pair of large flower'd ſilver ſhoe buckles,
a pair large knee ditto, a black Barcelona handkerchief, and a pair of white leather gloves.
Whoever ſhall take up and ſecure ſaid thief in
any of his Majeſty's Goals ſo that he may be
dealt with according to law, and the goods re-
covered, ſhall have ſix dollars reward, and all
neceſſary charges paid by
                              Joſiah Goodrich.
Wetherfield, July 3 1772.

Wollaston, Robert Feke, John Hesselius, Joseph Blackburn, and Jeremiah Theus for having achieved a genuine "likeness."

What seemed to have most satisfied the people who purchased these portraits was the extraordinarily detailed delineation of the garments worn by their friends and relatives. In Great Britain such artists would have been known somewhat derisively as "drapery painters." They were the ones employed by large London studios after a master court painter had completed the face and hands, in other words, the hard bits. The struggling limners who accepted American commissions were thus peculiarly prepared to provide the colonists with exactly what they wanted, paintings celebrating their acquisition of fashionable garments. What a man like Wollaston may have lacked in ability to render the depth of individual character, he made up—in the words of one student of mid-eighteenth-century American art—"by his skill in painting laces, silks, and satins."[38] This successful itinerant knew his market. He produced over three hundred portraits. As in other societies, the portrait in colonial America asserted one's claim to status. What made this culture unusual was that status was negotiated through the quality and character of the fabric that the provincial consumer chose to wear at the moment of carefully staged self-fashioning.

Even in so-called folk or primitive paintings, one encounters the same concern for presenting the sitter in relation to consumer objects, especially to imported British cloth. A painting from the Garbisch collection, *Susanna*

Susanna Truax seems quite at ease among her imported possessions. *The Gansevoort Limner Portrait, 1730 (possibly by Pieter Vanderlyn), Gift of Edgar William and Bernice Chrysler Garbisch. Photograph © 2002 Board of Trustees, National Gallery of Art, Washington, D.C.*

Truax, provides a splendid example of this phenomenon. This portrait by an unknown artist shows a young girl outfitted in a bright, striped dress, obviously a garment made of the type of fabric just then flooding into the colonies from England. On a table one sees a teapot, sugar cubes, and a cup and saucer. The picture situates the girl within a vibrant Anglo-American economy. The tea set and a fashionable dress support her claim to social standing. What gives this painting special charm is the fact that Susanna Truax is so demonstrably at ease among her possessions.

When we view Susanna Truax, it probably does not seem possible that she might have been a fake. No doubt, she was exactly what she appeared, a pleasant middle-class girl. But one could not always be so sure. Behind the shrill rhetoric lamenting the loss of clear status markers were tales of unpleasant moments resulting from colonists interpreting apparel as an external badge of personal worth only to discover that the owner was in fact a counterfeit.[39] One cannot help feeling a little sorry for a struggling Maryland farmer who became the butt of a class joke that turned on an erroneous translation of cultural symbols. The man had journeyed across the Potomac River to have his grain ground into flour at a mill operated by the

Carters, one of the wealthiest families in Virginia. Young "Bob," the son of the owner of Nomini Hall, decided to have a bit of sport with the simple visitor. Standing next to his own clerk, who "wore a red Coat," Bob pretended that he was the Carters' paid assistant at the mill. The Marylander took the measure of the person wearing the "scarlet Coat," judging him to be a gentleman, and then inquired who "is the other [fellow] in a frowsled Wig?" The shabbily dressed Bob responded by identifying himself as "my father's Clerk." That night the tale "entertained" the patriarch of Nomini Hall over dinner. The "Colonel" may have felt that it was about time that a great planter fooled a poor farmer rather than the other way round.[40] After all, as the story reveals, it was not very hard to obtain a scarlet coat in this society.

One of the more dramatic accounts of how hard the new consumer marketplace had made sorting out status occurred in Maryland not far from the Carter plantation. Dr. Alexander Hamilton entered a rural tavern called Curtis's, located on the Maryland-Pennsylvania border. There he met William Morison, an individual to whom the Scottish physician took an immediate dislike. Morison, it seems, was "a very rough spun, forward, clownish blade, much addicted to swearing, [and] att the same time desirous to pass for a gentleman." The proprietor certainly did not think Morison merited special treatment. She took one look at his clothes—"a greasy jacket and breeches and a dirty worsted cap"—and concluded that Morison must be a "ploughman or carman." At Curtis's such persons received only weak tea and "scraps of cold veal."

When the owner placed this insulting meal before him, Morison protested loudly that it was only the presence of another gentleman that kept him from throwing "her cold scraps out at the window and break[ing] her table all to pieces should it cost him 100 pounds for damages." The other "gentleman" was, of course, Hamilton. Morison judged the doctor's status the same way that the tavern's proprietor had judged his, on the basis of the style and quality of his garments. In any event, like an irate terrier, Morison began digging wildly in his own baggage, pulling out various trophies which until that moment had been hidden from sight. He quickly exchanged "his worsted night cap" for a "linen one out of his pocket" and went on to perform a change of clothes worthy of a modern superhero, and then announced to the amazed onlookers, "Now . . . I'm upon the borders of Pennsylvania and must look like a gentleman." Even after the two men had departed Curtis's, Morison remained defensive, as if he suspected that the traveling Scot really did rate him as no more than a common laborer. As Hamilton recounted with characteristic hauteur, Morison declared "that tho' he seemed to be but a plain, homely fellow, yet he would have us know that he was able to afford better than many that went finer: he had good linnen in his bags, a pair of silver buckles, silver clasps, and gold sleeve buttons, two Holland shirts, and some neat nightcaps." And to support further his demand for respect, Morison bragged that "his little woman at home drank tea twice a day."[41] Hamilton thought the entire performance vulgar. Morison may have been about to cross the border into Pennsylvania, but he had a long way to go before he could traverse the boundaries that separated the laborer from the gentleman. At least, that would have been Hamilton's interpretation. Since class and status are relative categories established through human interaction, we may assume that Morison rode north from Maryland convinced that Hamilton knew nothing about the workings of American society.

The question posed by the likes of Morison—at least for the wealthier sort—was how to control choice in an open, liberal society. History suggested some answers. Earlier societies had experimented with sumptuary laws, which prohibited men and women from wearing garments that allowed them to present themselves as persons of a higher status than that recognized by their social betters. These statutes seldom achieved the ends for which they were intended. But during the eighteenth century sumptuary legislation seemed little more than a risible attempt to lock the barn after the horse had fled. Ambitious colonists such as Morison were not about to surrender the store-bought items that helped persuade them that they were really as good as those gentlemen who defended their own status in the social order on the basis of largely invisible attributes related to character and breeding. Franklin understood the realities of the new marketplace. Writing as "Father Abraham," he asked an imagined crowd of eager buyers, "What would you think of that Prince, or that Government, who should issue an Edict forbidding you to dress like a Gentleman or a Gentlewoman, on Pain of Imprisonment or Servitude? Would you not say that you are free, have a Right to dress as you please, and that such an Edict would be a Breach of your Privileges, and such a Government tyrannical?"[42]

The effort to keep consumer goods out of the hands of those who desired them even failed when the "uppity" persons involved were African American slaves. In a "Negro Act" passed by the South Carolina legislature in 1735, lawmakers complained that black people wore "clothes much above the condition of slaves, for the procuring whereof they use sinister and evil methods." No evidence indicates that the slaves paid the slightest attention to the act. A Charleston Grand Jury seemed amazed to discover in 1744 that black women in the city dressed "in Apparel quite gay and beyond their Condition." The local newspaper added with a hint of romantic conspiracy that "there is scarce a new mode [of fashion] which *favourite* black and mulatto *women slaves* are not immediately *enabled* to adopt." The situation in Virginia appeared to mock attempts to restore an imagined social order in which every person obediently fashioned himself or herself according to an arbitrary hierarchy that took no account of the force of novelty. One telling example of the impossibility of coercing consumer desire appeared in an advertisement for a runaway slave named Bacchus. At the moment of flight from his master, Bacchus had in his possession

> two white Russia Drill Coats, one turned up with blue, the other quite plain and new, with white figured Metal Buttons, blue Plush Breeches, a fine Cloth Pompadour Waist-coat, two or three thin or Summer Jackets, sundry Pairs of white Thread Stockings, five or six white Shirts, two of them pretty fine, neat Shoes, Silver Buckles, a fine Hat cut and cocked in the Macaroni Figure, a double-milled Drab Great Coat, and sundry other Wearing Apparel.[43]

One cannot help speculating what kind of conversation Bacchus might have had with Morison. The feisty white traveler who resisted Hamilton's efforts to define him as a mere laborer would most likely not have been amused by Bacchus's efforts to reinvent himself as a free person. But in point of fact, both colonists—however separated by their consciousness of racial difference—understood that clothes could indeed make the man. In a curious essay advocating strict legal controls on how black people dressed, "A. B." addressed the complex relation between the new material culture and what might be termed the psychology of self-presentation. He equated a recent crime wave in Maryland with the almost insatiable desire of the local blacks "to raise Money to buy fine Cloaths," for "when dressed in them, [they] make them so bold and impudent that they insult every poor white Person they meet." A. B. appealed for upper-class support for his proposed legislation by extending the argument to "poor whites," another group over which the elite seemed to exercise minimal control. "I am fully convinced of the Efficacy of such a Law," he explained to the readers of the *Maryland Gazette,* "from what I have seen of some of our own Colour, for I have been in Company with Men when they have been meanly dressed, and they have been as still and humble as a Bee, and at other Times have seen them with their Sunday or Holyday Clothes on, and they have been as impudent and bold as a Lion." His conclusion from an excursion across the boundaries of class and race was that "such is the Difference fine Cloaths make in the Vulgar, and such is the Difference, I am sure, they make in the Negroes."[44]

Coercion obviously could not preserve an ordered society in which people of genuine worth ruled over those who remained vulgar and lower class no matter how tasteful the cut of their garments. At issue was power. At mid-century, those Americans who so desperately wanted servants and laborers to remain in their assigned places—indeed, to show proper deference to their betters—began to imagine a different way to legitimate their own claims to privileged status. Since they could not effectively outpurchase ordinary colonists, and since the strutting peacocks of Williamsburg and New York might in reality be impostors, those who styled themselves the rightful leaders of provincial society reasoned that they might reduce social instability by curtailing their own fashionable excesses. If gentlemen and ladies were supposed to set examples of acceptable public behavior for the less affluent and the base-born, then they should do so by forgoing the acquisition of fashionable goods. Playing upon the theme of elite self-sacrifice, a Boston writer insisted that the extravagance in "Buildings, Furniture, Apparel, and Tables . . . can never be remedied until they who find most Fault with these Things remedy them at home, and set their Inferiours a good Example."[45] The *Independent Reflector* of New York joined in, exclaiming that there was no hope of reducing wasteful spending on imported goods unless persons in "the higher and middle Stations of Life" provided guidance. Surely they must know that "as People in the inferior Stations of Life, are extremely apt to imitate those who move in a more elevated Sphere: It ought to be the Endeavour of the latter to set them the laudable Example."[46]

For many centuries moral writers in Europe had been giving similar advice. They had long hectored courtiers about cutting back lavish expenditures. With peasants starving in the streets, it seemed objectionable for aristocratic toffs to consume quite so conspicuously. Scripture sustained the critique, and although the elite classes of Europe more or less politely ignored such counsel, the notion that rulers might demonstrate genuine concern for the common good by curtailing their own purchase of material goods became woven into religious and political discourses that became part of the cultural baggage of the eighteenth century. These inherited ideas—be they Stoic or classical republican in character—were like modern investments that rise and fall in relation to changing market conditions. The sudden expansion of consumer choice—an unprecedented phenomenon that touched the lives of even the poorest people in this society—activated older notions about the link between self-sacrifice and responsible leadership. In fact, in this social context, perceptions of a growing threat to the traditional social order made it increasingly plausible to think of simplicity and sobriety in the marketplace as a way to reinforce and authenticate claims to political authority. As one newspaper observed, "Let the principal gentlemen but set the example, [and] they will be quickly followed by the bulk of the people."[47]

IV

For entirely understandable reasons, historians of the eighteenth century have tended to depict colonization as an awkward stage of development to be overcome—like adolescence—so that the American people could get on with the serious business of nation building. Colonization suggests political dependence, perhaps calling to mind those nineteenth-century outposts of empire where Europeans mixed uneasily with the native peoples. We imagine such outsiders sipping tea in a secure compound, gossiping about current events in England and France and all the while frightened that somehow by simply living in India or Africa they would become not quite European.[48] Such conditions, we assume, surely did not pertain in America; our colonization was not the colonization of that later empire. But, of course, it was. To be sure, the dynamics of settlement were different, and most white Americans had not the slightest interest in leaving their homes for a new life in England. In terms of culture, however, they were not unlike those nineteenth-century colonial officers and their families who waited impatiently on the edge of empire for the arrival of a ship bringing news from what they would have regarded as civilized society. Although New York and Philadelphia were not the Nairobi or Calcutta of colonial America, they contained many men and women who defined taste as English taste, fashion as English fashion, and polite conversation as but a provincial echo of the learned and witty talk they believed regularly occurred in cosmopolitan centers. The shopkeepers who advertised in the colonial newspapers appre-

THE CORROSIVE LOGIC OF CHOICE   → 167

ciated the allure of Britishness. Like George Bartram, a Philadelphia dry-
goods merchant, they issued to all Americans the Siren call, "Just imported
in the last ships from Britain and Ireland."[49] The construction of a new cultural identity within an "empire of goods" is generally known as Anglicization, an admittedly awkward term that carries the sense that even in
isolated colonial American communities men and women saw themselves
increasingly as fully British. Like most broad concepts intended to advance
our understanding of social change in earlier times, Anglicization had been
stretched to its explanatory limits, for if it is meant to convey the notion
that the colonists were absolute slaves to English models and incapable of
modifying imported goods in interesting and original ways, then it has taken
us further than the evidence can bear. Many colonists were openly ambivalent about the impact of English culture on their lives, and it was not uncommon for such figures at one moment to sound more English than the
English and at the next to proclaim aggressively the superiority of American ways. This is not a surprising phenomenon. A kind of relatively harmless cultural schizophrenia has long been associated with the experience of
colonization.[50]

But, even if we recognize the capacity of the colonists to develop cultural forms outside the penumbra of Anglicization, we must acknowledge
that after 1740 London and to a lesser extent the rest of England acted as a
powerful magnet pulling the colonists ever closer to the defining center of
the good life. The force worked its magic as strongly in South Carolina as in
Massachusetts. Charleston may have been the most sophisticated city in
mid-century America, but to the disconsolate Eliza Pinckney, a woman credited with successfully promoting indigo as a commercial export crop, it might
have been located on the dark side of the moon. In 1762 she wrote to a
friend living in England, begging for news of George III's new queen, Char-
lotte Sophia of Mecklenburg. "If, Madam, you have ever been witness to the
impatience of the people of England about a hundred mile[s] from London to be made acquainted with what passes there," lectured the forgotten
provincial, "[then] you may guess a little at what our impatience is here
when I inform you that the curiosity increases with the distance from the
Center of affairs; and our impatience is not to be equaled with any peoples
within four thousand mile[s]." In another cranky letter, Pinckney described
herself as "an old woman in the Wilds of America" and assured her correspondent in Great Britain, "You people that live in the great world in the
midst of Scenes of entertainment and pleasure abroad, of improving studies and polite amusement at home, must be very good to think of your
friends in this remote Corner of the Globe."[51]

Colonists learned about English fashions in predictable ways. They read
novels depicting themes with which they were all too familiar, especially ones
recounting the perils that awaited innocent women who misinterpreted the
well-dressed seducer as a gentleman. In addition to the advertisements, newspapers carried stories about the comings and goings of the royal family; they
perused up-market magazines that informed them about the character of

English country life.[52] The cultural messages issuing forth from the cosmopolitan center percolated down through provincial society, from major port cities to small farming villages, until the latest intelligence about good taste and polite behavior eventually reached corners of the globe far more remote than Eliza Pinckney had ever seen. An anonymous writer who appeared in a Connecticut journal mapped out the progress of Anglicization as well as any of his contemporaries. Through an elaborate network of emulation, he explained, "the Fashions of London, are communicated to the poorest, meanest Towns of Connecticut." It was quite a sight "to behold the Manners and Fashions of the Ladies walking in St. James's Park, copied by the Female Quality of S–ff–d and N–F–d in Connecticut. From the Metropolis of Great Britain, these Manners and Fashions are conveyed to Bristol [England], from Bristol they are transported to Boston in New England, from Boston they travel to Hartford; thence to C–w–l and N–F–d."[53] A powerful imagination was required to conflate the demimonde display found at St. James's Park with the more modest shows encountered at Cromwell, but then, we must remember, it probably did not take much glitter to persuade commentators that the poor farmers of America had forsaken their homespun garments for the fancy styles of London.

As might be expected of a person so attuned to the offerings of the consumer marketplace, Franklin put a different interpretation on the colonists' preference for English goods. He did not believe that their presence in the little villages of Connecticut was necessarily a matter of great concern. Rather, the arrival of the latest styles in the provincial shops indicated a special fondness for the nation that had provided so many choices. What triggered Franklin's remarks was a report by a British traveler who allegedly had just returned from America. It declared that in terms of their apparel the colonists had been a disappointment. Americans not only had selected somewhat duller colors for their clothes than the visitor had expected but also dressed so much alike that one could hardly tell one colonist from another. Writing in a London journal under the pen name "A New Englandman," Franklin brilliantly turned the critique into testimony for a kind of consumer nationalism. "All I know of it is," Franklin observed in his disarming way, "that they [the Americans] wear the manufactures of Britain, and follow its fashions perhaps too closely, every remarkable change . . . making its appearance there within a few months after its invention here." He assured English readers that it was to be expected that the colonists would see fashion as an expression of their Britishness, for, in point of fact, their sense of style was "a natural effect of their constant intercourse with England, by ships arriving almost every week from the capital, their respect for the mother country, and admiration of every thing that is British."[54]

One can never quite tell whether Franklin is pulling one's leg, but in this matter—at least, before the imperial crisis over taxation—his assessment seems right on the mark. Colonial booksellers would surely have agreed. They learned that colonial readers preferred an English imprint to an American edition of the same title. "Their estimate of things English was so high," discovered one historian, "that a false London imprint could seem an effective way to sell a local publication."[55] The standardization of the colonial consumer marketplace, a function of the availability of the same general range of imported British goods from Georgia to New Hampshire, created a paradoxical situation.[56] As Americans purchased the same kinds of British manufactures—in other words, as they had similar consumer experiences—they did in fact become more Anglicized. This cultural process has sometimes been referred to as "the colonization of taste," a phrase that seems as useful for provincial America as for India and Scotland.[57]

As commentators like Franklin revealed, the ubiquitous items imported from Great Britain transformed the visual landscape of everyday life in provincial America. About color, the English traveler who provoked the riposte from Franklin was simply wrong. We have already seen how shopkeepers demanded certain colors from their suppliers. One of them candidly announced that "only an unfashionable colour is a sufficient reason for our rejecting various goods."[58] He knew his business. After 1740 the new consumer marketplace presented American consumers with an unprecedented range of colors, in cloth and paint, and so, if nothing else, Britishness suddenly brightened how ordinary people appeared in public. Flashy color became a badge of participation in the empire of goods, and although it is difficult to quantify such cultural developments, the imaginative use of color in some significant way made Americans feel as if they were British people who just happened to live in America.[59] It certainly transformed drab household interiors from New England to South Carolina into Technicolor displays that seem to modern eyes so extraordinary—indeed, so garish—that those in charge of preserving the material culture of the eighteenth century have been reluctant to restore the late colonial homes to their true radiance. They feared that a clash of colors—crimson mock-flock wallpaper struggling against the arresting verdigris of an adjacent room, for example— would horrify visitors who assumed that colonial Americans would have rejected the possibility of such colorful self-fashioning out of hand.[60]

Drawing attention to the mid-century as the moment when Americans initially discovered the possibilities of color in their lives helps us to recapture the constant sense of surprise—even wonder—that accompanied the rapid Anglicization of the late colonial landscape. Changes associated with the new British imports meant that men and women could not take for granted what the interior of a house might look like. John Adams, for example, was not a person easily bowled off his feet, but when he entered the home of a successful Boston merchant, he could not believe his eyes. "Went over [to] the House to view the Furniture," the young lawyer confided to his diary, "which alone cost a thousand Pounds sterling. . . . [T]he Turkey Carpets, the painted Hangings, the Marble Table, the rich Beds with crimson Damask Curtains and Counterpanes, the beautiful Chimney Clock, the Spacious Garden, are the most magnificent of any Thing I have ever seen."[61] This was not a typical dwelling, of course, and such "magnificent" things may have inspired in a latter-day Puritan like Adams a mixture of jealousy and condemnation. But however the Britishness of the new material culture was received, it could not be ignored. It was something to be discussed and then, long afterward, remembered. During the 1820s John Fanning Watson, an antiquarian, interviewed several citizens who had lived in Philadelphia before independence. After the passage of so many years, these older people still talked about fine English imports of mid-century with as much excitement as had Adams. "T. Matlack, Esq., when aged 95, told me he had a distinct recollection of meeting with the first carpet he had ever seen about the year 1750, at the house of Owen Jones, at the corner of Spruce and Second streets," Watson explained. "Mrs. S. Shoemaker, an aged Friend of the same age, told me she had received as a rare present from England a Scotch carpet; it was but twelve feet square, and was deemed quite a novelty."[62]

Anglicized provincials who knowingly or not had experienced a colonization of taste insisted on receiving the "latest" English goods. They became remarkably attuned to even subtle changes in metropolitan fashion. "And you may believe me," a young Virginia planter named George Washington lectured a British merchant in 1760, "when I tell you that instead of getting things good and fashionable in their several kinds we often have Articles sent Us that could only have been us[e]d by our Forefathers in the days of yore."[63] Since most of the imports that Washington demanded had not been available in Virginia before 1740, his sense of the "days of yore" must be taken as the hyperbole of a disappointed consumer. Washington may have envied his neighbors in Annapolis, who seemed to obtain the latest British fashions faster than he. The people of New York were as alert in the interpretation of these cultural cues as were the consumers in Virginia and Maryland. "In the city of New-York," wrote William Smith in 1762, "through the intercourse with the Europeans, we follow the London fashions."[64] And in Boston the almost desperate desire to keep up to date within the empire was equally manifest. One woman told an English friend—perhaps protesting a bit much—that "here we follow the fashions in England & have made great strides in Luxury & Expense within these three years Esp[ly] in that of Dress & the young Ladies seem as smart as those we left in England."[65]

Tea provides an especially revealing example of the impact of Anglicization on consumer taste. Early in the eighteenth century this hot drink became the preferred beverage of gentry households. As in England, in America polite ladies—perhaps as a device to lure gentlemen away from tavern society—organized elaborate household rituals around the tea service. The purchase of tea necessitated the acquisition of pots, bowls, strainers, sugar tongs, cups, and slop dishes. As Mrs. Franklin might have noted, once one decided to keep up with neighbors in the contest for British goods, one thing inevitably seemed to lead to another. A writer in a New York City newspaper suggested the need for a special school that could instruct uncertain colonists in proper tea etiquette. The young men of the city, finding themselves "utterly ignorant in the Ceremony of the Tea-Table," were advised to employ a knowledgeable woman "to teach them the Laws, Rules, Customs, Phrases and Names of the Tea Utensils."[66]

Although less well-to-do Americans did not possess the entire range of social props, they too demanded tea. To be sure, tea did not originate in England, but it did—a few smugglers excepted—generally find its way to the colonies through British ports. More than any other item, tea became the signature of a new polite society. As early as 1734 one New Yorker exclaimed, "I am credibly informed that tea and china ware cost the province, yearly, near the sum of £10,000; and people that are least able to go to the expense, must have their tea tho' their families want bread. Nay, I am told, [they] often pawn their rings and plate to gratifie themselves in that piece of extravagance."[67] It did not take long for this alleged luxury to become a necessity. "Our people," wrote another New York gentleman in 1762, "both in town and country, are shamefully gone into the habit of tea-drinking."[68] And when Israel Acrelius visited the old Swedish settlements of Delaware at mid-century, he discovered people consuming tea "in the most remote cabins."[69] During the 1750s even the inmates of the public hospital of Philadelphia, the city's poorhouse, insisted on having tea. Indeed, they made it a non-negotiable demand.[70] All these colonists drank their tea out of imported cups, not necessarily from china ones but rather from ceramics that had originated in the English Midlands, where they had been fired at very high temperature and thus made resistant to the intense heat of the Americans' new favorite drink. It does not require a great stretch of imagination to appreciate that the custom of taking one's tea could under certain circumstances become a locus of fierce contest over political identity and culture.

We must not exaggerate the colonization of taste. Ordinary Americans certainly adopted tea for reasons other than social emulation. After all, it was a mild stimulant, and a hot cup of tea perhaps laced with a little sugar probably helped the laboring poor to endure hard work and insubstantial housing. Nevertheless, in some isolated country villages the desire to keep up with the latest English fads led to bizarre results, the kind of gross cultural misunderstanding that anthropologists encounter in places where products of an alien technology have been introduced into a seemingly less developed society.[71] In 1794 a historian living in East Hampton, New York, interviewed a seventy-eight-year-old woman. "Mrs. Miller," he discovered, "remembers well when they first began to drink tea on the east end of Long Island." She explained that none of the local farmers knew what to do with the dry leaves: "One family boiled it in a pot and ate it like samp-porridge [cornmeal mush]. Another spread tea leaves on his bread and butter, and bragged of his having ate half a pound at a meal, to his neighbor, who was informing him how long a time a pound of tea lasted him." According to Mrs. Miller, the arrival of the first teakettle was a particularly memorable day in the community. "It came ashore at Montauk in a ship (the *Captain Bell*)," she recounted. "The farmers came down there on business with their cattle, and could not find how to use the tea-kettle, which was then brought up to old 'Governor Hedges.' Some said it was for one thing, and some said it was for another. At length one, the more knowing than his neighbors, affirmed it to be the ship's lamp, to which all assented." Mrs. Miller may have been having some fun at the historian's expense, but whatever the truth of her tale, it reveals the symbolic importance of tea in this remote eighteenth-century village. Like so many other colonists, the people of East Hampton wanted to keep up with English customs; they just were not too sure how to go about it. The same sort of thing could even happen to affluent colonists. Virginia's royal governor gave Mrs. William Nelson, the wife of a wealthy merchant, a set of modish dessert dishes, but the woman had no idea how to use them. Her amused husband thanked the governor: "Mrs. Nelson is obliged for your present of the Necessaries for a Desert: tho' I Fancy she will be puzeled [how] to bring them into use."[72]

With so many colonists trying so hard to be English in America, it was quite logical for Franklin—the master consumer of the era—to accentuate the link between identity and market experience. We have already heard him give soothing assurances to the readers of a London journal about the profound sense of Britishness engendered by "constant intercourse with England." A few years later he expanded the argument about provincial loyalty. On this occasion he wanted to persuade a victorious government that had just driven the French out of Canada to hold on to these vast territories. No one in England need be concerned, he explained, that the Americans would now entertain thoughts of independence simply because they no longer had to worry about the French threat. Sounding a lot like Edmund Burke, Franklin insisted that commerce would ensure American obedience.[73] Because of the pervasiveness of consumer trade, many Americans "must 'know,' must 'think,' and must 'care' about the country they chiefly trade with." He painted a word-picture of the perfect marketplace. Unlike Ireland, which regularly sent its wealthiest inhabitants to live in England, the Americans remained in the colonies. And there, they spent their money on British imports. "If the *North American* gentleman stays in his own country," Franklin asked rhetorically, "and lives there in that degree of luxury and expense with regard to the use of *British* manufactures, that his fortune entitles him to; may not his example (from the imitation of superiors so natural to mankind) spread the use of those manufactures among hundreds of families around him, and occasion a much greater demand for them, than it would do if he should remove and live in *London*?"[74] No contemporary global capitalist could imagine a more favorable situation: consumer colonies consuming at a robust rate and thanking British authorities for the benefits of the relationship.

V

Eighteenth-century commentators knew who was chiefly to blame for what they perceived as the confused state of society. Women were responsible. The colonial Jeremiahs found that they could hardly discuss the challenge of the consumer economy without immediately denouncing the legions of

wives and daughters who had compromised the common good in the interests of satiating their own selfish desires. The mocking humor of many
attacks barely disguised the misogyny that energized the surging public
rhetoric. A single example captures the rhetorical climate. In 1743 a little
poem entitled "The Ladies' Complaint" appeared in a South Carolina newspaper. Devoid of literary merit, the piece advocated greater equality between the sexes. The final couplets summarized the argument:

> Then equal Laws let Custom find;
> And neither Sex oppress.
> More Freedom give to Womankind,
> Or to Mankind give less.[75]

The very next issue of the journal ran a response from a person identified
as a man, expressing the hope that the female poet would not in the future
conspire "to diminish our [male] Liberty."[76] As many exchanges of this type
made clear, those most anxious about maintaining order associated dis-
ruptive change with too many assertive women making too many choices
in the consumer marketplace. Country shopkeepers certainly could not afford to ignore their demands. Even the visitor to the Moon encountered the
women of Lunar City parading through the streets in fancy clothes they
had no business wearing.

At almost any time, accelerated economic change strains a culture's assumptions about gender roles. But in the mid-eighteenth century, real market conditions heightened the sense—at least among males—that something
had gone terribly wrong. As Albert O. Hirschman, an economic historian,
explains, "antagonism toward material culture comes to the fore in periods
of economic expansion when consumer goods, frequently of a new kind, become more widely diffused."[77] And so it was in colonial America after 1740.
Just as modern critics of consumption complain that an influx of electronic
gadgetry will corrupt the youth of the nation, so too did colonial censors
couple the flood of British goods with the appearance of new kinds of women
who seemed bent on taking control of their own self-fashioning.

Colonial women had the great misfortune to become ensnared in one
of the major controversies of the eighteenth century, the so-called luxury
debate.[78] Although a few audacious writers such as Bernard Mandeville
claimed that self-indulgence in the marketplace would probably not destroy Western civilization, most of his contemporaries on both sides of the
Atlantic passionately disagreed, describing luxury as a toxin so powerful
that it could, in fact, undermine the course of empire and deprive free citizens of their liberties. The frenzied reaction to this cultural threat, no doubt,
reflected an uneasy accommodation within the wealthier European states
to the more liberal conditions of getting and spending found in modern
commercial societies. Having witnessed a growing disjuncture between class
and status, luxury's adversaries vowed to halt its spread before the age irre-
deemably abandoned itself to what one commentator labeled "*vain, luxurious,* and *selfish* EFFEMINACY."[79]

The critique took various forms, but the dominant one iterated themes put forward by early Christian theologians. Within this moral discourse luxury not only qualified as a sin but also invited a host of attendant evils such as avarice, intemperance, vanity, and pride. People who worshiped the fine objects of material culture obviously had set up a false idol. "It is a time in which mankind in general are much concerned to be adorn'd with the most agreeable ornaments, & dress'd in the best fashion," explained the Reverend Jonas Clarke of Lexington, Massachusetts, but before the young people of New England set their hearts on appearing "most amiable and engaging," he warned, they should "learn the best *fashion* [is] from the *pulpit*, and the *art of dress* from the *word of GOD.*"[80] The Reverend Andrew Eliot gave a Boston congregation a lesson on luxury from Scripture. Addressing his own "evil and adulterous generation," he asked, "Shall I speak of *Luxury,* or that Propensity there is in us, to gratify our sensual Appetites? Poor as we are, we live high, and *fare sumptiously every Day.* This destroys our Health, consumes our Substance, enfeebles the Mind, feeds our Lusts, and stupifies Conscience. While we feed and pamper our Bodies, we starve our Souls."[81] A little bit of this kind of rhetoric must have gone a long way. Even without his guidance, Eliot's auditors already knew that the most effective antidotes to extravagance were frugality and industry.

A second line of attack on luxury involved a didactic reading of history. As any educated person in this period could testify, the past demonstrated unequivocally that luxury sapped the public virtue, the fighting spirit, and even the freedoms enshrined by people who had once celebrated the simple life. Rome had taken this ruinous path, and if Great Britain did not quickly mend its ways, it would suffer the same fate. In 1753 an anonymous American writer could take the lessons of history for granted, noting in his appeal for "Industry & Frugality" that only "a few Pages of History" would be sufficient to demonstrate the threat of luxury to commercial states.[82] The editor of the *Independent Reflector* announced, as if he were sharing a self-evident truth, that luxury is "a great and mighty Evil, carrying all before it, and crumbling States and Empires, into slow, but inevitable Ruin.— Like sweetened Poison, it is soft but strong, enervates the Constitution, and triumphs at last, in the Weakness and Rottenness of the Patient." Curiously, the New York journal aimed this particular judgment not at the sybaritic courts of Europe but at neighboring New England, where, according to the report, men and women "attempt to outlive each other, in Dress, Tables, and the like." Boston was on the edge of a great fall. Indeed, it was said that a traveler in Massachusetts could tell how far he was from the city "by the Length of the Ruffles of a Belle of the Town he was in."[83] Each nation apparently had a weakness for a different sort of luxury. The Italians liked "pompous" palaces, the French fine suits, the Poles a "splendid Equipage," the Germans a "capacious Cellar," and the Spanish a "Bead-Roll of Titles." But the British provincials outdid them all, for "our Taste is universal; and there is scarce a little Clerk among us, who doth not think himself the Outcast of

Providence, if not enabled by his Salary, Fees, &c. to out-live the rich Man in the Gospel."[84]

Among the dry leaves of these older discourses rustled a more recently minted critique of luxury, which, while no less inimical to self-indulgence in the consumer marketplace, staked out a more secular ground. Put simply, luxury beggared the people, especially those who happened to live in the colonies. Within the provinces this argument took onboard much of the rhetoric associated with a loosely defined economic position known as mercantilism.[85] To be sure, by making unwise choices, Americans revealed a worrisome inability to control what one writer called their "Horseleech Desires." But more than being a sign of moral deficiency, expensive purchases of imported goods sucked hard currency out of the colonies, leaving them debtors. As one newspaper declared, "a *Community* may be view'd in the same Light as a *private Man*: However extensive and profitable his Trade is, yet his Gains large as they are may be swallow'd up and annihilated by *Prodigality* and *Extravagance*."[86] Whether one regarded luxury as a badge of sin or just bad economics, it raised the possibility that the totality of private consumer decisions in the marketplace—thousands of colonial strangers indulging their "Horseleech Desires"—could have major, quite negative consequences on the common good. The luxury debate also revealed a well-developed capacity to blame someone else for one's own lack of control.

Women, of course, had been accused of disorderly conduct for a very long time. As the daughters of Eve, they regularly led unsuspecting males into temptation. During the seventeenth century, they often found themselves embroiled in religious controversies, and the more assertive among them, like Anne Hutchinson, had voiced the possibilities of dissent from the established churches.[87] But the Jezebels of the consumer revolution beguiled men—husbands and lovers—not into theological error but into effeminate luxury. They spoke of heresies in the marketplace; they beckoned innocent males into purchasing imported British goods beyond their means. As a Charleston article entitled "NEW THOUGHTS upon LUXURY" warned, "The manners of women merit . . . a singular attention. When everything is allowed them, and we shut our eyes to their conduct, they give into finery and bagatelle with fury, and fill up the very measure of luxury."[88] The complaint against women derived its force from the fact that real women from New England to the Carolinas were suddenly making decisions about how to allocate family resources. In other words, the castigating rhetoric that appeared in the newspapers and the sermons of the period was a particularly shrill response to a changing market culture. As "Atticus" explained in the *Pennsylvania Gazette,* colonists were trying to make sense of a flood of new items "which were unadmitted in the happy days of our forefathers."[89]

The downfall of eighteenth-century American women was a tale told in terms of cloth. Everywhere colonial males looked, they were confronted by females decked out in gayly colored "Silks and Lawn" tailored to the latest fashion. Their bodies had become a highly visible index to the advance of luxury, and judging from the reports found in colonial newspapers, the prospects of avoiding the kind of catastrophe that had befallen Rome must not have seemed promising. According to "Intonsus Cato," a beleaguered Connecticut male, it did not require much intelligence to predict the future of a society in which men allowed their wives and daughters to "use Cambrick, and Velvet, for their ordinary Wear, and spend more than Half their time in Cards, Visits, Dances, Talk and Tea."[90] Another writer, who appeared originally in the *American Magazine,* put forward a more imaginative argument, explaining that most of what had gone wrong in contemporary society could be attributed to "Female Dress." At the dawn of time, it seems, people had apparently been quite content to go about their business covered only in animal skins. But the age of commerce—and here he meant the rise of a consumer economy—had generated entirely new tastes. "As Men grew rich and ingenious," he lectured, "something new always presented [itself], wherewith to decorate and oblige the Ladies." However patronizing the generous males may have been, the women took advantage of the situation to make consumer decisions of their own. In an effort to please the men in their lives, they "became studious how to apply their Gifts, so as [they] might at once render themselves more amiable, and express their Regard for the kind Donors. This naturally enough produc'd an Attention to Dress." Indeed, it did, at an almost explosive pace. Women had worn basically the same sorts of garments from the Norman conquest to the seventeenth century. But within living memory, fashion had kicked into high gear, and almost overnight women had become "the Slaves of *French* Whims, Fancies, and Conceits."[91] No one could tell how far these trends would go. In 1755 a Boston newspaper predicted that women would soon appear in public with "no other Covering than the original Fig-Leaf." Why, the writer asked, should anyone be shocked? After all, he exclaimed, "considering the present Dress of our Women of Fashion, there remains no further Step to be taken except absolute Nakedness."[92]

What made the situation even harder for men to accept was that these female slaves to fashion seemed to have minds of their own. They expressed a troubling assertiveness precisely by selecting one color over another, one fabric over an alternative. The author of an essay in the *Pennsylvania Chronicle,* identifying himself as "A Sincere Admirer, but no Flatterer of the Fair-Sex," concluded that self-fashioning had gone far enough. Honest men, he maintained, detested false ornamentation and painted faces. Women who ignored this good advice from concerned males had only themselves to blame for whatever disappointment might befall them. "If it is the ambition of the ladies to appear handsome *in their own eyes only,*" he observed defensively, "they are at liberty, without doubt, to do it in what manner they think proper, and to follow their own fancy, *in the choice* of their dress and ornament."[93] It sounded like a dare, one that John Brown, a popular moral commentator in the colonies, assumed that modern women would surely accept. His own interpretation of recent cultural history concluded: "The Sexes have now little other apparent Distinction, beyond that of Person and Dress: Their peculiar and characteristic Manners are confounded and lost: The one Sex having advanced into *Boldness*, as the other have sunk into *Effeminacy*."[94]

These new bolder women drank tea. So too did a rapidly growing number of other colonists, but by the middle of the eighteenth century the complex ritual associated with serving tea in one's home—the proper use of "Cups, Saucers, Slop-Basin, etc."—had become closely associated with independent women making decisions in the marketplace.[95] In 1746 one female writer complained that the "Male Readers" of the local newspaper had described tea as "a *Female Luxury.*" She rightly observed that her male friends were as "great *Tea-Sots* as any of us," but that was not exactly the point.[96] The afternoon tea parties represented more than social events where friends sipped a faddish hot drink. Within the framework of a developing consumer economy, such gatherings allowed women to carve out a gendered space in which they exercised a measure of control. In these situations, they determined the rules of engagement; they defined the character of a cultural moment already known at mid-century as "the Ceremony of the Tea-Table."[97] Men could be taught how to behave in the salon, but, as a New York writer observed, the instructor would most certainly have to be a woman. One male had the temerity to tell "those dear Creatures" how best to brew tea. "Publicolus" convinced himself that copper kettles—as opposed to those made of iron—were "prejudicial to their Health," but his cautious tone suggests that he knew he was fighting a losing battle. Health hazard or not, tea was the province of women. As the author declared, if the modern women did not believe him about the copper, then "your Grandmothers will tell you."[98]

Tea talk raised other concerns. Within a discourse of threatened masculinity, men worried that the gaily dressed tea drinkers might be gossiping about manly affairs, such as which local merchants were most worthy of credit.[99] In 1754 another male commentator wondered whether the female tea drinkers ever bothered with heady matters such as the pernicious attacks "upon *English Liberty.*" In an effort to enlist their support, he expressed a patronizing "hope [that] the Tea-Tables and other *Female Associations* will take this Affair into their serious Consideration, and use their Influence, as the *Roman* Matrons did formerly, to save the State."[100] All this rhetoric, of course, has a distinctly middle-class ring. But the symbolic link between women and tea extended to the lower orders, and while they may have organized cultural space around breakfast rather than afternoon levees, they too understood how to manipulate the props of the new material culture for their own purposes.[101] Peter Kalm, for example, the respected Swedish scientist who toured colonial America at mid-century, thought that tea explained why ordinary American women had such bad teeth. "I then began to suspect the tea," Kalm reported from New York, "which is drunk here in the morning and afternoon, especially by women, and is so common at present that there is hardly a farmer's wife or poor woman who does not drink tea in the morning."[102]

The tea ceremony brought family members together in complex rituals involving an impressive array of imported goods. *"A Family Being Served Tea." Artist unknown, ca. 1740–5. Courtesy of the Yale Center for British Art, Paul Mellon Collection.*

Skirmishes over the gendered etiquette of the tea service had a counterpart in ongoing negotiations over the nature of marriage. How men and women expect spouses to behave in a relationship has been a bone of contention for at least as long as societies have kept records. The character of the cultural debate has evolved over the centuries, but in general it would be fair to state that the battle of the sexes has usually been waged over issues of freedom and control. In this respect, mid-eighteenth-century America was no exception. What distinguished the sparring between men and women was not the clash between authority and independence but rather how the participants so self-consciously defined these tensions within the context of a rapidly changing consumer culture. An economy organized increasingly around the distribution and sale of household goods imported from Britain invited women to imagine new social opportunities, in other words, to think of their life chances in terms of choice.

In 1740 a Boston newspaper published an essay entitled "A New Method for Making Women as Useful and as Capable of Maintaining Themselves, as the Men are. . . ." Although one can never be certain about the identity of an anonymous author, the piece claimed to be the work of "a Lady." The article began conventionally enough by observing that the education that women received was not appropriate to the needs of an expanding commercial society. The skills that women acquired as children amounted to "Trifles." But such an ill-conceived curriculum could easily be remedied if young girls of fifteen or sixteen years of age were encouraged to apply their knowledge of needlework to real business situations. Instead of indulging themselves in idleness and luxury—as many contemporary males complained—they could take positions as "Apprentices to genteel and easy Trades, such as Linen or Woollen Drapers, Haberdashers of small Wares, Mercers, Glovers, Perfumers, Grocers, Confectioners, Retailers of Gold and Silver Lace, Buttons, etc." This was a brilliant rhetorical move. Since women were so identified in the popular culture with consumer goods, then "a Lady" did not see why they should not apply what they had learned specifically as women to the marketplace.

> Why are not these as credible Trades for the Daughters of Gentlemen as they are for their Sons; and all of them more proper for Women than Men? Is it not as agreeable and becoming for Women to be employ'd in selling a Farthing's worth of Needles, a Halfpenny of Lace, a Quarter of a Yard of Silk, Stuff, or Cambricks, as it is absurd or ridiculous to see a Parcel of young Fellows, dish'd out in their Tie Wigs and Ruffles . . . busied in Professions so much below the Honour and Dignity of their Sex?

"A Lady" anticipated resistance to her proposal. But she would have none of it, for, in fact, women could not only "weigh and measure" as well as men but also "buy as cheap, and perhaps cheaper." The reason for their relative success in business was that men spent too much time in "Taverns and Coffee houses" after completing a deal, while women "go directly Home, and follow their Affairs."[103] The slaves of fashion had devised a way to transform an alleged weakness into freedom.

"A Lady" probably represented the worst nightmare for many colonial males during this period. Beware, one explained, of women who view marriage as "the gilded pill of liberty, authority, privilege and equality." The quotation came from an essay fetchingly entitled "A Letter from an Uncle to his new married Niece, with Advice how to conduct herself in her present state." The editor of the *Boston Evening-Post* had apparently come across the piece in the *New Universal Magazine* and immediately concluded that it spoke truth to "uppity" American women. "This most excellent Letter is now published," he noted, "for the Perusal of our *Female Readers*, [and] ... we could not think of a more valuable or a more seasonable Present."[104] He knew that his male subscribers did not want the objects of their affections either working in retail shops or spending their husbands' hard-earned money on more British baubles.

The ideal marriage partner in a society that presented so many choices would without doubt possess "*Industry, Frugality,* and *Religion.*"[105] That logic seemed to energize "U. Loverule" as he penned "Offences Against Common Sense in the Ladies, Particularly Wives." In his opinion, too many modern women approached social life with "immoderate Zeal." He begged his readers in South Carolina to consider the long-suffering husband of "Phillis." This invented figure "is the discontented Mate of a sober honest Tradesman, but would fain to pass upon the World for a Woman of Fashion: She *dyes, alters,* and *turns* her little Stock of Finery into all the Changes of Fancy and Affection." One might conclude that Phillis should be congratulated for so cleverly mixing and matching within a small wardrobe, but U. Loverule knew better. He insisted on full patriarchal authority. Colonial women should give up even trying to be "the finest" or "the best dress'd." Indeed, there could be no compromise. "I would banish every violent Attachment, whatever be the Object of it," he growled. "Lap-Dogs or Children, female Friends, or, what is often the Disguise of bad Purposes, the innocent Desire of public Approbation; For every attachment, when indulg'd, will engross too much of the female Mind, and leave too little Room for domestick Care." Virtuous men like U. Loverule longed to find a kind of classical republican woman, obedient, self-sacrificing, inured to "Magnificence," and dedicated to "elegant Frugality." Wives of this sort would stand by their men—the Catos of South Carolina—and, in the political sphere, help them restore the community's "lost Spirit of Independence." The only problem was that republican women were probably a little boring, and one can understand why the honest tradesmen of America went for "Phillis" every time.[106]

In Connecticut, women of Phillis's temperament had participated in a courtship conspiracy. They regularly trapped naive and trusting lads. " 'Tis well known," a Hartford newspaper announced, "that the principal Design of the unmarried Part of Womankind (the Part most addicted to extravagant Expense) is, to make themselves amiable in the Eyes of the other Sex." The expense, of course, went to pay for consumer goods, and it was the women who were making the decisions about which items to purchase. The prospect was daunting: legions of calculating although highly desirable women whose consumer activities threatened to bankrupt the entire Connecticut economy. This is a curiously ironic argument, considering that in contemporary novels it was usually the innocent women who became the victims of improvident men. The author of this desperate admonition decided to give the seducers a basic lesson in domestic bookkeeping. "All these Ladies cannot expect to obtain Husbands able to support them and their Children in Grandeur and Inactivity, for which a Husband must be worth £200 per Annum." Could women of such luxurious tastes not see the unhappy future that awaited their sons and daughters? The writer even raised the specter of "Children who are to have Poverty entailed on them by their Parents' Idleness and Pride, to be tainted by their Parents' bad Example; who are likely to be left in such a Condition as to be necessitated either to starve, or procure their Livelihood in some dishonest Way."[107]

Even a respected clergyman such as Jonathan Mayhew felt compelled to take up the complaint about the rising material expectations that seemed to be undermining the institution of marriage. Although he did not depict the issue in terms of a female conspiracy, he did think that the children of the colonial middle class faced a serious problem. "Among the numerous bad effects of pride and luxury in life," Mayhew observed, "the prevention of MARRIAGE is not the least." The young demanded instant gratification, not, as one might predict, in terms of physical fulfillment but rather in terms of a luxurious style of life to which they had become accustomed. They wanted all the nice things that they had enjoyed while growing up, and when they discovered that the normal expenses connected with marriage and children might deprive them of such pleasurable goods, they refused marriage, thus failing to "comply with the order of God and nature." Like an aging and angry King Lear confronting a generation of yuppies, Mayhew pilloried the "irrational" insistence of young men and women that they "should expect to begin the world with as much equipage and grandeur, or to live *at first* in as sumptuous a manner as their parents could well do *at last,* after having, by the blessing of God on many years industry, acquired riches." What, he asked the children, did they want the parents to do? "Can any expect that their parents should either make away with themselves, or give up all to them while they live?" The representatives of what Mayhew called the "amiable sex" were as bad as the men, for the women preferred the single state over marriage to a person who could not maintain them "in as genteel and grand a manner as that, in which they were brought up in their fathers' houses; or that in which they see some of their contemporaries live."[108]

For all their fulminations against the women who purchased the alluring objects sold on the "Proud-lanes" of colonial America, the males who criticized female consumers do not seem to have made the slightest dent in the everyday practices of getting and spending. The rhetoric about bankruptcy and celibacy, about moral weakness and fatal luxury, about working women and the dangers of the tea ceremony, represented doomed attempts to control a new generation of women who had grown accustomed to making choices in the marketplace. We should not overinterpret this evidence.

Access to an exciting range of imported British goods most certainly did not radically change the social and political life of American women, either as daughters or as wives, for, whatever they managed to acquire, they remained under stifling legal constraints. But participation in the empire of goods could have unanticipated consequences for women, indeed, for some even a growing sense of empowerment. As we turn to the mobilization of a colonial people against the power of Great Britain—a protest that organized itself around massive consumer boycotts—we can appreciate the need to include women in an expanded story of revolutionary politics, for if the men who led the movement had been unable to persuade colonial women to sacrifice the pleasures of the marketplace, independence would have remained but a dream.

VI

Other people, fighting on other rhetorical grounds of battle, sought to contain the spreading consumer culture. In this losing battle against a new consumer culture, Protestant ministers played a curiously ineffective part. Worldly pleasures generally struck ordinary Americans as more attractive than religious asceticism. On this point, people drinking in Connecticut taverns told an amusing story about a clergyman who had tried to turn back the flood of imported British fineries. Early in 1743 the Reverend James Davenport had brought the full blast of the Great Awakening to the colony. Other evangelical ministers who followed in the footsteps of the Reverend George Whitefield criticized the established clergy of New England, but none of them went quite so far in stirring up religious passions as Davenport. The itinerant visited New London, and there, according to a person who claimed to have witnessed what occurred, he informed the people who flocked to hear him that they had "made Idols of their Gay Cloaths." The anxious sinners debated among themselves whether the offending garments ought to be consigned to a large bonfire in the center of the town. Some people seeking the New Birth did not initially comprehend the logic behind the appeal to burn their possessions. One man declared that "he could scarce see how [Davenport's] disliking the Night-Gown that he had on his Back, should render him guilty of Idolatry." But such concerns were quickly brushed aside. The true believers began stripping, women as well as men. "The Women brought in their Scarlet Cloaks, Velvet Hoods, fine Laces, and every Thing that had two Colours," a Boston journal reported, "so that it is supposed the Heap of *Women's Idols*, and the Men's Wigs, Velvet Collars, &c. &c. is worth three or four hundred Pounds." Davenport consulted the Lord, and having satisfied himself that he was purging New London of sin, he took off all that he had been wearing. He then ordered the conflagration to start. Only nothing happened. At the last possible second, the people in the crowd had second thoughts, and just before the fire was lit, the semi-nude citizens rushed to rescue their clothes. A newspaper observed that the items were "*Reprieved* from the Flames . . . and that every Bird has taken its own Feather[s] again."[109]

About a year later Dr. Alexander Hamilton found himself in a New London tavern, where he "sat drinking of punch, and telling of droll stories" with some of the locals. One of them informed Hamilton about Davenport, whom he called "a fanatick preacher." And, indeed, by that time the Connecticut government had declared the minister *non compos mentis.* The narrator confirmed that the women had enthusiastically supported the call to burn the false idols of the marketplace, only in this telling of the story the list of consumer goods had expanded. "The women," Hamilton learned, "made up a lofty pile of hoop petticoats, silk gowns, short cloaks, cambrick caps, red-heeled shoes, fans, necklaces, gloves, and other such apparel." At that moment, Davenport took off his pants and placed them on the very top of the collection. But reason miraculously prevailed. A "moderate" managed to persuade his neighbors that "making such a sacrifice was not necessary for their salvation." And that was probably a lucky turn of events for Davenport, since if his own breeches had gone up in flames, he "would have been obliged to strutt about bare-arsed."[110] The final line surely sparked a hearty laugh. It impressed Hamilton enough that he took down every word of the anecdote in his personal journal.

What made the story funny was the force of common sense. Only persons who had completely lost their senses could possibly throw their clothes onto a bonfire of vanities. It was one thing to walk many miles in the snow to hear an evangelical preacher describe the New Birth. It was quite another to sacrifice all those consumer goods that had cost so much to acquire. The moderate enthusiast who saved Davenport's pants probably spoke for the great majority of the American people. They listened more or less politely to social superiors who told them that indulging themselves in so much finery overturned the proper order of society. And then they returned to the stores. They heard those who said that consuming women were a threat to male authority. And then they ordered more imported goods from Great Britain. The rhetoric of denial that has captured the imagination of so many modern historians—discourses of moral reform—appears at the end of the day not to have made much impact on the colonists themselves. Stories similar to the one repeated in New London echoed in other places, suggesting that consumers in Pennsylvania and South Carolina shared the logic of the Connecticut moderate. When a Philadelphia Quaker, described in the newspaper as a "Pythagorean-cynical-Christian Philosopher," decided to bear public witness against the vanity of tea drinking by destroying a huge assemblage of china in a central square, he was immediately "interrupted by the Populace." They stormed the "stall on which he had placed the Box of Wares" and grabbed whatever could be saved. They offered to pay him for the pieces, but, being quite insane, he refused to negotiate.[111] And when an itinerant minister arrived in Charleston, eager to condemn "the splendid Equipage" of that city, he received a cool reception. One hard-nosed consumer announced that it was not in the preacher's power to persuade "any rational Man from a clean Shirt on his Back, and a warm House o'er his Head, or a good Dish of Meat and a Bottle of Wine for his Dinner, if he has either Money or Credit to procure them."[112] Colonists who did have money and credit continued to go about their business, preferring the good life to the simple life, and, as we shall discover, while most of them did not bother to comment directly on their activities, a few began to speak of *choice* as a *right,* a development that indicated that the daily experience of making selections from among competing goods and of spending one's money however one desired was acquiring an ideological voice.

If evangelical pronouncements against an idolatrous material culture fell on deaf ears, so too did hectoring by the members of the ruling elites. However strenuously the colonial gentry railed against luxury—and by this, they generally meant other people's buying habits—they found that the market itself undermined the very categories they employed to control the consumer demand of those consigned to the lower and middling orders. In theory, it was easy enough to identify a luxury item. An object such as a diamond necklace or a gold ornament was so expensive that only the most wealthy, and presumably the most cultivated men and women in society could possibly afford it. Indeed, those who tried so hard to check other people's spending divided the goods of the marketplace into three deceptively neat categories: superfluities, necessaries, and conveniencies.

The critics of luxury who importuned the poorer sorts to content themselves with basic needs soon discovered, however, that the categories would not hold. The language itself was quicksand. The market moved too swiftly to allow anyone to distinguish with confidence the difference between a superfluity and a convenience, for what was perceived at one moment as a luxury could within a short time be seen by consumers as a necessity. This instability presented a real interpretive challenge. After all, if the upper classes accused everyone else of corrupting the public virtue and called them back to industry and diligence, it helped to know just what kind of sacrifice they had in mind. Many developments explained the difficulty of pinning down the meaning of words that allegedly carried such far-reaching moral significance. The language problem was exacerbated by new manufacturing technologies that lowered prices, access to cheaper copies of more expensive imports, rising real wages that made it possible for ordinary people to acquire more goods, and a willingness in even modest households to forgo the purchase of plain objects in favor of a few exceptional pieces.[113]

A writer in the *Independent Advertiser* tried unsuccessfully to negotiate the shifting categories. He began with a thunderous attack on "LUXURY AND EXTRAVAGANCE," the capital letters reinforcing the message that these were terms of opprobrium. Luxury was a vice capable of destroying the commonwealth. "Especially does this appear likely to happen," he warned, "when this Contagion has infected the lower Sort of People (as it has apparently among us) by whose Labour and the Sweat of whose Brows the Community should draw its chief Support." But then, when it actually came to defining the evil indulgence, the writer had to admit, "There is indeed (it must be allowed) a *certain Degree* to which *Luxury* may be tolerated, and in which it contributes its Part toward Happiness and Support of the State, especially a trading one; and it may perhaps be difficult to fix the precise Boundaries; or to determine exactly the *very Point* where it becomes exorbitant and dangerous."[114] This loose definition would not have been very helpful to "the lower Sort of People," anxious presumably about the charge of promoting vice. The author's treatment of luxury was a little like the United States Supreme Court's of pornography; the justices have been unable to determine precisely what pornography is, but they insist that they would be able to identify it if they ever saw it.

Other colonists eager to stamp out the degeneracy associated with extravagance found that they were chasing a moving target. "Mentor"—a writer who appeared in a number of different newspapers—complained that in a rapidly changing marketplace luxury goods soon became items of everyday consumption. "Thus," he announced, "a whole nation habituates itself to look upon the most superfluous things as the necessaries of life; and thus every day brings forth some new necessity of the same kind." The problem in a nutshell was that "men can no longer live without things, which but thirty years ago were utterly unknown to them."[115] He was speaking from experience. Once china ranked as a luxury in the colonies, but, as we have seen, it became common enough in Philadelphia that a deranged person could take a hammer to a crate of cups and saucers in a public square. Once the women of New London had not been able to afford two-color fabrics, but by the 1740s such cloth was merely one of many imported goods that had reached a modest farming community on the edge of empire.

Although the moral critics of luxury pounded away in sermons and newspaper essays, they did not carry the day. Other colonial writers began to suggest that, far from leading to universal vice, extravagance might under some circumstances yield real benefits. "Publius Agricola" ridiculed the "*abstemious Sages*" who abstracted morality from actual market expectations and who tried to persuade ordinary people that their desire for expensive imports was "*unreal and imaginary,*" in other words, an artificial and irrational inflation of human need. The author dismissed such cultural theory as out of touch with "the numerous Herd of Mankind." To claim that the wants of the middling sorts of people were invented—a figment of commercial fantasy— missed the central psychological elements driving eighteenth-century consumers. "When Industry has furnished any Person with the indispensable Necessaries of Life, such as *Food, Raiment,* and *Lodging,* he rests not there, but proceeds to *Luxury,* the *Bane* of Wealth, to create new Wants, which are so far real, as they prompt and excite us to Action and Industry; without it, Life would be tasteless, and a heavy Burden." "Publius Agricola" could well ask the moralists—be they civic humanists of the republican tradition or traditional religious spokesmen—why anyone would bother to work if there were no prospect of supplying "the Delicacies and Conveniences of Life." The answer, of course, was that the true end of labor was "to acquire Wealth, and [to] have it in his Power to gratify every Appetite, and Every Desire."[116]

Another author known to his readers only as "X" saw no justification for prohibiting people from buying whatever they could afford. "Man in his nature," he explained, "is a progressive being, with the rude materials put into his hands, he naturally rises, from the necessaries of life, to the conveniences, the delicacies, and the luxuries."[117] Reckless and irresponsible spending on imported goods could become addictive; it could ruin families and reveal a need for greater self-control. But turning the exceptional case into an excuse for restricting the normal ambition for a better life made no sense. One essay even insisted that consumers promoted the common good. As he argued, "Whilst things are in their own Nature necessary to us, or, from Custom and Fancy, made necessary, we will be turning every thought to come at them; and where they cannot be got by Violence and Rapine, Recourse will be had to Invention and Industry."[118]

And, indeed, the desire to obtain imported British goods did promote

Like so many other colonial Americans, this man from central Massachusetts took pride in his material possessions, many of which had been imported from England. *Overmantel panel from the mid-eighteenth-century house owned by Mose Marcy in Southbridge, Massachusetts. Unidentified artist, oil on wood panel. Collection of Old Sturbridge Village, 20.19.1. Photography by Henry E. Peach.*

a surge of invention and industry in colonial America before the final constitutional crisis fractured the empire. We have concerned ourselves mostly with the acquisition of goods. It would be misleading, however, to leave the impression that provincial farmers did not appreciate the close relationship between consumption and production. As Jan de Vries, a comparative economic historian of the eighteenth century, has discovered in western Europe and North America, ordinary men and women were willing to work harder so that they would have more household resources to spend on manufactured goods. Families reallocated labor so that women and children who at an earlier time had devoted themselves to producing basic items such as cloth in the home turned increasingly to assisting the adult males in the fields or in commercial activities that would generate hard currency. This radical shift—de Vries calls it the "industrious revolution"—expanded income, which in turn enhanced the buying power of each family unit. With more money in their pockets, colonial Americans were able to indulge new tastes and acquire goods of their own choosing.[119] The Reverend Jared Eliot, a Connecticut essayist who urged contemporaries to develop more productive farming techniques, imagined his audience as made up of people already fully accommodated to a commercial mentality. Whenever they sensed a market opportunity, they exploited it until it could absorb no more colonial staples. "We glut the markets every where," Eliot observed, "if we hear of a market, if we can come at it by land, we run, ride, and drive, till we have overstocked it; by sea we are all afloat, sailing till provisions may be purchased cheaper there, than at home." To pay for their ever growing consumption of British imports, Eliot told the converts to the industrious revolution to experiment with new products. He recommended silk, not only because it represented a potentially lucrative export but also because "the raising [of] silk may, in all its parts, be performed by women, children, cripples, and aged persons."[120] The women who were described in the moral discourse on luxury as idle and frivolous appeared in the literature of industry and invention as a large, untapped labor force. In 1754 the Society for Encouraging Industry in Massachusetts explained that because the colony could not sustain sufficient flocks of sheep—the climate was too harsh—it had to import large quantities of woollen goods from Great Britain. The problem extended to "pewter, Brass, and other Commodities bro't from thence, that we cannot subsist without, nor produce our selves, [and which] will require all we can procure for Exportation to make Returns." The Society thought the answer was linen. The new enterprise seemed especially appropriate, since it would "employ our own Women and Children, who are now in a great measure idle."[121]

During the 1740s intellectual issues associated with the luxury debate spilled over into the political sphere. Many colonies, chronically lacking a sufficient supply of hard currency with which to conduct normal commerce, began to print paper money. This response to the problem sparked a firestorm of protest from the merchant community as well as from royal officials convinced that the British government would take a dim view of the issuance of provincial bills unsecured by either gold or silver. The controversy raged most fiercely in Massachusetts, where opponents of the paper currency trotted out a number of arguments ridiculing plans for soft money. This colony had in fact long circulated limited amounts of paper bills, but the new scheme permitting private banks to issue many more notes provoked a crisis. The paper currency, opponents claimed, would only increase the colony's growing indebtedness to Great Britain, lead to explosive inflation, and bankrupt honest merchants, who expected proper payment in specie. These well-worked themes did not go to the cultural and ideological heart of the dispute, however, for woven into much of the acrimonious rhetoric was the assumption that a larger, more accessible supply of money would further stimulate the consumption of imported goods.

From the perspective of the hard-money advocates that seemed a most unwelcome development, and while no persuasive evidence demonstrates that the public battle pitted the haves against the have nots, the language employed by the adversaries suggests that they saw paper money in terms of a struggle between freedom and control in the consumer marketplace.

"Philalethes," for example, blamed "*the Floods of European Goods imported,* [on] . . . the *Floods of Paper Bills emitted.*"[122] The logic was simple: The more paper money the colonies printed, the more the people would flock to the stores. Another writer pointedly asked, "What has produc'd our Extravagancy so much for these 20 or 30 Years past, as our Paper Money? . . . It is that which in a great Measure has encourag'd the vast Import of Commodities more than we want, & prevented People's improving & Wearing their own Manufactures; & so long as they can be furnish'd with it for almost nothing at all, it never will be otherwise."[123] When one reads a passage of this sort, one wonders why the author distinguished between the "we" and the "people." Surely the men and women who wanted to curtail the currency supply, and thereby deny the people a chance to purchase additional imported goods, did not propose to sacrifice their own pleasures in the market. Presumably they possessed characters strong enough to resist the debilitating consequences of luxury. The others were best advised to restrict their desires to those objects that could be made in the home or by local craftsmen.

Pitted against the champions of hard money were colonists of various backgrounds who had become accustomed to making choices and fashioning themselves as they alone saw fit. For them the value of things on the market was determined not by the supply of gold and silver but rather by decisions taken by innumerable consumers. As one writer in the midst of the currency controversy explained, the real value of an item was a function of what a person was willing to pay for it. Articles such as colorful imported cloth were not intrinsically cheap or expensive. "These [consumer goods] have their Value or Estimation from the *voluntary Choice* of Mankind, guided either by Reason, or mere Humour & Fancy, in choosing one thing and neglecting or refusing another at one Time, and again choosing what they before neglected or refused." The prose was awkward, but there could be no doubt about the author's sentiments. Since market values "change with the Fashion for the Year or a particular Season," it was proper state policy to let the people act openly and freely and without concern for currency restrictions that denied them the chance to make meaningful choices.[124]

In Boston, at least, a strange quirk in how imported goods were actually merchandised exacerbated political tensions. Because the city had long suffered from an insufficient supply of money—too little specie, not enough paper—the merchants resorted to something called the "Truck-Trade" or "Shop Notes." Laborers brought to retail stores various products, which they then exchanged for "Shop Notes," certificates allowing the holder to demand goods at some future date. They received the certificates in lieu of a full cash payment. When these workers later presented their "Shop Notes" at the local stores, however, they discovered that the notes had been heavily discounted, perhaps by as much as a quarter, so that they did not purchase as many items as a cash customer would have obtained with the same nominal amount of money. Moreover, the shopkeepers pushed goods onto the

Jolley Allen fully appreciated the importance of consumer choice for mid-century colonial Americans. *Boston Post-Boy*, 4 July 1768. *Courtesy of the Massachusetts Historical Society.*

vulnerable laborers that they did not necessarily want, often things so outrageously inappropriate that the moral critics accused the urban poor of being fools for luxury. As one writer observed, however, there were "Hundreds of honest House-keepers, who, if they were paid in Cash for their Work, would many times look on their Money before they would give it to buy their Wives and Daughters Velvet Hoods, red Cloaks, or Silk Garments."[125] In 1741 the caulkers of Boston—men who labored on the ropewalks—announced that they would no longer accept "Notes on Shops for Money and Goods." These laborers would take only "good lawful publick bills of Credit," promissory notes from established merchants, or farm commodities "at the Price currant, or Market Price." The caulkers hoped that "this good and commendable Example will soon be follow'd by Numbers of other Artificers and Tradesmen."[126] At stake in this protest was not a call for more money or better working conditions, however important such considerations may have been. Like so many other men and women just getting by in Boston, the caulkers insisted simply on enjoying genuine and equal consumer choice.[127]

Within this contentious environment some colonists took an ideological step of immense significance. They started discussing the "*voluntary Choice* of Mankind" within a regime of human rights. The language of rights had been around for a long time, and even if mid-eighteenth-century Americans did not closely analyze the political philosophy of John Locke, they understood fully the thrust of his thinking. The rights discourse had begun to influence how people worked out the meaning of religious toleration in this society.[128] The claim made here, therefore, is not that the experience of living in a robust consumer marketplace caused liberalism or that it directly explains the subsequent popularity of Locke's *Second Treatise* among the revolutionary generation. Whatever the long-term possibilities may have been, however, it seems clear that within this particular context—a colonial society dependent on imported consumer goods—the concept of freedom of choice was elevated into a right, and within that mental framework, choice no longer had to be defended on purely prudential or historical grounds. From this perspective, rights talk not only gave ordinary men and women an effective language with which to resist the controlling logic of classical republican and traditional theology but also made it possible to conceive of the pursuit of happiness as something more exalted than a vulgar concern for economic self-interest.[129]

Within this interpretive context, one text brilliantly captured the move from experience to ideology. We do not know the identity of the author of *The Good of the Community Impartially Considered, in a Letter to a Merchant in Boston.* He called himself "Rusticus." Writing in 1754 during a dispute over a proposed excise tax that would have allowed inspectors appointed by the colonial government of Massachusetts to monitor the private consumption of certain items, he explored the liberating assumptions that the new commercial society had brought into play. To an imaginary disputant who favored the excise, he responded, "I am really afraid, Sir, the most discerning Sort of Men will think you are aiming to throw the Burthen of the Taxes upon the poorer Sort of People, while you yourself are desirous of *wallowing freely* in all the Luxuries of Life." In other words, the issue was not consumption itself, but rather, the conditions under which others would be allowed to pursue material happiness. "Rusticus" conceded that all citizens had an obligation to work for the common good. They should pay taxes. What was unacceptable was an assessment that hit the "poorer Sorts" harder than it did the upper classes.

> To what Purpose is it, that Mankind *Work*, and *Toil*, and *Slave* themselves, unless they may be allow'd to enjoy all the Comforts of Life, they had as good be in a State of Nature, and eat and drink nothing but the natural Fruits of the Earth?

The answer was that no one would volunteer to be a member of such a joyless society. Without real incentives people would lose direction, becoming idle and despondent. After all, "the Enjoyment of Property is the Aim of all Mankind; and the Foundation of their ent[e]ring into Societies." We note that the author has not said that it is a concern over the security of property that draws people into a social contract. In this American version of Locke, "Enjoyment" has been silently substituted for security, and we find ourselves suddenly engaged in a pursuit of happiness. The next move in the argument elegantly employs the defiant language of rights as a means to resist the claims of class:

> Surely, a poor Man's Liberty is as dear to him, as a rich Man's; how unjust is it then for the Government, to burthen them with a Tax, which the Rich are not burthen'd with? Every Man has a *natural Right* to enjoy the Fruit of his own Labour, both as to the *Conveniencies*, and *Comforts*, as well as the *Necessaries* of Life; *natural Liberty* is the same with one Man, as another; and unless in the Enjoyment of these Things they hurt the Community, the Poor ought to be *allow'd* to use them as freely as the Rich.—But such is the Perverseness of human Nature, that when a Man arises to any tolerable Degree of Fortune, he begins to think all below him were made for his Service, and that they have no Right to any Thing but what is despised & refused by him. We could very well be contented with this, if these Gentlemen would but let us enjoy such Things as we were able to purchase, *freely*; or with the same Freedom [that] they are allow'd to do it.[130]

"Rusticus" managed in a short pamphlet to link a political crisis to the purchase of consumer goods. He demonstrated that behind the seeming benign cultural vocabulary of politeness and gentility lurked philosophic concerns about power, equality, and freedom. And although he did not anticipate the coming of the American Revolution, he did suggest how ordinary people might communicate to each other about natural rights through the experience of making choices in a consumer marketplace. As a modern anthropologist might say, for them, goods were good to think.[131]

VII

At the end of the day, an empire of goods came to impede the pursuit of personal happiness. As we turn our attention in the second half of this study to the sudden and dramatic politicization of a vast colonial market—to the organization of massive boycotts—we must remind ourselves that only people who had experienced within their own families the pleasures and frustrations of so many consumer choices could possibly have come to appreciate how a disruption of that market might be an effective weapon in a contest against a Parliament that appeared to rate its own sovereignty above commercial prosperity. In these chapters, we have demonstrated from different perspectives how British imports transformed everyday life in colonial America for the great mass of middling men and women who would soon be asked to sacrifice their own common goods for a common good which none of them could have imagined before 1763. When the crisis arrived, these consumers more than met the challenge.

Part Two

"A Commercial Plan of Political Salvation"

6

Strength out of Dependence: Strategies of Consumer Resistance in an Empire of Goods

No one knows when precisely American public opinion first realized that imported goods provided powerful political leverage within the empire. Such discoveries usually result from a slow, cumulative conviction that the taken-for-granted of everyday life has possibilities that no one only a few years earlier quite perceived. But insomuch as there was a moment when inchoate thoughts about consumer dependence crystallized into firm belief, it occurred in mid-February 1766. On the eleventh of that month the rulers of Great Britain received a lecture from a celebrated American about the radical potential of the goods exported across the Atlantic. The British House of Commons, sitting as a committee of the whole, had just launched a painful review of what seemed to many members a flawed colonial policy. Violent American resistance to the Stamp Act had taken them by surprise, and now, confused and angered by the turn of events, they gathered information on how best to respond to an imperial crisis brought on by their own decision to collect new revenues in America.[1] Not until the third day of the proceedings did they summon Dr. Benjamin Franklin. Everyone knew in advance that he would be the star witness.

On this stage Franklin performed brilliantly, as, of course, he knew he would. He had carefully rehearsed his lines. The initial question—a seemingly straightforward declaration of identity—set the theatrical tone for a marathon exchange.

Q. What is your name, and place of abode?
A. Franklin, of Philadelphia.

The ambitious provincial had long ago learned how to play the part of the authentic American before an audience of English gentlemen of the sort elected to Parliament. His claim to be "Franklin, of Philadelphia"—a plain-speaking man from the colonies—betrayed a rhetorical strategy more artful than disingenuous. The people present that chilly afternoon recognized him for what he was: a distinguished scientist, prosperous entrepreneur, and cosmopolitan philosopher. Had he been anything less—had he not already crafted the character of the successful representative of an expansive Anglo-American culture—Franklin would probably have not been called at that critical moment to speak for the colonies.[2]

Whatever his qualifications, Franklin experienced rough handling from the House of Commons. Over several grueling hours, he endured some 174 questions, 89 of which he classified as antagonistic.[3] Try as they would, however, his interrogators could not control the proceedings. The nimble witness painted before their skeptical eyes a portrait of an expansive commercial empire, unprecedented in world history. Franklin warned Britain's rulers that unless they reconsidered taxing the colonists without representation and reformed new coercive modes of enforcement, they risked destroying the American goose that had laid so many golden eggs.

After an initial period of sparring, Franklin took charge of the exchange. The House of Commons wanted to know, for example, whether the colonists had merely used the passage of the Stamp Act as a convenient excuse to challenge imperial authority. Perhaps the Americans had long contemplated steering an independent political course. Perhaps recent revenue policies had only exacerbated tensions already present. Franklin dismissed that line of thought as nonsense. Before 1763, he insisted, the "temper" of the colonists toward Great Britain had been "the best in the world." What made their loyalty all the more impressive in his opinion was that it cost the Exchequer so little. Obedience never depended on "forts, citadels, garrisons or armies." The mere communication of command generated swift results in distant provinces, for, as the members of Parliament had obviously forgotten, the Americans "were governed by this country at the expense only of a little pen, ink and paper. They were led by a thread."

The image of imperial authority as a mere thread was inspired. This most gentle form of social and political control—English threads, not Spanish or French chains—explained the extraordinary might of the British Empire. The entire system drew strength not from military force but rather from shared values. The colonists, Franklin confessed, had "an affection, for Great-Britain, for its laws, its customs and manners, and even a fondness for its fashions, that greatly increased the commerce." And then, in a flash of rhetorical legerdemain, Franklin leapt from metaphorical "threads" of authority to the real manufactured threads that sustained the Atlantic economy, to the wool and cotton fibers woven into fashionable cloth which for a generation or more had transformed the very bodies of ordinary Americans into colorful emblems of a flourishing commercial empire. Statistics told a story of success. "I think the inhabitants of all the provinces together, taken at a medium, double in about 25 years," he explained. Stunning demographic growth only began to suggest the true potential of colonial trade. American demand, Franklin assured the members of Parliament, "increases much faster, as the consumption is not merely in proportion to their numbers, but grows with the growing abilities of the same numbers to pay for them. In 1723, the whole importation from Britain to Pennsylvania, was but about 15,000 Pounds Sterling; it is now near Half a Million."[4]

Commercial figures of this sort were, of course, old news. But Franklin interpreted the numbers in a strikingly innovative manner, pushing the political logic of everyday consumer demand in a direction that suggested that colonial buyers were neither as vulnerable nor as dependent as their British rulers may have imagined. In fact, the Stamp Act crisis had cast relations between Great Britain and the American colonies, between colonial consumers and English producers, in an entirely new light. No one had planned such a dramatic shift in political perspective. Reassessment of imperial identity simply evolved out of a confrontation with an aggressive House of Commons, an unintended consequence of an ill-conceived policy. And now, as a result of these events, the Americans began to appreciate that Britain's extraordinary commercial success in the New World had given them a voice in imperial affairs.

According to Franklin, those eager colonial customers who had been so willing for so long to part with their money, who accepted ever higher levels of debt as the inevitable burden of fulfilling material desire, and who had come to regard the exercise of choice in the marketplace as a right rather than a privilege could without a second thought reject the manufactured goods that flowed across the Atlantic. Indeed, the process had already begun. In some major port cities, American dry-goods merchants responding to popular political anger had canceled orders for imported manufactures. The market protests were growing. The colonists in a commercial empire had somehow forged a brilliantly innovative strategy. Before this time no other dependent people had so fully come to appreciate that their own economic dependence could be effectively translated into organized resistance, uniting anonymous consumers from Portsmouth to Savannah in a common enterprise that was itself a product of a commercial empire.

Some members of Parliament that February afternoon must have wondered whether they had heard the American expert correctly. Surely, Franklin must have exaggerated the ability of so many colonial buyers to withhold their traditional custom. What was the meaning of the Pennsylvania trade statistics that he had just read into the official record if not to expose the colonists' utter reliance on imported British manufactures? But on this point Franklin remained adamant, insisting that "I do not know a single article imported into the Northern Colonies, but what they can either do without, or make themselves."

The astounding claim that the Americans might be willing to forgo the pleasures of fashion sparked a predictable exchange, one well worth quoting in full since it marked a critical historical moment when British legislators explicitly confronted a new element in the imperial equation, one that the colonists themselves had just begun to appreciate: Private consumer decisions made thousands of miles away from the source of manufacture might under certain political circumstances become an engine of organized popular resistance.

Q. Don't you think cloth from England absolutely necessary to them?

A. No, by no means absolutely necessary; with industry and good management, they may very well supply themselves with all they want.

Q. Will it take a long time to establish that manufacture among them? And must they not in the mean while suffer greatly?

A. I think not. They have made a surprising progress already. And I am of opinion, that before their old clothes are worn out, they will have new ones of their own making.

Q. Can they possibly find wool enough in North-America?

A. They have taken steps to increase the wool. . . . The people will all spin, and work for themselves, in their own houses.

Q. If the act is not repealed, what do you think will be the consequences?

A. A total loss of the respect and affection the people of America bear to this country, and of all the commerce that depends on that respect and affection.

Q. How can the commerce be affected?

A. You will find, that if the act is not repealed, they will take very little of your manufactures in a short time.

Q. Is it in their power to do without them?

A. I think they may very well do without them.

Q. Is it their interest not to take them?

A. The goods they take from Britain are either necessaries, mere conveniences, or superfluities. The first, as cloth, &c. with a little industry they can make at home; the second they can do without, till they are able to provide them among themselves; and the last, which are much the greatest part, they will strike off immediately. They are mere articles of fashion, purchased and consumed, because the fashion in a respected country, but will now be detested and rejected. . . .

Q. Is it their interest to make cloth at home?

A. I think they may at present get it cheaper from Britain, I mean of the same fineness and neatness of workmanship; but when one considers other circumstances, the restraints on their trade, and the difficulty of making remittances, it is their interest to make every thing.

Q. What used to be the pride of the Americans?

A. To indulge in the fashions and manufactures of Great-Britain.

Q. What is now their pride?

A. To wear their old cloaths over again, till they can make new ones.[5]

Whether Franklin changed the minds of any members of Parliament during his presentation can never be known with certainty. No doubt, he confirmed much of what they had heard from well-placed constituents such as the cloth manufacturers of the Midlands who worried about the loss of American business and who petitioned against the government's new revenue policies.[6] But, whatever its immediate impact, Franklin's interrogation was a bravura performance, linking familiar commercial arguments in new ways suggesting that the colonists' putative economic dependence could be interpreted as a source of political strength. This line of reasoning had been implicit in the standard eighteenth-century writing on the British Empire, volumes that repeatedly drew attention to the central role the colonies played in Britain's—read England's—stunning economic growth.[7] Until the early 1760s, however, no one had so brilliantly seen the threat of organized market disruption as an effective device for gaining the full attention of England's ruling class. Within several weeks, the House of Commons repealed the hated Stamp Act. As Franklin's friend William Strahan said of Franklin's contribution to the decision, "In Truth, I almost envy him the inward Pleasure, as well as the outward Fame, he must derive from having it in his Power to do his Country such eminent and seasonable Service."[8]

As so many Americans discovered during the imperial crisis, however, preaching the language of market sacrifice was a lot easier than actually adopting the simple life. Basking in the political victory he had done so much to bring about, a relaxed Franklin dashed off a letter to his long-suffering wife, Deborah, who had never left Philadelphia. The contrast between this short note and the formal testimony before Parliament was striking. The correspondence revealed with surprising candor the fragility of the strategy of self-reliance and commercial denial that Franklin had just trumpeted before the House of Commons. "As the Stamp Act is at length repeal'd," he declared, "I am willing you should have a new Gown, which you may suppose I did not send sooner, as I knew you would not like to be finer than your Neighbours, unless in a Gown of your own Spinning." Still maintaining a jolly tone, Franklin reflected that if the hated revenue act had remained in force, he would have been forced to wear either homespun clothes or, more likely, old garments that he had long ago consigned to storage. "I told the Parliament," he recounted, "that it was my Opinion, before the old Cloaths of the Americans were worn out, they might have new ones of their own making. And indeed if they had all as many old Clothes as your old Man has, that would not be very unlikely; for I think you and George [Franklin's black servant] reckon'd when I was last at home, at least 20 pair of old Breeches." Personal decisions made over a long period—choices of color, texture, and cut—suddenly acquired different symbolic possibilities. The "old Cloaths" had taken on new meaning; the private choices in the marketplace spoke of shared public sacrifice in a political cause.

Or so it seemed. At precisely the mid-point of his letter, Franklin suddenly assumed an entirely different tone. The wording of his abrupt transition—"Joking apart"—called into question the character of much of his testimony a few weeks earlier before Parliament. What exactly was Franklin's colonial joke? That American consumers were really prepared to produce gowns of their own spinning? That men such as Franklin would actually agree to appear in public in breeches long since gone out of fashion or were a bit tight around the belly? Franklin seemed relieved that events had saved him and the members of his immediate family from having to make such hard market decisions, and the man who found it nearly impossible to resist the "Baubles of Britain" informed Deborah that a ship from London would soon deliver "a fine Piece of Pompador Sattin, 14 Yards cost 11s. per Yard. A Silk Negligee and Petticoat of brocaded Lutestring for my dear Sally, with 2 Doz. Gloves. . . . I send you also Lace for two Lappet Caps, 3 Ells of Cambrick . . . 3 Damask Table Cloths, a Piece of Crimson Morin for Curtains, with Tassels, Line and Binding. A large true Turkey Carpet cost 10 Guineas, for the Dining Parlour." The list contained many other exciting consumer items, including "some oil'd Silk, and a Gimcrack Corkscrew."[9]

As Franklin had observed not many years earlier writing as "Father Abraham," given the choice the colonists would happily rush to the marketplace. As individuals they celebrated the comforts of a new and expanding material culture. Franklin was no exception. Of course, as he warned

the House of Commons, it was possible for the colonists to imagine denying themselves the manufactured goods that had made them feel prettier,
warmer, cleaner, more fashionable, even more British. But it was not a welcome sacrifice. Indeed, what his letter to Deborah indicated—and what it
would take many ordinary American consumers a decade fully to comprehend—the manufactured threads that held the commercial empire together
were much stronger than even the most fervent colonial protesters understood at this early stage of political controversy. The desire to experience
private pleasure always strained against the appeal to support a common
cause. Until the colonists forged a greater sense of confidence that other
colonists living in other places could be trusted to forgo British imports,
they found it hard to translate rhetoric about the renunciation of the market into genuine self-denial and seriously to join utter strangers throughout America in resisting a powerful military adversary.

The interpretation of the coming of the American Revolution advanced
in this section invites a thoroughgoing reconsideration of popular mobilization. Parliament's attempts to raise revenue in the colonies sparked a profound symbolic transformation in which objects of everyday life—the myriad
"Baubles of Britain"—suddenly acquired new shared meanings.[10] Within this
political environment private decisions about mundane purchases became
matters of public judgment. Or, as one might state in a more familiar modern vocabulary, American men and women slowly, often painfully discovered
that highly personal actions carried inescapable political significance, so that
what once had seemed no more than matters of individual choice about comfort and appearance provided the cultural resources necessary during the run-
up to independence to forge effective revolutionary solidarities. The argument
is most definitely not that the language of liberty and rights failed to resonate
across traditional boundaries of class and geography. It obviously did so. But
such rhetoric was not a sufficient cause of revolution. Without a foundation
of widespread trust—a bond linking distant strangers and tested repeatedly
through rituals of consumer sacrifice—the principled declarations that domi-
nate our own memory of national independence would not have been able to
sustain broad structures of political resistance or have produced a meaningful sense of common purpose.

II

Even before Franklin warned Parliament about the economic power of self-
sacrificing American consumers, indeed, well before the colonists seriously
entertained the possibility of separation from the mother country, everyday imported goods from Great Britain had begun to take on new political
possibilities. The manufactured articles that flooded the imperial marketplace after 1740 had always symbolized a mutually advantageous commercial relationship between English producers and colonial consumers.
Sometime during the late 1750s, however, the social context in which goods

acquired shared meanings changed. It was during the period immediately following the successful conclusion of the Seven Years' War that Americans developed a fuller consciousness of their status as colonists within the British Empire, and in this more uncertain climate, they interpreted the articles of consumer experience with new eyes.

The transformation of colonial identity within a larger imperial structure occurred incrementally, almost without anyone being fully aware that a far-reaching shift was taking place. But whatever the pace of change, personal reassessments of empire gradually gathered momentum in public debate. People who had for a very long time taken membership in the British Empire for granted or had viewed it uncritically as the wellspring of liberty, prosperity, and security began to appraise in unprecedented language the burdens as well as the benefits of being British subjects. It was in this period of initial reassessment, roughly from 1757 to 1764, that many Americans concluded that they were in fact simply colonists—perhaps *nothing more* than colonists—subjects of the crown who did not quite measure up to the men and women who happened to reside in England. Put another way, the study of revolutionary mobilization forces a recognition that colonists could not have imagined national independence until they had first experienced the psychological burden of political dependence.

A new, more sober sense of colonial identity surfaced in the wake of extraordinary military triumph. The stunning victory over the French forces in Canada in 1759 raised popular expectations about America's central role within the empire to an extravagant pitch. It was against this inflated background that colonists would later express such bitter disappointment when a prosperity artificially fueled by war suddenly collapsed following the cessation of hostilities. Their reactions to the news of Britain's successes on the battlefield had been almost entirely positive. Ignoring the threat of a post-war cooling of the economy, Americans gloried in a highly flattering self-image. By their own lights they had done their part in turning back the French, and if the colonists could not quite claim full partnership within an ascendant British Empire, they reasoned plausibly that they deserved a kind of junior membership that awarded them unquestioned respectability.

Although no evidence survives suggesting that colonists belted out the lyrics of James Thomson's recently composed song "Rule, Britannia" with the same gusto as did contemporary English patriots, Americans who shared in the burst of post-war euphoria enthusiastically adopted what some historians have termed the rhetoric of "colonial nationalism" or "emulative patriotism." It was an aggressive language of Britishness that resonated with equal persuasiveness among the Protestants of Ireland as well as the Scots.[11] As one exuberant colonial newspaper editor of this period declared in his inaugural issue, it was the responsibility of provincial journals such as the *New-Hampshire Gazette* to reinforce, perhaps even to construct from whole cloth, a compelling sense of an American imperial identity "as *British Brothers*, in defending the Common Cause."[12] For some Americans, imperial patriotism merged with the prophesies of evangelical ministers. The war had taken on the trappings of a religious crusade. Major General James Wolfe's victory over a French army on the Plains of Abraham (1759) sparked widespread millenarian hopes, since, as the Canadian victory appeared abundantly to confirm, the Lord favored the interests of his Protestant subjects over those of their authoritarian, Catholic rivals.[13]

The bombast of mid-century colonial nationalism coexisted uneasily with a different theme. Behind the Americans' bold declarations of shared Britishness lurked a gnawing suspicion that their putative "British Brothers"—in other words, an English public—would never accept the colonists as equals within the empire. As various cabinet members sketched plans for a more rigorous regulation of colonial affairs, the provincial celebration of a common imperial identity increasingly rang hollow. It was in this political environment that some writers proposed that being colonial meant in fact being regarded by the English as somehow inferior to those people who enjoyed the good fortune of having been born in the mother country.[14] The prospect of possible relegation to second-class status within the British Empire was deeply humiliating. Indeed, the threat of rejection so nettled several highly educated colonists that they protested in crudely racist language that the English now thought of the Americans as little more than black Africans. Only wounded pride could explain such an extreme reaction. "We won't be their negroes," snarled a young, ambitious John Adams, writing in the *Boston Gazette* as "Humphrey Ploughjogger." Like others of his generation, Adams maintained that Providence had never intended white Americans "for Negroes . . . and therefore never intended us for slaves. . . . I say we are as handsome as old English folks, and so should be as free."[15] James Otis Jr., the brilliant Boston lawyer, inquired, "Are the inhabitants of British America all a parcel of transported thieves, robbers, and rebels, or descended from such? Are the colonists blasted lepers, whose company would infect the whole House of Commons?"[16] Like the anonymous author of a piece that appeared in the *Maryland Gazette*—an essay originally published in a Boston journal—colonists throughout America found themselves asking an embarrassing question of immense political and cultural consequence: "Are not the People of *America*, BRITISH Subjects? Are they not *Englishmen*?"[17]

The sense of doubt animating these rhetorical questions invites further explanation, especially if we are to grasp the context in which private decisions about consumer objects took on new political meaning. After all, colonial Americans had not always complained about comparative standards of good looks or fears of English rejection. Although their extraordinary sensitivity about such matters may strike us as absurd, Adams was in fact quite serious. If nothing else, his plaintive words remind us how difficult it is for modern Americans to comprehend what it meant for people of his generation to imagine themselves as *colonists*. It is a category that we take for granted.[18] The problem is that we do not really regard the colonists in this country as ever having been colonists, certainly not in the same way that twentieth-century Ghanaians or Nigerians, for example, were once colonists. Unlike them, we downplay the burden of a colonial past, real or imagined, electing rather to treat it as a period during which colonists—hearty yeomen all—were somehow preparing for nationhood. Within this narrative, American colonialism has lost its sting. It evokes a popular form of architecture, a quaint Georgian world that we have lost, or perhaps merely an invitation to enjoy a patriotic vacation.

For our purposes, such benign images of early American society serve largely to obscure a significant shift in popular political consciousness that occurred only at the very end of the so-called colonial era. To give colonialism a harder edge, therefore, let us stipulate that the 1780s were in fact a genuine *post-colonial* period in the history of the United States.[19] This possibility represents a kind of thought experiment designed to drive home the point about the relation between political consciousness and perceptions of dependence. As with Europe's former colonies in Asia and Africa, our post-colonial moment would have been a time of profound cultural strain in American society when a newly empowered people struggled to free themselves from the weight of imperialism and to establish an authentic voice with which to express national aspirations. Historians of the United States have seldom welcomed the analytic vocabulary of post-colonialism.[20] Instead, they have generally situated the years following the Revolution within a progressive political story that anticipates a burgeoning new republic, and few have seen much value in asking exactly how the citizens of this independent nation may have confronted—as did the peoples of India and Kenya, for instance—their recent colonial past.

Whatever the merits of this unfamiliar framework, we must accept that it raises provocative questions about the relationship between popular political ideas about power on the eve of independence and traditional assumptions about a long, largely undifferentiated era known commonly as the colonial period of American history. For example, had a genuine post-colonial mentality expressed itself in the United States after 1783, we might now feel obliged to determine more accurately than we do at present the precise content of America's colonial experience. We might want to know more about the defining characteristics of the colonial society against which the revolutionaries reacted. From the perspective of a post-colonial culture, it would surely make little sense to define the colonial period as everything that happened between the founding of Virginia in 1606 and the Declaration of Independence in 1776. Rather, in terms of the history of political consciousness, our colonial period would shrink to a few years following the defeat of the French in 1757. We would recognize that it was during these years that ordinary Americans became more fully aware of themselves as being colonists, as being politically and economically dependent on a powerful European state. Of course, one might properly observe in passing that the rulers of eighteenth-century Great Britain did not bring to white colonists the same oppressive violence that their nineteenth- and twentieth-century successors would visit on the indigenous peoples of Africa and Asia. But comparative repression is not our project. We must remember that however mild the hand of imperial power may now seem, we still have to explain how—and why—these particular colonists managed to organize what was in fact a successful colonial rebellion.

As John Adams and James Otis appreciated, it was only within a relatively short span of time that the term *colonist* had acquired ominous possibilities. It had suddenly ceased to be a relatively innocuous category, a mere geographic designation. The discovery of colonial dependence after the Seven Years' War forced itself onto the political imagination, requiring accommodation and negotiation even by those men and women who, unlike Adams and Otis, did not fret so much about English measures of handsomeness. The reassessment of exactly what counts as the "colonial experience" is of paramount importance to our reinterpretation of popular mobilization, since it was within this intense, newly problematic setting that imported manufactured articles, what Samuel Adams would label the "Baubles of Britain," crystallized previously inchoate assumptions about colonial dependency and compelled colonial Americans to reassess the implications of liberal choice in an imperial marketplace.[21] Store-bought goods served as what Michel Foucault has labeled "dense transfer points," sites of the production of meaning about relations of power.[22]

III

The grimmer face of colonialism first appeared in many households in the form of tighter family budgets. As one historian has observed, "the single most significant factor" in shaping the colonists' reaction to British regulatory policies "was the depression that by 1764 had fastened a clammy grip on trade in every colony, and which would not fully release it until the decade had ended."[23] The withdrawal of so many British troops from the American theater of war depressed local commerce, for without the soldiers—the very men who had sustained "the tale of the hospitable consumer"—the demand for goods and services decreased quite rapidly.[24] The colonists had to adjust not only to a contracting domestic market but also to heavy taxation levied to pay off debts incurred during the long conflict. After the French surrender, British officials grumbled that the colonists had failed to provide the level of funding needed to ensure victory, thus leaving the hard-pressed English rate payers with a huge public debt. The charges were unfair. Colonies such as Massachusetts had spent large sums during the war, and it was not until the late 1760s that the provincial governments were able to liquidate public obligations taken on a decade earlier.[25]

To make matters worse, during the post-war period international trade stagnated, forcing some prominent merchant houses into bankruptcy. A tightening of credit throughout the Atlantic world contributed to a lowering of commodity prices. Among the hardest hit was tobacco. In 1764, according to one Maryland newspaper, "The bankruptcies in Europe has made such a scarcity of money, and had such an effect on credit, that all our

American commodities fall greatly."[26] As with most economic reverses, everyone predicted that business conditions would soon return to normal, restoring the prosperity of former times, but recession gradually settled into genuine depression. These developments exacerbated chronic problems associated with an insufficient money supply.[27] By the middle of the decade the situation had become bleak, especially in the major port cities, where higher rates of unemployment and rising prices for basic supplies such as firewood created severe social pressures.[28] Although few Americans feared starvation, the prolonged downturn touched their everyday lives in many different ways. Some may have been disappointed in the results from the sale of a crop; others may have known a tradesman thrown out of work. Even ordinary people found that personal debts often outpaced income. As the frustrated members of Maryland's assembly explained, unless the colony's planters found new sources of revenue—something that seemed to the representatives highly unlikely—they would have no means of "discharging a continually increasing Debt contracted by Woollens and [Britain's] other Manufactures, so that should the Trade of the Colonies, even that which we have no immediate Hand in, be continued to be cramped, the evident Consequence must be that we should not have Credit to purchase such considerable Quantities of British Manufactures as we now do."[29] Or, as a writer in the *Providence Gazette* stated, "It is seldom, indeed very seldom, that any people have had more at stake than we at present have."[30]

At stake for the colonists, of course, were the many material comforts to which they and the members of their parents' generation had become accustomed. How best to preserve their newfound well-being turned on how Britain's empire of goods was supposed to operate, a subject that came to preoccupy many American writers. They accepted the fact that within recent memory a profound division of labor had evolved. On the one hand, the mother country purchased raw staples from America; on the other hand, the colonies provided a closed market for British manufactures. Any policy that disturbed this delicate economic structure—additional commercial taxes or the growth of consumer debt—threatened the entire balance of Atlantic trade and all the cultural and political expectations that the relationship sustained. In 1764 Oxenbridge Thacher, author of a pamphlet published in Boston, patiently reviewed the recent economic experience of the colonies. One can almost feel his sense of frustration. What had happened to notions of commercial reciprocity within the empire? Why are we being treated so poorly? What more can the Americans do? "Everybody knows," he declared, "that the greatest part of the trade of Great-Britain, is with her colonies. . . . The colonists, settled in a wide and sparse manner, are perpetually demanding the linen, woollen and other manufactures of Great Britain. . . . And while they can pay for those of Great Britain, with any proper remittances, their demands will be perpetually increasing. Great Britain besides, is the mart which supplieth the colonies with all the produce of the other countries in Europe, which the colonies use." With a nice touch of irony, Thacher added, "[D]oubtless even the luxury of the colonists is the gain of G. Britain."[31]

In fact, the British really did have the best of the deal. Thomas Fitch, governor of Connecticut, stated the terms of the colonial trade-off as well as any American during this period. "The Colonies and Plantations in *America*," he wrote in 1764, "are, indeed, of great Importance to their Mother Country and an Interest worthy of her most tender Regard." As the colonists grew in number and in prosperity, they would inevitably purchase more British imports. Rightly considered, therefore, imperial trade implied reciprocity, not dependency. "In the Colonies there is a Vent for and a Consumption of almost all Sorts of *British* Manufactures . . . whereby the Revenue of the Crown and Wealth of the Nation are much increased, at the Expense of the Colonies."[32] From the American perspective, the wisest imperial policy—well before the crisis over the Stamp Act in 1765—was not one that interrupted the flow of consumer goods but one that allowed the colonists the freedom and opportunity to earn the money they needed to pay for them. And, as people like Fitch explained, rising debts and new regulations were making that goal harder every year. Something had to be done.

The economic slump did not immediately translate into organized market strategies of protest. It did, however, draw attention to the politics of individual consumer decisions. Indeed, changing commercial conditions persuaded many Americans that their relationship with Great Britain—their status as colonists within an empire—may have come at a higher personal cost than earlier generations had appreciated. They were not receiving value for money. The private pleasures associated with consuming imported manufactures now raised disconcerting issues directly connected to a growing level of colonial indebtedness, to a constant drain of hard currency to the mother country to pay for an ever increasing volume of goods, to the enforcement of the Navigation Acts, which prohibited British colonists from entering foreign markets, and to a rising number of bankruptcies.[33] Imported items themselves were, of course, just as desirable as they had ever been, bringing color, warmth, and beauty to men and women who had worked hard for their money. But private enjoyments had a social price. Each purchase—no matter how justified in terms of the finances of a given household—spoke not simply of self-fulfillment but also of responsibilities to communities of local purchasers who happened to be experiencing straitened times.[34] As "The Farmer" argued with reference to Pennsylvania, the very survival of the colony hung in the balance. "Whether this province will continue to languish," the writer declared, "or whether folly, luxury, and vanity have taken such deep root, that wisdom and reason cannot eradicate, must be left to time only to make manifest; the best is to be hop'd for, and every honest man, no doubt, wishes that the good sense of the people will rouse them from their lethargy."[35] The people of good sense apparently reasoned dispassionately about consumer desire. "Philo Publicus" echoed the plaintive cry. "We have taken wide Steps to Ruin," insisted the Boston author, "and as we have grown more Luxurious every Year, so we run deeper and deeper in Debt to our Mother Country. . . . Industry and Frugality are Virtues which have been buried out of Sight; 'tis Time, High Time to revive them."[36]

What we are witnessing is the first stage of a shift in how ordinary people interpreted consumer goods within an imperial environment which before they had largely taken for granted or regarded as an altogether good thing. This was the moment during which imported manufactures took what might be called a political turn. The initial impulse was not to blame the British government or even the major importers for the economic depression. Rather, colonists began asking whether they—as individual consumers— actually needed so many yards of cloth, such a wide selection of weights and colors, indeed, whether it might make more sense to curtail personal expenditures before acquiring new debt. In this context, goods did not cause a change in collective behavior. They did, however, act as a catalyst for reassessment, a mental link between the personal and the political, a framework in which to reinterpret a shifting imperial landscape.[37]

As colonists brought a rough form of cost-benefit analysis to membership in a commercial empire, they focused not so much on the details of their own debts—in other words, on the pounds and pence actually owed to local storekeepers for imported goods—but rather on everyday patterns of market behavior that in a depressed economy suddenly threatened to turn independent consumer choice into slavish dependence. As "Pelopidas" explained to readers of the *Boston Gazette*, "it is known to every man in business, that our trade with Great-Britain is greatly against us, that our money is daily exported to pay for manufactures, that our debt to them is notwithstanding annually increasing, and will, if suffered to go on, be the instrument of making us slaves to that people."[38] Decisions made by individuals increasingly became matters of public concern; consumer desire could not so neatly be separated as it once was from its political consequences. To appreciate just how quickly private acts had become matters for legitimate public review, one only has to look at a letter published in the *Boston Gazette* in 1754—in other words, well before the onset of the postwar depression—for in this piece it was forcefully maintained that no group had a right to monitor household consumer habits. "Now I would ask," the writer announced, "whether it be consistent with that Honour which every English Householder claims as his Right, to oblige him to expose the private Œconomy of his Family, to the View of the World?—Has it not always been justly deem'd Impertinent for one Man to busy himself with the Family Concerns of Another? Would it not be an intolerable Insult for him to demand of his Neighbour an Account of his private Conduct & Family Expenses?"[39] Less than a decade after these words appeared in print, people raised a quite different question. How, if the common good is at stake, could a neighbor refuse to bear witness against private excess?

Americans initially pinned responsibility for the economic downturn on ordinary men and women who purchased so many goods without properly reflecting on the moral and political effects of their actions. In an article published in several different newspapers in 1764, "The Farmer" lamented that "luxury and extravagance abound, and have taken deep root, even to such a degree, that when two hundred pounds, about ten years ago, would have maintain'd a common family for the current year, three times that sum is now become necessary." If the economy had not turned sour, the colonists might have gone on spending at a high rate, even enjoyed doing so. But, according to this commentator, as "trade droops and sinks her head; wisdom cries alou'd to retrench and use our utmost industry, frugality and economy."[40] The situation called for reform of personal values, not government intervention nor the mobilization of entire communities. Consumers who had apparently once taken "luxury and extravagance" in their stride now had to adjust their buying habits in ways that echoed the mandates of an earlier Puritan ethic but during a post-war recession represented a largely secular remedy for an unwelcome reversal of fortune.

That appeals for economic reform merged so easily with conventional moral values is not surprising. Before the start of the Seven Years' War, when the prospects for the colonists looked considerably brighter, American writers employed an emotionally charged condemnation of luxury to discourage ordinary people from buying so many imported goods, especially high-quality textiles, which allowed them to reinvent themselves in a marketplace that celebrated choice and to assume airs that belied their humble origins. In this provincial setting insistence on frugality was a kind of class rhetoric intended to reinforce a traditional social hierarchy.[41] As the colonial economy lost momentum, however, Americans found that the moral vocabulary of an earlier era could serve other ends. Retrenchment was viewed less as a means of keeping ordinary people in their place than as a vehicle for reviving the general prosperity. Consumer virtue even acquired a patriotic tone, for men and women who saved their money during a difficult patch thereby contributed to an imagined common good. The colonists insisted that "Our enemies very well know that dominion and frugality are closely connected; and that to impoverish us, is the surest way to enslave us. Therefore, if we mean still to be free, let us unanimously lay aside foreign superfluities, and encourage our own manufacture. SAVE YOUR MONEY AND YOU WILL SAVE YOUR COUNTRY!"[42]

A writer in the *Pennsylvania Chronicle* who signed his contributions with the pen name "Œconomicus" developed these themes in particularly persuasive prose. He noted that "the expenses of living, which have of late increased among us much faster than our abilities to defray them," had reduced many families in "the foremost rank" to "real poverty and distress." Œconomicus did not think that such hardship resulted solely from self-indulgence in the consumer marketplace, but sybaritic habits were surely a large part of the problem. In fact, an objective observer could see that "in some instances" rising personal indebtedness could be traced to "idleness and the pursuit of pleasure." This author was most familiar with conditions in Pennsylvania. In that colony "a temperate, industrious, religious people, with money at command for every emergency, are now become voluptuous, idle, profligate, involved in debt, and almost left without the prospect of recovery." The solution to this sad state of affairs called for nothing less than a moral recommitment to consumer virtue, a call for each man and woman to practice within individual households "industry and frugality, a disuse of foreign superfluities, and a limitation of our desires to the real necessaries and comfortable conveniencies of life."[43]

This type of discourse represented a significant shift in how people thought about luxury in the marketplace. If the older rhetoric condemning consumer self-indulgence aimed to preserve the proper order of society and to dissuade ordinary people from participating too enthusiastically in the new empire of goods, this more patriotic appeal had the potential to generate a quite different interpretation. For if the lower orders of society really had it in their power to effect such marvelous results—nothing less than balancing trade between Great Britain and the colonies—they could not be treated as marginal actors in the politics of empire. Ordinary people may not have counted for much, but they were beginning within this commercial context to count for something. As men and women would soon discover, moral power in the consumer marketplace was no less effective for being moral. No one planned to invite other social groups into a public conversation over debt. But language has its own peculiar logic, suggesting at moments of social strain consequences that contemporaries never intended. And so the call for frugality in a secular sphere sparked thoughts about a more expansive political culture, not one defined in traditional terms of suffrage but rather one best described as a kind of politics out-of-doors, which was driven by consumer choice. It would be some time before calls for personal sacrifice spawned large-scale boycotts. So much as a historian can ever confidently declare that a popular movement originated at a particular moment, however, this is surely one of them.

The popular rhetoric surrounding what we might call the character of the virtuous consumer fits uneasily in an impressive historical literature that has sought to define a dominant ideology that enabled the colonists to make sense of a changing imperial environment.[44] Much of what the Americans had to say about the challenge of a depressed provincial economy sounds like the language of Reformed Protestantism. Like the early New England Puritans, colonists during the post-war years advocated a bundle of traditional religious values. From their perspective, it seemed quite clear that ordinary men and women should encourage frugality, simplicity, and diligence. But this eighteenth-century moral vocabulary had been drained largely of religious content. The goal of social reform in the marketplace was the restoration of general prosperity, not the defeat of idolatry. It was not that these people no longer concerned themselves with spiritual matters. They cared very much about such topics, and most attended churches of one denomination or another.[45] When they discussed the decayed state of the imperial economy, however, they employed a familiar religious vocabulary in strikingly secular ways. After all, anyone with money in his or her pocket could qualify as a virtuous consumer, even if that person happened to be an unlikely candidate for admission into a religious group.

The market discourse of the period also echoed key assumptions about a commercial economy and the spread of capitalist values that historians have come to associate with civic humanism or Classical Republicanism.[46] The fear of losing one's independence, a condition that seemed to promote corruption and threaten liberty, haunted writers of republican persuasion. These authors, we are told, feared commerce, especially the highly speculative variety that became more common during the eighteenth century, arguing that it brought on a culture of luxury, which in time would surely deprive self-indulgent and effeminate citizens of their ability to resist tyranny.

While it is true that colonists who appeared in the public journals demanded public virtue, they did not define virtue in the same way as the republican theorists who, we are told, played such a central role in the coming of revolution. Colonial commentators situated virtue solidly within the new consumer marketplace; it was preeminently a bourgeois virtue. When "A Farmer" praised the "honest man," he had in mind a person able to exercise self-restraint when tempted by a brilliant array of imported British goods. Virtue was a function of liberal choice—in this case, of consumer decisions to forgo private pleasures in order to advance the public welfare. The virtuous consumer did not reject the market, much less capitalism, but he or she had the strength of character to appreciate that private vices such as buying more than the purchaser could afford might compromise the larger public virtue of the community.[47] From this perspective, consumer debt was a problem not because it exposed a weakness for exciting imported goods— after all, it was quite natural to want to look prettier, feel warmer, and keep up with popular fashion—but rather because consumer excess reduced colonial buyers to slavish dependence on their creditors. Daniel Dulany, a prominent Maryland lawyer who protested the constitutionality of the Stamp Act in 1765, provided insight into the mentality of the virtuous consumer. "A prudent Man," Dulany explained, "constrained to abridge his Outgoing, will consider what Articles of Expense may be retrenched or given up, without Distress or Discomfort, and if, after this saving, he still finds that his Expenses exceed his Income, he will then consider of what Articles he can provide a Supply by the Application of domestic Industry."[48]

IV

Even before the outbreak of violent resistance to the Stamp Act in 1765, colonists had begun to discuss strategies that would ensure a continued access to the basic comforts of material life and, at the same time, reduce their dependence on imported goods from Great Britain. It was a tall order. They appreciated the need to reform participation in the consumer marketplace in ways that increased their political leverage within a commercial empire. But like anyone intent on having one's cake and eating it too, Americans were not yet prepared to contemplate radical changes in a comfortable style of life. In this situation some colonists trumpeted the kind of defiant arguments that Franklin would echo before the members of Parliament. Americans pledged to become more frugal, more diligent, and more self-reliant; they would search out alternative sources of goods. The challenge was clear enough. As one contributor to the *New-Hampshire Gazette* asked a local audience of virtuous consumers, "What then must be done?—Can we give up our Favourite Diversions, our Luxury either in eating or drinking, and take care of our Families?—Can we go plainer in Clothes, lay by our Laces, Ribbons, gaudy Flowers, and that most trifling of all Things, GAUZE[?] . . . Can we in New-England do without this?"[49]

Although it is premature in our discussion of the politicization of manufactured goods to explore the gendered aspects of consumer reform, one can see that brave talk of economic self-reliance was bound over time to focus public opinion on the household, on the ability and willingness of women to produce a supply of cloth sufficient to free colonial families from dependence on store-bought textiles. When the boycott movement reached its height later in the decade of the 1760s, women discovered that they had a voice in revolutionary politics, which modern historians interested largely in the activities of official committees and elected assemblies have failed to hear. By the same token, however, one might note that attacks on "Laces, Ribbons, [and] gaudy Flowers" touched the lives of women more directly than it did men, and it is perhaps not surprising that male writers almost unthinkingly assumed that it was up to their wives and daughters to make the greatest sacrifices in the consumer marketplace.

Indeed, from the first stirring of discontent, American consumers found it hard to define with confidence the precise content of self-denial. Even as the colonists began associating a flood of British imports with their own political dependency, they encountered a problem with the elusive language of the marketplace. As we have seen in our discussion of the traditional moral condemnation of luxury, the descriptive categories of eighteenth-century consumption were distressingly fluid.[50] One family's necessities often struck the members of other families as extravagance or as opulence, certainly as examples of the kinds of self-indulgence that might easily be dropped from a shopping list for the welfare of the community. As colonists devised various responses to post-war depression, they struggled to distinguish between superfluities and conveniences, between fineries and necessities. Someone was bound to claim that he or she could not do without a certain item. "What are called in North America luxuries," Daniel Dulany confessed, "ought for the most part to be ranked among the comforts and decencies of life." He predicted that however Americans defined the lexicon of demand, they would be willing to relinquish everyday goods that brought them pleasure if they could be guaranteed "a supply of necessaries . . . by domestic industry."[51] Like Franklin, who during his interrogation before Parliament struggled with such semantic distinctions, Dulany attempted to give precise meaning to what was in fact a highly unstable vocabulary of popular consumer sacrifice.

Whatever confusions bedeviled popular discourse, the colonists had no trouble seeing the commercial advantage that would undoubtedly result from the development of domestic manufacturing. The goal, of course, was to make the very articles that drained so much hard currency away from the American market. At least initially, colonists talked most excitedly of real centers of production, and it took several years before political decisions made in London forced them to refocus attention on the need to increase productivity within the home. In the post-war discussions, however, they dreamed bold dreams, ignoring the lack of sufficient capital and technological expertise required to launch large-scale ventures. In their desire to achieve greater self-sufficiency in the manufacture of basic items such as cloth, optimistic predictions of success far outran the possibility of satisfying an ever expanding consumer demand. Newspapers regularly encouraged a "recourse to domestic economy."[52] This type of reform, they believed, would shift the colonial workforce away from agriculture toward manufacturing. And confronted with a chronic imbalance of Atlantic trade, Americans seemed to have no other rational choice. "Tho' our Abilities to pay for the Manufactures of England greatly decrease," explained one writer in the *New-Hampshire Gazette*, "yet the Price, especially of Woolens, rise upon us, and the Importation and Consumption increase beyond Imagination."[53]

Observers bravely searched the provincial landscape for examples of the new self-reliant economy. Experiments of this sort were thin on the ground. Several journals praised a "Company of Gentlemen" for establishing "a New Woolen Manufactory" on Long Island, and reports from the site assured readers from "any of the Provinces ... [that] they may be supplied with Broad-Cloths, equal in Fineness, Colour, and Goodness, and cheaper than any imported." With no apparent sense of contradiction, the owners announced that they would welcome "any Persons who are [in] any Way vested in the Woolen Manufacture." The list of current job openings included "Woolcombers, Weavers, Clothiers, Shearers, Dyers, Spinners, Carders, or [people] understanding any Branch of the Broad-Cloth, Blanket, or Stroud Manufactory."[54] The large number of positions for skilled laborers suggested that perhaps the colonists would have to wait a long time before realistically competing with the makers of British textiles, and although an occasional advertisement informed "the Publick" of the availability of a variety of locally produced articles such as "Linen, Stockings, Mittens, Men's Caps ... &c., &c.," the patriotic rhetoric betrayed defensiveness about quality as well as availability. The reformers were simply not sure that ordinary American consumers would accept a cheap substitute even if by so doing they would be helping to restore the prosperity experienced during the height of the Seven Years' War. As one promoter of "HOME MANUFACTURED GOODS" exclaimed nervously, "Happy Country! That can supply itself with these Articles, and a People so public spirited as to encourage and be satisfied with them."[55]

During this early stage in the debate over the appropriate character of public sacrifice in the marketplace, Dulany expanded on the argument for local manufacturing. Even he seemed to be straining to make the case. "Let the manufactures of America be the symbol of dignity, the badge of virtue," he insisted, "and it will soon break the fetters of distress. A garment of linsey-woolsey, when made the distinction of real patriotism, is more honorable and attractive of respect and veneration than all the pageantry and the robes and the plumes and the diadem of an emperor without it. Let the emulation be not in the richness and variety of foreign productions, but in the improvement and perfection of our own."[56] The problem was that most colonial consumers knew quite well the difference between inferior goods made in America and the finer weights and colors from Great Britain they saw in the stores. "O. Z.," a writer from Rhode Island, summed up the situation with extraordinary bluntness. "The People of this Colony are daily taught," he noted, "from innumerable Lessons or Instances that are but too conspicuous in the numerous Shops, Stores, and Warehouses, how backward and ignorant we are in the manifold Branches of Manufacture, necessary or superfluous."[57] In such circumstances, abstract appeals about the state of the economy, even those invoking a new language of economic patriotism within the empire, were not capable of breaking long-standing habits of consumer desire. An organized sacrifice of pleasure in the marketplace—in other words, a strategy capable of uniting colonists across the boundaries of class and region—required more than reminders of hard times.

However quixotic the hope for a rapid build-up of domestic manufacturing in provincial America—one writer even claimed that "all these different branches [of manufacturing] have little or no existence but in news-papers"—the rising concern over the politics of consumer spending for British imports did have a curious impact on one aspect of public life.[58] For a very long time, especially in New England, moralists had complained that funerals had the unfortunate effect of beggaring poor and middling families. In anthropological terms these rituals had become scenes of intense, often vulgar competition, as surviving relatives attempted to outspend other families on the accoutrements that fashion deemed essential for such occasions. It fell to the widows and widowers to supply a host of mourners with rings, gloves, and scarves, all of which had come from England. Moreover, those concerned with social appearances at wakes purchased lavish amounts of imported wine.

These extraordinary episodes of conspicuous consumption occurring at moments of genuine bereavement came to the attention of the Massachusetts House of Representatives. In 1741 this body concluded that since "the giving of scarves, gloves, wine, rum and rings, at funerals is a great and unnecessary expense," the government had no other choice but to intervene. Henceforth, there would be no more distribution of scarves or rings, and the representatives insisted that only six people attending a funeral, in addition to the minister and six pallbearers, could receive special gloves. If the members of any family ignored these guidelines, or if they served imported wine or rum, they risked paying the state an enormous fine of fifty pounds sterling.[59] As with many reforms of this type, ordinary people in Massachusetts seem to have taken their chances on being caught, and they organized funerals in a manner they viewed as a reflection of their own gentility. In 1753 a newspaper that made a name for itself by criticizing the governing elite ran an essay entitled "Of the Extravagance of our Funerals," a piece that railed against the general insistence upon "a pompous Intern- ment." The author, who identified himself as "Shadrech Plebianus," seemed offended by "the fashionable Apparatus [which was now required to be] buried Alamode." He laid the blame for consumer excess at the feet of the colony's wealthier families. Since "People in the inferior Stations of Life are extremely apt to imitate those who move in a more elevated Sphere: It ought to be the Endeavour of the latter to set them the laudable Example of sup- pressing this fantastical and inconvenient Piece of Luxury."[60]

Such appeals to bury the dead "with suitable Decency and Decorum" seem to have fallen largely on deaf ears. That is, they did so until economic depression threatened the prosperity of Britain's post-war commercial em- pire. Suddenly, in this altered imperial context, calls for the reform of fune- real customs acquired unmistakable political overtones, and warnings about the moral implications of luxury were woven into a broader discourse that now included uneasiness about colonial economic dependency. Contem- poraries understood that the terms of the local debate had shifted. In 1764 "P. P." lectured readers of the *Boston Gazette* that the general decay of com- merce necessitated a reduction of the cost of funerals. If people could be persuaded to practice frugality at such moments, thus merging concerns about the common goods with private expressions of grief, then "each indi- vidual being ransomed from the tyranny of fashion, will be free to act as his circumstances may require, and such *freedom* can scarce be purchas'd too *dear*, as it has the necessary tendency to deliver a community from *bond- age*."[61] The major issue before the public was the colony's growing debt to Great Britain. Although no one thought that retrenchment of expenses for memorial rings and scarves would in itself restore the balance of imperial trade, such measures represented a welcome start; they communicated a shared commitment to solving a problem that affected everyone, rich and poor. As "Incola" explained, colonists must avoid "unnecessary Consump- tions, particularly in Funerals." The new "*Frugal*" methods of burying the dead would benefit many families by saving "some Thousands [of pounds] Sterling . . . which would otherwise be Remitted to Great-Britain for those Expensive and *Superfluous Habits* formerly used at Funerals."[62]

Advocates of less expensive interments turned the language of an eigh- teenth-century consumer society against itself in innovative ways that only a people fully engaged in the pleasures of the market could appreciate. No one claimed that "frugal funerals" represented a return to old customs; no one invoked memories of thrifty members of a founding generation. Rather, according to the people who contributed to the local newspapers, simple burials represented a new fashion. "It is now out of Fashion to put on Mourn- ing at the Funeral of the nearest Relation," announced one Boston writer, "which will make a Saving to this Town of Twenty Thousand Sterling per Annum.—It is surprising how suddenly, as well as how generally an old Custom is abolished."[63] Others, sounding a lot like newspaper advertisers for trendy goods, praised funerals staged "in the new establish'd Method."[64]

More than any other item associated with this ritual, gloves seem to have symbolized an incipient revolt against consumer dependency. The imported white gloves that families provided for mourners not only cost a lot of money but also represented a colossal waste. After all, a pair of funeral gloves could only be worn a single time. If New Englanders insisted on distributing gloves at funerals, then they ought to purchase those made in America. Such gloves would not reflect the cosmopolitan tastes of contemporary London. They would be warm, sensible, "suitable to the Climate." In fact, if one wanted to demonstrate a genuine commitment to the restoration of a balanced trade with Great Britain, one might affix on the funeral gloves "some peculiar Mark of Distinction." One person recommended that a proper emblem of colonial self-sufficiency might be "a Bow and Arrow, or a Pine Tree, in *lieu* of the usual stitching on the Back."[65] Pallbearers in Dorchester received special commendation for refusing "the usual Present of Gloves, to prevent a needless Expense to the Relations."[66]

However radical the New England funeral reformers may have sounded in terms of the manipulation of fashion, their instincts about social class remained solidly traditional. They assumed that the poorer sorts would naturally follow the lead of their betters, so that it was the responsibility of local gentlemen to set a model of frugality which the less fortunate could emulate. "S. A." revealed how during a period of imperial adjustment one might condemn the errors of the past—adopting a standard trope of Enlightened discourse—and at the same time preserve the prerogatives of the ruling elite. Noting how quickly the people of Boston had apparently accepted the new mode of interment, he could not ignore "the *stupidity of former times! And what amazing treasures have been thrown away,* in 100 years past, to support a *needless,* a *foolish* and *hurtful custom!*—Surely then, those *worthy gentlemen,* who have been instrumental in *shaking off* a *senseless & impoverishing fashion,* deserve the esteem & thanks of the public." In fact, S. A. believed that the wisdom of the well-born had saved those in the *"lower stations of life"* from *"inevitable ruin."*[67] It is not clear whether Boston's poor interpreted the changing fashion in funerals in these terms. In time, as we shall see, quite ordinary people took the lead in demanding consumer sacrifice in the name of liberty. For the moment, however, colonists seem to have agreed that the dead deserved equal treatment at bargain rates. According to "Hannah Prudence," "People of all Ranks and Conditions have come into the new Mode of attending the Funerals of their deceased Friends."[68]

To state with certainty how many New England families adopted the new guidelines for politically correct funerals is not possible. The newspapers, of course, reported a remarkably wide-spread rejection of the old customs. In January 1765 one commentator declared, "It is, I think about four months since this prudent regulation took place in *Boston;* in which time, I suppose there have been more than 100 funerals, and among that number (so far as I can learn) there has been but one or two families that have not strictly conformed to the new and laudable custom." Such impressive results provided a clear message. "It may fairly be concluded, that all ranks and orders of persons among us, do highly approve of it [the new frugal funerals], as a *prudent*, a *necessary*, and a *saving article* of reformation."[69] However many proper funerals may have been organized during this period, observers took the opportunity to introduce an entirely new figure into the realm of popular opinion. They celebrated the deceased man or woman not simply for having led a pious and honest life but also for holding a frugal and patriotic interment. At the moment of death, they revealed themselves as politically sensitive consumers. Mrs. Elizabeth Clarke was such a person. "Her Remains were decently interred on Friday last," announced the *Boston Evening-Post*, "in the frugal and laudable Manner lately introduced among us, and which prevails beyond Expectation in the Colonies."[70] A report from Concord declared, "This Day the Funeral of a Person of distinction was attended here in a new Mode, which gave universal Satisfaction to Persons of Character and others who attended the same. It's hoped other Country Towns will follow the Example which Boston has set us."[71] But these events paled in comparison to the burial of the Reverend Mr. Callender, the minister of the Baptist church in Boston. Whatever his virtues in life, Callender enjoyed a noble passing.

> The Town had the Satisfaction of seeing in this Instance, a Funeral conducted conformable to an Agreement lately entered into, by a great Number of the most respectable of its Inhabitants.—A long Train of Relations followed the Corpse (which was deposited in a plain Coffin) without any sort of Mourning at all:—Mr. Andrew Hall, the chief Mourner, appeared in his usual Habit, with a Crape round his Arm; and his Wife, who was Sister and nearest Relation to the Deceased, with no other Token of Mourning than a black Bonnet, Gloves, Ribbons, and Handkerchief.—The Funeral was attended by a large Procession of Merchants and Gentlemen of Figure, as a Testimony of their Approbation of this Piece of Œconomy, and as a Mark of their Esteem for a Family who have shown Virtue enough to break a Custom too long established, and which has proved ruinous to many Families in this Community.[72]

Although this new consumer ritual drew most support from Massachusetts, it had cultural significance far beyond the number of frugal funerals actually held. Local newspapers carried tales of the reform; they advocated the need for immediate retrenchment. The stories of simple burials and groups of "respectable" people who had encouraged them appeared in the journals of Connecticut and Philadelphia.[73] Readers in Charleston, South Carolina, may have learned from the Boston paper how New England families responded to the growing colonial indebtedness and, by extension, to the sting of dependence by refusing to wear imported gloves. An author in the *New-Hampshire Gazette* informed his audience that "The public Prints of a neighbouring Province have presented us with a *Frugal*, truly laudable, and now usual Manner of *Burying their Dead*."[74]

Reports of this kind are not usually the stuff of traditional political history. But for our purposes, it would be a mistake to adopt such a perspective. We should enlarge our sense of the political. Certainly, for ordinary people the shared news of heroic self-denial, especially as it affected the members of families not unlike their own, was profoundly political.

The journals of the period spoke of voluntary collectivities of Americans adopting innovative strategies of resistance. In this setting it did not really matter that the new mode of funerals had little direct impact on the overall imbalance of colonial trade. Tales of reform took on histories of their own, connecting distant strangers through a common language of consumer sacrifice. In this spirit one Boston commentator announced, "[A]s the present wise establishment relating to *funerals,* has taken deep root in this town, so it is likely it will spread not only through *our country towns,* but also through all the *neighbouring provinces.*"[75]

Short-lived strategies of funereal retrenchment as well as airy dreams of domestic manufacturing were like so many dry leaves stirring restlessly before an autumn storm. For all their discontents, Americans did not really want to forgo the pleasure of the consumer marketplace. We might describe their anticipation of material happiness as the Franklin dilemma, for, like the cosmopolitan figure who informed the members of Parliament that Americans might easily do without so many imported goods, they hoped that the current crisis would quickly pass. The good times would return. And, at that moment, the hard-pressed colonists would not have to recycle their old clothes, now perhaps a little snug around their waists, or join with other Americans whom they had never met in sacrificing the articles that had come to define their relationship with Great Britain. They would somehow avoid being "cloathed like their predecessors the Indians, with the skins of beasts, and sink into like barbarism."[76]

Events took a different course. The Sugar Act of 1764 represented an ominous hint of a regulatory policy that would reduce the colonists to a status that they found most objectionable. It reminded them that they were indeed becoming second-class subjects of the crown, in a word, colonists but not partners in a robust empire of goods. The legislation outlawed the colonists' lucrative trade with the French Caribbean and thus destroyed a triangular exchange that had become a vital source of the hard currency needed to pay English merchant houses for imported consumer goods. Britain's rulers, it seemed, did not fully comprehend the workings of the American market.

The burden of unconstitutional taxes and additional commercial regulations would in time suggest to the colonists new, more effective strategies of resistance and spark innovative forms of popular mobilization. Driving these collective responses was the firm conviction—first planted, ironically, by mid-eighteenth-century British commercial writers—that the colonists derived political strength in part through their own dependence upon the imported consumer goods.[77] From their perspective, it was Britain, not America, that had the most to lose if the colonists ever managed to curtail their own demand. Before anyone spoke of a declaration of independence, they consoled themselves in the knowledge that if Parliament did in fact break the commercial bonds that had linked them for so long, then "America, after many revolutions, and perhaps great distresses, will become a mighty empire."[78]

V

The vaguely defined though persistent imperial malaise that pervaded the post-war period suddenly came into sharper focus on March 22, 1765. It is no exaggeration to state that passage of the Stamp Act instantly transformed the political landscape of Britain's Atlantic world. After that date, colonists would never again view their imperial connection quite the same way as they had at mid-century. It was not that they espoused ideas of national independence. Rather, from their perspective, Parliament's shocking decision to levy taxes without representation called into question political assumptions about shared political identity—the stuff of colonial nationalism—and replaced these inchoate feelings of pride and loyalty with harsher emotions such as anger, confusion, and disappointment. The Stamp Act brought home to many Americans, already nervous about accumulating consumer debt and tighter commercial regulation, the full burden of colonial dependency. Indeed, the details of the statute—a stamp duty collected by crown officials on a wide variety of papers used in everyday business and legal transactions—seemed less significant to the colonists than did the rude discovery of a doctrine of inequality that now apparently informed imperial policy. In major provincial ports men and women protested what they interpreted as a direct attack on liberty and property; newspaper articles warned of dreadful conspiracies designed to reduce all free Americans to slavery. As William Smith Jr. of New York announced, "This single stroke has lost Great Britain the affection of all her Colonies."[79]

Others echoed Smith's reaction. Like more modern people who have experienced what they regard as a break in the flow of time—the destruction of the World Trade Center or the assassination of President John Kennedy, for example—colonists felt the sudden weight of history upon their shoulders. In their own lives, the Stamp Act forced an immediate and difficult reassessment of the meaning of empire. Few responses were as poignant as those of John Hancock, then an ambitious young Boston merchant. In his private letterbook where he preserved copies of commercial correspondence, Hancock recorded in turn waves of fear and defiance, dismay and uncertainty. On October 14, 1765, he informed the partners of a London firm that supplied him with consumer goods, "I have come to a Serious Resolution not to send one Ship more to Sea, nor to have any kind of Connection in Business under a Stamp. . . . I am Determin'd as soon as I know that they are Resolv'd to insist on this act to Sell my Stock in Trade & Shut up my Warehouse Doors & never Import another Shilling from Great Britain." Hancock insisted, "I am free & Determined to be so & will not willingly & quietly Subject myself to Slavery." One might conclude that Hancock's intemperate rhetoric was intended merely to alarm the English businessmen. But, in fact, he was genuinely disturbed by the sudden crisis. In a moving personal postscript to this letter, Hancock added a pledge that his correspondents could not have read: "This Letter I propose to remain in my Letter Book as a Standing monument to posterity & my children in particular, that I by no means Consented to a Submission to this Cruel Act, & that my best Representations were not wanting in the matter."[80]

The Reverend Jonathan Mayhew also appreciated the need to bear witness against the radical new imperial legislation. This respected Boston minister who had long served a wealthy congregation blasted the Stamp Act, and in a sermon entitled *The Broken Snare,* Mayhew reviewed exactly how Parliament's breach of trust had affected colonial society.

> This continent, from Canada to Florida, and the West-India Islands, most of them at least, have exhibited a dismal mixed scene of murmuring, despondence, tumult and outrage; courts of justice shut up, with custom-house and ports; private jealousies and animosities, evil furnishings, whisperings and back-bitings, mutual reproaches, open railing, and many other evils, since the time in which the grievous act . . . was to have taken place.[81]

Another thoughtful contemporary, the Reverend Jeremy Belknap, agreed with Mayhew's analysis, ruefully noting that news of the passing of the Stamp Act had produced despair throughout the colonies. As he explained, "The direct and violent attack on our dearest privileges at first threw us into a silent gloom; and we were at a loss how to proceed. To submit, was to rivet the shackles of slavery on ourselves and our posterity. To revolt, was to rend asunder the most endearing connexion, and hazard the resentment of a powerful nation."[82]

How many other colonial Americans shared such a profound sense of anger and betrayal at this moment is difficult to gauge. Leading clergymen and lawyers, merchants and planters, registered their opinions in public debates. They drew up formal petitions to the king and Parliament; they organized a gathering known as the Stamp Act Congress, which attempted, albeit unsuccessfully, to give voice to the grievances of all the colonies. But ordinary people made the depth of their own hostility to the new imperial legislation abundantly clear as well. They thoroughly intimidated crown officials appointed to distribute the stamped papers; they rioted in the streets of several American cities, sometimes pulling down entire houses. As members of a mob, they burned effigies of government agents associated with the hated duties. While colonists had occasionally employed violence to protest policies that they deemed obnoxious—the pressing of local seamen into the Royal Navy, for example—they had never before demonstrated such destructive passions. For a brief period rank-and-file resistance closed the courts of law and brought normal commerce to a standstill. Moreover, American newspapers and pamphlets displayed remarkable ideological conviction. There was no question that colonists who refused to pay the revenue did so on the basis of coherent political principles. They assured themselves as well as their friends in England that Parliament had acted in an unconstitutional manner that effectively annulled the natural and charter rights of all Americans. They knew exactly what they meant when they cried out, "No taxation without representation."[83]

However widespread the popular anger may have been, the Revolution did not in fact occur in 1765. This curious non-event begs explanation. After all, the elements that one assumes were necessary to transform colonial protest into full-scale rebellion seem to have been present at that moment: a radical ideology of colonial resistance, organized violence against the established government, and widespread anxiety that new taxes would exacerbate economic hardship. But, instead of provoking a general call to arms, the crisis passed, and we now interpret the protest against the Stamp Act as simply an early chapter in an eleven-year run-up to national independence. Several factors may account for the revolutionary dog that did not bark in the night. First, Parliament repealed the hated legislation on March 18, 1766, and for those Americans who cherished the opinion that compromise might stave off more serious confrontation, the retreat seemed to suggest a possible return to happier imperial relations. Second, a political culture shared time-out-of-mind with the English people—a stock of symbols and traditions associated with Britain's balanced constitution and the Glorious Revolution of 1688—proved impressively resilient, and many Americans clung to the hope that a compassionate king would at the end of the day intervene in their behalf.

But there is more than this to the story of the timing of revolution. Although a conservatism born of hope and tradition may go a long way toward explaining why popular defiance to the Stamp Act did not spark a full-scale revolt, it tends to obscure another equally persuasive account of why it took so long to translate what William Smith Jr. in 1765 called a momentous "stroke" into a broad-based continental cause. However much Americans may have detested the new revenue act and however passionately they defended their rights and liberty, they had not yet learned to reach out effectively to each other across the boundaries of social class and physical geography, so that while the Boston mob destroyed buildings and the rioters in New York City terrified crown officials, the protesters in neither locality had developed a sense of mutual trust that would allow them to assume almost reflexively that other Americans living in other places would support them if Great Britain decided to crush colonial resistance. In other words, what was missing from the equation in 1765 was a structure of political mobilization that would sustain solidarity among virtual strangers separated by bad roads and historical experience.

Imported manufactured goods played a central role in the process of reimagining the boundaries of political community. From our perspective, of course, it is easy to take a strategy of resistance based on the voluntary non-importation of British goods for granted. We recognize boycotts as a legitimate means of bringing pressure on those who would ignore popular grievances. But during the Stamp Act crisis the notion that imported items could be made to speak to power was entirely new. Consumer articles that had flooded into American households after 1740 provided colonists of entirely different backgrounds with a means of conversing about common political problems. No doubt, in other colonial situations over the last two centuries other aspects of shared experience—a common religion and ethnic identity spring to mind—served a similar function as did imported goods

in British North America. But it is extremely important in understanding
the various forms of resistance to colonial dependency to maintain a sharp
focus on the particular historical context in which solidarities developed.
Imported goods resonated with political possibilities precisely because they
had come to define so persuasively Britain's mid-century relationship with
its "consuming colonies." In an imperial economy in which colonists worked
ever harder to produce exports to pay for a rising demand for essential consumer items manufactured in England itself, it seemed almost inevitable
that imported goods would come to symbolize economic dependence and
political complaint. Or, put another way, colonial Americans learned, however slowly, to talk to each other about politics through organized disrup-
tions of the consumer marketplace.

As we have seen, these goods had already begun to take on new, increasingly problematic meanings during the period following the Seven
Years' War. After 1765 the reinterpretation of the articles of everyday material culture acquired a more overt political character. Consider, for example,
a seemingly straightforward list of goods that appeared in a Boston newspaper shortly after a mob had destroyed a house owned by Thomas
Hutchinson, an extremely wealthy Boston merchant who had been appointed lieutenant governor of Massachusetts Bay. The *Evening-Post* asked
subscribers to be alert for certain items that had gone missing on the night
of the attack.

> A Silver Hilt of a Sword which had been wash'd with Gold . . . two mourning Swords:
> a chafed Gold Head of a Cane, with the Lieut. Governor's Crest; a Lady's chafed Gold
> Watch, Hook & Chain; a new fashion'd Gold Chain and Hook for a Lady's Watch: a Set
> of large Silver Plate Buttons for a Coat & Breeches; 2 Sets ditto covered with Silver
> Wire, and very uncommon; several Funeral Rings . . . Gauze Handkerchiefs & Sattin
> Apron, both flowered with Gold; Silk Shoes; brocaded Silk, Padusoy Damask Lustring
> Gowns & Petticoats; laced Petticoats . . . Bundles of old Gold and Silver Lace . . .[84]

What catches the eye is not the traditional moral condemnation of luxury.
A new element has been introduced. The objects of desire have taken on an
unmistakable political character, so that the possession of various goods
that might once have reflected cosmopolitan taste or economic success now
present themselves to ordinary readers as badges of political corruption.
They understood the new critical language of "Funeral Rings."

Other colonial voices made even more explicit the link between imported goods and political dependence. The author of *A Discourse, Addressed
to the Sons of Liberty* (1766) compared the situation in which Americans
found themselves to that of "a young raw gamester sitting at a table between sharpers." On the one side of the colonist sat the "statesman," on the
other, the merchant. Both wanted nothing more than "to strip and plun-
der" the naive provincial consumer in this unequal game. But alas, the
American brought so little hard money to the contest that it made no sense
for the other two players to divide the spoils. Both aimed at taking the entire stake. There was hope, however. As "Pro-Patria" explained, the American consumer could avoid being fleeced, if only he would act. The writer

asked "a Solemn Assembly" gathered "Near the Liberty-Tree, in Boston," "What if the youth should discover their designs, resolve to keep better company, and take up his hat and walk off?" He could in effect boycott the commercial game. And if he did, could anyone blame the poor American "cully" for such resolve? "Whatever you may think," Pro-Patria continued, "this conduct, and no other, can bring about our deliverance; [for] as long as our backs are cloathed from *Great-Britain*, they [the imperial statesman and merchant] will lay what burthens upon them they please." *A Discourse*—a work clearly aimed at a popular audience—did not advocate revolt against consumer goods. The point was that "at a table between sharpers" Americans would be best advised to make these necessary articles for themselves. As he confessed, "[We have] trafficked so long abroad, for what could be found at home, that we are upon the point of selling, like *Esau*, our valuable and inestimable birthright for a mess of pottage."[85]

Another writer, who identified himself as "a Friend to the Liberty of his Country," took a more sober view of the challenge. He warned that the dreaded Stamp Collectors would soon demand whatever hard currency the colonists had managed to put aside for their own enjoyment. Without money the daughters of America would have to "sacrifice your gold beads, jewels, ear-rings, &c. until you are made bare and naked to your shame." Like Franklin, this writer did not welcome the sacrifice that unconstitutional taxation had forced on the colonists. The Stamp Act shattered the old symbols of empire. They once had represented a shared British identity. But by compromising the Americans' ability to purchase the goods they desired, Parliament had revealed an intention to treat the colonists like second-class subjects, in other words, like colonists. "For being called Englishmen," complained this Friend of Liberty, "without having the privileges of Englishmen, is like a man in a gibbet, with dainties set before him, which would refresh him and satisfy his craving appetite, if he could come at them, but being debarr'd of that privilege, they only serve for an aggravation to his hunger." He concluded, "O my poor brethren in the gibbet of America, that cannot come at the dainties of Europe, I pity you with all my heart and soul."[86] The Stamp Act had obviously put a heavy price on the pursuit of material happiness.

Any attempt to establish with precision the origins of non-importation as a mode of political resistance would be futile. During the 1720s the famed Irish satirist Jonathan Swift published "A Proposal for the Universal Use of *Irish* Manufacture, &c." in which he asked rhetorically, "What if . . . [the Irish Parliament] had thought fit to make a Resolution, *Nemine Contradicente*, against wearing any Cloath or Stuff in their Families, which were not of the Growth and Manufacture of this Kingdom?"[87] Nothing came of the suggestion. Nor was there a positive response to an appeal in a Boston newspaper in 1746 for the formation of an association whose members would pledge "not directly or indirectly, [to] buy or procure, or cause or permit to be bought or procured any Tea into our respective Families."[88] Rather than search for possible precedents for a consumer boycott movement, we should recognize that the creation of groups dedicated to achieving specific social, religious, or economic goals had a long history in British America. The colonists regularly formed associations to discuss new scientific ideas, to raise money for libraries, to finance the building of churches, and to fight fires. None of these communal efforts received support from local governments.[89] And although the non-importation movement that took root during the Stamp Act crisis was larger and less exclusive than were these earlier endeavors, it may have seemed quite unexceptional for men and women angry about taxation without representation to think in terms of voluntary organizations, in other words, of a framework of neighbors joining neighbors to address a common problem. Sacrifice in the consumer marketplace—like the acquisition of goods in the first place—required a conscious choice.

Although Parliament passed the Stamp Act in March 1765, news of this event did not reach American ports for almost two months. Popular protest against the statute and even more specifically against the local agents appointed to collect the stamp duties took many forms, one of which, as we have seen, was rioting in the streets. The urban merchants quickly found themselves at the center of a political controversy that threatened to spin out of control. If they elected to conduct normal commercial relations with their counterparts in England, they would be forced to purchase the stamped papers now required to get goods through customs. Organized resistance in the major colonial cities made capitulation of this sort a virtual nonstarter, and while some leading American merchants wanted desperately to avoid further involvement in the imperial dispute, others sanctioned elaborate non-importation agreements. Signed at meetings where only members of the merchant community had a voice, these resolutions may have been intended to head off the possibility that people not identified with commerce would push for non-consumption, a protest strategy that would have awarded to ordinary men and women a large measure of direct control over the sale of British goods in America. A group of New York merchants seized the initiative. On October 31 about two hundred of them gathered at the Long Room of George Burns's tavern, where they pledged to cancel all orders for manufactured articles until Parliament repealed the Stamp Act. They also persuaded local retailers of dry goods to join them in declaring that if the British government did not back down, New Yorkers would not accept any British imports after January 1. Merchant assemblies in other cities soon adopted the central provisions of the New York plan, and within only six weeks commercial leaders in Philadelphia, Albany, Boston, Salem, Marblehead, Newburyport, Portsmouth, and Plymouth had formally endorsed a limited non-importation plan.[90] On November 25 an appeal published in a Boston newspaper urged the "Merchants and Traders of the Massachusetts Bay" to emulate "the patriotic Conduct of the Gentlemen in Trade in New-York." If they came forward, the writer announced, the New Englanders would find themselves participating in a movement that was spreading rapidly, for, "a beginning being made, the Spirit will ketch from Town to Town, and Province to Province, than which nothing can more contribute to a speedy Redress of our Grievances."[91]

As the imperial crisis unfolded, the merchant community advanced various arguments in support of non-importation, some of which, not surprisingly, sounded transparently self-serving. Even before passage of the Stamp Act, many colonial merchants found themselves running up ever larger debts to their British suppliers, and if nothing else, an organized boycott of imported goods held out the possibility of reducing outstanding obligations while also providing a welcome opportunity to unload inventories that because of dull colors or unfashionable designs had been rejected by the consumer. One writer in Pennsylvania reported that "there is a full sufficiency of English goods now on the continent for a least seven year's consumption, and it would be for our advantage (the Stamp Act aside), if none were imported for half that time; then we might collect and pay our debts, which are already so heavy that we groan under them."[92] It is doubtful that colonial warehouses actually contained such a huge stock, but even in more guarded moments merchants assured commercial colleagues that it made sense in an uncertain business climate not to order new goods for at least twelve months.[93] In fact, in a perverse way the hated legislation benefited the American people, since the taxes prevented "an increase of our debt to the mother country, which we have now no means of defraying."[94]

A second justification for limited non-importation—in other words, a commercial effort that would cease as soon as Parliament repealed the act—was the merchants' assurance that the strategy would put serious economic pressure on British manufacturers. The argument turned on an insightful analysis of the new consumer marketplace. When prospects for exporting goods to the colonies dried up, British producers would be forced to lay off workers, and as the situation in England's industrializing centers deteriorated, unemployed laborers would join the Americans in protest against unconstitutional stamp duties. An article in the *Boston Evening-Post* explained exactly how the process would operate. Everyone knew that "we have enough [people] in Great Britain to plead our case," the journal reported. Although these allies were not powerful aristocrats or members of Parliament, they represented a "*respectable body*" of the English public. And it was certain "they will appear in our behalf . . . [since] if the trifling offence of wearing a piece of French silk can raise so large a body as 100,000 Spitalfield weavers that would attack the very P——t, what will be the consequence, when a very large part of the manufacturers of Great-Britain have nothing to do?"[95] If the workers took to the streets over non-importation, imperial reform could not be far behind.

In some accounts the notion that closing off the American market would have an adverse effect on the British economy took a sharper edge. "A Son of Liberty," for example, insisted that "such a measure might distress the manufacturers and poor people in *England,* but that would be their misfortune. Charity begins at home . . . and besides, a little distress might bring the people of that country to a better temper, and a sense of their injustice toward us."[96] Assertions that a hard-pressed working class in England would aggressively come forward in defense of American rights were generally unfounded. To be sure, some groups did lobby Parliament. While petitions from manufacturers and merchants who feared that non-importation did not have as great an impact on government policy as American enthusiasts claimed, it did spark a modest outcry, just enough grumbling, in fact, to sustain a colonial fantasy that Americans really did have friends in England.[97]

Champions of non-importation laced an older, more religious rhetoric about the virtues of self-sufficiency with bold new interpretive possibilities. Americans had been raised on the belief that diligence and hard work were positive attributes; individuals who applied themselves to their callings prospered. Their economic success freed them from dependence on others. While some critics of the Stamp Act echoed these familiar arguments, urging ordinary men and women to "a disuse of all foreign superfluities, and a limitation of our desires to the real necessaries and comfortable conveniencies of life," others began to link the emergence of American manufacturing to colonial independence.[98] No one, of course, anticipated the creation of a separate republic. Rather, within communities already worried about the burdens of colonial status within a commercial empire, appeals for home industries took on a political character. This construction was surely an unintended consequence of public discussion about non-importation. The merchants wanted American consumers to flock back to the dry-goods stores as soon as Parliament repealed the stamp duties.

Whatever their intentions, however, the seeds of new meanings had been planted. "Colbert" asked readers of the *Pennsylvania Gazette* seriously to reflect "on the dependent State they must ever be in, if they do not engage in, or encourage Manufactories."[99] A person identified only as "A Friend to *this* Colony" announced in the pages of the *New-London Gazette* that the "floods of English goods [that] have been poured in upon us" revealed a far-reaching conspiracy to destroy the local economy. To add insult to injury, these imports were apparently not worth the sacrifice required to obtain them, for "if [we] examine them we shall find them poor and miserable, such as could find no buyers in Great-Britain, but they are, it seems, good enough to be sent here to cheat *this* country with." The message to second-class colonial consumers was clear. "'Tis time we begin to prefer the goods of our country to the pride and vanity of individuals."[100] Other newspapers picked up this theme. A New Hampshire journal observed, "[W]e are told that the people of a neighboring government are setting us the example, having in bodies declared against wearing or consuming any thing but what is manufactured in America." This was an idea whose time had come. After all, "we shall have little reason to continue any trade that has hitherto brought poverty and a scourge upon us." Even more significant, economic independence might be the harbinger of an even grander destiny, for, as everyone knew, "all states and empires have been raised and have flourished by their œconomy and industry; but have declined and sunk into poverty and contempt by indolence and luxury. May it then be the business of America, to raise herself to opulence and wealth by the internal power she has of doing it."[101]

Doubts about the capacity of Americans to produce all the consumer goods that they desired—and no one really believed that homespun cloth would make a difference—persuaded some advocates of non-importation to turn weakness into strength. Drawing upon a mid-century commercial literature popular in Great Britain and upon arguments initially advanced during the general recession following the Seven Years' War, colonists assured each other during the Stamp Act crisis that the English actually needed them more than they needed the English.[102] The key element in this inspired line of reasoning was the Americans' utter dependence on British manufactures for the comforts of everyday life. Although few colonists welcomed the prospect of even a limited experiment with consumer sacrifice, they came to the conclusion that the indisputable statistical evidence of their growing indebtedness to Britain and their insatiable craving for fashionable products translated into real power within the British Empire. Indeed, their heady sense of themselves as vital agents in sustaining England's prosperity convinced colonists that repeal of the stamp duties was just a matter of time. It was in the mother country's best interest, one New Englander insisted, to guarantee that the Americans' hard-earned monies would be safe from unconstitutional taxes, for then "we should always send for as many goods as we could consume." Moreover, rising colonial imports would cement political loyalty, since "this demand for the English manufactures would increase as our numbers, and our union with, and subjection to Great-Britain would be the being of this trade."[103]

Left unspoken in this piece, of course, were the negative implications of the proposition. Others were more blatant. Writing in a Philadelphia journal, "Philoleutherus" scoffed at those who feared that commercial resistance might bring British "ships of war . . . [which would] seize and make prizes of all our vessels." To such nattering, he responded, "Those who imagine this an objection of any weight, shew great ignorance of our strength. Whatever courtiers may pretend, Great-Britain is in fact more dependent on us than we on her. . . . It is well known that by our consumption of her manufactures we maintain a large proportion of her people."[104] Even the lawyer John Dickinson appreciated the newfound powers of the colonial consumer. At the height of the Stamp Act resistance, he declared boldly, "I think it may justly be said, that THE FOUNDATIONS OF THE POWER AND GLORY OF GREAT BRITAIN ARE LAID IN AMERICA."[105] The point is not that non-importation turned people's thoughts as early as 1766 to political independence. That most certainly did not occur. But by the same token, we should consider that at moments of severe political tension writers—the sort of persons who contributed to the popular press—constructed the best case they could from the rhetorical materials at hand. And, whatever their immediate agenda, they surely made it seem almost inevitable that this colonial tail might soon wag the imperial dog.

In these several different ways non-importation encouraged colonists to reimagine their place within an empire of goods. For our purposes, however, it did a great deal more. It invited provincial consumers to think of the objects of market desire—the things in themselves—increasingly in terms of political principle. This mental link is fundamental to an understanding of how imported goods in this context became emblematic of abstract notions such as freedom. In other words, during this early phase of protest it gradually became apparent that consumer sacrifice would help Americans preserve what they defined as their basic rights and liberties. Although those who promoted non-importation focused almost exclusively on the behavior of the merchants, monitoring the willingness of these leaders to stop new orders for British goods, they began in published pieces to equate the pleasures of possession with broader, more public issues of constitutional misrule, a move that accelerated a symbolic process that would in time allow discontented Americans to conflate a perceived loss of freedom with their own participation in the consumer marketplace. As one Philadelphia essayist observed, whatever the ill effects of the Stamp Act, it had at least "awakened a whole continent, till then, going on in luxury, and sinking into a forgetfulness of their liberty."[106] In another journal "Œconomicus" warned that individual consumer purchases that spiraled into irresponsible debt threatened the common good. The stress here is on the political rather than the moral aspects of the issue. "Every person who owes more than he can certainly pay," declared the author, "is in a state of thraldom, and cannot, in speech or action, exercise the rights of a freeman. How carefully then should we, who entertain such high sentiments of the blessings of liberty, avoid every step that may involve us in debt, and thereby deprive us of this boasted liberty!"[107]

Not surprisingly, the non-importation efforts had a haphazard quality. Enforcement never matched public declarations of intent. The fact of the matter was that, despite lip service to moral reform and political fortitude, the merchants of the northern ports never found the new strategy of resistance particularly appealing. From the start of the controversy they worked to mend imperial fences, knowing full well that serious, sustained violence would only compromise accounts already strained to the limit. "A Trader" in Boston warned of the terrible consequences of a long-term boycott of British goods. "This [action]," he announced, "will involve a very great number of honest and industrious mechanics in want and misery, and their misfortune and want will spread to the next class, which is the day labourers and of great utility to the public." Unrest would spread to the mariners and finally "destroy the interest of the farmer." Soon a stand on principle in the marketplace would generate anarchy.[108]

Perhaps as a means to head off such unrest, the merchants—as a group—drew attention to their social standing as gentlemen, in other words, as representatives of the local elite who felt empowered to speak *to* and *for* ordinary Americans. It was no accident that newspaper reports during the height of the Stamp Act protest emphasized the respectability of the members of various urban merchant committees. In an announcement typical of the period, the *New-York Mercury* noted, "We hear that most of the Gentlemen in Town, have entered into a Resolution not to buy any European Manufactures." And, as gentlemen, they were not inclined to open their books for public examination. They did, however, present themselves as models of proper behavior, as examples of integrity in a time of troubles, and if someone of lower social standing registered doubt, that person was likely to be informed that good merchants were men of good character. Lest skeptics dismiss such tautology as nonsense, popular writers counseled their readers on how to identify the bad merchant. Ostentatious living was a telltale sign. "When I enter the Doors of a Gentleman in Trade," insisted "Philo Publicus," "and observe the Decorations of the Parlour, the shining Side Boards of Plate, the costly piles of China . . . [and when I] see the Mistress of [the house] dress'd in Apparel which can be worn by none with Propriety but those who live on their Income; I say when I observe all this . . . I wonder not when I hear of frequent Bankrupts."[109] A "Plain American" informed readers in Connecticut that bad traders were those who "put on this gay Attire to allure our Countrymen to buy their Trifles." The writer, it seemed, was just warming to his task.

> The industrious, frugal, and exemplary Trader, who sends the Produce of his own Country to foreign Ones, and imports in Exchange Gold and other Things which our Soil does not produce, is a [William] PITT to his Country. But the lazy, gay, designing Fop is a Pest to our Land: By the Help of Friends he gets Credit for a Shop of Fineries, Nicknacks, and Toys; in the Folds of which he latently imports our Shackles; he opens his Shop of Rarities, puts a Quantity on his Back, struts about with his Ruffles, Silks and Satins, a large Box full of the Snuff of Deceit and Flattery to bate well meaning People.[110]

Even the "good" merchants were unenthusiastic supporters of non-importation. That they laid the foundation for a later, much broader mobilization of ordinary colonists seems counterintuitive, if not simply incredible. After all, the merchants were by the very nature of their calling suspicious of competitors, especially those based in other American ports where the arrival of British imports could not be directly monitored. Under these unpromising conditions, political cooperation at a distance was bound to be fragile, for what appeared to one group of merchants as fair market advantage was likely to strike others as betrayal of the common interest. To reduce uncertainty, the merchants did what other Americans were doing with ever increasing attentiveness. They read the newspapers. These provincial journals, which were themselves the creatures of the new eighteenth-century consumer marketplace, provided intelligence about commercial agreements negotiated in other places. They reproduced the exact wording of every resolution touching upon trade; they announced the precise number of merchants who signed pledges of non-importation. A reader in Boston, for example, could learn from a single issue of the *Evening-Post* that the merchants of New York had taken the lead in halting normal trade with Great Britain. Another section of the same paper carried news that the "merchants and traders" of Philadelphia had passed five resolutions aimed at bringing about the Stamp Act's repeal.[111] Readers in New York and Philadelphia scoured the local press for reports of merchant agreements in Boston.[112]

Doubts about enforcement persisted, of course, but the newspapers made it possible for Americans to imagine that virtual strangers were actively supporting each other in ways that would substantially intensify the commercial and political pressure on Parliament.[113] For our purposes, it is important to remember that the topic of the day was the disruption of the consumer trade; the language focused on the transit of goods. But at stake was the first, highly tentative attempt to establish networks of trust, a necessary pre-condition of effective political resistance against a powerful empire. Contemporaries fully appreciated the role of the newspapers in promoting larger solidarities. In 1766 "A Son of Liberty" writing in a Philadelphia journal declared that "the PRESS hath never done greater service since its first invention." He recognized the value of pamphlets, to be sure, but these publications hardly had the widespread impact of the newspapers. "The argumentative pieces, letters, and addresses in the News Papers," he claimed, "have had a singular use in the great and good cause."[114]

However well the newspapers served the short-term concerns of the merchant communities, they also brought the latest news of the day to ordinary Americans, most of whom were fully literate. In this way they helped open up colonial political debate, for the journals implicitly invited their readers to assess the performance of the extra-legal bodies—in this case, self-selected groups of urban merchants—that had taken on responsibility to work for the common good, however defined. The non-importation agreements drafted during the autumn of 1765 were intended to persuade the members of Parliament and the friends of American commerce in England that they had made a dreadful mistake by accepting the Stamp Act. The merchants had in effect situated themselves within an Atlantic conversation. They concentrated their effort as provincial lobbyists on a British audience that actually determined the character of imperial policy. But within the American cities another group was taking shape, one that would be known simply as the "public," and at this early stage of colonial protest it focused its attention on the merchants who claimed that non-importation was a strategy that would bring about the swift repeal of the Stamp Act.[115] It was the public who watched for evidence of cheating: perhaps spotting a shipment of English dry goods that no one had anticipated or perhaps noting a warehouse that seemed to be the center of unusual consumer activity. That was as far as it went. Nothing about the non-importation efforts could rightly be described as democratic or even, in terms of inter-colonial organization, dependent on the popular will. Nevertheless, the reluctant merchants of 1765–66 had inadvertently opened the door to wider popular participation in resistance to an empire of goods.

Advocates of non-importation soon realized that if the new strategy of resistance had any chance of success, it would have to enjoy the full support of the women of colonial America. Perhaps no one at the time should have been surprised by this political discovery. After all, as we have seen in our discussion of mid-eighteenth-century consumer culture, women played a central part in making decisions about the purchase of British manufactures. Jan de Vries, a leading economic historian of this period, has demonstrated persuasively that families throughout western Europe and North America restructured household labor so that ordinary men and women could obtain a wide range of goods that had just appeared on the market, and as they did so "the wife [found herself] in a strategic position, located . . . at the intersection of the household's three functions: reproduction, production, and consumption."[116] In a social environment in which imported manufactures suddenly came to symbolize the burden of colonial dependence, therefore, women were inevitably thrust into the political debate. As one Pennsylvania writer explained in 1767, without the support of "the *American* Ladies"—single and married—the non-importation movement would surely fail. After all, their "approbation and assistance would give spirit to our efforts . . . for we all know how much it is in their power to retrench superfluous expenses."[117]

Whatever the political payoff, the males of colonial society do not seem to have welcomed the inclusion of their wives and daughters in the public forum. Men adopted a defensive, sulky tone in print, as if unforeseen events had forced them to issue an invitation about which they felt profoundly ambivalent. Some statements echo an earlier, religiously charged rhetoric depicting women as more likely than men to give in to temptation: Had they not insisted on purchasing crimson capes and other items of gaudy apparel, they would not now be recruits in the protest against the Stamp Act. Once people had linked consumer pleasure with colonial dependence, however, the provincial gentlemen had grudgingly to accept new voices in the public forum. "Country-women," "Philo Publicus" intoned, "will allow me to wish a general Reformation among them.—May they lay aside their Fondness for Dress and Fashions, for Trinkets and Diversions, and apply themselves to manage with Prudence the Affairs of the Family within, which their Husbands are busied in providing the Means. May none think themselves above looking into every Article of Expense,—nor exempt from performing any Part of Family Business, when properly called to it."[118]

That such frivolous Eves might tear themselves away from the joys of consumer life seemed a lot to ask, but "The Farmer" tried, employing none too subtle language in the attempt. "Tell the fair Ladies . . .," he announced, "how much more amiable they will appear in decent plain dresses made in their own country, than in the gaudy, butterfly, vain, fantastick, and expensive dresses brought from Europe, to pay for which (did they know the whole truth) their industrious parents or husbands must greatly labor and toil."[119] In New Hampshire more practical arguments apparently carried the day. "H. J." told the "Fair Sex . . . that it is high Time to lay aside all Extravagancies in Apparel." Some women had bravely accepted the challenge, for it was reported that "some even of the *delicate Madams* . . . actually have made up

Cotton Shifts, of our own Manufacture which is vastly preferable in this Cold Climate, to the finest of Hollands, besides much cheaper and stronger." And surprise, surprise, "what is still a greater Inducement to them to go on, they say that their Husbands like them full as well or better in a Cotton Smock, as in a Holland one."[120]

In this defensive political climate, some men felt compelled to describe the "good" wife. She was a person who would sacrifice her pleasures for the general welfare without thereby upsetting gender relations within the household. Again, we must remember that colonial Americans would probably not have raised these issues with such force had they not selected non-importation as the preferred strategy of protest in an empire of goods. In 1767 "Atticus" explained to the readers of the *Pennsylvania Chronicle* that "the mistress" of the household should properly serve as the guardian against promiscuous consumption. Such a marvelous helpmate "has [it] much in her power, towards preventing the entrance or growth of luxury." It was a major responsibility. She oversaw "the management of the table, the furniture, and the feminine part of the apparel [which] are more particularly within her province; and, those are articles in which, in this young country, there is no small danger; besides these, her willingness to be content with moderate things, in all other instances, will often have great influence." Fortunate indeed was a man to have a wife who demonstrated such self-restraint in the face of so many consumer temptations. He would be wise to expand her area of influence within the family, pronouncing judgment "in every branch where her observations can be proper!"[121]

How American women responded to these instructions within the privacy of their own families cannot easily be determined. In public, however, they participated in much-publicized spinning meetings, where, among other things, they celebrated the domestic production of cloth. These rituals often drew large crowds, for people of all sorts seem to have enjoyed assemblies that were at once patriotic and non-violent. The social standing of the spinners seems to have been important in giving legitimacy to the event. A Boston newspaper, for example, reported that the eighteen "Daughters of Liberty" who had gathered recently in Providence, Rhode Island, were all "young Ladies of good Reputation." Not only that, they were well chaperoned. According to various New England journals, the women "assembled at the House of Doctor *Ephraim Brown* . . . in Consequence of an Invitation of that Gentleman, who hath discovered a laudable Zeal for introducing Home Manufactures." Safely situated in the doctor's house, they worked all day, from "Sunrise until Dark," and amazed everyone by their reluctance even to take a break from spinning. Readers throughout the region learned that the gracious host had "provided an elegantly plain Dinner, and other Refreshments for the fair Company; but they expended but very little Time in dining." Such industry in such a good cause inspired other women; spinning meetings became a kind of contest to discover which group could produce more cloth over the course of a day. "We hear another Meeting of these *Daughters of Liberty*, with many more, is intended to be held at the Court House ...," noted the *Connecticut Courant*, "there to spin a handsome Piece of Linen."

But whatever the likes of Doctor Brown may have had in mind when they organized these gatherings, the local women "of good Reputation" sensed that the occasions provided them a measure of power in personal as well as political affairs. Before the meeting at Providence broke up for the day, the "Daughters of Liberty" unanimously resolved that "the Stamp Act was unconstitutional, [and] that they would purchase no more *British* Manufactures unless it be repealed." They also admonished the young men who no doubt were mooning around the assembly that consumer sacrifice involved more than just women. In fact, the spinners pledged that they would "not even admit the Addresses of any Gentlemen should they have Opportunity, without [unless?] they determined to oppose its [the Stamp Act's] Execution in the last Extremity, if Occasion required."[122] Out of genteel settings came amazingly radical demands. In any case, the times were changing for America's *"delicate Madams"*; at least they were for members of the middle class. In a widely circulated newspaper story, a woman who had experienced "the Spirit of Patriotism"—almost in evangelical terms—made a remarkable decision about political resistance. "A Lady of this Town [Newport, Rhode Island]," a New York journal exclaimed, "though in the Bloom of Youth, and possessed of Virtues and Accomplishments really engaging, and sufficient to excite the most pleasing Expectations of Happiness in the marriage State, has declared, that she should choose rather to be an Old Maid than that the Operation of the illegal Stamp Act should commence in these Colonies."[123]

Colonial males did not quite know what to make of charming women willing to forgo marriage and all its pleasures for the sake of political principle. From time out of mind, only men could rightly claim to be patriots, persons like the Roman hero Cincinnatus who put down the plow and gave his all to defend the common good. American women had not taken up the sword in the cause of liberty, but they were so determined to have their voices heard that some writers concluded that they too could be genuine patriots, a revision of gender stereotypes that reveals just how much the men in this traditional society needed the women to make non-importation actually work. In a curious letter entitled "An Address to the Ladies— From an Inferior," an author who adopted the name "Tabitha Strawbonnet" insisted, "Since the Days of the Romans, I have heard my Master say no so spirited and noble an Example of Patriotism, Male or Female, can be found as the Ladies in North America have shown." Strawbonnet may well have been a man, for later in the piece the writer observed—again suggesting how sexual politics and imperial politics had become confused—that the young males of Boston "love & admire you not half so much for your Beauty, and in gaudy Apparel, as for plain good Sense, Virtue, and Neatness."[124] But if this scribbler thought he was poking fun at women consumers, the Reverend Jonathan Mayhew, Boston's most respected Congregational minister, was quite serious about female patriotism. In a review of the Bay Colony's efforts to render the Stamp Act inoperative, he had special praise for the many "devout women" who were, "I imagine, so far metamorphosed into men on this sad occasion, that they would have declined hardly any kind of manly exertions, rather than live to propagate a race of slaves, or to be so themselves. In short, such was the danger, and in their opinion, so great and glorious the cause, that the spirit of Roman matrons in the time of the Commonwealth, seemed to be now equaled by the fairer daughters of America."[125]

The most tough-minded declaration of the political aspirations of colonial women during this period appeared originally in the *New-York Mercury* early in 1765. Signed "Sophia Thrifty," this piece achieved unusual persuasive power by drawing upon the real experiences of ordinary colonists. Whoever the author may have been, she rejected the kind of nervous playfulness that informed so many essays touching on the relation of the sexes. She welcomed the spread of colonial "patriotism" through "all ranks of people." And at such a critical historical moment, it genuinely annoyed her to hear Americans—presumably males—declare that women were by nature addicted to extravagance. In what kind of households did critics like this live? Had they come into contact with real women? "I can assure you," the writer continued, "that we Matrons, who are mothers and mistresses of families, and know that our husbands and sons must prosper or decline, with our flourishing or sinking country, will not hesitate a moment about resigning every thing inconsistent with the general welfare. On the contrary, we will sacrifice, cheerfully sacrifice the most darling appurtenances of the toilet on the altar of public emolument." And what was more, "Sophia Thrifty" rejected as utterly specious the argument that young women were empty-headed consumers whose only goal in life was snagging a man. If women behaved in this manner it was "not so much to please themselves, as to dazzle some of yours. While you men will be silly enough to admire a brilliant figure beyond a prudent girl, and prefer external ornament to intrinsic merit; we women will be polite enough to spread the most alluring snare." In fact, the patronizing tone of so many public statements about the inability of women to resist consumer temptation struck this writer as insulting twaddle.

> What should induce you to think, gentlemen, that those of us who are daily witnesses to the difficulty of procuring an estate, or even of providing for a large family, should be incapable of feeling for our country, for our husbands, for our offspring, amidst the impending distress universally apprehended.—You all allow us to have a good deal of spirit. Let me inform you, we have a good deal of publick spirit. We are not unconcerned spectators of the general calamity. We are not indifferent whether our native country sinks or swims. We don't set our trinkets and baubles in competition with the prosperity of North-America.

The looming imperial crisis required that for every "Cato" who stood up for colonial rights and liberty, the women of America would produce a "Cornelia."[126] In a way that no one could have predicted, a protest that organized itself around the rejection of consumer goods was encouraging some people, some of the time, to entertain rebellious thoughts about the shape of society. And in the coming years the door that the "Daughters of Liberty" had pried open, just a little, would open further, inviting into the public forum other Americans who just happened to be consumers.

VI

The predictable question to ask about non-importation is whether it actually worked. Did the canceling of so many orders in Boston, New York, and Philadelphia force the members of Parliament to reconsider an imperial policy that took for granted their right to tax the colonists without representation? The answer is no. The trade statistics show no appreciable drop in the value of British imports shipped to American ports during this period. But it would be a mistake to claim that because the colonists still loved fashionable consumer goods—because, like Benjamin Franklin, they did not want to squeeze into old breeches that no longer fit—that the whole enterprise had been a failure. The experience had taught some valuable lessons. It had not been a good idea to place so much responsibility for enforcement on the merchant community, a group that had every interest in encouraging Atlantic commerce.

If Americans really hoped to redefine their relationship with Parliament and with an empire that seemed increasingly to insist on colonial dependence, then they had to find a means to move from non-importation agreements to broader, more inclusive forms of popular mobilization. The people had to take charge of enforcement. It was a daunting challenge, and in the days following repeal of the Stamp Act, few colonists were willing to

contemplate sacrificing the manufactured goods that made life so enjoyable. When Parliament again passed taxes that the Americans deemed unconstitutional, however, they returned once more to the consumer marketplace, forging new links with distant strangers who understood, now more than ever, how thinking about goods invited ordinary men and women also to think about politics.

A celebratory artifact manufactured in England for the American market. *Teapot with lid. "Stamp Act Repeal'd." English, 1766. Cream colored earthenware, lead-glazed and hand-painted. Photograph by Mark Sexton. Courtesy of the Peabody Essex Museum, Salem, Massachusetts.*

7

Making Lists—Taking Names: The Politicization of Everyday Life

The Townshend Revenue Act of 1767, a bundle of taxes levied on imported articles such as glass, painter's colors, paper, and tea, triggered a frenzy of list making throughout colonial America. The lists themselves testify to how Parliament's tough stand on revenues brought about an extraordinary reordering of the symbolic meaning of British goods in this society. The reassessment of an older material culture had begun during the prolonged economic depression following the Seven Years' War, acquiring sharper articulation during the Stamp Act protests, but at this urgent moment the mental process rapidly accelerated, compelling colonial consumers quite literally to invent new forms of local knowledge. In this highly charged atmosphere, lists of imported manufactures that had once suggested only personal pleasures acquired overtly political possibilities.

Within a very short period of time—perhaps no more than the years from 1767 to 1771—private decisions in the consumer marketplace came to be widely reinterpreted as acts meriting close public scrutiny. As "Philo Patriae" announced in the pages of a Connecticut journal:

> Certainly, 'tis ten thousand times more eligible to enjoy freedom in this state, than to be slaves in large and well *glazed* houses, with fine cloaths, tea, wine or punch; and to have the pleasure of swallowing English beer and cheese; rustling in silks and ribbons, or glittering with jewels: all which we shall neither use nor wear any longer than our [British] masters judge they need them to *protect, defend and secure us.*[1]

Throughout America, committees and voluntary associations, many of them extra-legal groups claiming to speak in the name of the "public," constructed lists of prohibited goods as well as lists of people who purchased them; subscription lists favoring non-importation circulated door to door. Consumer polls were taken. These innovative strategies designed to gauge and enlist public support for non-importation unwittingly opened up political participation to persons—women, for example—whose only entitlement to a voice in such affairs was that they were potential consumers of imported British manufactures.

A remarkable list drawn up on October 28, 1767, by the "Freeholders and other Inhabitants of the Town of *Boston*" captured the instant when one group of colonists confronted the symbolic reordering of a culture of goods. Eligible voters gathered at Faneuil Hall, the city's commercial center; the fiery lawyer James Otis served as moderator. How many people attended is not known; since the proceedings lasted a full day, there must have been a lot of coming and going. Otis explained that the town had received a petition urging passage of "some effectual Measures" to be adopted as a means not only of revitalizing a stagnant local economy but also of countering "the late additional Burthens and Impositions on the Trade of the Province, which threaten the Country with Poverty and Ruin." To this end, the body put together an impressively detailed inventory of "enumerated" articles currently imported from Britain that it expected patriotic men and women to boycott after December 31. The full list, which appeared in several Boston newspapers, read much like the advertisements that shopkeepers regularly ran announcing the arrival of fresh shipments of goods from abroad. Only now, the language of marketing was employed self-consciously for different purposes, to stigmatize the objects of desire and to link consumer experience to political resistance.

> Loaf sugar, cordage, anchors, coaches, chaises, carriages of all sorts, horse furniture, men and women's hats, men and women's apparel ready made, house furniture, gloves, men and women's shoes, sole leather, sheathing and deck nails, gold and silver and thread lace of all sorts, gold and silver buttons, wrought plate of all sorts, diamond, stone and paste-ware, snuff, mustard, clocks and watches, silversmith and jeweler's ware, broad cloths that cost above 10 shillings per yard, muffs, furs and tippets, and all sorts of millenery ware, starch, women's and children's stays, fire engines, china ware, silk and cotton velvets, gauze, pewter, hollow ware, linseed oil, glue, lawns, cambricks, silks of all kinds for garments, malt liquors, and cheese.[2]

Unlike the general non-importation agreements published during the Stamp Act crisis, the Boston town meeting's list provided remarkable specificity about different products. The inclusion of each item seemed to have resulted from close analysis of the actual colonial marketplace, from knowledgeable conversations among merchants, store owners, and ordinary consumers about the meaning of certain goods in a changing provincial world. In fact, the meeting attempted to mobilize a public in a political cause through decisions about prosaic articles such as muffs and mustard seeds. And in this way, it effectively connected the defense of American rights and liberty to consumer self-sacrifice. As an author who assumed the name "Miles Standish" told readers of a Boston journal, "You who can be comfortably and decently cloathed with your own manufactures cannot think it an intolerable hardship to abstain from the unmeaning superfluities of foreign countries, when you discover that your fondness for them is the engine intended to be used to destroy the free constitution of your country."[3]

Other groups throughout America protested the Townshend duties by constructing lists of enumerated British imports. In Charleston, South Carolina, for example, protesters carefully distinguished what local consumers might properly purchase from what they should avoid. In this case, acceding to the special demands of a slave economy, South Carolinians exempted from a non-importation plan "Negro cloth, blanketing, ... plantation tools, and other tools necessary for our several occupations." They recommended that angry citizens in the region refuse articles such as silks and ribbons, India goods, and woollens, and since people could not go naked, organizers asked patriots to limit themselves to "coarse cloth" valued at not more than fifty shillings a yard, always, of course, "giving the preference to blue."[4]

The subscribers of a non-importation agreement in Annapolis rivaled the inhabitants of Boston and Charleston in their attention to detail. Until such time as Parliament repealed the Townshend Program, the signers promised not to buy scores of items, including such politically sensitive imports as "pickles," "trinkets," "playing cards," and "frying pans."[5] The leaders of Virginia also vowed to drop "pickles" from their shopping lists along with some fifty other categories of British manufactures.[6] The townsmen of Windham, Connecticut, a small, struggling agricultural community, echoed Boston's inventory, as did the list makers of nearby New London. Even in the smaller towns, people gave serious attention to the precise character of their proposed market sacrifice.[7] A meeting "of the major Part of the Merchants & Traders of the Colony of Connecticut & a Number of the respectable inhabitants convened at Middletown" decided to halt commerce in "fish hooks and lines, tin plates and hatter's trimming, salt petre [saltpeter], bar lead, pins and needles."[8] While some lists proscribed the goods specifically mentioned in the Townshend Revenue Act—tea, painter's colors, paper, and glass—most read like general shopping guides.

However these various lists may have been constructed, as a collective statement they revealed much about how Americans forged political solidarities on the eve of independence. First, although local groups promised to deny themselves the pleasures of the consumer marketplace, they communicated their decisions through newspapers, so that men and women living in other, often distant communities could learn how colonists whom they had never met were responding to a common threat. Newspapers had originally served as handmaidens to a rapidly expanding commercial empire, carrying information about the transit of goods throughout the Atlantic world, and now, as the meaning of things shifted, the same journals disseminated appeals which served to disrupt the very commercial ties that had once been seen as the special signature of enlightened eighteenth-century British authority.

Second, without giving much thought to the matter, colonists who began to reach out to other Americans during this period simply assumed that distant strangers—people on whom they would have to depend in any coordinated resistance to Parliament—were as dependent as they upon access to British manufactures. The language of the consumer marketplace, expressed in detailed lists, helped bridge differences of religion, ethnicity, and labor systems that might have immediately cut off the possibility of making common cause. Ironically, the market itself allowed Americans to accommodate difference, since, whether they recognized it or not, colonial consumers had been purchasing the same basic range of British goods for a very long time—a reflection of a growing standardization of weights, colors, and styles—and it was not hard for someone living in New England or New York to appreciate the construction of non-importation lists produced in Virginia and South Carolina.

Of course, the call for consumer sacrifice did not in itself guarantee that at a moment of military danger New Englanders could automatically trust South Carolinians nor that Virginians might without second thought count on the patriotic support of New Yorkers. But however tentative the movement toward broader imagined horizons—toward what some modern voices of nationalism have called a country of the mind—a shared hostility to their dependency on Britain for the key articles of the good life provided the ligaments for political union in the years to follow. Individual self-sacrifice gave palpable demonstration that one was willing to act for the public good. It gave force to high-sounding words that were easy to mouth and even easier to disavow when the going got tough. As one hard-nosed New Englander explained:

> Now let me lay down this plain undoubted Principle, That a State of Dependence is a State of Subjection, and Servitude. We may then project, resolve, vapor and threaten, as much as we please; 'tis all in vain, and we make but a ridiculous Figure, while we are dependent upon Great-Britain for a warm Coat to save us from freezing in the Winter.[9]

And finally, as the lists suggested, from Georgia to New Hampshire, Americans appreciated the link between liberty and consumption, between the enjoyment of political rights and the sacrifice of market pleasures. Goods were made to speak to power. "Atticus," appearing in a New York newspaper, understood the relationship. Once Great Britain had enjoyed a "grand-market for all her various manufactures," he observed, but instead of cherishing its loyal American customers, it had brought tyranny to the colonies. And, "since a contrary, and unaccountable system of politics, has been adopted, and we are not allowed to purchase the manufactures of our Mother-Country, unless loaded with taxes to raise a revenue from us, without our consent," there was no other recourse open to Americans but to refuse "their manufactures . . . until our grievances are redressed."[10] Even more poignantly, a Rhode Island "Son of Liberty" asked: Could Americans after more than a century in the New World give up the "liberty, which [their forefathers] purchased at so dear a rate, for the mean trifles and frivolous merchandise of *Great-Britain*"?[11]

In 1770, as it had done in 1765, Parliament retreated from violent confrontation, repealing all of the obnoxious duties except that on tea. Colonial consumers responded to the news by running back to the goods they so dearly loved, accepting political dependence when it no longer seemed so directly tied to unconstitutional forms of taxation. They did so as a changed people, however, for whatever disappointments they had suffered, they had in fact refined an entirely new strategy of resistance that survived in the memories of all consumers who had learned that lists now carried serious political implications.

II

Rightly or wrongly, Charles Townshend bore much of the blame for the crisis that engulfed the empire. As chancellor of the exchequer, he provided the catalyst for the second great wave of non-importation throughout the North American colonies. Perhaps the members of Parliament could have avoided what appears with hindsight to have been an unnecessary aggravation of imperial tensions, but a reconciliation would have required inspired political leadership. Townshend and his followers in the House of Commons were not up to the challenge, so that instead of preserving the bonds of a commercial empire, they encouraged partisan, seemingly vindictive legislation designed to assert the sovereignty of Parliament without acknowledging the colonists' legitimate complaints.

Like so many figures of modest talents who find themselves thrust into positions of authority, Townshend promised more than he could deliver. During the spring of 1767 he boldly announced that he could reduce the land taxes so hated by the English ruling class while at the same time compelling recalcitrant Americans to obey explicit orders to contribute to the housing and maintenance of British troops still stationed in the colonies. Predictably, the political establishment greeted his proposals with enthusiasm; it too wanted to show restive Americans how tough Parliament could be. But alas, for all his braggadocio, Townshend had no real plan. His so-called program offered little more than a grab bag of legislation, and, as his colleagues must surely have understood, the new duties on glass, paper, tea, and painter's colors that sparked so much resentment in the colonies would have covered only a small fraction of the total cost of the British army in America, that is, if they had actually been collected.[12]

Although the Townshend Program did not ignite the kind of street violence that had greeted the Stamp Act, the colonists made clear their implacable hostility to all legislation of this sort. They rejected out of hand the notion that Parliament could tax them without their consent; they dismissed claims that an unrepresentative body in England exercised absolute sovereignty over their domestic affairs.[13] On an emotional level, however, the popular contempt for the new Revenue Act involved more than abstract principles about the character of the British constitution. Townshend poignantly reminded Americans of the heavy burden of colonial dependence. It was not that in 1769 or 1770 they wanted to free themselves from British rule. What fueled anger was rather the lack of respect for the colonists that seemed increasingly to inform imperial policy. And most people appeared to have equated the sting of insult with the consumer market-place. In his widely admired *Letters from a Farmer,* John Dickinson noted that since articles such as glass and paper were "absolutely necessary for us," the colonists would end up paying the duties whether they liked it or not. In an irate outburst worthy of Jonathan Swift, Dickinson observed, "I think it evident, that we *must* use paper and glass; that what we use *must* be *British;* and that we *must* pay the duties imposed, unless those who sell these articles, are so generous as to make us presents of the duties they pay."[14] In other words, commercial necessity had forged the shackles of dependence, and although to modern ears such rhetoric may seem excessive, even conspiratorial, that is in fact how many colonists came to appraise their commercial entrapment.[15]

Other, lesser-known writers took up the theme. After rejecting the possibility of confronting "the military force of Great Britain," for example, a Connecticut writer concluded darkly that "We will either make our own cloaths, go naked, or augment our debt with Great Britain to a sum which will in the end enslave the country."[16] A South Carolinian excoriated market dependence in even blunter terms: "Our continuing to buy British manufactures then, under our present situation, is as weak, as unnatural, as it would be to buy a rod for our own breech; 'tis, in fact, doing the very same thing."[17] New Englanders expressed similar sentiments in the language of the Old Testament. According to "Philo Patriae" of New London, "[I]f we continue to purchase foreign [i.e., British] goods as in times past, 'tis easy to see that we shall be very soon in the case of the Egyptians, we shall have nothing left to pay for them, but our bodies and our lands."[18] The colonial situation had encouraged a bondage of pleasure; it was time to rethink consumer desire. "Philo Libertatis" reflected on the American dilemma. "Will not all mankind say," he asked the readers of a Connecticut newspaper, "we are an inconsistent people? Crying to heaven, and crying to the king against being made slaves, when at the same time we are struggling hard to make ourselves so, and to rivet our chains?"[19] It is not insignificant that with rare exception the most bitter protests against market dependence were found in the local newspapers, not in the formal pamphlets of the period, an indication perhaps that ordinary people almost reflexively grounded discontent in their personal experiences as consumers.

So effortlessly did Americans come to champion non-importation that it appears that what was in fact a highly innovative strategy of resistance sprang forth into the political world fully formed, as if an organized, popular disruption of normal trade required no serious justification. But, of course, it did. One of the first statements calling for an organized market protest appeared in the *Boston Gazette* on August 31, 1767, and even though it relied heavily on raw passion, it put forward a reasoned case for boycotting British goods. "My blood is chilled, and creeps cold through my stiffened veins," the author cried. "To what alas! is America reduced. This land for which our fathers fought and bled, must now become the den of slavery." The only hope for political salvation was to "put a stop to the importation of all English goods" and to demonstrate to Parliament that the colonists could "freely part with the gay trappings of a butterfly."[20]

One common argument stressed what might be described as Great Britain's breach of contract. For Americans, trade was never just trade; the sale of goods within an imperial framework implied mutual obligations.[21] In exchange for the enjoyment of a non-competitive market—the Navigation Acts dating back to the seventeenth century prohibited ships of foreign nations such as Holland or France from entering Britain's American ports—the mother country had agreed to give the colonists the best manufactures available at the best prices. Colonists saw no reason why British merchants should take advantage of a privileged market situation—a naive opinion, perhaps, or simply a reflection of bargaining weakness within the empire, but an interpretation that made sense to the Americans nonetheless.

One particularly thoughtful rendering of this point of view appeared in a South Carolina journal. The author, identified as "A Member of the Assembly and Signer of the Resolution"—probably Christopher Gadsden—analyzed the colonists' commercial connection with Great Britain. On their side, he observed, the British claimed "a right, to an absolute exclusive trade with her American colonies; and hath so confined them in their imports and exports . . . that the manufactures they want, they are not permitted to receive directly from any other nation but herself." It was widely accepted that the same goods could be had "from fifteen to twenty per cent cheaper than they *can* have from her, and better in quality than what *she sends* to them." Why, a reader might ask, would English businessmen engage in such offensive practices? "It is no secret," the writer confided, "that her manufacturers and wholesale dealers, put off their worst goods this way, many of them making scruple to say, anything will do for America." There was a solution to this problem, of course, one that had radical implications for an empire nurtured on protected markets. "This disadvantage to us, arises merely from Great-Britain having an exclusive trade to her colonies. Were it otherwise, by our ports being freely open to all nations, she would then, soon find it [in] her interest, to take the same care to please us, as well with regard to the quality as price of her wares, as she is obliged to do at the markets [where] she expects to meet any rival."[22]

Whether hawking second-rate goods represented a genuine conspiracy against American interests or merely reflected the colonists' structural dependence was not clear. Whatever the full implications of such reports may have been, people living in other colonies found them entirely credible descriptions of recent commercial experience. In Providence, Rhode Island, "A Friend" reminded readers of the local journal that "since floods of English goods have been poured in upon us . . . family economy is at an end. . . . 'Tis true goods are sold something cheaper than formerly but if we examine them, we shall find them poor and miserable, such as could find no buyers in Great Britain; but they are it seems good enough to be sent here, to cheat *this* country with."[23] Again, authors who advanced these views were not advocating political independence. It would be remiss, however, not to point out that at a moment of widespread anger over unconstitutional taxation, Americans raised the highly corrosive proposition that the "consumer colonies" had been sold a bill of goods, and if that was the case, then non-importation might not be as painful as one had imagined.

Several other arguments in support of a general boycott of British goods were more predictable. Writers explained, for example, that traditional remedies for political grievances simply had not worked. The Anglo-American legal culture had long recognized the petition as a legitimate means for bringing a complaint to the attention of crown or Parliament, but during the current controversies over taxation, formal appeals of this sort had fallen on deaf ears. Faced with indifference as well as hostility, a New Yorker known as "A. B." concluded, "we [have] no other peaceable Way left, but to use some effectual Measures to prevail with those who *are* represented in the British Parliament, and may be supposed to have *some* Influence there, to exert themselves in our Behalf and make our Cause their own."[24] Short of armed resistance, the most promising "effectual Measures" on offer were non-importation agreements. Organized consumer protests not only would serve to broadcast discontent but also seemed likely to promote manufacturing in America. As many colonists knew full well, this was a tenuous proposition. Manufacturing schemes had received an optimistic reception for some time, and even though there was almost no evidence that the colonists were really prepared to make cloth, glass, and metal objects on a scale commensurate with popular demand, they spoke of a boycott as a bitter although welcome medicine that would at last excite domestic industry. "The way then to get redress for our wrongs," insisted a Hartford writer, "is to render ourselves unprofitable to Great Britain, by industry. We must begin sooner or later; the increase of the inhabitants of this country being so great as to put it out of the power of Great Britain to cloath us a century hence."[25] As a plan to achieve a measure of economic independence by the 1870s, it had merit, but as a strategy to gain swift repeal of the Townshend Program, it left a lot to be desired.

More encouraging for the short term, newspaper essays throughout America assured colonists that non-importation would succeed precisely because it would make conditions intolerable for England's poorest industrial workers. The argument turned on pragmatism. A South Carolina author announced as a certainty that the only reason why British merchants exported so many goods to America was their desire "to prevent the Clamours of the People at Home." The colonial market was in fact little more than a mechanism for maintaining full employment in urban centers like Birmingham, and it did not take much intelligence to appreciate that "it is from the Loss of Business these [laborers] will FEEL, [and therefore] that we must originally look for Redress of our Grievances."[26] Another colonist asked rhetorically, "Must not such a number of idle hands, in the heart of any country, be extremely alarming?"[27] A New Yorker concurred with this tough line of reasoning:

The corrupt Authors of the comprehensive System of Mischief, which has thrown one of the most prosperous, powerful and happy Empires the World ever produced, into Discontent, Confusion, and Distress, are well aware of the powerful Influence that our Non-importation Scheme, duly prosecuted, would give us over the manufacturing and trading Part of the Nation, and consequently over themselves at second Hand.[28]

However absurd notions of consumer tails wagging British dogs may have sounded to English authorities, they only had themselves to blame. After all, since the middle of the eighteenth century self-styled commercial experts had been announcing as an uncontested fact that the American market was absolutely essential to the continued prosperity of the mother country. The colonists came to believe what they read.

Another argument offered in support of non-importation drew attention to the actual men and women who purchased British goods, in other words, to the ordinary colonists who believed that they had a right to make choices from among contending products in a consumer marketplace. Selections reflecting personal preferences for color, weight, and texture were expressions of a cultural process known as self-fashioning. But as Americans discovered during this period, they could exercise the right of choosing by not doing so, by withholding their custom, and by engaging in a kind of political self-fashioning that probably would never have suggested itself as a strategy of resistance had they not come of age in a commercial empire in which colonists were extravagantly described as consumers of goods manufactured in the mother country. After all, provincial writers observed, the American people could do with their money exactly as they pleased. This definition of freedom sounds a bit crude, but in the context of the colonial experience it translated individual decisions about British articles into a political weapon, for the "it's your own money" justification for boycotts placed ultimate responsibility for success directly on anonymous shoppers. As one South Carolinian explained, "[E]very American has an indisputable right to lay his money out as sparingly as he pleases, and to give preference to American manufacturers, when to be had, [or] to any other whatever; and it is particularly his duty, to do so at this extremity."[29] The energizing spirit behind this statement was not a protest against the consumer market per se, or against commercial capitalism, but rather against specific British imports that now symbolized dependence. The *Virginia Gazette* reminded colonists that no imperial official, neither royal governors nor parliamentary leaders, "can oblige us to buy goods, which we do not choose to buy."[30] A New Englander universalized the claim, pointing out that "no power on earth can make us buy what we will not buy."[31]

Transforming arguments for non-importation—many of them really expressions of annoyance and hope rather than certainty—into an effective strategy of political resistance represented a formidable challenge. In 1767 few colonists probably appreciated the full immensity of the task that lay before them, for, like coaches for a team of untested players, they had no assurance that they could overcome even the more obvious obstacles to a continental boycott. Modern historians have tended to ignore these organizational problems, assuming apparently that since ideological principles of one sort or another drove the engine of American protest, it was not all that important to work out the evolution of large-scale political mobilization. But this lapse is surely a mistake. Even the most high-minded ideas about liberty and representation would have amounted to little more than sputtering anger without an organizational structure capable of sustaining a sense of unity and purpose.

Confronted with the Townshend Program, therefore, the colonists faced four major difficulties, and the failure to address any of them would have reduced non-importation to a hollow gesture of discontent. First, there was the matter of coordinating various local protests. The movement depended on grassroots agitation, but of course, if the various communities did not act together, the targeted imports would inevitably flow to the port or regions that had not yet come onboard, effectively destroying any real chance of putting pressure on British manufacturers or the members of Parliament. Drawing upon the lessons of the Stamp Act protest, one South Carolina writer observed, "If the alarm was so high in Great Britain, when only two or three of the Northern governments commenced their salutary and patriotic measures; what must it be, when she finds Pennsylvania, Maryland, and Virginia, together with our province, have adopted them too?"[32] Second, since any colonist was in fact a potential consumer of British goods, organizers had to persuade quite different sorts of people—women as well as men, gentlemen as well as farmers and laborers—to support the boycott. Third, as the colonists had discovered during an earlier wave of protest, non-importation agreements that lacked teeth were easily ignored, and they had to establish extra-legal means of enforcing a huge disruption of the market without thereby alienating moderate supporters. And finally, as the protest spread from colony to colony, from city to city, issues related to cooperation across vast distances forced them to imagine themselves in broader, more inclusive terms than they had ever done before, as "Americans," as members of an ill-defined "union," or as spokesmen for a "continent." Like other rebellious groups throughout history, they had to decide for themselves just who spoke for whom. What precisely was the character of the larger community to which they professed to belong? Who was the "we" urging ordinary people to hold steady in the face of danger? This was uncharted cultural ground, and within an experimental framework of political identity words such as *virtue, corruption,* and *patriotism* acquired special, historically specific meanings that resonated persuasively among defiant provincials.

III

The non-importation movement got off to a rocky start. With hindsight the reason seems clear enough. Like addicts, the colonists looked to someone else to protect them from their own dangerous habits—in this case, purchasing British goods whose price tag was political dependence—and in this situation, they demanded more of the merchants than they could deliver.[33]

It was not surprising, therefore, that as soon as Americans learned of the new duties, they insisted that local merchants organize an effective boycott of British manufactures. After all, the merchants provided the link between producer and consumer, and if they stopped their orders, the rulers of Great Britain would soon realize the stupidity of their attempts to bring the colonists to heel. It was widely believed that the merchants had forced Parliament to repeal the Stamp Act, and there seemed no cause to doubt that the merchants could bring about a second major victory.

The problem was that the merchants no longer wanted to play the part that other Americans had scripted for them. They dragged their heels, hoping that somehow the imperial problems would be resolved before they had to take a public stand on non-importation. Perhaps they understandably feared that they were being asked to ride the tiger of popular protest. In Boston the leading merchants—a few such as John Hancock excepted—refused to sign an agreement until March 1768, and even then they made clear that they would support non-importation only so long as the merchants of New York and Philadelphia followed their example. This decision set off a nervous dance. The New York merchants went along, but their counterparts in Philadelphia would not join, and so for lack of mutual trust the entire boycott in the northern colonies seemed fatally ill organized. But the tide of public opinion was running swiftly against the commercial community, and, bowing to the growing pressure to act, the merchants of Boston, New York, and Philadelphia in 1768 finally signed non-importation agreements. As Francis Bernard, royal governor of Massachusetts, observed of the Boston agreement, "The merchants are at length dragged into the cause; their intercourse and connection with the politicians and the fear of opposing the stream of the people have at length brought it about." The governor added that refusal to support non-importation would "be obnoxious to the lower sort of people."[34]

The major southern colonies—Maryland, Virginia, and South Carolina—did not adopt non-importation agreements until the summer of 1769. During the Stamp Act protests they had evinced little enthusiasm for interrupting the consumer trade with the mother country, but, faced with mounting opposition to British imperial policy, they gradually warmed to the proposition that cutting back on expenditures for a wide range of manufactured goods, especially luxury items, might force Parliament to repeal the hated Revenue Act. George Washington, who loved imported goods as much as any other American, accepted the strategy, noting that the colonists had to do something to resist "our lordly Masters in Great Britain." His neighbor on the Potomac River, George Mason, bravely tried to fortify Washington's resolve. "Our All is at Stake," Mason explained, "& the little Conveniencys & Comforts of Life, when set in Competition with our Liberty, ought to be rejected not with Reluctance but with Pleasure."[35] Another Chesapeake planter concurred. "These are the proper Means to use upon the present interesting Occasion," he wrote. "These are the Arms with which GOD and Nature have furnished us for our Defense."[36]

As leaders of the region discovered, however, in staple economies dependent on the export of tobacco, rice, and indigo, it was hard to put pressure on the merchant community. Unlike the northern colonies, where merchants generally came from respected local families and identified with the culture of the communities in which they worked, the southern colonies relied heavily on the employees of large Scottish or English merchant houses.[37] These transient factors, whom one South Carolinian dubbed "birds of passage," seldom gained acceptance into planter society.[38] Thus when it became apparent in 1769 that a united movement to boycott British goods might actually succeed, the southern colonies had to devise somewhat different ways to mobilize support. Usually, representatives of the dominant planter class took charge. These men either drafted agreements to halt most trade on a certain date or persuaded resident merchants that it would be wise for them to do so.

In Virginia, for example, a distinguished body of elected representatives including the likes of Washington, Mason, and Thomas Jefferson walked out of the House of Burgesses, reassembled in a nearby Williamsburg tavern, and, acting on their own authority, signed their names to a long list of British imported goods which they now renounced. Washington wondered whether his gentry friends could really count on the many insecure planters throughout Virginia who might complain that self-sacrifice of this sort would compromise their social ambitions. Such a person might cry out, Washington observed, that "an alteration in the System of my living, will create suspicions of a decay in my fortune, & such a thought the World must not harbour."[39] Washington, of course, might well have been describing himself, but whatever reservations he may have had, he too added his signature to the document. In Baltimore and Annapolis the principal gentlemen of Maryland joined local tobacco merchants in proclaiming non-importation, and eventually South Carolina came around, forging, in the words of one leading rice planter, "A happy Coalition of our Interest, and that of the Merchants, into ONE *immediate* SELF-INTEREST."[40]

However the early non-importation associations and committees constituted themselves throughout colonial America, they quickly exposed structural weaknesses that could well have compromised the growth of popular political mobilization. Since the agreements reflected the sentiments of particular communities—Boston or Williamsburg, New York or Charleston, for example—the colonists initially found it hard to coordinate consumer protest over large geographic areas. Different groups joined the cause when local conditions allowed. But the difficulties ran deeper, especially in the northern colonies. Reliance on the merchants to bring about political ends was probably doomed from the start. The world of commerce guarded its secrets carefully, and successful merchants seldom shared intelligence about credit, price, and supply with competitors. During this imperial crisis, merchants let normal suspicion about rivals develop into a kind of professional paranoia, and, under extreme pressure to make non-importation work, they projected onto other merchants schemes to gain market advantage. The argument was not without merit. If Boston's merchants canceled their orders for British goods while those in Philadelphia did not, then it seemed entirely plausible—at least, to the Boston traders—that their counterparts in Philadelphia must be cheating.

Consider just a single case. A group of merchants in Wethersfield, Connecticut, suspected the "Committee of Merchants of Boston" of having imported some highly questionable goods. Responding defensively to charges of bad faith, John Hancock and eight other Boston merchants insisted that they had confined "their Importations to the repeal of the Duty on Tea, paper, glass & Colors . . . & we Positively are now more firm, united & resolute than ever; We shall be glad at all Times to Concur with you in every legal measure to promote this Valuable purpose."[41] As in many exchanges of this type, the accusing merchants could not force the issue; they could not insist that the other merchants open their ledgers for inspection. And despite effusive expressions about the need to work together for the common cause, doubts festered. Between 1767 and 1770 the merchants of the northern ports spent a lot of anxious time watching the merchants of other colonies, trying to learn for sure whether competitors had really halted the sale of proscribed consumer goods. Commercial self-interest did not provide a credible foundation on which to build broad political trust.[42] Stated in different terms, during the heat of imperial controversy the merchants found that they could not convincingly speak for collectivities such as "America," or "our country," or the "people."

But others in colonial society managed to do so. During this period, Americans began to imagine allegiances that extended beyond the local communities which time out of mind had been the basis of political identity. Ultimately what allowed scattered colonists to overcome merchant suspicion and parochial loyalties and to communicate with each other across traditional boundaries of space and class, perhaps even of gender, was a profound shift in the character of popular political rhetoric. So long as broad mobilization in support of non-importation depended on narrowly defined interest groups such as the merchants, ordinary people did not have much incentive to participate actively in putting pressure on the British government. As one colonist explained, "The farmers and tradesmen in the country have vainly hoped that the virtue and public spirit of the merchant would be their relief, and that they [the merchants] would not import these things. But have we not had sufficient conviction, that this is not to be depended on? Why should we expect they should have more virtue than we?"[43]

The discovery that the interests of the colonial merchants were not necessarily those of the people helped to transform largely ineffectual bursts of anger into a mass protest. The process occurred slowly, in fits and starts, but during the course of mounting resistance against British duties on imported goods, the authors of broadsides and newspaper essays began to speak *to* and in the name *of* a powerful abstraction known as "the public." Colonial writers addressed the public, inviting it to take part in pressing political concerns which until very recently had been the purview of the provincial gentry, the great planters and well-connected lawyers who assumed that they spoke for the rest of society. But after 1769 it was clear that the times were changing, and the catalyst of change was the almost universal experience of making choices and voicing opinions in the new consumer marketplace of the eighteenth century. At this crucial moment, an imperial dispute triggered by parliamentary taxes on imported goods encouraged middling sorts of people who generally had little impact on the shape of the political culture to participate in the affairs of the day. Not surprisingly, Benjamin Franklin understood this transformation earlier and more clearly than did most contemporaries. Writing in a London newspaper, he explained, "I say, the generality of the people in America . . . have now taken the lead in a great degree, out of the hands of the Merchants, and in town and country meetings are entering into solemn resolutions not to purchase or consume British commodities: . . . if any Merchants do import before that time, they will mark them as enemies to their country, and never deal with them when the trade shall be opened. This is now become a restraint upon the Merchants."[44]

This shift in perception about the true locus of political power represented a genuinely radical development. In fact, protest against the Townshend Program activated what one might describe as a consumer public sphere.[45] With a rising sense of urgency, writers urged ordinary people— now defined as members of a colonial public—to judge for themselves whether the merchants had properly defended the public interest against its many enemies. Thus, to offer an example of this innovative rhetorical strategy, a New York City broadside appealed "To the PUBLIC." The street flier exhorted "the Inhabitants of this CITY . . . to meet at the Coffee House, on Monday next, precisely at twelve o'Clock, to give their Sentiments relative to the article of TEA."[46] On another occasion, the authors of a Philadelphia "CIRCULAR LETTER, from the COMMITTEE OF THE City to the COMMITTEES of other Colonies," praised "the Voice of the Public" which had recently exposed the schemes of clandestine importers.[47] What one encounters in such passages is anonymous persons invoking the public as a source of empowerment, thereby arrogating to themselves the high moral ground in political exchange. Although on some level everyone knew that the public was a convenient fiction, an invented category, it trumped the counter-arguments of special interests.[48] It was a construction that facilitated conversations about non-importation between distant strangers who came to accept the fact that they too belonged to a consumer public sphere which had acquired responsibility to preserve the freedom and liberty of all Americans.

Provincial newspapers sustained the public as an imagined moral force in colonial politics.[49] Ordinary people—the majority of whom were fully literate—turned to weekly journals for intelligence about what was happening in distant communities, and in the pages of what tellingly were called the "public Prints" they learned that the public was busy monitoring the non-importation of British goods. Governor Moore of New York lamented this state of affairs, informing the earl of Hillsborough in May 1768, "It would give me great pleasure if I could boldly assert that the inflammatory Publications in the printed News Papers . . . had been treated with the contempt they really deserve, but I am afraid the bad effects of them are but too sensible already, and that the doctrine they would endeavour to establish is without the least reluctance adopted by all Ranks and conditions of People here."[50]

Like modern televison viewers who marvel how rapidly the details of distant tragedies now reach their homes, the colonists appreciated the capacity of newspapers to expand their knowledge of events taking place in American cities and towns as foreign to their own experience as happenings in Afghanistan or Bangladesh are to most modern Americans. The *Boston Evening-Post*, for example, ran an item during this period in which the writer confessed, "We, who are at a distance from the metropolis, have no other way of being conversed with the political world than the News-Papers; therefore it is our constant practice to peruse them."[51] And when country readers did not find what they anticipated, they complained. "A Tradesman" reported that he was tired of articles about "Poles or Corsicans," preferring to learn more about the state of the domestic economy. The editors of the papers must know that "surely it is high time for the middling People to abstain from *every Superfluity*, in *Dress, Furniture,* and *Living*."[52] In 1770 one aspiring Connecticut poet celebrated the role of the journals in providing news that was, in fact, genuinely new, and in a piece entitled "The News-Paper" the author declared:

> 'Tis truth (with deference to the college)
> News-papers are the spring of knowledge,
> The general source throughout the nation,
> Of every modern conversation.
> What would this mighty people do,
> If there, alas!, was nothing new?[53]

What was new in colonial America, of course, was not accounts of herbal medicines, or the doings of the royal family, or advertisements of "the Latest Goods Just Arrived from London," but rather reports about a "public" putting pressure on merchants to hold the line against the importation of British manufactures. A reader living in New England or New Jersey might not have ever actually visited New York City, but he or she could ascertain from "A CITIZEN," who published in a New York paper circulating throughout the region, that the public should turn a deaf ear to the self-serving cries of the merchants, because "the private Interest of such Persons ought not to stand one Moment in Competition with the Common Good. They [the merchants] ought to wait patiently, till the Circumstances of the Times alter in their Favour; or if they cannot do this, then to apply themselves to other Employments."[54] Newspaper writers may have exaggerated local resistance; they may have even been blatantly disingenuous about the character of protest. Such considerations do not much matter here, since the distant reader, perhaps frightened about challenging British authority even by boycotting consumer goods, took a measure of assurance from the knowledge that he or she might be working in concert with persons who would never be identified more precisely than as members of the public. And it was consoling to be told that one's sacrifice—doing without the pleasures of the marketplace—really did advance the common good.

The question that one might ask, of course, was: Whose common good? For whom did the public speak? Although no one at the time consciously set out to reconceive colonial political identity, that was exactly what happened, for the accelerating swirl of communication in the weekly journals about non-importation provoked ordinary people to imagine themselves within larger political frameworks which had been formed of necessity in opposition to British imperial policy. The newspapers encouraged men and women who perhaps had never given much thought to what was happening in neighboring communities, let alone in distant colonies, to situate themselves within a larger community. Public journals kept people scattered over a vast territory informed about what other Americans were doing to curtail the sale of British goods, and it was not unusual, for example, to encounter in the newspapers of South Carolina or New York detailed stories recounting how the people of Boston or Pennsylvania had sustained the boycott.[55] Sir Henry Moore, the beleaguered royal governor of New York, complained to superiors in London that "extracts of a letter" about the success of non-importation sent to one person in a particular colonial city soon reached almost everyone in America, since "as soon as one of these letters appears in any public paper, it is copied into the Gazettes of all other Provinces, and propagated throughout the whole Continent." Moore exaggerated the reach of the journals, but he was correct to draw attention to the danger that an expanding audience for political intelligence posed for the British administration. As he observed, the "chief tendency of them [the letters in the journals] is to encourage Union among the Provinces, and to distress Great Britain by not importing any English manufactures."[56]

Everywhere Americans reached out to each other through the channel of print. Soon, even in small, relatively isolated communities, people began to situate themselves within a continental conversation that assumed that the members of local committees and associations belonged to an American public that spoke for the interests not of a single village or county, not even of a particular colony, but of something greater, a solidarity created originally by the rhetoric of resistance and soon taken for granted by the very people it was meant to persuade. In this extraordinary political environment, the "respectable inhabitants" of Middletown, Connecticut, together with "the major Part of the Merchants & Traders of the Colony" could declare with remarkable insouciance, "This meeting taking into Consideration the unmerited Distress which the People of America and the Inhabitants of this Colony in particular suffer and are further exposed to from the operation of several Acts of Parliament Imposing Duties." No one doubted, apparently, that "the People of America" actually existed or that they might suffer as one. Perhaps even more revealing, the Middletown group inserted in "the public News Papers of the Colony" an announcement of its intention to cooperate with "our Sister Colonies, in preserving just natural rights, Liberty, and the Welfare of America, & this Colony."[57]

Similar meetings throughout the colonies responded to the imperial challenge in precisely the same manner as did the inhabitants of this Connecticut community. They published their decisions; they protested their uncompromising resolve. And increasingly, they thought of themselves as Americans. A sudden proliferation of collective nouns and phrases reflected a pressing need among people who previously had not had much to do with each other to describe what they were becoming. This development in the political language of the day did not signal that the colonists had replaced older, local identities with a new sense of self. They still thought of themselves as New Englanders or Virginians, as rice planters or urban mechanics, as Lutherans or Congregationalists. Rather, an inventive terminology suggested that the extraordinary difficulties of coordinating a massive consumer boycott over such a large territory had raised a tough question of diction for those many popular newspaper writers who now presumed to speak within the consumer public sphere about a much broader although as yet ill-defined collectivity that seemed to be taking shape. They found themselves trying to project a political entity commensurate with the huge transatlantic market that it intended to disrupt.

The tentative choice of words employed to meet this challenge reflected the problem of representing a people who were not really a people who lived in a country that was certainly not a country. These were men and women who had no desire for independence from Great Britain and who would have been shocked to learn that they were on the high road to forming a nation of the mind. Some authors used the word country. Others seemed more comfortable referring to the "British Colonies in America," but however the union with the "Sister-Colonies" originated, the goal of the whole was the promotion of "American Happiness." After all, "Every Lover of Liberty on the Continent" strove to advance "the general Cause of American Liberty" or the "Common Cause of American Liberty." If "Our brethren in North-America" did anything less, they would be incapable of defending "The present and future INTEREST, LIBERTY AND WELL-BEING OF AMERICA."[58] A leading Boston paper reported that other colonists had urged that "we become one DETERMINED PEOPLE."[59] A New York City author went over the top, advocating in 1769 an "*American Magna Charta and a Bill of Rights.*" As this person explained in screaming capital letters, "every SON AND DAUGHTER OF LIBERTY IN AMERICA, must inevitably, FIRMLY RESOLVE NOT TO BE SLAVES FOR CONTINUANCE, but immediately subscribe to, and immediately PRACTICE the wearing of the *cheapest Cloathing,* THE VERY CHEAPEST CLOATHING that can possibly be invented. AMERICAN REPRESENTATIVES should immediately begin and set the EXAMPLE; it must strongly be promoted, become *fashionable,* and universally be esteemed POPULAR, till the Time shall arrive that EVERY GRIEVANCE IN AMERICA is justly removed."[60] Equating patriotism with fashion was a nice touch in a consumer economy.

Another perspective on the fabrication of political identity was to see it as an aspect of the formation of trust. It was all well and good for colonists living in different regions and separated by often impassable rivers and roads to champion the rhetoric of "the general Cause of American Liberty," but if those distant strangers failed to do more than talk the language of mutual purpose, there was no incentive for any group to take the lead in promoting consumer sacrifice. Trust of this sort is easily taken for granted. Anthropologists have long described, often nostalgically, the sense of trust that is frequently a characteristic of face-to-face relations or defines life in small, traditional communities. The colonial phenomenon was different. It involved trust established across space, impersonally, a product of a print culture, and it was absolutely essential for the development of the popular mobilization on which any successful revolutionary action depended. It had to be learned and relearned, nourished, proclaimed, and reaffirmed, for unless firmly grounded in public opinion, trust could not possibly survive rumors of betrayal.

And so, like inexperienced lovers, the colonists in 1769 and 1770 tentatively reached out to each other, afraid of having expressions of interest spurned and worried that the objects of their attention might turn out to be less reliable than had been assumed. The Sons of Liberty in North Carolina, for example, declared that the "People of this Province have bound themselves, in the general Cause of American Liberties, by extending their Resolutions [not to import British goods], until the Whole of their complaints is removed. It would be a capital Crime in us, to suspect the public Virtue of our Countrymen."[61] But, of course, the virtue of other Americans had to be taken on trust, at least until it had been affirmed in no uncertain terms by refusing British manufactures. After applauding "the spirited behavior of our Boston, New-York and Philadelphia brethren, in renouncing all commerce," the "Freeholders, Merchants, and Traders" of Elizabeth Town, New Jersey, bravely announced "That we are determined that we will at all times, be ready to join in any measure that shall be entered into by the colonies in general, to carry the design of said agreement into the fullest execution." To these people who were creatively expanding their political horizons it seemed worthwhile to take a chance on trust, for they had convinced themselves that "these are the general sentiments of all the freeholders and inhabitants of this Province; and we will readily concur with them in any further measures they may propose, for the support of an agreement, upon which the preservation of the liberties of America so essentially depend."[62] The general sentiments of the entire free population of New Jersey had to be accepted on faith; if one resided in Elizabeth Town, one simply assumed the best of political strangers. This was also the message of a Charleston writer who reminded the public that what was "wholesome" for South Carolina "politically speaking" must be so for the northern colonies as well, for although "our circumstances are, in some respects, dissimilar to theirs," they were potential allies. "And," the essayist continued, "the man, who endeavors to suggest any thing at this time, which may cause any jealousy or division amongst the American colonies, can be no friend to *any* of them."[63] Declaring trust in this manner did not in itself make the northern colonies more trustworthy, but certainly, if one wanted to promote non-importation in Charleston, it helped to imagine they were.

Expansion of political horizons throughout colonial America occurred most strikingly within a framework of consumer experience. This is a point of considerable significance, and one that historians have tended to underrate. Although a cherished language of rights and liberty played a central part in the process of reaching out to strangers, it almost always found expression in a strategy of non-importation. Abstractions about political freedom were thus woven into the fabric of everyday life, so that in this social climate one's relation to enumerated British objects became a concrete measure of commitment to rhetorical principle. Mobilization across traditional boundaries, therefore, should not be put forward as an either/or proposition: *Either* Americans constructed a larger sense of community through a shared political vocabulary of rights and liberty, *or* they assembled meaningful trust through the strategy of non-importation. The process of reimagining identity tapped both possibilities. People who were committed to the defense of rights and liberty were precisely those men and women who were most likely to support the boycott movement, and by publicly demonstrating their willingness to sacrifice manufactured British goods— the items so carefully inventoried on the lists—they communicated to others a deep commitment to political principle.

Communities did not talk to other communities through the newspapers simply about rights and property, about ideas in the abstract, but rather about the rights and property that they were actively defending by supporting non-importation. The men attending a town meeting at Ashford, a small farming village in eastern Connecticut, understood the connection. In 1770 they declared, "[I]f the people of America properly attend to the concern of salvation and (unitedly) resolve upon an unshaken perseverance in the affair of non-importation till there is a total repeal of the revenue acts and an ample redress of American grievances, we shall be a free and flourishing people!"[64] "Philo Patria," a New London writer, agreed. "The truth is we have no occasion for British manufactures; they are rank poison to the constitution of this country," to which he added, "Let us save our money in order to save our country."[65] A gathering of "freeholders, merchants and traders" in New Brunswick, New Jersey, endorsed the same logic, voting "That the Non-Importation Agreement which was generously and uniformly entered into, by the merchants and traders in the several colonies, is the best and most reasonable scheme that could have been fallen on, to prevent the direful effects of the act of parliament . . . calculated to enslave this country."[66] And finally, a group in Newbern, North Carolina, concluded that non-importation was a "momentous business, wherein we may now clearly perceive, entirely hinges American liberty."[67]

IV

The colonists rapidly learned that the rhetoric of protest unsupported by the means of enforcement amounted to little more than bombast. Between 1768 and 1770 Americans formed hundreds of groups to monitor the behavior of local merchants. In each community the composition of the oversight committees differed slightly. In some regions—especially in the New England colonies—town meetings put pressure on the merchants to uphold agreements not to import enumerated goods. In other places, such as Virginia and South Carolina, the source of authority in these matters was less clear. But however people decided to police the flow of British manufactures, they almost always focused attention on the activities of the merchants, a fact of some significance in understanding the precise timing of the final separation from king and Parliament. The Stamp Act had sparked furious passions, and if rebellion within the empire had depended solely on venting emotion, the despised legislation would have surely generated armed conflict. But however enraged the colonists may have been, they lacked in 1765 an infrastructure capable of sustaining a coordinated sense of purpose over large distances. If the Townshend Revenue Act did not quite ignite the same heated response, it did invite Americans of different backgrounds to explore the possibilities of trust, and while this development encouraged the invention of new, more expansive identities, it did not yet address the central question posed by the need to mobilize a population in a political cause: Were ordinary men and women willing to take direction and personal responsibility for their own actions, in this case, in the marketplace? During the second wave of boycotts, the answer was generally negative. They tried to pin blame for spotty enforcement of non-importation upon the merchants, insisting that those who sold and distributed British imports must cut off the flow of merchandise, a strategic move that temporarily masked their own political obligations as consumers.

In modern political terms one might conclude that "non-governmental organizations" had assumed authority over the enforcement of non-importation throughout colonial America. The analogy provides insight into the distribution of power on the local level. Even when town meetings exerted themselves, they did so more as groups of concerned citizens than as formal legal bodies. The Boston town meeting, for example, issued a report in May 1769 that "unanimously expressed their high Satisfaction on being informed that the Merchants had so strictly adhered to their late Agreement relative to a Non-importation of European Merchandise." In other words, a significant number of Boston merchants had previously agreed among themselves—whether out of love of country or fear of bankruptcy was not stated—to halt the sale of enumerated British goods until Parliament repealed the Townshend duties. Orders that arrived while the agreement was in effect were supposed to be stored in a public warehouse, and from time to time representatives of the town checked to discover if articles had mysteriously gone missing. The purpose of the May report was to warn

all "Inhabitants" against doing business with those merchants who had refused to sign the agreement and who were rumored to have imported a new
shipment of dry goods on "the Vessels lately arrived from Great-Britain."
Confronted with a fresh inventory of imported manufactures, inhabitants
were urged—not ordered—to give their custom only to merchants who
had signed the original agreement and who, thereby, had "freely preferred
the future Welfare of their Country and all North-America, to any present
Advantage of their own."[68] The pressure on the merchants was obviously
very great, and to make matters worse from their perspective, the self-appointed monitors of trade published their findings in newspapers that
quickly reached other cities and towns. The effectiveness of these non-governmental organizations amazed General Thomas Gage, who in December
1769 wrote from New York City:

> Committees of Merchants at Boston, N: York, and Philadelphia contrive to exercise
> the Government they have set up to prohibit the Importation of British Goods, ap-
> point Inspectors, tender Oaths to the Masters of Vessels, and enforce their Prohibi-
> tions by coercive Measures. In times less dissolute, and licentious, it would be a matter
> of Astonishment, to hear that British Manufactures were prohibited in British Prov-
> inces, by an illegal Combination of People . . . and surely wonderful, that such an
> Imperium should be set up, and at length established, without the least Show of Op-
> position.[69]

Quasi-legal modes of enforcement served different ends. However they
may have constituted themselves, local authorities clearly wanted to disrupt consumer trade with Great Britain. Less obvious but no less important in mobilizing political resistance, the mechanisms devised for keeping
the merchants in line functioned to distinguish persons who supported
protest from those willing to compromise principle in the name of private
advantage. Rituals of enforcement exposed people who might have mouthed
the right words, urging others to defend liberty, but did not really want to
sacrifice personal well-being in order to reform imperial policy. And finally,
enforcement of non-importation helped indoctrinate the general public—
not just the members of the merchant community—about the issues that
energized the controversy with Great Britain.

Discipline and instruction in the marketplace thus developed hand in
hand. In a Philadelphia broadside arrestingly entitled *To the Public* (1770), a
writer complained of the "pathetic" and presumably not fully sincere merchants who were recently caught selling enumerated goods. Every reader
should see through the charade, for "the gentlemen censured have meanly
and from pecuniary motives, endeavored to subvert the grand, the glorious
cause of Liberty; long ably, virtuously and successfully supported by our
Brethren on the continent in general, and the truly patriotic *Philadelphians*
in particular."[70] Such merchants had revealed themselves to be "*Enemies to
American Liberty*; their Names will be made public; their Companies
avoided; and every Stigma fixed upon them to make them *despicable*."[71]

The point is not that ordinary people did not understand the language
of rights or the arguments against unconstitutional taxation. They did.

To the PUBLIC.

NOTWITHSTANDING the generous and pathetic Confeſſion, publicly made and ſigned before the *Committee* of *Merchants*, at the *Coffee-Houſe*, by the unfortunate Violaters of the Non-importation Agreement, who have ſhewn all the marks of ſchool-boys penitence, by begging pardon for the crime they have committed, and promiſing heartily and ſincerely never again to commit the like, it is with a ſympathzeing concern, I hear numbers of our fellow citizens ſtill continue to cenſure thoſe penitential Gentleman, and are ſo hard-hearted as to declare they as juſtly merited taring and feathering as a late informer; but I hope the more ſenſible and cool-thinking amongſt us, are of a very contrary opinion---For though the gentlemen cenſured have, *meanly* and from pecuniary motives, endeavoured to ſubvert the grand, the glorious cauſe of Liberty; long ably, virtuouſly and ſucceſsfully ſupported by our Brethren on the continent in general, and the truly patriotic *Philadelphians* in particular; though they have baſely and treacherouſly deſerted the common cauſe, and ignominiouſly violated their moſt ſacred promiſes; though we have all the reaſon imaginable to believe (and indeed we have) that they would have acted in the ſame unwarrantably villainous manner, were they certain that the whole continent muſt inevitably have been enſlaved, from the ſucceſs of their *Nocturnal Enterprize*; nay more, though we are really ſenſible that they would ſacrifice their GOD, their Country and their King to private emolument; ſurely the greateſt patriot amongſt us, will not be ſo ſenſeleſs, as to ſay thoſe Gentlemen, Merchants, and Men of real Property, ſhould be put on a level with, and expoſed like an informer; a fellow not worth a groat, a poor wretch, of as little conſequence as a *Scotch-Pedler*. The apparent abſurdity of ſuch an opinion, muſt refute every argument offered in ſupport of it.---But as I have the conſolation to believe that the greater part, if not all thoſe who adviſe ſuch a ſevere and indecent mode of puniſhment, either have not ſeen the confeſſion of the unfortunately avaricious culprits, publiſhed in Meſſrs. *Bradford's Journal*, of *Thurſday* laſt, or believe it to be ſpurious, from their names not being annexed---I have in vindication of thoſe unhappy men, at my own expence got five thouſand copies thereof (ſigned with their names) printed, which I ſhall have carefully circulated in this, and the neighbouring provinces, for the *ſatisfaction* of ſuch as may not have an opportunity of ſeeing the original at the *Coffee-Houſe*; and doubt not, but every good man will conſider it a ſufficient attonement for their tranſgreſſion; eſpecially as it was committed againſt the intereſt and proſperity of *only* every freeborn ſubject in *ONE* quarter of the Globe.

(Above)
This 1770 Philadelphia broadside was addressed *To the Public*, an ill-defined but newly empowered group of colonial consumers. 4 July 1770. *Philadelphia. Courtesy of the American Antiquarian Society.*

(Right)
This public notice urged "the Sons and Daughters of LIBERTY" not to purchase goods from William Jackson, "an IMPORTER" who had refused to sign the Boston non-importation agreement. *Reproduced from the Prints Division, Library of Congress.*

[January, 1770]

WILLIAM JACKSON,

an IMPORTER; at the

BRAZEN HEAD,

North Side of the TOWN-HOUSE,

and Oppoſite the Town-Pump, *in*

Corn-hill, BOSTON.

It is deſired that the SONS and DAUGHTERS of *LIBERTY*, would not buy any one thing of him, for in ſo doing they will bring Diſgrace upon *themſelves*, and their *Poſterity*, for *ever* and *ever*, AMEN.

Rather, enforcement provided a rough index of commitment, and when respected commercial leaders—the type of man one might instinctively look up to in a society that encouraged dreams of upward mobility—were compelled by local committees of inspection to defend the common political good, ordinary people saw for themselves the power of ideas about rights and liberty. It was in this spirit that the author of a 1768 broadside published under the banner *The True Sons of Liberty and Supporters of the Non-Importation Agreement* decried those who purchased from William Jackson, a wealthy Boston merchant who had refused to sign the boycott agreement. "It is desired," announced this writer who spoke to the public in the name of the public, "that the Sons and Daughters of LIBERTY would not buy any one thing of him [Jackson], for in so doing they will bring Disgrace upon *themselves,* and their *Posterity,* for *ever* and *ever,* AMEN."[72]

In an unsettled political environment, colonists invented what might best be described as rituals of consumer protest. This surge of creativity comes as something of a surprise. Historians have long been aware that the Reform Protestant societies planted in North America lacked the kind of rich folk culture that one associates with early modern Catholic Europe. Within that customary world, peasant communities celebrated in the appropriate manner saints' days that structured the annual calendar. The highlight of the year may have been Carnival, held just before Lent, when the normal expectations of gender and class were often suspended. And when people strayed from the conventions of the community—for example, when an old man took a very young wife—they could find themselves targets of charivaris, highly threatening expressions of what was known as "rough music." The European migrants who traveled to the New World seemed largely to have discarded such expressions of traditional life.[73] And yet, when confronted with a political crisis within the empire, the colonists quickly devised popular rituals which like the charivaris of Europe attempted to shame those who defied the will of the community. Although in general form the rituals of consumer protest may have drawn upon knowledge of similar events in Europe, they did not in fact have much to do with religion. These were secular, market-inspired occasions intended to articulate the community's commitment to non-importation. Shaming mechanisms dramatically separated friends from enemies and thus made it ever harder for ordinary people to remain neutral in the cause of liberty.

The mere risk of public censure was frequently sufficient to neutralize opposition to the boycott. George Mason explained to a fellow Virginia planter, Richard Henry Lee, how the public might compel obedience. "Experience [has] too fully proved," wrote Mason, "that when the Goods are here, many of our People will purchase [them], even some who affect to be called Gentlemen. For this Purpose, the Sense of Shame & the Fear of Reproach must be inculcated & enforced in the strongest Manner; and if that can be done properly, it has a much greater Influence upon the Actions of Mankind than is generally imagined. Nature has impress'd this useful Principle upon every Breast: it is a just observation that if Shame was banished

At a Meeting of the Merchants & Traders,
at *Faneuil*-Hall, on the 23d *January* 1770.

The following Votes were paffed, viz.

WHEREAS in *Purfuance of a Vote on Thurfday laft, the Body affembled as above-mentioned repaired to the Houfes or Places of Abode of divers Perfons, requiring them to fulfill their own voluntary Contract made with the Merchants and Traders aforefaid, with whom they agreed to have their Goods ftored under the Care of the Committee of Infpection, to be by them kept until a general Importation might take Place*——*And whereas* William Jackfon, Theophilus Lillie, John Taylor *and* Nathaniel Rogers, all of Bofton, *did refufe, and yet delay to comply with the faid Requifition :*

Therefore it was *Voted,* That the faid *William Jackfon, Theophilus Lillie, John Taylor,* and *Nathaniel Rogers,* in thus refufing and delaying to comply with fo reafonable and juft a Demand, have abufed the Lenity and Patience of their Fellow Citizens ; and have confirmed this Body in their Opinion that they are obftinate and inveterate Enemies to their Country, and Subverters of the Rights and Liberties of this Continent : And we think it our indifpenfible Duty to Ourfelves and Pofterity, for ever hereafter, to treat them as fuch, by withholding not only all commercial Dealings, but every Act and Office of common Civility : Hoping that they may be forever fruftrated in this and in every other Attempt to counterwork the generous Intentions of the patriotic Merchants of this Metropolis, and of all America : And we do fervently wifh that all who with us are exerting themfelves to maintain and fecure the invaluable Rights of our Country, may refufe to fell to, buy of, or have any Intercourfe with the faid *William Jackfon, Theophilus Lillie, John Taylor* and *Nathaniel Rogers,* not only during the prefent Struggle for Liberty, but *for ever* hereafter.

"A Meeting of the Merchants & Traders, at Faneuil-Hall, on the 23d January 1770" called upon "the Friends to Liberty and their Country's Cause" to display this announcement "over the Chimney Piece of every public House, and on every other proper Place, in every Town, in this and every other Colony . . . as a Monument of the Remembrance of the detestable Names above-mentioned." *FMs Sparks 10, vol. 3, p. 62, by permission of the Houghton Library, Harvard University, Cambridge, Massachusetts.*

out of the World, she wou'd carry away with her what little Virtue is left in it."[74] Errant merchants, of course, had the most to fear. The public threatened to ostracize them, for, as "Civis" announced in a Boston journal in 1770, "Any man, I should think, must be lost to all sense of remorse, who from a consideration of commercial advantages, can be *unfeeling* to so high a censure of his fellow-citizens . . . [as well as the] additional resolution to withhold all *social* intercourse with him *forever* hereafter." By merchandising enumerated goods, the enemies of liberty "severed themselves from the Commonwealth." Civis thought such a fate almost too terrible to contemplate. "I know not what ideas some persons may have of happiness," he wrote, "[but] I cannot think of any greater misfortune in this life, than for a man to be *cursed by his Country.*"[75]

A chilling reminder of just what it might have meant for a person to be shunned in this manner came from a "Farmer," who claimed to have lived in Connecticut. After railing against Americans who might "value liberty at so small a price as a ribbon, a paper of pins or a silk neckcloth," the Farmer put forward his plan for enforcing non-importation:

> [I]f the principal part of the towns on the continent would vote it at their public town meetings not to purchase any goods imported from Great-Britain contrary to the agreement formerly held to, nor allow any to be had in their families, and that all such as purchase such goods or wares, shall incur the displeasure of the town, and be treated as enemies and betrayers of their country, and their names together with the offences committed, be recorded in the public records of the town. And further that they shall not be allowed the honor of any office of public trust in said town, nor have any privileges that they lawfully could withhold from them, it would greatly discourage the importing of British goods into America, and perhaps for the present put a stop to it.[76]

Several cases of people actually brought to the bar of public censure revealed how commercial shaming operated. Only the printed record survives. Notorious importers may have received private warnings to change their ways; rumors of their greed may have circulated in the taverns. But eventually, the local press exposed the more brazen offenders. During the summer of 1769 a broadside—revealingly labeled an "ADVERTISEMENT" by its anonymous author—was distributed on the streets of New York City under a sensational headline: "Of greater IMPORTANCE to the PUBLIC, than any which has yet appeared on the like Occasion." The problem was Simeon Cooley, a "Haberdasher, Jeweler, and Silversmith," who had established a solid business venture, purchased a house, and once even voiced sympathy for the rights of the American people. But ideological appearances were deceptive. First, Cooley took enumerated goods out of storage after promising that he would return them. He lied. "The vile Ingrate," the broadside proclaimed, ". . . took Advantage of the Lenity and Credulity of the Committee," and soon Cooley openly offered British imports for sale. Unless the public acted immediately, the "Reptile and Miscreant" might succeed. Indeed, the public must not allow him "to baffle or defeat the united virtuous Efforts, in the Support of so righteous a Cause, not only of this City, but of the whole Continent." Henceforth, Cooley should "be treated on all Occasions and by all legal Means as an Enemy to his Country, a Pest to Society, and a vile Disturber of the Peace, Police, and good order of this City." Perhaps Cooley could endure "the Loss of a little Reputation," but for most colonial shopkeepers, the "Hatred of the Public" was a real concern.[77]

John Taylor also suffered the pain of being ostracized. According to a Boston newspaper, he had joined "the TRUE HEART Fire-Club," an exclusive fraternity that served the community while bestowing a measure of distinction on its members. But whatever his qualifications for election, Taylor's public behavior angered his associates. A meeting of the society "unanimously Voted" to dismiss Taylor, since in the opinion of his colleagues he seemed "unworthy [of] being a Member of it, for not complying with the Agreement of the Merchants." Taylor apparently promised to mend his ways, and after three months the club readmitted him. Like Simeon Cooley, however, Taylor had not learned the desired ideological lesson. Six months after the first confrontation, the "TRUE HEART Fire-Club" lost patience, announcing that Taylor had "grossly affronted the Body of Merchants and this Society, by perfidiously violating his Agreement with them, and his Promise to us, not to vend any British Goods contrary to the universal Sense of the Friends of this oppressed CONTINENT, by which he has rendered himself justly obnoxious to all good Men, and more especially to every well wisher to AMERICA." It is striking that the firefighters claimed to represent the will of a country that was not a country, but, as Taylor discovered, by merchandising British imports he had shown himself no supporter of liberty. The fire club dropped him from the organization, denying him "all the Benefits of this Society, even in Times of Greatest Distress; and [voted] that he NEVER *be Re-admitted upon any Terms whatever.*"[78] How many other people endured public shame on this order is impossible to discern. Perhaps of greater significance is the fact that by debating Taylor's betrayal the members of the "TRUE HEART Fire-Club" gained a much clearer sense of their own colonial rights—and of exactly how selling British goods put those rights in jeopardy.

Shaming worked presumably because the likes of Taylor and Cooley did not want to lose face. Although men of modest standing in this society, they cared about honor and reputation. For time out of mind, honor had been at risk in small face-to-face communities where everyone quickly learned who had violated local custom. Exposure required only a word on the street, and soon neighbors shunned the rule breaker in church and tavern. But late eighteenth-century colonial ports were not intimate communities of this sort. As commercial centers they hosted many transient workers—sailors and day laborers—and cities like Boston, New York, and Philadelphia supported hundreds of shops, large and small. Almost no one could possibly have had dealings with more than a tiny fraction of the merchants and store owners in such a place, and the increasingly impersonal quality of public life made it hard to shame particular men and women who imported British goods. In these matters, the public needed guidance.

Not surprisingly, the popular press provided the remedy. It regularly published lists of names of those merchants who either refused to sign a non-importation agreement or broke their promise after signing. A "Committee of Inspection" in Boston, struggling to keep up with rumors of infractions, vowed "that the names of such persons shall be published constantly in the news-papers, and also in hand bills dispersed through the province, that the public may know them."[79] Ordinary readers combed through these lists, sometimes discovering that local figures whom they had previously held in high esteem were actually enemies of American liberty. A person from Long Island wrote to a New York City journal recounting that "In perusing a List of the infamous, untimely Importers, I observed the Names of a Number of respectable Gentlemen, who I thought would have suffered almost any Thing that might have been laid on them, rather than to have entered into such a Measure; a Measure which if persisted in, will entail Infamy and Disgrace upon themselves and their Posterity."[80] If nothing else, monitoring names eroded traditional deference. Even so-called gentlemen could not hide from the public their preference for their own "little private advantage [over] . . . the common Interest of all the Colonies."[81]

Exposure in print was not restricted to major cities. In remote towns along the North Carolina coast, the Sons of Liberty challenged the honor of violators, announcing that "Should those gentlemen still persist in a practice so destructive in its tendency to the liberties of the people of this colony, they must not be surprised, if hereafter the names of the importers and purchasers should be published in the Cape-Fear MERCURY."[82] The publication of names seems to have worked even over long distances. A South Carolina merchant accused of not supporting the boycott—wrongly, in his estimation—complained that by including his name on a list public enforcers had tarnished his reputation "in other Parts of the Continent," and that was bad for business.[83]

Rituals of consumer enforcement ended most satisfactorily when an accused merchant confessed to crimes against the political community. As extra-legal bodies, the committees of inspection could not arrest or jail brazen importers. In any case, disciplining traders represented only part of the challenge. Public admission of commercial misbehavior also provided a dramatic mechanism for indoctrinating ordinary people who for one reason or another had not given much thought to the ideological implications of non-importation. As performance, therefore, confessions might be compared to execution sermons, a popular form of entertainment in early America. At the moment of death, a minister often lectured the condemned man or woman about the moral deficiencies that had brought the person to the scaffold. Whatever their worth for the individual about to be hanged, these occasions served to legitimate normative religious values. The lesson was clear. If one lived according to Scripture, one might well avoid swinging at the end of a rope.

In an analogous setting, Alexander Robertson, a New York City merchant caught red-handed selling enumerated goods, presented just the kind of statement that the political culture demanded. In a broadside appropriately addressed "To the PUBLICK," Robertson proclaimed the legitimacy of non-importation. "As I have justly incurred the Resentment of my Fellow citizens, from my Behavior, as set forth in an Advertisement *Of great Importance to the Publick*," he confessed, "I beg Leave to implore the pardon of the Publick, assuring them that I am truly sorry for the Part I have acted; declare and promise that I never will again attempt an Act contrary to the true Interest and Resolutions of a People zealous in the Cause of *Virtue* and *Liberty*." After swearing that he had returned the objectionable British goods once in his possession, Robertson beseeched "the Public in general to believe me."[84] Whether it did so is hard to assess.

General Thomas Gage could not believe what was happening. Colonists were extorting confessions from merchants engaged in perfectly lawful trade. In a letter dispatched from New York to London, Gage sputtered, "A man brought by Threats and Violence from his House into the most open Part of the Town under a Gallows, and forced to read a Paper put into his Hands, to make Excuses for importing British manufactures: His Goods taken from him & put into Storage. You would from these Proceedings suppose this to be rather a French or Spanish Province, instead of Part of the British Territories."[85] What the general failed to appreciate was that in an empire of goods market protest was the most effective way to resist authority that increasingly seemed as autocratic as that of France or Spain.

The situation in New York was not exceptional. In another confession directed "To The Public," four Philadelphia merchants acknowledged "with shame and confusion" that they had acted "contrary to the sentiments of the inhabitants" by taking some goods out of storage "under the cover of night." They now admitted that they had acted "privately and clandestinely," and like Robertson, they declared, "[W]e are sincerely and heartily sorry and ask pardon of the Public."[86] In the small Connecticut village of Windham the process of discipline and indoctrination took a different turn. A "Committee of Inspection" found two traders guilty of knowingly bringing enumerated goods from Providence, Rhode Island, into Connecticut. Called before the members of the committee, James Flint and Shubel Abbe were asked to justify their actions. The men may not have understood exactly what was expected at that moment. Whatever their thoughts, they received a remarkable lecture on American rights. The traders should have appreciated "the mischievous Tendency of such Measures, and their threatening Aspect upon the Rights of America. . . . It was then urged, that the Body of Merchants in Providence had violated their explicit Agreement, counteracted the Spirit and Sense of the Country relative to Non-Importation, basely betrayed their Trust, and sold their Birthright Privileges for a Mess of Potage." Flint and Abbe were further reminded that "if such Dissimulation and Duplicity in Dealing was countenanced by the People in general, we should soon be grasped in the Iron Arms of Oppression, kicked about by the Tools of arbitrary Power, and plundered of every thing dear and valuable in Life."

Modern Americans who like to believe that independence came effortlessly, certainly painlessly, might reflect on such episodes, for if they are familiar with more recent revolutionary movements in Soviet Russia and Maoist China they might recognize in this colonial American town the voice of tough-minded political activists. Flint and Abbe certainly got the point. They wanted nothing to do with arbitrary power. And perhaps with a sigh of relief, they "freely and cheerfully" surrendered the objectionable British goods, and in the process of schooling the malefactors, the people of Windham reaffirmed their own political correctness.[87]

Some importers endured far worse than an impromptu lecture on liberty. How many so-called dishonest traders suffered tar and feathers during the Townshend protest cannot be accurately discerned, but the number was probably less than frightened British officials imagined. It would not have required many incidents of this sort to persuade fence-sitters among the merchants to sign a non-importation agreement. In any event, contrition, not physical violence, was the goal. A Boston case supports this hypothesis. According to someone calling himself "A Resolutionist," the trouble began one afternoon, between two and three o'clock, when a small-time merchant identified as McMasters was apprehended selling British goods. A group of angry people immediately seized him "at the South part of the town, and put [McMasters] into a cart, with some tar in a barrel, and a bag of feathers." A growing crowd then dragged the cart to King Street in the center of Boston, "where it was said he was to undergo the indignity of this modern punishment." By this time the trader was overcome by fear. Even his tormenters acknowledged that McMasters "appeared to be greatly frightened, which the humanity of some persons present, imagin[ed] might produce a fainting." Obviously, this exercise in street justice was not supposed to bring on a fatal heart attack. "A Resolutionist" explained that McMasters "was thereupon permitted to go into a gentleman's house for a short time, properly attended, in order to recover himself, where he soon after solemnly promised, that if he might be spared from being tarred and feathered, he would *immediately* leave the town, and never come into it again." The offer resolved a situation that seemed to be getting out of hand. The enforcers agreed "upon condition that he should be carried out in the cart." To this, McMasters "readily consented, and a chair being placed therein in lieu of the tar-barrel, he was then carted out of town as far as [the] Roxbury-line."[88]

What dishonest merchants such as McMasters lacked and what the vigilant public possessed was *virtue*. This word came close to defining the ideology of the entire non-importation movement. Indeed, at the time, almost everyone agreed that without popular virtue the cause of American liberty had no chance at all. Consumer virtue, however, must be clearly distinguished from two of its distant cousins, both of which have received a lion's share of attention from historians of eighteenth-century political thought. Perhaps the most celebrated virtue of the period was associated with a republican tradition which modern scholars have traced back to the Renaissance Italian city-states of Niccolo Machiavelli. This philosophy of civic power undoubtedly influenced some highly educated colonial American leaders who wrote formal pamphlets. It schooled them to depict the virtuous citizen as a man—never as a woman—whose landed property enabled him to rise above the corrupting influence of commerce and thereby to preserve the integrity of republican government. Cincinnatus, the noble Roman who famously put down the plow to defend the republic, was a model of classical republican virtue. Such a figure could not be bribed. His agrarian wealth guaranteed the independence of his political judgment and, of course, afforded him an opportunity unavailable to most other people in society of cultivating virtue.[89] A second language of virtue available to the colonists was solidly grounded in Christian morality, and at least one historian has insisted that the so-called Puritan ethic energized the rhetoric of popular protest. This claim was undoubtedly true. A population that had recently flocked to hear the Reverend George Whitefield expatiate on the New Birth, promoted a huge evangelical movement known as the Great Awakening, and described the future development of the American colonies in glowing millenarian terms almost unthinkingly brought the vocabulary of Scripture to political discussion.[90]

While both languages of virtue helped colonists make sense of an ever more threatening imperial crisis, neither rivaled the impact of consumer virtue on the mobilization of the American people. Indeed, the virtue that resonated through the entire boycott movement was closer to what one scholar has provocatively labeled "bourgeois virtue."[91] Unlike Christian virtue, it was essentially a secular quality whose origins could be found in the experience of participating in an advanced commercial economy rather than in the Bible. And unlike republican virtue, consumer virtue did not assume that one owned a great landed estate or could bring an unsullied independent judgment to civic debate. Anyone could possess consumer virtue. All one needed was the capacity to purchase goods in the marketplace, a qualification so elementary that women as well as men, urban dwellers as well as yeomen farmers, the poorer sorts as well as the well-to-do, could dare openly to invoke its name in the public sphere.

A virtuous person was one who voluntarily exercised self-restraint in the consumer marketplace. No one denied the desirability of the exciting new manufactured items imported from Great Britain; consumer virtue did not represent a revolt against the tenets of eighteenth-century commercial capitalism. But however appealing the imports were, the virtuous colonists exercised self-control for the common good. It was in this spirit that "a large body of respectable inhabitants" in one colonial city resolved to promote "virtuous self-denial."[92] In another case, the delegates to a New Haven boycott meeting in 1770 assumed without fear of contradiction that "the non-importation agreement come into by the colonies in general, and by this [one] in particular . . . were founded on free, virtuous, peaceable, manly and patriotic principles."[93] And "Juris Prudens," writing in a popular New York City newspaper, urged all Americans: "[L]et us import no Goods whatsoever from Great-Britain, and we shall be crowned Victors; we shall be free forever."[94]

The rather straightforward sense of market virtue that developed throughout the colonies on the eve of independence had powerful implications for political mobilization. Anyone who regularly purchased manufactured goods from Great Britain could become virtuous simply by curtailing consumption. The concept thus linked everyday experience and behavior with a broadly shared sense of the general welfare. What one did with one's money suddenly mattered very much to the entire community, for in this highly charged atmosphere economic self-indulgence became a glaring public vice. Unlike Cincinnatus, the bourgeois patriot did not reach immediately for the sword. He first examined the household budget, asking how each member of the family might contribute to the cause of liberty. "I laugh at a man who talks of facing cannon and red coats," asserted one Boston writer, "who cannot conquer his foppish empty notions of grandeur. What is true grandeur, but a noble patriotic resolution of sacrificing every other consideration to the Love of Country! And can he be a true lover of his country . . . who would soon be seen strutting about the streets, clad in foreign fripperies, than to be nobly independent in russet gray!"[95] Wherever they lived, bourgeois Americans instructed their "children . . . to practice virtue and industry with good economy, which will naturally supply the individuals . . . with abundance, and enable them to improve in all kinds of learning and science and render them useful, respectable and independent."[96]

Virtue of this sort encouraged ordinary people to join with distant strangers—consumers of the continent—in making a genuine sacrifice for their rights within the empire. To give up a personal item of comfort and beauty was something that they all could do. It was a realistic request, a call for sacrifice that touched the lives of colonists who perhaps had never heard of Cincinnatus but nevertheless wanted to make a palpable contribution to the American cause. To be sure, the individual consumer could exercise his or her free will and ignore appeals from those who supported the general boycott. But one thereby surrendered one's right to blame others for political oppression. Membership in a commercial society implied responsibilities to a large collectivity. As "Pro Aris Et Focis" wrote in 1769, "Our merchants have done worthily; but it is the body of the people, who must, under GOD, finally save us. For while there are debauched consumers of foreign luxuries, there always will be, in this depraved state, mercenary creatures enough to import the *bane of their country.*" The author refused to let the vicious consumer sit complacently. Victory over an autocratic Parliament required "the virtue of the people," all of them.[97]

In the formation of new political solidarities, it was of no little importance that the virtuous consumer actually look virtuous. Although it was not always advisable to judge people by appearances alone, a patriotic style of dress accompanied the celebration of bourgeois virtue. Fashion became a measure of ideological commitment; it certainly beat other ways of discerning what was going on inside people's heads. "Philo Americanus" could hardly contain himself when he reflected "on our political virtue." "I am almost transported," he exclaimed in 1769; "my heart distends with generous pride because I am an American. Others may extol Roman greatness or Corsican bravery, but the impartial must think American patriots fall behind neither." And what had the patriotic Americans done to deserve such praise? They had visibly changed their consumer habits. "America, from one end to the other, can now boast of Gentlemen and Ladies, used to all the delicacies of life, encouraging industry, and submitting to eat and drink and wear, what every peasant may procure. These are efforts of patriotism that Greece and Rome never yet surpassed, nay not so much as equaled."[98] Another Virginian who happened to share with Philo Americanus a penchant for grandiloquence assured newspaper readers that virtuous colonists had completely reformed the face of colonial society. Everyone could see that "our present Wants may be supplied, by importing only a *few* Articles from Great Britain; and that in a very short Time we can live *without them*. . . . The *whirling of our Spinning Wheels* affords us the most delightful *Music;* and that Man is the most respected who appears clad in Homespun, as *such* Dress is a sure Evidence of *Love to his Country*."[99] Journal authors even counseled Americans against giving their votes to candidates who failed to achieve the proper look of virtue. "A. Y.," for example, vowed not to support any person in an upcoming election "who do[es] not appear principally Clothed in Cloth made either in this Colony or some Part of America." As A. Y. explained, "Let a Man's Zeal for his Country appear ever so Flaming, if he is Attired in Foreign Fineries, I can't believe his Patriotism is sincere, for his very Apparel gives him the Lie."[100] A report from South Carolina echoed this logic: A Charleston writer insisted on halting all commerce with Georgia and Rhode Island until the merchants in those colonies showed more enthusiasm for non-importation. There should be no trade with them "till they have Virtue enough to *cloath* themselves in the humble Dress of public Virtue, preferable to the Chains of Oppression, or dirty Allurements of Self-Interest."[101]

The call for the public display of homespun had an unmistakable class edge to it. In fact, it represented an inversion of an earlier consumer rhetoric. At mid-century moral writers had employed the language of luxury to keep less affluent colonists in their places. If such people purchased goods beyond their means, they would soon call into question a traditional status system in which gentlemen were supposed to look like gentlemen, middling farmers like middling farmers. The problem was that the ordinary colonists with a little money in their pockets bought whatever they pleased, and they sometimes passed themselves off as belonging to a higher social class than the one into which they had been born.[102] But the politicization of fashion allowed the lower orders to turn the tables on their putative betters. It was now the wealthy gentlemen who had to rein in their expenditures, who had to give the appearance of consumer virtue, and who had to wear homespun garments however unappealing they may have seemed. As one contributor to the *Boston Gazette* complained, "The greatest Difficulty, with Regard to wearing Homespun Garments is, that the rich, the polite & fashionable do not wear them." Since the ordinary American allegedly loved "to mimic his Superiors," it seemed advisable "for our fine Gentlemen . . . instead of declaiming and writing in Favor of our own Manufactures, to appear in Public clothed all over in Homespun." If that happened, virtuous dress would become good for business. The shops would redouble their efforts to obtain homespun cloth. "For my Part," this writer concluded, "I never will believe that our great Folks are in earnest desirous of a Reformation in this Particular, till they bring Homespun into Fashion by wearing it themselves."[103]

One Henry Lloyd, Esquire, had apparently learned the lesson of visible equality. In March 1770 the *Boston Gazette* noted that this true American patriot had just set out on a journey to "New-York, Philadelphia and the

Southern Colonies." Lloyd won high marks since his "whole Apparel and Horse Furniture were of American Manufacture. His Clothes, Linen, Shoes, Stockings, Boots, Gloves, Hat, Wig . . . were all manufactured and made up in New-England—An Example truly worthy of Imitation."[104] Lloyd still looked like a proper gentleman, and as the public could now attest, his consumer heart was obviously in the right place.

V

A narrative of the non-importation movement might well be organized around a series of unintended consequences. Just as the need to coordinate consumer protest over a huge geographic area forced colonies to think of themselves in innovative collective terms—most typically, as Americans—so too a market strategy of resistance created unanticipated situations in which non-importation substantially transformed the character of political life, encouraging persons with little or no personal experience in formal elections to record their opinions on the most pressing issue of the day. From New England to South Carolina ordinary people scribbled their names on subscription rolls, pledging support for a boycott. These documents were carried through the neighborhoods, and although modern Americans may think nothing of signing their names to various petitions, colonists rightly understood that putting one's name on a list of this sort was a very serious act. Subscriptions taught middling people that *the public* was not simply a rhetorical device. It described the will of the majority. Numbers mattered. No one involved in these innovative procedures consciously set out to make colonial political culture more democratic. But whatever their goals may have been, organized non-importation rewarded ordinary consumers angered by recent parliamentary policy with a voice in public affairs, and once they discovered that they counted for something, they found it hard to return to an older, deferential system of political expression. Subscription politics figured in different areas at different moments. First observed in Boston, they later appeared in most major port cities and many smaller country towns, everywhere generating lists of the names of America's virtuous consumers, women as well as men.

The idea that ordinary people might sign up to support non-importation seems to have originated during a Boston town meeting held on October 28, 1767. After discussing possible explanations for a sharp downturn in the local economy, the most urgent of which was "the late additional Burthens and Impositions on the Trade of the Province, which threaten the Country with Poverty and Ruin," the city government voted to recommend cutting back on a long list of consumer items imported from Great Britain. But, instead of resting content with a statement of good intentions, the meeting decided that some kind of general subscription affirming popular support for non-importation should be drawn up for "individuals and householders" to sign. A committee drafted a document, which it then sent to a printer for distribution throughout Boston. Every person who affixed his or her name to one of these forms did "promise and engage, to and with each other, that we will encourage the Use and Consumption of all Articles manufactured in any of the British American Colonies, and more especially in this Province; and that we will not, from and after the 31st of December next ensuing, purchase any of the following Articles, imported from abroad." The inventory contained about fifty separate entries, many of them luxury goods. Pleased with their innovative plan to mobilize popular support for non-importation, town leaders ordered that the basic subscription form "relative to the enumerated Articles, be immediately Published; and that the Selectmen be directed to distribute a proper Number of them among the Freeholders of this Town; and to forward a Copy of the same to the Select-Men of every Town in the Province; as also to the principal City or Town Officers of the chief Town in the several Colonies on the Continent."[105]

The issuance of the subscription papers set off a buzz of excitement. The Boston selectmen reminded the public that they "strongly recommend this Measure to Persons of all Ranks, as the most honorable and effectual way of giving a public Testimony of their Love to their Country." The effort to obtain as many signatures as possible seems to have expanded the normal definition of politics. The call to "individuals and householders" became an appeal to "Persons of all Ranks." Town leaders were clearly worried about possible loss of face, for if few people bothered to sign the subscription, critics of organized non-importation—in this case, prominent merchants and crown appointees—could legitimately claim that relatively few Boston consumers were prepared to sacrifice comfort for principle. Market resistance, however, forced both sides to concede a significant point. Since anyone could qualify as a potential consumer, it made no sense to pretend that a narrowly defined group such as the "householders" could speak for "Persons of all Ranks." Grumbling about the subscription movement did not intimidate the selectmen. They observed that the town clerk had a good supply of forms, and "we especially recommend it [signing the pledge] at this Time, as malicious Persons venture, in the public Prints, falsely to insinuate that the above mentioned Subscription is merely a Party Business, and the Proposal only of a Junto; notwithstanding so many Gentlemen of the first Credit, Character, and Reputation have already encouraged it by their Subscription."[106]

Local newspapers cheered on the effort, providing regular updates on the number of people coming forward to sign. "We hear the Subscription Papers for encouraging our own Manufactures, and laying aside certain enumerated Articles," recounted the editor of the *Boston Gazette*, "fill up surprisingly, and that [the] said Measure is so well approved of in the Country, that Town Meetings are now calling in order to agree upon similar measures." Several issues later the journal announced that "the Subscription Rolls are daily filling up at the Town Clerk's Office." The *Evening-Post* had it on good authority from the "Gentlemen" who carried the forms through the neighborhoods that "it appeared that a great Part of the Freeholders had subscribed." Both newspapers reported that in the nearby communities of Charleston and Dedham consumer forms modeled on Boston's were "filling up fast," and in Providence and Newport, Rhode Island, subscription lists made the rounds.[107]

Although surviving records do not make it possible to know for certain how many people actually signed the rolls in Boston, British officials feared for the worst. Their comments suggested that "Persons of all Ranks" did in fact take this occasion to voice contempt for recent British legislation. Consumer politics was eroding traditional assumptions about the privileges of class. The royal governor of Massachusetts somewhat nervously assured a British correspondent that it was safe to dismiss the entire subscription drive, since, as he had apparently learned, most of the signers were marginal men and women. An even more revealing assessment of the new consumer politics came from Peter Oliver, a crown official who later penned a delightful though dyspeptic history of the American Revolution. Poking fun at Boston's radical spokesmen, people such as Samuel Adams and James Otis, Oliver declared that "they entered into non-importation Agreements. A Subscription Paper was handed about, enumerating a great Variety of Articles not to be imported from *England*, which they supposed would muster the Manufacturers in *England* into a national Mob to support their Interests. Among the various prohibited Articles, were *Silks, Velvets, Clocks, Watches, Coaches & Chariots*, & it was highly diverting, to see the names & marks, to the Subscription, of Porters & Washing Women." But surely Oliver missed the point. If these poor laborers had no prospect of purchasing a clock or coach, they fully appreciated the symbolic significance of these imports, and while a self-styled "True Patriot" could insist in a newspaper "that the most wealthy & respectable among us, have treated the thing in the ludicrous light it deserves," one suspects that however desirous the porters and washing women of Boston may have been of one day owning such fine objects, they also recognized that consumer dependence translated into a loss of liberty.[108]

In Connecticut non-importation also heightened popular participation in political affairs. Although no one seems to have done more than to suggest the circulation of subscription lists in this colony, commentators noted that a lot more people were turning out for town meetings.[109] In 1770 voters were especially agitated by rumors coming out of New York City that the merchants of that port had unilaterally decided to resume normal trade with Great Britain. Suddenly, previously indifferent persons felt compelled to record their resolute support for a continued boycott of imported goods. In Norwich, for example, it was reported that "there was as full a town Meeting as ever known, when the Town voted, almost unanimously, to adhere to their former Non-Importation Agreement." The "Inhabitants" of Norwich were remarkably well informed about the relation between consumer resistance and parliamentary oppression, and at this moment they wanted "to give their Sentiments upon the State of the general Agreement, as it now stands in this and the neighboring Colonies."[110] In Lyme a gathering of townsmen announced that they were "fully sensible of the necessity of Union and Harmony among the American Colonies at this Time especially when our Liberties are attacked in the most unjust and high-handed Manner, by the wicked Influence of a haughty and tyrannical Minister."[111]

The people of Connecticut did more, however, than simply give voice to a determination to uphold their non-importation agreements. They elected delegates—two from each town—to a completely unprecedented "General Meeting," which was in fact held in New Haven on September 13. The convention went by several different names, "general Congress of the Merchants," "Meeting of the Mercantile and Landed Interest of the Colony," and "General Congress of the Merchants and Landholders of the Colony of Connecticut," but whatever it was called, it operated outside the normal channels of government. Some evidence suggests that Connecticut voters experimented with an innovative form of representation based on economic interest, so that one representative from each town was supposed to be a merchant or trader, the other a farmer.[112] As "X" explained, "The Plough and the Sail" must unite for the common good, since in an advanced economy like Connecticut's, "Land, the capital of the husbandman, is of little or no value (however fertile) if no market offer for its produce, and ever rises, and becomes valuable, in proportion to the increase of trade, and commerce."[113] A majority of Connecticut's towns selected delegates, and while the elections may not have drawn into consumer politics persons of all ranks, their inventive character convinced "A Freeman," writing in a Hartford newspaper, that extra-legal meetings of this sort might be part of a conspiracy aimed at overthrowing traditional authority.[114]

In Maryland printed forms helped mobilize popular support for non-importation. In June 1769 colony leaders concluded that they needed a "general Resolution," precisely laying out in nine separate sections their expectations for political resistance. Although the wording of the Maryland statement was much like those drafted in other regions, it stipulated that the final document should be circulated throughout the various counties. Even before they got down to the business of passing resolutions, the delegates to the Annapolis meeting agreed that "Twelve Copies should be printed and transmitted to each County, to be signed by the People, which it is expected, will be done with great Readiness throughout the Province." The language of the Maryland statement did not define "the People," and since the great tobacco planters—designated in the documents as "the Gentlemen of the different Counties"—were not eager to expand the political culture, one may assume that an appeal to the people was not intended to encourage radical forms of participation. Still, once the genie was out of the bottle, one could not predict what might happen. As in other colonies attempting to generate popular enthusiasm for non-importation, Marylanders found that numbers counted, and a local newspaper proudly announced that some 840 people had signed their names to a list pledging "to promote Frugality and lessen the future Importation of Goods from

Great-Britain." And, of course, the printed resolutions served to indoctrinate the populace, to make trimmers uncomfortable, and to remind all consumers that failure to abide by the new rules would make them "Enemies to the Liberties of *America*," who would be treated "on all Occasions, with the Contempt they deserve."[115]

Non-importation thoroughly unsettled the politics of South Carolina. For many decades a group of wealthy and complacent rice planters had run the colonial assembly like a private club, and had Parliament left well enough alone, these men might have voiced their unhappiness with the Townshend Acts in ways that did not upset business as usual. But even before the British government enacted new duties, crown appointees in Charleston had managed to alienate powerful leaders in South Carolina, and agitation for an effective non-importation agreement during the summer of 1769 exacerbated festering tensions. In June two men claiming to speak for Charleston's "mechanics"—Christopher Gadsden and Peter Timothy, editor of the *South-Carolina Gazette*—put forth a list of resolutions related to non-importation. Although it enjoyed considerable popular support, the merchants objected to several details, and in July they issued their own agreement. Since having competing non-importation agreements made no sense, the mechanics and merchants—as well as an impressive crowd of prominent planters—gathered under Charleston's Liberty Tree to negotiate an uneasy alliance. Some 268 people took the occasion to sign the joint agreement.[116]

For the likes of Gadsden and Timothy that number, however impressive, was not sufficient. A lot of people living in other sections of South Carolina had not been present at the Liberty Tree, and so, like the organizers in Boston, they circulated subscription papers throughout the colony. As quickly became apparent, they not only wanted additional signatures but also demanded accurate reporting of the names. It was important to know precisely who was a "Subscriber" and who a "Non-Subscriber." Timothy reminded the "Gentlemen in the country [who are] possessed of these Forms . . . to transmit the names subscribed thereto, as frequently as possible."[117] As soon as the information on the new names reached Charleston, it was placed in "an exact Register," which anyone could examine. What few foresaw was that insistence on precision was intended more to punish non-subscribers than to identify the colony's virtuous consumers. The names of the resisters—a kind of negative list—appeared in the newspapers. An enforcement committee carefully monitored commercial dealings throughout South Carolina in an ongoing effort to isolate subscribers from non-subscribers. In November, for example, it spotted a problem. It seemed that some people who had signed the original non-importation papers had sold a parcel of rice belonging to a "Non-Subscriber" "contrary to the TRUE INTENT AND MEANING of the said Resolutions":

> The General Committee therefore think it necessary, to publish the first Breach of that solemn Agreement; and at the same Time, to remind every SUBSCRIBER, that the PURCHASING FROM, OR SELLING FOR, NON-SUBSCRIBERS, ANY GOODS OR MERCHANDISE WHATEVER, will be deemed an Infringement of the said Agreement.[118]

WE, His Majesty's dutiful and loving Subjects, the Inhabitants of SOUTH-CAROLINA, being sensibly affected with the great Prejudice done to GREAT-BRITAIN, and the abject and wretched Condition to which the BRITISH COLONIES are reduced by several Acts of Parliament lately passed; by *some of which* the Monies that the Colonists usually and chearfully spent in the Purchase of all sorts of Goods imported from GREAT-BRITAIN, are now, to their great Grievance, wrung from them, without their Consent, or even their being represented, and applied by the Ministry, in Prejudice of, and without Regard to, the real Interest of GREAT-BRITAIN, or the Manufacturers thereof, almost totally, to the Support of new-created Commissioners of Customs, Placemen, parasitical and novel ministerial Officers; and *by others of which Acts,* we are not only deprived of those invaluable Rights, Trial by our Peers and the Common Law, but are also made subject to the arbitrary and oppressive Proceedings of the Civil Law, justly abhorred and rejected by our Ancestors, the Freemen of England; and finding, that the most dutiful and loyal Petitions from the Colonies ALONE, for the Redress of those Grievances, have been rejected with Contempt; so that no Relief can be expected from that Method of Proceeding; and, being fully convinced of the absolute Necessity, of stimulating our Fellow Subjects and Sufferers in GREAT-BRITAIN to aid us, in this our Distress, and of our joining with the Rest of the Colonies, in some other loyal and vigorous Methods, that may most probably procure such Relief, which we believe may be most effectually promoted by strict OECONOMY, and by encouraging the MANUFACTURES of AMERICA in general, and of this Province in particular: WE THEREFORE, whose Names are underwritten, do solemnly, promise, and agree to and with each other, That, until the Colonies be restored to their former Freedom; by the Repeal of the said Acts, we will most strictly abide by the following RESOLUTIONS.

I. That we will encourage and promote, to the utmost of our Power, the Use of NORTH-AMERICAN MANUFACTURES, in general, and those of this Province in particular.

II. That we will upon no Pretence whatsoever, import into this Province, any of the Manufactures of GREAT-BRITAIN, or other Goods and Wares usually received from thence, other than such as may have been shipped in consequence of former Orders; and we do solemnly promise and declare, that we will immediately countermand all Orders to our Correspondents in GREAT-BRITAIN for shipping any such Goods, Wares and Merchandizes, excepting only NEGRO CLOTH, DUFFIL BLANKETS, OSNABRUGS, PLANTATION and WORKMENS TOOLS, POWDER, LEAD, SHOT, CANVAS, NAILS, SALT, COALS, WOOL CARDS, CARD WIRE, printed BOOKS and PAMPHLETS: Nor shall this Agreement influence us, to raise the Prices of the British Manufactures or other Goods and Wares any of us have now to dispose of, or of such as may arrive before our countermanding Orders get to Hand.

III. That we will use the utmost OECONOMY, in our Persons, Families, Houses and Furniture; particularly that we will use NO MOURNING, nor give Gloves and Scarves at Funerals.

IV. *That we will not, upon any Pretence whatsoever, directly or indirectly import, or purchase, any NEW NEGROES or Slaves, brought into this Province for Sale, from and after the 1st Day of January, 1770.*

AND, LASTLY, That we will look on every Inhabitant of this Colony, who refuses or neglects to sign this Agreement within one Month from the Date hereof, as no Friend to the true Interest of the Colony, and we will, upon no Account, at any Time thereafter, purchase from, or sell to such Person, any Goods or Merchandize whatsoever: *Nor will we purchase any British Manufactures, or other Goods usually imported from Great-Britain, from any transient Persons importing the same from any Place whatever.*

GIVEN under our Hands, the Twenty-Eighth Day of June, 1769.

Blank Copies of the above Agreement may be had, by any Gentlemen desirous of promoting so laudable and at this Time evidently necessary a Measure, at TIMOTHY's *Office in Broad-Street: Where, and at Mr.* ISAAC MOTTE's *on the Bay, and* CHRISTOPHER GADSDEN, *Esq's; a List of the Names of many respectable Gentlemen that have already set their Hands thereto may be seen, and where all that incline may add theirs.*

Gentlemen in the Country possessed of the Form without the Additions, are desired to return them, and to transmit the Names that shall be subscribed to this, as frequently as possible, to either of the above Gentlemen, or said TIMOTHY's Office, where an exact Register of them is intended to be kept.

☞ In the above Form a FOURTH ARTICLE has been introduced, by the unanimous Desire of a great Number of the Inhabitants collected together, with an EXPLANATORY ADDITION to the last, which are distinguished by being printed in *Italicks.*

As the signing ONE *and the* SAME FORM *by all the Inhabitants of the whole Province, will manifest their* UNANIMITY, *and must of Course have the greater Weight; so it may be proper, that Gentlemen should be particularly cautious not to subscribe any but* THIS; *for although others might vary little or not at all in Substance, yet artful and designing Men might thence take Occasion to insinuate a* DIVISION *in Sentiments.*

Non-importation resolutions circulated throughout South Carolina during the summer of 1769. Supporters obtained "Blank Copies" of the general agreement, collected as many signatures as possible, and then returned the lists to the leaders of the boycott. *South-Carolina Gazette,* 13 July 1769. *Courtesy of the Charleston Library Society, Charleston, South Carolina.*

By December life for the non-subscribers had become extremely difficult. One Charleston newspaper claimed that the "List of Non-Subscribers" had dropped to only twenty names. Even some of these people, it was reported, seemed to be trying to uphold the patriotic resolutions "by not dealing with other Non-Subscribers, and not even offering the Produce for Sale, but shipping it off." In South Carolina, at least, the public had been transformed into an extra-legal police force, and by expanding the scope of politics, the keepers of the Charleston lists reduced British imports by more than 50 percent in a single year.

A few voices protested the actions of the protesters. For them, it seemed absurd to claim that the public was a repository of consumer virtue. In Charleston, this self-constituted body had become an authoritarian instrument designed to strip honest merchants of their constitutional rights as British subjects. Drawing on his knowledge of the common law, William Wragg insisted that the July non-importation agreement represented an illegal combination in constraint of trade. As a non-subscriber he thought he should be allowed to sell his goods to whomever he pleased.[119] William Drayton agreed. A prosperous merchant who enjoyed family ties with the sitting lieutenant governor, Drayton blasted Gadsden's pretentious claim to speak for the popular will. "This Committee," Drayton fumed, "hath *violated* the first Principles of Liberty. Its Members act in a *despotic* and *unjust* Manner . . . for they have assumed a Power unknown to the Constitution." If Drayton enjoyed the same rights as any other Englishman, then he should not have to suffer seeing his name "printed and dispersed through North-America, with Design to prejudice my Countrymen against me." And in a direct challenge to his tormentors, he suggested that the heading appearing in the newspapers over the list of non-subscribers be revised: "A List of the Names of those Freemen, who, by being possessed of a proper Idea of Liberty, and the Constitution of Government under which they live, have the Courage and Integrity to persist, in acting in Conformity to the Dictates of their Reason."[120]

New Advertisements.

SOME Persons in this Town, Subscribers to the Resolutions entered into by the Inhabitants of this Province on the 22d Day of July last, have, contrary to the TRUE INTENT AND MEANING of the said Resolutions, sold a Parcel of R I C E, belonging to a Non-Subscriber : The General Committee therefore think it necessary, to publish the first Breach of that solemn Agreement; and at the same Time, to remind every SUBSCRIBER, that the PURCHASING FROM, OR SELLING FOR, NON-SUBSCRIBERS, ANY GOODS OR MERCHANDIZES, WHATEVER, will be deemed an Infringement of the said Agreement, and looked upon as not acting according to the TRUE INTENT AND MEANING thereof; and that the Names of such Violators, in future, will be published.

The Gentlemen in the Country, who have not yet returned the Subscription-Papers to the General Committee, are requested to do it as speedily as possible, that a correct List of Non-Subscribers in the several Parishes may be made known.

Local organizers of the South Carolina boycott maintained up-to-date lists of those who had subscribed to the "Resolutions" concerning commerce with Great Britain. The activities of "Non-Subscribers"—now easily identified—were exposed to constant public scrutiny. *South-Carolina Gazette,* 23 November 1769. *Courtesy of the Charleston Library Society.*

Gadsden rejected these cries out of hand. After all, the enemies of liberty had driven virtuous people into a corner. He reminded critics that the Americans had been "reduced to a necessity of associating together, in order to discover, and unite in, some common means, for the recovery and preservation of their rights and liberties." Gadsden never doubted that "the means they have actually fixed upon, for that purpose, are justifiable, upon natural and constitutional principles; and will, probably be productive of the end they aim at." In other words, pragmatism warranted the printing of the names of the non-subscribers. If the public did not know their identities, these secret foes might continue selling imported British goods to unsuspecting patriots, thus profiting from the noble sacrifice of those subscribers who had halted trade. But more, Gadsden had numbers on his side. He could point to the "exact Register" of names. When the majority determined how best to respond to a political threat—in this case, parliamentary legislation—the minority was obliged to accept that course of action. Although Gadsden possessed a tenuous grasp of syntax, his defense of the popular will revealed dramatically how the pressure to make non-importation work had affected colonial political discourse:

> And further, if we consider, that in the carrying on of all kinds of human transactions, of whatever nature or consequence, where the consent of a community or body of men is required, from the lowest club up to the parliament of Great-Britain, or to the people of the greatest nation upon earth, that, when an indubitable majority of such bodies of men, have deliberately determined upon any business within their several spheres, and fixed upon the manner of doing it, the minority . . . are, and ought to be, bound of course: And were this not the case, it would be next to impossible, to complete any business of this sort amongst mankind.[121]

Perhaps not surprisingly, Drayton left for England, to the last depicting himself a martyr to an extra-legal consumer public.

Subscription lists should be seen as a highly innovative instrument through which colonists explored the limits of democratic participation.[122] Appearing on the margins of mainstream political discourse, the popular lists addressed the issue of political exclusivity. Did the men and women who signed the papers, for example, necessarily represent the public? If they did not, then for whom did they speak? These were the sorts of questions that "Cato" examined in the *Pennsylvania Chronicle* in 1770. For him, the colonial political crisis was too important to be left in the hands of a minority pretending to speak for a majority. "This is a point," he wrote, "in which every freeholder of this province is highly interested, and in which every one of them has a right to a voice." He was irritated by inflated claims to political authority advanced by a select group of local "subscribers to the non-importation." These people assumed "an exclusive right to determine this matter." If they did possess such a privilege, Cato warned, "it follows that the subscribers to the non-importation have the sole right to determine a question of liberty, that most nearly concerns every freeman of this province. For if it is the only mode of opposition of any force, and those two or three hundred subscribers have a right to make the agreement voice whenever they please, it is a plain inference that they have a right to decide on a point which affects the liberties of the people of this province." Cato wanted to open up the process. Votes, not signatures, reflected the popular will, and he trusted that "every freeman, whether he be farmer, merchant, or mechanic, will insist upon his right to a vote in so important an affair."[123]

The question of political inclusion also flared in New York, sparking a debate that echoed those of the other colonies. During the summer of 1770 spokesmen on both sides of the boycott movement hotly debated the issue of democratic participation. After Parliament repealed most of the Townshend duties, the major import merchants of New York City agitated to renew trade as soon as possible. Delays in reestablishing English contracts, it was feared, might give competitors in Philadelphia or Boston a huge advantage. But however much the New York merchants wanted to turn a profit, they could not bring themselves unilaterally to break the local non-importation agreement. What they needed at this decisive moment was authorization from the public, and this they determined to obtain through a public opinion poll of consumers, perhaps the first such consumer plebiscite conducted in America. The merchants knew they would be safe if they could demonstrate with quantitative evidence that the public wanted to rescind the boycott. The tactic worked. Polling papers carried through the city wards revealed that a majority of the people of New York supported a greatly modified boycott that allowed the merchants to import virtually everything from Great Britain except tea.

Leaders of more radical persuasion in New York found themselves confronted with a quandary that had haunted democratic theorists since ancient Greece. How does a minority respond when it is certain that the majority has made a mistake? The obvious ploy was to declare the entire poll a fraud, and over several months the supporters of a continued total boycott did just that. They hammered away at the merchants' sham democracy. The author of "A Protest" in the *New-York Mercury* argued that the reported numbers were not credible. "It appears from the Ward-Lists," the writer charged, "that only 794 Persons in this populous City, including all Ranks, and both Sexes; declared for the Affirmative of the Question."[124] It is particularly significant that this writer assumed that a true canvass of colonial consumers—even one involving complex political issues—required inclusiveness, full participation by women as well as men, the poor as well as the rich. One South Carolina newspaper thought that the New Yorkers had already opened the floodgates, reporting that in New York City "The Sense of the People was taken by Subscription, and near 800 Names got, about 300 of the People without a single Shilling Property."[125]

"A Son of Liberty" also challenged the merchants' democratic claims. In the *New-York Advertiser* he ridiculed the assertion that "*a majority appeared for importation.*" The merchants had not even approached most of the men and women who composed the consumer public. "A Son of Liberty" observed that "there were not quite twelve hundred persons who signed for importing (notwithstanding the diligence and indefatigable industry of those who went about for the purpose), and I am well assured that they do

FORASMUCH as it is manifeft, that there is a moft unnatural and pernicious Confpiracy, formed by the Enemies of the Britifh Empire in general, and of America in particular, to deprive his Majefty's North-American Subjects, of the peculiar Benefits refulting from a full Enjoyment of the Britifh Conftitution, and thereby alienate their Affections ;———To which there can nothing have a greater Tendency, than the keeping up of a Military Force, at the Expence of the People,———and that without there Confent, fairly obtained, in order to exact in the moft rigorous Manner, Such Taxes, Duties and Impofitions, as they and their Creatures may from Time to Time infidioufly impofe.———All which, is directly contrary to a well known fundamental Maxim of the Conftitution,——— " That no Man is or can be, rightfully, bound by any Law, to which he has not given his Confent or Affent, either in Perfon or by Proxy :"——— And this with an avowed Intention of rendering all the Offices of Government independent of the People, to whom, they are of Right, and ought to be accountable for their public Conduct.———Which if accomplifhed, will inevitably deprive the governed, of a juft and neceffary Reftraint on legiflative and judicatory Affairs.———And, as that muft end in a total Deprivation of their moft valuable inherent Rights, as Britifh Subjects ; and finally fubjugate them and their lateft Pofterity, to the tyrannick Controul and capricious Infolence of their Fellow Subjects, both here and in Great Britain,———Than the very Apprehenfion of which, —there cannot be any Thing more painful and infupportable, to a People, animated with a juft Senfe of their natural Rights.———THEREFORE, we, the SUBSCRIBERS, whofe Minds are deeply impreffed with a due Senfe of the foregoing weighty Confiderations ; do, in Imitation of our Brethren, the Supporters of the Bill of Rights, in Great Britain,———legally confent and promife, to meet, and affociate with People of all reputable Ranks, Conditions, and Denominations ; within the City and County of New-York, at fuch Times and Places, as fhall be hereafter afcertained.———And that for the fole Purpofe of fupporting the Rights of America, which we conceive to be fimilar to thofe of his Majefty's Subjects of Great Britain :—And that we have, juftly, as indefeafible a Right to them, as we have to the Air we breathe : Juftice being every where immutable, whatever the Circumftances and Situation of Life may be.———In order theretore to promote thefe our juft Intentions, ———We do further agree and confent, that immediately after a fufficient Number of the Freeholders, and other creditable Inhabitants, have fubfcribed this Agreement ;———that then we will proceed to nominate and appoint, by plurality of Voices, or otherwife, as fhall appear the moft eligible,—nine difcreet Perfons, being Subfcribers hereto, who are to be a ftanding Committee of Correfpondence and occafional Conventions,— for the Space of one whole Year, from the Time of their being chofen.——— The Majority of whom, to be a Quorum, and invefted with full Power to communicate the Intentions of this Society, to all fuch Places, within his Majefty's acknowledged Dominions ; as they fhall think moft conducive, to the End propofed ; unlefs otherwife, particularly inftructed by the Majority of their Conftituents then met.———

Subscribers in New York pledged to support an association of like-minded people "of all reputable Ranks, Conditions, and Denominations" in defense of "the Rights of America." *Broadside. New York, 1770. Courtesy of the John Carter Brown Library, Brown University.*

not amount to above one third of the inhabitants of this city (not to mention the counties, who have an undoubted right to give their voices upon this very interesting and important subject)."[126]

During this contest, "A Citizen" produced a pointed defense of open, egalitarian procedures in a politicized consumer marketplace. To appreciate fully his contribution to a discussion of the meaning of the public, one must remember that "A Citizen" was exploring civic responsibility within a commercial public sphere of quite recent invention—in other words, within a popular political arena that was just beginning to express itself apart from traditional institutions of governance. The merchant canvass of New York brought theory into contact with events, helping ordinary men and women better to appreciate the interdependence of liberty and commerce. "Will it excuse this City to the rest of the World," "A Citizen" asked, "if it should appear that a Majority of the Inhabitants concurred in desiring to break through the [non-importation] Agreement?" He argued through interrogation, with hard questions leading to harder ones until the logic of the performance seemed irrefutable. "Supposing there is a Majority, (which is not admitted)," he inquired of the merchants,

> was it fairly and properly obtained? Was that Opinion given and subscribed with due Deliberation, Knowledge and Freedom? Or were not a very considerable Number of the Subscribers, influenced and determined, by your Persuasions and Representations, or by submitting their Opinions to be guided by your Advice and superior Judgment? Can opinions so given and obtained, properly be called the Voice of the People, or given a Sanction to the Dissolution of an Agreement of such immense Weight and Importance?[127]

The breaking of the New York boycott in 1770 came to a curious conclusion that prefigured America's eventual separation from Great Britain. As in the larger imperial contest, the failure of local authorities to expand representation, to listen to a newly empowered "Voice of the People," ended in violence. When "Gentlemen" sought to rationalize the resumption of trade, they were confronted by a group of forty or fifty people who gathered at the "house of Mr. Jasper Drake, inn-keeper." The *New-York Mercury* reported that "they erected a flag, as a signal of the place appointed for their rendezvous, and after carousing and drinking very plentifully . . . they sallied out in the evening, . . . carrying with them music, colors and staffs, upon which were labels fixed with the inscription of, *Liberty and Non-Importation*." The mob marched through the streets "crying out, *No Importation*." The leading merchants and their allies could not endure the provocation. The popular protest ended when "a Number of principal People . . . applied to an Alderman to go and stop those People, and take the Flag from them, upon which the Alderman headed a considerable Number with Canes and Clubs, and attempted to take their Colors, upon which a Scuffle ensued, and a few got hurt."[128]

The British could never quite comprehend why taxes on a few inconsequential consumer goods had sparked such intense debate. Nor, for that matter, did many privileged Americans understand where the popular currents were carrying them. But long before anyone dared to speak openly of independence, ordinary consumers had challenged several basic assumptions about colonial politics, inviting men and women of all ranks into a conversation about liberty and declaring that the act of signing one's name to a subscription list or carrying a banner in the streets of New York City was as fully political as were elections to the colonial assemblies. Experimental politics had demonstrated to those who had opposed the public will "what an evil thing and bitter it is to set up against the universal judgment of the people."[129] The narratives of consumer resistance remind modern Americans, once again, that it was "on the level of day-to-day life, rather than on the rarefied plateau of theoretical debate, that the opinions of most men were formed."[130]

VI

During the summer of 1770 an exchange occurred in the *Pennsylvania Chronicle, and Universal Advertiser* that revealed from yet another perspective how the politics of non-importation encouraged new voices to speak to power in a consumer public sphere. Two readers identified only as "Fidelia" and "Constantia" reported an argument provoked by an essay in the newspaper. In that piece "Atticus" claimed to have quoted directly from a letter written specifically by a woman, and Fidelia and Constantia challenged the authenticity of the correspondence. They demanded Atticus confess whether he had actually fabricated the material for his own editorial purposes. "Pray Mr. ATTICUS," demanded the inquisitive pair, "be so kind as to decide a dispute between two girls, who pretend to know something of style, by telling us whether you wrote the letters signed *Betty Telltruth,* or that they were really wrote by a female hand." Like advice columnists, then and now, Atticus responded coyly, assuring readers "that several of the letters which in the course of these essays, I have published, were not of my own composition . . . and by the delicacy of the sentiment, and handwriting, I believe them to have been wrote by a polite female."[131]

Atticus's evasive response probably failed to settle the quarrel. However unsatisfied the two women may have been, their aggressive interrogation draws attention to the fact that in this particular society women were speaking out. In the swirl of controversy over non-importation, they participated in the political life of American communities more fully, more expectantly, and more impatiently than at any previous time. During the Stamp Act crisis, men and women had sparred over the proper role of women in organized market resistance. As the political stakes were raised and as mere "Washing Women" signed their names to subscription lists, ongoing tensions between the sexes spilled over into the imperial debate, setting off a conversation within a conversation. Although colonial males may have hoped to contain the expansion of political participation—both in the streets and in print—it was clear that some women intended to make themselves heard, forcefully articulating what one historian has recently called "communal consciousness."[132]

About the centrality of women in determining the success of the non-importation moment, few American men disagreed. As consumers, women had long exercised broad discretion over day-to-day household expenditures, and even though the law formally awarded colonial males—as husbands and fathers—control over real property, women regularly dealt with the shopkeepers and itinerant traders who merchandised imported British goods. Without their enthusiastic support, a strategy of consumer sacrifice stood no chance. As a writer in a Boston newspaper declared quite matter-of-factly, "We must after all our Efforts, depend greatly upon the Female Sex for the Introduction of Economy among us."[133] An address entitled "To the Ladies of North America" made much the same point in an edgy, defensive style so characteristic of political commentary touching on questions of gender. "I am convinced," the male writer asserted, "that at this present [time] it is not only in your Inclination and Will, but also in your Power, to effect more in Favor of your Country, than an Army of a Hundred Thousand Men; and indeed more than all the armed Men on this vast Continent.—Can a Woman forget her Ornaments? Yes, I know she can."[134]

And, no doubt, the author was correct. Targeted market resistance depended on America's wives and mothers. Christopher Gadsden, the firebrand of Charleston, stated the proposition with typical bluntness. In a long speech urging an effective boycott of British manufactures, he told the audience, "I come now to the last, and what many say and think is the *greatest difficulty* of all we have to encounter, that is, to persuade our wives to give us assistance, without which 'tis impossible to succeed." After all, if the colonists were serious about abridging consumer spending, they would soon discover that "our political salvation" depended on establishing the principles of "strictest economy," a "management" skill associated in his mind with women. Gadsden was optimistic. However women in other colonies might react to the political crisis, he could declare of South Carolina women that "none in the world are better economists, make better wives and more tender mothers, than ours. Only let their husbands point out the necessity of such a conduct . . . [and] their affections will soon be awakened, and cooperate with their reason."[135]

Political urgency did not do much to promote male charm. Men professing to have the best interests of the country at heart fretted about the ability of their newly recruited female allies to make the kinds of sacrifices that genuine patriotism required. Part of the problem, male writers confessed, was that women were weaker vessels and therefore constitutionally less able to resist consumer temptation. If truth be known, they bore much of the responsibility for colonial dependency, since it was they who had insisted on purchasing so many faddish British imports in the first place and thereby had added immensely to the load of debt that weighed so heavily on the provincial economy. Newspaper commentators never had much to say about the flood of consumer goods acquired by other members of American families, nor did they seem much concerned that if women did in fact buy more British manufactures than did their husbands, then the women's sacrifice for liberty would be proportionally greater than the men's. Rather, like "Mahalaleel" of New London, male commentators whined that "Tea drinking is a female sin. Eve is represented as first in the transgression, so Eve's daughters are first in and most attached to this vice. They are most violently addicted to it, and use all their persuasions to entice their Adams to perpetuate the like folly, or at least to countenance them in it." One should not mistake the tone of such complaint for gentle teasing. A nasty streak was undeniable. "Eve's fair daughters, or sordid self-interest, encourage our merchants to the importation of this fatal plant."[136]

Although a contributor to a New York City journal known as "A. B." avoided outright belligerence, he still wondered whether the females of this society were up to the political challenge. It has been declared, he snidely reported, "that an Opinion prevails in England, among the Enemies of our Liberty, that the American Ladies, through an inordinate attachment to European Superfluities, will not be possessed of a sufficient Share of Virtue to discontinue their Use, under our present unconstitutional Impositions." In a classic backhanded compliment, A. B. announced that he never believed all the bad things people were saying about American women. After all, as "a real Friend to the Ladies," he felt comfortable advising "the married Ladies, [to] unite in one general Agreement, that they will respectively use their Influence (which is not a little) with their Husbands, not to rescind from that noble Resolution of Non-Importation." They might start, he thought, by "quitting the Use of those Tinsels, Gewgaws, and exuberant Fineries, which cost their Husbands much Toil in the Acquisition, and a serious Sum of Money in the using."[137]

The evidence against self-indulgent women was disturbing. In Connecticut, "Incutius Americanus" noted that "the ladies instead of attending the true interest of their families . . . have expended their estates in imitating the customs and dress of foreigners in adorning themselves according to the newest taste, with silks, lawns, cambrics, gauzes, chintz, calicoes, ribbons of the newest cut, &c. &c. &c."[138] One might observe in passing that Incutius Americanus seems to have followed the newest foreign cuts very attentively, but apparently that dangerous consumer knowledge did not threaten his virtue. A writer "From the Country" echoed the evangelical style, lecturing women, "Throw aside your sloth & bury your pride in oblivion, and lay your hand on the spindle." The "virtuous woman" was a marvel, for like the woman "given by Solomon, she seeketh wool and flax, and maketh fine linen, and selleth it. . . . Her price is far above rubies; she will do a man good, and not evil, all the days of her life."[139]

Cultural conversations about non-importation had the capacity to transform colonial households into revolutionary cells. Within these domestic settings, men attempted to institute a new political aesthetic, instructing women exactly how genuine female patriots should appear in public. The female body literally became a battleground of imperial politics. Male writers seemed particularly fond of homespun cloth, for example, missing few opportunities to recommend it to Eve's American daughters. The rhetoric of consumer sacrifice sometimes took on a romantic quality as male writers imagined a brave society in which women dutifully resisted British oppression by saving their husbands' money. One New England writer celebrated this wonderful new world. "Let the [women] rich and poor join heart and hand together," he exclaimed, "and their only ambition be to see which can make the best and finest apparel. What a beautiful prospect will then open to our view, to see the young ladies both of city and country, clothed in garments of their own manufacturing. How will it inspire the young gentlemen with elevated thoughts!"[140]

The everyday appearance of an ordinary woman—one's own wife or daughter—communicated political commitment; she embodied the symbolic shift in a material culture. "I would," announced another colonist, "observe that a Homemade Dress, will ever have an advantage beyond the Boughten & Foreign [one]; even under all circumstances, the latter can only be an ornament as a plume of fine feathers, but the other serves to a more noble purpose, as a badge of Virtue and Industry in the family."[141] A South Carolina essayist agreed. Calling for strict non-importation, "Pro Libertate et Lege" reminded "the ladies" that "they certainly will be much the properest persons to manage an affair of so much consequence to the American world." To demonstrate their dedication to the cause, he counseled, they might "at least wear out your old silk gowns, purchase no new ones 'till this heavy storm is past (storms are apt to spoil new silks): this will please your economical husbands; it will certainly be a sacrifice worthy to them."[142] "A Bachelor" writing in a Pennsylvania newspaper thought that "pretty country women" would have a better chance of finding honest suitors if they left off "those superfluities of dress, which their native beauty should teach them are unnecessary, and by this patriotic measure remove all complaints of their *would be admirers*."[143]

Colonial women apparently found patronizing advice as insufferable in the late 1760s as they had during the Stamp Act crisis.[144] Indeed, in stinging retort to Pro Libertate, "Philanthropos" observed that his condescending "kind of address to the Ladies . . . will, prove as unsuccessful, as he has already done, in some others made to that beautiful sex." Other women challenged their so-called lords and masters in ways that suggested that the non-importation movement had given them a greater sense of independence in the consumer public sphere, and the more that male writers insisted that women were politically indispensable, the more the women strove to renegotiate the taken-for-granted of domestic life.[145] On one level, the males who preached about the sensual allure of homespun clothes were hypocrites. They knew from their own experience that it was they who had encouraged women to dress like fashionable peacocks. One Connecticut author reminded male readers that for a very long time the women had "plumed ourselves only to please you. We baited our hook according to your humors. We found you was in chase of gay feathers, when you came into company with us. You respected our finery more than our persons; if one of us was loaded or even over-loaded with Silks, Ruffles and Lace, above the rest, she was your Phoenix." And now, confronted with a new round of British taxes, the eager suitors of yesterday had changed their tune. They chose to forget that had the women actually "appeared in Home Spun dress, we should have been treated as kitchen maids by you; had you respected our Persons, Comage and Virtue, or even our Tongues as you did our Dress, you would never have seen your Country at this pass."[146]

On another level of engagement, women resented men offering gratuitous advice about consumer choices. Three Boston women—"Aspatia," "Belinda," and "Corrinna"—rounded on a man who had urged them to "'lay aside our present Clothing, and Dress' entirely and universally in the 'Manufactures of America.'" They felt that he did not know what he was talking about. "How far (if practicable) it is prudent," they explained, "we must take Liberty to judge ourselves, since we do, or at least ought to know, what our own Circumstances as to the Means of Purchasing are; or, in other Words, whether we can afford to let our Garments lay useless, and buy new in their Room." It was not that the three authors refused to support non-importation. They stood with a number of people prepared to "promote the Public Good" and to practice "Public Virtue." They just did not want to hear from "the little Wits and Foplings" of Boston about making consumer choices.[147]

Although the details remained nebulous, patriotic women advanced a vision of a better society in which men would radically change their ways. In another context such criticism might have sounded chimerical, but with so many male writers appealing to women to endorse non-importation, women realized that their own, more domestic concerns might receive more serious discussion. Many women took the opportunity to castigate the heavy drinking that threatened the integrity of the colonial family. Such self-indulgence not only drew men away from their homes but also wasted money. One writer noted that males were always blathering about boring afternoon tea assemblies, social gatherings over which women exercised unquestioned cultural authority. "You charge us with drinking at the Tea-Table," the author explained, ". . . and cannot we charge you with drinking more unnaturally at the Tavern?" Contemporary males had forgotten their manners. "When we were at the Tea-Table, you were as merry in the Chat as any of us, tho' you now cry, we were ruining you and ourselves together: pretty Lovers to sport with the destruction of their Country." This author recommended that until Parliament repealed the Townshend duties American women should dismiss "Proud and Foppish" males, condemn public drunkenness, and refuse salutations from any man who was obviously in his cups.[148]

Some women pushed the argument in surprising directions. "The Ladies" of Newport, Rhode Island, for example, offered besotted males a bargain that could only have made sense within a far-reaching public debate over the political meaning of imported British goods. "We are willing to give up our dear & beloved Tea, *for the Good of the Public*," they announced, "provided the Gentlemen will give up their dearer & more beloved Punch, renounce going so often to Taverns, and become more kind and loving Sweethearts and Husbands." In a not very subtle jab at the performance of intoxicated males, they added:

> Most gladly we aside our Tea would lay,
> Could we more Pleasures gain some other Way.[149]

In this spirit, "A Female" writing in the *Massachusetts Spy* reported that a male contributor in a different newspaper had described women as "the *softer sex*." To which she responded smartly, "[N]otwithstanding our weakness ... I believe there are a greater number of tories of the *male* than of the *female* kind. Pray how many of our sex joined and denied ourselves of what was an idol to us—*Tea*? How did we withdraw from the shops of the importers, and abhor them?" When it came to making sacrifices for the public welfare, she concluded, "I have thought there may be a *set of men* who may be styled '*the softer sex.*'"[150]

The most remarkable call for the reformation of males came from Charleston, South Carolina. A woman who adopted the pen name "Margery Distaff" demanded, if not equality, then healthy signs of respect. It seems that someone called "Pedes Œconomist" had urged local women to take up spinning. To which Margery Distaff asked: What about the men? Were they prepared to give up drinking, gambling, horse racing, and cockfighting? "Women think," she stated, "it would tend to but very little good Purpose were they to card and spin, whilst the Men are racking their Brains, in contriving how to dissipate their Time and Money, in what they call PARTIES OF PLEASURE." Women would never behave like this. In a thoughtful although obviously angry attack on her society's construction of gender, Margery Distaff observed:

> The Reverse of all these Prodigalities is the Case with Women, whose utmost Expectations are, to go sometimes to a Ball or an Assembly, or to spend a few Hours in the Evening with an Acquaintance or two, after having carefully attended the Concerns of their Families in the preceding Part of the Day. These innocent Amusements only serve to relax their Minds for a small Time, and also to support a friendly Sociability between Friends; nor are such Meetings ever attended with any Expense that can hurt one's Fortune, whereas the Men throw away Hundreds, nay Thousands Of Pounds, in one Evening without the least Remorse, however their helpless infants may suffer for the future, by their present Imprudencies.

The essay reversed gender stereotypes. Her female companions were strong, responsible, prudent, and frugal. In other words, they possessed all the "virtues" claimed by males of the classic republican persuasion. Margery Distaff concluded this remarkably tough-minded piece with a stern warning to all would-be male patriots. " 'Til such a Reformation is brought about by our Superiors, we shall not think ourselves obliged to wear out our Fingers, either by carding or spinning," she announced. And even more striking, she told the strut-about males of Charleston that wearing "a Homespun Coat only, will never pass with Women, for a Mark of thorough Amendment, unless they give up better Proofs thereof than this paltry outside Show of it."[151]

For some American women—some of the time—resistance to parliamentary taxation extended beyond relationships within the family. Although it is impossible to tell from surviving records just how many women participated in the new consumer politics, a few women announced that they wanted a more prominent role in the defense of liberty. A strongly worded poem published in the *Pennsylvania Gazette* captured an aggressive mobilizing spirit that had not been present during the Stamp Act Crisis. "A Female" informed the newspaper's editor that she had penned the piece merely for "the Entertainment" of male readers. Such a claim may have raised expectations of a bantering interrogation of polite society. But "A Female" had a more serious agenda. She entitled the work "The FEMALE PATRIOTS: Addressed to the Daughters of Liberty in America." And from the opening lines, the author called upon colonial women to make their voices be heard in the public forum.

> Since the Men, for a Party or Fear of a Frown,
> Are kept by a Sugar-plum quietly down,
> Supinely asleep—and depriv'd of their Sight,
> Are stripp'd of their Freedom, and robb'd of their Right;
> If the Sons, so degenerate! The Blessings despise,
> Let the Daughters of Liberty nobly arise;
> And tho' we've no Voice but a Negative here,
> The Use of the Taxables*, let us forbear:—
> (Then Merchants import till your Stores are all full,
> May the Buyers be few, and your Traffick be dull!)
> Stand firmly resolv'd, and bid Grenville to see,
> That rather than Freedom we part with our Tea.

The asterisk drew the reader's attention to a list of prohibited imports— "Tea, Paper, Glass and Paints"—and the despised British minister was George Grenville, former chancellor of the exchequer, author of the Stamp Act, and Townshend's ally in squeezing revenues out of the American colonies. A Female acknowledged the traditional exclusion of women from political life. They could not vote. But in this performance, she seized an indirect power over public affairs; the Daughters of Liberty in America spoke for the communal consciousness.

> Join mutual in this—and but small as it seems,
> We may jostle a Grenville, and puzzle his Schemes;
> But a Motive more worthy our Patriot-Pen,
> Thus acting—we point out their Duty to Men;
> And should the Bound-Pensioners tell us to hush,
> We can throw back the Satire, by bidding them blush.[152]

The patriotic women of Boston refused to hush their protest. Like the merchants and town committees, they drew up a binding non-importation agreement. In 1770 the signers not only pledged to stop drinking tea "until the Revenue Acts are repealed" but also summarized the ideological principles that energized the market protest against Great Britain. Nothing about this striking document suggests that women deferred to men on questions of "our invaluable Rights and Privileges." To be sure, by their own admission the

A non-importation agreement which circulated in Boston during the height of popular resistance against the Townshend Revenue Act. 31 July 1769. *Mss. Large. Image number 652. Courtesy of the Massachusetts Historical Society.*

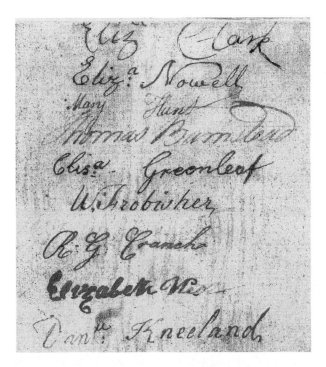

Women joined scores of male "Subscribers" in Boston in support of non-importation, a profoundly political act. Their signatures appear prominently on this 1769 agreement. 13 July 1769. *Mss. Large. Image number 652. Courtesy of the Massachusetts Historical Society.*

women had not taken the lead in the boycott movement, and their detractors suggested that they were unable to sacrifice consumer pleasures for the common good. The authors of this agreement, however, announced that they were now fully prepared to advance the colonial cause. "We think it our Duty," they asserted, "perfectly to concur with the true Friends of Liberty, in all the Measures they have taken to save this abused Country from Ruin and Slavery." Tea had become the seal of American oppression. And in these trying circumstances, Boston women wanted to support their husbands in resistance to the empire and to carve out a separate political space in which to operate. "We the Subscribers do strictly engage," they declared, "that we will totally abstain from the Use of the Article, (Sickness excepted) not only in our respective Families; but that we will absolutely refuse it, if it should be offered to us upon any Occasion whatsoever." The women's subscription immediately collected three hundred names. The organizers noted that they had obtained the signatures of a number of "worthy Ladies of the highest Rank and Influence," suggesting that a majority of the first signers had been ordinary women anxious to record a political opinion.

The Boston newspapers followed the subscription drive with great interest. Soon a hundred more women joined. Several weeks later the "young

Ladies of this Town" followed their mothers' example. "We [are] the Daughters of those Patriots who have and now do appear for the public Interest," they stated. "We as such do with Pleasure engage with them in denying ourselves the drinking of Foreign Tea, in hopes to frustrate a Plan that tends to deprive the whole Community of their all that is valuable in life." One hundred twenty-six "young Ladies" signed this second agreement.

The movement spread. Communication came in from Connecticut that "a Number of the principal Ladies" had discarded "foreign Tea." Nothing about this effort to mobilize consumers indicated that either the men or women of Boston regarded these activities as marginal to the cause of liberty. "The wise and virtuous Part of the fair Sex in Boston and other Towns," explained the *Boston Gazette*, ". . . being at length sensible that by the Consumption of Tea, they are supporting the Commissioners and other famous Tools of Power, have voluntarily agreed, not to give or receive any further Entertainments of that kind, until those Creatures, together with the Boston Standing Army, are removed, and the Revenue Acts are repealed."[153]

To exaggerate the numbers of women who actively engaged in organized consumer protests would be a mistake. The point is not that they transformed the character of the political culture. Rather, an increasingly intense conversation about British imports and American liberties invited people to think about political life in more inclusive terms. This was the society that inspired Abigail Adams to urge her husband, who was serving in the national legislature, to remember the ladies. Like his colleagues, John did not do so, and in the years following the Revolution some women looked back at this period with a sense of disappointment. Expectations had not been fulfilled.[154] After all, non-importation had unexpectedly raised hard questions about gender and politics. None reflected the radical mood better than an obscure New York poem entitled simply "A New Favorite Song for the Ladies."

> Though man has long boasted an absolute sway,
> While woman's hard fate was, love, honor, obey;
> At length over wedlock fair liberty dawns,
> And the Lords of Creation, must put in their horns;
> For Hymen among ye proclaims his decree
> When husbands are tyrants, their wives may be free.
>
> Away with your doubts, your surmises and fears,
> 'Tis Venus beats up for her gay volunteers;
> Enlist at her banner, you'll vanquish with ease,
> And make of your husbands what creatures you please;
> To arms then ye fair ones, and let the world see,
> When husbands are tyrants, their wives will be free.
>
> The rights of your sex wou'd ye e'er see restor'd
> Your tongues sho'd be us'd as a two-edged sword;
> That ear piercing weapon—each husband must dread,
> Who thinks of the marks you may place on his head;
> Then wisely unite, till the men all agree,
> That woman, dear woman, shall be free.

No more shall the wife, all as meek as a lamb,
Be subject to 'Zounds do you know who I am.'
Domestic politeness shall flourish again,
When women take courage to govern the men;
Then stand to your charter and let the world see,
Tho husbands are tyrants, their wives will be free.[155]

Whether the author of this piece was in fact male or female does not matter. For embattled consumers, the "Song" commented on a world turned upside down.

VII

The news from England might at another time have triggered wild celebrations throughout America. This was not such an occasion. During the summer of 1769 key members of the British cabinet decided to abandon the Townshend Program. It was not until March 1770 that Parliament finally repealed the legislation that had sparked colonial resistance. One nettlesome provision survived: A tax on tea remained on the statute books. The government's actions have been described as a retreat in face of mounting opposition. To call the elimination of duties on various consumer items a retreat, however, would leave the impression that the ministry had a coherent plan from which it was now retreating. None was in place. As the rulers of the greatest empire the world had ever known returned from London to their country seats that spring, they sensed that the country's leaders were floundering, and like so many regimes over the centuries that have lacked imaginative vision, this one mistook force and threats of force for a genuinely constructive policy.

The colonists shared the imperial fatigue. Another crisis had been averted. But the differences that had created the controversy had not been resolved, only temporarily tabled, and, of course, each gulp of tea represented an acceptance of taxation without representation. American merchants cried that they had had enough of non-importation. And however sincere their protestations about liberty and slavery, freedom and oppression, may have been, ordinary people interpreted partial repeal as an excuse for purchasing British goods in greater quantity than they had ever done before.

Colonists who had expended so much energy mobilizing the American people in support of non-importation found the sudden collapse of organized resistance devastating. They begged the merchants to abide by their agreements; they appealed to town committees to maintain their vigilance. They drew upon arguments that seemed to have worked so well only a few months earlier. "It is in the power of the people of New-York, and God be praised, of the people of the continent, by REFUSING TO PURCHASE, the *baubles* bought from the *Island* of Britain to prevent their future importation," insisted "An American," "and in doing this, they will save their money and their country at once."[156] "A Tradesman" asked poignantly, "Shall we exchange our birthright Privileges for the paltry Luxuries of Great-Britain, which impoverish and destroy us while we consume them?" Where were the *"real Lovers* of Liberty" at such a time?[157]

Cajoling rhetoric only inspired finger-pointing. Recriminations flowed from every region. It had been the New Yorkers who betrayed the cause. Rhode Island and Georgia were surely to blame. Everyone knew that the merchants of Boston cheated. The Philadelphia committees had always been lukewarm. On and on it went, a chorus of disappointment as the sinews of political trust dissolved. Whoever bore responsibility for defeat, it seemed clear that self-interest had thwarted consumer virtue in the marketplace. As "Cato" told the readers of several American journals, "The late Conduct of the Merchants of New-York, Philadelphia, &c. sufficiently proves that no Dependence is to be had upon any Combination or Agreement that can be entered into for the public Good, however well calculated to answer that End—if it interferes with the private immediate Interest of Individuals."[158] A statement originating in Charleston, South Carolina, employed heavy-handed irony to make the same point. "Thus disposed and situated," the author declared, "we pay little or no regard to the many reports and publications, of the whole Continent's having broken through their Non-Importation Agreements, or the infamous insinuations most industriously propagated, that none of them have played fair, but each endeavored to

New Advertisements.

Charles-Town, August 14, 1770.

THE PERFIDIOUS and WANTON Defection of those Inhabitants of the City of New-York, who have *deserted* the Cause of AMERICAN LIBERTY, requiring some spirited Resolutions to be immediately taken, by THOSE COLONIES who have sacrificed every particular Advantage for the PRESERVATION of that important Object: The GENERAL COM-MITTEE request a FULL MEETING of the People of this Province, for that Purpose, at LIBERTY-TREE, on WEDNESDAY the *Twenty-second* Instant, precisely at FOUR o'CLOCK in the Afternoon ; when some other Matters of Importance will also be laid before them.

Repeal of the more objectionable sections of the Revenue Act seemed to cool popular enthusiasm for "AMERICAN LIBERTY." Leaders of the non-importation movement bitterly accused those who had abandoned the cause of having sacrificed universal political rights for transient consumer pleasures. *South-Carolina Gazette,* 16 August 1770. *Courtesy of the Charleston Library Society.*

circumvent and take advantage of the other." After achieving such unprecedented cooperation, surely colonists would continue to sacrifice their personal pleasures for the common good. "We do not, nor can we believe, that the American Band of Union is broken or will be dissolved, merely because a few leading men in trade in each Northern Colony, have been so lost to every consideration, but their private emoluments."[159]

They did, of course, pay regard to such rumors in South Carolina. And so too did people in New England and the middle colonies. Partial repeal had tricked consumers into accepting partial freedom. One Connecticut writer concluded in 1772, "Ever since people's consciences have been released from the bonds of the non-importation agreement, we flow in goods; commerce not only meets with high encomiums, but is practiced upon as the health and wealth of the country."[160]

An occasional note of optimism emerged from the fog of gloom. One Boston writer dissented from those who insisted that non-importation had been a failure. "I am of a direct contrary opinion," he explained. "I am sensible it has produced great effects, and such as will be felt through ages. Great things rise from small beginnings. Industry, economy, and a resolution to inquire into and support our rights are visible through even the back settlements of America." Although this enthusiastic commentator did not express himself in terms of a symbolic shift in the meaning of material culture, he did remind his readers that in 1758 Americans had viewed with pride the scarlet coats worn by the soldiers in General Wolfe's army. Only a dozen years later the same brightly colored cloth from Great Britain had become an object of public disgust.[161] Such was a measure of progress. Lessons had been learned during the boycott, some more apparent than others. The lack of coordination had undermined the impact of the movement. Enforcement had been uneven, and despite heroic pledges to defend the common good, people had cheated, buying British imports that they knew had been enumerated.

Less appreciated at this moment of dejection was how Americans had constructed in their own imaginations a nation that was not yet a nation. A strategy of market protest had compelled colonists to think of their political futures in a language of union. Even as the house of cards came tumbling down, the Jeremiahs of non-importation unwittingly revealed how far they had come since the Stamp Act crisis. In his condemnation of the treachery of Philadelphia's erstwhile allies in the boycott, an anonymous writer inquired, "Do not the Importers in that province [Maryland] expect the same quantities [of imported goods] this Fall? Have not the Eastern-Governments most shamefully imported, notwithstanding their solemn declarations and resolves? Does not the conduct of the *Bostonians* sufficiently prove their perfidy, by re-shipping trunks and cases filled with rubbish, after gutting them of their British contents? In what manner have New-York and Rhode-Island behaved? Has Virginia ever entered into any agreement? Are not all the ports to the southward of South-Carolina open? Are not the ports of Quebec and Halifax, and other trading places in that

---

HARTFORD, June 6, 1770.

At a Meeting of the principal Merchants and Traders of the Colony of Connecticut. Taking into Consideration the late Extraordinary and unprecedented Conduct of a large Number of the Merchants and Traders of the Town of New-Port, in the Colony of Rhode-Island, in breaking Thro' & Violating the Non-Importation Agreement, come into, and observed elsewhere throughout America ; they by their Conduct declaring to the World the preference they give to their own present little sordid Views of self Interest, before the present and future Interest, Liberty and Well-being of America. That such a Conduct is justly alarming to the whole Continent, has tended to weaken that Union on which the Success of all our Efforts so much depends, has given our Enemies both at Home and Abroad an advantage against us, and justly incurred the Censure of every well-wisher to America.

Although effective political resistance dissolved after 1770, many Americans—such as those who attended a Connecticut meeting of "Merchants and Traders"—now thought in terms of the "present and future INTEREST, LIBERTY and WELL-BEING of AMERICA." In all the colonies, local decisions were seen increasingly as affecting "the whole Continent." *Connecticut Courant,* 6 June 1770. *Connecticut Historical Society.*

part of America open?"[162] This broadside offered up a list of betrayal, and however disconsolate its author may have been, he had begun almost reflexively to employ the language of continental identity. He took for granted shared interests that linked strangers from Canada to Georgia. To call this vision of a larger commercial and political solidarity the foundation for a later, more fully articulated American nationalism may seem premature. Nevertheless, it is hard to comprehend how colonists could have negotiated a common cause in 1776 without first having tasted this earlier promise of cooperation and union.

A second, more sobering lesson of non-importation was that the people were ultimately accountable for the common good. At the start of protest, men and women had turned to the merchants, believing that ordinary consumers like themselves could indirectly persuade, even compel, the leading importers to cancel their orders for British manufactures. In some communities the strategy worked well enough, but the merchants were a weak link on which to place such extravagant hopes. As "A Farmer" observed, "we see, that the Virtue of the Merchants, could not hold out, as was foreseen by our Enemies." But if the ordinary colonist could not count on the patriotic sacrifice of the merchants, then he or she had to face the fact that the success of a general boycott depended on a consumer public. During the dark days of 1770 when it seemed that the public had defaulted on its commitment to liberty, newspaper writers encouraged the American people to take responsibility for their own freedom. A boycott would only be politically effective if they made a total break with the store-bought objects that had made them at once more comfortable and more British. In his plea to the public,

> # To the PUBLIC.
>
> **T**HE Inhabitants of this CITY are defired, by the Committies of Infpection into the Importation of Goods, to meet at the Coffee-Houfe, on Monday next, precifely at twelve o'Clock, to give their Sentiments relative to the Article of TEA.
>
> NEW-YORK, *March* 8, 1770.

Protest leaders addressed appeals to a new imagined constituency, the "PUBLIC," a body of virtuous consumers whose sacrifice for political principle seemed the best hope for preserving American rights. *Broadside. New York,* 8 March 1770. *Courtesy of the Library Company of Philadelphia.*

"A Farmer" stated that if the people turned their backs on an empire of goods, "You will save your Country, and be as Healthy, as Easy and as Happy, as you need to be—God has put it in your Power: Improve that power: Help yourselves and God will help you."[163]

Could the colonists rise to the challenge? According to "Pro Aris Et Focis," the British had persuaded themselves that colonial consumers would never sacrifice the pleasures of the marketplace. It is blazed abroad, he declared, "that the mercantile endeavors would prove utterly abortive;—that no dependence was to be had upon the virtuous stability of the generality among us;—that the common people, or, as they disdainfully term it, the herd, were sunk in luxury, intemperance and degrading vice;—and that hence, any *commercial plan* of political salvation would prove, only, an amusing dream—a transitory phantom."[164] Whoever accepted the truth of this statement badly underestimated the political will of the American consumer.

8

Bonfires of Tea:
The Final Act

Colonial rebellion touched the lives of ordinary—and not so ordinary—Americans in surprising ways. For Ebenezer
Withington, a common "laborour" living in Dorchester, Massachusetts, the
moment of reckoning arrived one Saturday morning in late December 1773.
Without giving much thought to the political crisis then brewing in Boston, Withington took a walk "round upon the Marshes," and there he came
upon "part of a half chest" of tea bobbing in a tidal pool. He could not
believe his good fortune. Tea in such quantity, he knew, might fetch a handsome price, and, oblivious to the possibility that the Boston Sons of Liberty
dressed as Native Americans might have recently thrown this very chest
into the water, Withington decided to transport the treasure home. His
political ignorance was stunning. Only a few weeks earlier the members of
the First Provincial Congress in Massachusetts had strongly recommended
"to the people of this province an abhorrence and detestation of all kinds
of East India teas, as the baneful vehicle of a corrupt and venal administration, for the purpose of introducing despotism and slavery into this once
happy country; and that every individual in this province ought totally to
disuse the same."[1] But "old" Ebenezer Withington, as he was described in
later interrogations, seemed indifferent to the gathering storm.

Withington traveled only a short distance when he happened upon
"some Gentlemen belonging to the Castle." The encounter might have persuaded a more politically savvy person to drop the project. After all, the
Castle was the British fortification in Boston Harbor where royal office-
holders sought security when urban mobs threatened to get out of hand.
Withington did not know these gentlemen by name. He remembered only
that they "asked me if I had been picking up the Ruins." The question per-
plexed the laborer from Dorchester, and, expressing proper deference, he
inquired of these Tory sympathizers "if there was any Harm." They assured

him that he had nothing to fear, "except from my Neighbours." The warning seems not to have made the slightest impression on Withington, for, as he later explained, "Accordingly, I brought Home the same, part of which I disposed of." Another commentator might have observed, perhaps ungenerously, that Withington ran his mouth, bragging about his amazing piece of luck to the people who purchased a few ounces of tea.

Word of the tea spread quickly through the small agricultural community. Since the residents of Massachusetts had specifically been enjoined not to market this ubiquitous British import, "a number of the Cape or Narragansett-Indians" took it upon themselves to investigate the matter. Not imagining that "old" Withington might have been involved, the patriotic Indians first visited a house owned by Ebenezer's two sons "on the lower road from Boston to Milton." The owners offered no resistance when their disguised neighbors asked if they might search the building for contraband tea. None was discovered. Only then did suspicions turn to the father. And sure enough, the committee of pretend Indians soon found the parcel of tea, now a little lighter as a result of recent sales, and its members carried the trophy "to Boston Common where they committed it to the flames." On December 31, John Rowe, a leading Boston merchant, jotted in his diary: "There was found in the House of One Withington of Dorchester about half a Chest of Tea—the People gathered together & took the Tea, Brought it into the Common of Boston & Burnt it this night about eleven of Clock. This is supposed to be part of the Tea that was taken out of the Ships & floated over to Dorchester."[2]

The bonfire in Boston did not conclude Withington's ordeal. He had yet to atone for a crime against the common good. At a full meeting of the "Freeholders and other Inhabitants" of Dorchester—no doubt, many of them formerly "Cape or Narragansett-Indians"—the aged worker was made to confess his ideological sins. Before an audience of familiar faces, he recounted the entire story of finding the chest; while some of his listeners may have desired a more abject apology, they resolved that Withington's

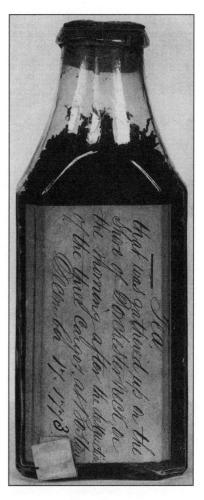

A bottle containing tea leaves allegedly "collected on the Shore of Dorchester Neck" soon after the Boston Tea Party. 17 December 1773. *MHS image number 106. Courtesy of the Massachusetts Historical Society.*

deplorable conduct had "proceeded from inadvertency." However unpleasant the episode may have been, full disclosure served to clear the community itself of wrongdoing. As the Dorchester farmers explained, "[I]t gives the greatest Satisfaction to this Town that he [Withington] hath been discovered selling said Tea; otherwise the Conspirators against our Rights and Liberties might have taken Occasion to have insinuated, as their Manner is, that the whole of the Tea said to have been destroyed was plundered and privately sold contrary to the most notorious Fact." The investigators determined to ferret out all persons who had done business with Withington. A chance purchase might have represented no more than error of judgment; it might have revealed the presence of a subversive group operating within Dorchester. The buyers of Withington's tea were ordered to surrender the remaining leaves for destruction, or to be "deemed as Enemies who have joined with the Tea Consigners and other Conspirators, to promote the use of the detested Article, and their Names shall be publicly posted accordingly." A final step remained. The townsmen voted that they would henceforth employ "all means in their Power [to] discountenance the use of Tea, while it is subject to a Duty imposed on it by the British Parliament." Withington went home a chastened although politically wiser man. Events he had little understood transformed his life. His inadvertent actions compelled neighbors publicly to reaffirm their commitment to the cause of liberty. Such was the process of revolutionary indoctrination.[3] In coercive settings throughout America, the doubters and fence-sitters, occasionally simple old men, were reminded that consumer sacrifice had become the signature of colonial patriotism in a contest against a commercial empire.

Less than a year after the Dorchester incident, a much more prominent American felt obliged to explain his passion for imported British goods. Despite his effusive praise for the simple life of the yeoman farmer, Thomas Jefferson could hardly restrain himself when he wanted a special object for Monticello, his beloved Virginia estate. After the Revolution, for example, Jefferson served the new nation in London and Paris, and when he was not performing official duties, he indulged his almost insatiable appetite for shopping. Upon his return to the United States in 1787, it required some sixteen pages just to inventory all the goods that he had acquired in Europe. Betraying a side of his character that often escapes modern comment, Jefferson informed Madame de Corney that the "splendor of their [the English] shops . . . is all that is worth seeing in London." His consumer frenzy embarrassed his old friend the marquis de Lafayette, who on one occasion admonished Jefferson to exercise more self-control in the stores. Jefferson responded weakly, "It is not from a love of the English, but a love of myself that I sometimes find myself obliged to buy their manufactures."[4]

An earlier expression of self-indulgence caused Jefferson's colleagues similar uneasiness. In late 1774 he informed local members of the Virginia Association, which had been charged with enforcing a total boycott of British goods, about an order to a London merchant house for "14 pair of sash windows" with glass. In a letter to Archibald Cary and Benjamin Harrison about the windows, Jefferson protested that he had intended to be "a conscientious observer of the measures generally thought requisite for the preservation of our independent rights," and he seemed quite unhappy that his purchase might "wear an appearance of contravening them." The order was all a misunderstanding, he reported. When the leaders of the House of Burgesses originally formed the Association, Jefferson assumed that it was aimed "against the future use of *tea only.*" Sounding increasingly defensive, Jefferson continued: "Tho' the proceedings of the [British] ministry against the town of Boston were then well known to us, I believe nobody thought at that time of extending our Association further to the total interruption of our commerce with Britain: or if it was proposed by any (which I do not recollect) it was condemned by the general sense of the members who formed that Association." And so, reasoning that tea was the only prohibited item, Jefferson dispatched a detailed request to London for the sash windows.

The months passed; political conditions in America changed. Jefferson became aware that many Virginians wanted a complete ban on British imports, but, diverted by the press of personal business and calls for a national congress, "I did not write to countermand my order, thinking I should have sufficient time, after the final determinations of the congress should be known, to countermand it." Finally, Jefferson received news that the windows were scheduled to land in Virginia. In a panic that his behavior might "give a handle for traducing our measures," he laid before the local members of the Association "a full state of the matter by which it might be seen under what expectations I had failed to give an earlier countermand and to shew that as they come within the prohibitions of the Continental Association (which without the spirit of prophecy could not have been foretold when I ordered them) so I mean they shall be subject to its condemnation."[5] That was the end of the affair. Perhaps, like Withington, Jefferson had made an inadvertent error of judgment. One wonders, however, why a person of such perspicacity about political affairs did not more fully appreciate how a purchase of this nature might appear to neighbors pushing for a total boycott on the eve of independence.

The experiences of two colonial consumers serve as poignant reminders to the complexities of popular mobilization. The Thomas Jefferson who is celebrated in so many modern histories of the period seems to have been a person motivated almost entirely by ideas about liberty and freedom, about the character of republican government, and it is easy to imagine that for the great majority of American people such abstractions, however dimly understood, were sufficient to explain their resistance to Great Britain. But principles without proof of commitment, ideas without structures of trust, thoughts without networks of communication, could not have sustained a revolutionary movement. As Jefferson discovered, the imperial crisis made private choices about domestic goods matters of legitimate public scrutiny. Without a willingness to sacrifice for a shared political cause, the rhetoric of protest rang hollow. Had Jefferson not been obliged to surrender the "14 pair of sash windows," he still would have been prepared to write nobly about rights and equality, but among his colleagues he might always have been regarded as a person who did not appreciate the full dimensions of personal responsibility. Visible acts of self-denial conveyed one's sincerity to strangers. Unlike Jefferson, Withington probably did not spend his days reading political philosophy. Within a world bounded by the Dorchester marshes, the tea acted as a converting mechanism, bringing him into a community of patriots who had already learned the relation between principle and sacrifice, between bonfires of tea and political solidarity. In both examples consumer goods provided the means for colonists not only to reassess their identity within an empire but also to forge political bonds with revolutionary neighbors.

Reflections on the structures of resistance raise once again questions posed at the beginning of this investigation. How does one explain the timing of revolution? Why did the break with Great Britain not occur at an earlier moment when passions ran high and mobs roamed the streets of the major colonial ports? A glib answer would be that the colonists were not ready to mount such a united effort in 1765 or 1770. The translation of local grievance into organized rebellion required the development of ways for Americans to reach out effectively to other Americans. That process of discovery took time. The colonists drew upon their participation in a vast new consumer marketplace, an experience that persuaded them that their dependence upon British manufactures might be turned by a colonial people into a powerful political weapon. During the Stamp Act agitation they took tentative steps toward non-importation. At first, it seemed reasonable to place responsibility for the success of this strategy on the merchants. Only slowly did ordinary colonists begin to appreciate that such a plan had little chance of success. The merchants marched to different drummers. More radical Americans such as Samuel Adams concluded that the protest against the Townshend duties had been a failure; after 1770 colonial consumers raced once again to the shops, buying British imports at record levels. In their disappointment, Adams and others undervalued changes in the political culture that were of profound significance for the character of later events. Between 1767 and 1770 Americans invented a "public" which monitored behavior in a consumer public sphere, experimented with new forms of extra-legal political participation, constituted themselves as a group with interests separate from those of the British, and forged channels of communication that promoted a sense of trust among distant strangers.

When Parliament passed the Tea Act in May 1773, the colonists were not the same people they had been in 1768. They drew upon a history of protest within the consumer marketplace, a history without precedent and entirely of their own making. Almost without fully comprehending the magnitude of their own achievement, Americans now almost instinctively moved from demands for *non-importation* to appeals for *non-consumption,* a shift of immense importance in the history of popular political protest. On this occasion they insisted that the people must take personal responsibility for their own political destiny. As one Connecticut writer observed in

1774, the former effort to make non-importation work had collapsed because "it stood on a rotten and unsolid basis. It was erected wholly on the virtue of the merchants, and rested its whole weight solely on this prop."[6] Just as the authors of the formal political pamphlets—documents that so often structure modern accounts of the American Revolution—were struggling to comprehend a republican polity founded on the will of the people, ordinary men and women were being asked in a parallel discourse to sacrifice personal comforts for the common good. Samuel Adams understood the challenge. In a letter written in June 1774 to Richard Henry Lee about the prospects for a total American boycott, Adams observed, "It is the virtue of the yeomanry we are chiefly to depend on."[7] In this atmosphere, the people no longer defined British imports such as tea as luxuries or as sources of debt but as poisons they had to purge in the name of liberty.

The argument is not that consumer goods caused the American Revolution. In Aristotelian terms, the claim is rather that British imports provided a necessary but not sufficient cause for the final break with Parliament. Other developments within late colonial society—the spread of evangelical Christianity, for example—helped ordinary men and women make sense of political events. And without an inspiring language of universal rights, non-importation would have been little more than a strategy in search of a proper goal. Still, imported goods invited colonists to think radical new thoughts about empire. British manufactures came to symbolize dependence and oppression. The mental link was so strong that when a small, very poor community in Massachusetts addressed the problem of the tea, it also raised questions about its place within a larger world. In response to news of the arrival of the tea ships in Boston Harbor, the inhabitants of the town of Harvard discussed the situation and found "it to be a matter of as interesting and important a nature when viewed in all its Consequences not only to this Town and Province, but to America in general, and that for ages and generations to come, as ever came under the deliberation of this Town."[8] The intensity of the reaction of these obscure farmers helps explain why colonists from South Carolina to New Hampshire stood with Boston during the terrible days following the destruction of the tea.

II

During 1773 the pace of events accelerated. Following the collapse of organized resistance three years earlier, many people on both sides of the Atlantic persuaded themselves that the time of troubles had ended and Humpty Dumpty had not in fact taken a great fall. But the House of Commons, now led by Frederick Lord North, second earl of Guilford, managed once again to roil imperial waters. The new crisis resulted not from tougher American policy but rather from a much overdue attempt to bring order to the chaotic affairs of the East India Company. This grossly mismanaged enterprise possessed a monopoly to import tea from South Asia into Great

Britain, but for many reasons—internal corruption being a prime candidate—the directors had run up huge operating debts, and to avoid bankruptcy they turned to the government for an emergency loan. Lord North offered to support such an arrangement, but only on condition that the Company reform its business practices. The directors argued that if they could sell their tea directly to the Americans without paying normal duties or going through wholesalers who ran up the price, they might be able to turn a profit. A concession from the government on duties would enable the Company to undersell the smugglers, who obtained their tea from the Dutch. Anxious that he not signal a retreat on the principle of parliamentary sovereignty, North refused to drop the last remaining Townshend Duty, a decision that still allowed the Company to cut prices substantially but also compelled the Americans to pay a tax which they labeled unconstitutional. When asked why he did not show greater flexibility on this point, North growled that "the temper of the people there is little deserving favour from hence."[9] If the minister really thought the colonists would accept the Tea Act, he was in for a shock. Although some modern Americans seem to accept the notion that the federal government should bail out failing corporations, the colonists branded the legislation venal, and they vowed to teach North that their love of liberty exceeded their love of tea.

During the fall of 1773 Americans scrambled to nullify the Tea Act. Learning that Company ships would arrive in the major colonial ports sometime in November, local protest groups pressured civil authorities to prohibit the unloading of the vessels. The Sons of Liberty did their best to intimidate newly appointed tea agents, many of them prominent merchants whose personal loyalties lay with the crown. In the newspapers and in cheap broadsides, patriotic voices sounded the alarm once again, urging the colonists to resist political oppression by refusing to buy imported goods. By now the mental link between consumer sacrifice and political ideology was well established. Still, at that moment, no one could confidently predict the popular response to the Tea Act. After all, between 1770 and 1773, in addition to the smuggled Dutch tea, Americans bought some 300,000 pounds of tea annually from British merchants, knowing full well that the purchase price included the Townshend duty. Of the many entreaties broadcast during this period, few were as strongly worded as a letter in the *Pennsylvania Packet* addressed to "the Freeholders and Freemen" of Pennsylvania. "Taking for granted . . .," the writer reasoned, "that the revenue acts are opposite to the very idea and spirit of liberty, it will naturally follow, that a ship, loaded with goods which come under one of those acts is the true and literal Pandora's box, filled with poverty, oppression, slavery, and every other hated disease." Colonial consumers should be forewarned that this legislation was only the start. "Whenever the Tea is swallowed, and pretty well digested, we shall have new duties imposed on other articles of commerce."[10] The Association of the Sons of Liberty in New York City prepared a stirring history of American non-importation from the "detestable Stamp Act" to the current campaign against tea.

What had been an imaginative although tentative strategy of consumer protest in 1765 had now evolved into the accepted mode of American resistance. If people embraced the tea, declared the Sons of Liberty, they would acquire a heavy burden of guilt. They would forever have to justify why they had failed "to defeat the pernicious Project" and thereby denied "to our Posterity, those Blessings of Freedom, which our Ancestors have handed down to us."[11] A New York newspaper wailed that "A SHIP loaded with TEA is now on her Way to this Port, being sent out by the Ministry for the Purpose of *enslaving* and *poisoning* ALL the AMERICANS." A later issue of the same journal provided readers with a secular catechism so that they might better understand the gravity of the crisis. Compared to the formal legal and constitutional pamphlets of the day, these productions may seem simple, even childish, but they expose a level of popular mobilization that intellectual histories generally ignore. The litany not only outlined the challenge but also advised ordinary men and women what they could do to demonstrate their commitment to the common good.

> QUERIES—Respecting the TEA ACT submitted to the most serious Consideration of every person in AMERICA.
>
> Query. As there is an Act of the British Parliament in Being, that would subjugate America to *Three Pence Sterling Duty* upon every Pound Weight of Tea imported from *Britain*; and as this Duty is *voted* independent of, and without the Sanction of any of *our American* Parliaments, what ought to be done unto every one of those *traitorous Persons*, who shall aid or abet the Importation of, *or landing*, the said Tea in any part of *America*, till the Act is totally repealed, *jointly, by King, Lords, and Commons?*
>
> Answer. Such base *Traitors* to this Country, without Exception, should immediately and *resolutely* be dragged from Concealment; they should be transported, or forced from every Place in *America*, loaded with the most striking Badges of Disgrace ...
>
> Query. What will be the most effectual Methods of Proceeding, to obtain a Repeal of the said oppressive, unconstitutional Act?
>
> Ans. TO USE NO TEA, *at least for the present,* for if any Persons should give the Sellers more than the usual Price for Tea, he ought to be held up as a mortal Enemy to *American Freedom*. And,—*brave Americans*.[12]

In New York City, Charleston, and Philadelphia last-minute negotiations helped prevent serious violence. Either the tea ships returned to London or crown officials prudently stored the tea in safe places where it could not be sold.[13]

In Boston events took a different turn. A crowd of five thousand men and women witnessed the arrival of the Company ships, carrying 342 chests of East India tea. Popular leaders begged the captains of these vessels to return to London, but perhaps to no one's surprise, local tea agents refused to compromise. The Hutchinson brothers, Thomas and Elisha, who represented the Company in Boston, insisted on landing the entire cargo. Samuel Adams and his friends pledged never to let that happen. The standoff pushed those who opposed the Tea Act to stake out ever more radical ground. One announcement signed by "The People" reminded "The Public, That it was solemnly voted by the Body of the People of this and the neighboring

Towns . . . that the said Tea never should be landed in this Province, or pay one Farthing of Duty." Anyone who dared to assist such an attempt, declared "The People," "must betray an inhuman Thirst for Blood, and will also in great Measure accelerate Confusion and Civil War. This is to assure such public Enemies of this Country, they will be considered and treated as Wretches unworthy to live, and be made the first Victims of our just Resentment."[14]

If crown officials and their supporters thought that such inflated rhetoric amounted to no more than bluster, they were mistaken. On December 16 Boston "Mohawks" spent much of the day throwing tea chests into the harbor, one of which, of course, found its way to Ebenezer Withington. Accounts of the Indian disguise have given this famous incident a slightly ludicrous character in American history, transforming the Tea Party into a kind of carnival event in which feathered citizens lightheartedly sparked the final confrontation with Parliament. It was nothing of the sort. As every participant understood, the destruction of the tea invited immediate and severe retaliation. They had violated private property, a provocation no British ruler could ignore. More to the point, the Tea Party represented not a break with the previous history of colonial resistance but rather an escalation of a tradition of consumer protest that had begun a decade earlier.

Boston's punishment staggered even those who expected the worst. Lord North could endure no more insolence from what seemed to him America's hotbed of radicalism. A well-placed London diarist, Matthew Brickdale, recorded the ministry's case against the community that had drowned the tea. Boston, scribbled Brickdale, "has been the ringleader of all violence and opposition to the execution of the laws of this country. New York and Philadelphia grew unruly on receiving the news of the triumph of the people of Boston. Boston had not only therefore to answer for its own violence but for having incited other places to tumults."[15] Thinking of this sort led in the spring of 1774 to a series of statutes known collectively in the colonies as the Intolerable Acts. These bills closed Boston Harbor to all commerce until the city reimbursed the East India Company for its loss. Other acts fundamentally altered the constitution of Massachusetts Bay. Perhaps the most intrusive measure was legislation limiting town meetings throughout the colony to a single session each year, a serious blow to a people who prized the rough-and-tumble debate of local government.

One Connecticut writer who styled himself the "Conciliator" explained the larger meaning of North's punitive policy. "At length," he declared, "the Harbor of Boston is blocked up, and the Business of Importation in that Town at an End. . . . Foreign Manufactures, it seems, are considered as pernicious to the Constitution of America, and we must either disuse them, or encounter the Horrors of Slavery." The Conciliator insisted that no colonist should be surprised to discover that common consumer goods now defined the battle lines of empire. "The Language of Great-Britain in Years past, in Accents loud as Thunder, has rung this solemn Peal in our Ears— Americans! Stop your Trade." But even in these dark hours, hope beckoned.

The British "know that Economy, Frugality and Virtue will raise us above the Reach of the envenomed Arrows of Oppression. . . . Our foolish Fondness for the Toys of that Country, provokes her Resentment." The message was clear. Americans might assist Boston with food and money. If they meant to be free, however, they had to rededicate themselves to consumer sacrifice. Sounding like an Old Testament prophet who believed that virtuous consumers must atone for past market sin, the Conciliator exclaimed, "It is our Treachery to ourselves, my Countrymen, that has brought these Burdens upon us."[16]

It did not require a miracle to persuade other Americans to pledge their support to Boston. They might, of course, have taken an easier path. After all, they might have reasoned, the Intolerable Acts did not directly affect them. Why not wait? Since Parliament had not closed their ports, they might continue to do business as usual. And yet, by and large, they stood firm when it counted most. The explanation for solidarity—a challenge informing this study from the start—was that by the summer of 1774 Americans had learned how to reach out to each other.[17] They had begun to think continentally. The experience of mounting ever more effective consumer protests against a commercial empire had encouraged them to imagine a new, geographically inclusive identity. A decade of protest in the marketplace had forced them to define themselves as not fully British. Indeed, in defiance of parliamentary taxation they increasingly saw themselves as Americans. The North government failed to appreciate that it was no longer dealing with a loose collection of colonies which might turn on each other to gain some transient advantage.

Parliament tried to make an example of Boston and, by so doing, aroused a nation. The reaction of the planters of Queen Anne's County, Maryland, to the Boston crisis was unusual only in its eloquence. In June 1774, they declared, "Duly considering, and deeply affected with the prospect of the unhappy situation of Great Britain and British America, under any kind of disunion, this Meeting think themselves obliged, by all the ties which ever ought to preserve a firm union amongst Americans, as speedily as possible, to make known their sentiments to their distressed brethren of Boston, and therefore publish [them] to the world." The planters' first decision reflected long years of experimentation with non-importation: "[T]hey look upon the cause of Boston, in its consequences, to be the common cause of America."[18] Resolutions of this sort poured forth from small, scattered communities. Their residents wanted to register a public commitment to a larger responsibility. At a "General Town Meeting" in Huntington, New York, for example, it was concluded that "we are of opinion that our brethren of Boston are now suffering in the common cause of British America."[19] The small farmers of Caroline County, Virginia, announced that they were prepared "not to import from Great Britain any commodity whatsoever . . . [until] the cruel Acts of the British Parliament against the Massachusetts Bay and the town of Boston are repealed."[20] The freemen of the lower part of Frederick County, Maryland, gathered in Hungerford's Tavern to resolve unanimously "That it is the opinion of this meeting that the town of Boston is now suffering in the common cause of America." After analyzing the current crisis, they concluded—as did people throughout the colonies—"that the most effectual means for the securing American freedom, will be to break off all commerce with Great Britain."[21]

To stake its demand for colonial obedience on tea represented a high-risk decision for Parliament. Had it chosen a different British import—perhaps porcelain or small metal items—it might have avoided such a firestorm of protest. But, as the leading English merchants of the day could have informed imperial legislators, tea had long ago made its way into the great majority of colonial households. A Philadelphia businessman calculated that Americans purchased almost six million pounds of tea a year. On the basis of this figure, he estimated that about a third of the entire population of British America drank tea twice a day. And, of course, although tea was not itself a durable good, its use sustained a huge market in related imported articles such as china cups and tea pots.[22] It had become the master symbol of the new consumer economy. By mid-century the tea service provided a standard of good manners and cosmopolitan taste. Women anxious to establish a social sphere of their own organized elaborate afternoon tea parties.

The question for Lord North as well as for American spokesmen was how consumer popularity might translate into political protest. In 1774 a Tory sympathizer offered an obvious answer. If the Americans really resented the tax on tea, he observed, they could simply stop buying it. They were free to choose what they consumed. To this proposition, a skeptical patriot writer responded with a story about a Philadelphia "madman" who some twelve years earlier had proclaimed himself "monarch of the country," a privileged position that allowed him to "tax the air." To which his subjects asked, "[M]ay it please your Majesty, will such a tax be right? Air was always common and free, in the time of your Majesty's royal progenitors and predecessors. Will not your subjects think this an arbitrary law, like the poll tax? Arbitrary! Cried the prince, enraged; and like the poll tax too! What rebels! Why unless they breathe, they don't pay the duty; therefore it is quite in their option whether they will pay it or no."[23] Enjoying a morning mug of tea may not have been quite the same thing as breathing, but the point hit the mark. It was hard to imagine maintaining the normal fabric of social relations without tea. A contributor to a South Carolina newspaper took it as a given that tea was a ubiquitous article of colonial life. "The Ministry too well know the Effect of long Habit. . . . It is Tea that has kept all America trembling for Years. It is Tea that has brought Vengeance upon Boston."[24]

Anyone quoting odds on how easy it would be to mobilize the American people around a boycott of tea would have been well advised to consider the product's recent history in the colonial marketplace. At the beginning of the eighteenth century, tea drinking had been an activity only affluent colonists could afford. Critics identified tea as a luxury item which threatened the morals of elite society. But like so many other consumer goods during this period, tea migrated from luxury to necessity. On the eve of revolution, people of very modest means drank tea, sometimes from porcelain cups. According to "A. B.," "At the introduction of TEA into America, it was considered as a luxury, and only used by the wealthy and extravagant, but since being more plentiful and cheaper, it is become a necessary and common diet for the *poor,* and as used by them will go further than any thing else of equal value."[25] A writer in the *New-York Mercury* echoed this commonplace. He rejected the notion that tea was "a mere Luxury." "By Habit it is become necessary, and it has been found as cheap as almost any Thing that could be substituted in its Stead."[26] This evidence might be interpreted as an indication of the great difficulty that patriot leaders faced in persuading ordinary men and women to sacrifice something deemed so essential to their well-being.

But there is another, more compelling possibility. If poor people did purchase so much tea, they then had an article in their possession that could actually be given up for a political cause. Calls for this kind of sacrifice, therefore, were neither abstract nor impossible. During an earlier subscription drive in Boston, an opponent of non-importation had chided the "Porters & Washing Women" for pledging not to purchase silks and velvets, coaches and chariots. He argued that one could not take the political commitment of these people seriously since they were not able to buy the goods that they publicly pledged to forgo. Tea, however, was a different matter. It appeared in modest homes; as a mild stimulant, it helped urban workers and marginal farmers endure hard physical labor. A voluntary promise from such people to do without tea in the name of liberty represented a genuine sacrifice, one that was perhaps even more difficult for them than it was for their social betters. And, of course, one should not forget that without their support—as soldiers, for example—the Revolution would have died aborning.

Consumer protest against the Intolerable Acts encouraged a strident, often hyperbolic language unprecedented in the evolution of non-importation. Earlier efforts to curtail the purchase of British goods had stressed the link between imported manufactures and American concerns such as the growing burden of colonial dependence, the rising level of colonial debt, and the moral dangers of self-indulgence in the marketplace. Within this context, British goods symbolized a strained although remediable imperial relationship. But few writers described tea in these terms. During the months following the closing of Boston Harbor, tea became emblematic of an emotional separation between a people who now regularly called themselves Americans and a distant English government that seemed to have squandered their trust and affection. Such a mental process—a psychological distancing from Great Britain—was an essential element not only for popular mobilization but also for the development of a broadly shared sense of American identity. Within this mental framework, tea sustained an inchoate spirit of nationalism.

By mid-1774 drinking tea had become equated in the popular mind with political sin. No longer could one pretend that private enjoyments within one's own family did not have public consequences. Anyone could see that tea, like an insidious drug, allowed conspirators in the mother country to erode colonial rights. As "A Woman" informed readers of a Massachusetts journal, "[I]n the present case the use of tea is considered not as a *private* but a *public* evil; so the arguments used against it should be of a public nature." It did not matter, she insisted, whether tea undermined personal health. The most salient fact was that since Lord North had "saddled [tea] with a tribute, &c. . . . we are not to consider it merely as the herb tea, or as what has an ill tendency as to health, but as it is made a handle of to introduce a variety of public grievances and oppressions amongst us."[27] A sermon on tea published in Lancaster, Pennsylvania, reminded all Americans that tea drinking was "a political absurdity. This baneful herb is the match by which an artful wicked ministry intended to blow up the liberties of America." People who believed that a sip of their favorite beverage would do no harm were wrong. "Continuing to purchase tea, under present circumstances, is high treason against three millions of Americans."[28] A colonist writing under the name "A Consistent Patriot" captured in powerfully persuasive prose the hardening of symbolic categories. For him, as a result of an alchemy driven by imperial politics, a former pleasure had been transformed into a dangerous poison.

> The importation and use of Tea, abstractly considered, may be innocent, and he who in ordinary times, has an inclination to import or use it, has a right to the protection of the laws. But when the importation is connected with the ruin of government, its trade—and what is infinitely more valuable, its liberty;—when it is designed for that purpose and will infallibly have that effect, we ought to consider and treat it as we would THE PLAGUE.[29]

In even stronger rhetoric, a South Carolina essay entitled "On Patriotism" explained that "the baneful chests" of tea forced on the Americans by the East India Company contained "in them a slow poison, in a political as well as a physical sense. They contain something worse than death—the seeds of SLAVERY."[30]

As the flow of events swept ever more colonists into the imperial maelstrom, popular writers revived an older discourse about the actual physical dangers of using tea. Even at the time some pseudo-scientific rhetoric about tea struck some readers as mere "scare crow stories."[31] But from the perspective of those determined to mobilize a population in support of renewed non-importation—not to mention American rights and liberty—reports about the deleterious impact of tea on normal men and women served to heighten public attention. Moreover, tales of contagious disease increased the pressure on individual households to sacrifice for the common good. Earlier in the century, social commentators often argued that tea undermined the moral health of its users. Women, it was claimed, were especially susceptible to the enervating effects of tea. As this import came to symbolize political oppression, however, the critique focused increasingly on the peril it represented for the well-being of the entire community.

The tea menace appeared in different forms. One widely reprinted article asserted that the habit of drinking tea made people smaller. Within a generation or two, observers had allegedly discovered that "our race is dwindled, and become puny, weak and disordered, to such a degree, that were it to prevail a century more, we should be reduced to meager Pygmies."[32] Another critic appealed to the lessons of history. "It is about 100 years since this herb, worse than Pandora's Box, was introduced into Europe," he declared. "In which time mankind had lost some inches in their stature, many degrees in their strength, and disorders have assumed a new complexion." The most serious menace was "Histeria." Once only women suffered from the nervous complaint, but now tea exposed able-bodied males to this wasting ailment. As anyone could document, tea had "reduced the robust masculine habit of men to a feminine softness—In short, it has turned men into women, and the women into—God knows what."[33] The point was clear. If patriotic colonists wanted to stand tall against the empire, they had better give up tea. And it was a decision that they could not postpone. A Boston physician warned that the spread of tea drinking had caused "spasms, vapors, hypochondrias, apoplexies of the serious kind, palsies, dropsies, rheumatisms, consumptions, low nervous, miliary and petechial fevers."[34] Rumors circulated that imported English tea bred insects, was packed in chests by people with dirty feet, and promoted smallpox.[35] No wonder that "An Old Mechanic" expressed nostalgia for "the time when Tea was not used, nor scarcely known amongst us." He testified that "people seemed at that time of day to be happier, and to enjoy more health in general than they do now." But then, what was one to expect of unreflective shoppers? "We must be every day bringing in some new-fangled thing or other from abroad, till we are really become a luxurious people. No matter how ugly and deformed a garment is; nor how insipid or tasteless, or prejudicial to our healths an eatable or drinkable is, we must have it, if it is the *fashion*."[36] As appeals for non-importation echoed loudly in the newspapers, Americans had to face the fact that a nation of puny tea drinkers could never hope to summon the manly virtue required to battle Great Britain.

Many Americans probably did not fully appreciate what a sacrifice giving up tea represented until they tried a substitute suggested by well-meaning experimenters. These alternative beverages seem as a group to have been so ill-tasting that every cup must have reminded ordinary colonists of the pleasure that they had renounced in a show of political solidarity. The only positive attribute of these replacements was that they were locally grown—in some cases, as weeds—and so, when patriotic persons drank these vile concoctions, they had the satisfaction of knowing that American plants did not carry parliamentary taxes. "If we must, through custom, have some warm tea, once or twice a day," queried a Pennsylvania author, "why may we not exchange this slow poison, which not only destroys our constitutions, but endangers liberty, and drains our country of so many thousand pounds a year, for teas of

A

SERMON

O N

TEA.

(❖❖❖❖❖❖❖❖❖❖❖❖❖❖❖❖❖❖❖❖❖❖❖❖❖)

" *Touch not, Taſte not, Handle not.*"
ST. PAUL.

(❖❖❖❖❖❖❖❖❖❖❖❖❖❖❖❖❖❖❖❖❖❖❖❖❖)

" *The Tea Pots full of warm Water, I ſee*
" *upon their Tables, put me in mind of* PANDO-
" RA's *Box, from whence all Sorts of Evil iſſue*
" *forth.*"

TISSOT.

(❖❖❖❖❖❖❖❖❖❖❖❖❖❖❖❖❖❖❖❖❖❖❖❖❖)

LANCASTER:
PRINTED BY FRANCIS BAILEY.

In this sermon even St. Paul warned American patriots against drinking tea. *A Sermon on Tea* (Lancaster, 1774). *Rare Book/Special Collections Reading Room (Jefferson LJ 239). Courtesy of the Library of Congress.*

our own *American Plants.*" He listed possibilities. In the Chesapeake colonies, for example, people were brewing "*Hairy Moss,*" a drink guaranteed to cure various illnesses.[37] Others advised boiling common herbs. In South Carolina it was reported that East India Tea had been dropped in favor of "Sage, Balm, Rosemary, and Cassina."[38] Northern colonists apparently preferred Labrador Tea, made from the leaves of red root, which according to individuals who had actually tried it was similar to wild rosemary with a very strong flavor and deep brown color. Some users confessed that they could barely swallow this disgusting liquid. North Carolinians recommended Hyperion Tea "as a succedaneum to that more pernicious and destructive plant Bohea, which annually drains America of thousands."[39] And then, for those suffering severe withdrawal, there was always Yeopann Tea. "This plant is much used among the lower sort," explained one newspaper; "[it] is of great efficacy when taken physically, being a powerful sudorific; is no exotic but a domestic of almost every sandy plantation in this province."[40] Having a powerful sudorific for breakfast, a medical treatment intended to produce heavy sweats, would undoubtedly have concentrated the mind on political affairs.

Colonists who refused to give up imported English tea for the common good faced increasing pressure from neighbors. This was a significant development, since what sustained colonial resistance in the face of intimidation from Parliament was the readiness of ordinary men and women to enforce the public will within their own communities. Traditional histories of the American Revolution that concentrate on the proceedings of colonial assemblies and the decrees of imperial administrators tend to take the participation of these people for granted. After being relegated to bit parts as urban rioters, they appear almost magically just in time to take up arms against the Red Coats. But a deep shift in popular allegiances was underway before New England militiamen flocked to Bunker Hill. If, as some have claimed, all politics are in some significant measure local politics, then it was within the small towns and scattered counties of provincial America that colonists finally decided that they were no longer subjects of the crown.

And, more often than not, the litmus test of commitment was the private citizen's relationship to common goods, initially to tea, but soon to all imported articles. During the protest against the Townshend duties, efforts to implement a strategy of non-importation had relied largely on shame and humiliation, and except for several notorious examples of the tarring-and-feathering of merchants who brazenly sold British manufactures, the worst an unrepentant consumer might fear was censorious looks and insulting language in the streets. No one advocated forcing obedience. But as Americans moved fitfully toward an endorsement of non-consumption, as opposed to non-importation, they employed more coercive techniques to expose the doubters and trimmers in their midst. Seizure of property—an extremely radical act in any social context—served the double function of punishing colonists defined as political enemies while at the same time quickening a spirit of solidarity among those who policed the possession of tea. Ebenezer Withington's ordeal provided a dramatic example of the process leading to effective mobilization—threat, indoctrination, and destruction—a community ritual which if nothing else made other Dorchester farmers think twice before violating the rules of patriotic consumption. As "A Carolinian" warned soon after Parliament shut down Boston Harbor, "[W]e need only fight our *own selves,* suppress for a while our Luxury and Corruption, and wield the Arms of *Self*-Denial in our own Houses, to obtain the Victory. . . . And the Man who would not refuse himself a *fine Coat,* to save his Country, deserves to be hanged."[41]

The colonists burned as much tea as they had tossed into the ocean. The drama surrounding the Tea Party dominates American memory, but in fact people anxious to pledge their solidarity not only with the Boston resistance but also with protest leaders of their own community carried small amounts of tea—often no more than a few ounces stored in a kitchen cupboard—to a central green where they consigned the package to the flames. Since they had come to regard tea as a pollutant, it was fitting that they organized collective rituals of this sort to purge local society of political sin. These bonfires served as the funeral pyres of empire. Only days after the destruction of the Boston tea, a newspaper "recommended to every inhabitant who is a friend to his country, to collect every atom of this poisonous herb, and sacrifice it to the flames in the Common[s], as an utter detestation of a mean[s] that may contribute to the support of tyrants, perjured traitors and those who insolently lord it over the liberties of a free people."[42] A Connecticut writer who identified himself as "Home Manufacture" wondered whether it was such a good idea to incinerate so much tea. He asked the organizers of the bonfires "whether when the duty was fix'd on *Glass* as well as *Tea,* it would not have been a very extraordinary resolution, to have determined on breaking all the glass in America, and to send round committees to put it in execution?"[43]

The point was lost on those who chose to define colonial patriotism in terms of ritual immolation. "The freeholders and other inhabitants" of Charleston, Massachusetts, for example, met on December 23, 1773, to cleanse their village of imported tea. After weighing "the advantages that will result to this community (in every point of light,) from the disuse of India tea," they voted not to use, sell, buy "or suffer [tea] to be used in our families" until Parliament repealed the Tea Act. It was not enough, however, to give up drinking tea. The physical evidence of oppression had to be removed. Those present selected a committee of neighbors to demand "from all the inhabitants of this town, all the tea they may have by them." The Charleston meeting then determined that "the tea so collected, be destroyed by fire, on Friday next at noon day, in the market place." Tea lovers who might have been tempted to squirrel away enough leaves for a last cup were admonished that "if any of the inhabitants of this town, shall do anything to counteract, or render ineffectual the foregoing votes, they are not only inimical to the liberty of America in general, but also show a daring disrespect to this town in particular." And finally, the group decided that "the above proceedings of this town, be published in the News-Papers," a reminder that communicating consumer sacrifice to other Americans may have been as significant in mobilizing popular support for rebellion as the deed itself.[44]

Other bonfires of tea invited ordinary people in Massachusetts to reflect on their political allegiance during the months following the Tea Party. Lexington received praise in the newspapers for its blazing display of patriotism. The *Massachusetts Spy* reported that the town had "unanimously resolved against the use of Bohea tea of all sorts, Dutch or English importation; and to manifest the sincerity of their resolution, they brought together every ounce contained in the town, and committed it to one common bonfire."[45] One can only speculate about a connection between this ritual purging of tea and the decision of Lexington's militia to confront the British army in April 1775. Perhaps they were simply unrelated events that happened to take place on the same village green. A month after the destruction of the Lexington tea, the journal learned that on a particularly chilly day the people of Exeter organized a similar sacrifice. "We hear . . . ," the paper announced, "that last Wednesday a number of ladies and gentlemen, met on Tower-Hill . . . and there consumed by fire a considerable quantity of that baneful and despised article, TEA." Their actions gave new meaning to the word *consume*. The writer could not resist a patronizing barb: "As the weather was very cold, the ladies were not backward in feeding the fire."[46]

Sometime later, Providence, Rhode Island, ignited a much more elaborate bonfire. At noon of the appointed day, the town crier gave notice to the public: "At five o'clock, this afternoon, a quantity of India Tea will be burnt in the market-place.—All true friends to their country and lovers of freedom, and haters of SHACKLES and HANDCUFFS, are hereby invited to testify their good disposition, by bringing, and casting into the fire, a needless herb, which for a long time has been highly detrimental to our liberty, interest, and health." Billed as "the funeral of Madam SOUCHONG," the event drew "a great number of inhabitants." They cheered as patriotic colonists brought forth "about three hundred pounds weight of tea" and fed it to the fire. For good measure, the people of Providence burned a barrel of tar, a speech recently delivered by Lord North, copies of newspapers that had taken a Tory stance, and "divers other ingredients." The destruction of "so pernicious an article" as tea apparently spurred individuals to come forward. Women, for example, made sacrificial offerings of imported leaves "from a conviction of the evil tendency of continuing the habit of tea-drinking." As the smoke from the bonfire rose, the bells of the city rang out. One particularly "spirited son of liberty" went through Providence with a brush and supply of lampblack, obliterating "the word TEA on the shop signs." No one could have predicted a few years earlier that Madam Souchong would come to such an ignominious end. Only forty years before, she had arrived in America, where she was "greatly caressed by all ranks." But the lady proved herself a prostitute, and over time "her price was so lowered that any one might have her company for almost nothing."[47] The funeral pyre concluded a long and passionate American relationship with an imported love.

Colonists also engaged in more spontaneous attacks on tea. In small country towns the provocation came in the form of a furtive peddler who thought that the locals would compromise political principle for a fresh supply of imported Asian tea. In Montague, Massachusetts, an inhabitant "inadvertently purchased a small quantity of tea" from a traveler. Several neighbors who witnessed the transaction immediately went to the man's house and "endeavored to convince him of the impropriety of making any use of that article for the present, while it continues to be a badge of slavery." Apparently, these self-appointed enforcers made a persuasive case, since the buyer "was easily induced to commit it to the flames."

The Montague story seems to have been intended as a general warning to peddlers or, as one journal explained, to "those gentry called peddlers, from selling this noxious herb, at a time when the shop-keepers have generally abandoned it." No doubt, it was not hard for the patriotic supporters of Boston to monitor business conducted in stores. Peddlers posed a different problem. They could appear at any hour of the day; they displayed their wares in the privacy of people's homes. But, as the residents of Montague knew, there were laws on the books "against hawking and peddling" that they were prepared to put into effect should strangers "offer any more of this politically poisoned herb for sale." "We can't say what their punishment would be," one person speculated ominously, "but [we] have reason to imagine they would bless themselves, should theirs be as light as was the peddler's last Friday se'night at Shrewsbury." He referred to an example of rough justice most certainly not countenanced by provincial law. The Shrewsbury peddler's tea "was taken from him by a number of people, at the tavern in that town, and carried into the road, where it was burnt to ashes; and had not [the] culprit very opportunely made his escape, he might have found himself soon enveloped in a modern dress."[48] Tarring and feathering was probably a messy affair, and most towns seem to have been content with an instructive fire.

The author of a letter published in a Massachusetts newspaper provided more detail about consumer rituals of political indoctrination in the countryside. Once again, a peddler triggered the crisis, this time in Leo-minster. Something about his demeanor aroused suspicion, and a search of his goods by local patriots—called Whigs—soon yielded "a Quantity of the destructive & detestable Weed Tea." Asked to explain himself, the man claimed that he had brought the tea back to America "in a late Foreign Voy-age" as a present for "his dear Wife." He persuaded no one in the village. "Ruth," who recounted the incident, observed that the peddler showed little regard for his wife's political welfare "by his giving her Poison." In any event, a few inhabitants of Leominister had actually witnessed the stranger's at-tempt to sell tea to a storekeeper, a bad move since everyone present in the shop identified himself as a "true Whig." When he realized his error, the "Tea-Merchant" started to tremble with fear. According to Ruth, it was "as violent an agitation in his knees as ever was in those of Belshazzar," the last king of Babylon, whose downfall was prophesied by mysterious writing on a wall. The traveling salesman begged to be spared a coat of tar, pointing out that the weather that day was excessively hot. The patriots of Leominister "granted his Petition, but repeatedly exhorted him to reform, and be no longer an Enemy to himself and Country." They urged him voluntarily to burn the tea, a proposal to which he readily agreed. He even "thanked them for their Kindness and Benevolence." But Ruth was in a less forgiving mood. She announced that such leniency "cannot, must not be exercis'd toward these Enemies much longer, [for] it is to be fear'd the direful Period is at Hand, when the Sons of Liberty will be bound by Duty, both to God and themselves, to hang, drown, or otherwise demolish these execrable Villains from the Face of the Earth, that Posterity may enjoy a peaceful and happy Land, preserv'd from utter Ruin, by the Noble Efforts of Freedom's Sons."[49]

The impact of the scattered local tea protests on women was hard to determine. They were certainly present, often making small contributions to the flames.[50] If nothing else, their participation in these extra-legal events obsessed some Tory sympathizers, in other words, those persons already persuaded that the times were out of joint. In these attacks, ridicule pro-vided a sharp weapon. Introducing himself as "Susanna Spindle," a Boston writer gave a tongue-in-cheek account of a recent "Meeting of the Matrons of Liberty." A "Moderatrix" appealed to the members of her audience "to take into consideration the distressed state [to which] the Females are re-duced, by the unreasonable and arbitrary procedure of their Husbands, under a pretense of defending their Liberties." The boycott strategy, she thought, had backfired. Had men not called for homespun cloth to replace British imported fabrics, and then, instead of weaving and spinning, or-dered their poor, overworked wives "to manufacture the wool and flax"? In the name of equity, the Matrons of Liberty concluded that "it is high time to exert ourselves, and to stand for our just Liberty (which is arbitrarily wrested from us without our consent)." The joke apparently was that women might really extend the kinds of arguments voiced regularly in the Boston town meeting by the likes of Samuel Adams and James Otis to domestic affairs. The Matrons advanced twelve profoundly silly proposals. The first

The British never quite understood that the boycott movement had given political voice to American women. This caricature by Philip Dawe poked fun at the women who organized the "Edenton [North Carolina] Tea Party." *North Carolina Collection. Courtesy of the University of North Carolina Library at Chapel Hill.*

proclaimed that "the Women in America, are entitled to all the Liberties which Women in Great-Britain enjoy, and particularly to drink Tea." The second announced that "we understood our Husbands did covenant (when we married) to provide us Tea, or we never would have joined our hands with theirs."[51] Not a few women rejected this lampooning of legitimate aspirations. "Prudence Vertue" responded to the condescending wits, explaining, among other things, that women were prepared to save America and, if their husbands failed to perform, to go it alone. "Be it known to all Men and Women," she stated, "that we will not still add Fuel to the Fire, by using foreign Teas, and make ourselves and children still greater Slaves to our Lusts and other tyrannical Masters; but as the Women once saved the Nation from the Tyranny of the Danes, so will we from the Tyranny of Bute and North, &c. &c."[52]

Everywhere the circle of politics was expanding. In small, largely self-contained agricultural communities, ordinary people found that tea focused attention as never before on the governance of an empire of goods. The catalyst for these local discussions may have been anxious letters from the Boston Committee of Correspondence, inviting colonists in outlying villages to hold open debates about the best way to resist parliamentary authority.[53] But whatever intelligence sparked confrontation with hard issues, the people themselves conducted their own conversations without outside interference. They could have ignored external appeals. In a letter to the historian Mercy Otis Warren written long after the American Revolution, John Adams chided her for taking a narrow, overly traditional view of politics. By concentrating her analysis on maneuvers in the colonial assemblies, she had missed what Adams called the other theaters of politics, one of which he identified as "every fireside."[54] One theater was surely the town meetings where inhabitants came to think about tea. Before this moment, local meetings had been generally ill attended. One suspects that neighbors bored each other, repeating the words of previous speakers and sometimes forgetting the motion on the floor. But during the first half of 1774 the public pulse beat faster. External events demanded attention, even in the absence of a devious peddler or a bonfire of tea. The townspeople voted resolutions which were a form of covenant, pledges of mutual obligation no less binding for being secular in character. As a community they promised to transform ideas into actions, and although the talk was about tea and the relief of Boston, the energizing theme was what it now meant not to be fully British.

Tea certainly had the capacity to mobilize an entire village. By their own admission, the inhabitants of Truro, an isolated village on Cape Cod, had not kept well informed about the gathering political storm in Boston. Then, one day, some tea apparently washed ashore near Provincetown, and, like Ebenezer Withington, the men who discovered it sold small quantities to a few Truro farmers. That purchase precipitated a local crisis. A town committee questioned these persons and concluded "that their buying this noxious Tea was through ignorance and inadvertence, and that they were induced thereto by the base and villainous example and artful persuasions of some noted pretended friends of government from the neighboring towns; and therefore this meeting thinks them excusable with an acknowledgment."

But individual confession was not sufficient to exonerate the community. The people of Truro had failed to educate themselves about the dangers to their constitutional liberties and, of course, had left themselves vulnerable to scheming persons who peddled tea, the symbol of oppression. The town meeting decided, therefore, to form a special committee which would draft a resolve "respecting the introduction of Tea from Great Britain subject to a duty, payable in America." After deliberating for half an hour, the members of the committee returned with a statement that was at once defensive and radical:

> WE, the inhabitants of the town of Truro, though by our remote situation from the center of public news, we are deprived of opportunities of gaining so thorough a knowledge in the unhappy disputes that subsist between us and the parent state as we could wish; yet as our love of Liberty and dread of slavery is not inferior (perhaps) to that of our brethren in any part of the province, we think it our indispensable duty to contribute our mite in the glorious cause of liberty and our country.

People asked immediately what in fact they could do to demonstrate that their ideological hearts were in the right place. "We think," the committee responded, that "the most likely method that we can take to aid in frustrating those inhuman designs of administration is a disuse of that baneful dutied article Tea."[55] The inhabitants of this village communicated their political commitment not only to the protest leaders in Boston and to the members of the Massachusetts general assembly but also to themselves through the disuse of tea. By dropping this popular beverage they overcame the peculiarities of local experience and linked up in their imaginations with other Americans, distant strangers whose crucial common bond with the farmers of Truro at this moment was their participation in an eighteenth-century consumer society.

Truro was unusual only in that the discovery of real tea on the beach sparked a debate about the community's political future. In other towns the stimulus for action was less spectacular, perhaps a letter from a Boston committee or a report in a provincial newspaper. But whatever concentrated public attention, these local discussions about tea rendered increasingly problematic long-held ideas about identity and obedience. The ideological foundations of commercial empire shook more violently in New England than in other parts of America, but within a short time the tremors would be felt in distant places where it also seemed that the common good might be in conflict with the purchase of common goods manufactured in Great Britain. In January 1774 the freeholders and inhabitants of Newbury concluded that the actions of the agents of the East India Company—men such as Thomas Hutchinson—threatened to reduce a free people to slavery. They agreed that "it is unmanly, mean and deserving of general contempt, for private persons, who are in affluent circumstances to endeavor the increase of their rights, by dealing in an article of commerce so circumstanced, as that the support or continuance of it, among a people, tends greatly to impoverish them, and bring them into bondage." What, the inhabitants of Newbury must have asked, can we do to demonstrate our sincerity? That we are worthy of trust? First, they agreed no longer to "buy other useful commodities of such traders, whether far or near, as shall be publicly known to supply themselves anew with the article TEA." And second, these people linked personal behavior to a shared commitment, everyday village experience to a world of fellow consumers, for, as they knew, if they could not practice virtue around "every fireside," the rhetoric of sacrifice meant little. "We will not use it [tea] ourselves," they resolved, "and with our best prudence discontinue the use of it in our families; and particularly that we will absolutely forbid the use of it in our houses as a species of entertainment for visitors, whether relations or others, until the act of Parliament imposing a duty upon it is repealed."[56]

In each community tea sparked a slightly different political conversation. A meeting of the inhabitants of Brookline, Massachusetts, for example, agreed with other towns that anyone who imported tea while it was still subject to a parliamentary tax should be "considered and treated by this Town as an Enemy to this Country." What struck these people as most offensive was the blatant inequity of the legislation. They were tired of being treated like second-class subjects of the crown. They had no doubt that a few well-placed individuals in England were getting richer at the expense of American rights, a kind of corporate profiteering that once had the capacity to inspire indignation. "Thus," the Brookline meeting observed, "have the Parliament discovered the most glaring Partiality in making one and the same Act to operate for the Ease and Convenience of a few of the most opulent Subjects in Britain on the one Hand, and for the Oppression of MILLIONS of Freeborn and most loyal Inhabitants of America on the other."[57] Only a few months later, the "votable inhabitants" of Bolton staged a seminar on tea and taxation, and after considering the issue of parliamentary sovereignty from various perspectives—they termed it a "free debate"—the assembly passed without a single negative voice a number of strongly worded resolutions, the most demagogic of which declared that "in order to counteract and render abortive (according to the utmost of our power) the British act, respecting the duty on Tea to be paid *here*, we will not take of this politically forbidden fruit, if even solicited thereto by the Eves of our own bosoms, nor any other consideration whatever, whilst it remains under the circumstance of taxation."[58]

Other towns added their views. The "freeholders and other inhabitants" of Falmouth took up the challenge of the tea on February 10, 1774. Although the possibility of military violence frightened these people, they concluded that it was time to make a united stand against British tyranny. "It is the opinion of this town," they reported, "that one of the most effectual means for obtaining a redress of our grievances, is for every town to make proof of their virtue, by desisting from the use of all India tea." The phrase "proof of their virtue" seems to have been their own invention, but even if they borrowed it, the wording captured the profoundly commercial character of American resistance. In their minds the sacrifice of consumer pleasures had become the seal of public virtue, the single action that broadcast to "the whole continent" their own devotion to freedom.[59] The "Freeholders and other Inhabitants" of Charlestown passed five resolutions, one of which revealed just how tenuous the hold of empire had become for the sorts of Americans most at risk to show up on revolutionary battlefields. "We are and will be on proper Occasions," they proclaimed, "ready in Conjunction with our oppressed American Brethren to risk our Lives and Fortunes in the Support of these Rights, Liberties and Privileges with which God, Nature and our happy Constitution has made us free."[60]

At the distance of over two centuries, public opinion can be measured only crudely through anecdotes. As colonial leaders were busy attempting to make sense of an official British policy of punishment, ordinary Americans sought as best they could to provide proof of consumer virtue. In a letter sent to Abigail during the summer of 1774, John Adams recounted a scene that warmed the heart of a weary patriotic traveler. After a hard ride of over thirty-five miles through the interior of Massachusetts, Adams finally arrived at the house where he intended to take a rest. "'Madam' said I to Mrs. Huston, 'is it lawful for a weary Traveller to refresh himself with a Dish of Tea provided it has been honestly smuggled, or paid no Duties?'" Mrs. Huston was shocked by the request. "'No sir,' said she, 'we have renounced all Tea in this Place. I cant make Tea, but I'le make you Coffee.' Accordingly I have drank Coffee every Afternoon since, and have borne it very well. Tea must be universally renounced. I must be weaned, and the sooner, the better."[61] About Adams's contribution to the revolutionary cause, there is not the slightest doubt. It is people such as Mrs. Huston who have been undervalued.

III

Tea was not enough to mobilize a nation. Transforming an imagined state into an actual one required a greater sacrifice from American consumers than forgoing their favorite beverage. To be sure, in the immediate aftermath of the Intolerable Acts, colonists from Georgia to New Hampshire wanted to express solidarity with Boston. But during the summer of 1774 the tide of public opinion was also running strong for a more demanding form of consumer resistance, one that would demonstrate to the British as well as the Americans that they were now capable of uniting in one great demonstration of popular virtue. A total denial of British imported goods was a necessary step on a long, difficult road from consumer colonies to an independent republic. Even before the recognized political leaders of the day were prepared to take such a radical decision, farmers and mechanics—the middling sort who had for so long enjoyed the fruits of the consumer economy—contemplated a complete cessation of trade with Great Britain. The exact number of people involved is impossible to estimate with precision. The figure could not have been small, however, and it was these men and women who were in the vanguard of the final push for independence.

John Dickinson, a savvy observer of such matters, sensed the change in the political climate. "What never happened before," he explained to Josiah Quincy in June, "has happened now. The country people have so exact a knowledge of [the] facts, and of the consequences attending the surrender of the points in question, that they are, if possible, more zealous than the citizens who lie in a direct line of information."[62] That same day, Samuel Adams reported from Massachusetts to his Virginia friend Richard Henry Lee, "The people of this Province are thoroughly sensible of the necessity of breaking off all commercial connection with a country whose political Councils tend only to enslave them. . . . [T]hey are urged to it by motives of self-preservation; and are, therefore, signing an agreement in the several towns, not to consume any *British* manufactures."[63] In a statement that might have served as an epitaph for an empire of goods, a Pennsylvania writer asked American newspaper readers:

> What could she [Britain] wish from us more than we freely gave? For whom have we toiled in this once uncultivated wilderness; For whose benefit do we rise up early and lye down late, is it not for Great Britain?—Are not our sails spread to every wind that blows under heaven, to bear away the dear earnings of the sweat of our brow, that they may at last center in Britain? Are we not her faithful generous customers, for all the various commodities of her industrious workmen? Do we clamor at the prices they exact? . . . What more, in a commercial way, has she a right to wish?[64]

Once the commercial link that had bound these two people together for so long came unraveled, the partners in the relationship suddenly discovered that they did not have as much in common as they may have thought.

Renewed appeals for non-importation came from local meetings throughout America. Their willingness to entertain the possibility of a total boycott of British goods, especially in New England, may have reflected attempts by the Boston Committee of Correspondence to push for a more aggressive strategy of resistance. But the influence of the Boston radicals has been exaggerated. People in other parts of America took the manifestos pouring out of Boston with a grain of salt. They certainly had minds of their own, and as they assessed the flow of events, they came to independent conclusions about a proper plan of action. Although Samuel Adams and his allies in the Boston town meeting initially dragged their heels on the wisdom of calling an "American Congress," others encouraged such a national gathering.[65] They remembered how the non-importation campaigns of 1769 and 1770 had collapsed amid charges of cheating and smuggling. If non-importation had any chance of persuading Parliament to reconsider its punishment of Boston, it would have to be a coordinated effort, a response commensurate to the resources of a global commercial empire. George Mason, the thoughtful Virginia lawyer, understood the problem. "The associations," he had explained in 1770, "almost from one end of this continent to the other, were drawn up in a hurry and formed on erroneous principles." The local organizers of those boycotts had expected Parliament to back down quickly, certainly within a year or two, but that had not happened. The colonists' inability to overcome parochial concerns did not discourage Mason, however, for, as he had posited then, "had one general plan been formed exactly the same for all colonies (so as to have removed all cause of jealousy or danger of interfering with each other) in the nature of a sumptuary law, restraining only articles of luxury and ostentation together with the goods at any time taxed," the results might have been more impressive.[66] In 1770 Americans had not yet discovered how to think continentally, how to compromise differences for a common cause.

By mid-summer 1774, however, public opinion had caught up with Mason. One newspaper called for a "Politico-Mercantile Congress," which it claimed "seems now to be the voice of all the Colonies from Nova-Scotia to Georgia; and New-York the place of [the] meeting."[67] This definition of the continent was perhaps overly expansive, but the report captured the kinds of conversations Americans were having with each other about their future. As was the case during the earlier non-importation drives of 1768 and 1769, public discussion about closing their markets pushed the colonists a little closer to accepting a political identity that was not British. The "Freeholders and Inhabitants" of Orange Town, New York, resolved that "it is our unanimous Opinion, that the stopping [of] all Exportation and Importation, to and from Great Britain, and the West-Indies, would be the most effectual Method to obtain a speedy Repeal."[68] The farmers of East Hampton, a village on the eastern tip of Long Island, voted to join other colonies to defend the "Liberties and Immunities of British America." They concluded that "a Non-importation Agreement through the Colonies is the most likely Means to save us from the present and further Troubles."[69] The concept of a united boycott became for these people a way both to bring pressure on Lord North's government and to voice a shared sense of political purpose with distant Americans who probably could not have located East Hampton on a map. The freeholders of Rowan County, a small Tidewater settlement on the coast of North Carolina, also weighed the issues, concluding that "this Colony ought not to trade with any Colony which shall refuse to join in any Union or Association that shall be agreed upon by the greater Part of the other Colonies on this Continent, for preserving their common Rights and Liberties."[70] The North Carolinians communicated their trustworthiness through consumer sacrifice; their ideology through common goods. A meeting of people in Queen Anne's County, Maryland, agreed that "the only effectual means for obtaining such repeal [of the Intolerable Acts] . . . is an association under the strongest ties, for breaking off all commercial connections with Great Britain." And they immediately dispatched a report of their decision to "the next Maryland and Pennsylvania Gazettes."[71]

A particularly poignant discussion of a small town's political future in a suddenly wider world occurred in Dartmouth, Massachusetts. By their own admission, the residents of Dartmouth had been slow off the mark,

A 1774 covenant binding subscribers in Lincoln, Massachusetts, not to "purchase or consume" British goods. *Courtesy of the American Antiquarian Society.*

neglecting even to hold a meeting about the crisis in Boston. But, adopting a better-late-than-never philosophy, they "moved at last in the common cause." For whatever reasons, they now felt themselves part of "a general American union." And in their eyes America was in deep trouble. "America we apprehend," the Dartmouth meeting announced, "has been exposed to ruin, by the excessive use of foreign commodities, therefore the late acts of the British Parliament, may be considered a loud call in providence, for a fast from those excesses." It was rare even in the late eighteenth century for a boycott to be labeled a fast, but Dartmouth had been consulting the Old Testament for insight about the present political situation. It thought that "similar to the preaching of Jonah to Nineveh, who, as he expressed himself, cried out of the belly of hell, yet his errand was designed by heaven, to prevent the destruction of multitudes: and if Americans will proclaim and keep a universal fast from English and India goods (which seems to be the

(Here and following page)
The actual signatures of some subscribers to the 1774 Lincoln covenant. *Courtesy of the American Antiquarian Society.*

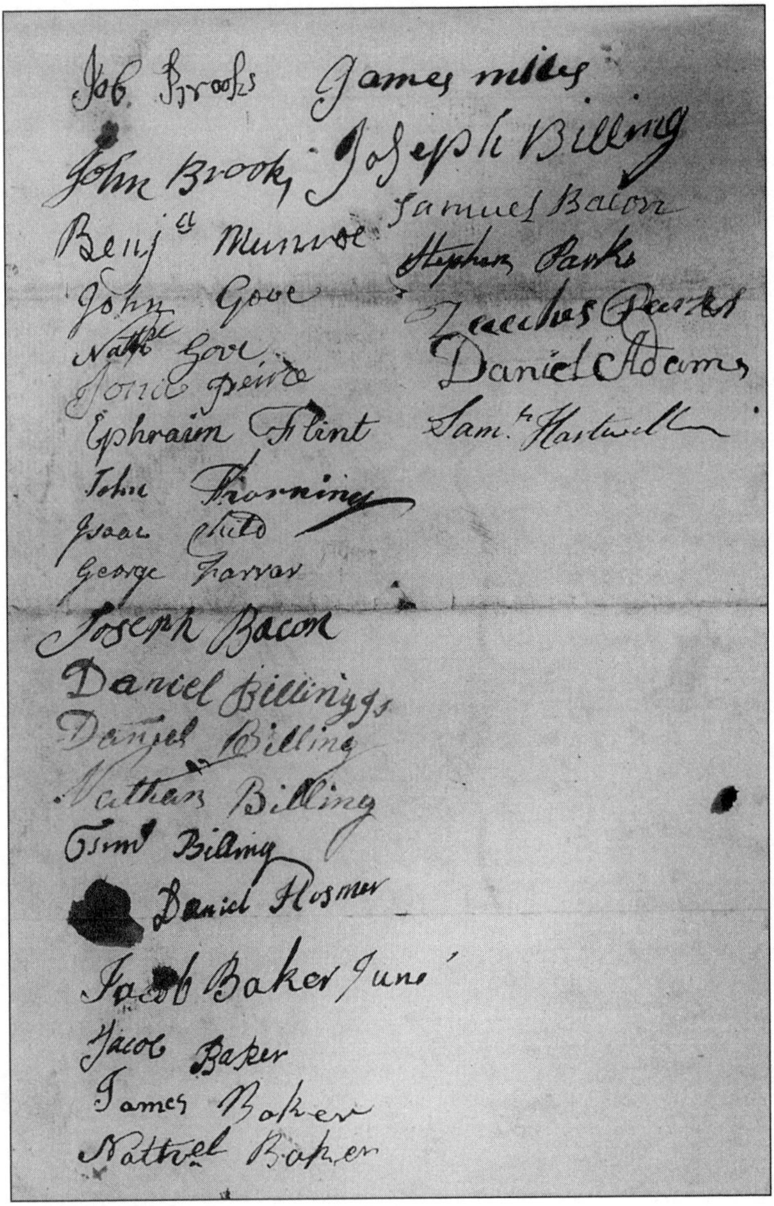

Job Brooks   James Miles

John Brooks   Joseph Billing

Benjᵃ Munroe   Samuel Bacon

John Gove   Stephen Parks

Nathˡ Gove   Jacobus Parkst

Jonᵃ Peirce   Daniel Adams

Ephraim Flint   Samˡ Hartwell

John Thorning

Isaac Child

George Farrar

Joseph Bacon

Daniel Billings

Daniel Billing

Nathan Billing

Samˡ Billing

Daniel Hosmer

Jacob Baker Junᵣ

Jacob Baker

James Baker

Nathˡ Baker

terms and conditions regarded for their salvation) no doubt their deliverance . . . will be complete."[72]

As momentum for a national congress accelerated, a few skeptics dared to speak out, arguing that non-importation could not possibly fulfill popular political expectations. They assembled an exhaustive list of reasons why a national boycott could not succeed. If Americans sealed their ports to imported goods, the British would simply develop new markets in other parts of the world. It was asserted that the Americans had grossly overestimated their commercial importance to Great Britain, and thus non-importation—even if rigorously enforced—would scarcely trouble Lord North and those setting imperial policy. To claim that American manufacturers could supply current market demand for consumer goods was a joke. A boycott would jeopardize civil society, "raising a most unnatural Enmity between Parents & Children & Husbands & Wives."[73] Moreover, the money supply would soon dry up. A New York Loyalist beseeched proponents of non-importation—a strategy often coupled with non-exportation—"Can you live without money? Will the shop-keeper give you his goods? Will the weaver, shoemaker, blacksmith, carpenter, work for you without pay? If they will, it is more than they will do for me."[74] The naysayers warned that colonists would cheat on their agreements, so that the sacrifice of honest merchants and consumers would amount to a hollow gesture.

Most of all, however, the scoffers could not believe that other Americans would voluntarily forgo the material pleasures which for more than half a century had brought them warmth, beauty, color, comfort, sanitation, leisure, and a heady sense of self-worth. Writing under the name of "The British American," a Virginian ridiculed those who advocated the simple life in the name of rights and liberty. They might be able to give up imported salt, he predicted, since "hickory ashes, though a poor substitute, may supply the place of it as well to you as it formerly did to the native *Indians.*" Getting by in such an environment would be an adventure, a little like summer camp for people who normally took modern appliances for granted. "Nails, without slitting mills, will be made with great difficulty, but logged cabins may be built without them; clothes for yours[e]lves and Negroes are not worth thinking of, because you may confine yours[e]lves and them to your houses in cold weather." But surely, even under the primitive conditions of self-sufficiency, the patriot would somehow survive. "Elegancies, and even luxuries," observed "The British American," "which many of you, by having been long accustomed to, now consider as the conveniencies, if not the nceessaries of life, may be resigned as baubles, beneath the consideration of men who either desire or deserve to be free."[75]

One skeptic gave the Loyalist game away when he urged Americans to ignore what they could read every day in the colonial press. The Reverend Jonathan Boucher begged the public in vain, "[f]or the Sake of common Humanity . . . [to] disdain to co-operate, with hand bills, with news papers, with the high menacing resolves of common town meetings."[76] But, of course, the conversations about non-importation that one heard in the streets and taverns shared none of his dark predictions of impending economic ruin. On the eve of a continental congress, popular writers assured American consumers that their huge demand for manufactured objects was actually a source of strength. "We can when we please," announced "Steel," "set up an independent commonwealth in America, and Britain would not dare to attack us, for her existence as a nation depends upon her union with America."[77] It is perhaps worthy of note that Steel put forward the incendiary idea of an independent commonwealth more than a year before Jefferson penned his famous declaration. By the summer of 1774 such notions were already in the air. In a dialogue with an imaginary Englishman, "Consideration" asked, "How can the colonists affect *your* [the British] interest, and the interest of *other* nations, for the grand purpose of securing the liberties of America?" The answer was obvious to those who had turned apparent economic dependence—the colonial burden—into political advantage. "The colonies," declared Consideration, "will withhold their trade from *you,* and give it to *other nations.* This stroke of policy will be effectual and decisive; and as it is seen to be the only thing which will answer the grand purpose of preserving LIBERTY, it will be pursued with ardor, and persevered in with firmness." Anyone who knew anything at all about international trade could state with assurance that "the TRADE of America is a prize for which the commercial states will all contend, and embrace every opportunity to acquire."[78] "An American" told South Carolinians that "we can do without her [Great Britain] forever, and be great gainers by it."[79]

These were radical statements for people who had never faced a Red Coat on the field of battle. Whether such rhetoric reflected ignorance or naïveté, hope or arrogance, it suggested that the seeds of a powerful new national identity were sprouting among colonial consumers who were still British subjects. The most elegant argument for taking a separate commercial road appeared under the name of "A Citizen of Philadelphia." Echoing however subtly the social contract theory of John Locke, "A Citizen" explained that "Our commerce with England being founded on mutual convenience, and voluntary compact, it certainly rests with us to determine how far it shall be extended, and when it shall cease; this is a right, which even Lord North, with all his arbitrary views, dare not deny." These remarks were aimed straight at the choicemaker in the marketplace who was now being recruited for rebellion. "No man can be obliged to purchase goods of another: the seller can do no more than expose his wares to public sale, the buyer is to determine what, when, and how much, he will buy; this being the case, it becomes now a question, whether this is not the time to make a general exercise of that power: as an individual, after having maturely weighed the subject, I give my voice for exerting it, in its fullest extent. I would recommend a general non-importation, as the most effectual means of convincing the people of England, of how much importance we are." Just in case American readers missed the central point, he added in bold letters, "It is A GENERAL NON-IMPORTATION HONESTLY ADHERED TO, that must work our deliverance."[80]

Delegates to the First Continental Congress opened their proceedings on September 5, 1774. As might be expected, they spent the early days learning more about each other. They were, in fact, a collection of strangers from distant places who had only a superficial understanding of the various cultures that had sent representatives to Philadelphia. They quickly overcame personal differences. Although many of them would have denied the charge, these men were engaged in a revolutionary act that challenged the authority of Parliament. They appreciated the possible consequences of their conduct. Anyone who knew even a little about recent Irish and Scottish history comprehended the cruel violence that Great Britain might visit upon them and their supporters. Bravely taking their chances on America, the delegates turned to the business at hand. Within a few weeks they devised a grand scheme for halting all trade with the mother country. The members of the congress argued about the details of the program, for, as they discovered, the southern colonies worried that colonial resistance too quickly implemented might cost them the sale of the annual harvest of tobacco and rice. But for all the grumbling about the particular needs of local economies, they accepted a complex package containing provision for non-importation, non-consumption, and non-exportation, a plan as radical in its implications for the American people as any passed by any legislature during the nation's entire history. It drew upon more than a decade of experience. It brought to fruition a brilliantly original strategy of consumer resistance to political oppression, one that had invited Americans to think of themselves as Americans even before they entertained a thought of independence. On October 20, the Continental Congress proclaimed:

> To obtain redress of these grievances, which threaten destruction to the lives, liberty, and property of his majesty's subjects, in North-America, we are of opinion, that a non-importation, non-consumption, and non-exportation agreement, faithfully adhered to, will prove the most speedy, effectual, and peaceable measure: And, therefore, we do, for ourselves, and the inhabitants of the several colonies, whom we represent, firmly agree and associate, under the sacred ties of virtue, honour and love of our country.[81]

Non-importation went into effect on December 1. Non-consumption, which the delegates described as "an effectual security for the observation of non-importation," started on March 1, 1775, and non-exportation was put off until September 1.

The delegates had also learned from the failure of earlier appeals for non-importation that enforcement held the key to success. Voluntary measures had not worked; the consumer marketplace held too many temptations for too many people. To remedy the problem, Congress called for the creation of the Continental Association. This action authorized the formation of local committees throughout America. Elected by voters in each town, city, and county, these groups of virtuous citizens were charged with monitoring the economic activities of their neighbors. Modern historians have generally discounted the significance of the Continental Association.[82] For whatever reasons, they have failed to see that these were genuinely revolutionary organizations, responsible under a ruling by an illegally convened national assembly to police and indoctrinate a public comprised of many individuals not yet prepared openly to disobey Parliament, nor for that matter to sacrifice the goods imported from Great Britain. In another context such as the French Revolution these local bodies would have been called committees of safety. The eleventh section of the congressional resolution declared:

> That a committee be chosen in every county, city, and town, by those who are qualified to vote for representatives in the legislature, whose business it shall be attentively to observe the conduct of all persons touching this association; and when it shall be made to appear, to the satisfaction of a majority of any such committee, that any person within the limits of their appointment has violated this association, that such majority do forthwith cause the truth of the case to be published in the gazette; to the end, that all such foes to the rights of British-America may be publicly known, and thenceforth we respectively will break off all dealings with him or her.[83]

The Association represented a profoundly bourgeois response to the policies of a commercial empire, and it was not a bit less revolutionary for being so.

To argue that the Association made the American Revolution inevitable would be unwarranted. Last-minute negotiations could have altered the course of events. Lord North might have rejected a military solution. But the formation of local committees altered the political chemistry in the cities, towns, and counties of America. It was on this level that ordinary men and women declared their independence. Lord Dunmore, the royal governor of Virginia, realized immediately how local committees were able to intimidate those subjects who still professed loyalty to the crown. The Associations spoke in the name of a new national authority. In December 1774 he reported to Lord Hillsborough, the British secretary of state for America, that "the Associations . . . recommended by the people of this colony, and adopted by what is called the Continental Congress," were enforcing their regulations "throughout this country with the greatest rigor. A committee has been chosen in every county whose business it is to carry the Association of the Congress into execution, which committee assumes an authority to inspect the books, invoices, and all the secrets of the trade and correspondence of the merchants, to watch the conduct of every inhabitant without distinction, and send for all such as come under their suspicion into their presence, to interrogate them." When Virginians put through this ordeal challenged the authority of the local committees, they were informed that they had violated what the enforcers "call the laws of Congress."[84]

The Reverend Samuel Seabury, an Anglican rector in New York, expressed shock at what he witnessed in his neighborhood. The colony's Association had called a general meeting in New York City of "freeholders and freemen . . . to chose eight persons out of every ward, to be a Committee, to carry the Association of the Congress into execution." Seabury predicted that these patriotic busybodies would soon invade the privacy of law-abiding men and women. They would ask impertinent questions. Do the families drink "any Tea or wine"? Have they imported garments manufactured in Great Britain or Ireland? And if the answer was affirmative, "their names are to be published in the Gazette, that they may be *publicly known*, and *universally condemned, as foes to the Rights of British America, and enemies of American Liberty.*" The threat of exposure marked the end of the old order as Seabury recognized it. The consumer revolt had spawned an ill-disciplined mob which had the audacity to declare purchasers of British goods "Out-laws, unworthy of the protection of civil society . . . to be *tarred, feathered, hanged, drawn, quartered, and burnt.—O Rare American Freedom!*"[85]

Seabury inflated the punishments dispensed for breaking the political rules of consumption.[86] Everywhere, however, one encountered a wave of excitement. As Henry Laurens of South Carolina explained in anticipation of the Association:

> From the best intelligence that I have received, my conclusions are, that, So. Carolina, No. Carolina, Virginia, Maryland, Pennsylvania, New Jersey, New York, Connecticut, Rhode Island, Massachusetts, New Hampshire, one Chain of Colonies extending upwards of 1,200 Miles & containing about three Millions of White Inhabitants of whom upwards of 500,000 [are] Men capable of bearing Arms, will unite in an agreement to Import no goods from Great Britain, the West India Islands, or Africa until those Acts of Parliament which Strike at our Liberties are Repealed.[87]

Laurens judged correctly. It has been estimated that local elections for the committees brought seven thousand men into the political process who had never before served in public office.[88] The committees monitored consumption, identifying local patriots by the garments they wore and by the beverages they drank, and demanded public confessions from those who erred. In Virginia counties everyone was expected to sign the Association, a promise before one's neighbors—almost a statement of one's new birth as a consumer—not to purchase the despised manufactures of the mother country. According to James Madison, these signings were "the method used among us to distinguish friends from foes and to oblige the Common people to a more strict observance of it [the Association]."[89]

As in earlier boycotts, people sorted themselves out politically through goods. A committee in Prince George's County announced "That to be clothed in manufactures fabricated in the Colonies ought to be considered as a badge and distinction of respect and true patriotism."[90] In Charleston, South Carolina, a committee sent children through the streets to collect tea, which was then burned publicly on Guy Fawkes Day.[91] The local associations also educated ordinary men and women about the relation between consumer goods and constitutional rights, in other words, about the relation between experience and ideology. A committee in Anne Arundel County, Maryland, helped Thomas Charles Williams understand that by importing tea he had "endangered the rights and liberties of America." Proceedings against Williams were dropped after he proclaimed that he was "sincerely sorry for his offense."[92] An Association in Farmington, Connecticut, forced Solomon Cowles and his wife to confess that secretly drinking tea after March 1, 1775,

The Association forced Americans such as the man signing a local agreement to support the general boycott of British goods. *"The Alternative of Williamsburg," Print, 1775. Courtesy of the Colonial Williamsburg Foundation.*

is a violation of the third article of said Association, contrary to the sense of the people of this town, derogatory of the character it sustains as firmly engaged in the interesting cause of liberty, and to the manifest injury of the public interest of British America: Which conduct of ours, we do voluntarily, in this public manner, utterly disapprove of and condemn, And further, we do promise and engage for the future, strictly to conform ourselves to the obvious sense and meaning of the said Association, in this and every other particular.[93]

Alas, Silas Newcomb of Cumberland, New Jersey, was more stubborn. The members of the local Association failed to convince the man of his error in drinking "East-India Tea in his family," and they were finally compelled "to break off all dealings with him, and in this manner publish the truth of the case, that he may be distinguished from the friends of American liberty."[94]

The colonists who responded to Boston's call in 1774 were consciously repudiating the empire of goods. Within barely a generation the meaning of the items of everyday consumption had changed substantially. At mid-century imported articles—the cloth, the ceramics, the buttons—had served as markers of a British identity, and as they flooded into the homes of yeomen and gentry alike, they linked ordinary men and women with the distant exciting culture of the metropolis. By participating in the marketplace, by making choices among competing manufactures, the colonists became in some important sense English people who happened to live in the provinces. By taxing these goods, however, Parliament set in motion a process of symbolic redefinition, slow and painful at first, punctuated by lulls that encouraged the false hope that the empire of goods could survive, but ultimately straining the colonial relationship to the breaking point. Americans who had never dealt with one another, who lived thousands of miles apart, found that they could communicate their political grievances through goods or, more precisely, through the denial of goods that had held this empire together. Private consumer experiences were transformed into public rituals. Indeed, many colonists learned about rights and liberties through common consumer items, articles which in themselves were politically neutral but which in the changed political atmosphere of the 1760s and 1770s became the medium through which ideological abstractions acquired concrete meaning.

When the colonists finally and reluctantly decided that they could do without the "Baubles of Britain," they destroyed a vital cultural bond with the mother country. "The country," explained James Lovell to his friend Joseph Trumbull in December 1774, "seems determined to let England know that in the present struggle, commerce has lost all the temptations of a bait to catch the American farmer."[95] Lovell may have exaggerated, but he helps us to understand why in 1774 the countryside supported the cities. Consumer goods had made it possible for the colonists to imagine a nation; the Association made it easier for Americans to imagine independence.

IV

David Ramsay possessed outstanding talent. The South Carolina physician not only fought in the Revolution with distinction but also wrote a wonderfully insightful history of that event. While the outcome of the war was still in doubt, Ramsay delivered "An Oration on the Advantages of American Independence," a statement that revealed that he was already contemplating the future of a new republic. He reminded the people of Charleston that they had rejected British tyranny for a country "for which we would choose to live, or dare to die." The struggle had been uphill from the start. "It was [in] the Interest of Great-Britain to encourage our dissipation and extravagance, for the two-fold purpose of *increasing the sale of her manufactures,* and of *perpetuating our subordination.*" Ramsay told the audience that Parliament had done everything it could to maintain special commercial privileges in the colonies, and the flow of imported goods, many of them luxury items, had come close to undermining American virtue. The British wanted the colonists to be more like the British. "The whole force of example was employed to induce us to copy the dissipated manners of the country from which we sprung." The temptations were so great, in fact, that had "[we] continued dependent, our frugality, industry, and simplicity of manners, would have been lost in an imitation of British extravagance, idleness, and false refinements." But good had triumphed over evil; Americans had made the sacrifices necessary to preserve liberty.

And then, with the swiftest of transitions, Ramsay turned his attention to the future. A free republic would open its harbors to the trade of the world. He foresaw a level of prosperity that could not have been grasped before the Revolution. "Our change of government," Ramsay asserted, "smiles upon our commerce with an aspect peculiarly benign and favorable. In a few years, we may expect to see the colors of France, Spain, Holland, Prussia, Portugal, and those of every other maritime power, waving on our coasts; whilst Americans unfurl the thirteen Stripes in the remotest harbors of the world. Our different climates and soils produce a great variety of useful commodities. The sea washes our coast along an extensive tract of two thousand miles; and no country abounds in a greater plenty of the materials for ship-building." Ramsay may have intended to raise the spirits of a war-weary city, but this was not simply a learned pep talk. Like him, the people who heard Ramsay's oration anticipated that "the wealth of Europe, Asia, and Africa, will flow in upon America: Our Trade will no longer be confined by the selfish regulations of an avaricious step-dame, but follow wherever Interest leads the way. Our great object, as a trading people, should be to procure the best prices for our commodities, and foreign articles at the most reasonable rates."[96] In a new, expansive continental environment the objects of material culture changed their meaning. No longer associated with oppression, they communicated hope; no longer equated with political slavery, they spoke of prosperity; no longer coupled with the destruction of morality; they invited all Americans to share in the common goods which they had always desired.

It has become fashionable among some commentators to condemn modern consumer culture, insisting that it sustains itself on the creation of false wants. Self-indulgence, one hears, erodes the bonds of civil society. The critics may be correct. Whatever the truth, they do sound a lot like those eighteenth-century moralists who fretted that ordinary people could not handle the temptations of the marketplace. This perspective underestimates the capacity of men and women to comprehend their own political situation. It is true that goods can corrupt. But in certain circumstances they can be made to speak to power. The choice is ours to make.

Notes

Introduction

1. Reprinted in Bernard Peach, ed., *Richard Price and the Ethical Foundations of the American Revolution: Selections from His Pamphlets, with Appendices* (Durham, N.C., 1979), 292.
2. The phrase "consumer revolution" appears in Neil McKendrick, John Brewer, and J. H. Plumb, *The Birth of a Consumer Society: The Commercialization of Eighteenth-Century England* (Bloomington, Ind., 1982), 9–33. Also see Martin Daunton and Matthew Hilton, eds., *The Politics of Consumption: Material Culture and Citizenship in Europe and America* (Oxford, 2001).
3. The mobilization of the people under Mahatma Gandhi and other nationalist leaders provides an interesting comparison. Like the Americans, Gandhi's followers believed that massive British imports, especially textiles, sustained colonial dependence and therefore that political freedom required ordinary consumers to boycott goods manufactured in the mother country. See Manu Goswami, "From *Swadeshi* to *Swaraj*: Nation, Economy, and Territory in Colonial South Asia, 1870 to 1907," *Comparative Studies in Society and History* 40 (1998), 609–36; and Bernard S. Cohn, "Cloth, Clothes, and Colonialism: India in the Nineteenth Century," in *Colonialism and Its Forms of Knowledge: The British in India*, ed. Cohn (Princeton, N.J., 1996), 106–62.
4. Quoted in John Shy, "Confronting Rebellion: Private Correspondence of Lord Barrington with General Gage, 1765–1775," in *Sources of American Independence: Selected Manuscripts from the Collections of the William L. Clements Library*, ed. Howard H. Peckham (Chicago, 1978), I, 37.
5. 27 November 1767.

Chapter 1

1. Benjamin Woods Labaree, *The Boston Tea Party* (New York, 1964).
2. Richard Price, *Observations on the Nature of Civil Liberty* (1776), in *Richard Price and the Ethical Foundations of the American Revolution: Selections from His Pamphlets, with Appendices*, ed. Bernard Peach (Durham, N.C., 1979), 99.
3. *Massachusetts Spy*, 15 July and 11 August 1774.
4. *Massachusetts Spy*, 28 July 1774.
5. "Proceedings of the Freeholders of Rowan County," in *The Colonial Records of North Carolina*, ed. William L. Saunders, 10 vols. (Raleigh, N.C., 1886–90), IX, 1025.
6. *Massachusetts Spy*, 16 June 1774.

7. Cited in Henry S. Nourse, *History of the Town of Harvard, Massachusetts, 1732–1893* (Harvard, Mass., 1894), 308.

8. *Massachusetts Spy,* 4 August 1774.

9. Charles Chauncy to Richard Price, 10 January 1775, in Peach, ed., *Richard Price,* 293.

10. John Adams to Hezekiah Niles, 13 February 1818, in *The Works of John Adams,* ed. C. F. Adams, 10 vols. (Boston, 1850–56), X, 283.

11. David Ramsay, *An Oration on the Advantages of American Independence . . .* (Charleston, S.C., 1778), 18.

12. Samuel McClintock, *A Sermon Preached on Occasion of the Commencement of the New Constitution* (Portsmouth, N.H., 1784) reprinted in *Political Sermons of the American Founding Era, 1730–1805,* ed. Ellis Sandoz (Indianapolis, Ind., 1991), 800.

13. Andrew Burnaby, *Travels Through the Middle Settlements in North America in the Years 1759 and 1760* (Ithaca, N.Y., 1963), 113.

14. Thomas Pownall, *The Administration of the Colonies,* 2d ed. (London, 1765), 64.

15. [Benjamin Franklin], *The Interest of Great Britain Considered . . .* (Philadelphia, 1760), 31. The best modern account of the Albany Congress is Timothy J. Shannon, *Indians and Colonists at the Crossroads of Empire: The Albany Congress of 1754* (Ithaca, N.Y., 2000).

16. Ezra Stiles, *A Discourse on the Christian Union . . .* (Boston, 1761), 99.

17. Clarke to Franklin, 6 May 1754, in *The Papers of Benjamin Franklin,* ed. Leonard W. Labaree, 35 vols. (New Haven, Conn., 1959–) V, 270.

18. Adams to Niles, in *Works of John Adams,* X, 283.

19. "Journal of Josiah Quincy, Jun., During His Voyage and Residence in England from September 28th, 1774, to March 3d, 1775," Massachusetts Historical Society *Proceedings* 50 (1917), 438.

20. Ramsay, *Advantages of American Independence,* 1.

21. See T. H. Breen, "Making History: The Force of Public Opinion and the Last Years of Slavery in Revolutionary Massachusetts," in *Through a Glass Darkly: Reflections on Personal Identity in Early America,* ed. Ronald Hoffman, Mechal Sobel, and Fredrika J. Teute (Chapel Hill, N.C., 1997), 67–95.

22. Quite a few excellent monographs address the coming of revolution within a specific colony, and although many of these studies are thorough and imaginative, they seldom explain how the issues that propelled one group or region toward independence might have resonated in other areas. This is the problem of micro explanations for a macro event. A list of some of the better monographs would include Rhys Isaac, *The Transformation of Virginia, 1740–1790* (Chapel Hill, N.C., 1982); Edward Countryman, *A People in Revolution: The American Revolution and Political Society in New York, 1760–1790* (Baltimore, Md., 1981); and Robert A. Gross, *The Minutemen and their World* (New York, 1976).

23. A good discussion of the problem of explaining popular mobilization can be found in John Shy, "The American Colonies in War and Revolution, 1748–1783," in P. J. Marshall, ed., *The Eighteenth Century,* vol. 2 of *Oxford History of the British Empire,* ed. William Roger Louis (Oxford, 1998), 300–324.

24. "Libertas at Natale Solum," *South-Carolina Gazette,* 20 August 1770 (italics omitted).

25. Bernard Bailyn, *Ideological Origins of the American Revolution* (Cambridge, Mass., 1967), iv. Also see J.G.A. Pocock, *The Machiavellian Moment: Florentine Political Thought and the Atlantic Republican Tradition* (Princeton, N.J., 1975), and "Virtue and Commerce in the Eighteenth Century," *Journal of Interdisciplinary History* 3 (1972–73), 119–34; Gordon S. Wood, *The Creation of the American Republic, 1776–1787* (Chapel Hill, N.C., 1969). For a useful review of the historiographic debate, one might look at "*The Creation of the American Republic, 1776–1787:* A Symposium of Views and Reviews," *William and Mary Quarterly,* 3d ser., 44 (1987), 549–640, and Ronald Hamowy, "Cato's Letters, John Locke, and the Republican Paradigm," *History of Political Thought* 11 (1990), 273–94. For the enthusiastic reception of Trenchard and Gordon's "Cato's Letters" in colonial America, see Bernard Bailyn, *The Origins of American Politics* (New York, 1968), 3–58.

26. James T. Kloppenberg, "The Virtues of Liberalism: Christianity, Republicanism, and Ethics in Early American Political Discourse," *Journal of American History* 74 (1987), 9–33. For a different analysis see T. H. Breen, *The Lockean Moment: The Language of Rights on the Eve of the American Revolution* (Oxford, 2001).

27. Gordon S. Wood posed the interpretive problem most forcefully in "Rhetoric and Reality in the American Revolution," *William and Mary Quarterly,* 3d ser., 23 (1966), 3-32.

28. See, for example, Edmund S. Morgan, "The American Revolution: Revisions in Need of Revising," *William and Mary Quarterly,* 3d ser., 14 (1957), 3–15.

29. Richard L. Bushman, *The Refinement of America: Persons, Houses, Cities* (New York, 1992). The English side of the story is detailed in Paul Langford, *A Polite and Commercial People: England, 1727–1783* (Oxford, 1989).

30. These interpretive issues are explored in T. H. Breen, "Can Goods Speak to Power? A Curious Silence in the History of the 18th-Century Atlantic World," a presentation for Going Abroad: British Art and Design in a Wider World, 1500–1900, a conference at the Victoria and Albert Museum, London, 6 December 2002; and Martin Daunton and Matthew Hilton, eds., *The Politics of Consumption: Material Culture and Citizenship in Europe and America* (Oxford, 2001), 1–32.

31. [Anonymous], *Considerations upon the Act of Parliament . . .* (Boston, 1764), 22. In his colonial history of New York, originally drafted in 1762, William Smith confirmed what British military officers had suspected: "Every man of industry and integrity has it in his power to live well, and many are the instances of persons who came here distressed by their poverty, who now enjoy easy and plentiful fortunes." Smith, *The History of the Late Province of New-York,* New-York Historical Society *Collections,* vol. 4, pt. 2 (1829), 277. Much of the discussion of the "Hospitable Consumer" appeared originally in T. H. Breen, "Narrative of Commercial Life: Consumption, Ideology, and Community on the Eve of the American Revolution," *William and Mary Quarterly,* 3d ser., 50 (1993), 471–501.

32. [John Dickinson], *The Late Regulations Respecting the British Colonies on the Continent of America Considered . . .* (Philadelphia, 1765), 23–24. The scholarly Dickinson footnoted his version of the consumer narrative, citing Malachy Postlethwayt, *Universal Dictionary of Trade and Commerce* (London, 1751–55), who claimed that since Sir Walter Raleigh's time, English writers "have found an interest in *misrepresenting,* or lessening the value" of the American colonies. During the eighteenth century, however, hostile commentators began alleging the Americans "were not *useful enough* to their mother country; that while we were loaded with taxes, they were absolutely free; that the *planters* lived like *princes,* while the inhabitants of *England* laboured hard for a tolerable subsistence"([Dickinson], *Late Regulations,* 23–24). To this, he added that especially heavy duties on Chesapeake tobacco in Great Britain were part of a "design to bring down the pride of these PRINCELY PLANTERS" (ibid.).

33. Josiah Tucker, *A Letter from a Merchant in London to His Nephew in North America . . .* (London, 1766) with Franklin's notes is reprinted in *Pennsylvania Magazine of History and Biography* 25 (1901), 315–21, 524–25.

34. *The Power and Grandeur of Great-Britain, Founded on the Liberty of the Colonies, and the Mischiefs Attending the Taxing of Them by Act of Parliament Demonstrated* (New York, 1768), 5, 7.

35. Ibid., 7–8.

36. [William Hicks], *The Nature and Extent of Parliamentary Power Considered . . .* (Philadelphia, 1768), 18–19.

37. *New-London Gazette,* 20 January 1769.

38. *Boston Evening-Post,* 2 January 1769.

39. *Connecticut Journal, and New-Haven Post-Boy,* 11 October 1771.

40. Ebenezer Baldwin, "An Appendix, Stating the Heavy Grievances the Colonies Labour Under . . . ," in Samuel Sherwood, *A Sermon, Containing, Scriptural Instructions to Civil Rulers* (New Haven, Conn., 1774), 45, 50–51.

41. *New-York Mercury,* 4 July 1774, reprint of "A Citizen of Philadelphia," *Pennsylvania Packet,* 27 June 1774.

42. David Ramsay, *The History of the American Revolution,* ed. Lester H. Cohen, 2 vols. (1789; reprint, Indianapolis, Ind., 1990), I, 51.

43. Jeremy Belknap, *The History of New-Hampshire,* 2 vols. (1784–92; reprint, New York, 1970), I, 327–28.

44. Carole Shammas, "How Self-Sufficient Was Early America?" *Journal of Interdisciplinary History* 13 (1982), 247–72. Also see Ann Smart Martin, "Makers, Buyers, and Users: Consumerism as a Material Culture Framework," *Winterthur Portfolio* 28 (1993), 141–57; and Martin, "Frontier Boys and Country Cousins: The Context for Choice in Eighteenth-Century Consumerism," in *Historical Archaeology and the Study of American Culture,* ed. Lu Ann De Cunzo and Bernard L. Herman (Winterthur, Del., 1996), 71–102.

45. John J. McCusker and Russell R. Menard, *The Economy of British America, 1607–1789* (Chapel Hill, N.C., 1985), 10–34. An example of production-driven analysis is Peter A. Coclanis, *The Shadow of a Dream: Economic Life and Death in the South Carolina Low Country, 1670–1920* (New York, 1989).

46. Jan de Vries, "Peasant Demand Patterns and Economic Development: Friesland, 1550–1750," in *European Peasants and Their Markets: Essays in Agrarian Economic History*, ed. William N. Parker and Eric L. Jones (Princeton, N.J., 1975), 206. Also see Eric L. Jones, "The Fashion Manipulators: Consumer Taste and British Industries, 1660–1800," in *Business Enterprise and Economic Change: Essays in Honor of Harold F. Williamson*, ed. Louis P. Cain and Paul J. Uselding (Kent State, Ohio, 1973), 198–226.

47. De Vries, "Peasant Demand," 236.

48. McCusker and Menard, *Economy of British America*, 277.

49. See, for example, T. H. Breen, *Tobacco Culture: The Great Tidewater Planters on the Eve of Revolution* (Princeton, N.J., 1985).

50. Samuel Adams to Arthur Lee, 31 October 1771, in *The Writings of Samuel Adams*, ed. Harry Alonzo Cushing, 4 vols. (New York, 1904–6), II, 267.

51. Neil McKendrick, John Brewer, and J. H. Plumb, *The Birth of a Consumer Society: The Commercialization of Eighteenth-Century England* (Bloomington, Ind., 1982).

52. See Linda Colley, *Britons: Forging the Nation, 1707–1837* (New Haven, Conn., 1992); J. L. McCracken, "Protestant Ascendancy and the Rise of Colonial Nationalism, 1714–60," in T. W. Moody and W. E. Vaughan, eds., *Eighteenth-Century Ireland, 1691–1800*, vol. 4 of *A New History of Ireland* (Oxford, 1986), 106–8; Joep Leersen, "Anglo-Irish Patriotism and Its European Context: Notes Toward a Reassessment," *Eighteenth-Century Ireland* (Dublin), 3 (1988), 7–24; Thomas Barlett, " 'A People Made Rather for Copies than Originals': The Anglo-Irish, 1760–1800," *International History Review* 12 (1990), 11–25; Isolde Victory, "The Making of the Declaratory Act of 1720," in *Parliament, Politics, and People: Essays in Eighteenth-Century Irish History*, ed. Gerard O'Brien (Dublin, 1989), 9–30; and S. J. Connolly, "Varieties of Britishness: Ireland, Scotland and Wales in the Hanoverian State," in *Uniting the Kingdom?* ed. Alexander Grant and Keith J. Stringer (London, 1995), 195.

53. T. H. Breen, "Ideology and Nationalism on the Eve of the American Revolution: Revisions Once More in Need of Revising," *Journal of American History* 84 (1997), 13–39.

54. Cited in Ned C. Landsman, *Scotland and Its First American Colony, 1683–1765* (Princeton, N.J., 1985), 72.

55. Nicholas Phillipson, "Politics, Politeness, and the Anglicisation of Early Eighteenth-Century Scottish Culture," in *Scotland and England, 1286–1815*, ed. Roger A. Mason (Edinburgh, 1987), 56. On Adam Smith's analysis of "luxury," see Neil De Marchi, "Adam Smith's Accommodation of 'Altogether Endless' Desires," in *Consumers and Luxury: Consumer Culture in Europe, 1650–1850*, ed. Maxine Berg and Helen Clifford (Manchester, Eng., 1999), 18–36. See also Colin Kidd, "North Britishness and the Nature of Eighteenth-Century British Patriotisms," *Historical Journal* (Cambridge) 39 (1996), 361–82; Kidd, *British Identities Before Nationalism: Ethnicity and Nationhood in the Atlantic World, 1600–1800* (Cambridge, 1999); and Tony Claydon and Ian McBride, eds., *Protestantism and National Identity: Britain and Ireland, c.1650–c.1850* (Cambridge, 1998).

56. T. C. Smout, *A History of the Scottish People, 1560–1830* (London, 1969), 287–97.

57. Francis Godwin James, *Ireland in the Empire, 1688–1770* (Cambridge, Mass., 1973), 207–8; and Sarah Foster, "Buying Irish: Consumer Nationalism in 18th-Century Dublin," *History Today* 47 (1997), 44–51.

58. Lynn Hunt discusses the "politicization of the everyday" in *Politics, Culture, and Class in the French Revolution* (Berkeley, Calif., 1984), 53–56.

59. *South-Carolina Gazette*, 9 November 1769.

60. Albert O. Hirschman, *Shifting Involvements: Private Interest and Public Action* (Princeton, N.J., 1982), 63–67.

61. See Benedict Anderson, *Imagined Communities: Reflections on the Origin and Spread of Nationalism* (London, 1983).

62. The most useful general discussion of this point is Robert D. Putnam, *Making Democracy Work: Civic Traditions in Modern Italy* (Princeton, N.J., 1993), 163–85. Also see Niklas Luhmann, *Trust and Power* (Chichester, Eng., 1973); Karen S. Cook, ed., *Trust in Society* (New York, 2001); and Fran Tonkiss and Andrew Passey, eds., *Trust and Civil Society* (New York, 2000).

63. [Christopher Gadsden], "To the Inhabitants of the Province of South-Carolina, About to Assemble on the 6th of July," reprinted in *American Archives . . .* , ed. Peter Force, 4th ser., 9 vols. (Washington, D.C., 1837–53), I, 511.

64. In his *Revolutionary People at War: The Continental Army and American Character, 1775–1783* (Chapel Hill, N.C., 1979), Charles Royster makes a similar argument about the relation between experience—in this case, the shared sacrifice of ordinary soldiers for the common good—and the acceptance of a political ideology. As Royster explains, the men who served in the Continental Army may not have joined the military because they were republicans, but after serving with other American troops for long periods and after keeping the dream of national independence alive when so many of their countrymen appeared to have had second thoughts, they became republicans. Solidarity nurtured a political language which helped explain to themselves and to the American people what they had endured.

65. "Aspatia, Belinda, and Corinna," *Boston Gazette,* Supplement, 28 December 1767. Also see Linda K. Kerber, "'History Can Do It No Justice': Women and Reinterpretation of the American Revolution," in *Women in the Age of the American Revolution,* ed. Ronald Hoffman and Peter J. Albert (Charlottesville, Va., 1989), 18.

66. On the timing of the development of nationalism, one should also see David Waldstreicher, *In the Midst of Perpetual Fetes: The Making of American Nationalism, 1776–1820* (Chapel Hill, N.C., 1997). Also Breen, "Ideology and Nationalism."

67. *Massachusetts Spy,* 14 October 1773.

68. Samuel Johnson, *A Journey to the Western Islands of Scotland . . .* , ed. R. W. Chapman (1775; reprint, London, 1924), 18–20.

69. Cited in Robert M. Weir, "The Role of the Newspaper Press in the Southern Colonies on the Eve of the Revolution: An Interpretation," in *The Press and the American Revolution,* ed. Bernard Bailyn and John B. Hench (Worcester, Mass., 1980), 100.

70. Isaiah Thomas, *The History of Printing in America: With a Biography of Printers and an Account of Newspapers,* ed. Marcus A. McCorison (1810; reprint, Barre, Mass., 1970), 267.

71. [Peter Annet?], *A Discourse on Government and Religion, Calculated for the Meridian of the Thirteenth of January* (Boston, 1750), 39–40.

Chapter 2

1. In 1756, for example, "Poor Richard" advised colonial readers, "When you incline to have new Cloaths, look first well over the old Ones." Moreover, "when you incline to buy China Ware, Chinces, India Silks, or any other of their flimsey slight Manufactures . . . *put it off.*" The author insisted that "*Superfluities,* or at best, Conveniences . . . you might live without for one little Year, and not suffer exceedingly." As we shall discover, neither Franklin nor many other wealthy Americans of this period were prepared to accept such counsel. Leonard W. Labaree, ed., *The Papers of Benjamin Franklin,* 35 vols. (New Haven, Conn., 1959–), VI, 323.

2. Carl Bridenbaugh, ed., *Gentleman's Progress: The Itinerarium of Dr. Alexander Hamilton, 1744* (Chapel Hill, N.C., 1948), 3, 54–55.

3. A good account of this debate can be found in David E. Shi, *The Simple Life: Plain Living and High Thinking in American Culture* (New York, 1985). A recent survey of early nineteenth-century American society celebrates the values of subsistence families, who although not wholly self-sufficient still managed to distance themselves from the market. "From the perspective of economic historians," writes Charles Sellers, "farm folk who bartered a few hams or a tub of cheese for a frying pan or piece of calico sometimes seem incorporated into the market. But from the perspective of the household devoting its labor overwhelmingly to subsistence, the market remained marginal" (*The Market Revolution: Jacksonian America, 1815–1846* [New York, 1991], 15). A rich, often contentious literature examining the economic culture of mid-eighteenth-century America includes Daniel Vickers, "Competency and Competition: Economic Culture in Early America," *William and Mary Quarterly,* 3d ser., 47 (1990), 3–29; James A. Henretta, "Families and Farms: *Mentalité* in Pre-Industrial America," ibid., 35 (1978), 3–32; Richard L. Bushman, "Family Security in the Transition from Farm to City, 1750–1850," *Journal of Family History* 6 (1981), 238–56; Michael Merrill, "Putting 'Capitalism' in Its Place: A Review of Recent Literature," *William and Mary Quarterly,* 3d ser., 52 (1995), 315–26; and John E. Crowley, *The Invention of Comfort: Sensibilities and Design in Early Modern Britain and Early America* (Baltimore, 2001).

4. Lord Cornbury, "Trade and Manufactures of the Province, 1705," reprinted in *The Documentary History of the State of New-York*, ed. E. B. O'Callaghan, 4 vols. (Albany, N.Y., 1849), I, 711.

5. Ibid., 712.

6. Ibid., 713–14.

7. Ibid., 717.

8. Ibid., 757–58.

9. Cited in Jean B. Lee, *The Price of Nationhood: The American Revolution in Charles County* (New York, 1994), 33.

10. Ibid., 33–42.

11. [James Glen], "A Description of South Carolina," in *Historical Collections of South Carolina . . .* , ed. B. R. Carroll, 2 vols. (New York, 1836), II, 227.

12. Ibid., 227–30.

13. "The Law Papers: Correspondence and Documents During Jonathan Law's Governorship of the Colony of Connecticut, 1741–1750: Volume III," Connecticut Historical Society *Collections* 15 (1914), 301.

14. *The Official Papers of Francis Fauquier, Lieutenant Governor of Virginia, 1758–1768*, ed. George Reese, 3 vols. (Charlottesville, Va., 1980–83), II, 1012.

15. Gottlieb Mittelberger, *Journey to Pennsylvania*, ed. and trans. Oscar Handlin and John Clive (Cambridge, Mass., 1960), 37, 88–89. The respected Swedish scientist Peter Kalm traveled through the middle colonies at roughly the same time as Mittelberger. When he visited New York City, he discovered that "cloth is imported from London and so is every article of English growth or manufacture, together with all sorts of foreign goods." (*Peter Kalm's Travels in North America*, ed. Adolph B. Benson, 2 vols. [New York, 1937], I, 134). In 1740 an English commercial visitor known only as "Mr. Bennett" penned a short account of "Boston in 1740." Like Kalm and Mittelberger, Bennett was impressed by how much the colonists relied on England for basic goods, "but more especially clothing for men, women, and children" ("Bennett's History of New England," Massachusetts Historical Society *Proceedings* 5 [1860–62], 111).

16. "Letters of Rev. Jonathan Boucher," *Maryland Historical Magazine* 7 (1912), 5.

17. William Eddis, *Letters from America*, ed. Aubrey C. Land (Cambridge, Mass., 1969), 57, 75, 51–52.

18. John M. Hemphill, ed., "John Wayles Rates His Neighbours," *Virginia Magazine of History and Biography* 66 (1958), 305. On the use of Turkey carpets in the British mainland colonies during this period, see Charels F. Hummel, "Floor Coverings Used in Eighteenth-Century America," in *Imported and Domestic Textiles in Eighteenth-Century America*, ed. Patricia L. Fiske (Washington, D.C., 1976), 61–92; and John F. Watson, *Annals of Philadelphia, and Pennsylvania, in the Olden Times*, ed. Willis P. Hazard, 3 vols. (1830; reprint, Philadelphia, 1884), I, 205. Another valuable discussion of the highly visible effects of economic change during the eighteenth century can be found in "Autobiography of the Rev. John Barnard," Massachusetts Historical Society *Collections*, 3d ser., 5 (1836), 239–40.

19. *Independent Reflector*, 14 June 1753.

20. William Smith, *The History of the Late Province of New-York*, New-York Historical Society *Collections*, vol. 4, pt. 2 (1829), 277. Another interesting commentary on consumer behavior in New York can be found in an anonymous pamphlet, *The Commercial Conduct of the Province of New-York Considered, and the True Interest of that Colony Attempted to be Shewn. In a Letter to the Society of Arts, Agriculture, and Œconomy* (New York, 1767). The author exclaimed, "That such a Country [New York] . . . should have Recourse to *Europe,* and even to some of the most despicable Corners of it, and through them to *Asia,* in order to clothe themselves, is such a Conduct of its Inhabitants, that a Stranger, unacquainted with these Facts, would pronounce it incredible. But would he not be astonished when he was told, that the Colonies of *North America* were near Five Millions . . . in Debt to *Great Britain,* not only for *British* Goods, but for Silks, Chintz, Callico, Muslin, Tea, &c. from *Asia,* and even for Linen from *Silesia* and *Austria,* via *London, Hamburgh,* and *Amsterdam;* Hemp, Diaper, and other Linen, through *England* from *Russia,* and even from *Arch-Angel,* when they have under their Feet a Country whose natural Fertility surpasses any in the World?" (9–10).

21. Jared Eliot, *A Continuation of the Essay upon Field-Husbandry, As it is or May be Ordered in New England* (New London, Conn., 1749), 20.

22. A marvelous introduction to this world of goods can be found in Michael Snodin and John Styles, eds., *Design and the Decorative Arts: Britain, 1500–1900* (London, 2002), 154–305.

23. Richard L. Bushman, *The Refinement of America: Persons, Houses, Cities* (New York, 1992), xi.

24. Cited in Edward A. Chappell, "Housing a Nation: The Transformation of Living Standards in Early America," in *Of Consuming Interests: The Styles of Life in the Eighteenth Century*, ed. Cary Carson, Ronald Hoffman, and Peter J. Albert (Charlottesville, Va., 1994), 216.

25. On the celebration of the colonial craftsman see Carl Bridenbaugh, *The Colonial Craftsman* (New York, 1950).

26. William M. Kelso, *Captain Jones's Wormslow: A Historical, Archaeological, and Architectural Study of an Eighteenth-Century Plantation Site near Savannah, Georgia* (Athens, Ga., 1979); James J. F. Deetz, "Ceramics from Plymouth, 1635–1835: The Archaeological Evidence," Marley R. Brown III, "Ceramics from Plymouth, 1621–1800: The Documentary Record," Garry Wheeler Stone, "Ceramics from the John Hicks Site, 1723–43: The Material Culture," and Arnold R. Mountford, "Staffordshire Salt-Glaze Stoneware," in *Ceramics in America*, ed. Ian M. G. Quimby (Charlottesville, Va., 1973), 15–40, 41–74, 103–40, 197–216. James Deetz provides a highly readable introduction to the entire field of historical archaeology in his *In Small Things Forgotten: The Archaeology of Early American Life* (Garden City, N.Y., 1977).

27. The interpretive problem is discussed in William M. Kelso, *Kingsmill Plantations, 1619–1800: Archaeology of Country Life in Colonial Virginia* (Orlando, Fla., 1984), 204–5. Also see Dennis J. Pogue, "The Archaeology of Plantation Life: Another Perspective on George Washington's Mount Vernon," *Virginia Cavalcade* 41 (1991), 76–78; and William Hampton Adams and Sarah Jane Boling, "Status and Ceramics for Planters and Slaves on Three Georgia Coastal Plantations," *Historical Archaeology* 23 (1989), 69–96. Similar discoveries have been made at other plantations throughout the South.

28. Francis Parkman, *France and England in North America*, 2 vols. (New York, 1983), II, 736.

29. Michael D. Coe, "The Line of Forts: Archaeology of the Mid-Eighteenth Century on the Massachusetts Frontier," in *New England Historical Archaeology*, ed. Peter Benes, Dublin Seminar for New England Folklife *Annual Proceedings* 2 (1977), 52, 54.

30. James Deetz, *Flowerdew Hundred: The Archaeology of a Virginia Plantation, 1619–1864* (Charlottesville, Va., 1993), 165.

31. Kelso, *Kingsmill Plantations*, 205, 213–4 (Appendix B).

32. Cornbury, "Trade and Manufactures of the Province," 757–58.

33. York County (Virginia), Wills and Inventory, Bk. #19, 1740–46, 86–87, Foundation Library, Colonial Williamsburg. For a splendid account of how one astonishingly complete inventory led to the reinterpretation of an entire building, see Graham Hood, *The Governor's Palace in Williamsburg: A Cultural Study* (Williamsburg, Va., 1991).

34. Gloria Lund Main, "The Correction of Biases in Colonial American Probate Records," *Historical Methods Newsletter* 8 (1974), 10–28; Main, "Probate Records as a Source for Early American History," *William and Mary Quarterly*, 3d ser., 32 (1975), 89–99; Peter Benes, ed., *Early American Probate Inventories*, Dublin Seminar for New England Folklife *Annual Proceedings* 12 (1987), 5–17; Margaret Spufford, "The Limitations of the Probate Inventory," in *English Rural Society, 1500–1800: Essays in Honour of Joan Thirsk*, ed. John Chartres and David Hey (Cambridge, 1990), 139–74.

35. Carole Shammas, *The Pre-Industrial Consumer in England and America* (Oxford, 1990), 52–194; Shammas, "Constructing a Wealth Distribution from Probate Records," *Journal of Interdisciplinary History* 9 (1978), 297–307; Shammas, "Consumer Behavior in Colonial America," *Social Science History* 6 (1982), 67–86; John J. McCusker and Russell R. Menard, *The Economy of British America, 1607–1789* (Chapel Hill, N.C., 1985), 286–87; and Cary Carson, "The Consumer Revolution in Colonial British America: Why Demand?" in *Of Consuming Interests: The Styles of Life in the Eighteenth Century*, ed. Cary Carson, Ronald Hoffman, and Peter J. Albert (Charlottesville, Va., 1994), 483–697.

36. Lois Green Carr and Lorena S. Walsh, "Changing Lifestyles and Consumer Behavior in the Colonial Chesapeake," in Carson et al., eds., *Of Consuming Interests*, 59–166; Carr and Walsh, "Inventories and the Analysis of Wealth and Consumption Patterns in St. Mary's County, Maryland, 1658–1777," *Historical Methods Newsletter* 13 (1980), 81–104; Carr and Walsh, "The Standard of Living in the Colonial Chesapeake," *William and Mary Quarterly*, 3d ser., 45 (1988), 137–43; Walsh, "Urban Amenities and Rural Sufficiency: Living Standards and Consumer Behavior in the Colonial Chesapeake, 1643–1777," *Journal of Economic History* 43 (1983),

109–17; Gloria Lund Main, *Tobacco Colony: Life in Early Maryland, 1650–1720* (Princeton, N.J., 1982), 239–44; Gloria Seaman Allen, "The Consumption of Delftware in Kent County, Maryland, 1740–1780," *Journal of Early Southern Decorative Arts* 9 (1983), 10–12.

37. Gloria Lund Main, "The Standard of Living in Southern New England, 1640–1773," *William and Mary Quarterly*, 3d ser., 45 (1988), 125–29; Main, "The Standard of Living in Colonial Massachusetts," *Journal of Economic History* 43 (1983), 101–8; Garry Wheeler Stone, "Ceramics in Suffolk County, Massachusetts, Inventories, 1680–1775," Conference on Historical Site Archaeology *Papers*, vol. 3, pt. 2 (1970), 73–90; and Rodris Roth, *Tea Drinking in Eighteenth-Century America: Its Etiquette and Equipage* (Washington, D.C., 1961).

38. *Pennsylvania Gazette*, 14 September 1752. Also see Harry D. Berg, "The Organization of Business in Colonial Philadelphia," *Pennsylvania History* 10 (1943), 157–77.

39. Benedict Anderson, *Imagined Communities: Reflections on the Origin and Spread of Nationalism* (London, 1991), 62–64. Kathleen Wilson explores the commercial character of English provincial newspapers in *The Sense of the People: Politics, Culture, and Imperialism in England, 1715–1785* (Cambridge, 1995), esp. 38–39.

40. Stephen Botein, "'Meer Mechanics' and an Open Press: The Business and Political Strategies of Colonial American Printers," *Perspectives in American History* 9 (1975), 127–225; and David A. Copeland, *Colonial American Newspapers: Character and Content* (Newark, Del., 1997), 23–41.

41. Clarence S. Brigham, *Journals and Journeymen: A Contribution to the History of Early American Newspapers* (Philadelphia, 1950).

42. *Virginia Gazette*, October 8, 1736, cited in Lawrence C. Wroth, *The Colonial Printer* (Portland, Me., 1938), 236.

43. James Parker to Benjamin Franklin, 24 December 1767, in Labaree, ed., *Papers of Benjamin Franklin*, XIV, 347.

44. Patricia Cleary, "'She Will Be in the Shop': Women's Sphere of Trade in Eighteenth-Century Philadelphia and New York," *Pennsylvania Magazine of History and Biography* 119 (1995), 181–202.

45. Brigham, *Journals and Journeymen*, 29.

46. Observations about the character and content of eighteenth-century American advertising found in this section are based on extensive research in the newspapers of Boston, New York, Philadelphia, Williamsburg, and Charleston (South Carolina), carried out by the author and Rebecca Becker, then a graduate student at Northwestern University. Starting with the year 1723, Becker constructed a decade-by-decade count of all British imports advertised in the New York papers over the next fifty years. She was also able to chart—again decade by decade from 1723 to 1773—the first appearance in the New York market of almost 2,000 separate consumer items.

47. *New-York Mercury*, 13 June 1763 and 14 June 1773. On the commercialization of medicine during this period, see Colin Jones, "The Great Chain of Buying: Medical Advertisement, the Bourgeois Public Sphere, and the Origins of the French Revolution," *American Historical Review* 101 (1996), 13–40.

48. Mountford, "Staffordshire Salt-Glaze Stoneware," 205; Leslie A. Clarkson, *The Pre-Industrial Economy in England, 1500–1750* (London, 1971), 106–14; Charles Wilson, *England's Apprenticeship, 1630–1763* (New York, 1965), 302–6; and Maxine Berg, "From Imitation to Invention: Creating Commodities in Eighteenth-Century Britain," *Economic History Review* 55 (2002), 1–30.

49. William Culliford's career and the later development of the customs accounts is the subject of G. N. Clark, *Guide to English Commercial Statistics, 1696–1782* (London, 1938), 1–42.

50. Ibid., 11–30. Some contemporaries and not a few modern scholars seem to have been unaware that the eighteenth-century figures did not reflect current values. The problems associated with interpreting the Customs House ledgers are treated in John J. McCusker, "The Current Value of English Exports, 1697 to 1800," *William and Mary Quarterly*, 3d ser., 28 (1971), 607–28; Jacob M. Price, "New Time Series for Scotland's and Britain's Trade with the Thirteen Colonies and States, 1740 to 1791," ibid. 32 (1975), 307–25; and McCusker and Menard, *Economy of British America*, 73–75.

51. Clark, *English Commercial Statistics*, 1–25; Price, "New Time Series," 307–17.

52. For an impressively full accounting of how the static figures employed in the Customs House records were recalculated to reflect an eighteenth-century consumer price index, see

McCusker, "The Current Value," and Price, "New Time Series." Although smuggling affected the import totals for Great Britain, it did not greatly influence figures for exports to the mainland colonies. As Thomas C. Barrow argues, the incidence of smuggling in late colonial America has generally been greatly exaggerated. See his *Trade and Empire: The British Customs Service in Colonial America, 1660–1775* (Cambridge, Mass., 1967), ch. 7.

53. The figures are taken from Appendix IIB ("British Exports to the Thirteen Colonies and States, 1740 to 1791") in Price, "New Time Series," 324–25. The numbers for the 1740s and 1760s reflect running averages, 1742–48 and 1762–68. It is true that the customs ledgers known as CUST 3 list goods that cannot be classified strictly as durable or semi-durable manufactures. They contain some foodstuffs, for example, but these items represent a very small percentage of the total exports to America. Moreover, because of the way the inspector-general's staff constructed these records, it would be almost impossible to separate this category of goods from the major articles such as cloth and metal ware. See Public Record Office, Board of Customs and Excise, CUST 3 ledgers, London, Great Britain.

54. Price, "New Time Series," 324–25.

55. Jacob M. Price, "What Did Merchants Do? Reflections on British Overseas Trade, 1660–1790," *Journal of Economic History* 49 (1989), 274; and Price, "Colonial Trade and British Economic Development, 1660–1775," in *La Révolution Américaine et L'Europe* (Paris, 1979), 221–42.

56. McCusker and Menard, *Economy of British America*, 283–286; Ralph Davis, "English Foreign Trade, 1700–1774," *Economic History Review*, 2d ser., 15 (1962), 285–303; and Bernard Bailyn, "1776: A Year of Challenge—A World Transformed," *Journal of Law and Economics* 19 (1976), 437–66.

57. The most accessible discussion of colonial population growth can be found in McCusker and Menard, *Economy of British America*, ch. 10. The quotation from Malthus appears on page 213. Also see Daniel Scott Smith, "Early American Historiography and Social Science History," *Social Science History* 6 (1982), 267–91; Bernard Bailyn, *The Peopling of British North America: An Introduction* (New York, 1986); and Aaron Fogleman, "Peopling of Early America: Two Studies by Bernard Bailyn," *Comparative Studies in Society and History* 31 (1989), 612–13.

58. "Estimated Population of American Colonies: 1610 to 1780," Series Z1-19 in *Historical Statistics of the United States: Colonial Times to 1970*, 2 vols. (Washington, D.C., 1975), 1168.

59. McCusker and Menard, *Economy of British America*, 279–80. Also, Price, "What Did Merchants Do," 276.

60. The calculation of a per capita income figure is explained in Carole Shammas, "How Self-Sufficient Was Early America?" *Journal of Interdisciplinary History* 13 (1982), 247–72. Also see Shammas, "Consumer Behavior in Colonial America," 67–86. In her examination of one colony, Shammas wrote, "From figures now available on per capita income and imports circa 1770, I would estimate that roughly one quarter of yearly expenditures went toward buying goods brought in from outside the province [Massachusetts]" (81). Shammas included all imports, including sugar from the Caribbean Islands and foodstuffs from other mainland colonies, and thus comes up with a much higher consumer percentage than I did by using the £12 figure found in McCusker and Menard, *Economy of British America*, 280 (Table 13.1).

61. "Achenwall's Observations on North America, 1767," *Pennsylvania Magazine of History and Biography* 27 (1903), 14. In his *Interest of Great Britain Considered* (Philadelphia, 1760), Franklin claimed that the consumption of British exports in colonial America was increasing faster than was the total population and explained that this phenomenon "must be owing to this, that the people having by their industry mended their circumstances, are enabled to indulge themselves in finer cloaths, better furniture, and a more general use of all our [British] manufactures than heretofore" (30).

62. Arthur L. Jensen, *The Maritime Commerce of Colonial Philadelphia* (Madison, Wisc., 1963), 89–90.

63. These comments are based on my analysis of CUST 3 (Customs Records).

64. Davis, "English Foreign Trade," 290.

65. On the limited domestic production of cloth during this period, see Carole Shammas, *The Pre-Industrial Consumer*, 61–62; and Shammas, "Consumer Behavior in Colonial America," 81–83. For a different interpretation of the extent of homespun production, at least in late eighteenth-century New England, see Laurel Thatcher Ulrich, "Wheels, Looms, and the

Gender Division of Labor in Eighteenth-Century New England," *William and Mary Quarterly*, 3d ser., 55 (1998), 3–38.

66. [Anonymous], *Industry and Frugality Proposed as the Surest Means to Make Us a Rich and Flourishing People* . . . (Boston, 1753), 11.

67. *Connecticut Journal, and New-Haven Post-Boy*, 6 January 1769. In *The Power and Grandeur of Great-Britain, Founded on the Liberty of the Colonies* . . . (New York, 1768), another anonymous American declared with considerable hyperbole that "[n]ew countries can seldom do more than support themselves: But a country that is not only new, but where every person consumes from three to twenty pounds sterling, of British manufactures, must necessarily be poor. All the exports of North-America, will scarce suffice to pay for their necessary cloathing" (18).

68. *Pennsylvania Gazette*, 6 July 1758.

69. *American Weekly Mercury*, 31 July 1740.

70. Much recent analysis of early modern consumer activity compares Europe and America without adequately considering precisely what segment of the various populations was at risk to participate in the new marketplace. Neither England nor Holland, the two most advanced manufacturing nations during this period, experienced rapid increases in the rate of population growth, and while Great Britain had a large servant class, it did not arbitrarily drop as much as a fifth of its population from the consumer economy. One reason that Adam Smith condemned the institution of slavery was that it excluded so many people from the world of goods and thus discouraged productivity. For general comparative purposes the best study of eighteenth-century English consumer behavior remains Neil McKendrick, John Brewer, and J. H. Plumb, *The Birth of a Consumer Society: The Commercialization of Eighteenth-Century England* (Bloomington, Ind., 1982). Also see Jan de Vries, "Between Purchasing Power and the World of Goods: Understanding the Household Economy in Early Modern Europe," in *Consumption and the World of Goods*, ed. John Brewer and Roy Porter (London, 1993), 85–132.

71. McCusker and Menard, *Economy of British America*, 270; Carole Shammas, "Changes in English and Anglo-American Consumption from 1550 to 1800," in Brewer and Porter, eds., *Consumption and the World of Goods*, 177–205; and Carr and Walsh, "Changing Lifestyles and Consumer Behavior," 104–5.

72. Carole Shammas, "The Decline of Textile Prices in England and British America Prior to Industrialization," *Economic History Review*, 2d ser., 47 (1994), 483–507.

73. See Shammas, "Changes in English and Anglo-American Consumption."

74. Lois Green Carr, Russell R. Menard, and Lorena S. Walsh re-create this stark material culture in *Robert Cole's World: Agriculture and Society in Early Maryland* (Chapel Hill, N.C., 1991).

75. On the broad geographic distribution of imported goods, see McCusker and Menard, *Economy of British America*, 279–82, 302–3; and Robert D. Mitchell, *Commercialism and Frontier: Perspectives on the Early Shenandoah Valley* (Charlottesville, Va., 1977), 152–54.

76. *Connecticut Courant*, 7 December 1767, originally published in *Providence Gazette*, 14 November 1767.

77. "Letters and Papers of Cadwallader Colden: Volume II, 1730–1742," New-York Historical Society *Collections* 51 (1918), 32–33.

78. Smith, *History of the Late Province of New-York*, 278.

79. "Gov. Moore to the Lords of Trade," in O'Callaghan, ed., *Documentary History of the State of New-York*, I, 735.

80. [Franklin], *The Interest of Great Britain*, 15.

81. Ibid., 30–31.

82. See Thomas Jefferson, *Notes on the State of Virginia*, ed. William Peden (Chapel Hill, N.C., 1955); and Drew R. McCoy, *The Elusive Republic: Political Economy in Jeffersonian America* (Chapel Hill, N.C., 1980).

83. Charles S. Olton, *Artisans for Independence: Philadelphia Mechanics and the American Revolution* (Syracuse, N.Y., 1975), 23–28.

84. Cited in Arlene Palmer, "Glass Production in Eighteenth-Century America: The Wistarburgh Enterprise," *Winterthur Portfolio* 11 (1976), 98.

85. Paul Leicester Ford, ed., *The Writings of John Dickinson, Vol. 1: Political Writings, 1764–1774*, (New York, 1970), 354.

86. Laurel Thatcher Ulrich makes this argument in "Wheels, Looms, and the Gender Division of Labor," 3–38.

87. *Connecticut Courant*, 17 August 1767.

88. "Pitkin Papers: Correspondence and Documents During William Pitkin's Governorship of the Colony of Connecticut, 1766–1769," Connecticut Historical Society *Collections* 19 (1921), 56.

89. Mary Beth Norton, "The Evolution of White Women's Experience in Early America," *American Historical Review* 89 (1984), 604–5.

90. O'Callaghan, ed., *Documentary History of the State of New-York*, I, 733–34.

91. McKendrick et al., *Birth of a Consumer Society*; John Brewer, *The Pleasures of the Imagination: English Culture in the Eighteenth Century* (New York, 1997); and Simon Schama, *The Embarrassment of Riches: An Interpretation of Dutch Culture in the Golden Age* (New York, 1987).

92. See Henretta, "Families and Farms," 3–32; and T. H. Breen, "Back to Sweat and Toil: Suggestions for the Study of Agricultural Work in Early America," *Pennsylvania History* 49 (1982), 241–58.

93. An ongoing debate over the meaning of "self-sufficiency" in early American history has generated some excellent articles. Among the most valuable are Winifred B. Rothenberg, "The Market and Massachusetts Farmers, 1750–1855," *Journal of Economic History* 41 (1981), 283–314; Shammas, "How Self-Sufficient Was Early America?" 247–72; Bettye Hobbs Pruitt, "Self-Sufficiency and the Agricultural Economy of Eighteenth-Century Massachusetts," *William and Mary Quarterly*, 3d ser., 41 (1984), 333–64; and Daniel Vickers, "Competency and Competition," 3–29. Ann Smart Martin, a respected interpreter of colonial material culture, makes some of the same points from a different perspective in her "Frontier Boys and Country Cousins: The Context for Choice in Eighteenth-Century Consumerism," in *Historical Archaeology and the Study of American Culture*, ed. Ann De Cunzo and Bernard L. Herman (Winterthur, Del., 1996), 71–102.

94. *Connecticut Courant*, 7 December 1767.

95. James P. Horn, "The Letters of William Roberts of All Hallows Parish, Anne Arundel County, Maryland, 1756–1769," *Maryland Historical Magazine* 74 (1979), 125.

96. Cited in Linda Baumgarten, *Eighteenth-Century Clothing at Williamsburg* (Williamsburg, Va., 1986), 11.

Chapter 3

1. The debate in early modern England over the meaning of "empire" is explored by David Armitage in *The Ideological Origins of the British Empire* (Cambridge, 2000).

2. *The Works of the Right Honourable Edmund Burke*, 8 vols. (London, 1854–56), II, 180, 170. See Frank O'Gorman, *Edmund Burke; His Political Philosophy* (Bloomington, Ind., 1973), 67–79; and Isaac Kramnick, *The Rage of Edmund Burke: Portrait of an Ambivalent Conservative* (New York, 1977), 106–25.

3. *Works of Edmund Burke*, II, 179.

4. Ibid., II, 180.

5. Ibid., II, 180–81.

6. Ibid., II, 183. Burke seems to have invented the phrase. See John Bartlett, *Familiar Quotations: A Collection of Passages, Phrases, and Proverbs Traced to their Sources in Ancient and Modern Literature*, rev. ed. (Boston, 1980), 372.

7. For a fuller discussion of the meaning of the phrase, see James A. Henretta, *"Salutary Neglect": Colonial Administration Under the Duke of Newcastle* (Princeton, N.J., 1972), 317–18, 323–25, 344. Also see T. H. Breen, "Ideology and Nationalism on the Eve of the American Revolution: Revisions *Once More* in Need of Revising," *Journal of American History* 84 (1997), 22–23.

8. *Works of Edmund Burke*, II, 119, 181. Edmund Burke, "Speech on American Taxation, 19 April 1774," in *Writings and Speeches of Edmund Burke*, ed. Paul Langford, 9 vols. (Oxford, 1981–), II, 432–33.

9. [William Douglass], *A Discourse Concerning the Currencies of the British Plantations in America . . .* (Boston, 1740), 4, 55.

10. See T. H. Breen, *Puritans and Adventurers: Change and Persistence in Early America* (New York, 1980).

11. Roy Porter develops this point in his *Creation of the Modern World: The Untold Story of the British Enlightenment* (New York, 2000). Several paragraphs on colonial nationalism included in this section originally appeared in Breen, "Ideology and Nationalism," 13–39.

12. Lawrence Stone, "The New Eighteenth Century," *New York Review of Books*, 29 March 1984, 42–48; Paul Langford, *A Polite and Commercial People: England, 1727–1783* (Oxford, 1989), 679; Kathleen Wilson, *The Sense of the People: Politics, Culture, and Imperialism in England, 1715–1785* (Cambridge, 1995), 4; Linda Colley, *Britons: Forging the Nation, 1707–1837* (New Haven, Conn., 1992); John Brewer, *The Sinews of Power: War, Money, and the English State, 1688–1783* (New York, 1989); and Brewer, "The Eighteenth-Century British State: Contexts and Issues," in *An Imperial State at War: Britain from 1689 to 1815*, ed. Lawrence Stone (London, 1994), 52–71.

13. See Linda Colley, *In Defiance of Oligarchy: The Tory Party, 1714–1760* (Cambridge, 1982); P. C. Corfield, *The Impact of English Towns, 1700–1800* (Oxford, 1982).

14. Patrick K. O'Brien, *Power with Profit: The State and the Economy, 1688–1815* (London, 1991).

15. Langford, *Polite and Commercial People*, 692.

16. Breen, *Puritans and Adventurers*, 134–35.

17. A fine assessment of this literature can be found in Joanna Innes, "Review Article: Jonathan Clark, Social History and England's 'Ancien Régime,'" *Past and Present*, no. 115 (1987), 196–97. On Britain's ability to finance modern warfare, see Peter G. Dickson, *The Financial Revolution in England: A Study in the Development of Public Credit, 1688–1756* (London, 1967); Brewer, *Sinews of Power*; Stone, ed., *Imperial State at War*; Nancy F. Koehn, *The Power of Commerce: Economy and Governance in the First British Empire* (Ithaca, N.Y., 1994); M. J. Braddick, *Parliamentary Taxation in Seventeenth-Century England: Local Administration and Response* (Woodbridge, Eng., 1994); and Mark Greengrass, ed., *Conquest and Coalescence: The Shaping of the State in Early Modern Europe* (London, 1991).

18. For useful discussion of the changing historical contexts in which different peoples experienced a heightened sense of national identity, see E. J. Hobsbawm, *Nations and Nationalism Since 1780: Programme, Myth, Reality* (Cambridge, 1990); Ernest Gellner, *Nations and Nationalism* (Oxford, 1983); and Benedict Anderson, *Imagined Communities: Reflections on the Origin and Spread of Nationalism* (London, 1991). For some splendid insights into the shifting intellectual frameworks in which various European nationalisms have found popular meaning, see Maurizio Viroli, *For Love of Country: An Essay on Patriotism and Nationalism* (Oxford, 1995). Less successful in dealing with these contextual issues is the ambitious comparative work of Liah Greenfield, *Nationalism: Five Roads to Modernity* (Cambridge, Mass., 1992), 27–87. On older expressions of national identity, see Richard Helgerson, *Forms of Nationhood: The Elizabethan Writing of England* (Chicago, 1992).

19. Colley, *Britons*, 86. Also see Colin Kidd, *British Identities Before Nationalism: Ethnicity and Nationhood in the Atlantic World, 1600–1800* (Cambridge, 1999).

20. Gerald Newman, *The Rise of English Nationalism: A Cultural History, 1740–1830* (New York, 1987).

21. As Roy Porter correctly reminds us in "Review Article: Seeing the Past," *Past and Present*, no. 118 (1988), "English patriotism during the Georgian century should not be passed off as nothing but hegemonic social control, the conspiratorial ideological imprint of the ruling order; rather it signified a positive and critical articulation of the political voice of the middle classes" (198). Also see Dror Wahrman, "National Society, Communal Culture: An Argument About the Recent Historiography of Eighteenth-Century Britain," *Social History* 17 (1992), 61–62; and Kathleen Wilson, "Empire, Trade and Popular Politics in Mid-Hanoverian Britain: The Case of Admiral Vernon," *Past and Present*, no. 121 (1988), 74–109.

22. Langford, *Polite and Commercial People*; and Lawrence Stone and Jeanne C. Fawtier Stone, *An Open Elite? England, 1540–1880* (Oxford, 1984), 408.

23. Langford, *Polite and Commercial People*, 59–121. See also Nicholas Rogers, "Review Article: Paul Langford's 'Age of Improvement,'" *Past and Present*, no. 130 (1991), 201–9.

24. B. G., Esq, *The Advantages of the Revolution Illustrated, by a View of the Present State of Great Britain . . .* (London, 1753), 17, 19–20, 20–21, 22, 23.

25. Jacob M. Price, ed., *Joshua Johnson's Letter Book, 1771–1774: Letters from a Merchant in London to His Partners in Maryland*, London Record Society *Publications* 15 (1979), 33. Also see

Kenneth Morgan, ed., *An American Quaker in the British Isles: The Travel Journals of Jabez Maud Fisher, 1775–1779* (Oxford, 1992).

26. Neil McKendrick, John Brewer, and J. H. Plumb, *The Birth of a Consumer Society: The Commercialization of Eighteenth-Century England* (Bloomington, Ind., 1982), 1. For a sampling of the large and growing literature on the development of a consumer economy in Great Britain and, by extension, in colonial America, see Roy Porter, *English Society in the Eighteenth Century* (Middlesex, Eng., 1982), 201–68; Frank O'Gorman, "The Recent Historiography of the Hanoverian Regime," *Historical Journal* (Cambridge), 29 (1986), 1005–20; John Brewer and Roy Porter, eds., *Consumption and the World of Goods* (London, 1993); Carole Shammas, *The Pre-Industrial Consumer in England and America* (Oxford, 1990); Joan Thirsk, *Economic Policy and Projects: The Development of a Consumer Society in Early Modern England* (Oxford, 1978); and Lorna Weatherill, *Consumer Behavior and Material Culture in Britain, 1660–1760* (London, 1988).

27. Josiah Tucker, "Instructions for Travellers" (1757), in *Josiah Tucker: A Selection from His Economic and Political Writings*, ed. Robert Livingston Schuyler (New York, 1931), 245–46.

28. P .J. Marshall, "Empire and Authority in the Later Eighteenth Century," *Journal of Imperial and Commonwealth History* 15 (1987), 105–22.

29. Several studies that provide a broader, more complex analysis of the eighteenth-century imperial connection are Jack P. Greene, *Peripheries and Center: Constitutional Development in the Extended Polities of the British Empire and the United States, 1607–1788* (Athens, Ga., 1986); Greene, *Pursuits of Happiness: The Social Development of Early Modern British Colonies and the Formation of American Culture* (Chapel Hill, N.C., 1988); Bernard Bailyn and Philip D. Morgan, eds., *Strangers Within the Realm: Cultural Margins of the First British Empire* (Chapel Hill, N.C., 1991); and J.G.A. Pocock, "British History: A Plea for a New Subject," *Journal of Modern History* 47 (1975), 601–21.

30. James Parker, *The Power and Grandeur of Great-Britain . . .* (New York, 1768), 3–4.

31. On the alleged "ensavagement" of European civilization in eighteenth-century America, see Bernard Bailyn, *Voyagers to the West: A Passage in the Peopling of America on the Eve of the Revolution* (New York, 1986).

32. Jack P. Greene raises many of these issues in "Search for Identity: An Interpretation of the Meaning of Selected Patterns of Social Response in Eighteenth-Century America," in his *Imperatives, Behaviors, and Identities: Essays in Early American Cultural History* (Charlottesville, Va., 1992), 143–73. As John Clive and Bernard Bailyn explain, the Scots faced many of the same problems in relation to an imperial English culture ("England's Cultural Provinces: Scotland and America," *William and Mary Quarterly*, 3d ser., 11 [1954], 200–13).

33. The striking development of Marblehead and the Reverend Mr. Barnard's impressive entrepreneurial skills are examined in Christine Leigh Heyrman, *Commerce and Culture: The Maritime Communities of Colonial Massachusetts, 1690–1750* (New York, 1984).

34. "Autobiography of the Rev. John Barnard," Massachusetts Historical Society *Collections*, 3d ser., 5 (1836), 200.

35. Breen, "Ideology and Nationalism," 13–39.

36. James Otis, *The Rights of the British Colonies Asserted and Proved . . .* (1764), reprinted in Bernard Bailyn, ed., *Pamphlets of the American Revolution, 1750–1776* (Cambridge, Mass., 1965), 436.

37. See Anthony Pagden, *Lords of All the Worlds: Ideologies of Empire in Spain, Britain and France, c. 1500–c. 1800* (New Haven, Conn., 1995).

38. Cited in McKendrick et al., *Birth of a Consumer Society*, 122. Also see Ralph Davis, *A Commercial Revolution; English Overseas Trade in the Seventeenth and Eighteenth Centuries* (London, 1967), 3–14.

39. Cited in McKendrick et al., *Birth of a Consumer Society*, 108.

40. Joyce O. Appleby, *Economic Thought and Ideology in Seventeenth-Century England* (Princeton, N.J., 1978); William Letwin, *The Origins of Scientific Economics: English Economic Thought, 1660–1776* (London, 1963); and E.A.J. Johnson, *Predecessors of Adam Smith: The Growth of British Economic Thought* (New York, 1937).

41. Daniel Defoe, *The Complete English Tradesman*, vols. 16 and 17 of *The Novels and Miscellaneous Works of Daniel Defoe* (Oxford, 1841), XVI, 260.

42. John Campbell, *A Political Survey of Britain: Being a Series of Reflections on the Situation, Lands, Inhabitants, Revenues, Colonies, and Commerce of this Island . . .* , 4 vols. (Dublin,

1775), IV, 565. Johnson quoted in *The Dictionary of National Biography*, ed. Leslie Stephen and Sidney Lee, 2d ed., 22 vols. (London, 1908–9), III, 827.

43. A valuable discussion of market expansion in this period can be found in David Ormrod, "English Re-Exports and the Dutch Staplemarket in the Eighteenth Century," in *Enterprise and History: Essays in Honour of Charles Wilson*, ed. D. C. Coleman and Peter Mathias (New York, 1984), 89–115.

44. See Jürgen Habermas, *The Structural Transformation of the Public Sphere: An Inquiry into a Category of Bourgeois Society*, trans. Thomas Burger (Cambridge, Mass., 1989), 1–26.

45. See the entry entitled "Britain—Great" in Richard Rolt, *A New Dictionary of Trade and Commerce, Compiled from the Information of the Most Eminent Merchants . . .* (London, 1756), n.p.

46. B. G., Esq, *Advantages of the Revolution*, 30.

47. See Albert O. Hirschman, *The Passions and the Interests: Political Arguments for Capitalism Before Its Triumph* (Princeton, N.J., 1977).

48. Rolt, "Britain-Great," *New Dictionary of Trade*, n.p.

49. Malachy Postlethwayt, *Universal Dictionary of Trade and Commerce*, 2 vols. (London, 1751–55), I, 533.

50. [Benjamin Franklin], reprinted in *Boston News-Letter*, 7 August 1760.

51. Thomas Pownall, *The Administration of the Colonies*, 2d ed. (London, 1765), 26.

52. Bernard Bailyn, *The Origins of American Politics* (New York, 1968), 40–41, 54–55. See also Bernard Bailyn, *The Ideological Origins of the American Revolution* (Cambridge, Mass., 1967), 35–45.

53. John Trenchard and Thomas Gordon, *Cato's Letters; or, Essays on Liberty, Civil and Religious, and Other Important Subjects*, ed. Ronald Hamowy, 2 vols. (Indianapolis, Ind., 1995), I, 474.

54. The fullest discussion of the development of England's commercial policy can be found in Charles M. Andrews, *England's Commercial and Colonial Policy* (New Haven, Conn., 1938).

55. The phrase comes from Jacob M. Price, "What Did Merchants Do? Reflections on British Overseas Trade, 1660–1790," *Journal of Economic History* 49 (1989), 270–71. Also see Jacob Price, "Who Cared About the Colonies? The Impact of the Thirteen Colonies on British Society and Politics, circa 1714–1775," in Bailyn and Morgan, eds., *Strangers Within the Realm*, 395–436; and Ralph Davis, *Commercial Revolution*, 15.

56. Cited in *Boston Evening-Post*, 11 January 1742.

57. Pownall, *Administration of the Colonies*, 27.

58. Adam Smith, *An Inquiry into the Nature and Causes of the Wealth of Nations*, ed. R. H. Campbell and Andrew S. Skinner, 2 vols. (Indianapolis, Ind., 1981), II, 661.

59. Rolt, "British Islands," *New Dictionary of Trade*, n. p.

60. Campbell, *A Political Survey*, IV, 567.

61. Pownall, *Administration of the Colonies*, 26.

62. [Robert Dodsley], *The Preceptor: Containing a General Course of Education . . .* , 4th ed., 2 vols. (London, 1763), II, 445–48.

63. Ibid., II, 447, 450.

64. *New-York Mercury*, 24 September 1764.

65. [Amicus Reipublica], *Trade and Commerce Inculcated in a Discourse . . .* (Boston, 1731), 2–4.

66. *Independent Reflector*, 3 May 1753.

67. Mason to Washington, 5 April 1769, in *The Papers of George Mason: Volume I, 1749–1778*, ed. Robert A. Rutland (Chapel Hill, N.C., 1970), 100.

68. *Letters from a Pennsylvania Farmer to the Inhabitants of the British Colonies* (1768), in *The Writings of John Dickinson: Vol. 1, Political Writings, 1764–1774*, ed. Paul Leicester Ford (New York, 1970), 337. Many leading figures of the Scottish Enlightenment analyzed economic progress in similar although more sophisticated developmental terms. See Hirschman, *Passions and Interests*.

69. John M. Murrin, "Political Development," in *Colonial British America: Essays in the New History of the Early Modern Era*, ed. Jack P. Greene and J. R. Pole (Baltimore, 1984), 432.

70. Jared Eliot, *The Sixth Essay on Field-Husbandry . . .* (New Haven, Conn., 1759), 12–13.

71. Ibid., 16–17.

72. William Douglass, *A Summary, Historical and Political, of the First Planting . . . of the British Settlements in North-America* (Boston, 1749), 227–28.

73. [Anonymous], *Four Dissertations, on the Reciprocal Advantages of a Perpetual Union Between Great-Britain and Her American Colonies . . .* (Philadelphia, 1766), 55–57.

74. Ford, ed., *Writings of John Dickinson*, I, 213–15.
75. *New-England Weekly Journal*, 18 November 1740.
76. *The American Magazine, or a Monthly View of the Political State of the British Colonies*, no. 1 (1741), 5.
77. "Observations Concerning the Increase of Mankind" (1755), in *The Papers of Benjamin Franklin*, ed. Leonard W. Labaree, 35 vols. (New Haven, Conn., 1959–), IV, 229.
78. Rolt, "Excise," *New Dictionary*, n.p.
79. [Archibald Kennedy], *Observations on the Importance of the Northern Colonies Under Proper Regulations* (New York, 1750), 10.
80. Cited in *New-York Mercury*, 11 January 1768.
81. *Connecticut Journal, and New-Haven Post-Boy*, 2 February 1770.
82. William Smith, *The History of the Late Province of New-York . . .* , New-York Historical Society *Collections*, vol. 4, pt. 2 (1829), 281.
83. [Kennedy], *Observations on the Importance of the Northern Colonies*, 9–10.
84. Cited in the *New-York Mercury*, 24 September 1764.
85. On the parallel development of different colonial discourses during this period, see T. H. Breen and Timothy Hall, "Structuring Provincial Imagination: The Rhetoric and Experience of Social Change in 18th-Century New England," *American Historical Review* 103 (1998), 1411–38.
86. Cited in the *South-Carolina Gazette*, 23 February 1769. The piece originally appeared in *Pennsylvania Journal*, 12 January 1769.
87. David Ramsay, *An Oration on the Advantages of American Independence . . .* (Charleston, S.C., 1778), 2.
88. Cited in Henry S. Nourse, *History of the Town of Harvard, Massachusetts, 1732–1893* (Harvard, Mass.,1894), 304–5.
89. *South-Carolina Gazette*, 23 February 1769.

Chapter 4

1. [Thomas Prince], *The Vade Mecum for America; or a Companion for Traders and Travellers* (Boston, 1731), i–iii.
2. *Pennsylvania Chronicle, and Universal Advertiser*, 17 February 1772.
3. Cited in A. Roger Ekirch, *Bound for America: The Transportation of British Convicts to the Colonies, 1718–1775* (Oxford, 1987), 13–14. Also see Beverley Lemire, *Dress, Culture, and Commerce: The English Clothing Trade Before the Factory, 1660–1800* (New York, 1997), ch. 5.
4. *Boston Evening-Post*, 2 October 1738; *New England Weekly Journal*, 14 March, 8 August, and 27 September 1738.
5. *New-York Journal; or, General Advertiser, Supplement Extraordinary*, 12 February 1767; also 22 January and 14 February 1767.
6. *An Account of the Robberies Committed by John Morrison, And his Accomplices, in and near Philadelphia, 1750: Together with the Manner of their being discover'd, their Behaviour on their Tryals, in the Prison after Sentence, and at the Place of Execution* (Philadelphia, 1750/1).
7. [Isaac Frasier], *A Brief Account of the Life, and Abominable Thefts, of the Notorious Isaac Frasier, who was Executed at Fairfield, Sept. 7th, 1768, Penned From His Own Mouth, And Signed by Him, A Few Days Before His Execution* (New London, Conn., 1768). Also see Noah Hobart, *Excessive Wickedness, the Way to an Untimely Death* (New Haven, Conn., 1768). After breaking out of the jail in Worcester, Massachusetts, Frasier briefly worked with a small gang of young black and white men. One of these associates was Arthur, a slave whose own curious story is recounted by T. H. Breen, "Making History: The Force of Public Opinion and the Last Years of Slavery in Revolutionary Massachusetts," in *Through a Glass Darkly: Reflections on Personal Identity in Early America*, ed. Ronald Hoffman, Mechal Sobel, and Fredrika J. Teute (Chapel Hill, N.C., 1997), 67–95.
8. The newspapers carried stories of other burglars who seem to have had a well-trained eye for quality goods. See *Boston Weekly Post-Boy*, 27 March 1738, for the "country woman" who successfully stole goods from a shop where "there were six Men present." For the story of the man who turned a piece of expensive green velvet pulpit cloth into a pair of breeches, see Dell Upton, *Holy Things and Profane: Anglican Parish Churches in Colonial Virginia* (Cambridge, Mass., 1986), 153. Also *Connecticut Courant*, 23–30 June 1772 and 17–24 August 1773.

9. Daniel A. Cohen, *Pillars of Salt, Monuments of Grace: New England Crime Literature and the Origins of American Popular Culture, 1676–1860* (New York, 1992).

10. Jared Eliot, *God's Marvellous Kindness* . . . (New London, Conn., 1745), 5. The sermon gave thanks for the victory of Anglo-American forces over the French at Louisbourg.

11. [Jacob Duché], *Observations on a Variety of Subjects* . . . (Philadelphia, 1774), 3–4.

12. Lynn Glaser, *Engraved America: Iconography of America Through 1800* (Philadelphia, 1970), 56.

13. On the changing eighteenth-century skylines, see Jon Butler, *Awash in a Sea of Faith: Christianizing the American People* (Cambridge, Mass., 1990), 107–16.

14. See Patricia A. Cleary, " 'She Merchants' of Colonial America: Women and Commerce on the Eve of the Revolution" (Ph.D. diss., Northwestern University, 1989), as well as her *Elizabeth Murray: A Woman's Pursuit of Independence in Eighteenth-Century America* (Amherst, Mass., 2000).

15. Richard L. Bushman, "Shopping and Advertising in Colonial America," in *Of Consuming Interests: The Style of Life in the Eighteenth Century*, ed. Cary Carson, Ronald Hoffman, and Peter J. Albert (Charlottesville, Va., 1994), 239–46. Historian Bruce H. Mann claims, on the basis of an analysis of legal documents, that "[a]s trade expanded [in colonial Connecticut], so did the ranks of the merchants, whose numbers by mid-century were increasing both absolutely and relative to other occupational groups." *Neighbors and Strangers: Law and Community in Early Connecticut* (Chapel Hill, N.C., 1987), 126.

16. See R. C. Nash, "The Organization of Trade and Finance in the British-Atlantic Economy, 1600–1830," paper presented at a conference on North Atlantic Economic History held by the Institute for Early American History and Culture, Charleston, S.C., October 1999. Also see Thomas M. Doerflinger, *A Vigorous Spirit of Enterprise: Merchants and Economic Development in Revolutionary Philadelphia* (Chapel Hill, N.C., 1986), 90–93.

17. A good account of the structure of the British export market can be found in Kenneth Morgan, "Business Networks in the British Export Trade to North America, 1750–1800," in *The Early Modern Atlantic Economy*, ed. John J.McCusker and Kenneth Morgan (Cambridge, 2000), 36–64.

18. Cited in Philip L. White, *The Beekmans of New York in Politics and Commerce, 1647–1877* (New York, 1956), 387.

19. Ibid., 372–73.

20. Ibid., 370.

21. A valuable account of merchant practices can be found in Doerflinger, *A Vigorous Spirit of Enterprise*, esp. 86–88. Also see Harry D. Berg, "The Organization of Business in Colonial Philadelphia," *Pennsylvania History* 10 (1943), 157–77; and James Blaine Hedges, *The Browns of Providence Plantations*, 2 vols. (Providence, R.I., 1968), I.

22. Cited in White, *The Beekmans*, 381. See W. T. Baxter, *The House of Hancock; Business in Boston, 1724–1775* (New York, 1965).

23. This theme is developed in T. H. Breen, *Tobacco Culture: The Mentality of the Great Tidewater Planters on the Eve of Revolution* (Princeton, N.J., 1985).

24. Cited in John W. Tyler, *Smugglers and Patriots: Boston Merchants and the Advent of the American Revolution* (Boston, 1986), 113. Also see Marc Egnal and Joseph A. Ernst, "An Economic Interpretation of the American Revolution," *William and Mary Quarterly*, 3d ser., 29 (1972), 15–16.

25. John Hancock to Harrison, Barnard & Spragg, 16 October 1767, in the Hancock Papers (JH-6), Baker Library, Harvard University School of Business, Cambridge, Mass.

26. Berg, "The Organization of Business," 172–73.

27. John J. McCusker and Russell R. Menard, *The Economy of British America, 1607–1789* (Chapel Hill, N.C., 1985), 71–88.

28. William Eddis, *Letters from America*, ed. Aubrey C. Land (Cambridge, Mass., 1969), 51–52.

29. Cited in Christopher P. Bickford, *Farmington in Connecticut* (Canaan, N.H., 1982), 148.

30. Madam Knight, "Journal," in *Narratives of Colonial America, 1704–1765*, ed. Howard H. Peckham (Chicago, 1971), 31.

31. *The Journal of Nicholas Cresswell, 1774–1777* (New York, 1924), 17.

32. Bickford, *Farmington in Connecticut*, 141–44.

33. Robert D. Mitchell, *Commercialism and Frontier: Perspectives on the Early Shenandoah Valley* (Charlottesville, Va., 1977), 154–59. For a full discussion of British retailing practices during this period, see Hoh-cheung Mui and Lorna H. Mui, *Shops and Shopkeeping in Eighteenth-Century England* (Kingston, Ont., 1989).

34. Cited in Baxter, *House of Hancock*, 188. See also White, *The Beekmans*.
35. Thomas Hancock to Mr. John Rowe, 13 June 1737, in Thomas Hancock Letterbook [TH-3], Baker Library, Harvard University School of Business, Cambridge, Mass.
36. Cited in Kenneth Wiggins Porter, *The Jacksons and the Lees: Two Generations of Massachusetts Merchants, 1765–1844*, 2 vols. (Cambridge, Mass., 1937), I, 179.
37. Glenn Weaver, *Jonathan Trumbull, Connecticut's Merchant Magistrate, 1710–1785* (Hartford, Conn., 1956), 32–40; and Hedges, *The Browns of Providence Plantations*, I, ch. 3.
38. Cited in T. H. Breen, *Imagining the Past: East Hampton Histories* (Athens, Ga., 1996), 150.
39. Knight, "Journal," 31–32. On the shortage of currency see Curtis Nettels, *The Money Supply of the American Colonies Before 1720* (Madison, Wisc., 1934).
40. These changes are documented in James Hoffman Lewis, "Farmers, Craftsmen, and Merchants: Changing Economic Organization in Massachusetts, 1730 to 1775" (Ph.D. diss., Northwestern University, 1984).
41. Quoted in Margaret E. Martin, *Merchants and Trade of the Connecticut River Valley, 1750–1820*, vol. 24 of *Smith College Studies in History* (Northampton, Mass., 1939), 19.
42. Breen, *Imagining the Past*, 154–55; Bickford, *Farmington in Connecticut*, 144; and Richard I. Melvoin, *New England Outpost: War and Society in Colonial Deerfield* (New York, 1989), 280.
43. The best account of these turbulent years is Edmund S. Morgan, *American Slavery, American Freedom: The Ordeal of Colonial Virginia* (New York, 1975).
44. Among the most valuable titles are Philip D. Morgan, *Slave Counterpoint: Black Culture in the Eighteenth-Century Chesapeake and Lowcountry* (Chapel Hill, N.C., 1998); Gloria L. Main, *Tobacco Colony: Life in Early Maryland, 1650–1720* (Princeton, N.J., 1982); Allan Kulikoff, *Tobacco and Slaves: The Development of Southern Cultures in the Chesapeake, 1680–1800* (Chapel Hill, N.C., 1986).
45. The classic study of the eighteenth-century tobacco trade is Jacob M. Price, *Capital and Credit in British Overseas Trade: The View from the Chesapeake, 1700–1776* (Cambridge, Mass., 1980). Also see T. M. Devine, *The Tobacco Lords: A Study of the Tobacco Merchants of Glasgow and Their Trading Activities, c. 1740–90* (Edinburgh, 1975).
46. Devine, *Tobacco Lords*. Also helpful is T. M. Devine, *The Scottish Nation: A History, 1700–2000* (New York, 1999), 24–26, 52–59, 120–22.
47. Paul G. E. Clemens, *The Atlantic Economy and Colonial Maryland's Eastern Shore: From Tobacco to Grain* (Ithaca, N.Y., 1980), 82–97.
48. Lois Green Carr and Lorena S. Walsh, "Inventories and the Analysis of Wealth and Consumption Patterns in St. Mary's County, Maryland, 1658–1777," *Historical Methods Newsletter* 13 (1980), 96.
49. See Nash, "The Organization of Trade and Finance."
50. Breen, *Tobacco Culture*.
51. Charles Carter to Charles Gore, 10 August 1764, cited in Charles Royster, *The Fabulous History of the Dismal Swamp Company: A Story of George Washington's Times* (New York, 1999), 62. See also Harry Roy Merrens, *Colonial North Carolina in the Eighteenth Century: A Study in Historical Geography* (Chapel Hill, N.C., 1964), 168–69.
52. Francis Jerdone to Neil Buchanan, 4 August 1743, cited in Lois Green Carr and Lorena S. Walsh, "Changing Lifestyles and Consumer Behavior in the Colonial Chesapeake," in Carson et al., eds., *Of Consuming Interests*, 108.
53. Jerdone to Messrs. Buchanan and Wilson, 7 May 1739, ibid.
54. Carr and Walsh, "Inventories and the Analysis of Wealth," 96; Marc Egnal and Joseph Ernst, "An Economic Interpretation of the American Revolution," *William and Mary Quarterly*, 3d ser., 29 (1972), 25–27.
55. John Mair, *Book-Keeping Modernized . . .* , 6th ed. (Edinburgh, 1793), 497.
56. James Robinson to Bennet Price, 7 October 1767, in T. M. Devine, ed., *A Scottish Firm in Virginia 1767–1777: W. Cuninghame and Co.*, Scottish History Society *Publications*, 4th ser., 20 (1984), 1–2, 12.
57. Robinson to John Turner, 22 April 1769, ibid., 12.
58. Edward C. Papenfuse, *In Pursuit of Profit: The Annapolis Merchants in the Era of the American Revolution, 1763–1805* (Baltimore, 1975), 15–17, 52–57; Clemens, *The Atlantic Economy and Maryland's Eastern Shore*, 88–96.
59. Jacob M. Price, "Buchanan & Simson, 1759–1763: A Different Kind of Glasgow Firm Trading to the Chesapeake," *William and Mary Quarterly*, 3d ser., 40 (1983), 3–41.

60. Nash, "Organization of Trade and Finance," 5–7; Rachel N. Klein, *Unification of a Slave State: The Rise of the Planter Class in the South Carolina Backcountry, 1760–1808* (Chapel Hill, N.C., 1990), 30.

61. Walter B. Edgar, ed., *The Letterbook of Robert Pringle*, 2 vols. (Columbia, S.C., 1972), I, 30–31, 56, 224, 249.

62. Tryon to the Board of Trade, 30 January 1767, in *The Correspondence of William Tryon and Other Selected Papers*, ed. William S. Powell (Raleigh, N.C., 1980–81), I, 410. See also Merrens, *Colonial North Carolina*, 168–69.

63. Daniel B. Thorp, "Doing Business in the Backcountry: Retail Trade in Colonial Rowan County, North Carolina," *William and Mary Quarterly*, 3d ser., 48 (1991), 387–408.

64. See Arthur L. Jensen, *The Maritime Commerce of Colonial Philadelphia* (Madison, Wisc., 1963), 70–71; James Floyd Shepherd and Samuel H. Williamson, "The Coastal Trade of the British North American Colonies, 1768–1772," *Journal of Economic History* 32 (1972), 783–810.

65. Edgar, ed., *Letterbook of Robert Pringle*, I, 392; II, 567–68. Also Baxter, *House of Hancock*, 189.

66. Baxter, *House of Hancock*, 189.

67. Allan MacLean, Account Book 1741–6, Merchant Hartford, Connecticut Historical Society, Hartford, Connecticut. Almost every colonial archive has a few records of this sort. Others that I examined were Mss. Samuel Grant, Account Book, 1737–1760, Folio vols. G, American Antiquarian Society, Worcester, Massachusetts; and Gay Fisher, Account Book 1768–1774, Connecticut Historical Society.

68. Doerflinger, *Vigorous Spirit of Enterprise*, 92–93.

69. Cited in Carl Bridenbaugh, *Cities in Revolt: Urban Life in America, 1743–1776* (New York, 1964), 275.

70. *Boston Evening-Post*, 21 August 1749.

71. *South-Carolina Gazette*, 2 September 1732.

72. Knight, "Journal," 31–33.

73. Cited in Carr and Walsh, "Changing Lifestyles and Consumer Behavior," 110.

74. Thomas Clifford to Abel Chapman, 25 July 1767, cited in Anne Bezanson, Robert D. Gray, and Miriam Hussey, *Prices in Colonial Pennsylvania* (Philadelphia, 1935), 263. Also Baxter, *House of Hancock*, 185–87.

75. Edgar, ed., *Letterbook of Robert Pringle*, I, 30.

76. Doerflinger, *Vigorous Spirit*, 92–93.

77. "Letters from Letter-Book of Richard Hockley, 1739–1742," *Pennsylvania Magazine of History and Biography* 28 (1904), 31.

78. Carr and Walsh, "Changing Lifestyles and Consumer Behavior," 110. Also see Richard L. Bushman, "Shopping and Advertising in Colonial America," 233–51; Jean B. Lee, *Price of Nationhood: The American Revolution in Charles County* (New York, 1994), 32–42; and T. H. Breen, "An Empire of Goods: The Anglicization of Colonial America, 1690–1776," *Journal of British Studies* 25 (1986), 467–99.

79. Cited in Jensen, *Maritime Commerce*, 103.

80. Cited in Ann Smart Martin, "The Role of Pewter as Missing Artifact: Consumer Attitudes Toward Tablewares in Late 18th-Century Virginia," *Historical Archaeology* 23 (1989), 6.

81. Edgar, ed., *Letterbook of Robert Pringle*, I, 392.

82. Thomas Hancock to Edward Cradock, 20 December 1736, TH-3.

83. Cited in Berg, "Organization of Business," 170.

84. Hancock to John Cooper, 27 September 1736, TH-3.

85. Cited in S. Botein, "The Anglo-American Book Trade Before 1776," in *Printing and Society in Early America*, ed. William L. Joyce (Worcester, Mass., 1983), 75.

86. Henry Callister to Foster Cunliffe, 2 October 1750, cited in Carr and Walsh, "Changing Lifestyles and Consumer Behavior," 108–9.

87. David Barclay and Sons to Mary Alexander, 10 July 1759, cited in Cleary, "'She Merchants' of Colonial America," 234.

88. Cited in Berg, "Organization of Business," 171. Also see Kenneth Morgan, "Business Networks," 46–50.

89. Cited in Porter, *The Jacksons and the Lees*, I, 181.

90. Hancock to John Rowe, 13 June 1737, TH-3.

91. Joshua Johnson of Maryland proposed that his agents circulate "patent cards" among storekeepers operating in the western parts of the colony. He seems to have anticipated what we

know as the catalogue store. Jacob M. Price, ed., *Joshua Johnson's Letter Book, 1771–1774: Letters from a Merchant in London to His Partners in Maryland,* London Record Society *Publications* 15 (1979), 37.

92. On the rapid changes in product design, see John Styles, "Product Innovation in Early Modern London," *Past and Present*, no. 168 (2000), 124–69.
93. Cited in White, *The Beekmans*, 455.
94. See Chapter 2 for a discussion of how mid-eighteenth-century advertising provides evidence for the development of a radically new consumer marketplace.
95. *South-Carolina Gazette*, 29 October 1753. Also see Robert Magnum Barrow, "Newspaper Advertising in Colonial America, 1704–1775," (Ph.D. diss., University of Virginia, 1967).
96. *South-Carolina Gazette*, 12 February 1753.
97. Joseph and Daniel Waldo, *Imported from London & Sold by Wholesale or Retail at the Cheapest Rates . . .* (Boston, 1749).
98. John Appleton, *Imported in the Last Ships from London . . .* (Salem, Mass., 1773).
99. Peter Mathias, "Risk, Credit, and Kinship in Early Modern Enterprise," in McCusker and Morgan, eds., *Early Modern Atlantic Economy*, 15–35. Although it deals with an earlier period, Craig Muldrew's *The Economy of Obligation: The Culture of Credit and Social Relations in Early Modern England* (London, 1998) challenges historians of eighteenth-century America to pay closer attention to the social and cultural role of credit.
100. [Anonymous], *The Ill Policy and Inhumanity of Imprisoning Insolvent Debtors* (Newport, R.I., 1754), 11.
101. Doerflinger, *Vigorous Spirit of Enterprise*, 90–92; Carole Shammas, *The Pre-Industrial Consumer in England and America* (Oxford, 1990), 269; White, *The Beekmans*, 394; Mann, *Neighbors and Strangers*, 5–62; Wilbur C. Plummer, "Consumer Credit in Colonial Philadelphia," *Pennsylvania Magazine of History and Biography* 66 (1942), 390–94; and Gregory H. Nobles, *Divisions Throughout the Whole: Politics and Society in Hampshire County, Massachusetts, 1740–1775* (Cambridge, 1983), 120–22.
102. *Boston Evening-Post*, 26 June 1738. Also *New-England Weekly Journal*, 1 May 1739.
103. *Postscript, to a Discourse Concerning the Currencies of the British Plantations in America,* republished in *Colonial Currency Reprints, 1682–1741, with an Introduction and Notes,* ed. Andrew McFarland Davis, 4 vols. (New York, 1964), IV, 53–54.
104. See John Brewer, "Commercialization and Politics," in Neil McKendrick, John Brewer, and J. H. Plumb, eds., *The Birth of a Consumer Society: The Commercialization of Eighteenth-Century England* (Bloomington, Ind., 1982), 208–16.
105. *South-Carolina Gazette*, 29 January 1732.
106. [Anonymous], *Ill Policy of Imprisoning Debtors*, 11.
107. [Benjamin Franklin], *Advice to a Young Tradesman* (Boston, 1762), 1–4. Also, "Rules Proper to Be Observed in Trade," *Pennsylvania Gazette*, 20 February 1750.
108. *New-York Weekly Journal*, 12 July 1736, reprinted from *South-Carolina Gazette*.
109. *Boston Evening-Post*, 16 March 1752.
110. Ibid., 1 September 1746.
111. Ibid., 6 April 1741.
112. *New-London Gazette*, 10 February 1769.
113. Ezra Gleason, *The Massachusetts Calendar, or, Wonderful Almanack for . . . 1773* (Boston, 1772), 4–5.
114. Samuel Johnson, *A Journey to the Western Islands of Scotland,* ed. Mary Lascelles (New Haven, Conn., 1971), 130.
115. Marc Egnal and Joseph A. Ernst, "An Economic Interpretation of the American Revolution," *William and Mary Quarterly*, 3d ser., 29 (1972), 15–16.
116. Knight, "Journal," 37.
117. Edgar, ed., *Letterbook of Robert Pringle*, II, 645.
118. Bridenbaugh, *Cities in Revolt*, 276.
119. *New-England Weekly Journal*, 6 December 1737.
120. *Pennsylvania Chronicle, and Universal Advertiser*, 17 February 1772.
121. [Anonymous], *A Few Reasons in Favour of Vendues* (Philadelphia, 1772).
122. Moore to the earl of Hillsborough, 26 May 1769, in *Documents Relative to the Colonial History of the State of New-York . . .* , ed. E. B. O'Callaghan, 15 vols. (Albany, N.Y., 1853–87), VIII, 167.

123. *Pennsylvania Chronicle, and Universal Advertiser*, 17 February 1772.

124. [Benjamin Franklin], *Father Abraham's Speech* . . . (Boston, 1758), 10–11, 13–14, 16.

125. Thomas Gage to Lord Barrington, 7 October 1769, in *The Correspondence of General Thomas Gage* . . . , ed. Clarence Edwin Carter, 2 vols. (New Haven, Conn., 1931), II, 527.

126. Carl Bridenbaugh, ed., *Gentleman's Progress: The Itinerarium of Dr. Alexander Hamilton, 1744* (Chapel Hill, N.C., 1948), 104, 150.

127. Darrett B. Rutman and Anita H. Rutman, *A Place in Time: Middlesex County, Virginia, 1650–1750*, 2 vols. (New York, 1984), I, 231; Merrens, *Colonial North Carolina*, 168–69; and Robert D. Mitchell, *Commercialism and Frontier*, 153–54.

128. Martin, *Merchants and Trade of the Connecticut River Valley*, 139.

129. H. R. McIlwaine, ed., *Journals of the House of Burgesses of Virginia, 1758–61* (Richmond, Va., 1908), 92, 189.

130. Peter Force, ed., *American Archives* . . . , 4th ser., 6 vols. (Washington, D.C., 1837–53), I, 1105.

131. William S. Sachs, "The Business Outlook in the Northern Colonies, 1750–1775" (Ph.D. diss., Columbia University, 1957), 249–50. A sample of these kinds of regulations can be found in *Acts and Resolves, Public and Private of the Province of the Massachusetts Bay* . . . , 21 vols. (Boston, 1869–1922) I, 720–21; II, 47, 232–33, 386.

132. Cited in William Nelson, ed., *Documents Relating to the Colonial History of the State of New Jersey* . . . , New Jersey *Archives*, 1st ser., 12 (1895), 677–78.

133. Quoted in Ellen D. Larned, *History of Windham County, Connecticut*, 2 vols. (Worcester, Mass., 1880), II, 119.

134. Bridenbaugh, ed., *Itinerarium of Dr. Alexander Hamilton*, 95, 160.

135. *Boston Weekly Post-Boy*, 26 February 1739.

136. Jonathan Trumbull Sr. Papers I (1653–1759), Connecticut Historical Society, Hartford, Conn. Also Jackson Turner Main, *Society and Economy in Colonial Connecticut* (Princeton, N.J., 1985), 280; and Richard Bushman, *From Puritan to Yankee: Character and Social Order in Connecticut, 1690–1765* (New York, 1967), 113.

137. White, *The Beekmans*, I, 356–57, 392–93.

138. Neal W. Allen Jr., ed., *Province and Court Records of Maine*, 6 vols. (Portland, Me., 1928–75), VI, 72–76.

Chapter 5

1. [Anonymous], *News from the Moon. Containing a Brief Account of the Manners and Customs of the Inhabitants: Very Suitable to the Present Times* (Boston, 1772), 1–15. There has been some ambiguity concerning the authorship of this pamphlet, and it should not be confused with an earlier work of a similar title, which was published in Boston in 1721. That piece, which ridiculed the prosecution of libel, was copied from Daniel Defoe's "A Review of the State of the *British Nation*," a serial publication in England. Some bibliographers, therefore, have entertained suspicions that this anonymous pamphlet might have also been a reprint of some Defoe material. While the author certainly drew inspiration from Defoe's style of satire, and imitated his use of the moon as a lunar setting for his critiques, the weight of evidence strongly suggests that Defoe was not in fact the author. There are no similar passages in either his popular work, *The Consolidator; or, Memoirs of Sundry Transactions from the World in the Moon, Translated from the Lunar Language* (London, 1705), or the various editions of "A Review of the State of the *British Nation*." There is also evidence from within the text itself that would seem to cast doubt upon Defoe's authorship. In a time of rapid change, new terms and vocabularies were emerging to describe the expanding consumer world. Words like "Jockey-cap," which the author employed to describe the new fashions he witnessed on the moon, were not even coined until mid-century, well after Defoe's death (J. A. Simpson and E.S.C. Weiner, eds., *Oxford English Dictionary*, 2d ed., 20 vols. [Oxford, 1989], VIII, 252). The thrust of the entire satire, moreover, would seem somewhat strange for Defoe, who always used the lunar world to criticize the political sphere, and who generally celebrated the new consumer world just beginning to emerge in his day. See Sandra Sherman, *Finance and Fictionality in the Early Eighteenth Century: Accounting for Defoe* (Cambridge, 1986).

2. Wallace Stevens, "Esthétique du Mal," in *Collected Poems* (New York, 1954), 320.

3. *New London Gazette*, 1 February 1771.

4. On the relevance of this particular debate for the study of eighteenth-century material culture, see John E. Crowley's provocative *Invention of Comfort: Sensibilities and Design in Early Modern Britain and Early America* (Baltimore, 2001).

5. Francis Hutcheson, *Reflections upon Laughter, and Remarks upon the Fable of the Bees* (Glasgow, 1750), 44, 49.

6. Richard Rolt, *New Dictionary of Trade and Commerce . . .* (London, 1756). This volume has no pagination. The quotations can be found under the heading "Fashion." On the importance of product innovation see John Styles, "Product Innovation in Early Modern London," *Past and Present*, no. 168 (2000), 124–69. Also see Neil McKendrick's essays on Wedgwood and other innovators in the marketplace in Neil McKendrick, John Brewer, and J. H. Plumb, *The Birth of a Consumer Society: The Commercialization of Eighteenth-Century England* (Bloomington, Ind., 1982), 100–94.

7. [John Brown], *An Estimate of the Manners and Principles of the Times . . .* , 5th ed. (London, 1757), 117–18, 125.

8. *Pennsylvania Chronicle*, 9 November 1767.

9. *Boston Weekly News-Letter*, 19 July 1750; continued 26 July 1750.

10. *The Commercial Conduct of the Province of New-York Considered, and the True Interest of that Colony Attempted to be Shewn . . .* (New York, 1767), 7.

11. *Massachusetts Gazette and Boston News-Letter*, 19 July 1767.

12. Cited in E. W. Gilboy, "Demand as a Factor in the Industrial Revolution," in *The Causes of the Industrial Revolution in England*, ed. R. M. Hartwell (London, 1967), 128.

13. Nathaniel Potter, *A Discourse on Jeremiah 8th, 20th* (Boston, 1758), 13. Potter is here quoting from an unnamed source.

14. Benjamin Franklin, *Autobiography*, intro. by Lewis Leary (New York, 1962), 80.

15. Benjamin Franklin to Deborah Franklin, 19 February 1758, in *The Papers of Benjamin Franklin*, ed. Leonard W. Labaree, 35 vols. (New Haven, Conn., 1959–), VII, 381–83.

16. Daniel Vickers, "Competency and Competition: Economic Culture in Early America," *William and Mary Quarterly*, 3d ser., 47 (1990), 3–29.

17. *Independent Advertiser*, 20 March 1749.

18. Stephen Foster, *Their Solitary Way: The Puritan Social Ethic in the First Century of Settlement in New England* (New Haven, Conn., 1971), and Perry Miller, "Religion and Society in the Early Literature of Virginia," in his *Errand into the Wilderness* (Cambridge, Mass., 1956), 99–140.

19. Roy Porter, *Enlightenment: Britain and the Creation of the Modern World* (London, 2000).

20. J. E. Crowley, *This Sheba, Self: The Conceptualization of Economic Life in Eighteenth-Century America* (Baltimore, 1974), 4. Also see Albert O. Hirschman, *Shifting Involvements: Private Interest and Public Action* (Princeton, N.J., 1982), 57.

21. The problem of how to sort people out in a fluid, open society also affected the structure of the churches. As the historian William McLoughlin explained, "Social boundaries were still in theory strict and definable, yet every time it became necessary to 'dignify the pews' by assigning seats around the pulpit proportionate in distance to the social and economic prestige of each parishioner, it became increasingly difficult to discern the lines of difference. Men born as bond servants or the sons of bondservants, rose in wealth to equal that of the oldest families and most respected leaders." "Such rapid fluctuations in society," he revealed, meant "that it was increasingly difficult to discover what God (who controlled it all) intended." *New England Dissent, 1630–1833: The Baptists and the Separation of Church and State*, 2 vols. (Cambridge, Mass., 1971), I, 334.

22. *Boston Gazette*, 7 January 1765.

23. Although this essay originally appeared in the *Gazetteer and London Daily Advertiser*, the Boston editor reprinted the piece with his "blessing." *Boston Evening-Post*, 6 January 1755.

24. *Connecticut Courant*, 10 June 1765.

25. *Boston Gazette*, 10 January 1763. The parallels between this debate and the one that swirled around the new evangelical religion are striking. See Timothy Hall, *Contested Boundaries: Itinerancy and the Reshaping of the Colonial American Religious World* (Durham, N.C., 1994).

26. William Tennent, *An Address, Occasioned by the Late Invasion of the Liberties of the American Colonies by the British Parliament* (Philadelphia, 1774), 13–16.

27. [William Douglass], *A Discourse Concerning the Currencies of the British Plantations in America* . . . (Boston, 1740), 29.

28. *Pennsylvania Packet*, 9 November 1772.

29. See Chapter 2.

30. Philopatria [Thomas Paine], *A Discourse, Shewing That the Real First Cause* . . . (Boston, 1721), cited in Margaret Ellen Newell, *From Dependency to Independence: Economic Revolution in Colonial New England* (Ithaca, N.Y., 1998), 147.

31. *Boston Evening-Post*, 16 March 1752. On the theme of clothes and status, see the anonymous pamphlet *The Miraculous Power of Clothes, and Dignity of the Taylors: Being an Essay on the Words, Clothes Make Men* (Philadelphia, 1772); and Jonathan Mayhew's advice to the young people of Boston on how to dress in *Christian Sobriety* . . . *Preached with a Special View to the Benefit of the Young Men* . . . (Boston, 1763), 150–55.

32. The statistics for the importation of mirrors are derived from *Customs 3: Ledgers of Imports and Exports, 1696–1780* (East Ardsley, Wakefield, Yorkshire, 1974), microfilm. See also Benjamin Goldberg, *The Mirror and Man* (Charlottesville, Va., 1985).

33. *Journal and Letters of Philip Vickers Fithian, 1773–1774: A Plantation Tutor of the Old Dominion*, ed. Hunter Dickinson Farish, 2d ed. (Williamsburg, Va., 1957), 29, 130–31.

34. Peter Collinson to John Bartram, 17 February 1737, quoted in T. H. Breen, *Puritans and Adventurers: Change and Persistence in Early America* (New York, 1980), 153–54.

35. Cited in Bernard Bailyn, "Voyagers in Flight: A Sketchbook of Runaway Servants, 1774–1775," in his *Voyagers to the West: A Passage in the Peopling of America on the Eve of the Revolution* (New York, 1986), ch. 10.

36. Gary Zaboly, "Descriptions of Military Uniforms and Equipage in North America, 1755–1764, Part I," *Military Collector and Historian* 39 (1987), 8.

37. Chris Bayly, "The Origins of *Swadeshi*: Cloth and Indian Society, 1700–1930," in *The Social Life of Things: Commodities in Cultural Perspective*, ed. Arjun Appadurai (Cambridge, 1986), 303–11.

38. The quotation is from Edgar P. Richardson, *American Paintings and Related Pictures in the Henry Francis du Pont Winterthur Museum* (Charlottesville, Va., 1986), 30. Also see George C. Groce, "John Wollaston (Fl. 1736–1767): A Cosmopolitan Painter in the British Colonies," *Art Quarterly* 15 (1952), 133–48; and Wayne Craven, "John Wollaston's Career in England and New York City," *American Art Journal* 7, no. 2 (1975), 19–31. The argument about the cultural significance of cloth for early American painting is more fully developed in T. H. Breen, "The Meaning of 'Likeness': Portrait-Painting in an Eighteenth-Century Consumer Society," in *The Portrait in Eighteenth-Century America*, ed. Ellen G. Miles (Newark, Del., 1993), 37–60.

39. The widespread fear of accepting a counterfeit object or a confidence man as the real thing is explored in T. H. Breen and Timothy Hall, "Structuring Provincial Imagination: The Rhetoric and Experience of Social Change in Eighteenth-Century New England," *American Historical Review* 103 (1998), 1411–39. A striking example of the fear of being fooled by upwardly mobile "sons and daughters of inferior mechanics" can be found in *New-Hampshire Gazette*, 11 November 1763.

40. Cited in Karin Calvert, "The Function of Fashion in Eighteenth-Century America," in *Of Consuming Interests: The Style of Life in the Eighteenth Century*, ed. Cary Carson, Ronald Hoffman, and Peter J. Albert (Charlottesville, Va., 1994), 232.

41. Carl Bridenbaugh, ed., *Gentleman's Progress: The Itinerarium of Dr. Alexander Hamilton, 1744* (Chapel Hill, N.C., 1948), 13–14.

42. [Benjamin Franklin], *Father Abraham's Speech* . . . (Boston, 1758), 13–14.

43. The quotations from South Carolina and Virginia come from Shane White and Graham White, "Slave Clothing and African-American Culture in the Eighteenth and Nineteenth Centuries," *Past and Present*, no. 148 (1995), 154–55, 159–61.

44. *Maryland Gazette*, 18 October 1770.

45. [Anonymous], *A Proposal to Supply the Trade with a Medium of Exchange* . . . (Boston, 1737), x. Also, *Boston Evening-Post*, 25 August 1746.

46. *Independent Reflector*, 14 June 1753.

47. *New-York Journal; or, General Advertiser*, 1 June 1769, reprinted from *Virginia Gazette*.

48. Two books that imaginatively develop this comparative perspective on empire are Linda Colley, *Captives: The Story of Britain's Pursuit of Empire and How Its Soldiers and Civilians*

Were Held Captive by the Dream of Global Supremacy, 1600–1850 (New York, 2002); and Kathleen Wilson, *The Island Race: Englishness, Empire, and Gender in the Eighteenth Century* (London, 2003).

49. *Pennsylvania Chronicle*, 6–13 January 1772. For more on the character of advertising during this period, see Chapter 2.

50. For an early discussion of the concept of Anglicization, see John M. Murrin, "The Legal Transformation: The Bench and Bar of Eighteenth-Century Massachusetts," in *Colonial America: Essays in Politics and Social Development*, ed. Stanley N. Katz (Boston, 1976), 415–49. Also see T. H. Breen, "Ideology and Nationalism on the Eve of the American Revolution: Revisions *Once* More in Need of Revising," *Journal of American History* 84 (1997), 13–40. The widespread cultural ambivalence of the period is stressed in Jack P. Greene, "Search for Identity: An Interpretation of the Meaning of Selected Patterns of Social Response in Eighteenth-Century America," in his *Imperatives, Behaviors, and Identities: Essays in Early American Cultural History* (Charlottesville, Va., 1992), 143–73. The American "ensavagement" that Bernard Bailyn highlights in his *Voyagers to the West* appears to have receded by the eighteenth century, when colonists like William Byrd II inhabited a cultural world that was assertively English and cosmopolitan. See Kenneth A. Lockridge, *The Diary and Life of William Byrd II of Virginia, 1674–1744* (Chapel Hill, N.C., 1987).

51. Elise Pinckney, ed., *The Letterbook of Eliza Lucas Pinckney, 1739–1762* (Chapel Hill, N.C., 1972), 175, 180–81.

52. David S. Shields, *Civil Tongues and Polite Letters in British America* (Chapel Hill, N.C., 1997); and Jay Fliegelman, *Prodigals and Pilgrims: The American Revolution Against Patriarchal Authority, 1750–1800* (Cambridge, 1982).

53. *Connecticut Courant*, 29 October 1764.

54. "To the Printer of the London Chronicle, 9 May 1759," in Labaree, ed., *Papers of Benjamin Franklin*, VIII, 342.

55. Stephen Botein, "The Anglo-American Book Trade Before 1776: Personnel and Strategies," in *Printing and Society in Early America*, ed. William L. Joyce et al. (Worcester, Mass., 1983), 79.

56. See Chapter 2.

57. Bayly, "Origins of *Swadeshi*," 303–11. See also Nicholas Phillipson, "Politics, Politeness, and the Anglicisation of Early Eighteenth-Century Scottish Culture," in *Scotland and England, 1286–1815*, ed. R. A. Mason (Edinburgh, 1987), 226–46; and Bernard S. Cohn, "Cloth, Clothes, and Colonialism: India in the 19th Century," paper presented at Wenner-Gren Foundation symposium, 1983.

58. *Boston Gazette*, 9 November 1767.

59. The symbolic importance of color is explored in T. H. Breen, "Discovering Color: Reconstructing a New Visual Landscape in the Age of Washington" lecture at the John Carter Brown Library, Providence, R.I., 13 April 2000.

60. Frank S. Welsh, "The Early American Palette: Colonial Paint Colors Revealed," Thomas H. Taylor Jr. and Nicholas A. Pappas, "Colonial Williamsburg Colors: A Changing Spectrum," and Matthew J. Mosca, "Paint Decoration at Mount Vernon: The Revival of Eighteenth-Century Techniques," in *Paint in America: The Colors of Historic Buildings*, ed. Roger W. Moss (New York, 1994), 68–85, 87–103, 105–27.

61. *Diary and Autobiography of John Adams*, ed. L. H. Butterfield, 4 vols. (New York, 1964), I, 294.

62. John Fanning Watson, *Annals of Philadelphia and Pennsylvania, in the Olden Times*, 2 vols. (Philadelphia, 1856–57), I, 205.

63. George Washington to Robert Cary & Co., 28 September 1760, in *The Writings of George Washington*, ed. John C. Fitzpatrick, 39 vols. (Washington, D.C., 1931–44), II, 350. According to one historian, Washington ordered "fine china and silver, fashionable clothing, furniture, books, decorative porcelains, statuary, and paintings. . . . The latest London fashions appeared at Mount Vernon within months of their introduction on the London market." Bruce A. Ragsdale, "George Washington, the British Tobacco Trade, and Economic Opportunity in Pre-Revolutionary Virginia," *Virginia Magazine of History and Biography* 97 (1989), 143.

64. William Smith, *The History of the Late Province of New-York . . .* , New-York Historical Society *Collections*, vol. 4, pt. 2 (1829), 277.

65. [Ann Hulton], *Letters of a Loyalist Lady* (Cambridge, Mass., 1927), 45.

66. Cited in Esther Singleton, *Social New York Under the Georges, 1714–1776* (New York, 1902), 380–81.

67. Ibid., 375.

68. Smith, *History of New-York*, 281.

69. Cited in Rodris Roth, *Tea Drinking in Eighteenth-Century America: Its Etiquette and Equipage* (Washington, D.C., 1963), 66.

70. Billy G. Smith, "The Material Lives of Laboring Philadelphians, 1750 to 1800," *William and Mary Quarterly*, 3d ser., 38 (1981), 168–70.

71. A wonderfully humorous example of this phenomenon can be found in H. A. Powell, "Cricket in Kiriwina," *Listener* 48 (1952), 384–85.

72. William Nelson to Francis Fauquier Jr., 16 August 1768, cited in Graham Hood, *The Governor's Palace in Williamsburg: A Cultural Study* (Williamsburg, Va., 1991), 132.

73. For Burke's views on commerce in the empire, see Chapter 3.

74. [Benjamin Franklin], *The Interest of Great Britain Considered . . .* (Philadelphia, 1760), 27–28.

75. *South-Carolina Gazette*, 15 August 1743. For the kind of over-the-top criticism of women that surged forth during this period, see the many so-called news stories found in the *Boston Evening-Post* for late 1752. These include a report of a jealous woman who cut off the genitals of her philandering husband with a knife. A poem entitled "Advice to a Young Lady Lately Married" (6 November 1752) counseled the woman:

> Be sure you ne'er for Pow'r contend,
> Nor try by Tears to gain your End. . . .
> Heaven gave to Man superiour Sway,
> Then Heaven and him at once obey.

This advice sparked a stinging rebuke from a woman, informing the males of Boston that reform of marriage should begin with the men. "If Honour and Generosity, Tenderness tempered with Resolution, Frugality and Industry, and such other Virtues as dignify Human Nature, and Contribute to the Happiness of Society, could once be brought into *Fashion* among them, I dare say we should hear very few Complaints against Ladies."

76. Ibid., 22 August 1743.

77. Hirschman, *Shifting Involvements*, 50.

78. A fuller examination of the "luxury debate" can be found in John Sekora, *Luxury: The Concept in Western Thought, Eden to Smollett* (Baltimore, 1977); Crowley, *This Sheba, Self*; and Christopher J. Berry, *The Idea of Luxury: A Conceptual and Historical Investigation* (Cambridge, 1994).

79. John Brown, *An Estimate of the Manners and Principles of the Times*, 7th ed. (Boston, 1758), 19.

80. Jonas Clarke, *The Best Art of Dress; or, Early Piety Most Amiable and Ornamental* (Boston, 1762), 7–8.

81. Andrew Eliot, *An Evil and Adulterous Generation* (Boston, 1753), 19.

82. [Anonymous], *Industry & Frugality Proposed As the Surest Means to Make Us a Rich and Flourishing People . . .* (Boston, 1753), 8.

83. *Independent Reflector*, 18 January 1753.

84. *Maryland Gazette*, 9 March 1748. The article originally appeared in the *Boston Gazette*, 19 January 1748.

85. On this policy, see John E. Crowley, *The Privileges of Independence: Neomercantilism and the American Revolution* (Baltimore, 1993).

86. *Independent Advertiser*, 27 February 1749.

87. See Jane Kaminsky, *Governing the Tongue: The Politics of Speech in Early New England* (New York, 1997), ch. 3; and Mary Beth Norton, *Founding Mothers and Fathers: Gendered Power and the Forming of American Society* (New York, 1996).

88. *South-Carolina Gazette; and Country Journal*, 2 November 1773.

89. *Pennsylvania Gazette*, 7 December 1767.

90. *Connecticut Courant*, 10 June 1765.

91. *Maryland Gazette*, 17 February 1747, reprinted from *American Magazine*, November 1746.

92. *Boston Gazette*, 2 June 1755.

93. *Pennsylvania Chronicle*, 17 April 1769 (emphasis added).

94. Brown, *Estimate of the Manners*, 51.

95. Cited in Singleton, *Social New York*, 381. Also see Elizabeth Kowaleski-Wallace, *Consuming Subjects: Women, Shopping, and Business in the Eighteenth Century* (New York, 1997), 19–36.

96. *Boston Evening-Post*, 25 August 1746.

97. Cited in Singleton, *Social New York*, 381.

98. *Boston News-Letter*, 18 February 1762.

99. *New-York Weekly Journal*, 12 July 1736.

100. [John Lovell], *Freedom, the First of Blessings* (Boston, 1754), 1, 3.

101. Roth, *Tea Drinking in 18th-Century America*, 66.

102. *Peter Kalm's Travels in North America*, trans. Adolph B. Benson, 2 vols. (New York, 1937), I, 190, also 346–47. For a broader European perspective on the demand for tea among the working classes, see David Ormrod, "English Re-Exports and the Dutch Staplemarket in the Eighteenth Century," in *Enterprise and History: Essays in Honour of Charles Wilson*, ed. D. C. Coleman and Peter Mathias (Cambridge, 1984), 89–115.

103. *Boston Gazette*, 17 March 1740. The newspaper editor explained to his subscribers that he especially recommended this piece, which he had taken from an unnamed magazine.

104. *Boston Evening-Post*, 6 April 1752.

105. *Boston Gazette*, 21 January 1765.

106. *South-Carolina Gazette*, 20 June 1748. On the republican discourse in eighteenth-century America, see Bernard Bailyn, *The Origins of American Politics* (New York, 1968), 3–58.

107. *Connecticut Courant*, 10 June 1765. Also see [John Barnard], *A Present for an Apprentice; or, A Sure Guide to Gain Both Esteem and Estate . . .* (Boston, 1747), 16.

108. Mayhew, *Christian Sobriety*, 197–99.

109. *Boston Evening-Post*, 14 and 21 March 1743. The best general history of the Great Awakening is Frank Lambert, *Inventing the "Great Awakening"* (Princeton, N.J., 1999).

110. Bridenbaugh, ed., *Gentleman's Progress*, 160–61.

111. *Boston Weekly Post-Boy*, 12 April 1742.

112. *South-Carolina Gazette*, 9 March 1738.

113. Dell Upton, *Holy Things and Profane: Anglican Parish Churches in Colonial Virginia* (Cambridge, Mass., 1986), 229; Cary Carson, "The Consumer Revolution in Colonial British America: Why Demand?" in Carson et al., eds., *Of Consuming Interests*, 504–47; and [Anon.], *Industry & Frugality Proposed*.

114. *Independent Advertiser*, 20 March 1749. Also see Colin Jones, "Bourgeois Revolution Revivified: 1789 and Social Change," in *Rewriting the French Revolution*, ed. Colin Lucas (Oxford, 1991), 88–89.

115. *Boston Gazette*, 10 January 1763; *Virginia Gazette*, 29 December 1752; and Nathaniel Ames, *An Astronomical Diary; or, An Almanack for 1773* (Boston, 1772). Also "Atticus," *Pennsylvania Chronicle*, 7 December 1767.

116. *Maryland Gazette*, 23 December 1746.

117. *Connecticut Journal, and New-Haven Post-Boy*, 16 February 1770.

118. *Independent Advertiser*, 26 June 1749. Also see Albert Hirschman, *The Passions and the Interests: Political Arguments for Capitalism Before Its Triumph* (Princeton, N.J., 1977).

119. Jan de Vries, "Between Purchasing Power and the World of Goods: Understanding the Household Economy in Early Modern Europe," in Carson et al., eds., *Of Consuming Interests*, 85–132; de Vries, "The Industrial Revolution and the Industrious Revolution," *Journal of Economic History* 54 (1994), 249–70. Also Eric Jones, "Agricultural and Economic Growth: Economic Change," in his *Agriculture and Industrial Revolution* (Oxford, 1974), 116–17.

120. Jared Eliot, *The Sixth Essay on Field-Husbandry* (New Haven, Conn., 1759), 12–17. Also see Lois Green Carr and Lorena S. Walsh, "Changing Lifestyles and Consumer Behavior in the Colonial Chesapeake," in Carson et al., eds., *Of Consuming Interests*, 109–11; Laurel Thatcher Ulrich, "Wheels, Looms, and the Gender Division of Labor in Eighteenth-Century New England," *William and Mary Quarterly*, 3d ser., 56 (1998), 16–17; and Kevin M. Sweeney, "From Wilderness to Arcadian Vale: Material Life in the Connecticut River Valley, 1635–1760," in *The Great River: Art and Society of the Connecticut Valley, 1635–1820*, ed. Gerald W. R. Ward and William N. Hosley Jr. (Hartford, Conn., 1985), 23.

121. *Articles of Incorporation of the Society for Encouraging Industry* (Boston, 1754), 1–2.

122. *Boston Evening-Post*, 9 December 1751.

123. *Boston Gazette*, 6 October 1740. See also [William Douglass], *An Essay Concerning Silver and Paper Currencies: More Especially with Regard to the British Colonies in New-England* (Boston,

1738), 12–13; and *Independent Reflector*, 24 May 1753. The best recent account of the currency controversy in Massachusetts is Newell, *From Dependency to Independence*, 181–240.

124. [Hugh Vans], *An Inquiry into the Nature and Uses of Money* (Boston, 1740), 2.

125. *Boston Weekly Post-Boy*, 8 December 1740; also 22 September 1740.

126. *New-England Weekly Journal*, 24 February 1741; also *Boston Evening-Post*, 22 September 1740 and 6 April 1741. There is no fully satisfactory historical account of the "Shop Notes."

127. *Boston Weekly News-Letter*, 20 December 1750; [Anonymous], *A Letter to the Merchant in London* (Boston, 1741), 7; and William Borden, *An Address to the Inhabitants of North Carolina* (1746), reprinted in *Some Eighteenth-Century Tracts Concerning North Carolina*, ed. William K. Boyd (Raleigh, N.C., 1927), 69–73. Breen and Hall explore the pre-revolutionary development of a "liberal self" in "Structuring Provincial Imagination," 1411–38.

128. See Edmund S. Morgan, ed., *Puritan Political Ideas, 1558–1794* (Indianapolis, Ind., 1965), xiii–xlvii; and John Dunn, "The Politics of Locke in England and American in the Eighteenth Century," in *John Locke: Problems and Perspectives, a Collection of New Essays*, ed. John W. Yolton (Cambridge, 1969), 45–80.

129. John J. McCusker, "Comment," *William and Mary Quarterly*, 3d ser., 45 (1988), 170; John Brewer, "Commercialization and Politics," in McKendrick et al., *Birth of a Consumer Society*, 200–206; and Michael Ignatieff, *The Needs of a Stranger* (New York, 1984), 122. Joyce Appleby has traced the development of an American language of liberal "self-interest" in "The Social Origins of American Revolutionary Ideology," in her *Liberalism and Republicanism in the Historical Imagination* (Cambridge, Mass., 1993), 161–87.

130. "Rusticus," *The Good of the Community Impartially Considered, in a Letter to a Merchant in Boston* (Boston, 1754), 5, 12, 18–19. Also [Anonymous], *The Ill Policy and Inhumanity of Imprisoning Insolvent Debtors* (Newport, R.I., 1754), 31; and *Boston Gazette*, 16 July 1754.

131. Jean-Christophe Agnew, "Coming Up for Air: Consumer Culture in Historical Perspective," in *Consumption and the World of Goods*, ed. John Brewer and Roy Porter (London, 1993), 19–39.

Chapter 6

1. The most satisfactory account of these events is Edmund S. Morgan and Helen M. Morgan, *The Stamp Act Crisis: Prologue to Revolution* (Chapel Hill, N.C., 1953), 282, 286–87. The Morgans stress the confusion that Franklin created for both the members of Parliament and many subsequent historians of the American Revolution over the alleged distinction between internal and external taxation.

2. A study that captures the complexities of Franklin's character is Edmund S. Morgan, *Benjamin Franklin* (New Haven, Conn., 2002).

3. Leonard W. Labaree, ed., *The Papers of Benjamin Franklin*, 35 vols. (New Haven, Conn., 1959–), XIII, 127–29.

4. Ibid., 135–36.

5. Ibid., 140–59.

6. The lobbies and factions that shaped colonial policy during this period are the subject of Peter D. G. Thomas's *British Politics and the Stamp Act Crisis: The First Phase of the American Revolution, 1763–1767* (Oxford, 1975).

7. See Chapter 3 for a discussion of consumer colonies in a commercial empire.

8. Cited in Labaree, ed., *Papers of Benjamin Franklin*, XIII, 125.

9. Benjamin Franklin to Deborah Franklin, 6 April 1766, ibid., 233–34.

10. Jean-Christophe Agnew discusses the "symbolic dimensions of goods" in "Coming Up for Air: Consumer Culture in Historical Perspective," in *Consumption and the World of Goods*, ed. John Brewer and Roy Porter (London, 1993), 32–33.

11. The striking development at mid-century of a heightened sense of English nationalism is the subject of Linda Colley's important book *Britons: Forging the Nation, 1707–1837* (New Haven, Conn., 1992). Also useful are John Brewer, "The Eighteenth-Century British State: Contexts and Issues," in *An Imperial State at War: Britain from 1689–1815*, ed. Lawrence Stone (London, 1994), 52–71; Colin Kidd, "North Britishness and the Nature of Eighteenth-Century British Patriotisms," *Historical Journal* (Cambridge), 39 (1996), 361–82; and Kathleen Wilson, "Empire, Trade, and Popular Politics in Mid-Hanoverian Britain: The Case of Admiral Vernon," *Past and Present*, no. 121 (1988), 74–109. A discussion of "colonial national-

ism" within the American colonies can be found in T. H. Breen, "Ideology and Nationalism on the Eve of the American Revolution: Revisions *Once More* in Need of Revising," *Journal of American History* 84 (1997), 13–39. Also valuable is Stephen Conway, "From Fellow-Nationals to Foreigners: British Perceptions of the Americans, circa 1739–1783," *William and Mary Quarterly*, 3d ser., 59 (2002), 65–100.

12. *New-Hampshire Gazette*, 13 July 1764.
13. Nathan O. Hatch, *The Sacred Cause of Liberty: Republican Thought and the Millennium in Revolutionary New England* (New Haven, Conn., 1977); and Ruth Bloch, *Visionary Republic: Millennial Themes in American Thought, 1756–1800* (Cambridge, 1985).
14. See Jack P. Greene, "Independence and Dependence: The Psychology of the Colonial Relationship on the Eve of the American Revolution," in his *Imperatives, Behaviors, and Identities: Essays in Early American Cultural History* (Charlottesville, Va., 1992), 174–80; and John Clive and Bernard Bailyn, "England's Cultural Provinces: Scotland and America," *William and Mary Quarterly*, 3d ser., 11 (1954), 200–13. On the mid-century tightening of imperial controls, see Jack P. Greene, *Peripheries and Center: Constitutional Development in the Extended Polities of the British Empire and the United States, 1607–1788* (Athens, Ga., 1986), 48–76.
15. *Boston Gazette*, 14 October 1765.
16. James Otis Jr., *A Vindication of the British Colonies* (1765), in *Pamphlets of the American Revolution*, ed. Bernard Bailyn (Cambridge, Mass., 1965), I, 568.
17. *Maryland Gazette*, 8 August 1765 (reprinted from *Boston Gazette*, 15 July 1765).
18. This theme is developed in greater detail in T. H. Breen, "Subjecthood and Citizenship: The Context of James Otis's Radical Critique of John Locke," *New England Quarterly* 71 (1998), 378–403.
19. These reflections on the meaning of *colonial* in American history were inspired by Michael Warner's essay "What's Colonial About Colonial America," in *Possible Pasts: Becoming Colonial in Early America*, ed. Robert Blair St. George (Ithaca, N.Y., 2000), 49–70. The literature on post-colonialism is huge. For comparative purposes, one might start with Leela Gandhi, *Postcolonial Theory: A Critical Introduction* (New York, 1998), and Howard J. Booth and Nigel Rigby, eds., *Modernism and Empire* (Manchester, Eng., 2000).
20. One historian recently rejected the notion that the American colonists were ever colonized, thus effectively dismissing comparisons between twentieth-century liberation movements against European imperialism and popular mobilization on the eve of American independence. See David Armitage, "The Declaration of Independence and International Law," *William and Mary Quarterly*, 3d ser., 59 (2002), 64.
21. Samuel Adams to Arthur Lee, 31 October 1771, in *The Writings of Samuel Adams*, ed. Harry Alonzo Cushing, 4 vols. (New York, 1904–8), II, 267.
22. Michel Foucault, *The History of Sexuality*, trans. Robert Hurley, 3 vols. (New York, 1978), I, 103. The relevance of Foucault's insight to my analysis was suggested by Ann Laura Stoler, "Tense and Tender Ties: The Politics of Comparison in North American History and (Post) Colonial Studies," *Journal of American History* 88 (2001), 831.
23. Fred Anderson, *Crucible of War: The Seven Years' War and the Fate of Empire in British North America, 1754–1766* (New York, 2000), 588.
24. See Chapter 1 for the peculiar history of this colonial conceit.
25. See William Pencak, *War, Politics, and Revolution in Provincial Massachusetts* (Boston, 1981), 149–58.
26. Cited in T. S. Ashton, *Economic Fluctuations in England, 1700–1800* (Oxford, 1959), 127.
27. The best discussion of the general economic crisis remains Charles M. Andrews, "The Boston Merchants and the Non-importation Movement," Colonial Society of Massachusetts *Publications* 19 (1916–17), 159–259.
28. Good accounts of the economic slump can be found in Gary B. Nash, *The Urban Crucible: Social Change, Political Consciousness, and the Origins of the American Revolution* (Cambridge, Mass., 1979), 246–63; and Anderson, *Crucible of War*, 588–89. A new culture of debt is explored in T. H. Breen, *Tobacco Culture: The Mentality of the Great Tidewater Planters on the Eve of Revolution* (Princeton, N.J., 1985).
29. J. Hall Pleasants, ed., "Proceedings and Acts of the General Assembly of Maryland 1764–1765," Maryland Historical Society *Archives* 59 (1942), 207–8.
30. *Boston Evening-Post*, 4 February 1765, reprinting article from the *Providence Gazette*, 21 January 1765.

31. [Oxenbridge Thacher], *The Sentiments of a British American* (Boston, 1764), 13.

32. [Thomas Fitch], *Reasons Why the British Colonies in America, Should Not Be Charged with Internal Taxes* (New Haven, Conn., 1764), 21–22.

33. John J. McCusker and Russell R. Menard, *The Economy of British America, 1607–1789* (Chapel Hill, N.C., 1985), 354–55.

34. A good example of this rhetoric can be found in the *Newport Mercury*, 24 September 1764.

35. *New-Hampshire Gazette*, 14 September 1764, taken from *Pennsylvania Journal*, 23 August 1764.

36. *Boston Gazette*, 1 October 1764.

37. My thinking on the hermeneutic aspects of the consumer marketplace owes much to Albert O. Hirschman's *Shifting Involvements: Private and Public Actions* (Princeton, N.J., 1982), 5–6.

38. *Boston Gazette*, 9 November 1767.

39. Ibid., 16 July 1754. For the context of this statement, see Paul S. Boyer, "Borrowed Rhetoric: The Massachusetts Excise Controversy of 1754," *William and Mary Quarterly*, 3d ser., 21 (1964), 328–51.

40. *New Hampshire Gazette*, 14 September 1764, taken from *Pennsylvania Journal*, 23 August 1764. Also Andrews, "The Boston Merchants," 191.

41. See Chapter 5 for a discussion of class and consumer choice.

42. *Boston Evening-Post*, 9 November 1767. Edmund S. Morgan develops a similar argument about the relationship between consumer virtue and the common good in "The Puritan Ethic and the American Revolution," *William and Mary Quarterly*, 3d ser., 24 (1967), 3–43.

43. *Pennsylvania Chronicle*, 28 December 1767.

44. In his "Virtues of Liberalism: Christianity, Republicanism, and Ethics in Early American Political Discourse," *Journal of American History* 74 (1987), 9–33, James T. Kloppenberg provides a thoughtful summary of the various positions in this ongoing debate over the character of revolutionary ideas.

45. See Patricia U. Bonomi, *Under the Cope of Heaven: Religion, Society, and Politics in Colonial America* (New York, 1986), chs. 4 and 7.

46. The main contributions to what has been labeled the "republican synthesis" are J.G.A. Pocock, "The Mobility of Property and the Rise of Eighteenth-Century Sociology," in his *Virtue, Commerce, and History: Essays on Political Thought and History, Chiefly in the Eighteenth Century* (Cambridge, 1985), 103–23; Pocock, *The Machiavellian Moment: Florentine Political Thought and the Atlantic Republican Tradition* (Princeton, N.J., 1975); Bernard Bailyn, *Ideological Origins of the American Revolution* (Cambridge, Mass., 1967); and Gordon S. Wood, *The Creation of the American Republic, 1776–1787* (Chapel Hill, N.C., 1969). For a general critique of this literature, see T. H. Breen, *The Lockean Moment: The Language of Rights on the Eve of the American Revolution* (Oxford, 2001).

47. Steve Pincus raises some of the same points about liberal virtue in "Neither Machiavellian Moment nor Possessive Individualism: Commercial Society and the Defenders of the English Commonwealth," *American Historical Review* 103 (1998), 705–36.

48. Daniel Dulany, *Considerations on the Propriety of Imposing Taxes in the British Colonies* (Annapolis, Md., 1765), 45. A valuable sketch of Dulany's public life can be found in Edmund and Helen Morgan, *The Stamp Act Crisis*, ch. 6.

49. H. J. in the *New-Hampshire Gazette*, 15 February 1765.

50. See Chapter 5.

51. Dulany, *Considerations on the Propriety of Imposing Taxes* (1765), in Bailyn, ed., *Pamphlets*, I, 648–49.

52. *Pennsylvania Journal*, 28 June 1764, reprinted in *Newport Mercury*, 16 July 1764.

53. *New-Hampshire Gazette*, 6 July 1764.

54. *Boston Evening-Post*, 8 October 1764.

55. *New-York Mercury*, 30 December 1765.

56. Dulany, *Considerations*, 649.

57. *Newport Mercury*, 17 September 1764.

58. *Boston Evening-Post*, 23 November 1767.

59. "An Act to Retrench the Extraordinary Expense at Funerals," reprinted in *Acts and Resolves Passed by the General Court of Massachusetts*, 72 vols. (Boston, 1920–), II, 1086.

60. *Independent Reflector*, 14 June 1753.

61. *Boston Gazette*, 1 October 1764.

62. *New-Hampshire Gazette*, 19 October 1764.
63. *Boston Gazette*, 1 October 1764.
64. *Boston Evening-Post*, 19 November 1764.
65. Ibid., 24 September 1764; also see *Boston Gazette*, 14 December 1767.
66. *Boston Evening-Post*, 19 November 1764.
67. Ibid., 21 January 1765.
68. *Boston Gazette*, 21 January 1765.
69. Ibid.
70. *Boston Evening-Post*, 4 February 1765
71. Ibid., 29 October 1764.
72. Ibid. Peter Oliver, a Tory placeholder in Massachusetts, wrote an acerbic account of the rising discontent in the Bay Colony, and among other things he accused the people of Boston of gross hypocrisy in their insistence on frugal funerals. Oliver claimed that however principled the rhetoric of retrenchment may have sounded, the colonists used these occasions to show off their most recent and expensive purchases. "Under Pretence of Œconomy," Oliver reported, "the Faction undertook to regulate Funerals, that there might be less Demand for English Manufactures. . . . But what at another Time would have been deemed œconomical, was at this Time Spite & Malevolence. One Extreme was exchanged for another. A Funeral now seemed more like a Procession to a *May Fair*; and Processions were lengthened, especially by the Ladies, who figured a way, in order to exhibit their Share of Spite, & their Silk Gowns. In short, it was unhumanizing the Mind, by destroying the Solemnity of a funeral Obsequy, & substituting the Gaiety of Parade in its Stead." (Douglass Adair and John A. Schutz, eds., *Peter Oliver's Origin and Progress of the American Revolution: A Tory View* [San Marino, Calif., 1961], 62). Robert A. Gross suggests that in the case of Concord, Oliver may have been correct. (See his *The Minutemen and Their World* [New York, 1976], 33). In a Boston newspaper devoted to the "new mode" of funerals, we note the following advertisement: "Bonnets and crapes for gentlemen in the 'genteelest Manner' can be obtained from Ame & Elizabeth Cummings" (*Boston Evening-Post*, 24 September 1764).
73. *Connecticut Courant*, 29 October 1764, and *Pennsylvania Gazette* cited in Labaree, ed., *Papers of Benjamin Franklin*, XII, 240.
74. *New-Hampshire Gazette*, 19 October 1764.
75. *Boston Evening-Post*, 21 January 1765.
76. [Thacher], *Sentiments of a British American*, 14–15.
77. See Chapter 3 for a full discussion of the importance of colonial consumers for general British prosperity.
78. [Anonymous], *The Power and Grandeur of Great-Britain, Founded on the Liberty of the Colonies* (New York, 1768), 23.
79. Cited in Gordon S. Wood, *The American Revolution: A History* (New York, 2002), 24.
80. John Hancock Papers, Baker Library, Harvard Business School, Letter Book 1762–83, Hancock to Barnard & Harrison, 14 October 1765.
81. Reprinted in Ellis Sandoz, ed., *Political Sermons of the American Founding Era, 1730–1805* (Indianapolis, Ind., 1991), 247.
82. Jeremy Belknap, *The History of New-Hampshire*, 3 vols. (Dover, N.H., 1812), II, 250.
83. For a full account of these events, see Morgan and Morgan, *Stamp Act Crisis*.
84. *Boston Evening-Post*, 2 September 1765.
85. *A Discourse, Addressed to the Sons of Liberty, at a Solemn Assembly, near the Liberty-Tree, in Boston, February 14, 1766* (Providence, R.I., 1766), 7–8.
86. [Benjamin Church], *Liberty and Property Vindicated, and the St——pm——n Burnt* (Boston, 1765), 11–12.
87. The essay can be found in Herbert John Davis and Louis A. Landa, eds., *Jonathan Swift: Irish Tracts, 1720–1723* (Oxford, 1963), 16.
88. *Boston Evening-Post*, 18 August 1746.
89. See, for example, Peter Clark, *British Clubs and Societies 1580–1800: The Origins of an Associational World* (Oxford, 2000), 389–404; David S. Shields, *Civil Tongues and Political Letters in British America* (Chapel Hill, N.C., 1997); and Benjamin L. Carp, "Fire of Liberty: Firefighters, Urban Voluntary Culture, and the Revolutionary Movement," *William and Mary Quarterly*, 3d ser., 58 (2001), 781–818.

90. Andrews, "The Boston Merchants," 159–259; Merrill Jensen, *The Founding of a Nation: A History of the American Revolution, 1763–1776* (New York, 1968), 129–30; Morgan and Morgan, *Stamp Act Crisis*, 264; Pauline Maier, *From Resistance to Revolution: Colonial Radicals and the Development of American Opposition to Britain, 1765–1776* (New York, 1972), 74; and Joseph S. Tiedemann, *Reluctant Revolutionaries: New York City and the Road to Independence,1763–1776* (Ithaca, N.Y., 1997), 69–71. Also *New-York Mercury*, 28 October 1765.

91. *Boston Gazette*, 25 November 1765.

92. *Pennsylvania Gazette*, 26 December 1765.

93. See, for example, John Chew's letter to Samuel Galloway (7 November 1765), cited in Ronald Hoffman, *A Spirit of Dissension: Economics, Politics, and the Revolution in Maryland* (Baltimore, 1973), 37.

94. *Pennsylvania Chronicle*, 28 December 1767.

95. *Boston Evening-Post*, 25 November 1765.

96. [Silas Downer] A Son of Liberty, *A Discourse, Delivered in Providence . . . at the Dedication of the Tree of Liberty* (Providence, R.I., 1768), 14–15.

97. See Thomas, *British Politics and the Stamp Act Crisis*.

98. *Pennsylvania Chronicle*, 28 December 1767. For the moral content of this discourse see Morgan, "Puritan Ethic and the American Revolution."

99. *Pennsylvania Gazette*, 9 January 1766.

100. *New-London Gazette*, 27 November 1767.

101. *New-Hampshire Gazette*, 10 August 1764, originally published in the *Pennsylvania Journal*, 28 June 1764.

102. For the history of this discourse, see Chapter 3.

103. *Boston Evening-Post*, 15 October 1764.

104. *Pennsylvania Journal and Weekly Advertiser*, 2 January 1766 (Supplement).

105. [John Dickinson], *The Late Regulations . . . Considered in a Letter from a Gentleman in Philadelphia to His Friend in London* (1765), reprinted in Bailyn, ed., *Pamphlets of the Revolution*, I, 687.

106. *Pennsylvania Gazette*, 26 December 1765.

107. *Pennsylvania Chronicle*, 28 December 1767.

108. *Boston Evening-Post*, 12 October 1767.

109. *New-York Mercury*, 16 December 1765; *Boston Gazette*, 1 October 1764.

110. *Connecticut Journal, and New-Haven Post-Boy*, 25 December 1767.

111. *Boston Evening-Post*, 25 November 1765.

112. See, for example, *Pennsylvania Gazette*, 26 December 1765. The journals played a similar role in spreading political news, and as Edmund S. and Helen Morgan have demonstrated, erroneous reports about radical resolves allegedly passed by the Virginia House of Burgesses spread throughout colonial America, persuading leaders in other colonies to phrase their grievances more aggressively than they might have done had the news out of Virginia been more accurate (*Stamp Act Crisis*, 92–107).

113. See Arthur M. Schlesinger, "Colonial Newspapers and the Stamp Act," *New England Quarterly* 8 (1935), 63–83.

114. *Pennsylvania Journal and Weekly Advertiser*, 10 April 1766 (Supplement).

115. On the concept of a "public" as it developed during the eighteenth century, see Jürgen Habermas, *The Structural Transformation of the Public Sphere: An Inquiry into a Category of Bourgeois Society*, trans. Thomas Burger (Cambridge, Mass., 1989); and Craig Calhoun, ed., *Habermas and the Public Sphere* (Cambridge, Mass., 1992).

116. Jan de Vries, "Between Purchasing Power and the World of Goods: Understanding the Household Economy in Early Modern Europe," in Brewer and Porter, eds., *Consumption and the World of Goods*, 119. A thoughtful discussion of women and revolutionary politics can be found in Linda K. Kerber, *Women of the Republic: Intellect and Ideology in Revolutionary America* (Chapel Hill, N.C., 1980), 15–67.

117. *Pennsylvania Chronicle*, 28 December 1767.

118. *Boston Gazette*, 1 October 1764.

119. *Pennsylvania Journal*, 23 August 1764.

120. *New-Hampshire Gazette*, 15 February 1765.

121. *Pennsylvania Chronicle*, 7 December 1767.

122. *Boston Gazette*, 7 April 1766 (Supplement), and *Connecticut Courant*, 7 April 1766. Also see Andrews, "The Boston Merchant," 193–94; Alfred F. Young, "The Women of Boston: 'Persons of Consequence' in the Making of the American Revolution," in *Women and Politics in the Age of Democratic Revolution*, ed. Harriet B. Applewhite and Darline G. Levy (Ann Arbor, Mich., 1990), 181–226; and Laurel Thatcher Ulrich, " 'Daughters of Liberty': Religious Women in Revolutionary New England," in *Women in the Age of the American Revolution*, ed. Ronald Hoffman and Peter J. Albert (Charlottesville, Va., 1989), 211–43.
123. *New-York Mercury*, 30 December 1765.
124. *Boston Gazette*, 6 January 1766. On the debate over female patriotism, see Kerber, *Women of the Republic*, 35–45.
125. Jonathan Mayhew, *The Snare Broken: A Thanksgiving Discourse* (1766), reprinted in Sandoz, ed., *Political Sermons*, 248.
126. Originally published in *New-York Mercury* and rerun in *Boston Evening-Post*, 4 February 1765.

Chapter 7

1. *New London Gazette*, 15 April 1768.
2. *A Report of the Record Commissioners of the City of Boston Containing the Boston Town Records, 1758–1769* (Boston, 1886), 220–21; *Boston Evening-Post*, 2 November 1767. Also see Merrill Jensen, *The Founding of a Nation: A History of the American Revolution, 1763–1776* (New York, 1968), 268–70.
3. *Boston Gazette*, 19 February 1770.
4. *South-Carolina Gazette*, 22 June 1769; *South-Carolina Gazette and Country Journal*, 25 July 1769.
5. *Maryland Gazette*, 29 July 1769.
6. *Virginia Gazette* [Purdie and Dixon], 25 May 1769.
7. Ellen D. Larned, *History of Windham County, Connecticut*, 2 vols. (Worcester, Mass., 1874–80), II, 115–17; *New-London Gazette*, 25 December 1767. Also see Charles M. Andrews, "The Boston Merchants and the Non-Importation Movement," Colonial Society of Massachusetts, *Transactions* (1916–17), 191–92.
8. Silas Deane Papers, 1753–1842: Correspondence 1761–76, Box I, Folder 2, in the Connecticut Historical Society, Hartford, Conn.
9. *Connecticut Journal, and New-Haven Post-Boy*, 6 January 1769.
10. *New-York Journal; or, General Advertiser*, 1 June 1769, originally published in *Virginia Gazette*, 11 May 1769.
11. [Silas Downer?], *A Discourse . . . at the Dedication of the Tree of Liberty by a Son of Liberty* (Providence, R.I., 1768), 14.
12. The most detailed account of the Townshend Program is Peter D. G. Thomas, *The Townshend Duties Crisis: The Second Phase of the American Revolution, 1767–1773* (Oxford, 1987). One should also see Jensen, *Founding of a Nation*, ch. 8.
13. Historians now reject an older interpretation of American resistance which argued that the colonists regularly redefined the principles that underlaid their political protest. Edmund S. Morgan has persuasively demonstrated that from the very beginning of the imperial controversy Americans rejected as fatuous distinctions between "internal" and "external" taxes. They rightly concluded that taxation without representation was unacceptable whatever the form it took. A good review of this debate can be found in Morgan, *The Birth of the Republic, 1763–1789*, 3d ed. (Chicago, 1992).
14. Paul Leicester Ford, ed., *The Writings of John Dickinson, Vol. 1: Political Writings, 1764–1774* (Philadelphia, 1895), 355.
15. Many years ago historian Gordon Wood drew attention to the oddly hyperbolic character of public rhetoric during this period. His analysis of the colonists' excessive language can be found in "Rhetoric and Reality in the American Revolution," *William and Mary Quarterly*, 3d ser., 23 (1966), 3–32, and although my response to Wood's interpretive challenge is not one that he himself has favored, I acknowledge a great intellectual debt to his original formulation of the problem. See also Wood, "Conspiracy and the Paranoid Style: Causality and Deceit in the Eighteenth Century," *William and Mary Quarterly*, 3d ser., 39 (1982), 401–41.

16. *Connecticut Courant*, 7 December 1767, reprinted from *Providence Gazette*, 14 November 1767. Ironically, General Thomas Gage, who had no sympathy for the calls for non-importation which appeared in the provincial newspapers, assured a member of the current cabinet that the colonists would never succeed, for "they must take them [imported manufactures] from Britain, or go naked." Had such a letter become public knowledge in the colonies, it would have persuaded many Americans that there was in fact a conspiracy in the marketplace. See Gage to Lord Barington, 10 March 1768, in *The Correspondence of General Thomas Gage . . .* , ed. Clarence Edwin Carter, 5 vols. (New Haven, Conn., 1931–), II, 450.

17. *South-Carolina Gazette*, 1 June 1769.

18. *New-London Gazette*, 15 April 1768.

19. Ibid., 20 January 1769.

20. *Boston Gazette*, 31 August 1767.

21. See Chapter 3 for a fuller discussion of the origins of this interpretation of colonial commerce.

22. *South-Carolina Gazette*, 26 October 1769.

23. *Providence Gazette*, 14 November 1767.

24. *New-York Journal; or, General Advertiser*, 23 November 1769.

25. *Connecticut Courant*, 7 December 1767. Also see *South-Carolina Gazette*, 30 November 1769, and "Amicus's" assertion, "I can prove almost all goods imported from home [England], may be made full as cheap, and many much cheaper than can be made in England," in the *Massachusetts Spy*, 27 October 1770.

26. *South-Carolina Gazette*, 8 December 1769 (Supplement).

27. Ibid., 26 October 1769.

28. *New-York Journal; or, General Advertiser*, 23 November 1769.

29. *South-Carolina Gazette*, 26 October 1769.

30. *Virginia Gazette*, 11 May 1769, as reprinted in *New-York Journal; or, General Advertiser*, 1 June 1769.

31. *New-London Gazette*, 15 April 1768.

32. *South-Carolina Gazette*, 26 October 1769. Also Arthur L. Jensen, *The Maritime Commerce of Colonial Philadelphia* (Madison, Wisc., 1963), 183–84.

33. Historian Merrill Jensen argues persuasively, against an older historiography, that "it is my view that the evidence demonstrates that the non-importation movement was actually begun by the popular leaders who forced or persuaded merchants to take part in it by threats of non-consumption, and even of physical violence" (*Founding*, 265). On this point, I do not disagree. What must be explained, it seems to me, is why the so-called popular leaders insisted that the merchants organize the boycott, when it was so clear that the merchants resisted the idea and were prepared to resume trade with Great Britain as soon as they had an opportunity.

34. Cited in Jensen, *Founding*, 270. For a fine account of the maneuvering among northern merchants, see 265–87; and Arthur M. Schlesinger Sr., *Colonial Merchants and the American Revolution* (New York, 1918), 106–31.

35. The exchange between Mason and Washington can be found in Robert A. Rutland, ed., *The Papers of George Mason, 1749–1778*, 3 vols. (Chapel Hill, N.C., 1970), I, 96–100.

36. *Maryland Gazette*, 11 May 1769.

37. See Chapter 4 for a full description of merchandising in the southern colonies.

38. *South-Carolina Gazette*, 1 June 1769.

39. Rutland, ed., *Papers of George Mason*, I, 98.

40. *South-Carolina Gazette*, 1 June 1769.

41. Silas Deane Papers, 1753–1842: Correspondence 1761–76, Connecticut Historical Society, Box I, Folder 2, "A Committee of Merchants at Boston to Mr. Silas Deane and others of the Committee of Merchants at Wethersfield," 15 February 1770.

42. See Richard Buel Jr., "Freedom of the Press," in *The Press and the American Revolution*, ed. Bernard Bailyn and John Hench (Worcester, Mass., 1980), 27.

43. *New-London Gazette*, 20 January 1769.

44. "To the PRINTER of the LONDON CRONICLE: 'The Rise and Present State of Our Misunderstanding,'" reprinted in *The Papers of Benjamin Franklin*, ed. Leonard W. Labaree, 35 vols. (New Haven, Conn., 1959–), XVII, 272.

45. The author acknowledges a debt to Michael Warner for helping him appreciate how the so-called public sphere, which transformed the character of political discourse in *ancien régime* France, Germany, and Great Britain in the late eighteenth century, took on a peculiar commercial character in the American colonies. The literature on the public sphere is large. One should start with Jürgen Habermas, *The Structural Transformation of the Public Sphere: An Inquiry into a Category of Bourgeois Society*, trans. Thomas Burger (Cambridge, Mass., 1989), and Craig Calhoun, ed., *Habermas and the Public Sphere* (Cambridge, Mass., 1992). Also helpful is Michael Warner, *The Letters of the Republic: Publication and the Public Sphere in Eighteenth-Century America* (Cambridge, Mass., 1990).

46. *To the PUBLIC . . .* (New York, 1770), a broadside dated 8 March 1770.

47. The statement appeared in *South-Carolina Gazette; and Country Journal*, 13 November 1770.

48. See Edmund S. Morgan, *Inventing the People: The Rise of Popular Sovereignty in England and America* (New York, 1988).

49. My debt here to Benedict Anderson is obvious. His *Imagined Communities: Reflections on the Origin and Spread of Nationalism* (London, 1983) reshaped how a generation of historians understands the relation between commercial print culture and new forms of political identity such as nationalism which appeared throughout the Euro-American world during the late eighteenth century. See also T. H. Breen, "A Framework for Interpreting Nationalism: Patriotism and Political Ideology During the Age of the American Revolution," paper presented at Nationalism in the New World, Vanderbilt University, Nashville, Tenn., Oct. 9, 2003.

50. E. B. O'Callaghan, ed., *Documents Relative to the Colonial History of the State of New-York . . . ,* 12 vols.. (Albany, N.Y., 1857), VIII, 68.

51. *Boston Evening-Post*, 12 October 1767.

52. *Connecticut Journal: and New-Haven Post-Boy*, 25 December 1767, copied from a New York journal.

53. *New-London Gazette*, 25 May 1770 ("The Poet's Corner").

54. *New-York Journal; or, General Advertiser*, 21 June 1770. Also see Buel, "Freedom of the Press," and Arthur M. Schlesinger Sr., "Politics, Propaganda, and the Philadelphia Press, 1767–1770," *Pennsylvania Magazine of History and Biography* 60 (1936), 309–22.

55. See Andrews, "The Boston Merchants," 191–92. It was a rare colonial newspaper that did not carry news of the success or failure of the non-importation effort in other cities. A few examples of this spreading interest and increased borrowing of material are *Boston Gazette*, 9 and 23 November 1767; *Boston Chronicle*, 10 July 1769; and *Massachusetts Spy*, 29 September 1770.

56. Moore to the earl of Hillsborough, 3 June 1769, in O'Callaghan, ed., *Documents Relative to . . . New York*, VIII, 171.

57. Silas Deane Papers, 1753–1842: Correspondence 1761–76, Box I, Folder 2, Connecticut Historical Society.

58. "To the Gentlemen Select Men of Leicester, Massachusetts, 25 December 1769," Revolution Collection, Box I, Folder 3: 1754–1773, American Antiquarian Society, Worcester, Mass.; [Anonymous], *At a Town-Meeting Called by Order of the Town-Council* (Newport, R.I., 1767); *Pennsylvania Gazette*, 31 May 1770; "John Neufville, Chairman, General Committee to the Sons of Liberty in North Carolina (25 April 1770)," in *Colonial Records of North Carolina*, ed. William J. Saunders, 9 vols. (Raleigh, N.C., 1890), VIII, 197–98; *South-Carolina Gazette*, 9 August 1770; "The New-Castle [Delaware] County COMPACT," ibid., 12 October 1769; "At a Meeting of the Principal Merchants and Traders of the Colony of Connecticut," broadside, Connecticut Historical Society.

59. *Boston Gazette*, 23 November 1767.

60. *New-York Mercury*, 29 May 1769.

61. Saunders, ed., *Colonial Records of North Carolina*, VIII, 198.

62. "At a Meeting of the FREEHOLDERS, MERCHANTS, and TRADERS of the county of Essex, at Elizabeth-Town," published in *South-Carolina Gazette*, 28 June 1770.

63. Ibid., 9 November 1769.

64. Town records quoted in Larned, *History of Windham County*, II, 119.

65. *New-London Gazette*, 7 April 1769.

66. Published in *Massachusetts Spy*, 16 August 1770.

67. Report found in ibid., 29 November 1770.

68. *Boston Post-Boy and Advertiser*, 15 May 1769.

69. Carter, ed., *Correspondence of General Gage*, II, 530.

70. [Anonymous], *To the Public . . .* (Philadelphia, 1770).

71. "A Letter from a Gentleman in Virginia," *New-London Gazette*, 3 August 1770.

72. Boston, 1768. When John Mein, a feisty Boston merchant who refused to sign the non-importation agreement, started publishing his own newspaper, called the *Boston Chronicle*, in which he listed by name patriot leaders who he said had cheated on the boycott, the accused declared that such a man had no right to speak for the public in these matters. Francis Green, for example, asked, "Who gave this Mushroom Judge, Authority, to summon even a Chimney-Sweeper to his ridiculous Tribunal? Or wantonly, presumptuously, and very fallaciously to assume the respectable Title of *The Public*, in his romantic and indecent Addresses to an affronted Community?" (*Boston Gazette*, 25 September 1769).

73. Morgan and Morgan, *Stamp Act Crisis*, ch. 4.

74. 7 June 1770, in Rutland, ed., *Papers of George Mason*, I, 116–17.

75. *Boston Gazette*, 5 February 1770.

76. *Massachusetts Spy*, 22 November 1770.

77. New York, 20 July 1769.

78. *Boston Gazette*, 19 February 1770. The *South-Carolina Gazette*, 15 February 1770, carried an article from the *Massachusetts Gazette* which claimed that Taylor had fooled the Boston "Committee of Inspection " and gained entrance to the public warehouse "by means of a false key." On the fire clubs of Boston see Benjamin L. Carp, "Fire of Liberty: Firefighters, Urban Voluntary Culture, and the Revolutionary Movement," *William and Mary Quarterly*, 3d ser., 58 (2001), 781–818.

79. Quoted in *South-Carolina Gazette*, 15 February 1770. Also see *New-London Gazette*, 24 August 1770; *Boston Gazette*, 12 February 1770; and *Boston Post-Boy and Advertiser*, 13 August 1770.

80. *New-York Journal; or, General Advertiser*, 9 August 1770.

81. *A Report of the Boston Town Records,* 297–98.

82. *South-Carolina Gazette*, 9 August 1770.

83. Ibid., 14 September 1769.

84. [Anonymous], *To the PUBLICK . . .* (New York, 1769).

85. Carter, ed., *Correspondence of General Gage*, II, 526.

86. Broadside, Philadelphia, 1770. Also see *Boston Gazette*, 29 January 1770.

87. *New-London Gazette*, 15 June 1770.

88. The story was reprinted in *South-Carolina Gazette*, 12 July 1770. See Benjamin H. Irvin, "Tar, Feathers, and the Enemies of American Liberties, 1768–1776," *New England Quarterly* 74 (2003), 197–229.

89. J.G.A. Pocock, *The Machiavellian Moment: Florentine Political Thought and the Atlantic Republican Tradition* (Princeton, N.J., 1975); Pocock, "Virtue and Commerce in the Eighteenth Century," *Journal of Interdisciplinary History* 3 (1972–73), 119–34; Bernard Bailyn, *The Ideological Origins of the American Revolution* (Cambridge, Mass., 1967); Gordon S. Wood, *The Creation of the American Republic, 1776–1787* (Chapel Hill, N.C., 1969); and James T. Kloppenberg, "The Virtues of Liberalism: Christianity, Republicanism, and Ethics in Early American Political Discourse," *Journal of American History* 74 (1987), 9–33. For a critical assessment of this interpretive tradition, see Daniel Rodgers, "Republicanism: The Career of a Concept," *Journal of American History* 79 (1992), 11–38.

90. Edmund S. Morgan, "The Puritan Ethic and the American Revolution," *William and Mary Quarterly*, 3d ser., 24 (1967), 3–43; Patricia Bonomi, *Under the Cope of Heaven: Religion, Society, and Politics in Colonial America* (New York, 1986); and Nathan O. Hatch, *The Sacred Cause of Liberty: Republican Thought and the Millennium in Revolutionary New England* (New Haven, Conn., 1977).

91. T. A. Horne, "Bourgeois Virtue, Property, and Moral Philosophy in America, 1750–1800," *History of Political Thought* 4 (1983), 317–40. Also see Jeffrey C. Isaac, "Republicanism Vs. Liberalism? A Reconsideration," ibid. 11 (1988), 349–77; Isaac Kramnick, *Republicanism and Bourgeois Radicalism: Political Ideology in Late Eighteenth-Century England and America* (Ithaca, N.Y., 1990), 260–88; and Colin Jones, "Bourgeois Revolution Revivified: 1789 and Social Change," in *Rewriting the French Revolution*, ed. Colin Lucas (Oxford, 1991), 78–96.

92. *Massachusetts Spy*, 13 October 1770.

93. *New-York Mercury*, 24 September 1770.

94. Ibid., 6 August 1770. See also *New-London Gazette*, 2 November 1770.

95. *Boston Evening-Post,* 7 December 1767.

96. *Connecticut Journal*, 11 October 1771.
97. *Boston Gazette*, 11 September 1769.
98. *Virginia Gazette*, 9 November 1769, Supplement [Purdie and Dixon].
99. "A Letter from a Gentleman in Virginia," *New-London Gazette*, 3 August 1770.
100. *Newport Mercury*, reprinted in *Boston Gazette*, 6 March 1769.
101. *South-Carolina Gazette*, 14 November 1769.
102. This argument is developed in Chapter 5.
103. *Boston Gazette*, 11 January 1768.
104. Ibid., 26 March 1770.
105. *Boston Evening-Post*, 2 November 1767; *Boston Gazette*, 2 November 1767.
106. Ibid., 30 November 1767. For an insightful discussion of the radical implications of the general subscription in Boston, see Gary Nash, *The Urban Crucible: Social Change, Political Consciousness, and the Origins of the American Revolution* (Cambridge, Mass., 1979).
107. *Boston Gazette*, 9 and 23 November 1767; *Boston Evening-Post*, 23 November 1767; *Newport* (R.I.) *Mercury*, 30 November and 7 December 1767; and [Anonymous], *At a Town-Meeting Called by Order of the Town-Council . . .* (Newport, R.I., 1767).
108. On the royal governor, see John W. Tyler, *Smugglers and Patriots: Boston Merchants and the Advent of the American Revolution* (Boston, 1986), 112; Douglass Adair and John A. Schutz, eds., *Peter Oliver's Origin and Progress of the American Rebellion: A Tory View* (San Marino, Calif., 1961), 61; *Boston Evening-Post*, 23 November 1767.
109. On a proposal to prepare a subscription list, see *Connecticut Journal, and New-Haven Post-Boy*, 21 December 1767.
110. *New-London Gazette*, 24 August 1770; *New-York Mercury*, 10 September 1770.
111. *New-London Gazette*, 7 September 1770.
112. Ibid., 24 August and 7, 21, 28 September 1770; *New-York Journal; or, General Advertiser*, 20 September 1770; *Connecticut Courant*, 17 September 1770; and Christopher P. Bickford, *Farmington in Connecticut* (Canaan, N.H., 1988), 141.
113. *Connecticut Courant*, 29 January 1770.
114. Ibid., 19 February 1770.
115. *Maryland Gazette*, 11 May, 15 and 29 June 1769.
116. See Jensen, *Founding of a Nation*, for a detailed account of these negotiations, 306–12.
117. *South-Carolina Gazette*, 23 November 1769.
118. Ibid.
119. Ibid., 16 November 1769.
120. Ibid., 21 September 1769. Also see Robert Wier's introduction to *The Letters of Freeman, Etc.: Essays on the Nonimportation Movement in South Carolina*, ed. Robert M. Wier (Columbia, S.C., 1977).
121. *South-Carolina Gazette*, 26 October 1769.
122. The following six paragraphs originally appeared in T. H. Breen, "Narrative of Commercial Life: Consumption, Ideology, and Community on the Eve of the American Revolution," *William and Mary Quarterly*, 3d ser., 50 (1993), 491–94.
123. *Pennsylvania Chronicle*, 4 June 1770.
124. *New-York Mercury*, 6 August 1770. See also *New-York Journal; or, General Advertiser*, 2 August 1770.
125. *South-Carolina Gazette*, 20 August 1770 (Supplement).
126. *New-York Journal; or, General Advertiser*, 21 June 1770.
127. Ibid.
128. Ibid., 27 September 1770; *New-York Mercury*, 23 July 1770; *New-London Gazette*, 20 July 1770.
129. "A Trader that will not Import," *Connecticut Courant*, 10 September 1770.
130. Jensen, *Founding of a Nation*, 306.
131. *Pennsylvania Chronicle*, 4 June 1770.
132. Nancy F. Cott, "What's in a Name? The Limits of 'Social Feminism'; or, Expanding the Vocabulary of Women's History," *Journal of American History* 76 (1989), 809–29. Also see Mary Beth Norton, *Liberty's Daughters: The Revolutionary Experience of American Women, 1750–1800* (Boston, 1980).
133. *Boston Gazette*, 2 November 1767; reprinted in *New-London Gazette*, 6 November 1767.
134. *Boston Gazette*, 2 November 1767.

NOTES TO PAGES 280-296

135. Richard Walsh, ed., *The Writings of Christopher Gadsden* (Columbia, S.C., 1966), 83. See Linda K. Kerber, *Women of the Republic: Intellect and Ideology in Revolutionary America* (Chapel Hill, N.C., 1980), 7–12, 35–45.

136. *New-London Gazette*, 9 June 1769. Also see [Anonymous], *The Female Patriot, No. 1. Addressed to the Tea-Drinking Ladies of New-York* (New York, 1770).

137. *New-York Journal; or, General Advertiser*, 29 June 1769; also see the much reprinted story of the middle-class husband nearly run into bankruptcy by his spendthrift wife. One day, when she was out visiting friends, he sold all her "fashionable" possessions to pay off his debts (*Boston Gazette*, 30 March 1767).

138. *New-London Gazette*, 10 February 1769.

139. *Boston Evening-Post*, 4 January 1768.

140. Ibid.; and [Anonymous], *A Verse, Occasioned by Seeing the North-spinning, in Boton [sic]* (Boston, 1769).

141. *Connecticut Journal, and New-Haven Post-Boy*, 8 April 1768.

142. *South-Carolina Gazette*, 13 July 1769.

143. *Pennsylvania Chronicle, and Universal Advertiser*, 20 August 1770.

144. See the discussion of women and non-importation in Chapter 6.

145. *South-Carolina Gazette*, 20 July 1769.

146. *Connecticut Journal, and New-Haven Post-Boy*, 8 April 1768.

147. *Boston Gazette*, 28 December 1767 (Supplement).

148. *Connecticut Journal, and New-Haven Post-Boy*, 8 April 1768.

149. *Newport Mercury*, 7 December 1767; reprinted in *Boston Evening-Post*, 28 December 1767.

150. *Massachusetts Spy*, 14 March 1771.

151. *South-Carolina Gazette*, 5 October 1769. "Cleora" in the *Pennsylvania Chronicle, and Universal Advertiser* accused males of a political double standard. "You think you may indulge yourselves with impunity, in such instances of indiscretion, avarice, and ambition, which in women you take liberty to censure with freedom and severity." But, as Cleora warned, women possessed an unerring "faculty" to spot true virtue (7 January 1771).

152. *Pennsylvania Gazette*, 18 December 1769.

153. *Boston Gazette*, 5, 12, 19, 26 February 1770.

154. See T. H. Breen, *The Lockean Moment: The Language of Rights on the Eve of the American Revolution* (Oxford, 2001), and see Kerber, *Women of the Republic*.

155. *New-York Journal; or, General Advertiser*, 25 October 1770 ["Poet's Corner"].

156. *New-York Journal; or, General Advertiser*, 9 August 1770; originally published in *Boston Gazette*, 23 July 1770.

157. "A Tradesman," *To the Tradesmen, Farmers, and Other Inhabitants . . .* (Philadelphia, 1770).

158. *New-London Gazette*, 5 October 1770, reprinted from a New York journal, 9 September 1770.

159. Report published in *Massachusetts Spy*, 31 December 1770.

160. *Connecticut Journal, and New-Haven Post-Boy*, 8 May 1772.

161. *Boston Evening-Post*, 23 July 1770.

162. [Anonymous], *To the Freeholders, Merchants, Tradesmen and Farmers of the City and County of Philadelphia . . .* (Philadelphia, 1770), broadside. Also, [Anonymous], *To the Inhabitants of the City and County of Philadelphia . . .* (Philadelphia, 1770), broadside.

163. *New-London Gazette*, 2 November 1770.

164. *Boston Gazette*, 11 September 1769.

Chapter 8

1. William Lincoln, ed., *The Journals of Each Provincial Congress of Massachusetts in 1774 and 1775, and of the Committee of Safety* (Boston, 1838), 26. The quotations describing Withington and his adventure come from *Massachusetts Spy*, 6 and 13 January 1774.

2. Anne Rowe Cunningham, ed., *Letters and Diary of John Rowe, Boston Merchant, 1759–1762, 1764–1779* (Boston, 1903), 259.

3. John W. Shy, *A People Numerous and Armed: Reflections on the Military Struggle for American Independence* (New York, 1976), 216–22.

4. Susan Stein, *The Worlds of Thomas Jefferson at Monticello* (New York, 1993).

5. To Archibald Cary and Benjamin Harrison, 9 December 1774, in *The Papers of Thomas Jefferson*, ed. Julian Boyd et al., 29 vols. (Princeton, N.J., 1950–), I, 154–55.

6. "A Friend to Port-Bills," *Connecticut Gazette*, 29 July 1774.

7. Peter Force, ed., *American Archives . . .* , 4th ser., 9 vols. (Washington, D.C., 1837–53), I, 447.

8. Henry S. Nourse, *History of the Town of Harvard, Massachusetts, 1732–1893* (Harvard, Mass., 1894), 308.

9. Cited in Peter D. G. Thomas, *Lord North* (New York, 1976), 74.

10. *Boston Gazette*, 8 November 1773, taken from *Pennsylvania Packet*.

11. [Anonymous], *The Association of the Sons of Liberty . . . November 29, 1773* (New York, 1773).

12. *New-York Journal; or, General Advertiser*, 2 and 9 December 1773.

13. Merrill Jensen, *The Founding of a Nation: A History of the American Revolution, 1763–1776* (New York, 1968), 440–52.

14. *Massachusetts Gazette and Boston Post-Boy*, 6 December 1773.

15. Cited in Thomas, *Lord North*, 76.

16. *Connecticut Courant*, 5 June 1774.

17. See Chapter 1.

18. *New-York Journal; or, General Advertiser*, 9 June 1774.

19. Force, ed., *American Archives*, I, 453.

20. Ibid., 540.

21. Ibid., 403. For Charleston, South Carolina, see *New-York Journal; or, General Advertiser*, 4 August 1774.

22. Francis S. Drake, ed., *Tea Leaves: Being a Collection of Letters and Documents Relating to the Shipment of Tea to the American Colonies in the Year 1773* (Boston,1884), 200. Lois Green Carr, "Diversification in the Colonial Chesapeake: Somerset County, Maryland, in Comparative Perspective," in *Colonial Chesapeake Society*, ed. Lois Green Carr, Philip D. Morgan, and Jean B. Russo (Chapel Hill, N.C., 1988), 379.

23. [Philip Livingston], *The Other Side of the Question; or, A Defense of the Liberties of North-America . . .* (New York, 1774), 10.

24. *South-Carolina Gazette; and Country Journal*, 2 August 1774.

25. *Pennsylvania Chronicle, and Universal Advertiser*, 29 January 1770.

26. *New-York Mercury*, 6 August 1770. See Rodris Roth, *Tea Drinking in Eighteenth-Century America: Its Etiquette and Equipage* (Washington, D.C., 1961), 66.

27. *Massachusetts Spy*, 6 January 1774.

28. [Anonymous], *A Sermon on Tea* (Lancaster, Pa., 1774), 6. Also see "Phileleutheros" in *New-York Journal; or, General Advertiser*, 21 October 1773.

29. *Massachusetts Spy*, 14 October 1773.

30. *South-Carolina Gazette.* 21 October 1773.

31. *Massachusetts Spy*, 23 December 1773. On claims that tea undermined public health, see Roy Porter, "Consumption: Disease of the Consumer Society?" in *Consumption and the World of Goods*, ed. John Brewer and Roy Porter (London, 1993), 58–81.

32. *Massachusetts Spy*, 27 January 1774, taken from the *Pennsylvania Journal*.

33. [Anonymous], *Sermon on Tea*, 4.

34. *Boston Evening-Post*, 25 October 1773.

35. *Massachusetts Spy*, 23 December 1773.

36. *Pennsylvania Journal and Weekly Advertiser*, 20 October 1773.

37. *Massachusetts Spy*, 27 January 1774.

38. *South-Carolina Gazette,* 19 September 1774.

39. Cited in Charles M. Andrews, "The Boston Merchants and the Non-Importation Movement," Colonial Society of Massachusetts *Publications* 19 (1916–17), 194.

40. *New-Hampshire Gazette*, 22 July 1768.

41. *South-Carolina Gazette*, 27 June 1774.

42. *Massachusetts Spy*, 23 December 1773.

43. *Connecticut Gazette* [New London], 25 February 1774.

44. *Massachusetts Spy*, 6 January 1774; *New-York Journal; or, General Advertiser*, 23 December 1773. An invaluable guide to local Massachusetts politics during this period is Richard D. Brown, *Revolutionary Politics in Massachusetts: The Boston Committee of Correspondence and the Towns, 1772–1774* (Cambridge, Mass., 1970).

45. *Massachusetts Spy*, 16 December 1773. The story also ran in *New-York Journal; or, General Advertiser*, 23 December 1773.

46. *Massachusetts Spy*, 27 January 1774.

47. *Connecticut Courant*, 13 March 1775.

48. *Massachusetts Spy*, 17 February 1774. Also see the odd case of a purchaser of tea who was "way-laid . . . in the Wellfleet woods," ibid., 10 February 1774.

49. *Boston Gazette*, 5 September 1774. Another case was reported in Lyme, Connecticut, *Massachusetts Spy*, 31 March 1774.

50. Ibid., 28 July 1774.

51. *Boston Evening-Post*, 7 February 1774; also ibid., 5 September 1774 (Supplement).

52. Ibid., 21 March 1774.

53. See Brown, *Revolutionary Politics in Massachusetts*.

54. Adams to Warren, 27 July 1807, reprinted in Massachusetts Historical Society *Collections*, 5th ser., 4 (1878), 354–55.

55. *Massachusetts Spy*, 31 March 1774.

56. Ibid., 20 January 1774.

57. *Massachusetts Gazette and Boston Post-Boy*, 29 November 1773.

58. *Massachusetts Spy*, 15 April 1774.

59. Ibid., 17 February 1774.

60. *Massachusetts Gazette and Boston Post-Boy*, 29 November 1773. For the debates and resolutions of some other towns, see *Massachusetts Spy*, 6 January 1774 (Harvard); 13 January 1774 (Haverhill, New Hampshire); 27 January 1774 (Salem); 15 April 1774 (Westford).

61. John Adams to Abigail Adams, 6 July 1774, in *Adams Family Correspondence*, ed. L. H. Butterfield, 6 vols. (Cambridge, Mass., 1963–93), I, 129–30.

62. Force, ed., *American Archives*, I, 434.

63. Ibid., 447.

64. *Pennsylvania Packet*, 20 June 1774; reprinted in *New-York Mercury*, 27 June 1774.

65. Jensen, *Founding of a Nation*, 464–82.

66. Kate Mason Rowland, *The Life of George Mason, 1725–1792*, 2 vols. (New York, 1892), I, 148–49.

67. *Massachusetts Spy*, 16 June 1774.

68. *New-York Journal; or, General Advertiser*, 14 July 1774.

69. Ibid.

70. William L. Saunders, ed., *The Colonial Records of North Carolina*, 10 vols. (Raleigh, N.C., 1886–90), IX, 1026.

71. *New-York Journal; or, General Advertiser*, 9 June 1774.

72. *Massachusetts Spy*, 25 August 1774. Also see "Lincoln, Massachusetts, 1774. Covenant Not to Purchase Goods from Great Britain." U.S. Revolution Collection, Box 1, Folder 4:1774, American Antiquarian Society, Worcester, Mass.

73. Douglass Adair and John A. Schutz, eds., *Origin and Progress of the American Rebellion: A Tory View* (San Marino, Calif., 1961), 104. Also "A. Farmer" [Samuel Seabury], *Free Thoughts, on the Proceedings of the Continental Congress . . .* (New York, 1774); and "A Philadelphian," *New-York Mercury*, 25 July 1774.

74. "A. Farmer" [Seabury], *Free Thoughts*, 14.

75. Force, ed., *American Archives*, I, 620.

76. [Jonathan Boucher], *A Letter from a Virginian . . .* (Boston, 1774), 22.

77. *Massachusetts Spy*, 9 September 1773.

78. Ibid., 30 June 1774.

79. *South-Carolina Gazette*, 20 June 1774 (Supplement), from *Boston Evening-Post*, 23 May 1774. Also see [Richard Wells], *A Few Political Reflections . . .* (Philadelphia, 1774); and Robert Carter Nicholas, *Considerations on the Present State of Virginia Examined . . .* (Williamsburg, 1774).

80. *Pennsylvania Packet*, 20 June 1774.

81. William MacDonald, ed., *Select Charters and Other Documents Illustrative of American History, 1606–1775* (New York, 1899), 363–64.

82. Two notable exceptions are David Ammerman, *In the Common Cause: American Response to the Coercive Acts of 1774* (Charlottesville, Va., 1974), 85, and Jensen, *Founding of a Nation*, 506.

83. MacDonald, ed., *Select Charters*, 366.

84. Cited in Thomas J. Wertenbaker, *Give Me Liberty: The Struggle for Self-Government in Virginia* (Philadelphia, 1958), 241.

85. "A. Farmer" [Seabury], *Free Thoughts*, 17–18.

86. The following four paragraphs originally appeared in slightly different form in T. H. Breen, "'Baubles of Britain': The American and Consumer Revolutions of the Eighteenth Century," *Past and Present*, no. 119 (1988), 73–104.

87. Henry Laurens to John Petrie, 7 September 1774, in *The Papers of Henry Laurens*, ed. George C. Rogers Jr., 10 vols. (Columbia, S.C., 1981), IX, 552.

88. J. G. Marston, *King and Congress: The Transfer of Political Legitimacy, 1774–1776* (Princeton, N.J., 1987), 124.

89. James Madison to William Bradford, 20 January 1775, in *The Papers of James Madison*, ed. W. T. Hutchinson and William M. E. Rachal, 3 vols. (Chicago, 1962), I, 135.

90. Force, ed., *American Archives*, I, 494.

91. Jensen, *Founding of a Nation*, 517.

92. Force, ed., *American Archives*, I, 1061.

93. *Connecticut Gazette*, 15 April 1775.

94. Force, ed., *American Archives*, II, 34.

95. Cited in Jensen, *Founding of a Nation*, 561.

96. David Ramsay, *An Oration on the Advantages of American Independence* . . . (Charleston, S.C., 1778), 2–8.

Index

Note: Page numbers in *italics* indicate photographs and illustrations.